Software Architecture with C# 14 and .NET 10

Fifth Edition

Build enterprise applications using microservices, DevSecOps, EF Core, and design patterns for Azure

Gabriel Baptista | Francesco Abbruzzese

<packt>

Software Architecture with C# 14 and .NET 10

Fifth Edition

Portfolio Director: Kunal Chaudhari
Relationship Lead: Dhruv J. Kataria
Project Manager: K. Loganathan
Content Engineer: Srishty Goyal
Technical Editor: Irfa Ansari
Indexer: Rekha Nair
Proofreader: Srishty Goyal
Production Designer: Ponraj Dhandapani
Growth Lead: Vinishka Kalra

First published: November 2019
Second edition: December 2020
Third edition: March 2022
Fourth edition: February 2024
Fifth edition: May 2026

Production reference: 1260526

Published by Packt Publishing Ltd.
Grosvenor House
11 St Paul's Square
Birmingham
B3 1RB, UK.

ISBN 978-1-80666-355-2
www.packtpub.com

I would like to dedicate this book to my wife, Denise, and my children, Murilo and Heitor, who give me the strength to keep moving forward. Special thanks to our Packt team, who continually help us grow throughout the incredible journey of bringing this book to life.

– Gabriel Baptista

To my beloved parents, to whom I owe everything, thank you very much. A special thanks to the whole Packt team and the reviewers, whose invaluable feedback greatly enhanced this edition of the book.

– Francesco Abbruzzese

Contributors

About the authors

Gabriel Baptista leads a research and development team focused on digital products, using Microsoft technologies to design solutions for industry and retail. In addition, he is a computing professor who has published many papers and taught subjects such as software engineering, software development, and software architecture. He has also presented his expertise at technology conferences over the past few years.

Francesco Abbruzzese has dedicated his entire life to his two great passions: software and powerlifting. He is the author of the Blazor Controls Toolkit library and contributed to the diffusion and evangelization of the Microsoft web stack since the first .NET version. His company, Mvcct Team, offers web applications, tools, and services for web technologies. His latest product, SimpleProcess, is a sophisticated Blazor and .NET microservices-based process management software. He has moved from working on AI systems for financial institutions to top-10 video game titles such as *Puma Street Soccer*.

About the reviewer

Kirk Larkin is an expert in C#, .NET, ASP.NET Core, and Microsoft Azure. With over twenty years of professional experience, he has been recognized twice as a Microsoft MVP in Developer Technologies and has also worked for Microsoft. Kirk is the top-ranked Stack Overflow contributor for ASP.NET Core. He lives in the UK with his wife and two daughters.

Table of Contents

Preface **xxiii**

Free benefits with your book ..... **xxviii**

Part 1: Organizational, Architectural, and Design Principles **1**

Chapter 1: Understanding the Importance of Software Architecture **3**

What is software architecture? **3**

Creating an Azure account **5**

Software development process models **7**

Reviewing traditional software development process models • 8

Understanding the waterfall model • 8

Analyzing the incremental model • 9

Understanding agile software development process models • 9

Scaling agile throughout a company • 14

Gathering the right information to design high-quality software **15**

Understanding the requirements-gathering process • 15

Detecting exact user needs • 16

Analyzing requirements • 17

Writing the specifications • 18

Understanding the principles of scalability, robustness, security, and performance • 20

Reviewing the specification • 20

Using design techniques as a helpful tool **21**

Design thinking • 21

Design sprint • 22

Common cases where the requirements gathering process impacts system results **22**

Case 1 – my website is too slow to open that page! • 22

Understanding backend caching • 23

Applying asynchronous programming • 23

Dealing with object allocation • 24

Getting better database access • 24

Case 2 – the user's needs are not properly implemented • 25

Case 3 – the usability of the system does not meet the user's needs • 25

Summary **26**

Questions 26
Further reading 27

Chapter 2: Non-Functional Requirements 29

Technical requirements 29
Enabling scalability, availability, and resiliency with Azure and .NET 10 29
Creating a scalable web app in Azure • 30
Vertical scaling (scaling up) • 33
Horizontal scaling (scaling out) • 34
Creating a scalable web app with .NET 10 • 35
Performance issues to be considered when programming in C# 44
String concatenation • 45
Exceptions • 45
Multithreading environments for better results: do's and don'ts • 47
Usability – why inserting data takes too much time 49
Designing fast selection logic • 50
Selecting from a huge number of items • 51
Interoperability with .NET 52
Tip – creating a service in linux • 54
Achieving security by design 55
Practices for achieving a safe architecture • 56
Authentication • 56
Sensitive data • 57
Web security • 57
Summary 58
Questions 58
Further reading 59

Chapter 3: Managing Requirements 61

Technical requirements 62
Introducing Azure DevOps 62
Managing system requirements in Azure DevOps • 64
Epic work items • 65
Feature work items • 65
Product backlog items vs. user story work items • 66
Connecting requirements to delivery artifacts • 66
Azure DevOps repository • 66
Package feeds • 70

Test plans • 72
Pipelines • 73
Introducing GitHub projects 74
AI impact on managing and implementing requirements 80
Summary 82
Questions 82

Chapter 4: Best Practices in Coding C# 85

Technical requirements 85
Why simple code matters 86
Maintainability index • 87
Cyclomatic complexity • 87
Depth of inheritance • 92
Class coupling • 94
Number of lines of code • 95
Using a version control system 96
Using a version control system with AI support • 96
Dealing with version control systems in teams • 100
Writing safe code in C# 102
Try-catch • 102
Try-finally and using • 104
The IDisposable interface • 105
.NET 10 tips and tricks for coding 106
Identifying well-written code 108
Understanding and applying tools that can evaluate C# code • 109
Applying extension tools to analyze code • 113
Applying SonarQube for Visual Studio • 114
Checking the code after static analysis tools • 115
Applying GitHub Copilot to analyze code • 117
Summary 120
Questions 120
Further reading 121

Chapter 5: Implementing Code Reusability in C# 123

Technical requirements 123
Understanding the principles of code reusability 123
What code reuse is not • 124
What code reuse is • 125

Reusability in the development lifecycle • 127

Using .NET for code reuse **127**

Creating a reusable class library • 129

How does C# deal with code reuse? • 130

Object-oriented analysis • 130

Generics • 132

What if the code is not reusable? • 133

I have my libraries. How do I promote them? • 134

Documenting and publishing .NET libraries • 135

Documenting a web API using Swagger • 139

Summary **140**

Questions **140**

Further reading **140**

Chapter 6: Design Patterns and .NET Implementation 143

Technical requirements **143**

Understanding design patterns and their purposes **143**

SOLID principles as guardrails for design patterns **144**

Single responsibility • 144

Open-closed • 144

Liskov substitution principle • 144

Interface segregation • 145

Dependency inversion • 145

Presenting well-known design patterns **146**

Builder pattern • 146

Factory pattern • 148

Singleton pattern • 150

Proxy pattern • 153

Command pattern • 155

Publisher/Subscriber pattern • 157

Dependency injection pattern • 158

Understanding the design patterns available in .NET **160**

Cloud computing design patterns **161**

AI agents design patterns **162**

Summary **162**

Questions **163**

Further reading **163**

Chapter 7: Understanding the Different Domains in Software Solutions 165

Technical requirements 166
What are software domains? 166
Understanding domain-driven design 169
Relations among bounded contexts • 171
Entities • 172
Entity-level validation in .NET • 173
DDD entities in .NET • 174
Value objects • 176
Aggregates • 177
Domain events • 178
Common DDD patterns and architectures 178
Classic layered architecture • 179
Onion architecture • 180
Repository pattern • 184
Unit of work pattern • 185
Command query responsibility segregation (CQRS) pattern • 186
Event sourcing • 189
Command handlers and aggregate events • 189
Summary 192
Questions 193
Further reading 193

Chapter 8: Understanding DevSecOps Principles and CI/CD 195

Technical requirements 196
Describing DevSecOps 196
Service Design Thinking 197
Understanding DevSecOps principles 198
Continuous integration (CI) • 198
Continuous delivery (CD) • 199
Continuous security (CS) • 200
Insecure code applied in the repository • 201
Applying continuous production deployment with control • 201
Incomplete features • 203
An unstable solution for testing • 207
Continuous feedback (CF) • 211
Tools to facilitate DevSecOps implementation 212

Azure DevOps • 212
GitHub • 213
Application insights • 213
Summary ... 217
Questions ... 218

Chapter 9: Testing Your Enterprise Application 221

Technical requirements ... 222
Understanding test organization ... 222
Automating unit and integration tests • 223
Writing automated unit and integration tests • 224
Acceptance tests: writing functional and performance tests • 225
Understanding test-driven development ... 226
Functional tests ... 230
Behavior-Driven development (BDD) • 233
Defining C# test projects in Visual Studio ... 235
Using the xUnit test framework • 236
Advanced test preparation and teardown scenarios • 238
Mocking interfaces with Moq • 240
Automatic generation of tests: GitHub Copilot • 242
Automating functional tests in C# ... 242
Testing the staging application • 244
Testing the staging application with Selenium • 245
Testing a controlled application • 246
Recording tests with Selenium IDE • 248
Summary ... 249
Questions ... 250
Further reading ... 250

Chapter 10: Deciding on the Best Cloud-Based Solution 253

Technical requirements ... 253
Different software deployment models ... 254
IaaS and Azure opportunities ... 255
Security responsibilities in IaaS • 257
PaaS – a world of opportunities for developers ... 258
Web apps • 259
SQL databases • 259
SaaS – just sign in and get started! ... 262

Understanding what Serverless means 263
Comparing IaaS, PaaS, SaaS, and FaaS 264
Why are hybrid applications so useful in many cases? 265
Summary 266
Questions 266
Further reading 267

Chapter 11: Applying a Microservice Architecture to Your Enterprise Application 269

Technical requirements 269
What are microservices? 270
Microservices and the evolution of the concept of modules • 272
Microservices design principles • 274
The independence of design choices • 274
Independence from the deployment environment • 275
Loose coupling • 275
No chained requests/responses • 276
When do microservices help? • 279
Layered architectures and microservices • 280
When is it worth considering microservices architectures? • 284
Containers and Docker • 285
How does .NET deal with microservices? 287
.NET communication facilities 288
Resilient task execution • 289
Using hosts in .NET • 292
Visual Studio support for Docker • 297
Analyzing the Docker file • 298
Publishing the project • 299
Which tools are needed to manage microservices? 301
Interacting with a container registry • 301
Summary 302
Questions 302
Further reading 303

Part 2: Technologies and Programming Solutions 305

Chapter 12: How to Choose Your Data Storage in the Cloud 307

Technical requirements 308

Repository options for different purposes 308

Relational databases • 309

NoSQL databases • 312

Redis • 314

Azure storage accounts • 315

Choosing between SQL and NoSQL document-oriented databases 316

Azure Cosmos DB – an opportunity to manage a multi-continental database 319

Creating an Azure Cosmos DB account • 320

Creating an Azure Cosmos container • 321

Accessing Azure Cosmos data • 323

Defining database consistency • 324

The Cosmos DB client • 328

The Cosmos DB Entity Framework Core provider • 329

Summary 330

Questions 330

Further reading 331

Subscribe to Deep Engineering 332

Chapter 13: Interacting with Data in C# – Entity Framework Core 333

Technical requirements 334

Understanding ORM basics 334

Configuring Entity Framework Core 337

Defining DB entities • 338

Defining the mapped collections • 341

Completing the mapping configuration • 342

Entity Framework Core migrations 346

Understanding stored procedures and direct SQL commands • 349

Compiled models 350

Querying and updating data with Entity Framework Core 351

Returning query results to the outer layer • 355

How to turn Entity Framework Core entities into aggregates • 357

Issuing direct SQL commands • 359

Handling transactions • 361

Deploying your data layer 361

Entity Framework Core and NoSQL databases: the Cosmos DB provider 363

Understanding Entity Framework Core advanced features 364

Summary 367

Questions 367

Further reading 367

Chapter 14: Implementing Microservices with .NET 369

Technical requirements 370

Communication and data serialization 371

Efficient and flexible binary serialization • 373

Protobuf serialization • 380

Efficient and flexible RPC • 381

Reliable data-driven asynchronous communication • 384

Distributed transactions • 386

Implementing worker microservices with ASP.NET Core 389

Implementing microservices with .NET worker services and message brokers 393

Installing RabbitMQ • 393

RabbitMQ basics • 394

Replacing internal queues with RabbitMQ • 395

Summary 399

Questions 400

Further reading 400

Chapter 15: Applying Service-Oriented Architectures with .NET 401

Technical requirements 402

Understanding the principles of the SOA approach 402

SOAP and REST Web services 405

SOAP Web services • 405

SOAP specifications • 406

The turning point toward the new REST standard • 408

REST web services • 408

Service type compatibility rules • 409

REST and native HTTP features • 410

Example of methods in the REST language • 413

The OpenAPI standard • 413

REST services authentication and authorization • 414

API versioning • 415

How does .NET 10 deal with SOA? 416

SOAP client support • 416

gRPC support • 417

REST services and ASP.NET Core • 418

Implementing REST services with ASP.NET Core • 419

ASP.NET Core service authorization • 423
ASP.NET Core support for OpenAPI • 425
.NET HTTP clients • 427
Summary 431
Questions 431
Further reading 432

Chapter 16: Presenting ASP.NET Core 433

Technical requirements 434
Understanding the presentation layers of web applications 434
Understanding the basics of ASP.NET Core 435
ASP.NET Core middleware • 436
Loading configuration data and using it with the options framework • 440
Default configuration files • 440
Other configuration sources • 441
Setting the environment name • 442
Using publish profiles and project files • 443
Accessing the environment at runtime • 444
Mapping configuration to .NET objects • 445
Defining the ASP.NET Core pipeline • 446
Defining controllers and ViewModels • 449
Understanding how ASP.NET Core MVC creates the response HTML 454
Razor Views • 454
Learning the Razor flow of control statements • 456
Understanding Razor View properties • 458
Using Razor tag helpers • 459
Reusing view code • 464
Layouts – Shared page structure • 464
Partial Views – Reusable HTML fragments • 466
View Components – Reusable components with logic • 467
Understanding the connection between ASP.NET Core MVC and design principles 468
Advantages of ASP.NET Core pipeline • 469
Server-side and client-side validation • 470
ASP.NET Core globalization • 471
The MVC pattern • 475
Summary 477
Questions 477
Further reading 477

Chapter 17: Implementing Frontend Microservices with ASP.NET Core 479

Technical requirements ... 480

Frontends and micro-frontends ... 480

Public web APIs • 481

HTML micro-frontends • 483

Defining the microservice architecture ... 485

Defining the Domain Layer ... 488

Defining the DB driver ... 490

Defining the application services ... 493

Defining the authentication strategy ... 495

Defining controllers ... 497

Summary ... 498

Questions ... 498

Further reading ... 498

Chapter 18: Client Frameworks: Blazor 501

Technical requirements ... 502

Comparison of the various types of client technology ... 502

Single-Page Applications • 503

Progressive Applications • 504

Native Applications • 505

Cross-platform Applications • 505

How to choose the Client Technology for your Application. • 505

Blazor WebAssembly architecture ... 506

Blazor and single-page applications • 507

Loading and starting the application • 509

Routing • 511

Blazor pages and components ... 514

Component structure • 514

Templates and cascading parameters • 519

Error handling • 522

Events • 523

Bindings • 525

How Blazor updates HTML • 527

Component lifecycle • 528

Blazor forms and validation ... 530

Modifying HTML content from Blazor components ... 533

Blazor advanced features 534

References to components and HTML elements • 535

JavaScript interoperability • 535

Globalization and Localization • 537

Authentication and Authorization • 538

Communication with the server • 542

AOT compilation • 544

Third-party tools for Blazor WebAssembly • 545

.NET MAUI Blazor 546

What is .NET MAUI? • 546

Developing native applications with Blazor 547

Summary 550

Questions 550

Further reading 550

Chapter 19: Orchestrators and .NET Aspire 553

Technical requirements 554

A Primer on Orchestrators 554

Why and how orchestrators use containers • 555

How orchestrators handle microservice replicas and their network addresses • 556

How orchestrators handle permanent storage • 557

How orchestrators ensure resiliency and zero downtime • 558

How orchestrators interface with the external world • 559

The most popular orchestrators • 559

Orchestrating your Microservices with Kubernetes 561

Kubernetes basics • 561

.YAML files • 563

ReplicaSets and Deployments • 564

StatefulSets • 566

Services • 567

Ingresses • 569

Using Docker Desktop Kubernetes and Kubectl • 572

Advanced Kubernetes concepts • 573

Requiring permanent storage • 573

Kubernetes secrets • 574

Liveness and readiness checks • 576

Developing Microservice applications with .NET Aspire 578

Service Discovery and its Role in .NET Aspire. • 582

Resources Integration and Automatic Resources Configuration • 585
Application Telemetry • 587
Configuring Microservices and Resources • 589
Deploying a .NET Aspire Project • 592
Summary 594
Questions 594
Further reading 594

Chapter 20: Securing Data and Applications 597

Technical requirements 597
A Primer on Cryptography 597
Encrypting for privacy • 600
Digital signature: preventing unauthorized modification • 601
Proof of identity and chains of certificate authorities • 602
Keeping our encryption safe • 604
Securing communications 604
Using server certificates with Kestrel • 606
Using client certificates with .NET HttpClient • 609
Preventing the execution of malicious scripts in the browser • 610
Authentication and Authorization 612
Tokens and Claims • 612
Cookie-based authentication • 616
Handling cookie authentication in ASP.NET Core • 617
Web token authentication • 618
Handling web token authentication in ASP.NET Core • 620
Client certificate authentication • 622
Handling client certificate authentication in ASP.NET Core • 622
OAuth authentication • 625
Handling OAuth authentication in ASP.NET Core • 627
Encrypting database fields in the Cloud 629
Summary 630
Questions 630
Further reading 630

Chapter 21: Hardening Cloud-Based Solutions 633

What is hardening and why does it matter in the cloud? 634
Hardening and Compliance 634
Shared responsibility drives hardening priorities 635

Establish a secure baseline with a landing zone 637
Organizational Structure • 637
Identity Baseline • 638
Logging Baseline • 638
Network Baseline • 639
Runtime hardening by the computing model • 640
Misconfiguration management and drift control using IaC 641
Incident readiness and operational resilience 642
Summary 643
Questions 643
Further reading 644

Chapter 22: Case Study: Practical Usage of .NET Aspire 645

Technical requirements 645
Introducing World Wild Travel Club 645
User needs and system requirements 647
Customer experience • 647
Expert collaboration • 647
Administrative operations • 647
Scalability and performance • 648
Security and compliance • 648
Localization and accessibility • 648
Main types of .NET projects used at WWTravelClub 648
Managing WWTravelClub requirements using GitHub 650
Code standard for WWTravelClub - DOs and DON'Ts when writing code 655
Applying SonarCloud at WWTravelClub APIs 656
Reusing code as a fast way to deliver good and safe software 659
Understanding the domains of the WWTravelClub application 660
The WWTravelClub DevSecOps approach 662
How to Choose Your Data Storage in the Cloud 663
Worker microservice based on RabbitMQ 664
Exposing WWTravelClub packages using Web APIs 673
A worker microservice with ASP.NET Core 679
The specifications and architecture • 679
The Domain Layer • 680
The DB driver • 684
Application services • 688
The Outermost Layer • 690

Processing the queued requests • 693
Testing the gRPC Microservice project with a fake purchase request generator • 696
A Frontend Microservice **699**
Defining application specifications • 699
Defining the application architecture • 700
The Domain Model • 703
Domain Services • 706
The DB driver • 706
Defining the application services • 711
Defining the ASP.NET Core MVC outermost layer • 714
Packages Management globalization • 715
PackageManagement authentication and authorization • 715
Defining controllers and views • 720
Using Client Technologies **724**
Preparing the solution • 724
Implementing the required ASP.NET Core REST APIs • 726
Implementing the client-side business logic in a service • 730
Implementing the user interface • 731
Adding a Blazor MAUI Version • 734
Testing the WWTravelClub application **735**
Testing a Worker microservice with .NET Aspire **738**
Deploying a Worker microservice on Kubernetes **742**
Creating Docker images • 743
Pushing images into Docker Kubernetes • 744
Defining Kubernetes objects • 744
Summary **748**

Part 3: Appendices 749

Chapter A: Answers 751

Chapter 1 .... **751**
Chapter 2 .... **752**
Chapter 3 .... **752**
Chapter 4 .... **753**
Chapter 5 .... **754**
Chapter 6 .... **756**
Chapter 7 .... **757**
Chapter 8 .... **757**

Chapter 9 759
Chapter 10 759
Chapter 11 760
Chapter 12 760
Chapter 13 761
Chapter 14 762
Chapter 15 763
Chapter 16 763
Chapter 17 764
Chapter 18 764
Chapter 19 764
Chapter 20 765
Chapter 21 765

Chapter B: Unlock Your Exclusive Benefits 767

Unlock this Book's Free Benefits in 3 Easy Steps 768

Other Books You May Enjoy 772

Subscribe to Deep Engineering 775

Index 777

Preface

This book is a practical guide to designing, building, securing, and delivering modern cloud-based and distributed applications with C# and .NET. It brings together the architectural patterns, engineering practices, and platform technologies needed to create enterprise applications that are scalable, resilient, maintainable, and secure.

You will begin with the foundations of software architecture, including architectural thinking, requirement analysis, and coding best practices. From there, the book explores the principles and techniques that shape successful enterprise systems, such as design patterns, Domain-Driven Design, testing strategies, and DevSecOps. It also examines key architectural styles, including layered architecture, onion architecture, service-oriented architecture, microservices, single-page applications, and cloud-native architecture, helping you understand when and how to apply each one to real business scenarios.

The book then moves from principles to implementation, covering the frameworks and tools that support modern distributed development in .NET. You will work with ASP.NET Core, Entity Framework Core, cloud data technologies, frontend microservices, and Blazor for building both browser-based and native client applications. You will also learn how to design, deploy, and operate distributed systems in modern cloud environments using containers, Kubernetes, orchestration technologies, and Azure.

This fifth edition expands the book with three important new chapters focused on some of the most relevant challenges in modern enterprise development. You will explore orchestrators with .NET Aspire to understand how distributed applications are configured, coordinated, observed, and prepared for deployment. You will learn how to secure applications and data through authentication, authorization, encryption, and transport security. You will also discover how to harden cloud-based solutions by applying secure baselines, identity controls, infrastructure automation, and operational safeguards that reduce risk in production environments.

Another important theme throughout this edition is the role of AI in the software development process. Modern software delivery increasingly involves AI-assisted tools that can support analysis, design, coding, testing, review, and documentation. This book reflects that shift by discussing the application of AI in contemporary software engineering practice, while emphasizing the importance of critical thinking, sound architectural judgment, and responsible adoption.

Throughout the book, the focus remains firmly on practical application. Rather than treating software architecture as a purely theoretical discipline, the chapters show how architectural decisions influence the success of software products in real projects. All concepts are reinforced through realistic scenarios and a case study that brings together the patterns, tools, and techniques discussed across the book in the implementation of a modern enterprise solution.

Fully updated for C# 14 and .NET 10, this edition features improved code samples, clearer explanations, and broader coverage of today's development landscape. By the end of the book, you will be able to design, develop, secure, and deliver enterprise-ready .NET applications that align with business goals and modern cloud practices, and you will be equipped to build robust software systems for today's distributed, cloud-first, and increasingly AI-assisted world.

Who this book is for

This book is for engineers and senior developers who are aspiring to become architects or wish to build enterprise applications with the .NET stack. It is also for any software architect who wishes to improve their knowledge related to enterprise solutions based on .NET and C#. Notably, experience with C# and .NET is required.

What this book covers

Chapter 1, Understanding the Importance of Software Architecture, explains the basics of software architecture. This chapter will give you the right mindset to face customer requirements and then select the right tools, patterns, and frameworks.

Chapter 2, Non-Functional Requirements, guides you in an important stage of application development, that is, collecting and accounting for all constraints and goals that the application must fulfill, such as availability, scalability, resiliency, performance, multithreading, interoperability, and security.

Chapter 3, Managing Requirements, describes techniques for managing requirements, bugs, and other information about your applications. While most of the concepts are general, the chapter focuses on the usage of Azure DevOps and GitHub.

Chapter 4, Best Practices in Coding C#, describes best practices to be followed when developing .NET applications with C#, including metrics that evaluate the quality of your software and how to measure them with the help of all the tools included in Visual Studio.

Chapter 5, Implementing Code Reusability in C#, describes patterns and best practices to maximize code reusability in your .NET applications with C#. It also discusses the importance of code refactoring.

Chapter 6, Design Patterns and .NET Implementation, describes common software patterns with .NET 10 examples. Here, you will learn the importance of patterns and best practices for using them.

Chapter 7, Understanding the Different Domains in Software Solutions, describes the modern Domain-Driven Design software production methodology, and related design patterns and architectures. There you will also learn how to use it to face complex applications that require several knowledge domains, and how to use it to take advantage of cloud and microservices-based architectures.

Chapter 8, Understanding DevSecOps Principles and CI/CD, describes the DevSecOps basis for software development and evolution, also guaranteeing continuous security. Here, you will learn how to organize your application's continuous integration/continuous security/continuous delivery cycle, discussing the opportunities and difficulties for reaching this scenario. It also describes how to automate the whole deployment process, from the creation of a new release in your source repository, through various testing and approval steps, to the final deployment of the application in the actual production environment. Here, you will learn how to use GitHub Actions to automate the whole deployment process.

Chapter 9, Testing Your Enterprise Application, describes how to test your applications. The various kinds of tests that must be included in the development lifecycle, and the test-driven development methodology. Here, you will learn also how to test .NET Core applications with xUnit and see how easily you can develop and maintain code that satisfies your specifications with the help of test-driven design. Here you will learn also how to use functional tests to verify automatically whether a version of a whole application conforms to the agreed functional specifications, and how to automate the functional tests with Selenium.

Chapter 10, Deciding on the Best Cloud-Based Solution, gives you a wide overview of the tools and resources available in the cloud, and more specifically, on Microsoft Azure. Here, you will learn how to search for the right tools and resources and how to configure them to fulfill your needs.

Chapter 11, Applying a Microservice Architecture to Your Enterprise Application, offers a broad overview of microservices and Docker containers. Here, you will learn how microservices-based architecture takes advantage of all the opportunities offered by the cloud, and you will see how to use microservices to achieve flexibility, high throughput, reliability, and selective maintenance. You will learn how to use containers and Docker to mix different technologies in your architecture, as well as make your software platform independent.

Chapter 12, How to Choose Your Data Storage in the Cloud, analyzes when to use a relational database and when to use a NoSQL database. Then it describes the main storage engines available in the cloud and in Microsoft Azure. Here, you will learn how to choose the best storage engines to achieve the read/write parallelism you need, how to configure them, and how to interact with them from your C# code.

Chapter 13, Interacting with Data in C# – Entity Framework Core, explains in detail how your application can interact with various storage engines with the help of Object-Relational Mappings (ORMs) and, in particular, with Entity Framework Core.

Chapter 14, Implementing Microservices with .NET, describes how to implement a worker microservice with .NET in practice, and how to design communication among microservices. There you will also learn how to use the gRPC communication protocol and the RabbitMQ message broker on your .NET projects.

Chapter 15, Applying Service-Oriented Architectures with .NET, describes service-oriented architecture, which enables you to expose the functionalities of your applications as endpoints on the web or on a private network so that users can interact with them through various types of clients. Here, you will learn how to implement service-oriented architecture endpoints with ASP.NET Core and how to self-document them with existing Open API packages.

Chapter 16, Presenting ASP.NET Core, describes in detail the whole ASP.NET Core framework. Here, you will learn also how to implement web applications based on the Model-View-Controller (MVC) pattern.

Chapter 17, Implementing Frontend Microservices with ASP.NET Core, is dedicated to frontend microservices, that is, to the microservices that fill the role of interacting with the world outside of the application. There, you will learn in detail how to implement a frontend microservice based on ASP.NET Core.

Chapter 18, Client Frameworks: Blazor, describes the various client technologies for implementing presentation layers. The chapter focuses on and describes in detail both the browser-based Blazor WebAssembly and the .NET MAUI-based native Blazor. Here you will learn how to implement single-page applications and native applications in C#.

Chapter 19, Orchestrators and .NET Aspire, explains how modern microservice applications are deployed, coordinated, and tested in distributed environments. The chapter introduces the role of orchestrators, with particular attention to Kubernetes, describing how they manage replicas, networking, storage, resiliency, and external access. It then focuses on .NET Aspire as a powerful development-time framework for simulating orchestration locally, configuring microservices and resources, enabling service discovery and telemetry, and preparing applications for deployment to platforms such as Kubernetes and Azure Container Apps.

Chapter 20, Securing Data and Applications, discusses the main security concerns of enterprise software and explains how to address them in .NET applications. The chapter begins with the fundamentals of cryptography, showing how encryption, digital signatures, and certificates can be used to guarantee privacy, integrity, and proof of identity. It then describes how to secure communications with TLS and mTLS, how to manage authentication and authorization in ASP.NET Core using cookies, JWTs, client certificates, and OAuth, and finally how to protect sensitive cloud data through database field encryption.

Chapter 21, Hardening Cloud-Based Solutions, explains how to secure cloud environments by reducing attack surface and enforcing safer defaults. The chapter discusses why hardening is essential in modern cloud systems, how responsibilities differ across IaaS, PaaS, Kubernetes, and serverless models, and how secure baselines can be established through landing zones, identity controls, logging, and network restrictions. It also describes how Infrastructure as Code helps prevent misconfigurations and drift and concludes with guidance on incident readiness and operational resilience to ensure cloud solutions remain secure and reliable over time.

Chapter 22, Case Study: Practical Usage of .NET Aspire, is dedicated to the book travel agency case study, which shows how technologies and architectural patterns learned in the book can be used in practice in the implementation of a microservice-based enterprise application using .NET Aspire.

To get the most out of this book

- Inform the reader of the things that they need to know before they start: spell out what knowledge you are assuming. Tell the reader anything they need to know before they start.
- Any additional installation and information they need for getting set up.

Download the example code files

The code bundle for the book is hosted on GitHub at . We also have other code bundles from our rich catalog of books and videos available at `https://github.com/PacktPublishing`. Check them out!

Download the color images

We also provide a PDF file that has color images of the screenshots/diagrams used in this book. You can download it here: `https://packt.link/gbp/978-1-80666-355-2`

> **Note**
>
> **Please note:** Some images in this book are intended primarily for visual representation purposes. Higher-resolution or zoomed-in versions of these figures are available in the accompanying image bundle for improved readability.

Conventions used

There are a number of text conventions used throughout this book.

`CodeInText`: Indicates code words in text, database table names, folder names, filenames, file extensions, pathnames, dummy URLs, user input, and Twitter handles. For example: " Asynchronous programming lets you do this simply, by giving you the keywords `async` and `await`."

A block of code is set as follows:

```
StreamWriter file = new StreamWriter(@"C:\sample.txt");
file.WriteLine("Just writing a simple line");
```

Any command-line input or output is written as follows:

```
sudo cp sample.service /lib/systemd/system
sudo systemctl daemon-reload
sudo systemctl enable sample
```

Bold: Indicates a new term, an important word, or words that you see on the screen. For instance, words in menus or dialog boxes appear in the text like this. For example: " One key practice is to define an **authentication method** for your web app."

> **Note**
>
> Warnings or important notes appear like this.

> **Tip**
>
> Tips and tricks appear like this.

Get in touch

Feedback from our readers is always welcome.

General feedback: If you have questions about any aspect of this book or have any general feedback, please email us at `customercare@packt.com` and mention the book's title in the subject of your message.

Errata: Although we have taken every care to ensure the accuracy of our content, mistakes do happen. If you have found a mistake in this book, we would be grateful if you reported this to us. Please visit `http://www.packt.com/submit-errata`, click **Submit Errata**, and fill in the form.

Piracy: If you come across any illegal copies of our works in any form on the internet, we would be grateful if you would provide us with the location address or website name. Please contact us at `copyright@packt.com` with a link to the material.

If you are interested in becoming an author: If there is a topic that you have expertise in and you are interested in either writing or contributing to a book, please visit `http://authors.packt.com`.

Free benefits with your book

This book comes with free benefits to support your learning. Activate them now for instant access (see the "*How to Unlock*" section for instructions).

Here's a quick overview of what you can instantly unlock with your purchase:

DRM-Free PDF Version

Download DRM-free PDF and ePub copies of this book.

7-Day Packt Library Access

Get 7-day unlimited access to 8,000+ books and videos. No credit card required.

Available for first-time Packt+ trial users only.

Next-Gen Reader Access

Read this book on Packt Reader with progress sync, dark mode and note-taking.

How to Unlock

Scan the QR code (or go to packtpub.com/unlock). Search for this book by name, confirm the edition, and then follow the steps on the page.

UNLOCK NOW

Note: Keep your invoice handy. Purchases made directly from Packt don't require one

Join us on Discord!

Read this book alongside other users, developers, experts, and the author himself.

Ask questions, provide solutions to other readers, chat with the authors via Ask Me Anything sessions, and much more. Scan the QR or visit the link to join the community.

Share your thoughts

Once you've read *Software Architecture with C# 14 and .NET 10*, we'd love to hear your thoughts! Scan the QR code below to go straight to the Amazon review page for this book and share your feedback.

https://packt.link/r/1806663554

Your review is important to us and the tech community and will help us make sure we're delivering excellent quality content.

Part 1

Organizational, Architectural, and Design Principles

In this first part of the book, you'll develop a solid understanding of the architectural and design principles of modern enterprise applications. By the end of this part of the book, you'll have the knowledge needed to start a new enterprise project, namely the best practices to follow, how to collect requirements, how to organize the teamwork, and how to architect the application.

This part of the book includes the following chapters:

- *Chapter 1, Understanding the Importance of Software Architecture*
- *Chapter 2, Non-Functional Requirements*
- *Chapter 3, Managing Requirements*
- *Chapter 4, Best Practices in Coding C#*
- *Chapter 5, Implementing Code Reusability in C#*
- *Chapter 6, Design Patterns and .NET Implementation*
- *Chapter 7, Understanding the Different Domains in Software Solutions*
- *Chapter 8, Understanding DevSecOps Principles and CI/CD*
- *Chapter 9, Testing Your Enterprise Application*
- *Chapter 10, Deciding on the Best Cloud-Based Solution*
- *Chapter 11, Applying a Microservice Architecture to Your Enterprise Application*

1

Understanding the Importance of Software Architecture

The need to keep the focus on creating effective enterprise solutions continuously increases. Users always need more new features in their applications. Moreover, the need to deliver frequent application versions (due to a quickly changing market) increases our obligation to utilize sophisticated software architecture and development techniques.

Considering this scenario, the following topics will be covered in this chapter:

- What software architecture is
- Software development process models that can help you as a software architect
- Gathering the right information to design high-quality software
- Design techniques for helping in the development process
- The impact of requirements on system results

By the end of the chapter, you will understand exactly what the mission of software architecture is. You will learn what Azure is and how to create your own account on the platform. In addition, you will gain an overview of a variety of software processes, models, and techniques that will enable you to lead your team.

> **Note**
>
> **Your purchase includes a free PDF copy + exclusive extras**
>
> Your purchase includes a DRM-free PDF copy of this book, 7-day trial to the Packt+ library (no credit card required), and additional exclusive extras. See the *Free benefits with your book* section in the *Preface* to unlock them instantly and maximize your learning.

What is software architecture?

For the fact that you are reading this book today, you should thank the computer scientists who decided to consider software development as an engineering area. This happened in the last century, more specifically at the end of the sixties, when they proposed that how we develop software should be quite like the way we construct buildings. That is why we have the name **software architecture**.

Software architecture is the set of fundamental design decisions that define a software system's structure and behavior. It describes the system's major building blocks (components/services), how they communicate, how data flows, and the key constraints and quality attributes the solution must satisfy, such as performance, security, availability, scalability, maintainability, and cost.

Just as an architect designs a building and oversees its construction based on that design, the main goal of a software architect is to ensure that the software application is implemented well, and good implementation requires the design of a great architectural solution.

In a professional development project, you must accomplish the following tasks:

- Define the customer requirements for the solution
- Design a great solution to meet those requirements
- Implement the designed solution
- Test the solution implementation
- Validate the solution with your customer
- Deliver the solution in the working environment
- Maintain the solution afterward

Software engineering defines these activities as the fundamentals of the **software development lifecycle** (SDLC). All the theoretical software development process models (waterfall, spiral, incremental, agile, and so on) relate somehow to this cycle. No matter which model you use, if you do not perform the essential tasks in the initial stages of your project, you will not deliver an acceptable software solution.

Designing great solutions is foundational to the purpose of this book. You must understand that great real-world solutions bring with them some fundamental constraints:

- The solution needs to meet user requirements
- The solution needs to be delivered on time
- The solution needs to adhere to the project budget
- The solution needs to deliver good quality
- The solution needs to guarantee safe and effective future evolution

Great solutions need to be sustainable, and sustainability comes from architecture first, and modern tools and environments make it possible to shape that architecture around real user needs.

For this reason, this book will use some great tools provided by Microsoft. We decided to write the book to always follow the **long-term support** (LTS) versions, and that is why we are now applying all the examples using .NET 10. This is the third LTS version as a unified platform for software development, and it gives us a great opportunity to create fantastic solutions.

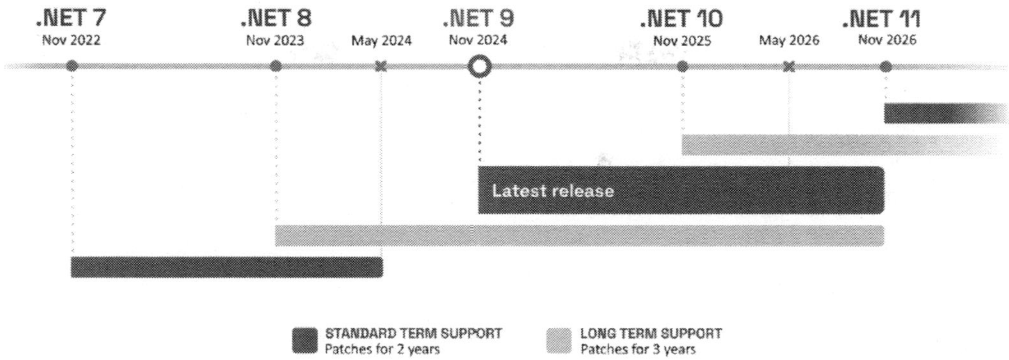

Figure 1.1: .NET support

As you can see in *Figure 1.1*, .NET 10 is delivered together with **C# 14**. It was released in November 2025, and it will provide support for 3 years, since it is an LTS version. The .NET approach of targeting many platforms and devices means that C# is now one of the most widely used programming languages in the world, running on everything from small devices up to huge servers, on different operating systems and in different environments.

> **Note**
>
> You can check details about the popularity of C# at `https://dotnet.microsoft.com/en-us/languages/csharp`

The book will also use **Microsoft Azure**, Microsoft's cloud platform, where you will find all the components the company provides to build advanced cloud-based software architecture solutions.

It is worth mentioning that the use of .NET 10 with Azure was just the option chosen by the authors. .NET can work just as well using other cloud providers, and Azure can handle other coding frameworks very well.

To be a software architect, you need to be familiar with these technologies, and many others too. This book will guide you on a journey where, as a software architect working in a team, you will learn how to deliver optimal solutions using these tools. Let us start this journey by creating your Azure account.

Creating an Azure account

During the entire book, we will need a Microsoft Azure Account to help us understand the technical aspects presented in the material. For this reason, we will guide you in creating it. Microsoft Azure is one of the best cloud solutions currently on the market. Inside Azure we find a broad range of components to help us define the architecture of twenty-first-century solutions.

> **Tip**
>
> If you want to check Azure's current state, structure, and updates in a compact, digestible way, just go to `https://azurecharts.com/`, developed by Alexey Polkovnikov. The content is continuously updated so you can revisit it to learn, evaluate, or even just have fun with the dozens of Azure components described in this Azure encyclopedia.

This subsection will guide you in creating an Azure account. If you already have one, you can skip this part:

1. First, go to `https://azure.microsoft.com`. There you will find the information you need to start your subscription. Translation to your native language is usually set automatically.
2. Once you have accessed this portal, it is possible to sign up. If you have never done this before, it is possible to **Start free**, so you will be able to use some Azure features without spending any money. Please check the options for free plans at `https://azure.microsoft.com/free/`.
3. The process of creating a free account is quite simple; you will be guided by a form that requires you to have a **Microsoft account** or **GitHub account**.
4. During the process, you will also be asked for a credit card number to verify your identity and to keep out spam and bots. However, you will not be charged unless you upgrade the account
5. To finish the task, you will need to accept the subscription agreement, offer details, and privacy statement
6. Once you have finished filling out the form, you will be able to access the Azure portal. As you can see in the following screenshot, the panel shows a dashboard that you can customize, and a menu on the left, where you can set up the Azure components you are going to use in your solution. Throughout this book, we will come back to this screen to set up the components needed to help us create modern software architecture. To find the next page, just select the hamburger menu icon and click on **All services**.

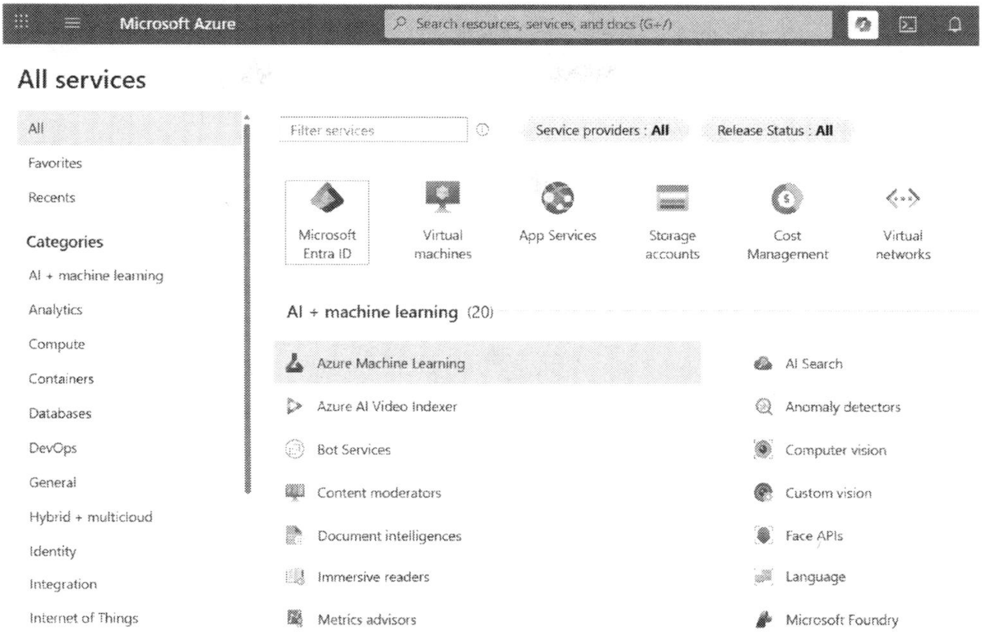

Figure 1.2: The Azure portal

Once you have created your Azure account, you are ready to find out how a software architect can lead a team to develop software, taking advantage of all the opportunities offered by Azure. *Figure 1.2* presents all available services provided by Microsoft Azure. However, it is important to keep in mind that a software architect needs to go beyond just technological choices, because they are expected to define how the software will be delivered.

Today, a software architect not only designs the overall structure and technical basis of a software solution but also determines how the whole software development and deployment process is conducted. The next section will cover some of the most widely used software development paradigms. We will start by describing what the community refers to as traditional software engineering. After that, we will cover the agile models that have changed the way we build software over the past 25 years.

Software development process models

As a software architect, it is important for you to understand some of the common development processes currently used in most enterprises. A software development process defines how people in a team produce and deliver software. In general, this process relates to a software engineering theory called a **software development process model**. Ever since software development was first defined as an engineering process, many process models for developing software have been proposed. Because architecture is shaped not only by technical decisions but also by how work is planned, built, reviewed, and released, choosing a development process becomes part of the software architect's responsibility. Let us review the traditional software models and then look at the agile ones that are currently common.

Reviewing traditional software development process models

Some of the models introduced in software engineering theory are already considered traditional and obsolete. This book does not aim to cover all of them, but here we will give a brief explanation of two that are still used in some companies: the **waterfall model** and **incremental model**.

Understanding the waterfall model

This topic may appear strange in a software architecture book from 2026, but yes, you may still find companies where the most traditional software process models remain the basis for software development. This process executes all fundamental tasks in sequence, resolving software development projects into the following steps:

1. ***Requirements***: where a product requirements document is created, which forms the basis for the software development process
2. ***Design***: where the software architecture is developed according to the requirements
3. ***Implementation***: where the software is programmed
4. ***Verification***: where tests are performed on the application
5. ***Maintenance***: where the cycle starts again after delivery

Let us look at a diagrammatic representation of this:

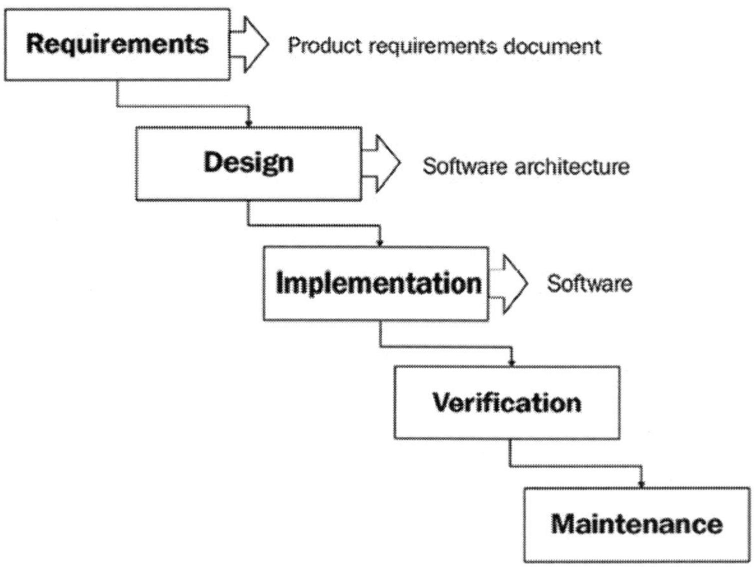

Figure 1.3: The waterfall development cycle (https://en.wikipedia.org/wiki/Waterfall_model)

Often, the use of waterfall models causes problems such as delays in the delivery of a functional version of the software and user dissatisfaction due to the gap between expectations and final product delivery. In addition, in our experience, having application tests start only after the completion of development always feels terribly stressful.

Analyzing the incremental model

Incremental development is an approach that tries to overcome the biggest problem of the waterfall model: the user can test the solution only at the end of the project. The idea of this model is to give the users opportunities to interact with the solution as early as possible so that they can give useful feedback, which will help during the development of the software.

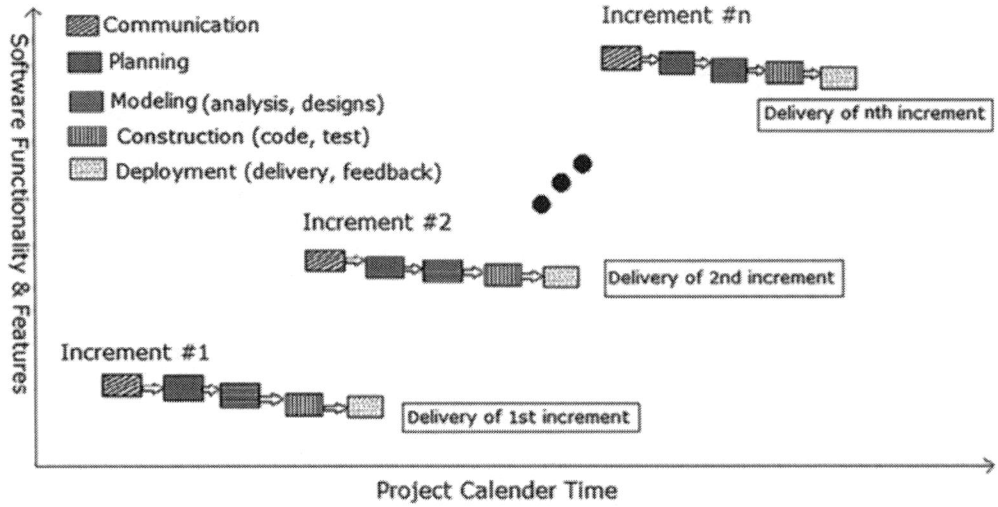

Figure 1.4: The incremental development cycle (https://en.wikipedia.org/wiki/Incremental_build_model)

The idea of the model, presented in *Figure 1.4*, is to run for each increment a set of practices related to software development (*communication*, *planning*, *modeling*, *construction*, and *deployment*). Although it mitigated problems related to the lack of communication with the customer, fewer increments were still a problem for big projects because the increments were still too long.

When the incremental approach was used on a large scale – mainly at the end of the last century – many problems related to project bureaucracy were reported, due to the large amount of documentation required. This clunky scenario brought about the rise of a very important movement in the software development industry: **agile**.

Understanding agile software development process models

At the beginning of this century, developing software was considered one of the most chaotic activities in engineering. The percentage of software projects that failed was incredibly high, and this fact proved the need for a different approach to dealing with the flexibility required by software development projects.

In 2001, the **Agile Manifesto** was introduced to the world, and from that time forward various agile process models were proposed. Some of them have survived up to now and are still very common.

> **Note**
>
> The Agile Manifesto has been translated into more than 60 languages. You can check it out at `https://agilemanifesto.org/`.

One of the biggest differences between agile models and traditional models is the way developers interact with the customer. The message behind all agile models is that the faster you deliver software to the user, the better. This idea is sometimes confusing for software developers who understand this as – *Let's try coding, and that's all, folks!*

However, there is an important observation included in the Agile Manifesto that many people do not read when they start working with agile: "*That is, while there is value in the items on the right, we value the items on the left more.*"

Figure 1.5: Manifesto for Agile Software Development

A software architect always needs to remember this: Individuals, interactions, working software, customer collaboration, and responding to change certainly are the most important aspects while developing software. At the same time, agile is inherently disciplined, so processes and tools, right-sized documentation, contract negotiation, and planning still matter. Moreover, when you use the agile process, you will quickly understand that there is no way to develop good software without discipline. On the other hand, as a software architect, you need to understand that *soft* means flexibility. A software project that refuses to be flexible tends to ruin itself over time.

The 12 principles behind agile are foundational to this flexible approach:

1. Continuously delivering valuable software to satisfy the customer must be the highest priority of any developer
2. Changing requirements need to be understood as an opportunity to make the customer more competitive
3. Use a weekly timescale to deliver software
4. A software team must be composed of businesspeople and developers
5. A software team needs to be trusted and should have the correct environment to get the project done

6. The best way to communicate with a software team is face to face
7. You can see the greatest software team achievement when the software is really working in production
8. Agile works properly when it delivers sustainable development
9. The more you invest in techniques and good design, the more agile you are
10. Simplicity is essential
11. The more self-organized the teams are, the better-quality delivery you will have
12. Software teams tend to improve their behavior from time to time, analyzing and adjusting their process

Almost 25 years after the launch of the Agile Manifesto, its importance, and connection to the current needs of software teams remain intact. Certainly, there are many companies where this approach is not fully accepted, but as a software architect, you should regard this as an opportunity to transform practices and evolve the team you are working with.

There are many techniques and models that have been presented to the software community with the agile approach. The following subsections will discuss **lean software development**, **extreme programming**, and **Scrum**, so that you can decide as a software architect which ones you might adopt to improve your software delivery.

Lean software development

After the Agile Manifesto, the approach of lean software development was introduced to the community as an adaptation of a well-known movement in automobile engineering, Toyota's model for building cars. The lean manufacturing method delivers a high level of quality even with few resources.

Mary and Tom Poppendieck mapped the following seven lean principles for software development, closely connected to agile and to the approach of many companies this century:

1. ***Eliminate waste***: You may consider waste to be anything that will interfere with the delivery of the real needs of the customer
2. ***Build quality in***: An organization that wants to guarantee quality needs to promote it in processes from the very beginning, instead of only considering it when code is being tested
3. ***Create knowledge***: All companies that have achieved excellence have a common pattern of generating new knowledge by disciplined experimentation, documenting the resulting knowledge, and guaranteeing that it is spread across the organization
4. ***Defer commitment***: Plan decisions at the latest possible moment without causing damage to the project
5. ***Deliver fast***: The faster you deliver software, the more elimination of waste you have. Companies that compete using time frequency have significant advantages over their competitors.
6. ***Respect people***: Giving reasonable objectives to the team, together with plans that will guide them to self-organize their routine, is a matter of respecting the people that you work with
7. ***Optimize the whole***: A lean company improves the cycle of value; from the moment it receives a new requirement to the point at which it delivers the software

Following the lean principles helps a team or company to improve the quality of the features that are delivered to the customer. It also reduces the time spent on features that will not be used by the customer. In lean, deciding what features are important to the customer guides the team in delivering software that matters, and this is exactly what the Agile Manifesto intends to promote in software teams.

Extreme programming

Just before the release of the Agile Manifesto, some of the participants who designed the document, especially Kent Beck, presented to the world the **Extreme Programming** (XP) methodology for developing software.

XP is based on the values of simplicity, communication, feedback, respect, and courage. It was considered later as a social change in programming, according to Beck in his second book about the topic. It certainly promotes a huge change in the flow of development.

XP has it that every team should simply do only what it was asked to do, communicating face to face daily, demonstrating the software early to get feedback, respecting the expertise of each member of the team, and having the courage to tell the truth about progress and estimates, considering the team's work as a whole.

XP also follows a set of rules. These rules may be changed by the team if they detect that something is not working properly, but it is important to always maintain the values of the methodology. The rules are divided into planning, managing, designing, coding, and testing. Don Wells has mapped XP at `http://www.extremeprogramming.org/`. Although some of the ideas of this methodology were criticized strongly by many companies and specialists, it incorporates many good practices that are still used today:

- ***Writing software requirements using user stories***: User stories are considered an agile approach to describing user needs, together with acceptance tests, which are used to guarantee correct implementation.
- ***Divide software into iterations and deliver small releases***: The practice of iterating in software development is defended by all methodologies after waterfall. The fact that delivering versions more frequently decreases the risk of not meeting the customer's expectations.
- ***Avoid working overtime and guarantee a sustainable speed***: Although this must be one of the hardest aspects a software architect may have to deal with, the need for overtime indicates that something is not working properly in the process.
- ***Keep things simple***: While developing solutions, it is quite common to try to anticipate features that the customer would like to have. This approach increases the complexity of the development and the time to market the solution. A different approach, creating complex software, will cause high costs and probably a low level of features that are used in the system you are developing.
- ***Refactoring***: Continuously refactoring code is good because it enables the evolution of your software and guarantees design improvements that will truly be necessary due to the normal technical changes of the platforms you use to develop on.
- ***Keep the customer always available***: If you follow XP, you should have an expert customer inside your team. This can be hard to do, but the main idea of this approach is to ensure that the customer is involved in all parts of development. As another bonus, having the customer close to your team means they understand the difficulties and expertise the team has, which is likely to increase trust between the parties.
- ***Continuous integration***: This practice is one of the bases of the current DevOps approach. The fewer differences that exist between your personal code repository and the main code repository, the better.

- ***Code the unit test first***: Unit testing is an approach where you program specific code for testing single units (classes/methods) of your project. This is a feature of the current development methodology called **Test-Driven Development** (TDD). The main goal here is to guarantee that every business rule has its own unit test case.
- ***Write code to agreed standards***: The need to determine standards for coding is connected to the idea that no matter which developer you have working on a specific part of the project, the code must be written so that any of them will understand it.
- ***Pair programming***: Pair programming is another approach that can be difficult to realize completely in a software project, but the technique itself—one programmer coding and the other actively observing and offering comments, criticism, and advice—is useful in critical scenarios.
- ***Acceptance tests***: The adoption of acceptance tests to meet user stories is a good way to guarantee that newly released versions of the software do not damage its ability to meet current needs. An even better option is to have these acceptance tests automated.

It is worth mentioning that many of these rules are today considered vital practices in different software development methodologies, including DevOps and Scrum. We will discuss DevOps later in this book, in *Chapter 8, Understanding DevSecOps Principles and CI/CD*. Let us get into the Scrum model right now.

Getting into the scrum model

Scrum is an agile model for the management of software development projects. The model comes from lean principles and is today one of the more widely used approaches for developing software.

> **Note**
>
> For more information about the Scrum framework, check out this link: `https://www.scrum.org/`.

As you can see in the following figure, the basis of Scrum is that you have a flexible backlog of user requirements (the Product Backlog) that needs to be discussed in each agile cycle, called a **Sprint**. The Sprint goals (Sprint Backlog) are determined by the **Scrum Team**, composed of the **Product Owner**, the **Scrum Master**, and the **Development Team**. The Product Owner is responsible for prioritizing what will be delivered in that Sprint. During the Sprint, this person will help the team to develop the required features. The person who leads the team in the Scrum process is called the Scrum Master. All the meetings and processes are conducted by this person.

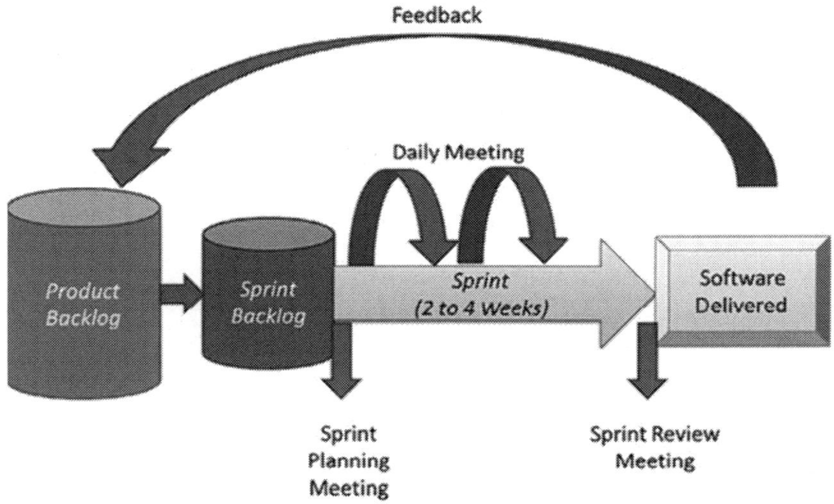

Figure 1.6: The Scrum process

It is common to apply Scrum together with another agile technique called **Kanban**, also developed by Toyota for manufacturing cars and commonly also used for software maintenance. The main purpose of Kanban is to enable a visual system to make sure everybody understands what is going on in the product that is being developed. The famous **Kanban board** is a fantastic way to do so, where you define what the team must do, what they are doing, and the things that are already done. We will learn how to set up this in *Chapter 3, Managing Requirements*, and we will be able to discuss a little bit more about how to create good Kanban boards.

It is important to note that the Scrum process does not discuss how the software needs to be implemented, or which tasks will be done to deliver this software. Again, you must remember the basis of software development, discussed at the beginning of this chapter; Scrum needs to be implemented together with a process model. DevOps is one of the approaches that may help you use a software development process model together with Scrum. Check out *Chapter 8, Understanding DevSecOps Principles and CI/CD*, to understand it better.

Scaling agile throughout a company

Today it is quite common to find companies where agility is being practiced and evolving in a good way, considering the results of the techniques presented in the previous sections. The mixture of Scrum, Kanban, and XP, together with the evolution and maturation of the software development process, has brought good results for companies, and we have a world where software development is one of the key strategies for business success. Some companies naturally need to scale up the number of teams, but the important question in this process is how to evolve without losing agility. And you can be sure that this question will be addressed to you, as a software architect. You may find in **SAFe® – Scaled Agile Framework** a good answer for this question:

> *"SAFe® for Lean Enterprises is a knowledge base of proven, integrated principles, practices, and competencies for achieving business agility using Lean, Agile, and DevOps."*
>
> *– Dean Leffingwell, creator*
>
> *© Scaled Agile, Inc.*

Based on the core values of alignment, built-in quality, transparency, and program execution, the framework provides a detailed path for delivering products with the agility needed in companies where you have one or more value streams. Its principles enable agility and incremental delivery, systems thinking, fast and economic decisions, and mainly, organization around value.

You may find opportunities for growth when agile is scaled using SAFe, considering you can work as a software architect in a system team, a system architect in an agile release train, or even an enterprise architect in the company. For sure, this will require a lot of study and dedication, but the use of SAFe, or something like it, is what you will find in big companies.

As with every framework, technique, or model in this book, the purpose of presenting SAFe to you is not to cover every single detail. You will find excellent material and training on the SAFe website at `https://framework.scaledagile.com/`. Understanding how to scale up a company's agile development efforts may be good knowledge to have in your toolbelt! Now that you know of it, and where to find out more, let us now return to the stages involved in designing high quality software, by discussing how to gather the right information to design it.

Gathering the right information to design high-quality software

Fantastic! You've just started a software development project. Now it's time to use all your knowledge to deliver the best software you can. Your first question is probably – *How do I start?* Well, as a software architect, you are going to be the one to answer that question. And you can be sure that your answer is going to evolve with each software project you lead.

Defining a software development process is the first task. This is generally done during the project planning process, or it might happen before it starts.

Another very important task is to gather the software requirements. No matter which software development process you decide to use, collecting real user needs is a difficult and continuous job. Of course, there are techniques to help you with this, and you can be sure that gathering requirements will help you to define important aspects of your software architecture.

These two tasks – defining the development process and gathering requirements – are considered by most experts in software development as key to eventual project success. You need to accomplish them to avoid as many problems as possible while guiding your team.

Understanding the requirements-gathering process

There are many ways to represent the requirements. The most traditional approach consists of writing a detailed specification before the beginning of the analysis. Agile methods suggest instead that you need to write user stories as soon as you are ready to start a development cycle.

Remember that you do not write requirements just for the user; you write them for yourself and your team too.

The truth is that no matter what approach you decide to adopt in your projects, you will have to follow steps to gather requirements. This is what we call **requirements engineering process**.

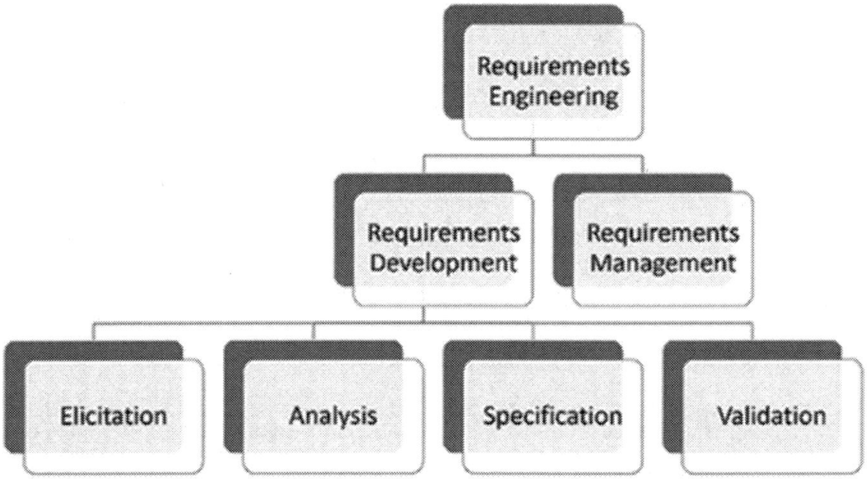

Figure 1.7: Requirements engineering process

During this process, described in *Figure 1.7*, you need to be sure that the solution is feasible. We call this *Requirements Development*. In some cases, the feasibility analysis is part of the project planning process too, and by the time you start the requirements elicitation, you will have the feasibility report already done. *Requirements Management* will be necessary once you have the requirements developed. We will discuss this topic further in *Chapter 3, Managing Requirements*. So, let us check the other parts of the requirements development process, which will provide you with a lot of important information about the software architecture.

Detecting exact user needs

There are many ways to detect exactly what the user needs for a specific scenario. This detection process is known as **elicitation**. In general, it can be done using a variety of techniques. Here, you have a list of the common ones:

- ***The power of imagination***: If you are an expert in the area where you are providing solutions, you may use your own imagination to find new user requirements. Brainstorming can be conducted together so that a group of experts can define the user's needs.
- ***Questionnaires***: This tool is useful for detecting common and important requirements such as the number and kind of users, peak system usage, and the most used operating systems (OS) and web browsers.
- ***Interviews***: Interviewing the users helps you as an architect to detect user requirements that perhaps questionnaires and your imagination do not cover.
- ***Observation***: There is no better way to understand the daily routine of a user than being with them for a day.
- ***Benchmarking***: A technique in which we compare current needs or existing solutions against industry competitors or best-in-class practices to identify gaps and define measurable improvement requirements.

As soon as you apply one or more of these techniques, you will have great and valuable information about the user's needs.

Tip

AI can evolve and accelerate this process. Why not have all the material you have obtained summarized by AI? Besides that, during meetings with stakeholders AI tools can be used to generate summarized records of the meetings as well as their transcripts.

Remember that you can use these techniques in any situation where the real need is to gather requirements, no matter whether it is for the whole system or just a single story.

At that moment, you will be able to start analyzing these user needs and detecting the user and system requirements. Let us see how to do so in the next section.

Analyzing requirements

When you have detected the user's needs, it is time to begin analyzing the requirements. To do so, you can use techniques such as the following:

- ***Prototyping***: Prototypes are fantastic to clarify and materialize the system requirements. Today, we have many tools that can help you to mock interfaces, with **Figma** (https://www.figma.com/) being the best-known tool for prototyping; a starter package is available that is free forever.
- ***Use cases***: The **Unified Modeling Language** (UML) use case model is an option if you need detailed documentation. Its main goal is to define how users interact with the functions of the system. Users or systems are called actors, while each function of the system is a use case. UML defines a standard for designing this model. The model is composed of detailed specifications and a diagram.
    - **DrawIO** is another good tool that can help you out with the documentation of the Use Case Diagram. You can access it at `https://www.drawio.com/`. You can see the model created in *Figure 1.8*:

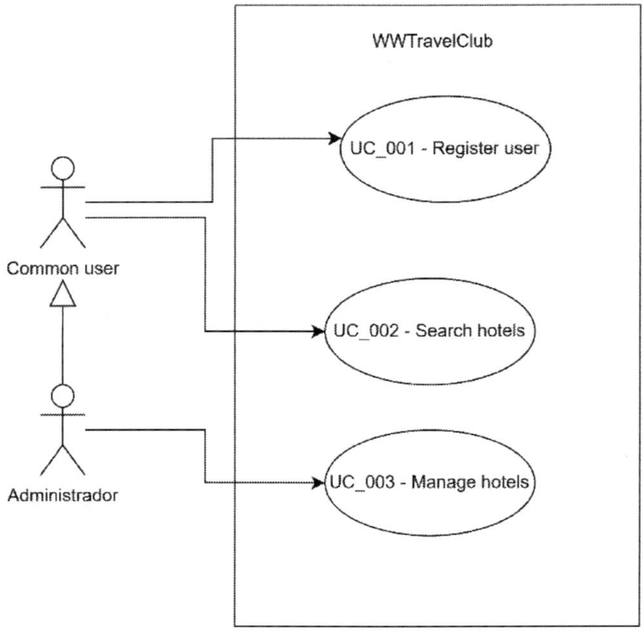

Figure 1.8: Use case diagram example

- **Mermaid** is another online diagramming platform built on the open-source Mermaid project that lets you quickly convert natural language or text/Markdown-style code into clear, editable visual diagrams (such as flowcharts, sequence diagrams, timelines, and more) with real-time collaboration and AI support. You can access it at `https://mermaid.ai/`.

> **Tip**
>
> There are some specific AI tools that can also help you out here. You might try some of them out to accelerate the prototyping phase. However, be careful about what you input to AIs, since otherwise you may encounter confidentiality issues.

While analyzing the requirements of the system, you will be able to clarify exactly what the needs of users are. This is helpful when you are not sure about the real problem you need to solve, and it is much better than just starting to program the system and hoping for the best. Time invested in requirements analysis is time invested in better code later.

Writing the specifications

After you finish the analysis, it is important to register it as a specification. The specification document can be written in terms of traditional requirements or as user stories, which are commonly used in agile projects.

A requirements specification represents the technical contract between the user and the team. There are some basic rules that this document needs to follow:

- All stakeholders need to understand exactly what is written in the technical contract, even if they are not technicians
- The document needs to be clear
- You need to classify each requirement, considering its complexity for implementation: small, medium, or high complexity
- Use simple future tense language to represent each requirement:
    - *Bad example*: A common user registers themselves
    - *Good example*: A common user shall register themselves
- Ambiguity and controversy need to be avoided
- Some additional information can help the team understand the context of the project they are going to work on. Here are some tips about how to add useful information:
    - Write an introductory chapter to give a full idea of the solution
    - Create a glossary to make understanding easier
    - Describe the kind of user the solution will cover
- Write functional and non-functional requirements:
    - Functional requirements are quite simple to understand because they describe exactly what the software will do.
    - Non-functional requirements, on the other hand, determine restrictions related to the software, which means scalability, robustness, security, and performance. We will cover these aspects in the next section.
- Attach documents that can help the user understand the rules

If you decide to write user stories, a good tip is to write short sentences that represent each point of interaction with the system for each user, as follows:

```
As <user>, I want <feature>, so that <reason>
```

This approach will explain exactly the reason why a particular feature will be implemented. It is also a good tool to help you analyze the stories that are most important and prioritize the success of the project. Obviously, you may want to use AI to accelerate the process here and, more than that, evolve the quality of what you will deliver. In *Chapter 3, Managing Requirements*, we will see how once you write a PRD (Product Requirements Document) you can apply it to the GitHub Copilot agent. Depending on the level of difficulty of the requirement, the agent can start implementing it for you! Finally, user stories can also be great for informing the automated acceptance tests that should be built. Now let's check out how scalability, robustness, security, and performance principles need to be discussed in a requirements specification.

Understanding the principles of scalability, robustness, security, and performance

Detecting requirements enables you to understand the software you are going to develop. However, as a software architect, you must pay attention to more than just the functional requirements for the system. Understanding the non-functional requirements is equally important, and one of the earliest activities for a software architect.

We are going to look at this in more detail in *Chapter 2, Non-Functional Requirements*, but at this point, it is important to know that the principles of scalability, robustness, security, and performance need to be applied in the requirements gathering process. Let us look at each concept in turn:

- ***Scalability***: The internet gives you the opportunity to have a solution with many users all over the world. This is fantastic, but you, as a software architect, need to design a solution that provides that possibility. Scalability is the ability for an application to increase its processing power as soon as necessary due to the number of resources that are being consumed.
- ***Robustness***: No matter how scalable your application is, if it cannot guarantee a stable and always-on solution, you are not going to get any peace. Robustness is important for critical solutions, where there is no opportunity for maintenance at any time due to the kind of problem that the application solves. In many industries, the software cannot stop, and lots of routines run when nobody is available (overnight, during holidays, and so on). Designing a robust solution will give you the freedom to live while your software is running well.
- ***Security***: This is another really important area that needs to be discussed after the requirements stage. Everybody worries about security, and different laws dealing with it are in place in different parts of the world. You, as a software architect, must understand that security needs to be provided by design. This is the only way to cope with all the needs that the security community is discussing right now.
- ***Performance***: The process of understanding the system you are going to develop will probably give you a good idea of how to obtain the desired performance from the system. This topic needs to be discussed with the user to help identify the bottlenecks you will face during the development stage.

It is worth mentioning that all these concepts are requirements for the generation of new solutions that the world needs. What differentiates good software from incredible software is the amount of work done to meet the project requirements.

Reviewing the specification

Once you have the specification written, it is time to confirm with the stakeholders whether they agree with it. This can be done in a review meeting, or it can be done online using collaboration tools.

This is when you present all the prototypes, documents, and information you have gathered. As soon as everybody agrees with the material, you are ready to start studying the best way to implement the reviewed specification of your project.

Tip

AI can also be considered in this process, especially if you use it to achieve completeness in the software requirements.

It is worth mentioning that you might use the process described here for either the complete software solution or for just a small part of it. Now that you have your software requirements, let's understand how design techniques can evolve the definition of your solution.

Using design techniques as a helpful tool

Defining a solution is not easy. Determining which technology to use is also difficult. It is true that, during your career as a software architect, you may encounter projects where your customer will bring you a solution *ready for development*. It is not a good idea to consider the solution brought by the customer *ready for development*. Most of the time, there will be architectural and functional mistakes that will cause problems with the solution in the future.

There are also cases where the problem is worse: when the customer does not know the best solution for the problem. Some design techniques can help us with this, and we will introduce two of them here: **design thinking** and **design sprints**.

What you must understand is that these techniques can be a fantastic option to discover real requirements. As a software architect, you are committed to helping your team use the correct tools at the correct time, and these tools may be the right options to ensure the project's success.

Design thinking

Design thinking is a process that allows you to collect data directly from users, focusing on achieving the best results to solve a problem. During the process, the team can discover all the *personas* that will interact with the system. This can have a wonderful impact on the solution, since you can develop the software by focusing on the user experience.

The process is based on the following steps:

1. ***Empathize***: In this step, you must execute field research to discover the users' concerns. This is where you find out about the users of the system. The process is good for making you understand why and for whom you are developing this software.
2. ***Define***: Once you have the users' concerns, it is time to define their needs to solve them
3. ***Ideate***: The needs will provide an opportunity to brainstorm some possible solutions
4. ***Prototype***: These solutions can be developed as mock-ups to confirm whether they are good ones
5. ***Test***: Testing the prototypes with users will help you to understand the prototype that is most connected to the real needs of the users

The focus of a technique like this is to accelerate the process of discerning the right product and considering the **Minimum Viable Product** (MVP). For sure, the prototype process will help stakeholders understand the final product and, at the same time, engage the team to deliver the best solution. Design thinking is not the only way to do so, so let's check another great technique called **Design sprint**.

Design sprint

A **design sprint** is a process focused on solving critical business questions through design in a five-day sprint. Created by Google, the technique allows you to quickly test and learn from an idea when you are looking to build and launch a solution to market.

The process involves stakeholders investing a week to solve the problem at hand, in a 'war room' prepared for that purpose. The week typically looks like this:

- ***Monday***: The focus of this day is to identify the target of the sprint and map the challenge to achieve it.
- ***Tuesday***: After understanding the goal of the sprint, participants start sketching solutions that might solve it. It is time to find customers to test the new solution that will be provided.
- ***Wednesday***: This is when the team needs to decide on the solutions that have the greatest chance of solving the problem. The team must draw these solutions as a storyboard, preparing a plan for the prototype.
- ***Thursday***: It is time to prototype the idea planned in the storyboard.
- ***Friday***: Having completed the prototype, the team presents it to customers, learning by getting information from their reactions to the solution designed.

As you can see, in both techniques, the acceleration of collecting reactions from potential customers comes from prototypes that materialize your team's ideas into something more tangible for the end user. In the next section we will discuss cases where the lack of requirements can cause problems with the system's results.

Common cases where the requirements gathering process impacts system results

All the information discussed up to this point in the chapter is useful if you want to design software following the principles of good engineering. The focus is on building software professionally.

It is also worth knowing about some cases in which failing to perform the activities you have just read about can cause trouble for a software project. The following examples are intended to describe what can go wrong and show how the preceding techniques can help a development team solve the associated problems.

In most cases, very simple actions can guarantee better communication between the team and the customer, and this easy communication flow can transform a big problem into a real solution. Let us examine three common cases where requirements gathering can impact software performance, functionality, and/or usability.

Case 1 – my website is too slow to open that page!

Performance is one of the biggest problems that you as a software architect will deal with during your career. The reason why this aspect of any software is so problematic is that we do not have infinite computational resources to solve problems. The cost of computation is still high, especially if you are talking about software with a high number of simultaneous users.

You cannot solve performance problems just by writing requirements. However, you will not end up in trouble if you write them *correctly*. The idea here is that requirements must present the desired performance of a system. A simple sentence describing this can help the entire team that works on the project:

Non-functional requirement: Performance – any web page of this software shall respond in at most *2 seconds, even when 1,000 users are accessing it concurrently.*

The preceding sentence lets everybody (users, testers, developers, architects, managers, and so on) know that any web page has a target to achieve. This is a good start, but it is not enough. A great environment for developing and deploying your application is also important. This is where .NET 10 can help you a lot. If you are talking about web apps, ASP.NET Core is considered one of the fastest runtimes we have today.

Note

You can check out Performance Improvements in .NET 10 at `https://devblogs.microsoft.com/dotnet/performance-improvements-in-net-10/`.

When it comes to performance, you, as a software architect, should consider the use of the techniques listed in the following sections, together with specific tests, to guarantee this non-functional requirement. ASP.NET Core, together with some **Platform as a Service** (PaaS) solution delivered by Microsoft Azure, will help you to use them easily.

Understanding backend caching

Caching is a great technique to avoid time-consuming and redundant queries. For instance, if you are fetching car models from a database, the number of cars in the database can increase, but the models themselves will not change. Once you have an application that constantly accesses car models, a good practice is to cache that information.

It is important to understand that a cache is stored in the backend and that the cache is shared by the whole application *(in-memory caching)*. When you are working on a scalable solution, you can configure a *distributed cache* using the Azure platform. In fact, ASP.NET provides both in-memory caching and distributed caching, so you can decide on the one that best fits your needs. *Chapter 2, Non-Functional Requirements,* covers scalability aspects in the Azure platform.

We should also mention that caching can happen in the frontend, in proxies along the way to the server, in CDNs, and so on.

Applying asynchronous programming

When you develop ASP.NET applications, keep in mind that your app should be designed for simultaneous access by many users. Asynchronous programming lets you do this simply, by giving you the keywords `async` and `await`.

The basic concept behind these keywords is that `async` enables any method to run asynchronously. On the other hand, `await` lets you synchronize the call of an asynchronous method without blocking the thread that is calling it. This easy-to-develop pattern will help your application run without performance bottlenecks and bring better responsiveness. We will cover this subject further in *Chapter 2, Non-Functional Requirements.*

Dealing with object allocation

One very good tip to avoid poor performance is to understand how the **garbage collector** (GC) works. The GC is the engine that will free memory automatically when you finish using it. There are some very important aspects to this topic, stemming from the GC's complexity.

Some types of objects are not collected by the GC if you do not dispose of them. The list includes any object that interacts with I/O, such as files and streaming. If you do not correctly use the C# syntax to create and destroy this kind of object, you will have memory leaks, which will deteriorate your application's performance.

The incorrect way of working with I/O objects is:

```
StreamWriter file = new StreamWriter(@"C:\sample.txt");
file.WriteLine("Just writing a simple line");
```

The correct way of working with I/O objects is:

```
using StreamWriter file = new StreamWriter(@"C:\sample.txt");
file.WriteLine("Just writing a simple line");
```

It might be worth noting that this correct approach also ensures the file gets written (it calls `FileStream.Flush()` before disposing of its resources gracefully). In the incorrect example, the contents might not even be written to the file. Even though the preceding practice is mandatory for I/O objects, it is recommended that you do this in all disposable objects. Indeed, using code analyzers in your solutions with warnings as errors will prevent you from accidentally making these mistakes! This will help the GC and will keep your application running with the right amount of memory. Depending on the type of object, mistakes here can snowball, and you could end up with other bad things happening on a bigger scale, such as port/connection exhaustion.

Another aspect you need to know about is that the time spent by the GC collecting objects can interfere with the performance of your app. Because of this, avoid allocating large objects and be careful with event handling and weak references; otherwise, you can find yourself always waiting for the GC to finish its task.

Getting better database access

One of the most common performance Achilles' heels is database access. The reason why this is still a big problem is insufficient attention being paid to writing the queries or lambda expressions that get information from a database. This book will cover Entity Framework Core in *Chapter 13, Interacting with Data in C# – Entity Framework Core*, which is a great framework for getting data from a database using C#, without the need to use SQL commands, and with great performance. But even without Entity Framework it is important to know what to query and the correct data information to read from a database. Filtering columns and rows is imperative to ensure that your application delivers on performance.

The good thing is that best practices related to caching, asynchronous programming, and object allocation fit completely into the environment of databases. Getting better-performing software is often just a matter of choosing the correct pattern.

Case 2 – the user's needs are not properly implemented

The greater the number of technologies that are used, the more difficult it is to deliver exactly what the user needs. Maybe this sentence sounds weird to you, but you must understand that developers, in general, study how to develop software, but they rarely study delivering the needs of a specific domain. Of course, it is not easy to learn how to develop software, but it is even more difficult to understand a specific need in a specific area. Software development nowadays delivers software to all types of industries. The question here is *how a developer, whether a software architect or not, can evolve enough to deliver software in the area they are responsible for?*

Gathering software requirements will help you in this tough task; writing them will make you understand and organize the architecture of the system. There are several ways to minimize the risks of implementing something different from what the user really needs:

- Prototyping the interface to achieve an understanding of the user interface faster
- Designing the data flow to detect gaps between the operations of the system and the user
- Frequent meetings to stay up to date on the user's current needs and remain aligned with incremental deliveries

Again, as a software architect, you will have to define how the software will be implemented. Most of the time, you are not going to be the one who programs it, but you will always be the one responsible for this. Still, high-quality implementation is a team outcome, and your role is to guide alignment and enable the team to deliver it. For this reason, some techniques can be useful to avoid bad implementations:

- Requirements are reviewed by the developers to guarantee that they understand what it is they need to develop.
- Code inspection to validate according to a predefined code standard. We will cover this in *Chapter 4, Best Practices in Coding C#*.
- Meetings to eliminate impediments.

Remember, making sure the implementation matches the user's needs is your responsibility. Use every tool you can to do so.

Case 3 – the usability of the system does not meet the user's needs

Usability is a key point for the success of a software project. The way the software is presented and how it solves a problem will determine whether the user wants to use it or not. As software architects, delivering software with good usability is mandatory nowadays.

There are basic concepts of usability that this book does not intend to cover, but a good way to meet the user's needs when it comes to usability is by understanding who is going to use the software. Design thinking can help you a lot with that, as was discussed earlier in the chapter.

Understanding the user will help you to decide whether the software is going to run on a web page, a cell phone, or even in the background, e.g. as a service. This understanding is very important to a software architect because the elements of a system will be better presented if you know who will use them.

On the other hand, if you do not care or pay attention about that, you will deliver software that may even work but does not truly deliver what the user needs. Delivering software that works can be enough for a short time, but it will not exactly meet the real needs that made a person ask you to architect the software. You must keep in mind the options and understand that good software is software designed to run on many platforms and devices.

You will be happy to know that .NET 10 is an incredible cross-platform option. So, you can develop solutions that run on Linux, Windows, Android, and iOS. You can run your applications on big screens, tablets, cell phones, and even drones! You can embed apps on boards for automation or in HoloLens for mixed reality. Software architects must be open-minded and design exactly what their users need.

Summary

In this chapter, we explained why software architecture matters for building sustainable systems, what architecture is, and what an architect does across the SDLC—making trade-offs among constraints like time, budget, quality, and long-term evolution, especially as systems and AI-assisted development increase complexity.

We also compared major development process models (waterfall, incremental, agile approaches such as Scrum/XP/lean, and scaling approaches such as SAFe), emphasizing that the delivery process shapes how architectural decisions are made, validated, and evolved over time.

Finally, we focused on requirements engineering and human-centered design practices (elicitation, analysis, specification, review; plus design thinking/sprints), showing that unclear requirements – especially missed non-functional requirements like performance, scalability, security, and usability – are a common root cause of project failure, and that AI can help speed up documentation and analysis when used responsibly.

In the next chapter, you will have the opportunity to understand more deeply how important functional and non-functional requirements are to software architecture.

Questions

1. What is the expertise that a software architect needs to have?
2. How can Azure help a software architect?
3. How does a software architect decide on the best software development process model to use in a project?
4. How does a software architect contribute to gathering requirements?
5. What kind of requirements does a software architect need to check in a requirement specification?
6. How do Design Thinking and Design Sprint help a software architect in the process of gathering requirements?
7. How do user stories help a software architect in the process of writing requirements?
8. What are some good techniques to develop very good performance software?
9. How does a software architect check whether a user requirement is correctly implemented?
10. How can AI help during the gathering requirements process?

Further reading

Here, you have some books and links you may consider using to gather more information about this chapter.

For information on Azure, check these out:

- `https://azure.microsoft.com/overview/what-is-azure/`
- `https://azure.microsoft.com/services/devops/`
- `https://azurecharts.com/`

More information on .NET 10 can be found here:

- `https://docs.microsoft.com/dotnet/`
- `https://docs.microsoft.com/aspnet/`
- `https://docs.microsoft.com/aspnet/core/performance/performance-best-practices`

Software development process model links are listed here:

- `https://agilemanifesto.org/`
- `https://www.amazon.com/Software-Engineering-10th-Ian-Sommerville/dp/0133943038`
- `https://www.amazon.com.br/Software-Engineering-Practitioners-Roger-Pressman/dp/1260548007`
- `https://scrumguides.org/`
- `https://en.wikipedia.org/wiki/Incremental_build_model`
- `https://en.wikipedia.org/wiki/Waterfall_model`
- `http://www.extremeprogramming.org/`
- `https://www.gv.com/sprint/`

Here you can find SAFe® information:

- `https://www.scaledagileframework.com/`
- `https://docs.microsoft.com/azure/devops/boards/plans/safe-concepts`

2

Non-Functional Requirements

Once you have gathered the system requirements, it is time to think about the impact they have on architectural design. This chapter focuses on how we shape architectural decisions, thinking about scalability, availability, resiliency, performance, multithreading, interoperability, security, and other aspects that need to be analyzed so that we can meet user needs. We refer to these aspects as non-functional requirements, which define the quality attributes and operational constraints of a system.

The following topics will be covered in this chapter:

- How .NET 10 and Azure enable scalability, availability, and resiliency
- Performance issues to be considered when programming in C#
- Software usability (i.e., how to design effective user interfaces)
- .NET 10 and interoperability
- Achieving security by design

The main purpose of discussing non-functional requirements here is that they are highly relevant to software architects. Even though they are not directly critical to getting software working, they can make all the difference when it comes to the usability and real-world effectiveness of solutions.

Technical requirements

The samples provided in this chapter require Visual Studio 2026 Community Edition with the .NET 10 SDK installed.

You can find the sample code for this chapter at `https://github.com/PacktPublishing/Software-Architecture-with-.NET-10-and-C-sharp-5E`.

Enabling scalability, availability, and resiliency with Azure and .NET 10

By the book, scalability means the ability of a system to keep working well when there is an increase in demand. When developers go by this definition, many of them incorrectly conclude that scalability just means adding more hardware to keep things working without stopping their apps.

Scalability relies on hardware solutions to some extent. However, as a software architect, you need to be aware that good software will keep scalability in a sustainable model, which means that well-architected software can save a lot of money. Hence, scalability is not just a matter of hardware but also a matter of overall software design. The point here is that the running costs of a system should also be a factor in architectural decisions. In practice, good architecture is not only about technical quality, but also about sustaining the solution economically over time.

In *Chapter 1, Understanding the Importance of Software Architecture*, while discussing software performance, we presented some tips to overcome performance issues. The same tips will help you with scalability too. The fewer resources we devote to each process, the more users an application can handle with the same computing capacity.

Although scalability is important, cloud computing applications must be designed to work with system failures. Every time you guarantee that your application can recover from a failure without exposing the failure to the end user, you are creating a resilient application.

> **Note**
>
> You may find more information on cloud architecture resiliency patterns at `https://docs.microsoft.com/en-us/azure/architecture/framework/resiliency/reliability-patterns#resiliency`.

The reason why resiliency is especially important in cloud scenarios is that the infrastructure provided to you may need a small amount of time to manage updates, resets, and even hardware upgrades. You are also more likely to have to work with multiple systems, and transient errors are likely to occur in communicating with them. That is why the non-functional requirement of resiliency has gained a higher profile in recent years.

The possibility of having scalable and resilient solutions gets more exciting when you can enable high availability in the system. It is worth mentioning that resiliency is the ability that a system has to recover from unexpected failures, while availability is the possibility of having a system online even when a component is down. All the approaches presented in this book will help you to design solutions with good availability, but in some cases, you will need to design specific alternatives to achieve your goal.

Rest assured that Azure and .NET 10 web apps can be configured to achieve these non-functional requirements. Now that we understand the concepts, let's see how they translate into practice in the following subsections.

Creating a scalable web app in Azure

It is simple to create a web app in Azure that is ready for scaling. The reason why you must do so is to be able to maintain different numbers of users during different seasons of the year. The more users you have, the more hardware you will need. Let us show you how to create a scalable web application in Azure.

As soon as you log in to your Azure account, you will be able to create a new resource (web app, database, virtual machine, and so on), as you can see in the following screenshot:

Figure 2.1: Microsoft Azure – Create a resource

After that, you can select **App Services** in Popular Options or even type it into the **Search resources, services, and docs** textbox. Then, you can select to **Create** a **WebApp**. This action will take you to the following screen:

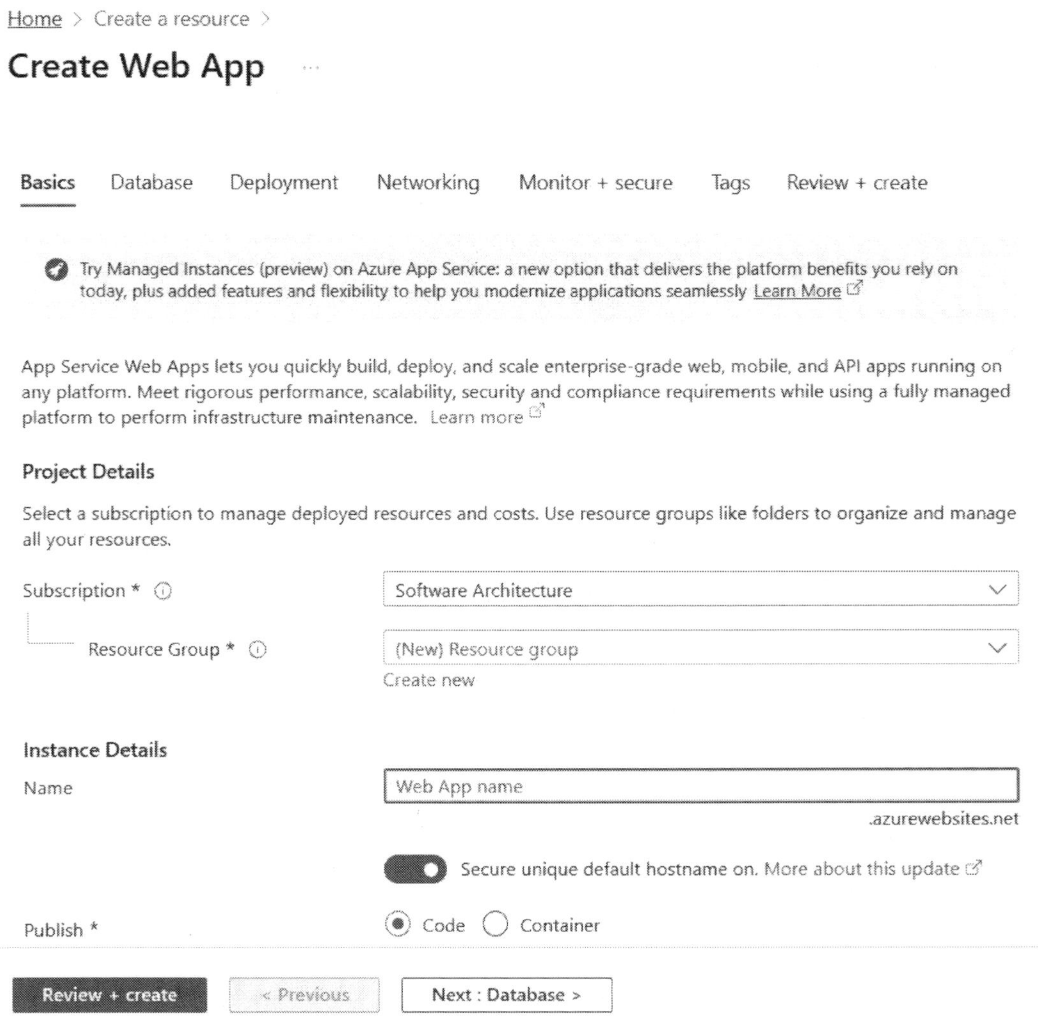

Figure 2.2: Microsoft Azure – Creating a web app

The required **Project Details** are as follows:

- **Subscription**: This is the account that will be charged for all application costs.
- **Resource Group**: This is the collection of resources you can define to organize policies and permissions. You may specify a new resource group name or add the web app to a group specified during the definition of other resources.

The **Instance Details** are as follows:

- **Name**: As you can see, the web app name is the URL that your solution will assume after its creation. The name must be globally unique and is checked to ensure that it is available.
- **Try a secure unique default hostname**: The main purpose of this feature is to guarantee that the hostname of your application is unique all over the world, protecting it from 'dangling DNS', where a bad actor may use the name of a known DNS record to take over the domain of a deleted app.
- **Publish**: This parameter indicates whether the web app will be delivered directly, or whether it is going to use container technology to publish content. Containers will be discussed in more detail in *Chapter 11, Applying a Microservice Architecture to Your Enterprise Application*. If you opt for container publication, you will be able to configure the **Image Source**, **Access Type**, and **Image** and tag information to have it deployed to the web app.
- **Runtime stack**: This option is obviously available only when you decide to deliver code directly. You can define stacks for .NET, Java, Node, PHP, and Python.
- **Operating System**: This is the option for specifying the OS that will host the web app. Both Windows and Linux may be used for .NET projects in the newest versions.
- **Region**: You may consider where you want to deploy your application; Azure has many different data centers all over the world.
- **Pricing Plans**: This is where you define the hardware plan that is used to handle the web app and the region of the servers. This choice defines application possibilities for scalability, performance, and costs.
- **Zone redundancy**: Starting with Premium Pricing Plans, you will be able to activate Zone Redundancy, which will increase the availability of the solution.
- **Database**: Another option that requires at least Basic Pricing Plans, this feature allows you to specify the Database and Cache Service for your application. The Database can be defined as Azure SQL, PostgreSQL, MySQL or Cosmos DB. The Cache Service used will be Redis. We will discuss more about databases and caches in *Chapter 12, How to Choose Your Data Storage in the Cloud*.
- **Deployment**: It is possible to define the GitHub repository responsible for continuously deploying the application using GitHub Actions. Continuous Deployment and GitHub Actions will be discussed in *Chapter 8, Understanding DevSecOps Principles and CI/CD*.
- **Networking**: You can select the network behavior of the application according to its requirements and proposal.
- **Monitor + secure**: This is a useful Azure toolset for monitoring and troubleshooting web apps. In this section, you can enable **Application Insights**. It is always recommended that you keep the same regions for the different components of your solution, since this will save costs in terms of traffic

exchange from one data center to another. Besides that, you can also enable **Microsoft Defender for Cloud**, which is a set of tools that enhance visibility and protection against cyberattacks.

- **Tags**: Tags enable you to categorize resources. This categorization is useful for understanding billing, since Azure consolidates the multiple resources that have the same tag applied.

Once you have created your web app, the application may be scaled in two conceptually different ways: vertically (**Scale up**) and horizontally (**Scale out**). Both are available in the web app settings, as you can see in the following screenshot:

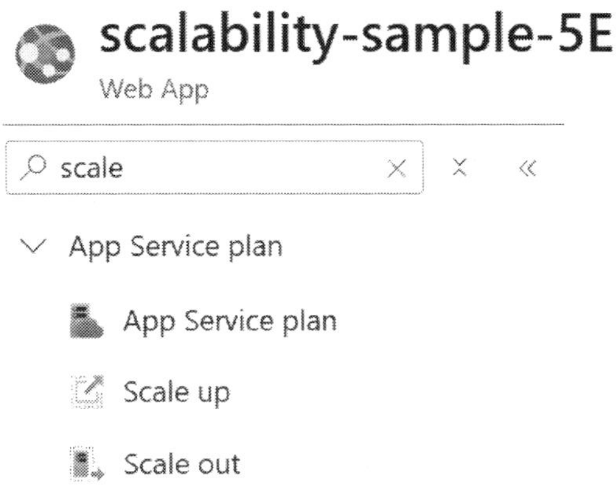

Figure 2.3: Scaling options for web apps

Let us check out these two types of scaling.

Vertical scaling (scaling up)

Scaling up, or **vertical scaling**, means changing the specification of the hardware that will host your application. In Azure, you have the opportunity to start with free, shared hardware, and move to an isolated machine with a few clicks. The following screenshot shows the user interface for scaling up a web app:

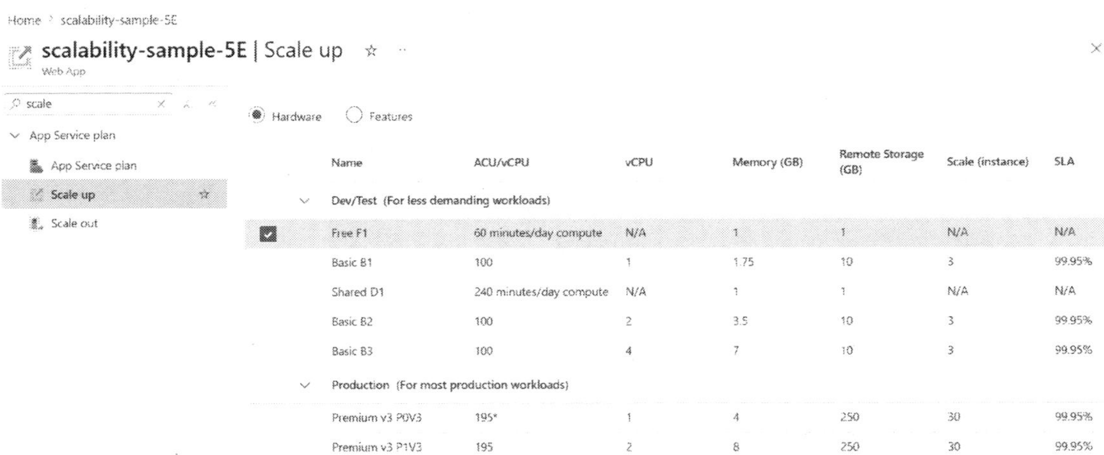

Figure 2.4: Vertical scaling options

By choosing one of the options provided, you can select more powerful hardware (machines with more CPUs, storage, and RAM). Monitoring your application and its **App Service plan** will guide you on how to decide the best infrastructure for running your solution. It will also offer key insights, such as possible CPU, memory, and I/O bottlenecks.

Horizontal scaling (scaling out)

Scaling out, or horizontal scaling, means splitting requests between more servers and using machines of the same capacity instead of using more powerful machines. The load on all the servers is automatically balanced by the Azure infrastructure. This solution is advised when the overall load may change considerably in the future, since **horizontal scaling** can automatically adapt to a given load. The following screenshot shows an automatic scale-out strategy defined by two simple rules, triggered by CPU usage:

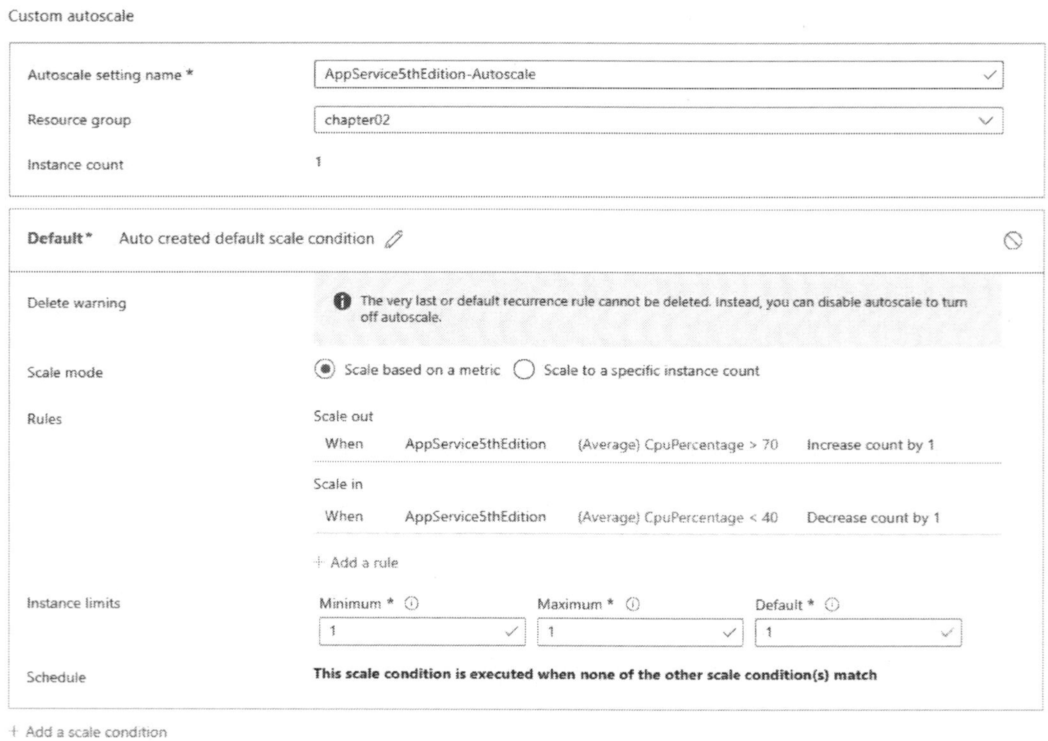

Figure 2.5: Horizontal scaling sample

It is worth highlighting that you can choose to have a hardcoded instance count or implement rules for automatic scale in/out.

A complete description of all the available autoscale rules is beyond the scope of this book. However, they are quite self-explanatory, and the *Further reading* section contains links to the full documentation.

> **Tip**
>
> Note that the scale-out feature is only available in paid service plans.

In general, horizontal scaling is a way to guarantee the availability of an application even with highly multiple simultaneous accesses. For sure, its use is not the only way to keep a system available, since we can make improvements in code and networking, but it does help. From an architectural decision perspective, vertical scaling is often more suitable for simpler or short-term scenarios, while horizontal scaling is usually the preferred option when the system requires higher availability, elasticity, and room for long-term growth. Now let's check how to create a scalable web app with .NET 10.

Creating a scalable web app with .NET 10

Among all the available frameworks for implementing web applications, ASP.NET Core in .NET 10 can provide good performance together with relatively low production and maintenance costs, depending on the architectural context and system requirements. The union of C#, a strongly typed and advanced general-purpose language, and the continuous performance improvements achieved in ASP.NET Core distinguish this option as one of the best for enterprise development.

The steps in this section will guide you through the creation of an ASP.NET Core Runtime 10-based web app. All the steps are quite simple, but some details require particular attention.

It is worth mentioning that .NET 10 gives you the opportunity to develop for any platform – desktops (WPF, Windows Forms, and UWP), web (ASP.NET), cloud (Azure), mobile (.NET MAUI), gaming (Unity), IoT (ARM32 and ARM64), or AI (ML.NET). So, the recommendation from now on is to favor .NET 10 in most new scenarios, while still evaluating the context of each solution. In this scenario, you can run your web app on either Windows servers or Linux servers, depending on compatibility, operational needs, and cost expectations.

Nowadays, Microsoft recommends classic .NET just in case the features you need are not available in .NET Core/5+ or you are deploying your web app in an environment that does not support .NET Core. In any other case, you should prefer .NET Core/5+ because it allows you to do the following:

- Run your web app in Windows, Linux, macOS, or Docker containers
- Design your solution with microservices
- Have high-performance and scalable systems

Containers and microservices will be covered in *Chapter 11, Applying a Microservice Architecture to Your Enterprise Application*. There, you will get a better understanding of the advantages of these technologies. For now, it is enough to say that .NET 10 and microservices were designed for performance and scalability, which is why you should prefer .NET 10 for all your new projects. Besides, .NET 10 is guaranteed by Microsoft as a Long-Term Support version, as we can see in *Figure 2.6*, which means three years of patches and free support.

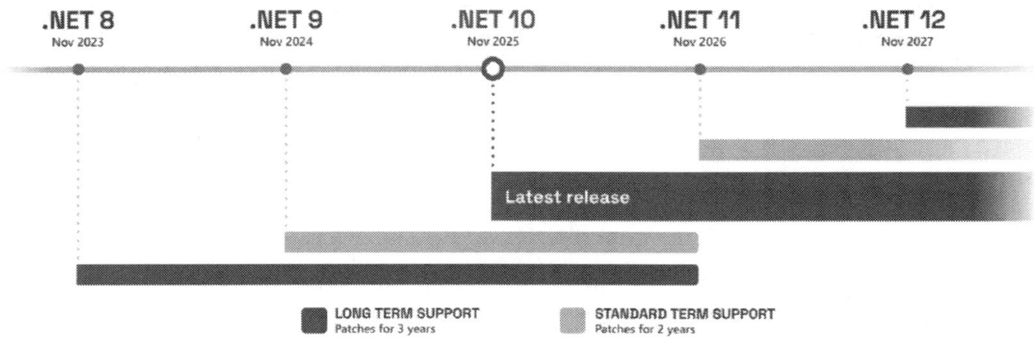

Figure 2.6: .NET 10 Support Policy

The following procedure outlines how to create an ASP.NET Core web app in Visual Studio 2026 with .NET 10:

1. As soon as you start VS 2026, you will be able to click on **Create a new project**
2. Once you select **ASP.NET Core Web App (Razor Pages)** you will be directed to a screen where you will be asked to set up **Project name, Location, and Solution name** as shown below:

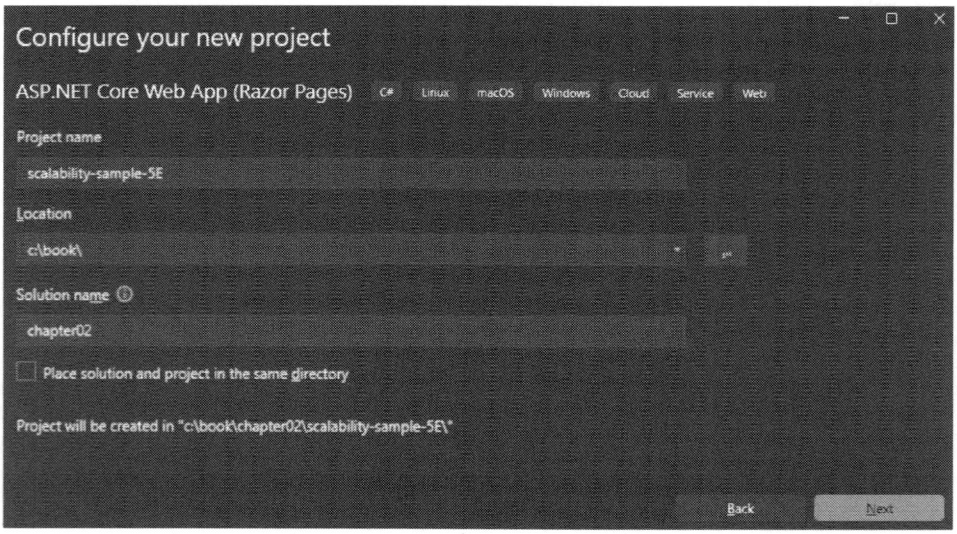

Figure 2.7: Creating an ASP.NET Core web application

3. After that you will be able to select the .NET version to use. Select **.NET 10.0** to get the most advanced and up-to-date platform.
4. Click **Create** to create your ASP.NET Core 10 web app
5. Having added the basic details, you can connect your web app project to your Azure account and have it published
6. If you right-click the project you created in Solution Explorer, you have the option to **Publish**

7. You will find different target options for where to publish your web app. Select **Azure** as the target as shown in the screenshot below:

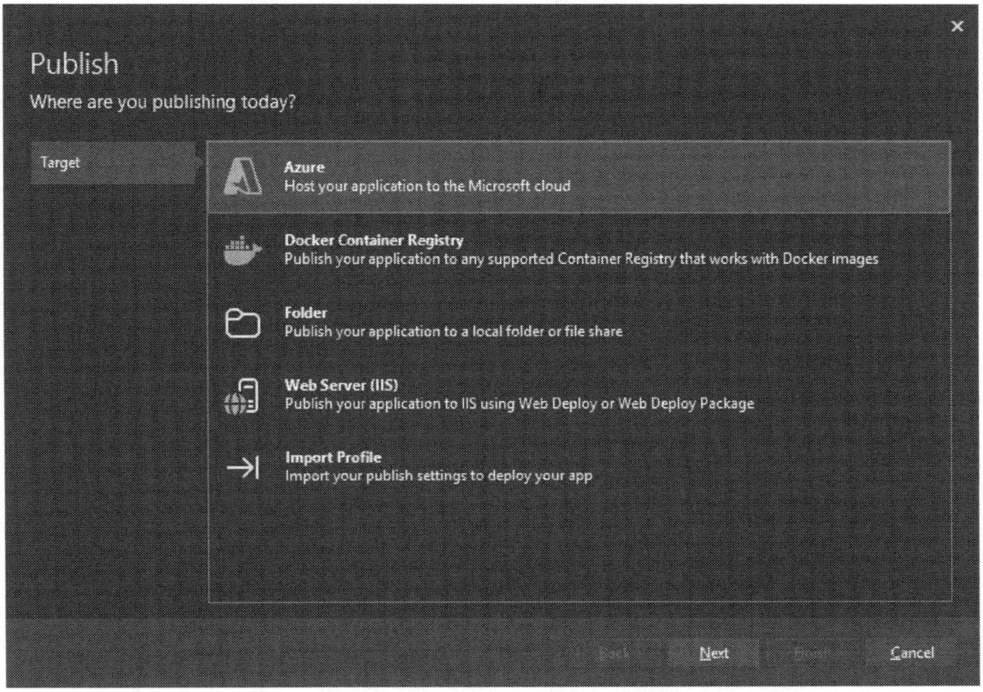

Figure 2.8: Targeting Azure to publish the app

8. Then you will be able to decide on the specific target to publish. Select **Azure App Service (Windows)** for this demo.

9. You may be required to define your Microsoft Account credentials at this time. This is because there is full integration between Visual Studio and Azure. This gives you the opportunity to view all the resources you created in the Azure portal in your development environment, as you can see in *Figure 2.9*.

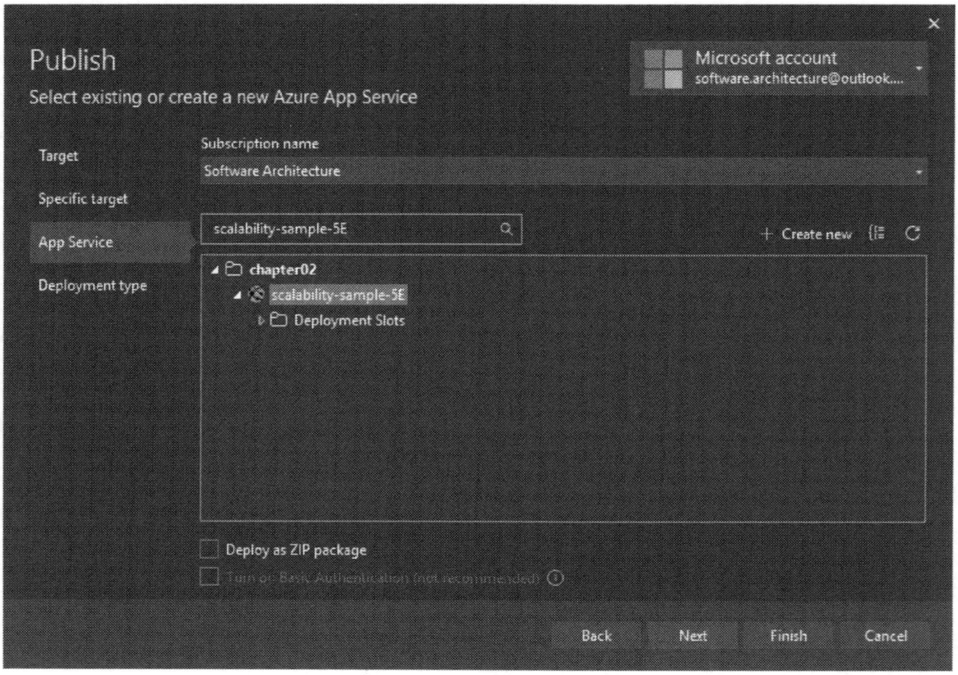

Figure 2.9: Integration between Visual Studio and Azure

10. If you want to create a new web app using Visual Studio, make sure during the App Service creation process to select the **Free Size** tier of pricing so that this does not incur any costs, as we can see in *Figure 2.10*

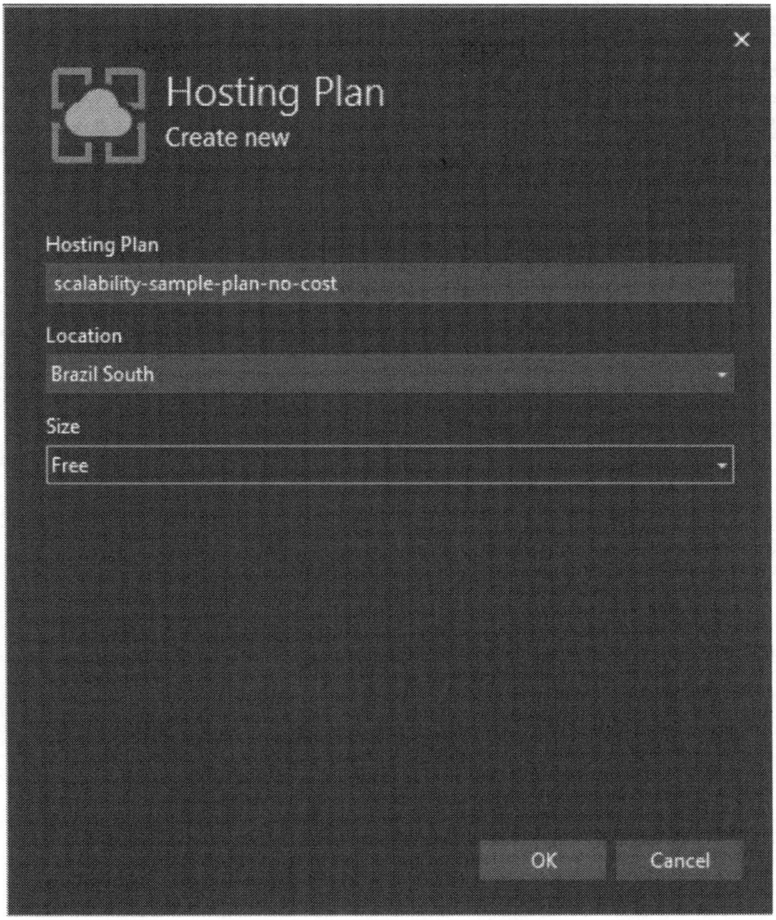

Figure 2.10: Creating a new hosting plan

11. The usual way to deploy using Visual Studio is by selecting **Publish Profile**, which generates a Visual Studio publish profile as a `pubxml` file. In this case, you currently have two modes for deployment. The first, **Framework-dependent**, will require a web app configured with the target framework. The second, **Self-contained**, will no longer need this feature since the binaries of the framework will be published together with the application. Once the file is created and the options selected, just click on the **Publish** button and the process will start:

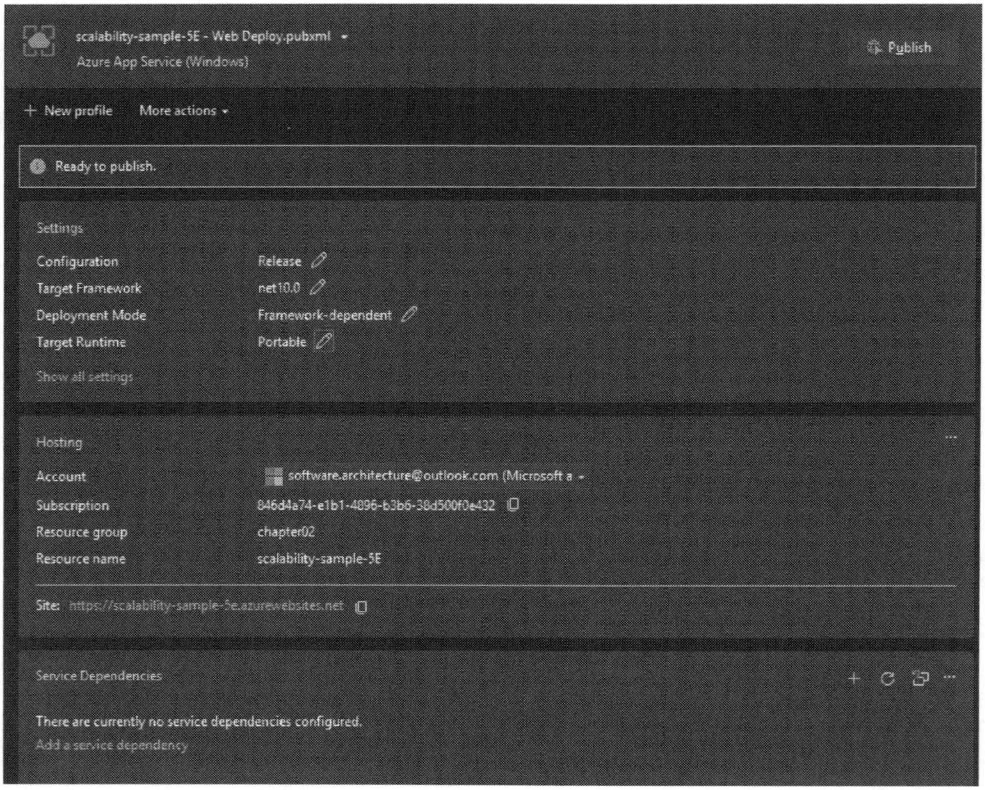

Figure 2.11: Publish Profile Web Deploy

Note

For more information on deploying ASP.NET Core 10 to Azure App Service, please refer to the following link: `https://learn.microsoft.com/en-us/aspnet/core/host-and-deploy/azure-apps/?view=aspnetcore-10.0`

12. Although publishing using Visual Studio 2026 may be considered a good option for demonstration, for the real world it is almost impossible to deliver your publishing strategy using it. For that reason, you might consider using a CI/CD flow based on GitHub Actions, which automatically enables deployment of the code being pushed to a GitHub repo. Note that you must be connected to a GitHub repo to access this new function. Let's use this new feature for this demonstration, shown in *Figure 2.12*. (We will discuss it further in *Chapter 8, Understanding DevSecOps Principles and CI/CD*.)

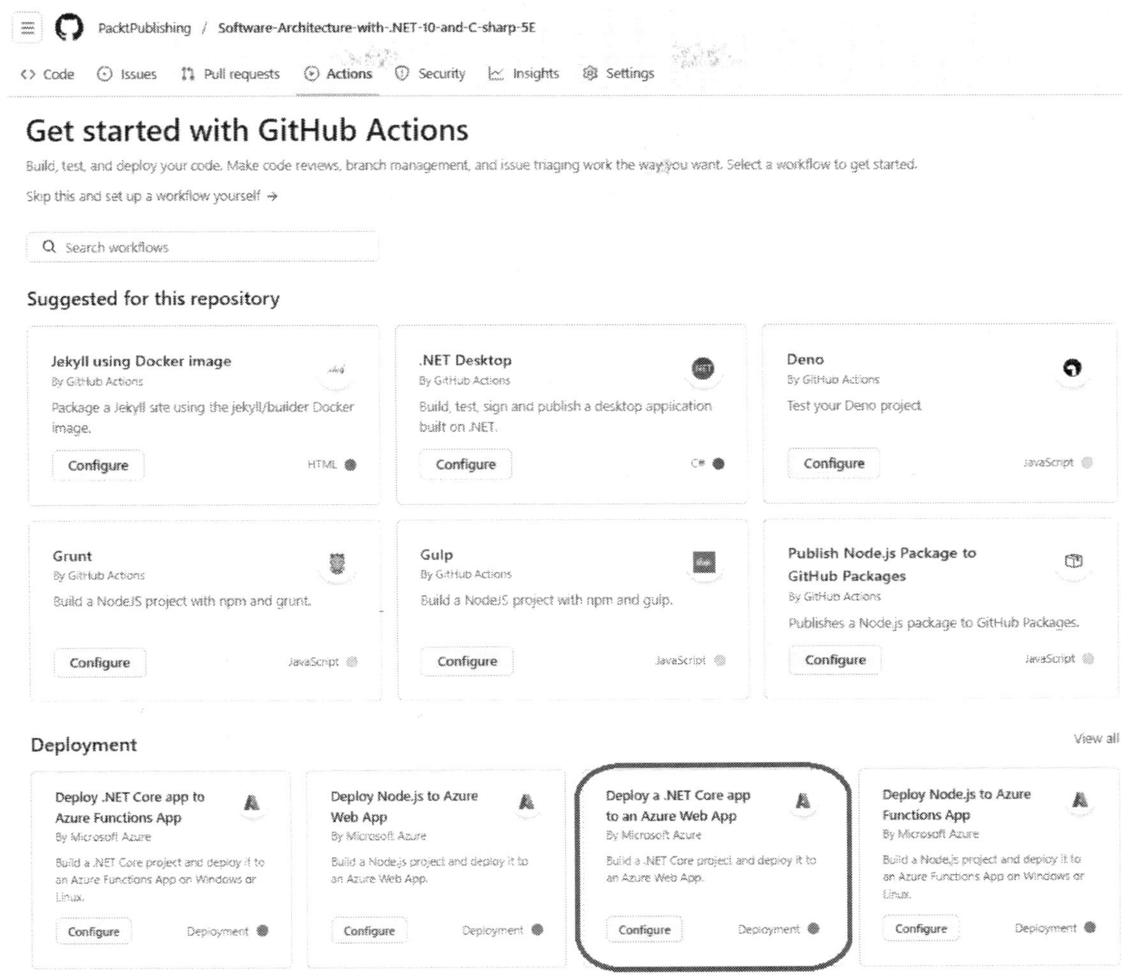

Figure 2.12: Deploying a Web App using GitHub Actions

13. Once you have pushed your code, you can go to the **GitHub Actions** pane and select how you want to deploy the Web App
14. For this second demo, you can select **Deploy a .NET Core App to an Azure Web App**. With this option, a YAML file will be created with all the instructions needed to connect your code to the Web App as shown in *Figure 2.13*.

Software-Architecture-with-.NET-10-and-C-sharp-5E / .github / workflows / scalability-sample-5E.yaml in main

Edit Preview

```yaml
# This workflow will build and push a .NET Core app to an Azure Web App when a commit is pushed to your default branch.
#
# This workflow assumes you have already created the target Azure App Service web app.
# For instructions see https://docs.microsoft.com/en-us/azure/app-service/quickstart-dotnetcore?tabs=net60&pivots=development-environment-vscode
#
# To configure this workflow:
#
# 1. Download the Publish Profile for your Azure Web App. You can download this file from the Overview page of your Web App in the Azure Portal.
#    For more information: https://docs.microsoft.com/en-us/azure/app-service/deploy-github-actions?tabs=applevel#generate-deployment-credentials
#
# 2. Create a secret in your repository named AZURE_WEBAPP_PUBLISH_PROFILE, paste the publish profile contents as the value of the secret.
#    For instructions on obtaining the publish profile see: https://docs.microsoft.com/azure/app-service/deploy-github-actions#configure-the-github-secret
#
# 3. Change the value for the AZURE_WEBAPP_NAME. Optionally, change the AZURE_WEBAPP_PACKAGE_PATH and DOTNET_VERSION environment variables below.
#
# For more information on GitHub Actions for Azure: https://github.com/Azure/Actions
# For more information on the Azure Web Apps Deploy action: https://github.com/Azure/webapps-deploy
# For more samples to get started with GitHub Action workflows to deploy to Azure: https://github.com/Azure/actions-workflow-samples

name: Build and deploy ASP.Net Core app to an Azure Web App

env:
  AZURE_WEBAPP_NAME: your-app-name    # set this to the name of your Azure Web App
  AZURE_WEBAPP_PACKAGE_PATH: '.'      # set this to the path to your web app project, defaults to the repository root
  DOTNET_VERSION: '5'                 # set this to the .NET Core version to use

on:
  push:
    branches: [ "main" ]
  workflow_dispatch:

permissions:
  contents: read

jobs:
  build:
    runs-on: ubuntu-latest

```

Figure 2.13: YAML file used to deploy the application

Tip

Depending on the WebApp you want to deploy, you may need a different script. These scripts are documented at `https://github.com/Azure/webapps-deploy`.

15. Considering you are going to create a connection between GitHub and Azure, there will be some secrets shared between these two portals. The best way to store them on GitHub is by using repository secrets.

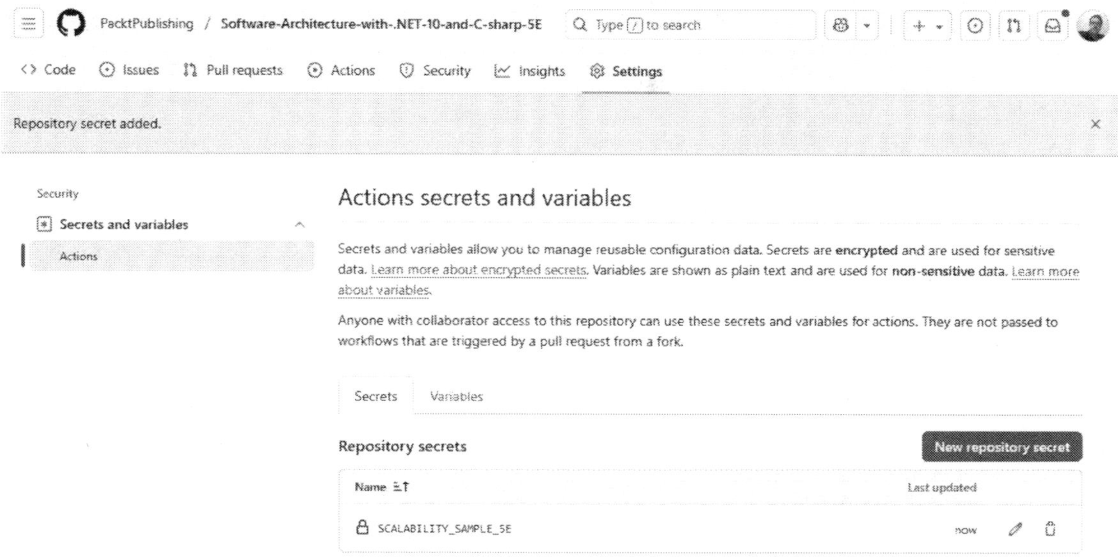

Figure 2.14: GitHub repository secrets

16. Once you have set the correct script, you will be able to check the execution of the GitHub Action

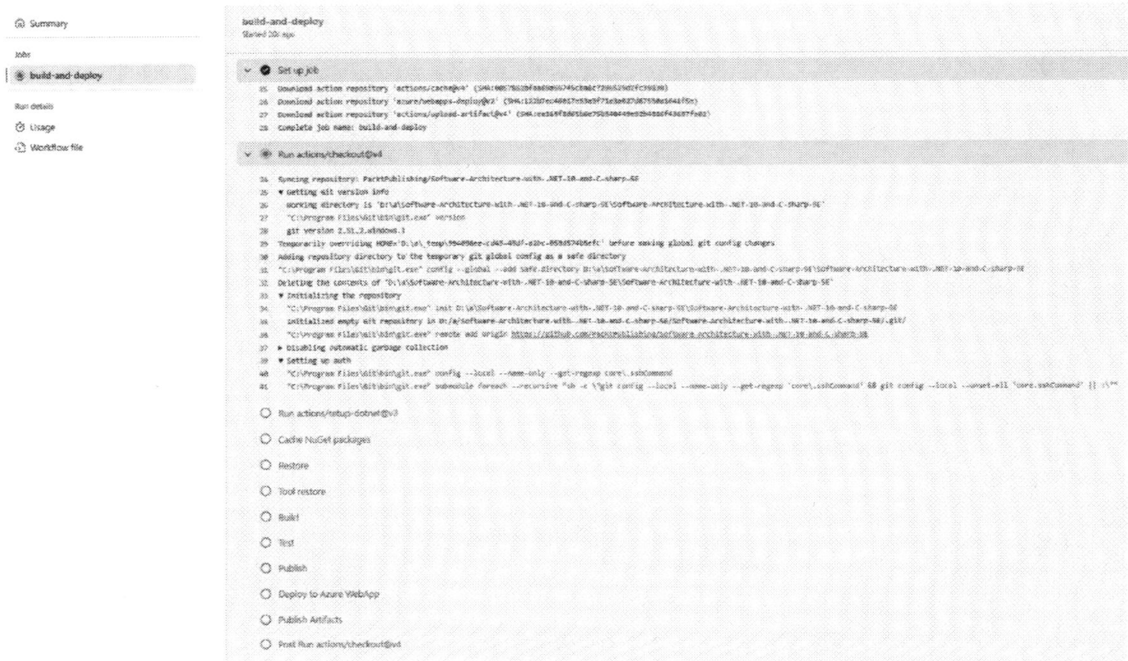

Figure 2.15: GitHub Actions tab

17. Here we have described two ways to deploy a web app. In *Chapter 8, Understanding DevSecOps Principles and CI/CD*, we will go further into *Continuous Integration/Continuous Delivery (CI/CD)* strategies to guarantee the occurrence of all the steps required to get an application to production: building, testing, deployment to staging, and deployment to production.

Now that you have learned a great way to make your WebApps run on Azure, with Visual Studio a good tool to help you achieve it, it is useful to understand performance issues that can affect scalability, responsiveness, and operational efficiency. So, the next section explores some of the challenges you may face while creating a solution.

Performance issues to be considered when programming in C#

Nowadays, C# is one of the most used programming languages in the world, so awareness of C# programming best practices is fundamental for the design of good architectures that satisfy the most common non-functional requirements.

The following sections mention a few simple but effective tips; the associated code samples are available in the GitHub repository for this book. It is worth mentioning that the .NET Foundation has developed a library dedicated to benchmarking, called BenchmarkDotNet, that you may find useful for your scenarios. Check it out at `https://benchmarkdotnet.org/`.

String concatenation

This is a classic one! A naive concatenation of strings with the + string operator may cause serious performance issues, since every time two strings are concatenated, their contents are copied into a new string.

If we concatenate, for instance, 10 strings that have an average length of 100 characters, the first operation has a computing cost of 200, the second one has a cost of `200+100=300`, the third one has a cost of `300+100=400`, and so on. It is not difficult to convince yourself that the overall cost grows as $m \times n^2$, where n is the number of strings and m is their average length. n^2 is not too big for small n (say, $n < 10$), but it becomes quite big when n reaches a magnitude of 100–1,000 and is unacceptable for magnitudes of 10,000–100,000.

Let us look at this with some test code that compares naive concatenation with the same operation but performed with the help of the `StringBuilder` class (the code is available in this book's GitHub repository):

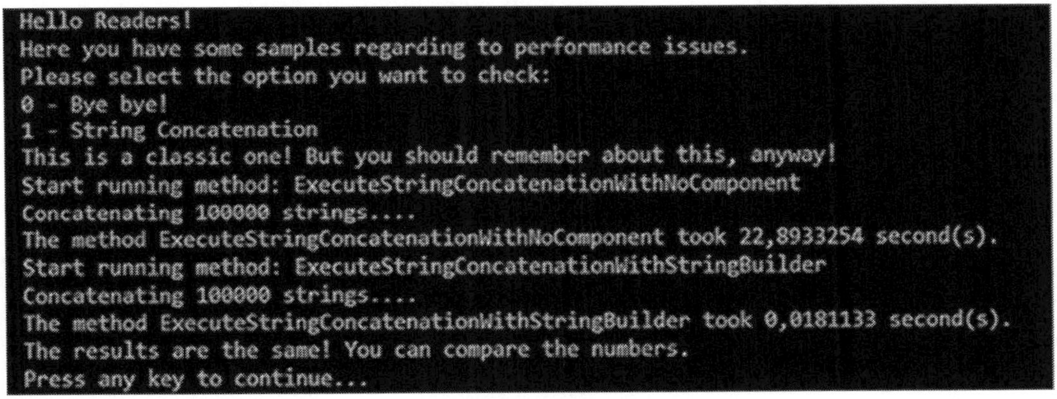

Figure 2.16: Concatenation test code result

If you create a `StringBuilder` class with something like `var sb = new StringBuilder()` and then add each string to it with `sb.Append(currString)`, the strings are not copied; instead, their pointers are queued in a list. They are copied in the final string just once, when you call `sb.ToString()` to get the result. Accordingly, the cost of `StringBuilder`-based concatenation grows simply as $m \times n$.

Of course, you will probably never find a piece of software with a function like the preceding one that concatenates 100,000 strings. However, you need to be alert for pieces of code where 0-100 strings, say, are concatenated simultaneously; in a web server that handles a great number of requests simultaneously, it might cause bottlenecks that damage your non-functional requirements for performance.

Now that we have covered the string concatenation case, let's move to exceptions, an important topic to consider when it comes to performance.

Exceptions

Always remember that exceptions are much slower than normal code flow! So, the use of `try–catch` needs to be concise and essential; otherwise, you run the risk of incurring big performance issues.

The following two samples compare the use of `try-catch` and `int.TryParse` to check whether a string can be converted into an integer:

```
private static string ParseIntWithTryParse()
{
    int? result;
    if (int.TryParse(string.Empty, out var value))
        result = value;
    else
        result = null;
    return $"Final result: {result}";
}
private static string ParseIntWithException()
{
    int? result;
    try
    {
        result = Convert.ToInt32(result);
    }
    catch (Exception)
    {
        result = null;
    }
    return $"Final result: {result}";
}
```

The second function does not look dangerous, but it is thousands of times slower than the first one:

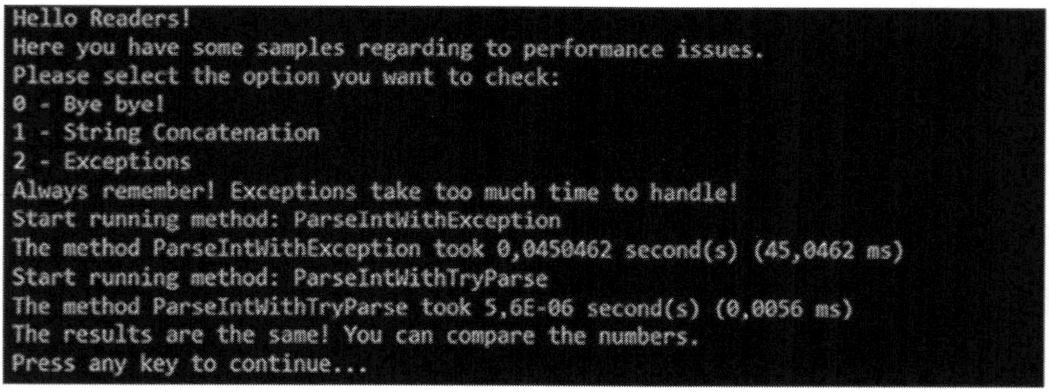

Figure 2.17: Exception test code result

To sum this up, exceptions must be used to deal with exceptional cases that break the normal flow of control, for instance in situations where operations must be aborted for unexpected reasons, and control must be returned several levels up the call stack. Now let's talk about multithreading environments, another challenging topic.

Multithreading environments for better results: do's and don'ts

To take full advantage of all the hardware provided by the system you are building, you must use multithreading. That way, when a thread is waiting for an operation to be completed, the application can leave the CPU to work on other threads instead of wasting CPU time.

On the other hand, no matter how hard Microsoft works to help with this, using parallel code is no piece of cake: it is error-prone and difficult to test and debug. The most important thing to remember as a software architect when contemplating the use of threads is: *does your system require them?* Non-functional and some functional requirements will answer this question for you.

As soon as you are sure that you need a multithreading system, you should decide which technology is most appropriate. Here are some options:

- ***Creating an instance of*** `System.Threading.Thread`: This is a classic way of creating threads in C#. The entire thread life cycle will be in your hands. This is good when you are sure about what you want, but you need control over every single detail of the implementation. The resulting code is hard to conceive and debug/test/maintain, so to keep development costs acceptable this approach should be confined to a few fundamental, performance-critical modules.
- ***Managing threads using*** `System.Threading.ThreadPool`: You can reduce the complexity of thread implementation by using the `ThreadPool` class. If you intend to develop a solution in which you will have many threads being executed, then this could be an especially good option. It is worth mentioning that the .NET thread pool has been re-implemented in .NET 6 as a C# class, bringing new possibilities for experimentation or customization.
- ***Using*** `System.Threading.Tasks.Task` ***and the Task Parallel Library (TPL)***: In most modern .NET applications, this is usually the preferred approach for concurrent work. Instead of explicitly creating and managing threads, developers define units of work as tasks and let the framework decide how they should be scheduled and executed. This reduces implementation complexity while improving readability, maintainability, and flexibility, and it usually represents a better default choice than manually creating threads.
- ***Programming using*** `System.Threading.Tasks.Parallel` ***classes***: Since .NET Framework 4.0, you have been able to use parallel classes to enable threads in a simpler way. This is good because you do not need to worry about the life cycle of the threads you create, but on the other hand, you have less control over what is happening in each thread.
- ***Developing using asynchronous programming***: This is, for sure, the easiest way to develop multithreaded applications, since the compiler takes on most of the work. Depending on how you call an asynchronous method, the task created may run in parallel with the thread used to invoke it. This way, asynchronous code mimics the behavior of classical synchronous code while keeping most of the performance advantages of general parallel programming.

The overall behavior is deterministic and does not depend on the time taken by each task to complete, so non-reproducible bugs are less likely to occur, and the resulting code is straightforward to test, debug, and maintain. Whether to define a method as an asynchronous task or not is the only choice left to the programmer; everything else is automatically handled by the runtime. The only thing you should be concerned about is which methods should have asynchronous behavior. It is worth mentioning that defining a method as `async` does not mean it will execute on a separate thread. There is useful information to be found at `https://docs.microsoft.com/en-us/dotnet/csharp/programming-guide/concepts/async/`.

Later in this book, we will provide some simple examples of asynchronous programming, and for further information about asynchronous programming and its related patterns, check out **Task-Based Asynchronous Patterns** in the Microsoft documentation (`https://docs.microsoft.com/en-us/dotnet/standard/asynchronous-programming-patterns/task-based-asynchronous-pattern-tap`).

> **Note**
>
> TAP is an evolution of EAP (*Event-based Asynchronous Pattern*), which in turn is the successor to APM (Asynchronous Programming Model pattern).

No matter which option you choose, there are some dos and don'ts to which, as a software architect, you must pay attention:

- ***Do use concurrent collections*** (`System.Collections.Concurrent`): As soon as you start a multithreading application, you must use these collections. The reason for this is that your program will probably manage the same list, dictionary, and so on, from different threads. The use of concurrent collections is the most convenient option for developing thread-safe programs.
- ***Do worry about static variables***: It is not possible to say that static variables are prohibited in multithreading development, but you should pay attention to them. Again, multiple threads taking care of the same variable can cause a lot of trouble. If you decorate a static variable with the `[ThreadStatic]` attribute, then each thread will see a different copy of that variable, hence solving the problem of several threads competing for the same value. However, `ThreadStatic` variables cannot be used for extra-thread communications, since values written by a thread cannot be read by other threads. In asynchronous programming, `AsyncLocal<T>` is the option for doing something like that.
- ***Do test system performance after multithreading implementations***: Threads give you the ability to take full advantage of your hardware, but in some cases, badly written threads can waste CPU time just doing nothing! Similar situations may result in almost 100% CPU usage and unacceptable system slowdowns. In some cases, the problem can be mitigated or solved by adding a simple `Thread.Sleep(1)` call in the main loop of some threads to prevent them from wasting too much CPU time, but you need to test this. A typical use case for this approach is a Windows service with many threads running in the background.
- ***Do not consider multithreading easy***: Multithreading is not as simple as it seems in some syntax implementations. While writing a multithreading application, you should consider things such as the synchronization of the user interface, thread termination, and thread coordination. In many cases, programs stop working well due to bad implementation of multithreading.

- ***Do not forget to plan the number of threads your system should have***: This is especially important for 32-bit programs. There is a limitation regarding how many threads you can have in any environment. You should consider this when designing your system.
- ***Do not forget to end each thread that you create***: If you do not use the correct termination procedure for each thread, you will probably have trouble with memory and handle leaks.

Scalability, performance tips, and multithreading are the main tools we can use to tune machine performance. However, the effectiveness of the system you design depends on the overall performance of the whole processing pipeline, which includes both humans and machines. For this reason, in the next section, we will spend a little time discussing how to design effective user interfaces.

Usability – why inserting data takes too much time

As a software architect you cannot improve the performance of humans, but you can improve the performance of man–machine interaction by designing an effective **user interface** (UI), i.e. one that ensures fast interaction with humans. That, in turn, means the following:

- The UI must be easy to learn, to reduce the time needed for the target users to learn how to operate it. This constraint is fundamental if UI changes are frequent, and for public websites that need to attract the greatest possible number of users.
- The UI must not cause any kind of slowdown in data insertion; data entry speed must be limited only by the user's ability to type, not by system delays or additional gestures that could be avoided.
- Today we must also consider accessibility aspects of our solutions, since by doing so we can be more inclusive of users.

It is worth mentioning that there are UX experts in the market. As a software architect, you must decide when their involvement is essential to the success of a project. From a practical perspective, easy-to-learn user interfaces usually depend on a few core principles:

- ***Learnability:*** Each input screen must state its purpose clearly and use the language of the user rather than the language of developers. When the interface matches the user's mental model, it becomes easier to understand and adopt.
- ***Efficiency and simplicity:*** Avoid unnecessary complexity. Design the UI with the average case in mind, while handling more advanced scenarios only when needed. Complex interactions can often be improved by splitting them into smaller steps or by progressively revealing additional inputs.
- ***Guidance and feedback:*** The interface should help users stay on the right path through appropriate suggestions, remembered inputs, and adaptive elements such as cascading drop-down menus. Error messages should not merely indicate that something is wrong, but should clearly explain how users can correct the input and continue their work.

Fast UIs result from efficacious solutions to the following three requirements:

- Input fields must be placed in the order in which they are usually filled, and it should be possible to move to the next input field with the **Tab** or **Enter** key. Moreover, fields that often remain empty should be placed at the bottom of the form. Simply put, usage of the mouse while filling in a form should be minimized. This way, the number of user gestures is kept to a minimum. In a web application, once the optimal placement of input fields has been decided, it is enough to use the `tabindex` attribute to define the right way for users to move from one input field to the next with the **Tab** key.

- System reactions to user input must be as fast as possible. Error (or information) messages must appear as soon as the user leaves the input field. The simplest way to achieve this is to move most of the help and input validation logic to the client side so that system reactions do not need to pass through both communication lines and servers.
- Efficacious selection logic: Selecting an existing item should be as easy as possible; for example, selecting one out of some thousands of products in an offer must be possible with a few gestures and with no need to remember the exact product name or its barcode. The next subsection analyzes techniques we can use to decrease complexity to achieve fast selection.

In *Chapter 18, Client Frameworks: Blazor,* we will discuss how this Microsoft technology can help us with the challenges of building web-based applications using C# code on the frontend.

Designing fast selection logic

When the number of possible choices is in the order of magnitude of 1-50, the usual drop-down menu is enough. For instance, take this currency selection drop-down menu:

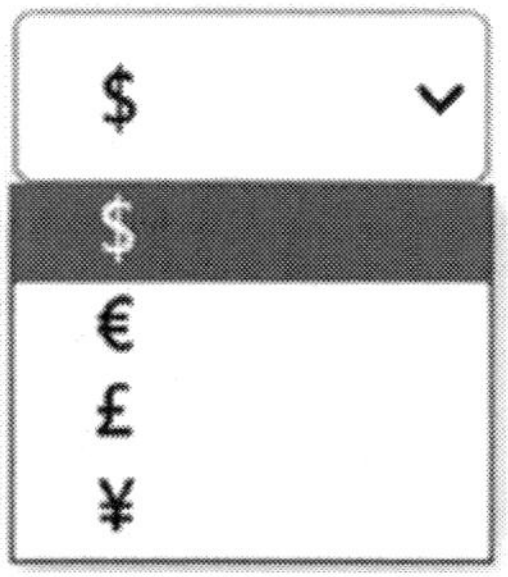

Figure 2.18: Simple drop-down menu

When the order of magnitude is higher but is less than a few thousand, an autocomplete that shows the names of all the items that start with the characters typed by the user is usually a good choice:

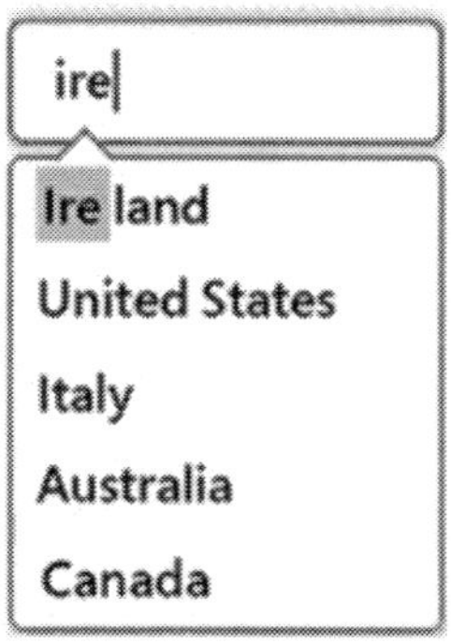

Figure 2.19: Complex drop-down menu

A similar solution can be implemented with low computational cost, since all the main databases can efficiently select strings that start with a given substring.

When names are quite complex, when searching for the characters that were typed in by the user, they should be extended inside each item string. This operation cannot be performed efficiently with the usual databases and requires ad hoc data structures, nor can we forget the debouncing aspect that can happen while typing, when we have a character typed repeatedly unintentionally, as a performance issue as well.

Finally, when we are searching inside descriptions composed of several words, more complex search patterns are needed. This is the case, for instance, with product descriptions. If the chosen database supports full-text search, the system can efficiently search for the occurrence of several words that have been typed by the user inside all the descriptions.

However, when descriptions are made up of names instead of common words, it might be difficult for the user to remember a few exact names contained in the target description. This happens, for instance, with multi-country company names like "Nordic–Ireland Holdings," "APAC–EMEA Shared Services Group," or "Canada–Colombia Trade Finance Partners." In these situations, the system needs a matching algorithm that can infer the best candidate from what the user types.

That typically means looking for partial strings across multiple positions within each description, not just exact prefix or token matches. In general, similar algorithms cannot be implemented efficiently with databases based on indexes but require all the descriptions to be loaded in memory and ranked somehow against the string that was typed by the user.

Now that we have checked some of the possible logics to enable fast selection of data, let's understand how to deal with huge numbers of items in this kind of scenario.

Selecting from a huge number of items

Here, *huge* does not refer to the amount of space needed to store the data, but to the difficulty the user has in remembering the features of each item. When an item must be selected from among more than 10,000–100,000 items, there is no hope of finding it by searching for character occurrences inside a description. Rather, the user must be driven toward the right item through a hierarchy of categories.

In this case, several user gestures are needed to perform a single selection: each selection requires interaction with several input fields. Once it is decided that the selection can't be done with a single input field, the simplest option is to implement cascading drop-down menus, i.e. a chain of drop-down menus whose selection list depends on the values that were selected in the previous drop-down menus.

For example, if the user needed to select a town located anywhere in the world, we might use the first drop-down menu to select the country, and once the country had been chosen, use this choice to populate a second drop-down listing all the towns in the selected country. A simple example is as follows:

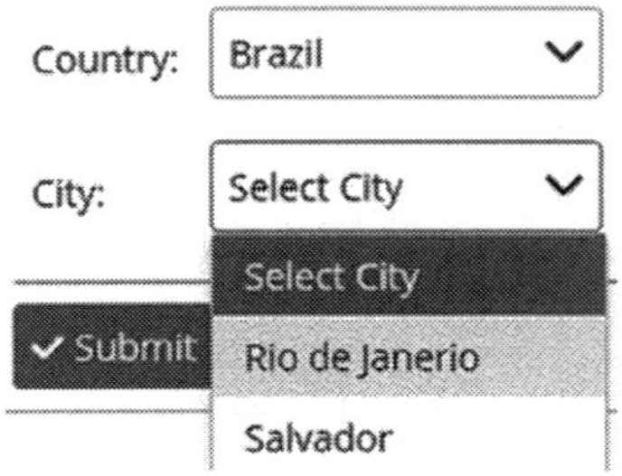

Figure 2.20: Cascading drop-down menu example

Clearly, each drop-down menu could be replaced by an autocomplete when required due to the high number of options.

If making the right selection requires the intersection of several different hierarchies then cascading drop-down menus become inefficient too, and we need a filter form, as follows:

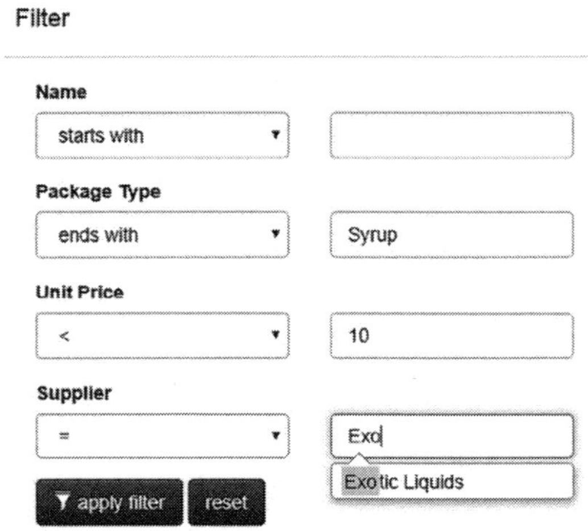

Figure 2.21: Filter form sample

The overall idea here is to enable better usability when you have too much information to present to the user. As a software architect, you will certainly be consulted about this topic. And remember that depending on the user interface decision, the impact on the access of the database can also cause performance issues. After that brief excursion into aspects of software usability, we now turn our attention to another common non-functional requirement: interoperability across different operating systems.

Interoperability with .NET

With .NET Core, Microsoft has given C# developers the ability to deliver their software to a range of platforms. As a software architect, you need to pay attention to this, considering that developing for operating systems like Linux and macOS is a great opportunity to expand the usage of a solution to your customers. Therefore, we need to ensure multi-platform support, a common non-functional requirement for many systems.

The good news is that both console applications and web apps designed with .NET 10 in Windows are almost completely compatible with Linux and macOS. This means you do not have to build the app again to run it on these platforms.

> **Note**
>
> Microsoft offers scripts to help you install .NET on Linux and macOS. You can find them at `https://docs.microsoft.com/dotnet/core/tools/dotnet-install-script`. Once you have the SDK installed, you just need to call `dotnet` the same way you do in Windows.

However, be aware of some features that are not fully compatible with Linux and macOS systems. For instance, no equivalent to the Windows Registry exists in these operating systems, and you must develop an alternative mechanism for storing various application parameters and settings. (An encrypted JSON config file can be a good option.)

Other important points include the fact that Linux is case-sensitive while Windows is not – remember that when you work with files – and that the Linux path separator is different from the Windows separator. You can use the `Path.PathSeparator` field and all the other `Path` class members to ensure your code is multi-platform-compatible, and `Environment.NewLine` can also be useful in some situations.

Note that you can adapt your code to the underlying OS by using the runtime checks provided by .NET 10, as follows:

```
using System.Runtime.InteropServices;
if (RuntimeInformation.IsOSPlatform(OSPlatform.Windows))
    Console.WriteLine("Here you have Windows World!");
else if(RuntimeInformation.IsOSPlatform(OSPlatform.Linux))
    Console.WriteLine("Here you have Linux World!");
else if (RuntimeInformation.IsOSPlatform(OSPlatform.OSX))
    Console.WriteLine("Here you have macOS World!");
```

This example shows that cross-platform development in .NET does not mean ignoring operating system differences. Instead, it means designing the application so that platform-specific behavior is isolated and handled explicitly where necessary. Runtime checks such as these are useful when a feature depends on OS-specific capabilities, file system conventions, native integrations, or external tools that are not uniformly available across environments. In practice, this allows developers to keep most of the codebase portable while still accommodating the differences that matter at execution time.

Although runtime checks are sometimes necessary, they should be used carefully. Excessive platform-specific branching can make the code harder to maintain, so the architect should always look for the right balance between portability and specialization. One area where this balance becomes especially important is background processing at the operating system level. On Windows, .NET provides a specific project type that supports this scenario more directly. On Linux, however, the approach is different and understanding it is an important practical consideration. The next section presents useful tips for creating a service on Linux.

Tip – creating a service in linux

As we have discussed at the end of the last topic, there are some good ways to create a service when you are developing on Windows, but how can we get the same result when developing for the Linux platform? The following script can be used to encapsulate a command-line .NET 10 app in Linux. The idea is that this service works like a Windows service. This service implementation in Linux can be useful, considering that most Linux installations are command-line-only and run without a user logged in:

1. The first step is to create a file that will run the command-line app. The name of the app is `app.dll` and it is installed in `appfolder`. The application will be checked every 5000 milliseconds (i.e., every 5 seconds). This service was created on a CentOS 7 system. Using a Linux terminal, you can type this:

```
cat >sample.service<<EOF
[Unit]
Description=Your Linux Service
After=network.target
[Service]
ExecStart=/usr/bin/dotnet $(pwd)/appfolder/app.dll 5000
Restart=on-failure
[Install]
WantedBy=multi-user.target
EOF
```

2. Once the file has been created you must copy the service file to a system location. After that you must reload the system and enable the service so that it will restart on reboots:

```
sudo cp sample.service /lib/systemd/system
sudo systemctl daemon-reload
sudo systemctl enable sample
```

3. Done! Now you can start, stop, and check the service using the following commands. The whole input that you need to provide in your command-line app is as follows:

```
# Start the service
sudo systemctl start sample
# View service status
sudo systemctl status sample
# Stop the service
sudo systemctl stop sample
```

The output of each command will depend on the way you program your service, but remember that we are talking about background execution, so the most important feedback needs to be delivered in a different way, like log files. Now that we have learned about a few concepts of background application in Linux, let's discuss another important non-functional requirement – security, especially about how to achieve it by design.

Achieving security by design

As is hopefully already apparent, the opportunities, and techniques we have for developing software are incredible. If you add all the information you will read about cloud computing in subsequent chapters, you will see that the opportunities just increase – as does the complexity involved in maintaining software in this computing environment.

As a software architect, you must understand that these opportunities come with many responsibilities. The world has changed a lot in recent years. The second decade of the 21st century has been dominated by technology. Apps, social media, Industry 4.0, big data, and artificial intelligence are no longer future objectives but current technologies that you will lead and deal with in your daily routine. However, the third decade of our century will require much more attention when it comes to cybersecurity.

The world now regulates companies that manage personal data. For instance, the GDPR – the General Data Protection Regulation – is not only mandatory for European territories; it has changed the way software is developed not only in Europe but all over the globe. There are many initiatives comparable to the GDPR that must be added to your glossary of techniques and regulations, considering that the software you design will be impacted by them. In architectural terms, this impact can be seen in decisions about data storage boundaries, retention policies, encryption strategies, logging practices, audit trails, and access control models.

Security by design must be one of your areas of focus for designing new applications. This subject is huge, and it is not going to be completely covered in this book, but as a software architect, you must understand the necessity of having a specialist in the information security area on your team to ensure conformance with the policies and practices needed to avoid cyber-attacks and maintain the confidentiality, privacy, integrity, authenticity, and availability of the services you architect. This is especially important because many architectural choices, such as defining authentication flows, authorization layers, observability mechanisms, and the exposure of APIs and integrations, may create risks if they are made without proper security guidance.

The ASP.NET Core application framework has many features to help you protect your application. For instance, it includes authentication and authorization patterns, and in the OWASP Cheat Sheet Series, you can read about many other .NET practices.

> **Note**
>
> The **Open Web Application Security Project®** (OWASP) is a nonprofit foundation that works to improve the security of software. Check it out at `https://owasp.org/`. For architects, OWASP helps translate security concerns into concrete design decisions, such as adopting secure defaults, reducing attack surfaces, strengthening access control, and addressing common vulnerability patterns from the beginning of the project.

ASP.NET Core also provides features to help you out with the GDPR, providing APIs and templates to guide you in the implementation of policy declaration and cookie usage consent. Although these framework features do not replace architectural responsibility, they help translate regulatory requirements into concrete application behavior. For the software architect, the key point is that compliance must not be treated as an isolated UI or legal detail, but as part of the overall design of data collection, consent management, request handling, and user transparency.

However, regulatory support and framework features alone are not enough to make an application secure. They must be combined with broader architectural practices that reduce risk and strengthen protection across the solution. The next section discusses practices for achieving safe architecture.

Practices for achieving a safe architecture

In this section we overview a starting point of the security-related practices that will help you, as a software architect, take an architectural approach to application safety.

Authentication

One key practice is to define an **authentication method** for your web app. There are many authentication options available nowadays, from ASP.NET Core Identity to external provider authentication methods, such as those provided by Facebook or Google. As a software architect, you must consider who the target audience of the application is. It could be worth considering using *Microsoft Entra* as a starting point if you choose to go down this route.

> **Note**
>
> Microsoft Entra is an *identity* product that manages *who can sign in* and *what can be accessed* across cloud and on-premises environments.

You may find it useful to design authentication associated with Microsoft Entra, a component for helping you manage access at the company you are working for. This alternative is pretty good in some scenarios, especially for internal use.

Depending on the context of the solution you are building, you might need to implement **MFA – Multi-Factor Authentication**. The idea of this pattern is to ask for at least two forms of proof of identity before allowing the solution to be used. It is worth mentioning that Microsoft Entra facilitates the implementation of MFA for you.

You may find it useful to base authentication on the *Microsoft Identity Platform* with *Microsoft Entra ID*. In that case, the **Microsoft Authentication Library (MSAL)** can significantly simplify token handling: it implements the standard OAuth 2.0 / OpenID Connect flows, manages token acquisition and refresh, and provides a built-in token cache so users don't have to sign in repeatedly. MSAL is especially helpful when your app needs to call protected APIs because it can obtain access tokens silently whenever possible and fall back to an interactive prompt only when required. For full implementation details and platform-specific samples, see the official documentation: `https://learn.microsoft.com/en-us/azure/active-directory/develop/msal-overview`.

Do not forget that you must decide on an authentication method for the APIs you provide. JSON Web Token is a pattern accepted worldwide, and its use is totally cross-platform.

You must also determine the authorization model you will use in your web app. There are four model options:

- ***Simple***, where you just use the `[Authorize]` attribute on the protected endpoint, page, class, or method
- ***Role-based***, in which you may declare roles that are allowed to access a given part of the application

- ***Claims-based***, where you define values that must be received during authentication to indicate that the user is authorized, such as `departament_id`, `region_id`, or `employee_id`
- ***Policy-based***, in which there is a policy established to define access requirements for a given resource or operation

You may also define an endpoint, page, class, or method as fully accessible to any user by applying the `[AllowAnonymous]` attribute. Be careful to ensure that this kind of implementation, if you use it, does not introduce vulnerabilities into the system you are designing.

The model you decide to use will define exactly what each user will be able to do in the application.

Sensitive data

While designing, as a software architect you will have to decide which elements of the data you store are sensitive and need to be protected. By connecting to Azure, your web app will be able to store protected data in components such as Azure Storage and Azure Key Vault. Storage in Azure will be discussed in *Chapter 12, How to Choose Your Data Storage in the Cloud.*

> Note
>
> It is highly recommended to check the Data Protection Framework (GDPR in the EU, LGPD in Brazil) that your solution will need to deal with, considering the countries where the application will be placed.

It is worth mentioning that **Azure Key Vault** can be used to protect any database passwords and API secrets your app may have. Consider using this Azure component when you have this kind of requirement.

Web security

It is totally unacceptable to have a production solution deployed without the HTTPS protocol enabled. Azure Web Apps and ASP.NET Core solutions have various possibilities to not only use but *enforce* the use of this security protocol.

There are many known attack methods and malicious patterns to be alert to, such as cross-site request forgery, open redirect, and cross-site scripting. ASP.NET Core provides APIs to solve them. You need to find the ones that are useful for your solution.

Good programming practices, such as avoiding SQL injections by using parameters in your queries, are also important.

> Note
>
> Further information on cloud architecture security patterns can be found at: https://docs.microsoft.com/en-us/azure/architecture/patterns/category/security.

To finish, there are some important structuring security principles that are worth mentioning now, but they are going to be discussed more in *Chapter 20, Securing Data and Applications* and *Chapter 21, Hardening Cloud-based Solutions.* First, security needs to be treated using the onion approach, which means that there are many layers of security to be implemented. Besides that, you must determine a policy to guarantee a process to access the data, including physical access for people who use the system you are developing. In addition, you also must develop a disaster recovery plan in case the system is attacked. The disaster recovery solution will depend on your cloud solution. We will discuss this later in *Chapter 10, Deciding on the Best Cloud-Based Solution*.

Summary

Functional requirements that describe the desired system behavior must be specified together with non-functional requirements that determine the desired parameters around system performance, scalability, availability, resilience, interoperability, usability, and security.

At this point, the architect plays a critical role in reconciling these concerns, because non-functional requirements often conflict and cannot all be maximized at the same time. Architecture therefore requires conscious trade-off decisions that align technical qualities with business priorities.

Performance requirements relate in the main to response times and system load capabilities. As a software architect, your concern is to obtain the required performance at the minimum cost, build efficient algorithms, and take full advantage of the available hardware resources with multithreading.

Scalability is the ability of a system to be adapted to an increasing load. Systems can be scaled vertically by providing more powerful hardware, or horizontally by replicating and load balancing the same hardware, which increases the availability. Cloud in general, and Azure specifically, can help us implement strategies dynamically, with no need to stop your application.

Tools such as .NET 10 that run on several platforms can ensure interoperability, that is, the ability of your software to run on different target machines and with different operating systems (Windows, Linux, macOS, Android, IOS, and so on).

Usability is ensured by taking care of field input order, the effectiveness of item selection logic, and how easy your system is to learn.

In addition, the more complex your solution is, the greater the need for it to be resilient. The idea of resilience is not to guarantee that the solution does not fail. Instead, the idea is to guarantee that the solution has an action defined when each part of the software fails.

As a software architect, you must consider security from the very beginning of the design process. Following the practices presented in the chapter for achieving safe architecture to determine the correct patterns and having a security specialist on your team are the best ways to comply with all the current regulations we have.

In the next chapter, you will learn how Azure DevOps and GitHub can help us when it comes to collecting, defining, and documenting solution requirements.

Questions

1. What are the two conceptual ways to scale a system?
2. Can you deploy your web app automatically from Visual Studio to Azure?
3. What is multithreading useful for?
4. What are the main advantages of the asynchronous pattern over other multithreading techniques?

5. Why is the order of input fields so important?
6. Why is the Path class so important for interoperability?

Further reading

The following are some links you may consider reading to gather more information in relation to this chapter:

- `https://learn.microsoft.com/en-us/azure/app-service/manage-automatic-scaling`
- `https://docs.microsoft.com/en-us/azure/architecture/best-practices/auto-scaling`
- `https://docs.microsoft.com/en-us/aspnet/core/host-and-deploy/azure-apps/`
- `https://docs.microsoft.com/en-us/dotnet/standard/parallel-processing-and-concurrency`
- `https://docs.microsoft.com/en-us/dotnet/standard/parallel-programming/`
- `https://devblogs.microsoft.com/dotnet/performance-improvements-in-net-10`
- `https://docs.microsoft.com/en-us/dotnet/standard/security/`
- `https://docs.microsoft.com/en-us/aspnet/core/security/`
- `https://owasp.org/`
- `https://cheatsheetseries.owasp.org/cheatsheets/DotNet_Security_Cheat_Sheet.html`
- `https://docs.microsoft.com/en-us/aspnet/core/security/gdpr`
- `https://docs.microsoft.com/en-us/azure/architecture/patterns/category/resiliency`
- `https://docs.microsoft.com/en-us/azure/architecture/patterns/category/availability`
- `https://dotnet.microsoft.com/platform/support/policy`
- `https://benchmarkdotnet.org/`
- `https://learn.microsoft.com/en-us/azure/active-directory/develop/msal-overview`

3

Managing Requirements

Based on what we covered in *Chapters 1 and 2*, the first step in software development is to create a software project. When it comes to software projects, the biggest challenge is how to organize them in such a way that every single participant understands what is needed. The best way to do that is to organize project requirements. But more than that, connecting a project's requirements to a code repository will deliver a more efficient and collaborative view of the project being worked on, while also enhancing traceability from requirements to code and deployment.

Good requirements management is not just about documenting what the system should do. It also requires clarity, traceability, and the ability to evolve requirements as the solution grows and changes. For years, Microsoft has invested in tools to support this process, with Team Foundation Server and Visual Studio Team Services being notable examples. Today, two strong approaches stand out and will be discussed in this chapter: Azure DevOps and GitHub.

Azure DevOps is an evolution of Visual Studio Team Services, and it offers a variety of new features that can help developers to document and organize their software. GitHub is well known as an online code repository, but following its acquisition by Microsoft, a bunch of great tools for application lifecycle management have been integrated into it. From the release of GitHub Copilot to the presentation of GitHub Copilot Coding Agent, the way developers create software has changed and, for this reason, as software architects, we must find different ways of using GitHub.

The following topics will be covered in this chapter:

- Azure DevOps approach to managing projects
- GitHub approach to managing projects
- Impact of AI on managing and implementing requirements

The first two sections of the chapter summarize the main functionalities offered by these tools, while the remaining sections focus specifically on tools for documenting requirements and supporting the overall development process. Most of the functionality introduced in the first two sections will be analyzed in more detail in other chapters.

Technical requirements

This chapter requires you to create a new free Azure account or use an existing one. The *Creating an Azure account* section in *Chapter 1, Understanding the Importance of Software Architecture*, explains account creation.

Introducing Azure DevOps

Azure DevOps is a Microsoft **Software-as-a-Service** (SaaS) platform that helps teams plan projects, store code safely, test solutions, and publish them across staging and production environments. From a requirements perspective, it also helps teams keep work organized, improve traceability, and maintain alignment between business needs and delivered software.

The automation of all the steps involved in software production greatly facilitates the continuous enhancement and improvement of an existing solution to adapt it to market needs.

You can start the process by accessing `https://dev.azure.com`. There you will be able to sign up using a new account or even sign in using your GitHub account. Once you have access to it, you will be asked to create an organization, as you can see in the following figure:

Figure 3.1: Creating an Azure DevOps organization

After the organization is created, you will be able to create a new project, as we can see in the following screenshot:

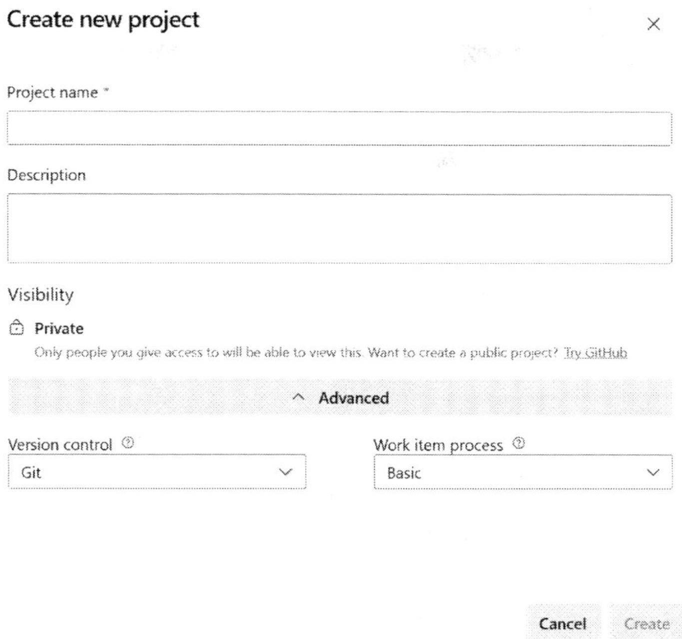

Figure 3.2: Creating a project using Azure DevOps

It is important to mention that public projects can be used, so long as you comply with the Azure DevOps code of conduct. Once you define the name of the project and its visibility, you will have the project created in seconds, as you can see from the following screenshot:

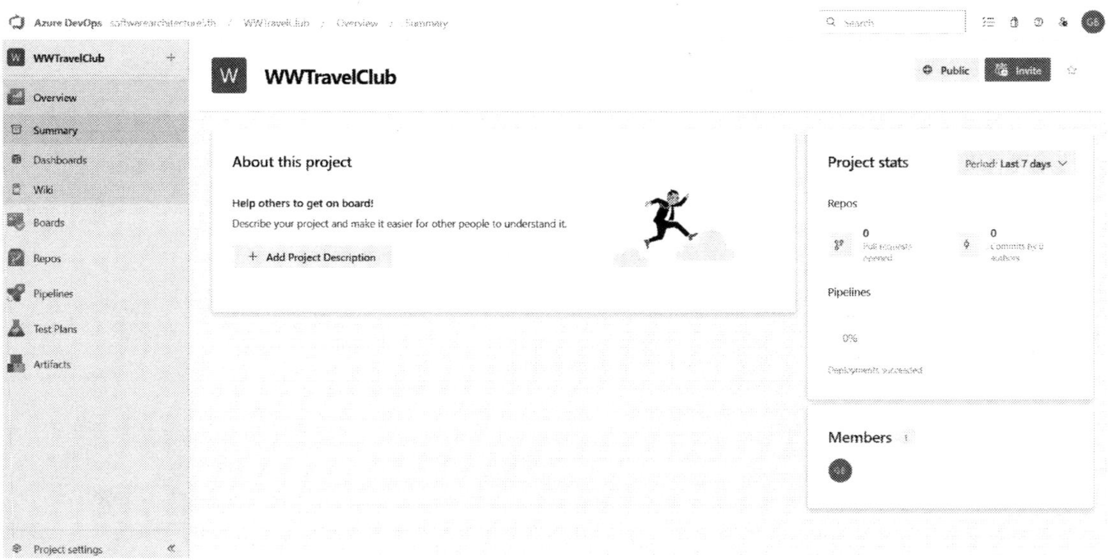

Figure 3.3: Azure DevOps project created

DevOps itself will be discussed in detail in *Chapter 8, Understanding DevSecOps Principles and CI/CD*, but for now you can understand it as a philosophy that is focused on delivering value to customers. It is the union of people, processes, and products, where the **Continuous Integration** and **Continuous Deployment** (CI/CD) methodology is used to apply continuous improvements to a software application delivered to the production environment. Azure DevOps is a powerful tool whose range of applications encompasses all the steps involved in both the initial development of an application and its subsequent CI/CD process.

Azure DevOps contains tools for collecting requirements and organizing the whole development process. They can be accessed by clicking the **Boards** menu option on the Azure DevOps page, as shown in *Figure 3.4*:

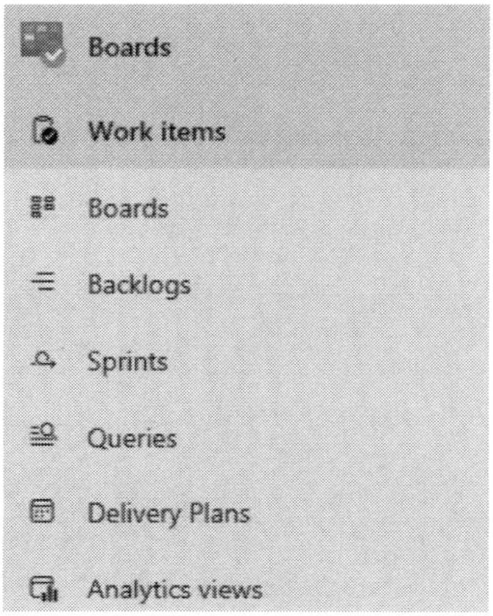

Figure 3.4: Azure DevOps Boards menu

All other functionalities available in Azure DevOps are briefly reviewed in the following subsections: they will be discussed in detail in later chapters. More specifically, DevOps principles and CI/CD are discussed in *Chapter 8, Understanding DevSecOps Principles and CI/CD*, and build/test pipelines in *Chapter 9, Testing Your Enterprise Application*. Now that we have the Azure DevOps Project set, let's understand how to manage system requirements on it.

Managing system requirements in Azure DevOps

In Azure DevOps, work items are the central structure used to transform requirements into manageable and traceable units of work. This makes them one of the main mechanisms through which requirements management happens inside the platform.

Work items are stored in your project as chunks of information that can be assigned to a person. They are classified into various types and can contain a measure of the development effort required, a status, and the development stage (iteration) they belong to. Principally they are tasks or actions that need to be completed to deliver a product or service. In this way, work items help ensure that requirements are not only documented, but also managed as deliverable and traceable parts of the solution.

DevOps is usually combined with agile methodologies, so Azure DevOps uses iterations, and the whole development process is organized as a set of sprints. The work items available depend on the **work item process** you select while creating the Azure DevOps project.

Note

You can check project types in Azure DevOps at `https://learn.microsoft.com/en-us/azure/devops/boards/work-items/guidance/choose-process`.

The following subsections contain a description of the most common work item types that appear when an **Agile** or **Scrum** work item process is selected (the default is **Agile**). The hierarchy presented in the following topics is how requirements evolve from high-level intent to executable work.

Epic work items

Imagine you are developing a system comprising various subsystems. You are probably not going to conclude the whole system in a single iteration. Therefore, we need an umbrella concept spanning several iterations to encapsulate all the features of each subsystem. Each Epic work item represents one of these umbrellas, which can contain several features to be implemented across several development iterations.

In the Epic work item, you can define the state and acceptance criteria as well as the start date and target date. Besides this, you can also provide priority and an effort estimate. All this detailed information helps the stakeholders follow the development process. The epic is useful as a macro view of the project, and now we will go a little bit deeper to another work item that is useful to define functionalities, called the feature work item.

Feature work items

All the information that you provide in an Epic work item can also be placed in a Feature work item. So, the difference between these two types of work items is not related to the kind of information they contain but rather to their respective roles and the goals your team aims to accomplish. A **feature** is a shippable software component. Epics may span several iterations and hierarchically are positioned above Features; that is, each Epic work item is linked to several child features, while each Feature work item is usually implemented in a few sprints and is part of a single Epic work item.

It is worth mentioning that all work items have sections for team discussions. There you can find a team member by typing the "@" character, as in many forums/social media applications. Inside each work item, you can link and attach various information. You can also check the history of the current work item in a specific section.

Feature work items are the places to start recording user requirements. This is because features usually represent user intent at a level that is detailed enough to guide implementation and planning, while epics are often too broad and better suited to grouping larger strategic objectives. For instance, you can write a Feature work item called **Access Control** to define the complete functionality needed to implement the system access control. Now let's check the difference between Product Backlog items and User Story work items in the next section.

Product backlog items vs. user story work items

Which of these work items is available depends on the development process selected. There are minor differences between them, but their purpose is essentially the same. They contain detailed requirements for features, described by the Feature work items they are connected to. More specifically, each Product Backlog/User Story work item specifies the requirements of a single functionality that is part of the behavior described in its parent Feature work item.

For instance, in a Feature work item for system access control, the maintenance of the users and the login interface should be two different User Story/Product Backlog items. These requirements will guide the creation of other child work items:

- ***Tasks***: These are important work items that describe the job that needs to be done to meet the requirements stated in the parent Product Backlog items/User Story work item. Task work items can contain time estimates, which help with team capacity management and overall scheduling.
- ***Test cases***: These items describe how to test the functionality described in the requirements.

> **Note**
>
> Considering that you will have many work items in a project, visualizing them is not an easy task. For this reason, you may consider *Work Item Visualization* to simplify your view. Check it out at `https://marketplace.visualstudio.com/items?itemName=ms-devlabs.WorkItemVisualization`.

The number of tasks and test cases you will create for each Product Backlog/User Story work item will vary according to the development and testing scenario you use.

Connecting requirements to delivery artifacts

Good requirements management does not end when requirements are documented as work items. To be truly useful, requirements must remain traceable as the project advances from planning to implementation, testing, and deployment.

In Azure DevOps, this means that requirements can be connected to the artifacts that bring them to life. A Feature, Product Backlog item, or User Story should not remain an isolated planning element; it should be associated with code changes, validation activities, and delivery steps. This traceability helps preserve alignment between business needs and the software being produced.

From an architectural point of view, this end-to-end visibility improves governance, collaboration, and impact analysis. It helps teams understand how a requirement evolves into working software and gives stakeholders greater confidence in the delivery process. The following sections present repositories, package feeds, test resources, and pipelines as mechanisms that extend requirements management across the software lifecycle.

Azure DevOps repository

There is no software without code, and the code implemented in response to a software requirement needs to be placed in a software repository. The **Repos** menu item gives you access to a default Git repository where you can place project code, as you can see below:

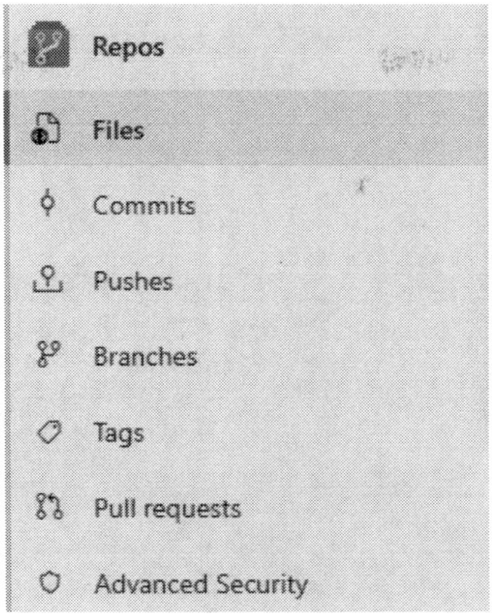

Figure 3.5: Azure DevOps Repos menu

By clicking the **Files** item, you enter the default repository's initial page. It is empty and contains instructions on how to connect to this default repository.

You can add further repositories through the drop-down menu at the top of the page:

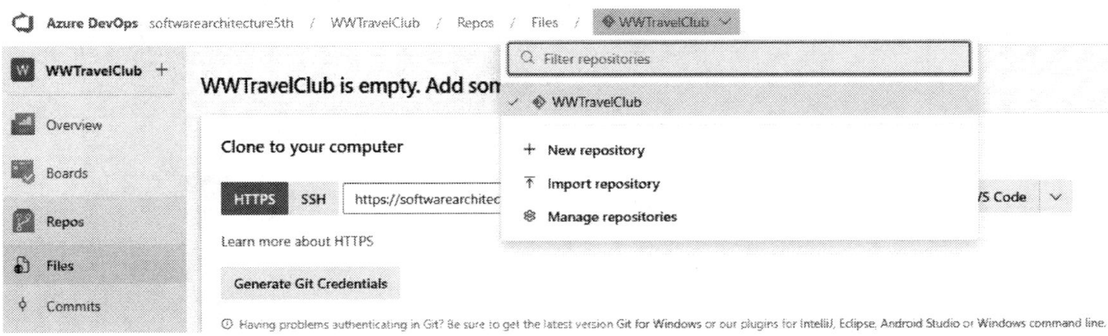

Figure 3.6: Adding a new repository

All repositories created are accessible through the same drop-down menu.

As shown in the preceding screenshot, each repository's initial page contains the repository address and a button to generate repository-specific credentials, so you can connect to your DevOps repositories with your favorite Git tools. However, you can also connect from inside Visual Studio in a very simple way:

1. Start Visual Studio and ensure you are logged in to it with the same Microsoft account used to define your DevOps project (or that was used to add you as a team member)
2. If the **Git Changes** window is not open, make it appear by going to the top menu in Visual Studio and selecting **View -> Git Changes**, as you can see in *Figure 3.7*

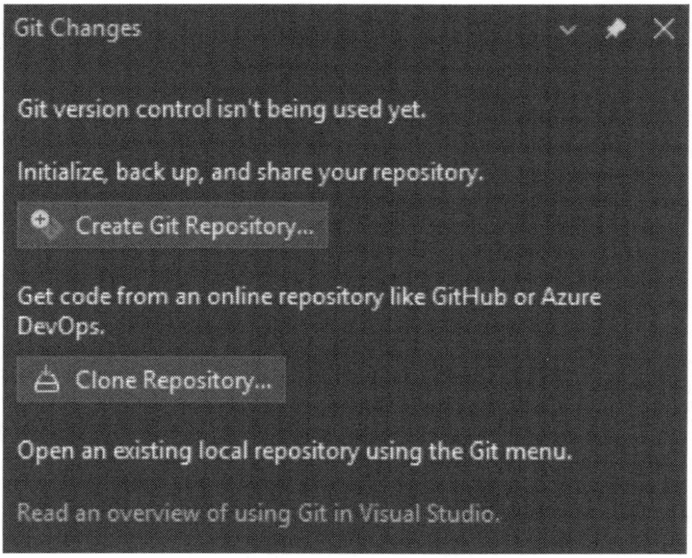

Figure 3.7: Git Changes window

3. Click the **Clone Repository...** button in the **Git Changes** window.
4. In the window that opens, select **Existing remote** and insert the URL of the DevOps repository you created. Then, click **Create and Push**:

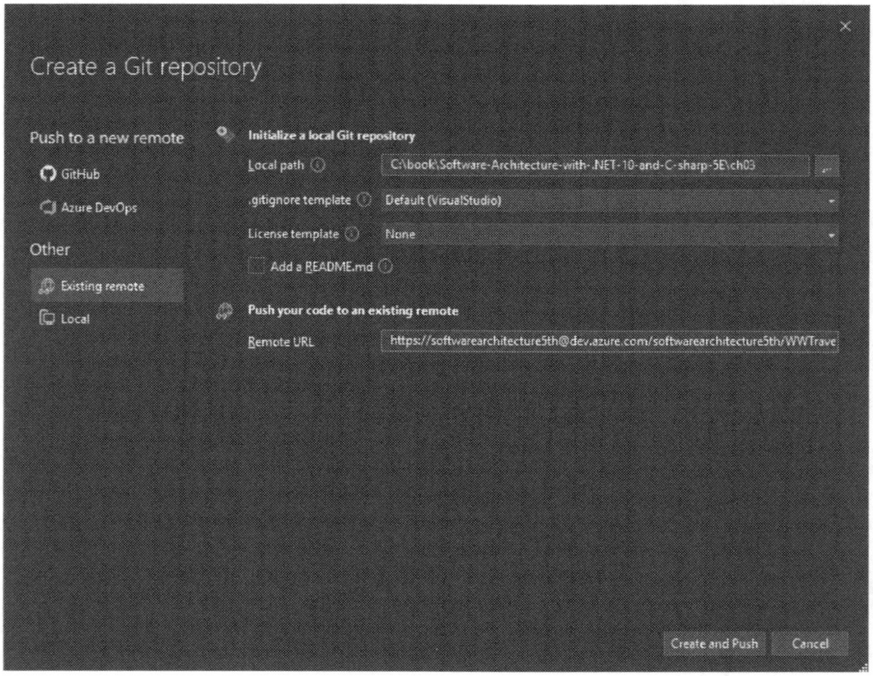

Figure 3.8: Connecting to the remote DevOps repository

Once connected to your DevOps remote repository, the **Git Changes** window will show several Git commands, as you can check in *Figure 3.9*. These commands are represented by downward and upward arrows.

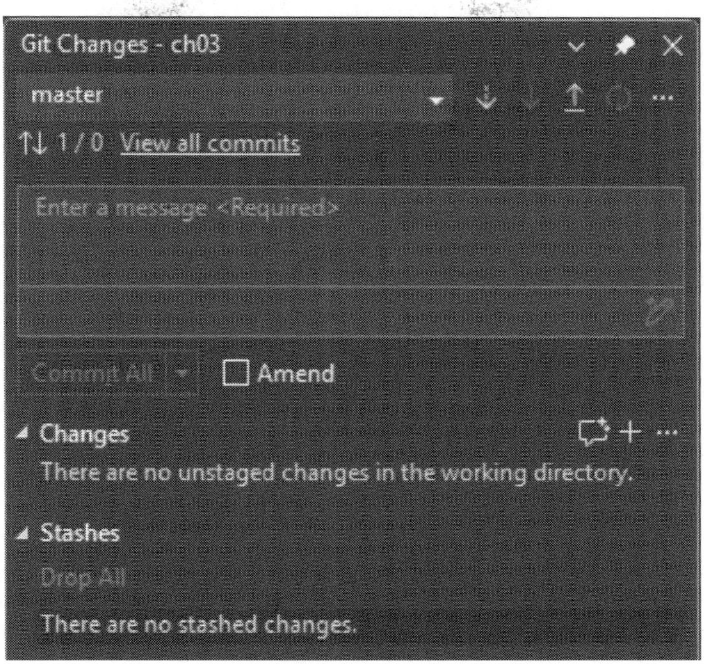

Figure 3.9: Git Changes window

When you have changes to commit, you can insert a message in the textbox at the top of the window and commit them locally by clicking the **Commit All** button, or you can click the dropdown next to this button to access more options:

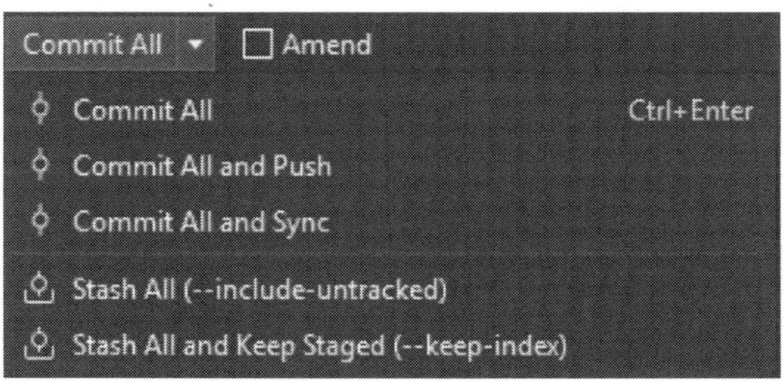

Figure 3.10: Commit options

You can commit and push or commit and sync, but you can also stage your changes. The three arrows in the top right of the **Git Changes** window trigger a fetch, pull, and push, respectively. Meanwhile, the dropdown at the top of the window takes care of operations on branches:

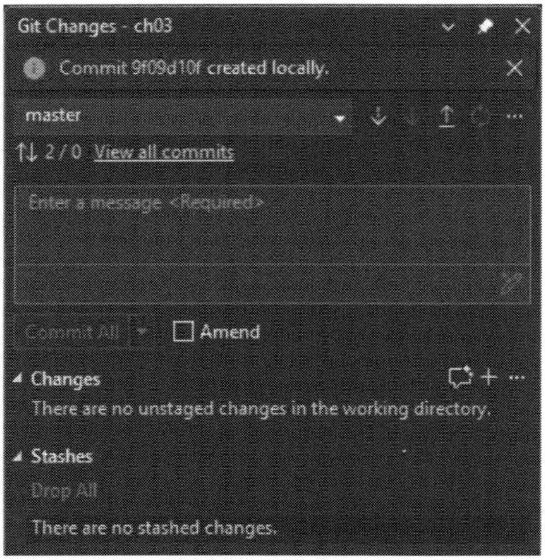

Figure 3.11: Branch operations

Between publication of the previous edition of this book and this new one, a very important feature was released to Azure DevOps Repository users: **code scanning**. This feature is focused on finding security issues in your code, using `CodeQL` – the GitHub code analysis engine. This option is available for projects that activate the Code Security for Azure DevOps feature.

> **Note**
>
> More information about Code Security for Azure DevOps is available at `https://learn.microsoft.com/en-us/azure/devops/repos/security/github-advanced-security-code-scanning`.

The complete tool enables alerts for vulnerabilities that affect your dependencies, alerts for vulnerabilities and coding errors, and alerts indicating secret exposures. Now let's check how to manage packages inside Azure DevOps.

Package feeds

A great way to accelerate software development is by reusing code components that meet user requirements. In general, these components are placed into packages. We will discuss this further in *Chapter 5, Implementing Code Reusability in C#*. The **Artifacts** menu handles the software packages used or created by the project. There you can define feeds for basically all types of package, including NuGet, Node.js, and Python. Private feeds are required since commercial projects also use private packages, and you need a place to put them. Moreover, packages produced during builds are placed in these feeds so that other modules which have them as dependencies can use them immediately.

Once in the **Artifacts** area, you can create several feeds by clicking the **+ Create Feed** button. Each feed can handle several kinds of packages, as shown in *Figure 3.12*.

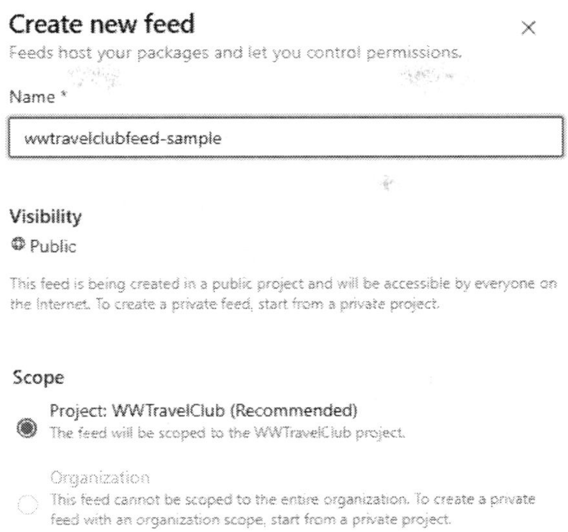

Figure 3.12: Feed creation

If you select the option to connect to packages from public sources, then by default the feed connects to `npmjs`, `nuget.org`, `pypi.org`, and `Maven`. However, you can go to the **Search Upstream sources** tab on the **Feed** settings page and remove/add package sources. The settings page can be reached by clicking the settings icon in the upper-right corner of the feed page.

A screenshot of the page of the newly created feed follows:

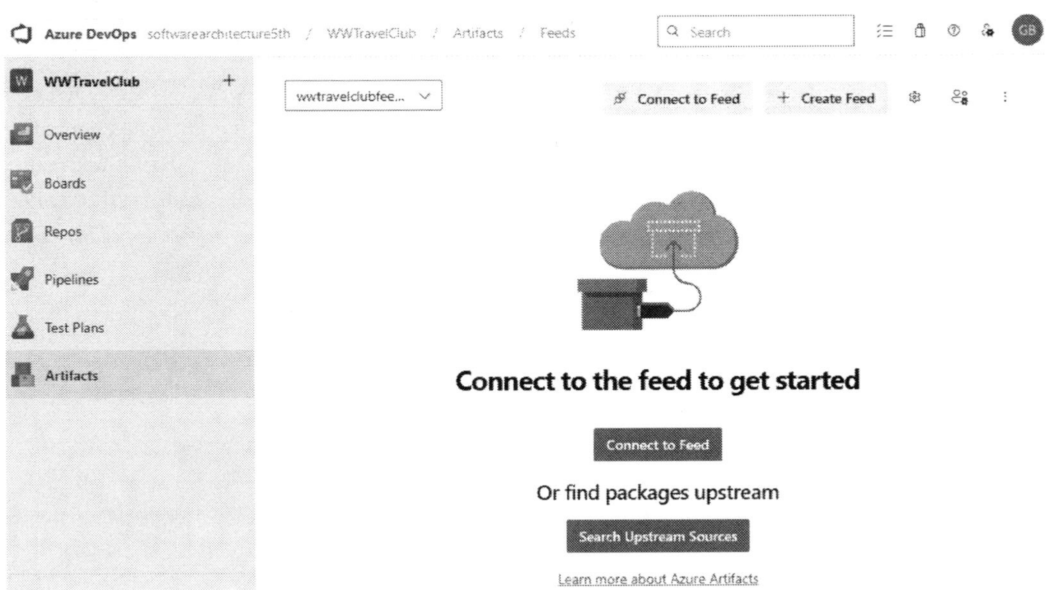

Figure 3.13: Feed page

The **Connect to Feed** button for each feed shows a window that explains, for each package type, how to connect to the feed, as you can see in *Figure 3.14*.

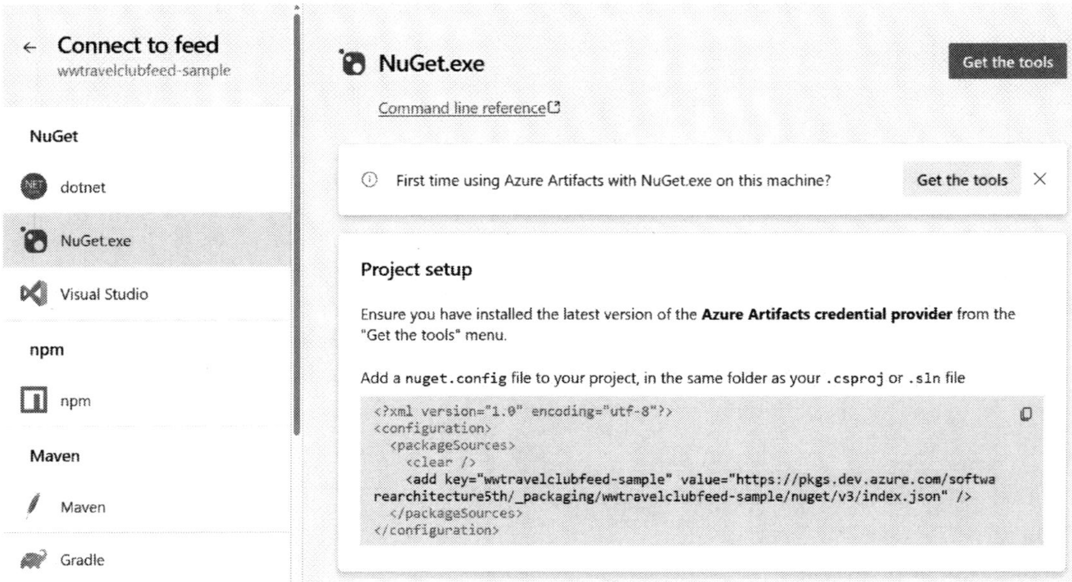

Figure 3.14: Feed connection information

For NuGet packages, you should add all project feeds to your Visual Studio projects or solutions `nuget.config` file so that local machines can also use them; otherwise, your local building will fail. Considering the packages are properly set, let's understand better how Azure DevOps deals with tests.

Test plans

The **Test Plans** section allows you to define the test plans you want to use and their settings. Tests are discussed in detail in *Chapter 9*, *Testing Your Enterprise Application*, but here we would like to summarize the opportunities offered by Azure DevOps. Test-related operations and settings can be accessed through the **Test Plans** menu item, as you can see in *Figure 3.15*. It is important to mention that you need a specific license to enable all the features of Test Plans in Azure DevOps. The full Test Plans feature set usually requires *Basic + Test Plans* access rather than the standard Basic license, although it may already be included for users with subscriptions such as *Visual Studio Enterprise*, *Visual Studio Test Professional*, or *MSDN Platforms*.

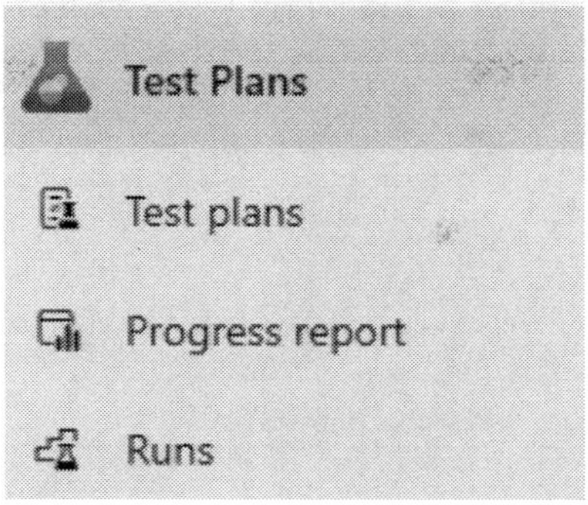

Figure 3.15: Test Plans menu

Here you may define, execute, and track test plans made up of the following:

- Manual acceptance tests
- Automatic unit tests
- Load tests

Automatic unit tests must be defined in test projects contained in the Visual Studio solution and based on a framework such as NUnit, xUnit, or MSTest (the .NET SDK has project templates for all of them, so you may find them in Visual Studio). Test Plans gives you the opportunity to execute these tests on Azure and to define the following:

- Several configuration settings
- When to execute them
- How to track them and where to report their results in the overall project documentation

For manual tests, you may define complete instructions for the operator in the project documentation, covering the execution environment (for example, an operating system) and where to report their results. You can also define how to execute load tests and how to measure the results. Once your test strategy is ready, let's move to pipelines, which will certainly enable automation to your DevOps cycle.

Pipelines

Pipelines are automatic action plans that specify all steps from the building of the code to the software deployment to production. They can be defined in the **Pipelines** area, which is accessible through the **Pipelines** menu item, as you can check in *Figure 3.16*:

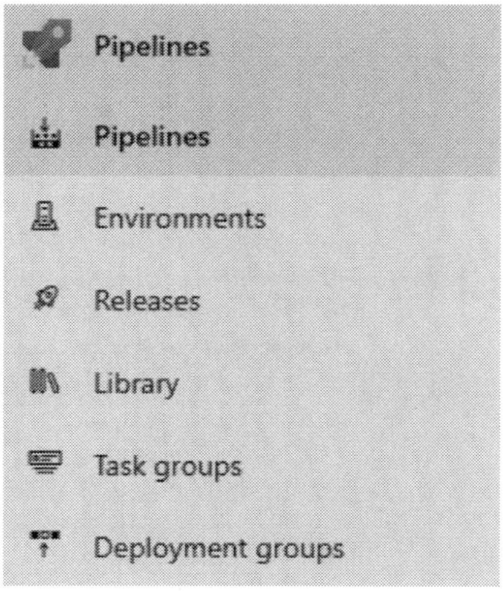

Figure 3.16: Pipelines menu

There you can define a complete pipeline of tasks to be executed, alongside their triggering events, which can encompass steps such as code building, launching test plans, and what to do after the tests have passed.

Typically, after the tests have passed, the application is automatically deployed to a staging area where it can be beta-tested. You can also define the criteria for automatic deployment to production. Such criteria include, but are not limited to, the following:

- The number of days during which the application was beta-tested
- The number of bugs found during beta-testing and/or removed by the last code change
- Manual approval by one or more managers or team members

The decision criteria will depend on the way the organization wants to manage the product that is being developed. You, as a software architect, must understand that when it comes to moving code to production, the rule is: the safer, the better.

As you can see from the preceding topics, the process for creating an Azure DevOps account is extremely simple. It is worth mentioning that you can start using this fantastic tool *at no cost* since you have no more than five developers on your team, plus any number of stakeholders. But even with all the benefits presented by Azure DevOps, there is another tool that is being extremely used and improved over the last years – GitHub. So, let's check how GitHub deals with projects in the next sections.

Introducing GitHub projects

Considering all the benefits of Azure DevOps that we've presented, you may now be asking why we need to explore another tool. The reason is simple: GitHub has become, over the years, a mainstay of the open-source world. So, we will find many initiatives and projects in the GitHub space that have changed the way we deliver software.

The main objective of GitHub is to manage code and guarantee that its users can create solutions in a collaborative way. For this, the platform presents features like version control, pull requests, code reviews, issue tracking, and CI/CD.

But it would be impossible to design great projects without a platform to support them. That is why we have GitHub Projects, an initiative that delivers an adaptable, flexible tool for planning and tracking work on GitHub.

> **Note**
>
> You can find more information about GitHub Projects at `https://docs.github.com/en/issues/planning-and-tracking-with-projects/learning-about-projects/about-projects`.

It is quite simple to set up a project on GitHub. Once you log in to the platform, you will find **Projects** in the left-side menu as shown in the following screenshot:

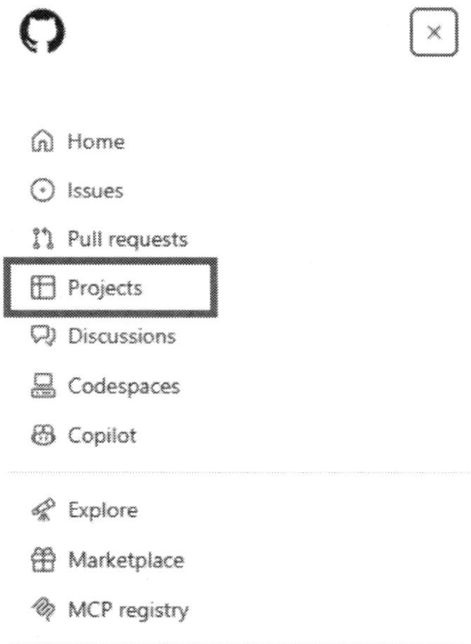

Figure 3.17: Accessing GitHub projects

You will find an option for creating a new project in the '+' menu on the right side. You will find different templates already provided by GitHub, as you can see in *Figure 3.18*.

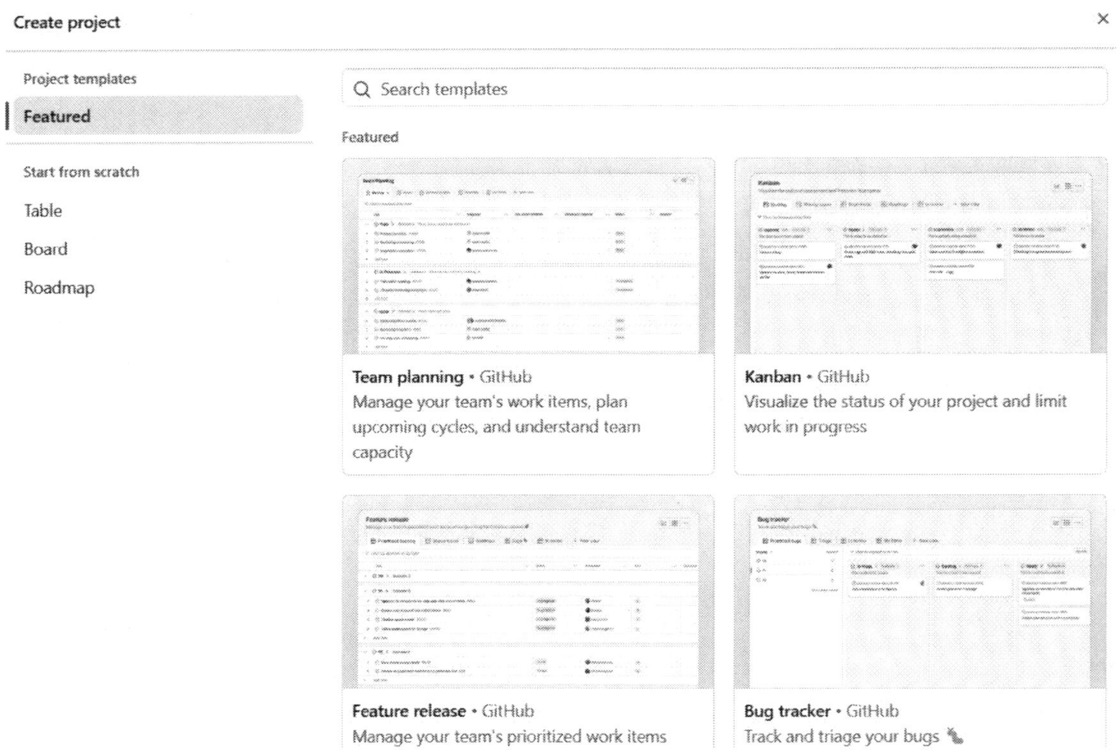

Figure 3.18: Creating a project on GitHub

The project needs to be linked to a repository. You can do this by accessing the **Projects** tab in your repo, as you can see in *Figure 3.19*. There you can also create a new project.

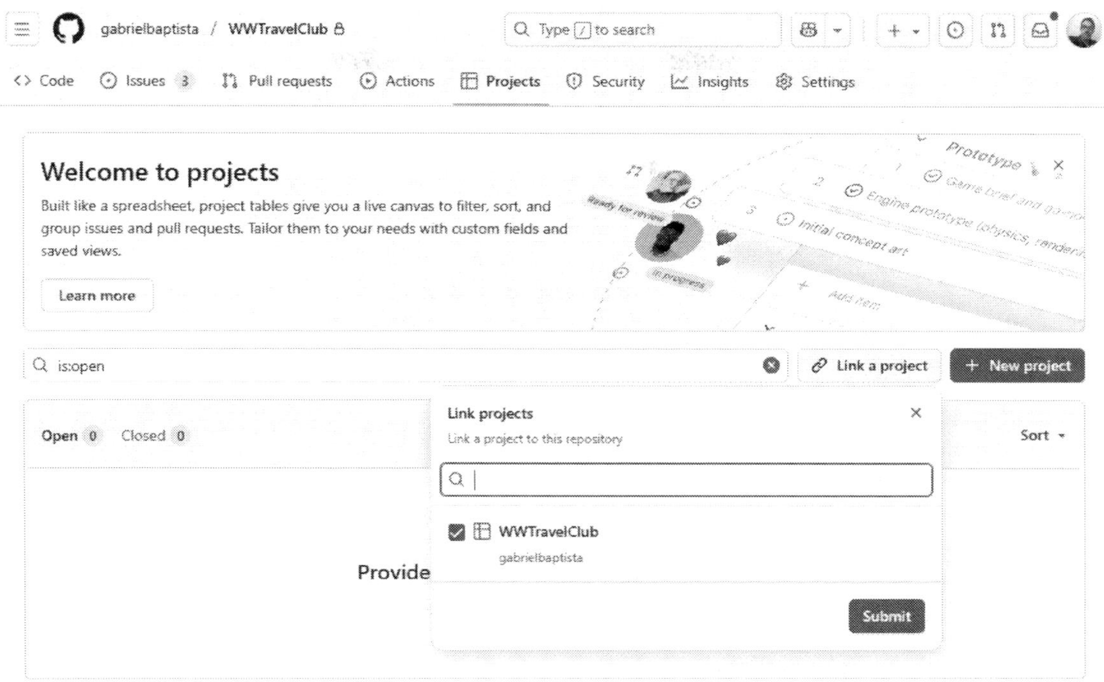

Figure 3.19: Connecting a GitHub repository to a project

It is worth mentioning that GitHub is more flexible than Azure DevOps, so you will find tools like the ones presented on Azure DevOps, but with different names/definitions. For instance, any task that you will need to define will be called an **issue**. Each issue can be placed in a *milestone*, as you can check in *Figure 3.20*, which is a good way to define a feature or user story, since it will describe a goal along with a target completion date.

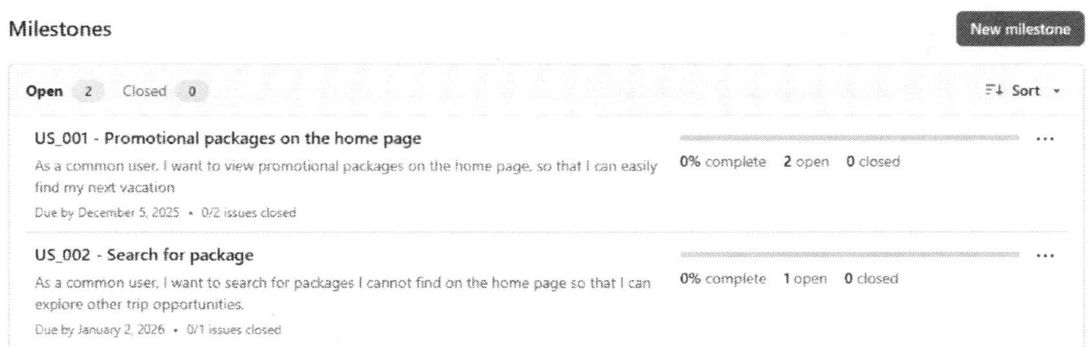

Figure 3.20: Setting milestones in a GitHub repository

Note

Check out more about using issues at `https://docs.github.com/en/issues/tracking-your-work-with-issues/about-issues` and milestones at `https://docs.github.com/en/issues/using-labels-and-milestones-to-track-work/about-milestones`.

The idea of projects on GitHub is to define useful information for each task that will be developed in the project, which is documented in an issue. By default, only *Title*, *Assignees*, and *Status* are required. But you can add labels, linked pull requests, reviewers, repositories, and milestones to each issue created. You can also define custom fields, like Iteration. For this you will need to access Project Settings, as you can check in *Figure 3.21*.

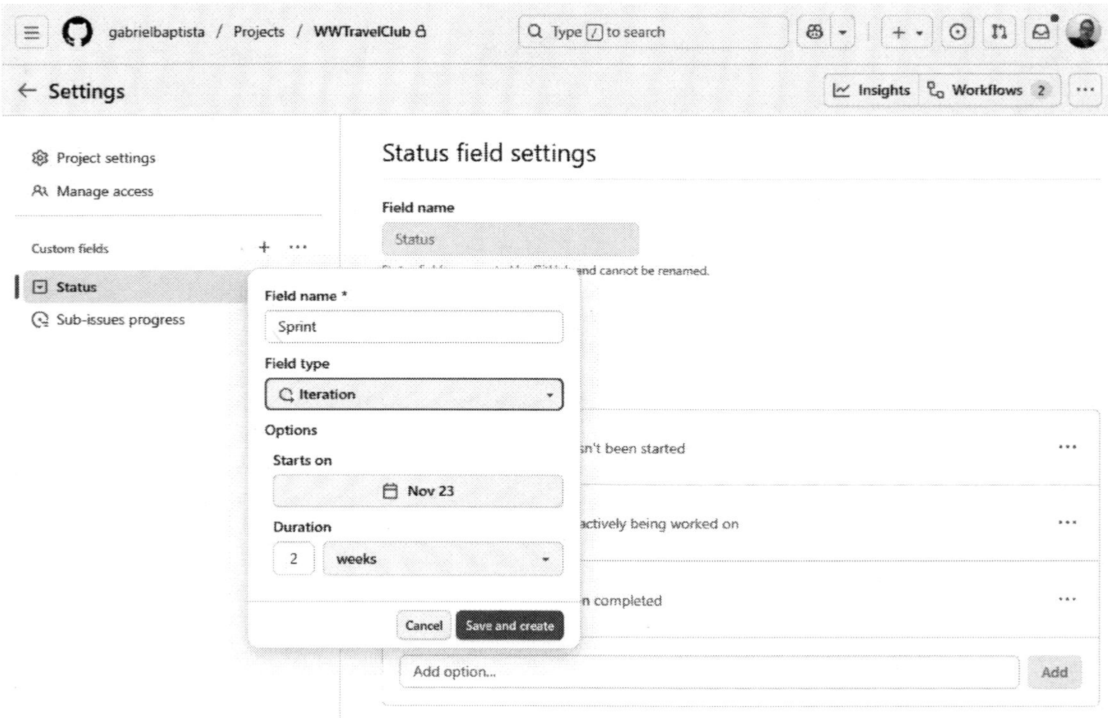

Figure 3.21: Creating custom fields for a GitHub project

In a GitHub project, you can also set different **Views**, such as **Table**, **Board**, or **Roadmap**. The **Table** view offers a quick and efficient method for entering this project-related information, including the custom fields you've created, into the project. In addition, the **Board** view supports requirement tracking through a visual workflow, while the **Roadmap** view helps the team align requirements with delivery plans and milestones. Once you've completed the design phase, you're ready to create issues for each item planned in your project.

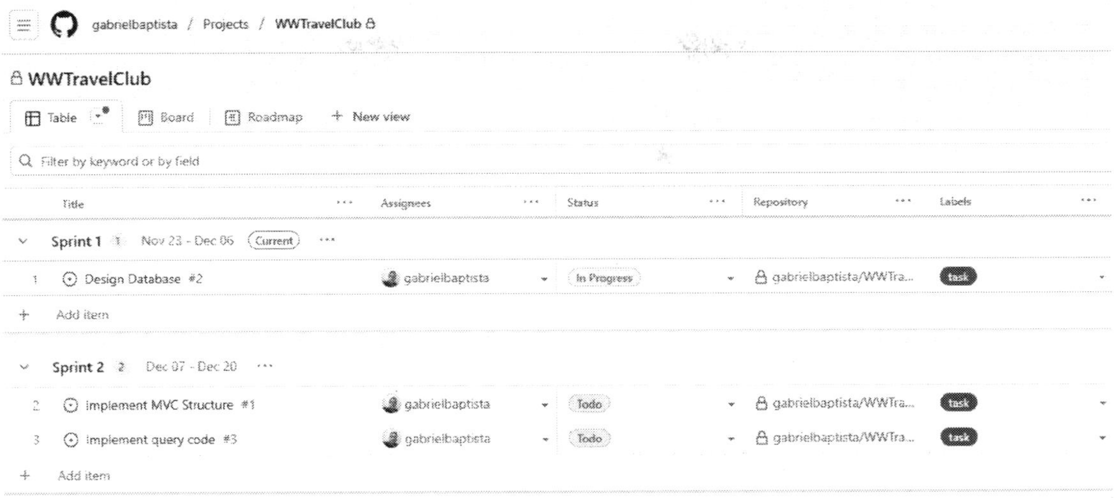

Figure 3.22: GitHub project Table view

The **Board** view, together with a filter related to iteration, is a perfect way to conduct daily meetings because you can see exactly what is happening to the project:

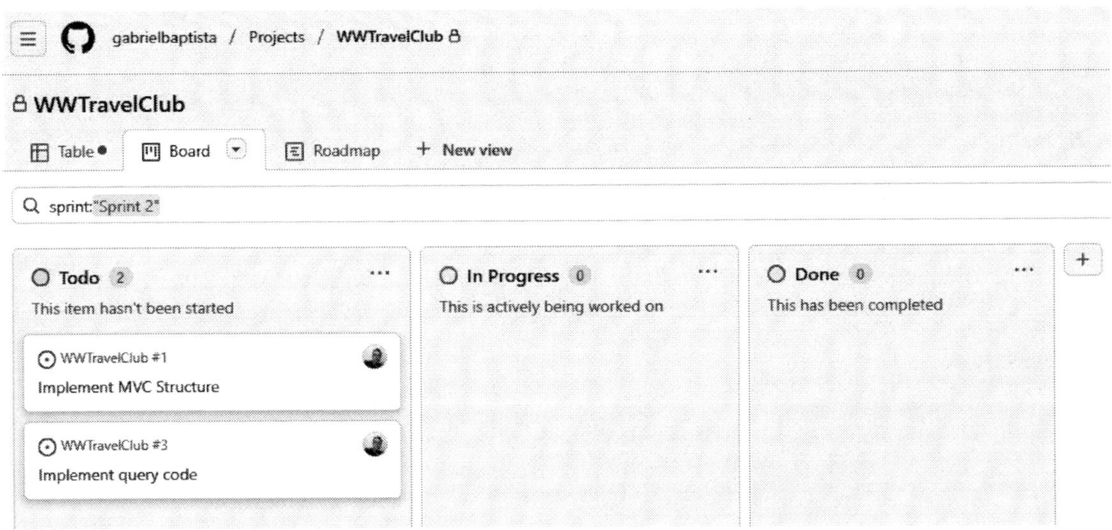

Figure 3.23: GitHub Board View

And to finish, the **Roadmap** view gives you a perspective of the entire project over time:

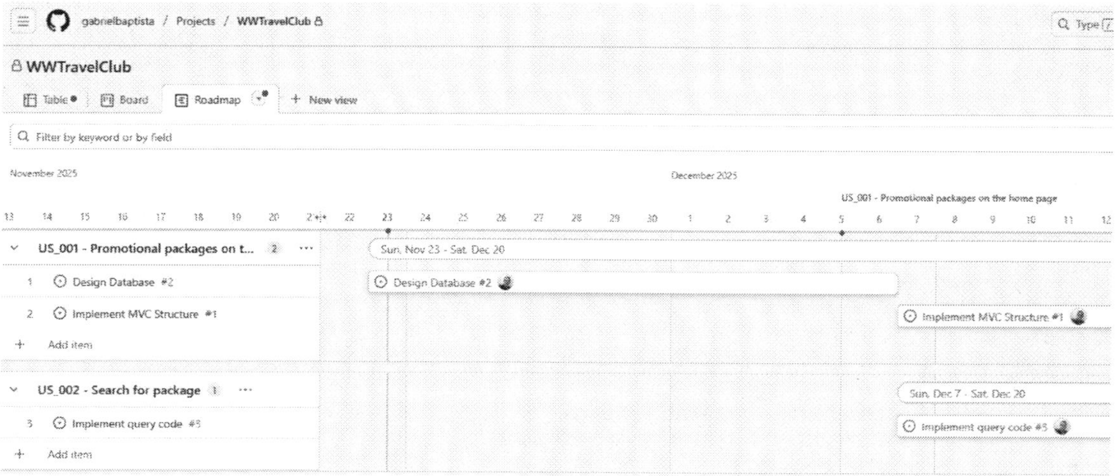

Figure 3.24: GitHub Roadmap view

As you can see, with GitHub projects, you will get almost the same results that we got when using Azure DevOps. Today we can say that GitHub Projects covers most of the planning and development workflow that we have in Azure DevOps, with a more flexible and simpler approach.

GitHub Projects brings requirements management closer to day-to-day software delivery by connecting planning, tracking, and implementation in the same collaborative environment. This makes it easier to preserve traceability and team alignment as requirements evolve. With this foundation established, we can now move on to the next topic, which will discuss the impact of AI on managing and implementing requirements.

AI impact on managing and implementing requirements

As we have seen in this chapter, a key aspect of delivering good software is proper requirements management. Both Azure DevOps and GitHub enable you to upload good product requirement data, and you will probably find them useful for doing so. However, there is one specific option that only GitHub supports—the use of Code Agents.

AI does not replace the responsibility of managing requirements. Instead, it increases the value of having requirements that are clear, structured, and traceable. When requirements are well written, AI can help transform product ideas into actionable backlog items, refine descriptions, suggest breakdowns into smaller units of work, and improve the consistency of project documentation. *GitHub Copilot*, for example, can help teams plan projects by turning ideas into epics, features, and tasks, and it can also generate structured issues from natural-language prompts or images.

From a requirements-management perspective, this is important because AI can support the evolution of requirements before implementation begins. Instead of using AI only to write code, teams can use it to make requirements more actionable, reduce ambiguity, and improve backlog quality. GitHub also provides AI-assisted issue triage, which helps identify whether an issue is actionable or still missing key information. In this way, AI starts contributing earlier to the lifecycle, not only at the coding stage.

Code agents is a much-discussed topic in this new era of AI. Microsoft has decided to focus on GitHub to provide code agents, so even for Azure DevOps users, the recommended path to enabling this important technology is by integrating Azure DevOps into GitHub.

> **Note**
>
> You can check detailed information about Azure DevOps and GitHub integration at `https://devblogs.microsoft.com/devops/azure-devops-and-github-repositories-next-steps-in-the-path-to-agentic-ai/`.

Once you have your repository integrated into a GitHub account that enables code agents, a new world will become available to you.

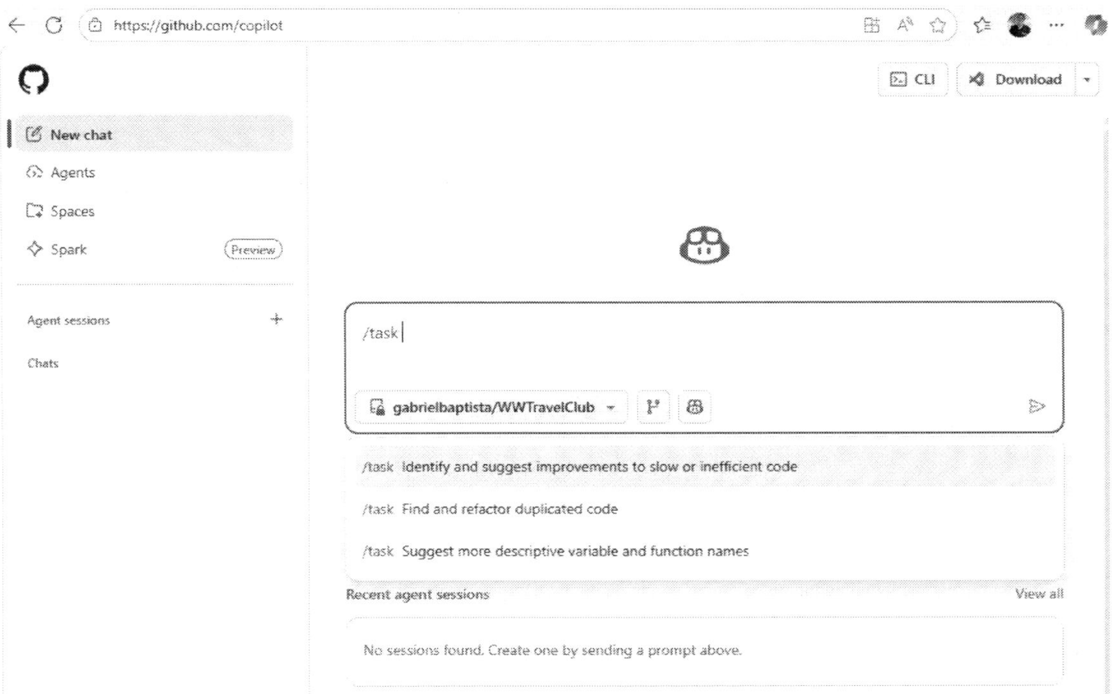

Figure 3.25: GitHub Copilot Interface

By accessing `https://github.com/copilot`, you can manage different agents in each repository. You can delegate different tasks to GitHub Code Agent, such as coding a new feature, reviewing a pull request, debugging an issue, or even documenting your solution.

GitHub Code Agent works as an autonomous development agent inside GitHub. In practice, you assign it a task through a GitHub issue or a Copilot prompt, and the agent then researches the repository, prepares an implementation plan, makes code changes on a branch, and can optionally open a pull request for human review. Unlike Copilot's agent mode in an IDE, this agent runs asynchronously on GitHub itself, in a GitHub

Actions-powered environment. It is worth noting that it is possible to specify different AI models for coding, like Claude and Gemini.

The key architectural point is that AI is most effective when requirements are already managed well. The better the requirement structure, context, and traceability, the more useful AI becomes in planning, implementation, validation, and review. Used in this way, AI does not weaken requirements management. Moreover, it strengthens it by helping teams move more quickly from intent to execution while preserving visibility and alignment across the lifecycle.

A practical example of this new approach is turning well-defined requirements into initial code drafts that developers can review and refine. The key takeaway is that AI is most effective when it operates on clear, structured, and traceable requirements, reinforcing the central idea of this chapter: better requirements management leads to better software delivery.

Summary

In this chapter, we have covered how you can create an Azure DevOps or GitHub account for a software development project, and how to start managing your projects with Azure DevOps or GitHub Projects. We have also given you a concise overview of all the main Azure DevOps functionalities, explaining how to access them through the Azure DevOps main menu.

To finish, we've presented the GitHub project view options for planning and managing a project. The chapter has also described in more detail how to manage system requirements, how to organize the necessary work using various kinds of work items or issues, and how to plan and organize sprints that will deliver epic solutions with rich features.

The decision of whether to use Azure DevOps or GitHub in a project will vary according to the expertise of the team and the objective of the project itself. If you are designing an open-source solution, GitHub will be a better option. On the other hand, if you are designing an enterprise solution and need everything to be connected, then Azure DevOps is a fantastic tool.

In the next chapter we look at some important approaches to adopt while writing code.

Questions

1. Is Azure DevOps only available for .NET projects?
2. What kinds of test plans are available in Azure DevOps?
3. Can DevOps projects use private NuGet packages?
4. Why do we use work items?
5. What is the difference between Epic and Feature work items?
6. What kind of relationship exists between Task and Product Backlog items/User Story work items?
7. How can GitHub projects be useful?
8. Which is the better option: Azure DevOps or GitHub?
9. How does GitHub Code Agent work?

Get this book's PDF version and more

Scan the QR code (or go to `packtpub.com/unlock`). Search for this book by name, confirm the edition, and then follow the steps on the page.

UNLOCK NOW

Note: Keep your invoice handy. Purchases made directly from Packt don't require an invoice.

4

Best Practices in Coding C#

When you are the software architect on a project, it is your responsibility to define and/or maintain a coding standard that will direct the team to program according to the expectations of the company. This chapter presents coding best practices that will help you establish guidelines for building safe, simple, and maintainable software. It also includes tips and tricks for coding in C#. From the lens of an architect, writing good code facilitates code maintenance and improves system performance. Although coding can be considered an art, writing understandable code is closer to a philosophy, because it directly affects readability, maintainability, and long-term collaboration. In this chapter, we also discuss practices that you, as a software architect, need to propagate to your developers, with techniques and tools for code analysis, so that you have well-written code for your projects.

The following topics will be covered in this chapter:

- How the complexity of your code can affect performance
- The importance of using a version control system
- Writing safe code in C#
- .NET 10 tips and tricks for coding
- Identifying well-written code

The impact of AI is enormous in the process of coding, and we are going to discuss the role of the software architect in this new era during the topics of the chapter. It is worth mentioning that C# 14 was launched together with .NET 10 and Visual Studio 2026. This last is presented with AI agents to guide us while coding. However, the practices presented here can be used in many versions of .NET, since they refer to the basics of programming C#. By the end of the chapter, you will be able to define which tools you are going to incorporate into your software development life cycle to facilitate code analysis.

Technical requirements

This chapter requires the Visual Studio 2026 free Community Edition or better.

Why simple code matters

Some people assume that writing complex code is a sign of programming skill, but in practice, the real challenge is solving complex problems with clarity and simplicity. The maturity of software development teaches us that good work is not measured by complexity, but by how clearly and simply a solution addresses a problem. Of course, complex problems can legitimately require complex solutions, and a skilled programmer is often one who *can* manage complexity effectively when the problem demands it. Some noteworthy scientists and researchers have confirmed this theory and emphasize that professional code needs to be focused on time, high quality, and budget.

Even when you have a complex scenario on your hands, if you reduce ambiguities and clarify the process of what you are coding, especially by using good names for methods and variables and respecting SOLID principles, you will turn complexity into simple code.

So, if you want to write good code, you need to keep the focus on how to do it, considering you are not the only one who will read it later. This is a good tip that changes the way you write code. This is how we will discuss each point of this chapter.

If your understanding of the importance of writing good code is aligned to the idea of simplicity and clarity while writing it, you should look at the Visual Studio tool **Code Metrics**. The access to the tool has changed in Visual Studio 2026, so you must go **View**, **Other Windows**, **Code Metrics**. As soon as the tool opens, there is a left button where you can execute the process for Calculating Code metrics, as you can see in *Figure 4.1*. It is worth noting that when clicking the button, the metrics are only shown for the project that's selected in the solution explorer. To see results for all projects, you have to select the solution itself.

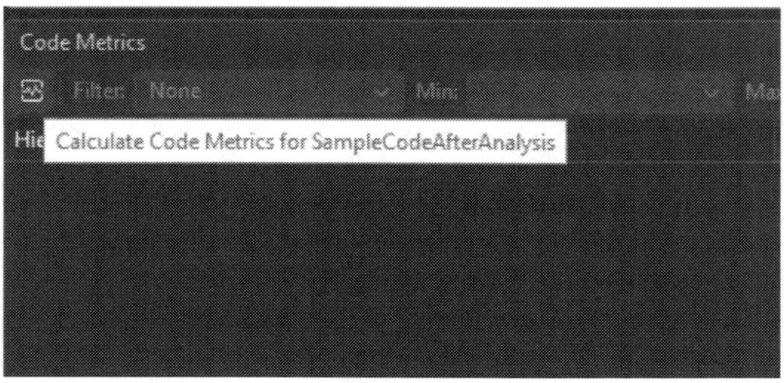

Figure 4.1: Calculating code metrics in Visual Studio

As a software architect, you should care about metrics because they support decision-making, strengthen governance, and provide early visibility into code health across the project. The **Code Metrics** tool will deliver metrics that will give you insights regarding the quality of the software you are delivering. The metrics that the tool provides can be found at this link: `https://docs.microsoft.com/en-us/visualstudio/code-quality/code-metrics-values`. The following subsections are focused on describing how **maintainability index**, **cyclomatic complexity**, **depth of inheritance**, **class coupling**, and the **number of lines of code** are useful in some real-life scenarios. For the architect, the real value of these metrics lies in the decisions they enable about refactoring, governance, risk reduction, and long-term maintainability.

Maintainability index

This index indicates how easy it is to maintain the code – the easier the code, the higher the index (limited to 100). Easy maintenance is one of the key points to keep software in good health. It is obvious that any software will require changes in the future since change is inevitable. For this reason, consider refactoring your code if you have low levels of maintainability. So, scores above 75 indicate highly maintainable code, while 50-75 indicates moderate maintainability, and scores below 50 indicate problematic code requiring refactoring. Writing classes and methods dedicated to a single responsibility, avoiding duplicate code, and limiting the number of lines of code of each method are examples of how you can improve the maintainability index. All these techniques will facilitate code legibility and reduce the number of bugs that the code can generate.

Cyclomatic complexity

The creator of the **cyclomatic complexity** metric is Thomas J. McCabe. He defines the complexity of a software function according to the number of code paths available (graph nodes). The more paths you have, the more complex your function is. McCabe considers that each function must have a complexity score of less than 10. That means that, if the code has more complex methods, you must refactor it, transforming parts of the code into separate methods. There are some real scenarios where this behavior is easily detected:

- Loops inside loops
- Lots of consecutive if-else statements
- Switch with code processing for each case inside the same method

For instance, look at the first version of this method for processing different responses of a credit card transaction. One reason this could be useful is to apply different processing rules for different credit card brands. As you can see, the cyclomatic complexity is greater than the number considered by McCabe as a basis. The reason why this happens is because of the number of if-else statements inside each case of the main switch:

```
/// <summary>
/// This code is being used just for explaining the concept of
/// cyclomatic complexity.
/// It makes no sense at all. Please Calculate Code Metrics for
/// understanding
/// </summary>
private static void CyclomaticComplexitySample()
{
  var billingMode = GetBillingMode();
  var messageResponse = ProcessCreditCardMethod();
  switch (messageResponse)
    {
      case "A":
        if (billingMode == "M1")
          Console.WriteLine($"Billing Mode {billingMode} for " +
            $"Message Response {messageResponse}");
        else
          Console.WriteLine($"Billing Mode {billingMode} for " +
```

```
            $"Message Response {messageResponse}");
        break;
      case "B":
        if (billingMode == "M2")
          Console.WriteLine($"Billing Mode {billingMode} for " +
            $"Message Response {messageResponse}");
        else
          Console.WriteLine($"Billing Mode {billingMode} for " +
            $"Message Response {messageResponse}");
        break;
      case "C":
        if (billingMode == "M3")
          Console.WriteLine($"Billing Mode {billingMode} for " +
            $"Message Response {messageResponse}");
        else
          Console.WriteLine($"Billing Mode {billingMode} for " +
            $"Message Response {messageResponse}");
        break;
      case "D":
        if (billingMode == "M4")
          Console.WriteLine($"Billing Mode {billingMode} for " +
            $"Message Response {messageResponse}");
        else
          Console.WriteLine($"Billing Mode {billingMode} for " +
            $"Message Response {messageResponse}");
        break;
      case "E":
        if (billingMode == "M5")
          Console.WriteLine($"Billing Mode {billingMode} for " +
            $"Message Response {messageResponse}");
        else
          Console.WriteLine($"Billing Mode {billingMode} for " +
            $"Message Response {messageResponse}");
        break;
      case "F":
        if (billingMode == "M6")
          Console.WriteLine($"Billing Mode {billingMode} for " +
            $"Message Response {messageResponse}");
        else
          Console.WriteLine($"Billing Mode {billingMode} for " +
            $"Message Response {messageResponse}");
        break;
      case "G":
        if (billingMode == "M7")
```

```
                Console.WriteLine($"Billing Mode {billingMode} for " +
                  $"Message Response {messageResponse}");
              else
                Console.WriteLine($"Billing Mode {billingMode} for " +
                  $"Message Response {messageResponse}");
              break;
            case "H":
              if (billingMode == "M8")
                Console.WriteLine($"Billing Mode {billingMode} for " +
                  $"Message Response {messageResponse}");
              else
                Console.WriteLine($"Billing Mode {billingMode} for " +
                  $"Message Response {messageResponse}");
              break;
            default:
              Console.WriteLine("The result of processing is unknown");
              break;
        }
    }
```

The code reveals several anti-patterns: nested conditionals within each case statement, repeated logic across branches, and no clear separation of concerns. These issues compound to create a complexity score of 67. If you ask to calculate the code metrics, you will find a bad result when it comes to cyclomatic complexity, as you can see in the following screenshot:

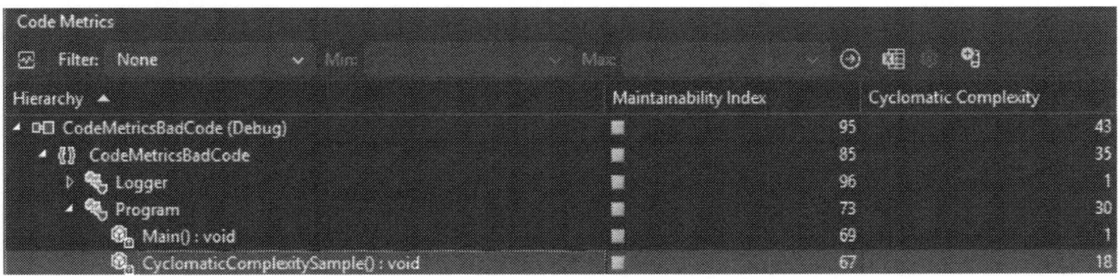

Figure 4.2: High level of cyclomatic complexity

It is important to say that the code is not the key here. The point here is to show you the number of improvements that can be made with a view to writing better code:

- The options from `switch-case` could be written using an Enum
- Each `case` processing can be done:
    - In a specific method

  - In a specific class, inheriting the action from the superclass, using the Polymorphism concept
  - In a specific class, implementing an interface to a contract
- `switch-case` can be substituted with `Dictionary<Enum, Method>` or by using the `switch expression`, introduced in C# 8.0

The main reason why we have chosen these techniques is code legibility. While we are reading code, the number of "ifs" provided by it will make our understanding more difficult and, as a consequence, we can create a bug in the code while maintaining it. Besides that, the responsibility of a piece of code must be unique, to facilitate its understanding. The use of object-oriented principles, like Polymorphism, will reduce the repeated number of lines, which can reduce bugs in the future in a specific modification of the code.

By refactoring this code with the preceding techniques, the result is a piece of code that is much easier to understand, as you can see in the following code snippet of its main method:

```
private static Dictionary<CreditCardProcessingResult, CheckResultMethod>
  GetMethodsForCheckingResult()
{
    var methods = new Dictionary<CreditCardProcessingResult,
        CheckResultMethod>();
    methods.Add(CreditCardProcessingResult.ResultA, CheckResultA);
    methods.Add(CreditCardProcessingResult.ResultB, CheckResultB);
    methods.Add(CreditCardProcessingResult.ResultC, CheckResultC);
    methods.Add(CreditCardProcessingResult.ResultD, CheckResultD);
    methods.Add(CreditCardProcessingResult.ResultE, CheckResultE);
    methods.Add(CreditCardProcessingResult.ResultF, CheckResultF);
    methods.Add(CreditCardProcessingResult.ResultG, CheckResultG);
    methods.Add(CreditCardProcessingResult.Succeed, CheckResultSucceed);
    return methods;
}

static void Main()
{
    var billingMode = GetBillingMode();
    var messageResponse = ProcessCreditCardMethod();
    Dictionary<CreditCardProcessingResult, CheckResultMethod>
        methodsForCheckingResult = GetMethodsForCheckingResult();
    if (methodsForCheckingResult.ContainsKey(messageResponse))
        methodsForCheckingResult[messageResponse](billingMode,
            messageResponse);
    else
        Console.WriteLine("The result of processing is unknown");
}
```

Using the `switch expression` available since C# 8.0, the code can be even simpler!

```
private static CreditCardProcessingResult
   CheckResult(CreditCardProcessingResult messageResponse, BillingMode
     billingMode) =>
messageResponse switch
{
    CreditCardProcessingResult.ResultA => CheckResultA(billingMode,
        messageResponse),
    CreditCardProcessingResult.ResultB => CheckResultB(billingMode,
        messageResponse),
    CreditCardProcessingResult.ResultC => CheckResultC(billingMode,
        messageResponse),
    CreditCardProcessingResult.ResultD => CheckResultD(billingMode,
        messageResponse),
    CreditCardProcessingResult.ResultE => CheckResultE(billingMode,
        messageResponse),
    CreditCardProcessingResult.ResultF => CheckResultF(billingMode,
        messageResponse),
    CreditCardProcessingResult.ResultG => CheckResultG(billingMode,
        messageResponse),
    CreditCardProcessingResult.Succeed => CheckResultSucceed(billingMode,
        messageResponse),
    _ => throw new ArgumentOutOfRangeException(nameof(messageResponse),
        $"Not expected value: {messageResponse}"),
};

static void Main()
{
    var billingMode = GetBillingMode();
    var messageResponse = ProcessCreditCardMethod();
    CheckResult(messageResponse, billingMode);
}
```

The full code can be found in the GitHub repository of this chapter at `https://github.com/PacktPublishing/Software-Architecture-with-.NET-10-and-C-sharp-5E/tree/main/ch04` and demonstrates how lower-complexity code can be achieved. The following screenshot shows these results according to Code Metrics:

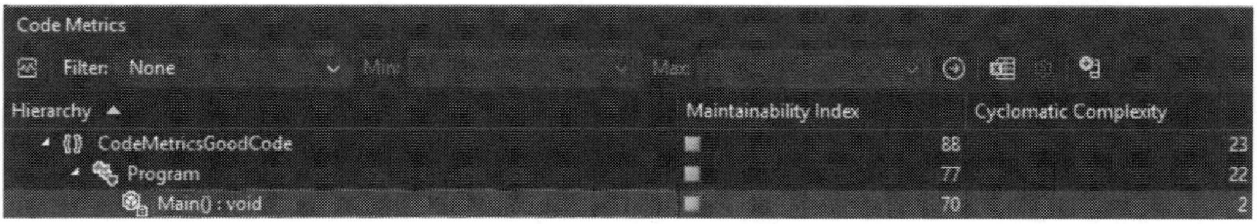

Figure 4.3: Cyclomatic complexity reduction after refactoring

As you can see in the preceding screenshot, there is a considerable reduction in complexity after refactoring. In *Chapter 5, Implementing Code Reusability in C#*, we will discuss the importance of refactoring for code reuse. The reason why we are doing this here is the same—we want to eliminate duplication.

The key point here is that with the techniques applied, the understanding of the code increased and the complexity decreased, proving the importance of cyclomatic complexity.

Depth of inheritance

This metric represents the *number of inherited classes you have from the class you are measuring to the root of the inheritance hierarchy*. The more classes you have inherited, the worse the metric will be. This is like class coupling and indicates how difficult it is to change your code. For instance, the following screenshot shows four inherited classes:

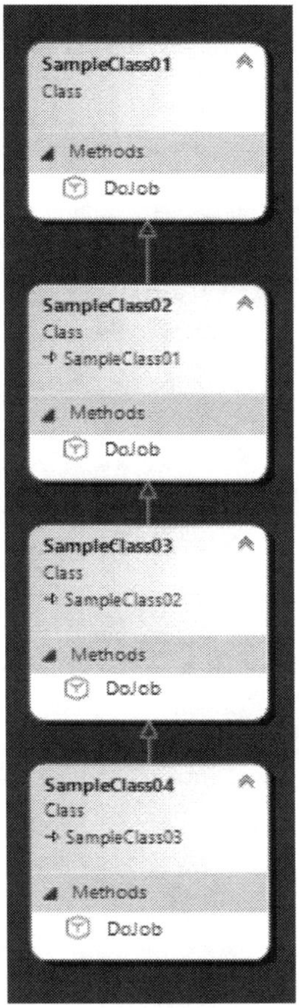

Figure 4.4: Depth of inheritance sample

You can see in the following screenshot that the deepest class has the worst metric value, so changing its behavior is more difficult, since you have many inheritances provided by the parent classes, considering there are three other classes that can change their behavior:

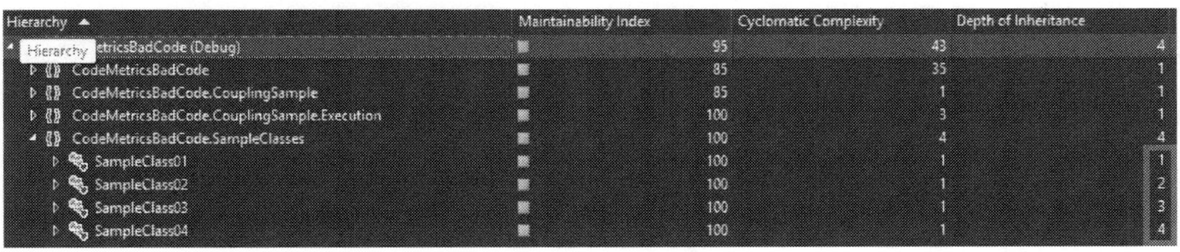

Figure 4.5: Depth of inheritance metric

Inheritance is one of the basic object-oriented analysis principles and it is fundamental to object-oriented programming. However, deep inheritance hierarchies create tight coupling between classes. So, if it makes sense to do so, instead of using inheritance, consider using composition, a design principle known as *composition over inheritance*. The reason we will consider this is to avoid class coupling, which we will explain in the following section.

Class coupling

When you connect classes in a single class, obviously, you will get tight coupling, and this can cause bad maintenance of your code. For instance, refer to the following screenshot. It shows a design where aggregation has been performed a lot. There is no sense to the code itself:

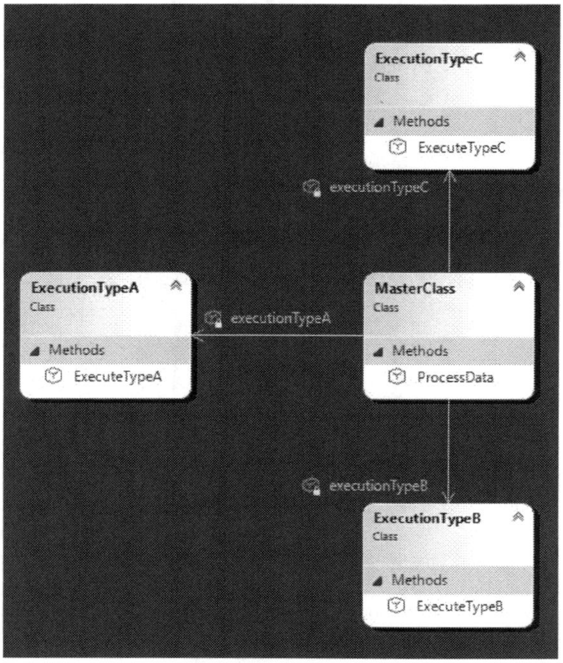

Figure 4.6: Class coupling example

Once you have calculated the code metrics for the preceding design, you will see that the number of class coupling instances for the `ProcessData()` method, which calls `ExecuteTypeA()`, `ExecuteTypeB()`, and `ExecuteTypeC()`, equals three (3) as shown in *Figure 4.7*:

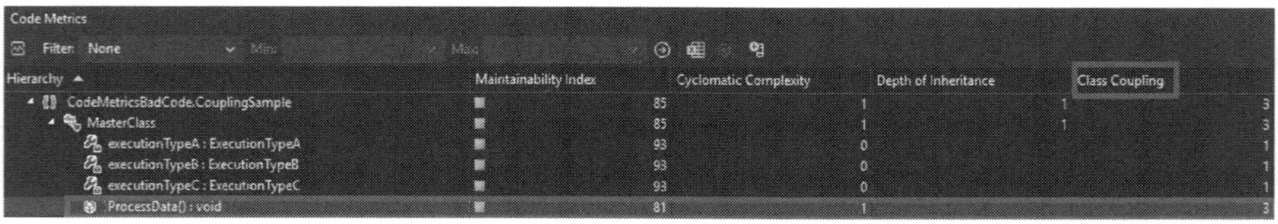

Figure 4.7: Class coupling metric

Recent Microsoft studies suggest that the maximum number of classes coupling instances should be nine (9). With aggregation being a better practice than inheritance, the use of interfaces will solve class coupling problems. For instance, the same code with the following design will give you a better result:

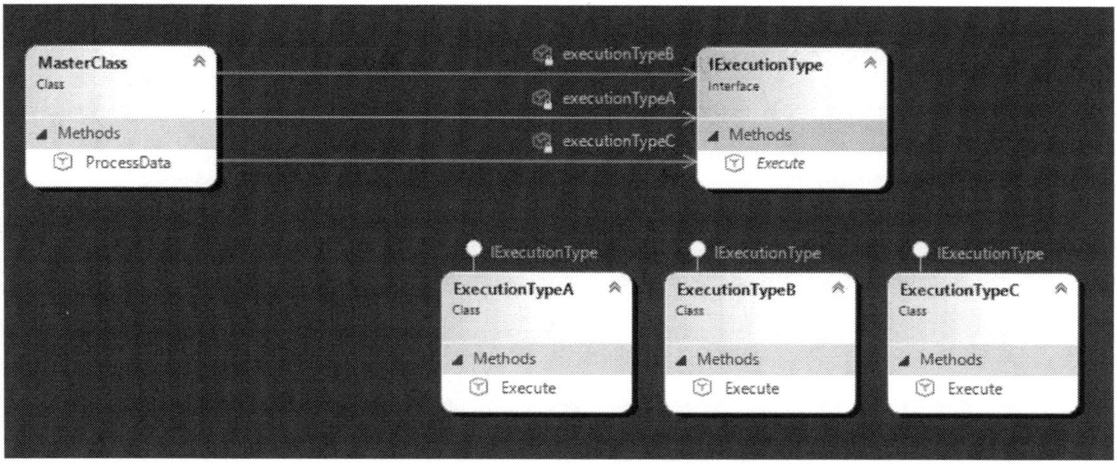

Figure 4.8: Reducing class coupling

Notice that using the interface in the design will allow you to increase the number of execution types without increasing the class coupling of the solution:

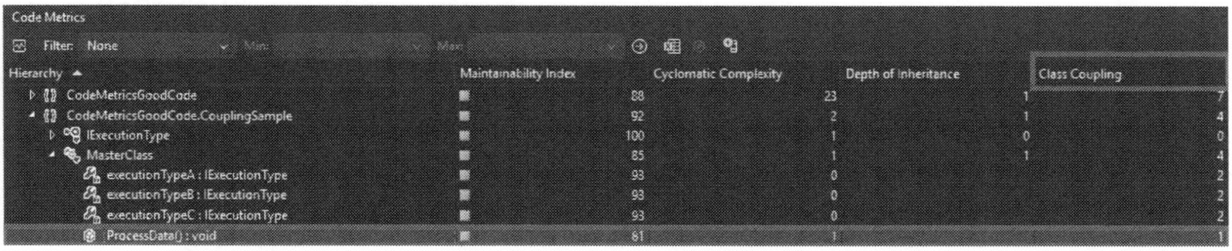

Figure 4.9: Class coupling results after applying aggregations

As a software architect, you must design your solution to have more cohesion than coupling. The literature indicates that good software has low coupling and high cohesion. In software development, high cohesion indicates that each class has its methods and data with good relationships between them. On the other hand, low coupling indicates that classes are not closely and directly connected. This is a basic principle that can guide you to a better architectural model.

Number of lines of code

This metric is useful in terms of making you understand the size of the code you are dealing with. Lines of code alone don't directly measure complexity, but they can indicate architectural problems since it does show the software size and software design. For instance, if you have too many lines of code in a single class (more than 1,000 lines of code – 1KLOC), this indicates that you probably have a bad design.

In Visual Studio 2026, this metric was divided into *Lines of Source code* and *Lines of Executable code*. They are similar but have different purposes. The first indicates the exact number of source lines, including blank lines. On the other hand, the second one estimates the number of executable code lines, the instructions the CPU executes.

As a software architect, you have the objective of delivering to your programmers a list of best practices that will enable each of them to improve their techniques for developing good software. Make sure they know the exact impacts of not achieving good metrics results in their code. The metrics presented above are certainly a great way to start to achieve this objective. But let us see how using a version control system can be the difference between amateur and professional software development.

Using a version control system

You may find this topic a bit obvious, but many people and companies still do not regard a version control system as an essential tool for software development! The idea of writing about it is to force you to understand our point! There is no architectural model or best practice that can save software development if you do not use a version control system.

Using a version control system is not only a matter of organizing source code changes, but also an important practice for preserving code quality and architectural control throughout a project. For a software architect, version control provides visibility into how the codebase evolves, supports safer collaboration among team members, and creates a structured process for reviewing changes before they become part of the product. When combined with pull requests, branch policies, and code review practices, it helps enforce coding standards, protect important architectural decisions, and reduce the risk of uncontrolled modifications that may degrade the design over time. In this way, version control becomes a key mechanism for maintaining consistency, traceability, and long-term software health.

In the last few years, we have been enjoying the advantages of online version control systems, such as Azure DevOps, GitHub, and Bitbucket. The fact is, you must have a version control system in your software development life cycle, and there is no reason not to have one anymore since most providers offer free versions for small groups. Even if you develop by yourself, these tools are useful for tracking your changes, managing your software versions, and guaranteeing the consistency and integrity of your code.

Modern version control systems have evolved beyond simple code storage. AI-powered tools now integrate directly with repositories to enhance code quality and developer productivity and that is exactly what we are going to check in the next topic.

Using a version control system with AI support

With the rise of AI for programming, it is worth noting that GitHub enables not only the repository for your team. AI Agents for coding certainly are changing the way we deliver good code.

For instance, using Visual Studio connected to a GitHub Copilot account, we can access Copilot chat directly in the code editor, as we can see in the picture below.

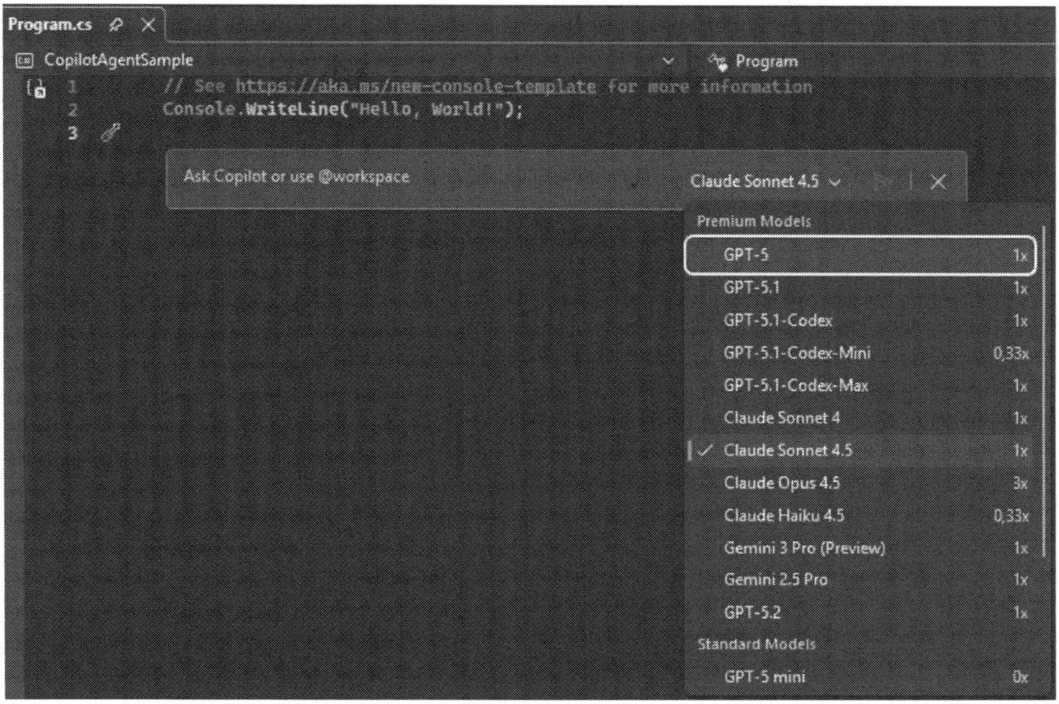

Figure 4.10: Accessing Copilot Chat using Visual Studio

The code below was totally created using *Claude Sonnet 4.5+*, using as prompt the message: *Create a sample code with bad alternatives. I will correct it in a demonstration.*

```
using System;
using System.Collections.Generic;
using System.Linq;

namespace CopilotAgentSample
{
    // Bad practice: Poor naming, tight coupling, no error handling
    public class proc
    {
        // Bad: Magic numbers, no encapsulation
        public List<string> data = new List<string>();
        public int x = 0;

        // Bad: Non-descriptive method name, no validation
        public void do_stuff(string s)
        {
            data.Add(s);
            x++;
```

```
}

// Bad: Nested loops, inefficient algorithm, poor readability
public string find(string val)
{
    for (int i = 0; i < data.Count; i++)
    {
        for (int j = 0; j < data[i].Length; j++)
        {
            if (data[i].Contains(val))
            {
                return data[i];
            }
        }
    }
    return "";
}

// Bad: Catching generic exception, swallowing errors
public void calc()
{
    try
    {
        int result = 10 / x;
        Console.WriteLine(result);
    }
    catch (Exception ex)
    {
        // Bad: Empty catch block
    }
}

// Bad: God method doing multiple responsibilities
public void ProcessData(List<string> items)
{
    // Validation
    if (items == null) return;

    // Processing
    foreach (var item in items)
    {
        data.Add(item.ToUpper());
    }
```

```
                // Logging
                Console.WriteLine("Processed " + items.Count + " items");

                // Persistence
                System.IO.File.WriteAllLines("output.txt", data);
            }
        }
    }
```

This is quite useful, but when you are working on a real project, the version control system that we currently have available can deliver more to you. In this same example, when I pull the code to GitHub, I can open an issue to correct it, as you can see in *Figure 4.11*.

Figure 4.11: Issue opened on GitHub

But more than opening an issue, with GitHub Copilot Agent, I can assign this issue to be solved by Copilot, as shown in *Figure 4.12*.

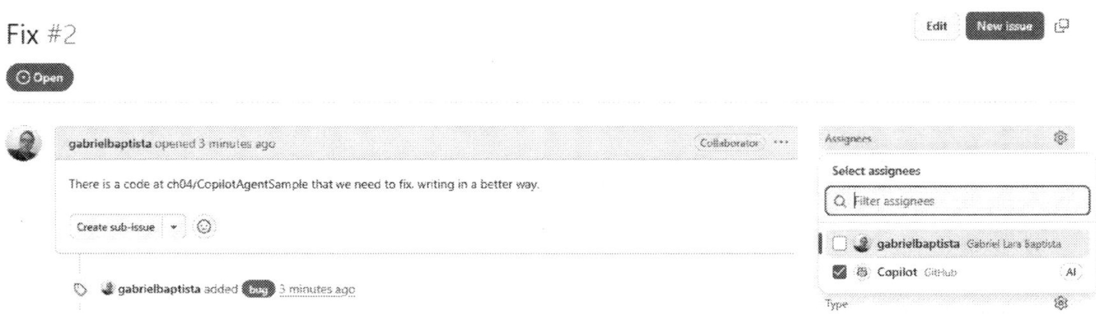

Figure 4.12: Assigning an issue to GitHub Copilot Coding Agent

This kind of approach completely changes the way we interact with a version control system! We are not only talking about saving our code to a repository. We are enabling a code velocity that will modify the next years of digital transformation.

You may think it is a bit strange to discuss this topic here while discussing bad or good practices of coding, but this essentially supports what a software architect must work on for the next months—we are not saying years

—using a version control system that supports this kind of AI technology for coding is going to be a game changer for the business you deal with.

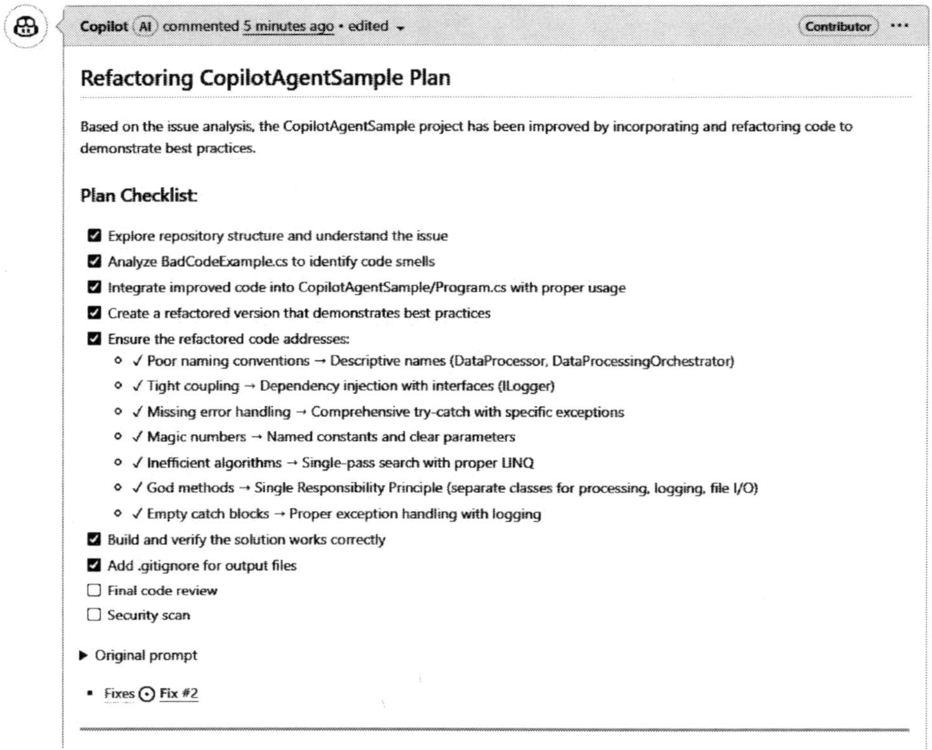

Figure 4.13: GitHub Copilot Coding Agent plan to solve the issue

As you can see in *Figure 4.13*, the agent not only solved the problem, but it created a plan that makes you understand its *chain of thoughts* before executing it. The chain of thought approach is valuable from an architectural perspective because it enhances the understanding and trustworthiness of AI systems. The result of this process is a *pull request*, where you can check all the changes made by the agent. If you ask for a change, the agent will start acting again, giving you back command as soon as it completes the task. You can check the detailed issue and the source code of this demo at `https://github.com/PacktPublishing/Software-Architecture-with-.NET-10-and-C-sharp-5E/issues/2`.

Version control has evolved beyond code storage and history tracking. With AI support, it becomes a strategic environment for improving code quality, guiding change, and reinforcing architectural governance through structured collaboration, automated assistance, and reviewable outcomes.

Dealing with version control systems in teams

The use of a version control system tool when you are working alone is purely related to your need to keep your code safely stored. But this kind of system was developed to solve team problems while writing code. For this reason, some features, such as branching and merging, were introduced to keep code integrity even in scenarios where the number of developers is quite large.

As a software architect, you will have to decide which branch strategy your team will adopt. As a software architect, your branching strategy choice affects deployment risk, release cadence, and team collaboration patterns. Microsoft and GitHub suggest different ways to deliver that, and both are useful in some scenarios.

Information about how the Microsoft teams deals with DevOps can be found here: `https://learn.microsoft.com/en-us/devops/develop/how-microsoft-develops-devops`. The branching strategy presented in this article describes an approach where a branch is created for each release. They call it **Release Flow**. The big difference here is that the master branch is not continuously deployed to production.

On the other hand, GitHub describes its process at `https://guides.github.com/introduction/flow/`. This process is called **GitHub flow** and can be defined as a lightweight, branch-based workflow, where each development is created in a specific branch that will be reviewed by collaborators as soon as a pull request is created for feedback. As soon as the pull request is approved, the new code is merged with the master branch, so you can delete the development branch created before.

Release Flow and GitHub flow are both branch-based approaches, but they optimize for different delivery rhythms and risk profiles. GitHub flow is built around short-lived branches, early pull requests, and frequent merges into main, with the ideal that main is always in a deployable state. Release Flow, in contrast, introduces an explicit release branch per release, so stabilization and production readiness happen at that release branch rather than assuming main is continuously shipped. In practice, that means GitHub flow tends to fit teams aiming for continuous deployment (or near continuous) and rapid iteration, while Release Flow fits organizations that need a clearly controlled release window, extra hardening time, or predictable release trains.

A practical way to choose between them is to look at cadence, operational maturity, and constraints. If you can keep main consistently releasable with strong automated tests, fast CI feedback, reliable rollback, and feature flags, GitHub flow minimizes overhead and keeps collaboration simple. If you must coordinate releases across many teams, support multiple versions, or operate under higher change-control expectations, Release Flow's *"branch for release stabilization"* provides a clearer place to lock scope, validate thoroughly, and ship with confidence. Many teams land on hybrids: they keep GitHub flow for day-to-day development (PRs into main) but cut periodic release branches for scheduled releases, or they reduce the need for long stabilization by using feature flags so incomplete work can merge safely without being exposed.

The CI/CD impact is significant because each flow changes what *green* means and where promotion happens. With GitHub flow, your strongest signal is typically *"main is green, so it can deploy,"* which pushes you toward strict PR checks, fast build/test pipelines, and automated deployments triggered by merges. With Release Flow, you usually end up with two tracks: CI on main to keep integration healthy, plus a tighter, more conservative pipeline on the release branch that produces release candidates and governs what goes to production (often with extra approvals, gates, and regression coverage).

Hotfix handling also differs: GitHub flow hotfixes commonly merge back into main and flow forward; Release Flow often requires explicit backport/forward-port discipline between the active release branch and main, which your pipelines and policies should support to avoid divergence.

As a practical decision heuristic, choose GitHub flow when your team can keep the main branch continuously releasable through strong automation, fast feedback, and disciplined pull request reviews. Choose Release Flow when your environment requires more controlled release cycles, additional stabilization time, or stronger separation between ongoing development and production readiness. The key architectural takeaway is that the best branching strategy is not the most popular one, but the one that best aligns with your delivery cadence, governance needs, and operational risk.

It is your choice: decide on the one that best fits your needs, but we do want you to understand that you need to have a strategy for controlling your code. In *Chapter 8, Understanding DevSecOps Principles and CI/CD*, we will discuss this in more detail. But now, let us see how to write safe code using C#, so that you can develop a list of best practices that will be shared with your developers.

Writing safe code in C#

Throughout this chapter, we've focused on simplifying coding using metrics that may help us to do so. Besides that, we need to write reliable code, and a key part of reliability is **code safety**: the ability to prevent avoidable failures, reduce undefined or unintended behavior, and make the application easier to evolve without introducing subtle defects.

C# can be considered a safe programming language by design. Unless you force it, there is no need for pointers, and memory release is, in most cases, managed by the garbage collector. Even so, some care should be taken so you can get better and safer results from your code. Let us have a look at some common practices to ensure safe code in C#.

Try-catch

Exceptions in coding are so frequent that you should have a way to manage them whenever they happen. It is also important to notice that some exceptions are expected outcomes of the environment, while others are bugs. `try-catch` statements are built to manage exceptions, and they are important for keeping your code safe. There are a lot of cases where an application crashes and the reason for that is the lack of using `try-catch`. The following code shows an example of the lack of usage of the `try-catch` statement. It is worth mentioning that this is just an example for understanding the concept of an exception thrown without correct treatment. Consider using `int.TryParse(textToConvert, out var result)` to handle cases where a parse is unsuccessful:

```
static int CodeWithNoTryCatch(string textToConvert)
{
    return Convert.ToInt32(textToConvert);
}
```

On the other hand, bad `try-catch` usage can cause damage to your code too, especially because you will not see the correct behavior of that code and may misunderstand the results provided.

The following code shows an example of an empty try-catch statement. It results in zero when any kind of exception happens, but there is no way to track why the exception is happening.

```
static int CodeWithEmptyTryCatch(string textToConvert)
{
    try
    {
        return Convert.ToInt32(textToConvert);
```

```
        }
        catch
        {
            return 0;
        }
    }
```

try-catch statements must be connected to logging solutions so that you can have a response from the system that will indicate the correct behavior and, at the same time, will not cause application crashes. The following code shows an ideal try-catch statement with logging management.

Note

When meaningfully needed, specific exceptions should be caught, since catching a general exception will hide unexpected behaviors.

```
static int CodeWithCorrectTryCatch(string textToConvert)
{
    try
    {
        return Convert.ToInt32(textToConvert);
    }
    catch (FormatException ex)
    {
        Logger.GenerateLog(ex);
        return 0;
    }
}
```

It is very important to say that exceptions are, computationally speaking, expensive. The exception process takes CPU time. No matter whether you are throwing them to indicate an error or catching them to manage errors, it takes a lot of computational processing. That is why we have mentioned considering using `int.TryParse(textToConvert, out var result)` to handle cases where a parse is unsuccessful. So, if there is not a good way to avoid an exception, it is common and preferable to rely on a higher-level exception handler instead of trying to handle everything everywhere, as the code might become hard to reason about.

However, it is also worth mentioning that exception errors delivered to the end-user (with or without stack traces) can cause the feeling that bad software was delivered. As a software architect, you should conduct code inspections to define the best behavior for the code.

Remember that instability in a system is often connected to the lack of try-catch statements in the code, so the goal is not to avoid exceptions but to handle them meaningfully.

Try-finally and using

Memory leaks can be considered as one of the worst software behaviors. They cause instability, bad use of computer resources, and undesired application crashes. .NET addresses managed memory with the **Garbage Collector** (GC), which automatically reclaims objects once they become eligible for collection, according to the GC's heuristics and schedule.

Objects that interact with I/O are the ones that generally are not managed by the Garbage Collector: the filesystem, sockets, and so on. The following code is an example of the incorrect usage of a `FileStream` object, considering the Garbage Collector will release the memory used, but it will not:

```
private static void CodeWithIncorrectFileStreamManagement()
{
    FileStream file = new ("C:\\file.txt", FileMode.CreateNew);
    byte[] data = GetFileData();
    file.Write(data, 0, data.Length);
}
```

Besides, it takes a while for the Garbage Collector to interact with objects that need to be released, and sometimes you may want to do it yourself. For both cases, the use of try-finally or using statements is the best practice:

```
private static void CorrectFileStreamManagementFirstOption()
{
    FileStream file = new ("C:\\file.txt",FileMode.CreateNew);
    try
    {
        byte[] data = GetFileData();
        file.Write(data, 0, data.Length);
    }
    finally
    {
        file.Dispose();
    }
}

private static void CorrectFileStreamManagementSecondOption()
{
    using (FileStream file = new ("C:\\file.txt", FileMode.CreateNew))
    {
        byte[] data = GetFileData();
        file.Write(data, 0, data.Length);
    }
}
```

```
private static void CorrectFileStreamManagementThirdOption()
{
    using FileStream file = new ("C:\\file.txt", FileMode.CreateNew);
    byte[] data = GetFileData();
    file.Write(data, 0, data.Length);
}
```

The preceding code shows exactly how to deal with objects that are not managed by Garbage Collector. You have both `try-finally` and `using` being implemented. In practice, there is no difference between these three approaches. As a software architect, you do need to pay attention to this kind of code. The lack of `try-finally` or `using` statements can cause huge damage to software behavior when it is running. It is worth mentioning that using code analysis tools, such as Sonar Lint and Code Analysis, will automatically alert you to these sorts of problems.

The IDisposable interface

Inside a method, you should dispose of `IDisposable` objects with `using` (or `try/finally`) so resources are released even when exceptions occur. The same principle applies at the class level. If a class *owns* long-lived `IDisposable` instances, typically stored in fields or properties backed by fields, it should implement `IDisposable` and dispose of those members. Otherwise, the application may hold unmanaged resources longer than intended and eventually run into resource exhaustion. For this reason, when you have a class that deals with and creates objects, you should implement the Disposable pattern to guarantee the release of all resources created by the class as shown below:

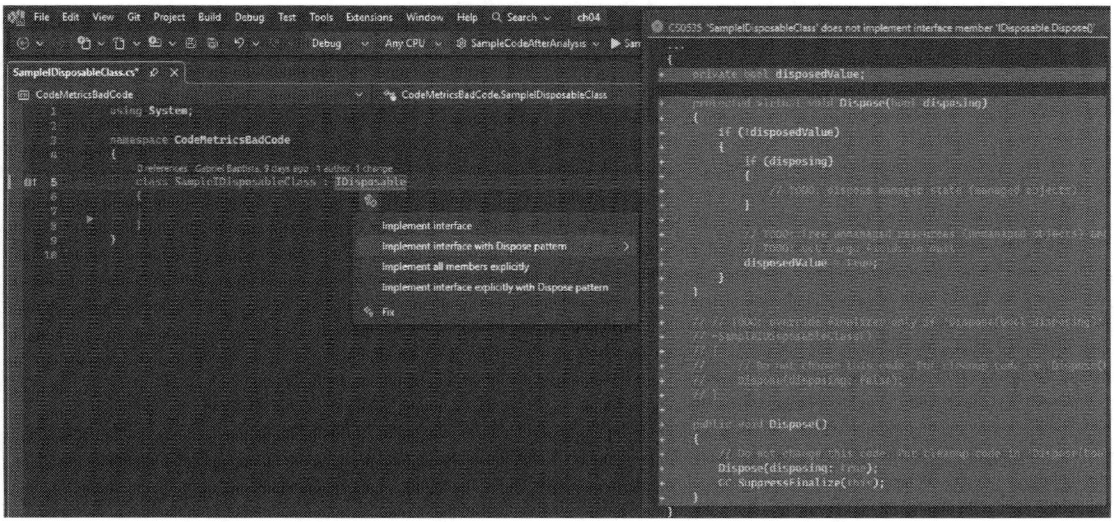

Figure 4.14: IDisposable interface implementation

The good news is that Visual Studio gives you the code snippet to implement this interface by just indicating it in your code and right-clicking on the *Quick Actions* and *Refactoring* options, as you can see in the preceding screenshot.

Once you have inserted the code, you need to follow the `TODO` instructions present in *Figure 4.14* so that you have the correct pattern implemented. The template Visual Studio generates for `IDisposable` guides you to concentrate all cleanup logic in `Dispose (bool disposing)`. It explicitly reminds you to dispose of the **managed resources** (other `IDisposable` objects your class owns) only when disposing is true, and to release any **unmanaged resources** (native handles, unmanaged buffers, OS resources) in a way that works even if the runtime calls cleanup through a finalizer. It also suggests optionally setting large fields to `null` to make memory eligible for collection sooner. Finally, it warns you not to modify the boilerplate in `Dispose()` or the (optional) finalizer stub. Instead, you implement the actual cleanup inside `Dispose(bool disposing)`, while `Dispose()` calls it and then uses `GC.SuppressFinalize(this)` to avoid unnecessary finalization once disposal is complete.

It is also worth noting that if the class is not intended to be inherited, declaring it as `sealed` can simplify the implementation. In that case, there is usually no need to expose an overridable `Dispose(bool disposing)` method, because no derived class will need to extend the cleanup behavior. This makes the disposable pattern easier to understand and implement in scenarios where inheritance is not required.

As a software architect, you will be responsible not only for the architecture defined in a system but also for how this system performs in operation. Memory leaks and bad performance in general are caused by errors related to `try-catch` strategy, lack of `try-finally/using`, and wrong or no implementation of `IDisposable`. So be sure your team knows how to deal with these techniques.

Now that we have discussed techniques for writing safe code in C#, let's move to some .NET 10 tips and tricks for coding in the next section.

.NET 10 tips and tricks for coding

.NET 10 implements some good features that help us to write better code. One of the most useful things for having safer code is **dependency injection** (DI) - a technique where a class receives its dependencies (services it uses) from the outside rather than creating them directly. DI will be discussed in *Chapter 6, Design Patterns and .NET Implementation*. There are some good reasons for considering this. The first one is that you will not need to worry about disposing of the injected objects since you are not going to be the creator of them.

Besides, DI enables you to inject `ILogger`, a useful tool for debugging exceptions that will need to be managed by `try-catch` statements in your code. Furthermore, programming in C# with .NET 10 must follow the common good practices of any programming language. The following list shows some of these. To make these practices easier to understand and apply, they can be viewed in three complementary groups: protecting the system from failures, keeping the codebase maintainable over time, and making the code easier for others to read and evolve.

1. ***Safety and correctness:*** This first group is focused on reducing the risk of defects, unexpected behavior, and resource misuse. These practices matter because software quality begins with code that behaves predictably and fails in a controlled way:
    - ***Objects should be checked before usage:*** Since null objects can exist, the code must have null-type checking. It is worth mentioning that since C# 8, we have nullable reference types to avoid errors related to nullable objects. You may refer to `https://docs.microsoft.com/en-us/dotnet/csharp/nullable-references` for more information about nullable reference types.

- ***Unsafe code should be avoided:*** Unsafe code enables you to deal with pointers in C#. Unless there is no other way to implement the solution, unsafe code should be avoided.
- `Try-catch` ***statements cannot be empty:*** There is rarely a reason for a `try-catch` statement without treatment in the `catch` area. More than that, the caught exceptions should be as specific as possible, and not just an "exception," to avoid swallowing unexpected exceptions.
- ***Dispose of the objects that you have created, if they are disposable:*** Even for objects where the Garbage Collector will take care of the disposed-of object, consider disposing of objects that you were responsible for creating yourself.
- `switch-case` ***statements must have a default treatment:*** Since `switch-case` statements may receive an unexpected value in some cases, the default treatment will guarantee that the code does not break in such a situation.

2. ***Maintainability and structure:*** The second group is related to long-term sustainability. These practices help architects and developers control technical debt, simplify future changes, and prevent code from becoming difficult to evolve:
    - ***Methods cannot have high complexity levels:*** Cyclomatic complexity should be checked to be under 10.
    - ***Avoid methods with many lines of code:*** Methods exceeding 50 lines of code often indicate excessive responsibility.
    - ***Members must have the correct visibility:*** As an object-oriented programming language, C# enables encapsulation with different visibility keywords. C# 10 has *init-only setters* so you can create `init` property/index accessors instead of `set`, defining these members as read-only following the construction of the object.
    - ***Duplicate code should be avoided:*** There is no reason for having duplicate code in a high-level programming language such as C#.
3. ***Readability and communication:*** The third group emphasizes clarity. Even correct and well-structured code loses value if other developers cannot quickly understand its purpose, intent, and proper usage:
    - ***Classes, methods, and variables should have understandable names:*** The name should explain everything that the reader needs to know. There should be no need for an explanatory comment unless these declarations are public.
    - ***Constants and enumerations should be used:*** A good way of avoiding magic numbers and text inside code is to transform this information into constants and enumerations, which are generally more understandable.
    - ***At least public methods should be commented on:*** Considering that public methods are the ones used outside your library, they must be explained for their correct external usage.

As a software architect, you should establish coding standards and provide templates that ensure consistency across your codebase. You can also use this code pattern as a checklist for coding inspection, which will enrich software code quality.

Identifying well-written code

It is not easy to identify whether code is well written. The best practices described up to here can certainly guide you to define a standard for your team. But even with a standard, mistakes will happen, and you will probably find them only after the code is in production. The decision to refactor code in production just because it does not follow all the standards you define is not an easy one to make, especially if the code in question is working properly. Some people conclude that well-written code is simply code that works well in production. However, this mindset can harm the long-term maintainability of the software, since developers may copy patterns from code that doesn't follow the agreed standards.

From an architectural perspective, this means that deciding whether code is "well written" cannot rely only on current behavior. Architects must also judge whether the code is aligned with the team's standards, whether it will remain understandable as the system evolves, and whether its patterns are safe to replicate across the codebase.

For this reason, as a software architect, you need to find ways to enforce adherence to the coding standard you've defined. Luckily, nowadays, we have many options for tools that can help us with this task. They are called static code analysis tools and using them is a great opportunity to improve both the software developed and the team's programming knowledge.

These tools are especially useful because they help transform architectural judgment into something more systematic. Instead of depending only on subjective code reviews, architects can use them to detect patterns that increase risk, reduce maintainability, or weaken consistency across the solution.

Code analysis tools facilitate knowledge sharing by providing consistent, immediate feedback that helps developers learn best practices. The tools that we have now have the same purpose. Better than that, with Roslyn, they do this task while you are writing the code. Roslyn is the compiler platform for .NET, and it enables you to develop some tools for analyzing code. It is designed as a set of open APIs that let tools access the same information the compiler uses (syntax trees, symbols, and semantic models). This is what enables IDE features like live diagnostics, refactoring, and custom analyzers that enforce coding standards automatically. These analyzers can check style, quality, design, and other issues.

For the software architect, the value here is not only technical automation, but decision support. Roslyn-based analysis helps identify when a problem is merely cosmetic, when it signals a weakness, and when it is serious enough to justify refactoring or stronger governance.

Now, with AI, you also have the possibility to add an AI assistant to work with your developer. GitHub Copilot for Visual Studio or Visual Studio Code can accelerate your development and can check if you are writing in the proper standard.

This adds another layer to architectural decision-making, because the architect is no longer deciding only which standards exist, but also which tools will reinforce them during daily development.

For instance, look at the following code. This example intentionally demonstrates several common code-quality problems: it declares an unused variable, relies on hard-coded values (like comparing `variable` to 10) that would be clearer as named constants, and uses a `switch` without a default `case`, so unexpected values may be ignored silently. Most importantly, it wraps the logic in a broad `try` and ends with an empty `catch`, which swallows every exception and hides failures, making troubleshooting and reliability much worse. Together, these issues show how code can "work" while still being fragile, hard to maintain, and unsafe in production.

```
try
{
    int variableUnused = 10;
    int variable = 10;
    if (variable == 10)
    {
        Console.WriteLine("variable equals 10");
    }
    else
    {
        switch (variable)
        {
            case 0:
                Console.WriteLine("variable equals 0");
                break;
        }
    }
}
catch
{
}
```

From an architectural viewpoint, examples like this are useful because they show the difference between code that merely executes and code that should be accepted as a repeatable pattern for the team. That distinction is central to architectural judgment.

The idea of this code is to show you the power of some tools to improve the code you are delivering. Let us study each of them in the next section, including how to set them up.

The key takeaway is that architects do not evaluate code only by asking whether it works, but by asking whether it is safe to maintain, safe to replicate, and worthy of becoming part of the team's standard.

Understanding and applying tools that can evaluate C# code

The evolution of code analysis in Visual Studio is continuous. This means that Visual Studio 2026 certainly has more tools for this purpose than Visual Studio 2022, and so on.

One of the strategic points that you (as a software architect) need to deal with is the *coding style of the team*. This certainly results in a better understanding of the code. For instance, if you go to **Visual Studio Menu, Tools->Options**, and then, in the left-hand menu, you go to **Languages -> C#**, you will find ways to set up how to deal with different code style patterns, and a bad coding style is even indicated as an error in the *Code Style* option, as we can check in *Figure 4.15*.

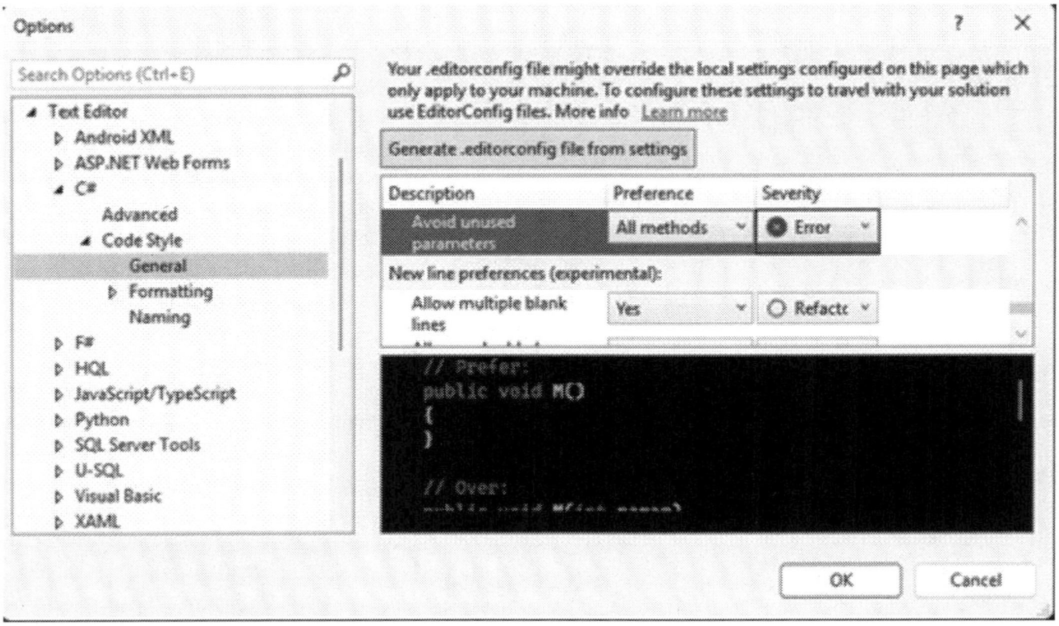

Figure 4.15: Code Style options

The preceding screenshot shows a change in the setup, considering that "*avoid unused parameters*" will be detected as an error.

After this change, the result of the compilation of the same code presented at the beginning of the chapter is different, as you can see in the following screenshot:

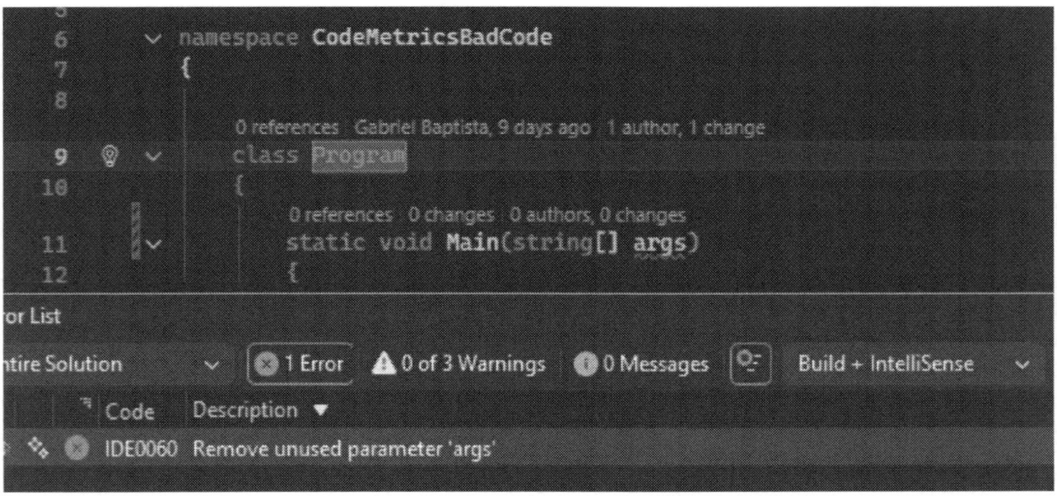

Figure 4.16: Code Style results

You can export your coding style configuration and attach it to your project so that it will follow the rules you have defined. In practice, this is often done through an `editorconfig file`, which keeps those rules versioned together with the project.

Note

Configuring code style options only in the IDE is not enough to guarantee team-wide consistency. A stronger recommendation is to apply the appropriate analyzers to the project and configure `TreatWarningsAsErrors` so that important style and quality violations are enforced during the build process itself. This makes the standard less dependent on individual developer configuration and more consistent across the entire team.

Another good tool that Visual Studio 2026 provides is **Code Cleanup**. Its usage is most effective when used as a *last mile* step before committing, so your PRs stay focused on real changes instead of whitespace and style churn, and during refactoring sessions when you're already reshaping code. With this tool, you can set up some code standards that can clean up your code. For instance, in the following screenshot, it was set to remove unnecessary code:

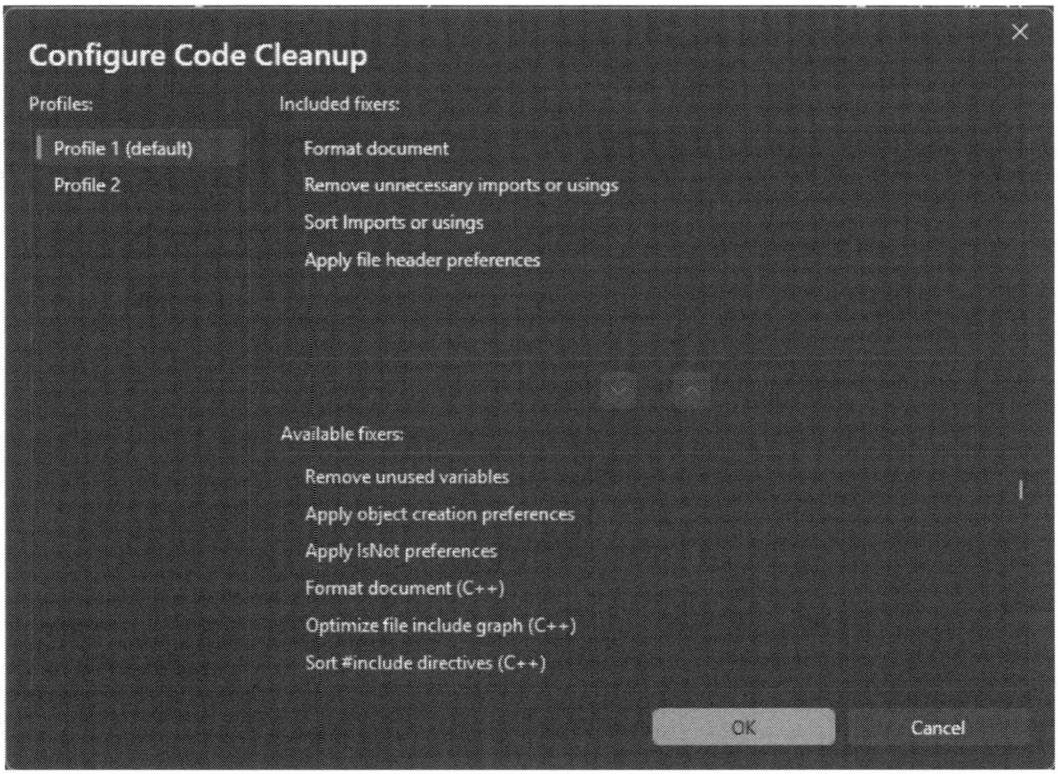

Figure 4.17: Configure Code Cleanup

The way you run Code Cleanup is by selecting it with the help of a right click in the **Solution Explorer** area, over the project where you want to run it. After that, this process will run in all the code files you have:

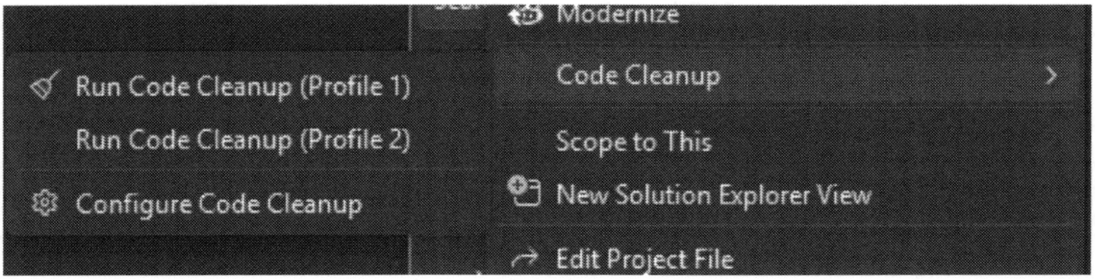

Figure 4.18: Run Code Cleanup

After solving the errors indicated by the Code Style and Code Cleanup tools, the sample code we are working on has some minimal simplifications, as follows:

```
using System;
try
{
    int variable = 10;
    if (variable == 10)
    {
        Console.WriteLine("variable equals 10");
    }
    else
    {
        switch (variable)
        {
            case 0:
                Console.WriteLine("variable equals 0");
                break;
        }
    }
}
catch
{
}
```

It is worth mentioning that the preceding code has many improvements that still need to be addressed, as we have presented earlier. Visual Studio enables you to add additional tools for the IDE by installing extensions to it. These tools can help you to improve your code quality, since some of them were built to perform code analysis. This section will list some free options so that you can decide on the one that best fits your needs. There are certainly other options and even paid ones. The idea here is not to indicate a specific tool but to give you an idea of their abilities.

To install these extensions, you will need to find the **Extensions** menu in Visual Studio 2026. Here is a screenshot of the **Manage Extensions** option:

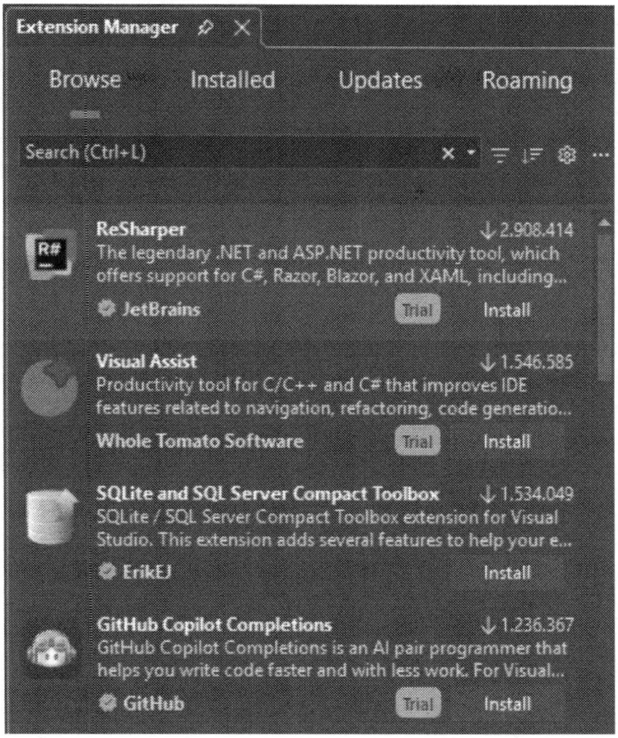

Figure 4.19: Extensions in Visual Studio 2026

There are many other great extensions that can improve the productivity and quality of your code and solution. Do a search for them in this manager.

After you have selected the extension that will be installed, you may need to restart Visual Studio. Most of them are easy to identify after installation since they modify the behavior of the IDE. However, they need to be set in each developer environment. To solve this, Visual Studio has introduced the option to include analyzers as NuGet packages, so all developers who work with the project will have their code analyzed. The key architectural idea is moving quality enforcement from the IDE to the codebase, so standards are versioned, repeatable, and enforced everywhere. Now let's check how these extensions properly work.

Applying extension tools to analyze code

Although the sample code delivered after the Code Style and Code Cleanup tools is noticeably better than the initial version, there are still opportunities to align it more closely with the best practices covered so far.

For this reason, we can divide analyzers into three groups:

- ***Code style analyzers***: Focus on consistent formatting and conventions (naming, `using` ordering, spacing, expression simplifications). They're typically configured in the repo via `.editorconfig`, so everyone sees the same rules. Updates come from changing the configuration and/or the IDE/.NET SDK version that contains the underlying analyzer behavior.

- ***Code quality analyzers (built-in in .NET 10)***: Ship with the .NET SDK and provide general correctness/quality guidance (e.g., common API misuse, reliability pitfalls, some performance-related patterns). Because they're part of the SDK, they're distributed and updated when you update your .NET SDK/runtime and teams usually control adoption by pinning the SDK version (for example, via `global.json`) and choosing rule severity.
- ***Third-party analyzers (NuGet packages or IDE extensions)***: Come from external vendors or the community and cover specialized rule sets (security-focused rules, domain-specific constraints, stricter style policies, etc.). If installed as NuGet packages, they travel with the project and are updated like any other dependency. If installed as Visual Studio extensions, they're updated per developer machine and may vary across the team unless standardized, so NuGet distribution is usually preferred for consistency and CI enforcement.

> **Note**
>
> You may find more information about the overview of source code analysis at `https://docs.microsoft.com/en-us/visualstudio/code-quality/roslyn-analyzers-overview`.

Let us study how these third-party analyzers can be useful, using the SonarQube package as a reference.

Applying SonarQube for Visual Studio

SonarQube for Visual Studio IDE is a free static analysis tool offered by the Sonar Source community to detect bugs and quality issues while you code. There is support for C#, VB.NET, C, C++, and JavaScript. The great thing about this extension is that it comes with explanations for resolving detected issues, and that is why we say developers learn how to code well while using these tools.

This extension can point out mistakes and, better than that, there is an explanation for each warning. This is useful not only for detecting problems but also for training developers in good coding practices, since the response for the developer is immediate after building the code.

In Visual Studio 2026, you can find the SonarQube for Visual Studio extension available. Besides that, you may also use the NuGet package, as we can see in the following screenshot.

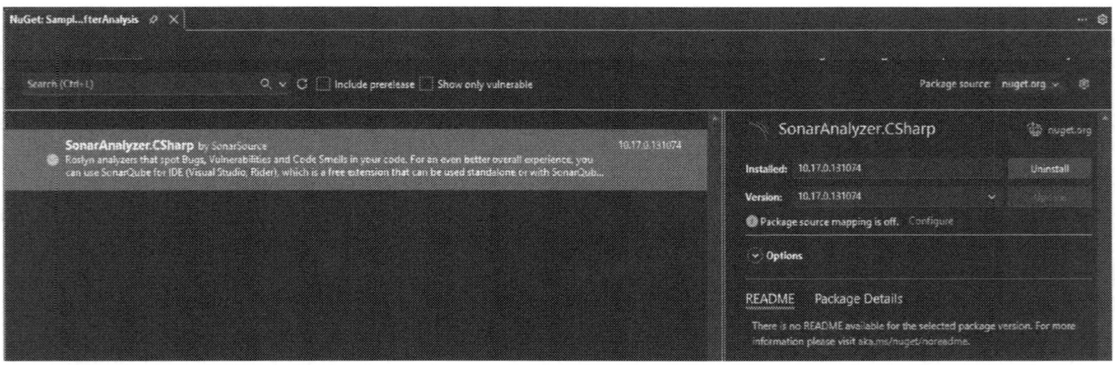

Figure 4.20: SonarAnalyzer.CSharp NuGet package

The result produced is the same as the one we got using the SonarQube extension, as we can check in *Figure 4.21*. But the good thing about this option is that any developer who needs to code this project will get their code analyzed.

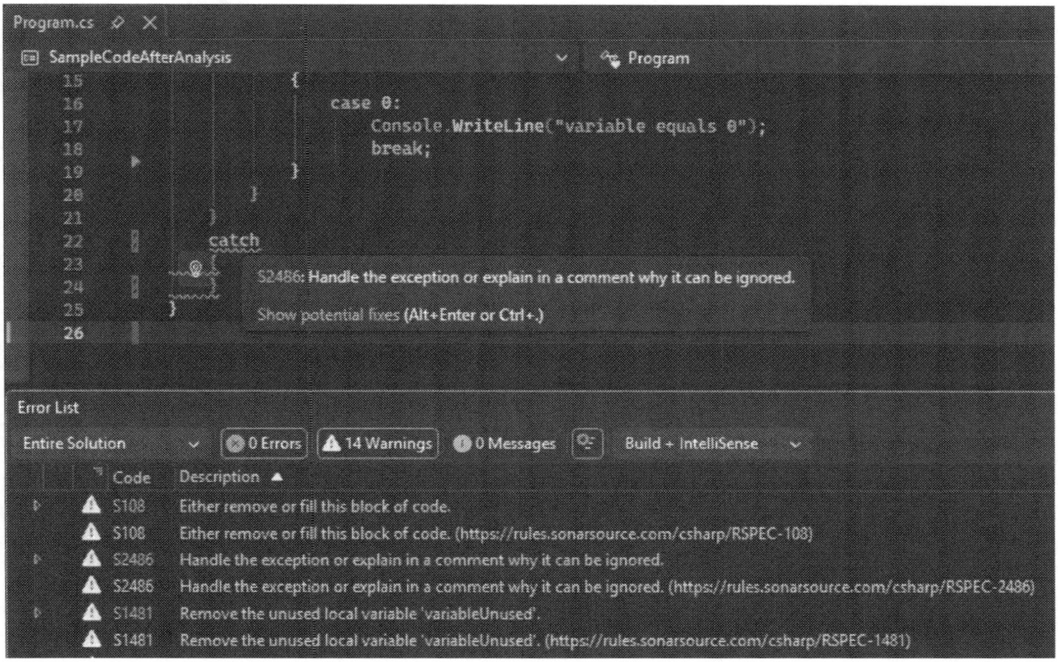

Figure 4.21: SonarAnalyzer.CSharp analysis result

As a software architect, you will always have to pay attention and take action to get the projects unified in the same code standard, so the NuGet option may be useful to achieve this goal. Let's now check the results after solving the outputs described by these static analysis tools.

Checking the code after static analysis tools

Following the analysis of Code Style and SonarQube analyzers, we have solved the issues from the original code. Here is the final code:

```
using System;

// Principle: exceptions should be handled at appropriate boundaries
// to avoid crashing unexpectedly.
try
{
    // (Cleanup) Removed the unused variable to reduce noise and
    // improve clarity.
    int variable = 10;
    if (variable == 10)
    {
```

```
            Console.WriteLine("variable equals 10");
        }
        else
        {
            switch (variable)
            {
                case 0:
                    Console.WriteLine("variable equals 0");
                    break;
                default:
                    // Principle: switch statements should be exhaustive.
                    // Adding a default case prevents silent fall-through
                    // for unexpected values.
                    Console.WriteLine("Unknown behavior");
                    break;
            }
        }
    }
    // Principle: avoid empty catch blocks
    // don't swallow failures silently.
    catch (Exception err)
    {
        // Principle: ensure exceptions are visible and diagnosable.
        // Logging/printing the exception is a minimal handling strategy.
        // In production, prefer structured Logging.
        Console.WriteLine(err);
    }
```

As you can see, the preceding code is not only easier to understand, but it is safer and is able to consider different paths of programming since the default for switch-case was programmed. This pattern was discussed earlier in this chapter, which brings us to the happy conclusion that best practices can easily be followed by using one (or all) of the options mentioned in this chapter.

But today we have more than analyzers available. With the advance of AI, we can improve a little bit more the code above. AI-assisted review can complement static analysis: instead of replacing analyzers, it builds on their foundation and adds a second layer of feedback that is more contextual, explanatory, and aligned with the team's conventions and architectural principles. Let's check this out in the next topic.

Applying GitHub Copilot to analyze code

With the possibility of AI Coding Agents, such as GitHub Copilot Coding Agent, you may give the list of instructions above as preliminary information for the agent that checks PRs, so it can check if all these statements are being fulfilled by the code you are writing.

AI usage for coding is certainly a way to accelerate the development of good software and you, as a software architect, cannot oppose this movement. Instead of it, a good option is to lead the way developers use AI, considering the importance of maintenance and delivery of good software.

As soon as you have a GitHub Copilot account available, there are two options to evolve your code using it. The first is by asking for assistance from Copilot using *Copilot Chat* inside the code editor. In Visual Studio, the command "Alt" + ";" will open this chat, as we can check in *Figure 4.22*.

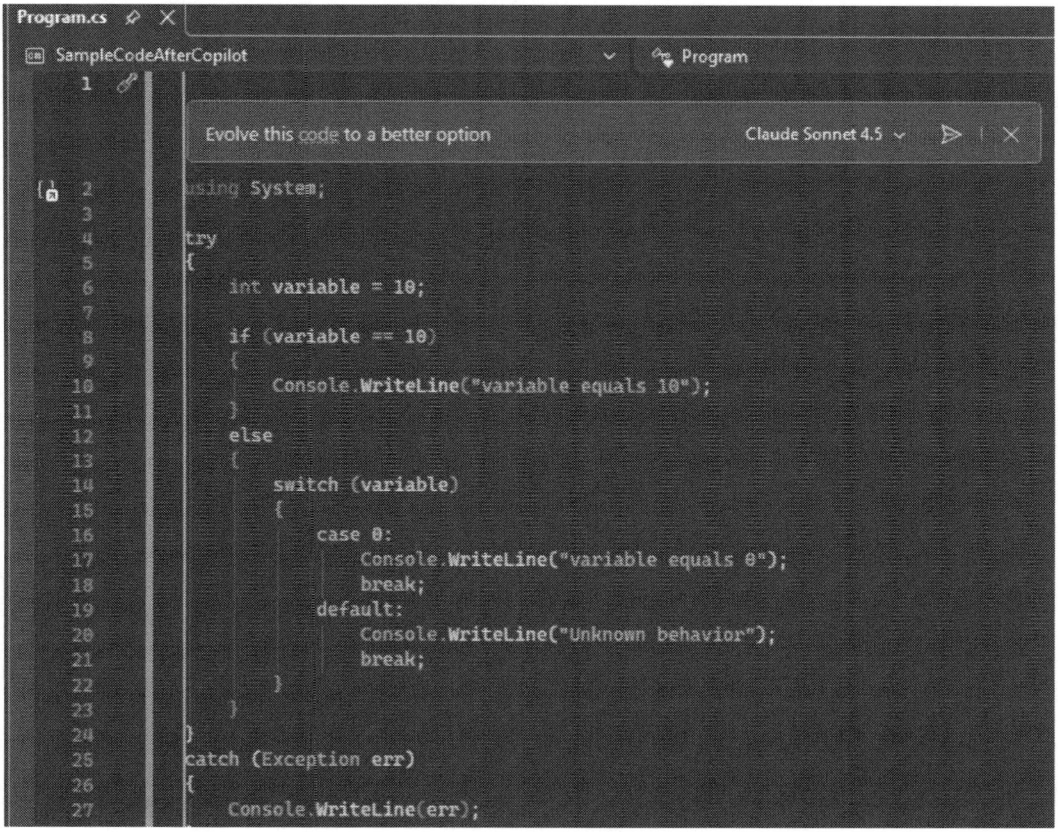

Figure 4.22: Copilot Chat in the Visual Studio Editor

The main idea of the command above is to check the evolution of the code AI will provide. The output of the command resulted in four alternatives, and we have selected the one below to present to you:

```
using System;

try
{
    const int expectedValue = 10;
    int variable = 10;

    if (variable == expectedValue)
    {
        Console.WriteLine($"variable equals {expectedValue}");
    }
    else
    {
        Console.WriteLine(variable switch
        {
            0 => "variable equals 0",
            _ => "Unknown behavior"
        });
    }
}
catch (Exception err)
{
    Console.WriteLine($"An error occurred: {err.Message}");
}
```

Although the result of the code will be the same, we cannot argue that the result presented by *GitHub Copilot* with *Claude Sonnet 4.5+* model has some details that can consider this code with more legibility.

We can also execute the same kind of prompt using GitHub Copilot Chat. In Visual Studio, the command "Ctrl" + "]" + "C" will open this chat, as you can see in *Figure 4.23*.

Figure 4.23: GitHub Copilot Chat Window

In this test, we have changed the model to GPT-5.2, but you can decide on the latest model at the moment you test it. It is worth mentioning that GitHub Copilot is constantly updating the models provided by them, so you need to keep updated, since the price and the versions of these models are changing very quickly. The output of the model has indicated some great information:

```
Updated Program.cs to a cleaner, more idiomatic .NET 10 / C# 14 style:
- Removed the broad try/catch (it wasn't adding useful handling here).
- Replaced the nested if/else + switch with a single switch expression.
- Used a const for the fixed value and emitted exactly one output path.
```

And below you have the result of the code.

```
using System;

const int value = 10;

Console.WriteLine(value switch
{
```

```
        10 => "variable equals 10",
        0 => "variable equals 0",
        _ => "Unknown behavior"
    });
```

As you can see in this example, the power of AI for analyzing code can significantly improve the speed and consistency of reviews by catching common issues early and providing actionable suggestions. As software architects, we need to promote the use of it to accelerate the delivery of the software we are designing, giving businesses the opportunity to reduce the time-to-market of the solutions.

Summary

In this chapter, we discussed some important tips for writing code using C#. It introduced code quality metrics so that you can manage the complexity and maintainability of the software you are developing. It also presented the importance of a version control system, especially today when we have integration with AI. It also discussed practices for having safe code, where we presented some good tips to guarantee that your software will not crash due to memory leaks and exceptions. In real life, a software architect will always be asked to solve this kind of problem.

The chapter also presented tools that can be used to apply the best practices of coding we discussed. We call them static analysis tools, and we have mentioned how the Roslyn compiler helps us out with it, enabling code analysis while the developer is coding.

To finish, we have also checked during the chapter how AI for coding is inevitable and is a must-use tool that will help us write simpler and better code.

You will find in *Chapter 22, Case Study: Practical Usage of .NET Aspire*, a way to evaluate C# code prior to publishing an application, which implements code analysis during the Azure DevOps building process using Sonar Cloud. We will also present how to do the same using GitHub Actions on GitHub.

When you apply all the content you have learned in this chapter to your projects, you will find that code analysis will give you the opportunity to improve the quality of the code you are delivering to your customer. This is a very important part of your role as a software architect.

In the next chapter, you will learn about Code Reuse, which is an incredible technique to guarantee quality and speed for your projects!

Questions

1. Why do we need to care about maintainability?
2. What is cyclomatic complexity?
3. List the advantages of using a version control system
4. How does garbage collector (GC) act and what are the implications of GC in unmanaged resources?
5. What is the importance of implementing the `IDisposable` interface?
6. What advantages do we gain from .NET 10 when it comes to coding?

7. What makes it possible for a piece of software to be described as having well-written code?
8. What is the importance of Roslyn for static code analysis tools?
9. What is the importance of code analysis?
10. How does Roslyn help with code analysis?
11. What are Visual Studio extensions?
12. What extension tools are available for code analysis?
13. How can AI-assisted tools complement static analyzers during coding and PR reviews?

Further reading

These are some books and websites where you will find more information about the topics of this chapter:

- Clean Code: A Handbook of Agile Software Craftsmanship, by Martin, Robert C. Pearson Education, 2012.
- The Art of Designing Embedded Systems, by Jack G. Ganssle. Elsevier, 1999.
- Refactoring, by Martin Fowler. Addison-Wesley, 2018.
- A Complexity Measure, by Thomas J. McCabe. IEEE Trans. Software Eng. 2(4): 308-320, 1976.
- `https://docs.microsoft.com/en-us/visualstudio/code-quality/code-metrics-values`.
- `https://github.com`.
- `https://bitbucket.org`.
- `https://azure.microsoft.com/en-us/services/devops`.
- `https://guides.github.com/introduction/flow`.
- `https://docs.microsoft.com/aspnet/core/fundamentals/logging`.
- `https://learn.microsoft.com/en-us/dotnet/csharp/whats-new`.
- `https://marketplace.visualstudio.com/items?itemName=SonarSource.SonarLintforVisualStudio2022`.
- `https://github.com/dotnet/roslyn-analyzers`.
- `https://docs.microsoft.com/en-us/visualstudio/ide/code-styles-and-code-cleanup`.

5

Implementing Code Reusability in C#

Code reusability is one of the most important topics in software architecture. From a strategic perspective, it impacts cost, coupling, and how safely a system can evolve over time. This chapter aims to discuss ways to enable code reuse, as well as help you understand how .NET solves the problem of managing and maintaining a reusable library. By the end of this chapter, you will be able to identify opportunities for strategic reuse, design reusable components with appropriate architectural trade-offs, and operationalize them through documentation, distribution, and lifecycle practices.

The following topics will be covered in this chapter:

- Understanding the principles of code reuse
- Best practices for enabling code reuse in the development life cycle
- The advantages of working with .NET
- Creating reusable libraries using .NET

Code reuse can be valuable, but architects should invest in reusability only when its benefits outweigh the added coupling, constraints, and maintenance overhead. Many good software architects agree that there is a lot of overengineering due to trying to make things reusable even though they are often single-use or not understood well enough, leading to unnecessary complexity and slowing down the development process.

Technical requirements

For this chapter, you will need the free Visual Studio 2026 Community Edition or better. You can find the sample code for this chapter at `https://github.com/PacktPublishing/Software-Architecture-with-.NET-10-and-C-sharp-5E/tree/main/ch05`.

Understanding the principles of code reusability

The fundamental justification for code reuse is efficiency – avoid reinventing solutions that already work well in other contexts. That is why many engineering domains rely on reuse-oriented principles: **modularity** (replace parts independently), **standardization** (shared interfaces and dimensions), **abstraction** (hide internal complexity behind a contract), and **documentation** (make correct reuse predictable). Consider light switches in your house. You can replace any switch without rewiring the entire electrical system because switches follow standardized specifications. This same principle – defining clear interfaces and separating concerns – enables software reusability.

Can you imagine the number of applications that can be made with the same interface components? The fundamentals of code reuse are the same. Again, it is a matter of planning a good solution so that part of it can be reused later.

In software engineering, code reuse is one of the techniques that can bring several advantages to a software project. It can increase confidence, since reused code has already been proven in production environments, and it can reduce design risk by encouraging the adoption of patterns and conventions that have already been widely used and validated in real-world systems. It can also enable more efficient resource allocation, allowing senior engineers and architects to focus on novel challenges rather than reimplementing solved problems, while increasing development velocity through the integration of existing, well-tested components. In addition, it can simplify maintenance, as fixes and improvements made to reusable components can benefit all applications simultaneously. Together, these advantages make code reuse a force multiplier for software teams, improving efficiency, consistency, and reliability across the project lifecycle.

These aspects suggest that code reuse should be done whenever it is strategically justified. However, creating reusable components does carry higher costs initially. That is why you need to focus on creating it in situations where you recognize that this piece of code will really be reused in the future, or where you are trying to reuse code that has not been created as a component. It is your responsibility, as a software architect, to ensure the preceding advantages are utilized and, more than that, that you incentivize your team to enable reuse in the software they are creating.

But remember that reuse creates the most value when it is treated as a strategic architectural decision, not as a default practice. In the next section, we will discuss what can be considered code reuse and what cannot. The main purpose of discussing it is to enable you to define a code reuse strategy that will transform the efficiency of your team.

What code reuse is not

The first thing you must understand is that code reuse does not mean copying and pasting code from one class to another. Even if this code was written by another team or project, this does not indicate that you are properly working with reusability principles. Let's imagine the case study of the book – *WWTravelClub* – presented in *Chapter 22, Case Study: Practical Usage of .NET Aspire*. There, we will have a software requirement for evaluating different kinds of travel subjects.

In this project scenario, where we have an online travel agency, you may want to evaluate different kinds of subjects, such as the *Package*, *DestinationExpert*, *City*, *Comments*, and so on. The process for calculating the evaluation average is the same, no matter which subject you are referring to. In this case it is calculated by aggregating all valid user ratings associated with that item and dividing the total score by the number of submitted evaluations.

Due to this, you may want to *enable* reuse by copying and pasting the code for each evaluation. The (bad) result will be something like in *Figure 5.1*, where you have the duplication of the method `CalculateEvaluationAverage` four times.

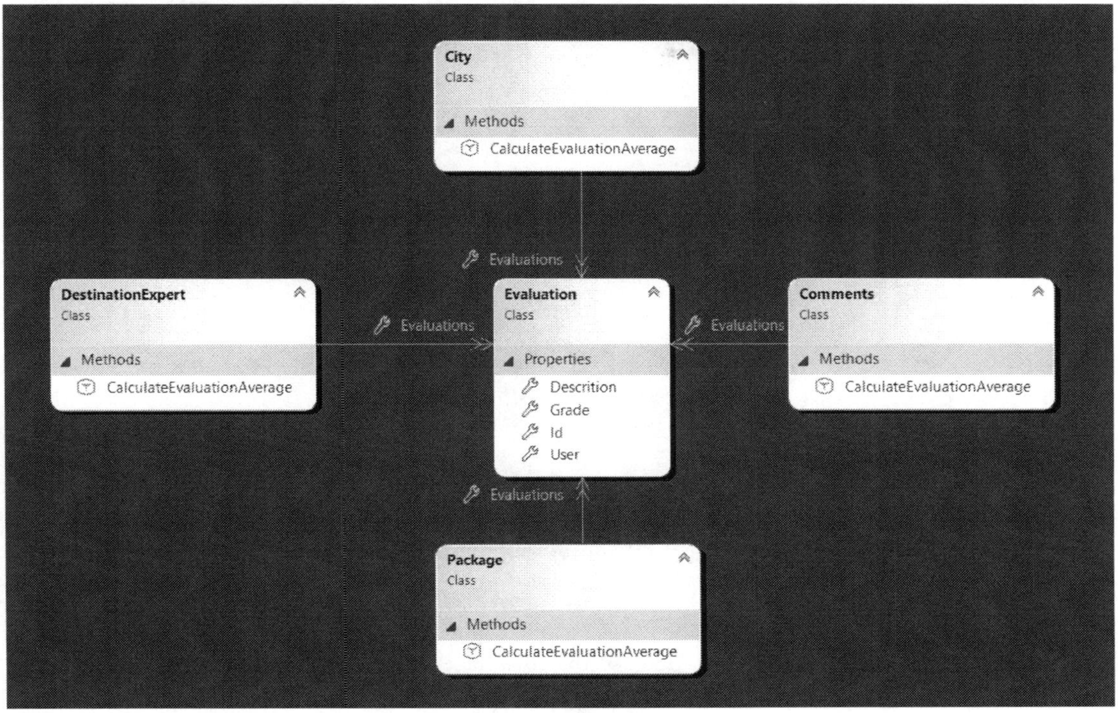

Figure 5.1: Bad implementation – there is no code reuse here

In the preceding diagram, the process of calculating the evaluation average is duplicated, which means that the same code will be duplicated in different classes. This will cause a lot of trouble, especially if the same approach is used in other applications. For instance, if there is a new specification covering how you must calculate the average, or even if you just get a bug in the calculation formula, you will have to fix it in all instances of the code. If you do not remember to update it everywhere, you will possibly end up with an inconsistent implementation.

So, copy-and-paste may look efficient at first, but it increases duplication, maintenance effort, and the risk of inconsistent behavior. In the next section, we will reorganize this code to respect the centralization principle, helping you avoid the issues we have mentioned here.

What code reuse is

The solution to the problem mentioned in the previous section is quite simple: you must analyze your code and select the parts of it that would be good to decouple from your application.

The most compelling reason you should decouple them is related to how you are sure that this code can be reused in other parts of the application or even in another application. This is exactly what Andrew Hunt and David Thomas present as the **DRY principle** (Don't repeat yourself). In short, the goal is not only separation, but reuse with confidence. With that in mind, we can now look at the main alternatives for achieving this, such as inheritance and composition as shown below:

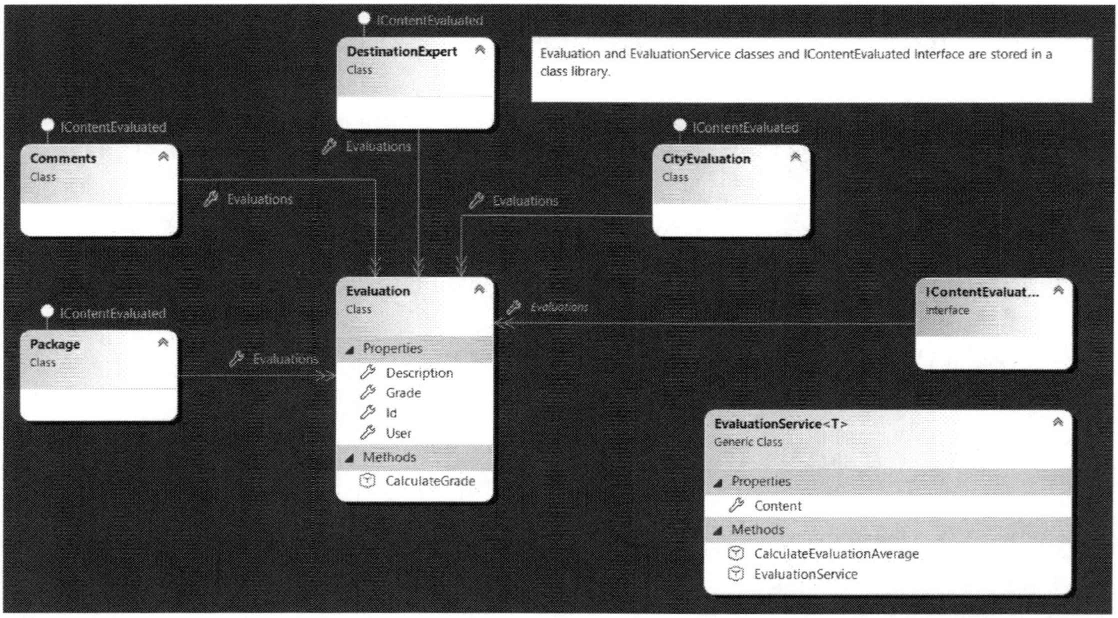

Figure 5.2: An implementation focused on code reuse

The centralization of the code brings with it a different responsibility for software architects like you. You must keep in mind that if there is a mistake or problem in this code, it can cause issues in many parts of the application or even other applications that use it. On the other hand, once you have this code tested and running, you will be able to reuse this code again in new projects with no worries. Besides, let's remember the use case we are implementing here: you may want to evaluate different kinds of subjects, such as the *Package*, *DestinationExpert*, *CityEvaluation*, *Comments*, and so on. The process for getting the evaluation average is the same, no matter which subject you are referring to. What if you need to evolve the average calculation process? In the design now provided, you will have to change the code in a single class. Considering what we have already learned, the centralized service isn't the only approach. Instead, this becomes a design decision that the software architect must evaluate according to the requirements, the expected flexibility, and the long-term maintainability of the solution. For example, you might consider:

- Making a base class implementing the logic of the method
- Inheriting all other classes from the newly created base class and eventually augment/modify the methods' behavior
- Turning the inheritance into an association (as discussed in *Chapter 4, Best Practices in Coding C#*)

Designing for reuse can cost more initially because it requires stronger abstractions, documentation, and long-term support. However, that investment pays off when the same component is used repeatedly, reducing implementation and maintenance effort across projects.

Always remember that effective reuse comes from centralizing stable behavior behind clear abstractions that can evolve safely over time. Now let's check how reusability can be handled in the development life cycle.

Reusability in the development lifecycle

If you understand that code reusability will take you to another level of coding, improving the way you write and use code, then it's time to think about how to make this technique available in your development life cycle.

As a matter of fact, creating and maintaining a component library is not very easy due to the responsibility you will take on and the lack of good tools to support the search for existing components.

To address these challenges, consider implementing these practices in your development process:

1. ***Use the already-implemented components from your reusable library***: Reuse existing components from your library whenever they meet the requirement with minimal adaptation. This avoids unnecessary engineering and reduces risk.
2. ***Identify library components***: Identify features that are likely to appear across products (e.g., authentication, auditing, device integration adapters) in the software requirements specifications. They are candidates to be designed as library components.
3. ***Modify the specification for reuse***: Considering that these features will be developed using reusable components, refine requirements to align with reusable capabilities (and constraints). Explicitly note what will be satisfied by the library versus what requires new development.
4. ***Design*** components for stable interfaces: Design the reusable components and be sure that they have the appropriate interfaces to be used in many projects
5. ***Build*** the project architecture with the new component library version: Build (or update) the solution architecture to use the new library version, ensuring compatibility, performance, and operational concerns are met
6. ***Document*** and socialize the library: Document the component library version and publish usage guidance so that every developer and team knows about it

The **use-identify-modify-design-build-document cycle** provides a framework for systematically incorporating reusability into your projects. As soon as you have the components you need to write for this library, you will need to decide on the technology that will provide these components.

During the history of software development, there have been many approaches to enable code reuse, from **dynamic link libraries** (DLLs) to microservices, as we will discuss in *Chapter 11, Applying a Microservice Architecture to Your Enterprise Application*, in the *Microservices, and the evolution of the concept of modules* section. The methodology explained in the section can be used by you, as a software architect, to implement this strategy to accelerate software development. Remember that reuse succeeds when it is built into the lifecycle through identification, design, adoption, and documentation practices. Now, let us check how .NET can help us with it.

Using .NET for code reuse

.NET has evolved a lot since its first version. This evolution encompasses API breadth, performance improvements, and dramatically expanded platform support. As we discussed in *Chapter 1, Understanding the Importance of Software Architecture*, you can run C# .NET on billions of devices, including Linux, Android, macOS, or iOS. For this reason, .NET Standard was first announced together with .NET Core 1.0, but .NET Standard became particularly important with .NET Standard 2.0 when .NET Framework 4.7.2, .NET Core, and Xamarin became compatible with it.

The key point is that .NET Standard is not only a type of Visual Studio project. It is a formal specification available to all .NET implementations. As you can see from the following table, **.NET Standard 2.0**, which is recommended by Microsoft, covers everything in .NET. You can find a full .NET Standard overview at `https://docs.microsoft.com/en-us/dotnet/standard/net-standard`.

.NET implementation	Version support
.NET and .NET Core	2.0, 2.1, 2.2, 3.0, 3.1, 5.0, 6.0, 7.0, 8.0, 9.0, 10.0
.NET Framework	4.6.1, 4.6.2, 4.7, 4.7.1, 4.7.2, 4.8, 4.8.1
Mono	5.4, 6.4
Xamarin.iOS	10.14, 12.16
Xamarin.Mac	3.8, 5.16
Xamarin.Android	8.0, 10.0
Universal Windows Platform	10.0.16299, TBD
Unity	2018.1

Table 5.1: NET Standard 2.0 support

This table shows that .NET Standard 2.0 enabled broad API compatibility across multiple .NET implementations. In practice, a library targeting .NET Standard 2.0 can be reused across many platforms that implement that standard. However, for modern development on unified .NET (5+ and later, including .NET 10), .NET Standard is best viewed as a **compatibility target**: prefer targeting netX.0 for new libraries and use .NET Standard only when you need to support older or more diverse consumers (for example, legacy .NET Framework).

Obviously, some components are not included in .NET Standard, but its evolution is continuous. It is worth mentioning that Microsoft's official documentation indicates that *the higher the version, the more APIs are available to you.*

The initiative of having a single framework for all platforms brought us to .NET 5. Microsoft indicated that from .NET 5.0, the framework would run everywhere. The next question you, as a software architect, might have is: *what is going to happen to .NET Standard?*

The answer to this question is well explained by Immo Landwerth at the dotnet blog: `https://devblogs.microsoft.com/dotnet/the-future-of-net-standard/`. The basic answer is that .NET 5.0 (and future versions) needs to be thought of as the foundation for sharing code moving forward.

Note

Considering that .NET 10 is an *LTS (long-term support)* version, we can now understand the framework as the best option for sharing code in new applications.

Bearing this scenario in mind, it is time to check how to create reusable class libraries. So, let's move on to the next topic.

Creating a reusable class library

If you want to make useful functionalities to be used by multiple applications, you will need to create a *class library* project. So, creating class libraries is the best way to reuse code using .NET. It is quite simple to create a *class library*. Basically, you need to choose the following project when creating the library:

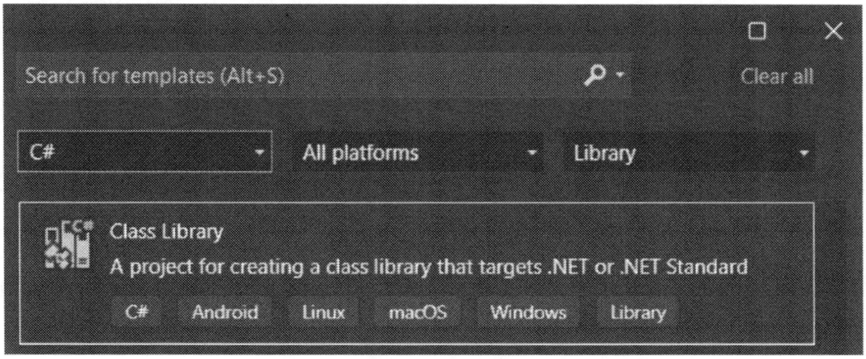

Figure 5.3: Creating a class library

Once you have concluded this part, you will notice that the project file keeps the information about the **target framework moniker** (TFM). The idea of the TFM is to define the set of APIs that will be available to the library. The TFM defines the library's available APIs so the compiler can validate compatibility and NuGet can choose the right assets for each consuming project. You can find the list of the available TFMs at `https://docs.microsoft.com/en-us/dotnet/standard/frameworks`:

```
<Project Sdk="Microsoft.NET.Sdk">
  <PropertyGroup>
    <TargetFramework>net10.0</TargetFramework>
    <ImplicitUsings>enable</ImplicitUsings>
    <Nullable>enable</Nullable>
  </PropertyGroup>
</Project>
```

As soon as your project is loaded, you can start coding the classes that you intend to reuse. The advantage of building a reusable class library this way is that you can consume the same code from multiple projects, if their target frameworks are compatible with the frameworks defined in the library project. On the other hand, you will find that some APIs that are available in .NET Framework do not exist in this type of project.

So, a class library is not just a code container. It is a packaging and compatibility decision that shapes how reuse happens across solutions. Considering that you already have the correct project type selected for creating reusable code, let us check how C# deals with code reuse in the next section.

How does C# deal with code reuse?

Considering you are writing class libraries using C#.NET, there are many approaches where **C#** helps us deal with code reuse. The ability to build libraries, as we did in the previous section, is one of them. One of the most important ones is the fact that the language is **object-oriented**. Besides this, it is also worth mentioning the facilities that generics brought to the C# language. This section will discuss object-oriented analysis and generics principles.

Object-oriented analysis

The **object-oriented analysis** approach gives us the ability to reuse code in different ways, from the facility of inheritance to the changeability of polymorphism. Complete adoption of object-oriented programming will let you implement abstraction and encapsulation too.

It is important to mention that in *Chapter 4, Best Practices in Coding C#,* we discuss how inheritance can cause complexity in your code. Although the following example presents a valid way to reuse code with no harm for real-life applications in this scenario, consider using composition over inheritance in scenarios with many levels of inheritance. Remember that deep inheritance hierarchies tend to increase coupling and rigidity, making the design harder to understand, maintain, and evolve.

The following diagram shows how using the object-oriented approach makes reuse easier. As you can see, there are different ways to calculate the grades of an evaluation, considering that you can be a basic or a prime user of this example system:

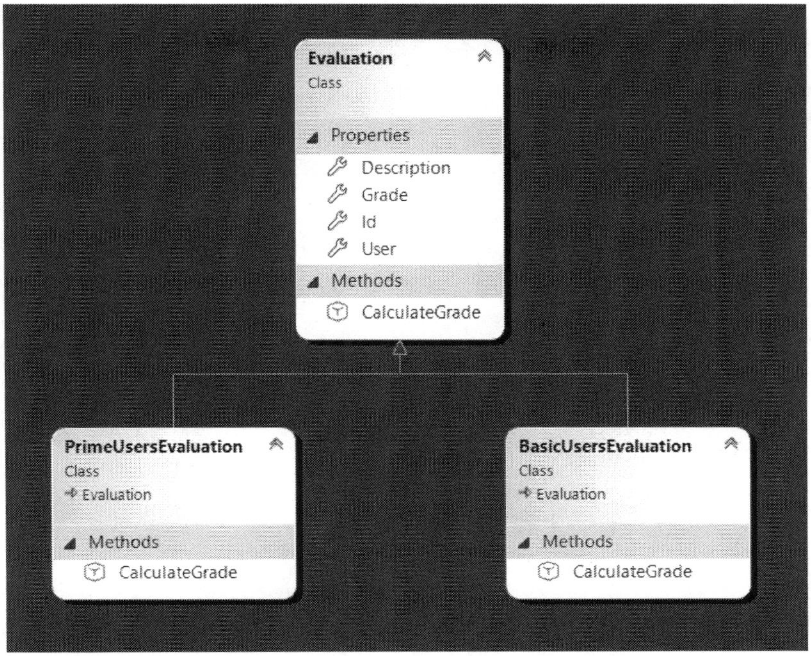

Figure 5.4: Object-oriented case analysis

There are two aspects to be analyzed as code reuse in this design. The first is that there is no need to declare the properties in each child's class since inheritance does it for you.

The second is the opportunity to use polymorphism, enabling different behaviors for the same method:

```
public class PrimeUsersEvaluation : Evaluation
{
    /// <summary>
    /// The business rule implemented here indicates that grades
    /// that came from prime users have 20% of increase
    /// </summary>
    /// <returns>the final grade from a prime user</returns>
    public override double CalculateGrade()
    {
        return Grade * 1.2;
    }
}
```

In the preceding code, you can see the usage of the polymorphism principle, where the calculation of evaluation for prime users will increase by 20%. Now, look at how easy it is to call different objects inherited by the same class. Since the collection content implements the same interface, `IContentEvaluated`, it can have basic and prime users too:

```
public class EvaluationService
{
    /// <summary>
    /// No matter the Evaluation, the calculation will always get
    /// values from the method CalculateGrade
    /// </summary>
    /// <param name="Content">Interface for enabling calculation</param>
    /// <returns>The average of the grade from
    /// Evaluations
    /// </returns>
    public double CalculateEvaluationAverage(IContentEvaluated Content)
    {
            return Content.Evaluations
                .Select(x => x.CalculateGrade())
                .Average();
    }
}
```

Object-oriented adoption can be considered mandatory when using C#. However, more specific usage requires study and practice. You, as a software architect, should always motivate your team to study object-oriented analysis. The more abstract abilities they have, the easier code reuse will become. Now let's understand the abstraction Generics provides.

Generics

Generics were introduced in C# in version 2.0 and are considered an approach that increases code reuse. It also maximizes type safety and performance.

The basic principle of generics is that you define a placeholder for a type. That placeholder is replaced with a specific type later, when the interface, class, method, property, event, or delegate is used. The opportunity you have with this feature is incredible since you can use the same code to run different versions of the type, generically.

The following code is a modification of `EvaluationService`, which was presented in the previous section. The idea here is to enable the generalization of the service, giving us the opportunity to define the goal of evaluation since its creation:

```
public class EvaluationService<T> where T: IContentEvaluated, new()
```

This declaration indicates that any class that implements the `IContentEvaluated` interface can be used for this service. The `new()` constraint indicates this class must have a public parameter-less default constructor. This matters because the service instantiates `T` internally. Without the constraint, the compiler would not allow `new T()`, and consumers would need to provide a factory or an instance instead.

The service will be responsible for creating the evaluated content:

```
public T Content { get; set; }

public EvaluationService()
{
    Content = new T();
}
```

It is worth mentioning that this code works because all the classes are in the same assembly. The result of this modification can be checked in the instance creation of the service:

```
var service = new EvaluationService<CityEvaluation>();
```

The good news is that, now, you have a generic service that will automatically instantiate the list object with the evaluations of the content you need. It's worth mentioning that generics will obviously need more time dedicated to the first project's construction. However, once the design is done, you will have good, fast, and easy-to-maintain code. This is what we call reuse!

To finish, it is worth mentioning that C# supports reuse through object-oriented design and generics, but these features create value only when applied with clarity and restraint. So let's check what to do if the code is not reusable.

What if the code is not reusable?

In fact, any code can be reusable. The key point here is that the code you intend to reuse must be well written and follow good patterns for reuse. There are several reasons why code should be considered not ready for reuse:

- ***The code was not tested before***: Before reusing code, it is a good approach to guarantee that it works. Remember, a bug in reused code becomes a system-wide bug.
- ***The code is duplicated***: If the same logic exists in multiple places, consolidate it into a single reusable implementation. If you don't do so, fixes and changes become inconsistent and expensive, because you must hunt down every copy.
- ***The code is too complex to understand***: The code that is reused in many places needs to be written with simplicity to enable easy understanding. Without it, teams will probably avoid using it, leading to shadow implementations and new duplication.
- ***The code has tight coupling***: This is a discussion related to composition versus inheritance when building separate class libraries. Classes (with interfaces) are usually much easier to reuse than base classes that can be inherited. In a reuse process, a tightly coupled library will force developers to adapt their code to the same dependencies and architecture, reducing autonomy and portability.

In any of these cases, considering a refactoring strategy can be a great approach. When you refactor code, you improve the code's structure without changing behavior, guaranteeing the code standards, reducing complexity, and respecting the input and output data that this code will process. This enables more comprehensive and lower-cost changes to be made to the code when the time comes. Martin Fowler, in his book *Refactoring* from 2018, indicates some reasons why you should consider refactoring:

- ***It improves software design***: The more expert your team becomes, the better the design will be. A better software design will deliver not only faster coding but also bring us the opportunity to process more tasks in less time, which is essential for reusable software.
- ***It makes the software easier to understand***: Regardless of whether we are talking about juniors or seniors, good software needs to be understood by every developer in your team, promoting the possibility of reusing it more.
- ***It helps us find bugs***: While you are refactoring, you are reviewing code. During this process, you will find business rules that may not have been well programmed, so you will probably find bugs. However, do not forget that the basis of refactoring is keeping the behavior, so be sure that it is the correct moment for fixing issues and make sure the code is stable before reusing it.
- ***It makes us program quicker***: The result of refactoring will be code that will enable faster development in the future, since you will be able to reuse it more times.

When refactoring, we can guarantee good results and minimize the errors that occur during the journey by following these steps:

- ***Be sure you have a set of unit tests to guarantee correct processing***: This set of unit tests will eliminate the fear of breaking the code.
- ***Eliminate duplication***: Refactoring is a good opportunity to eliminate code duplication.
- ***Minimize complexity***: Given that one goal is to make the code more understandable, following the best practices of programming, as mentioned in *Chapter 4*, *Best Practices in Coding C#*, will help you reduce the complexity of your code.
- ***Clean up the design***: Refactoring is a good time to reorganize the design of your libraries too. Do not forget to update the libraries you use as well. This can be a great way to eliminate bugs and security issues.

As a software architect, you will receive many refactoring demands from your team. The incentive for refactoring must be continuous, but you must remind your team that refactoring without following the preceding steps might be risky, since it may cause bugs during the process. AI can be a good partner here also, but be careful on this point, since we are talking about code that has already been tested. Refactoring should be guided with responsibility, not accidentally. Your role is to ensure it accelerates development and reduces the risk of regression. Remember that code is not ready for reuse when it is untested, duplicated, overly complex, or tightly coupled, and refactoring is often the path to making reuse safe. That's how it delivers real business value. Once you have value in your reusable libraries, let's understand how to promote them.

I have my libraries. How do I promote them?

Once you have made the necessary effort to create libraries that can be reused across projects, another difficult situation arises. Enabling reusability also requires making developers aware that these libraries exist and are ready to use.

Documenting is a good way to help developers take notice of the libraries they have. There are two approaches to documenting reusable code that we would like to mention in the following subsections.

Documenting and publishing .NET libraries

It is quite simple to document .NET libraries. We have the possibility to add XML Documentation to each class, and there are a lot of ways to use these comments later. You may find useful information about it at `https://learn.microsoft.com/en-us/dotnet/csharp/language-reference/xmldoc`.

Today, with GitHub Copilot using Agent Mode inside Visual Studio, documenting the code has become a simple task. For the library that we have created for demonstrating this chapter, you can check in the picture below the result of a prompt asking for this documentation.

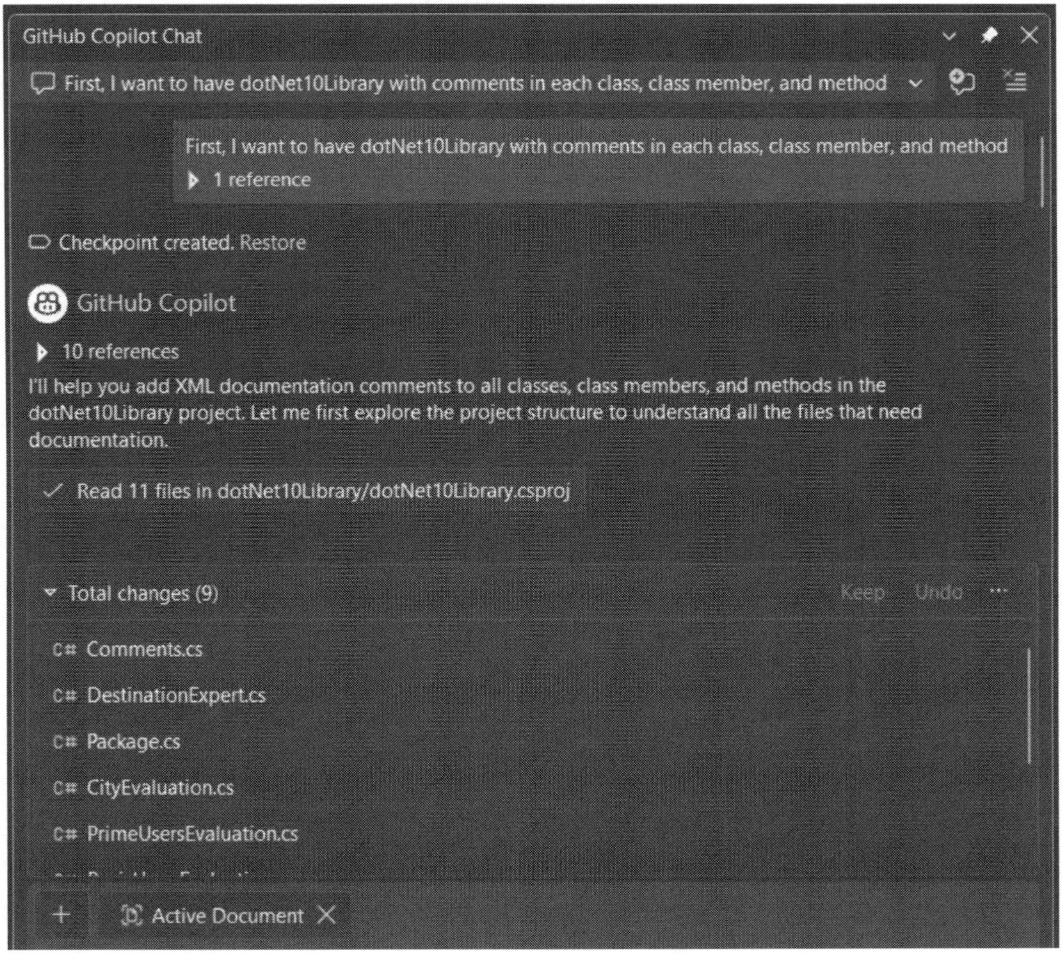

Figure 5.5: Using GitHub Copilot Chat to create comments in a library

But with this tool, there are a lot of other good approaches that we may use. For instance, it is possible to ask Copilot to generate a readme file for instructions about the library.

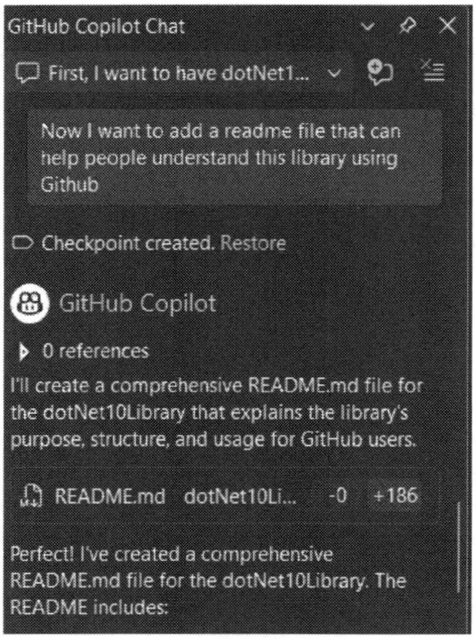

Figure 5.6: Using GitHub Copilot Chat for creating a README.md file

You can check the result of this prompt at `https://github.com/PacktPublishing/Software-Architecture-with-.NET-10-and-C-sharp-5E/tree/main/ch05/dotNet10Library`.

But documenting may not be enough, and you may want to publish your libraries. In this case, NuGet (`https://www.nuget.org/`) is a great alternative to do so. The process of creating an account is quite simple, and after that, you will need to create an API key:

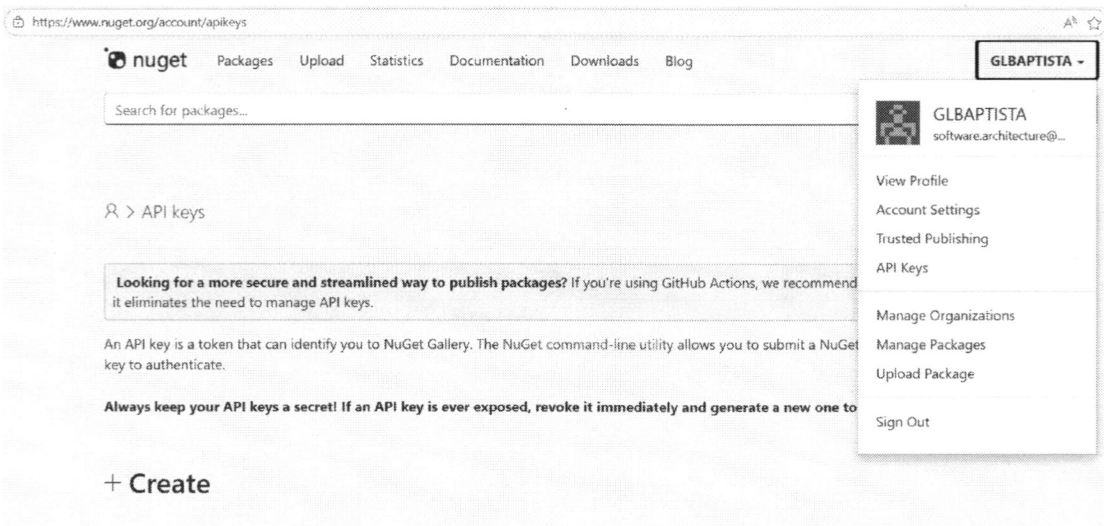

Figure 5.7: Creating an API Key at NuGet.org

Again, GitHub Copilot chat can help you in this process, where you will need to add some metadata at your `csproj`:

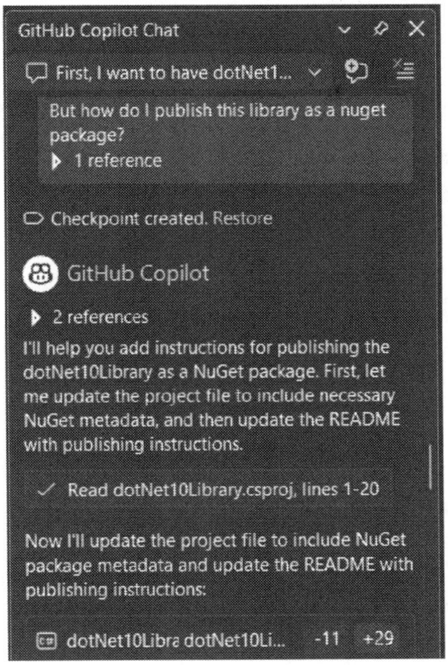

Figure 5.8: Using GitHub Copilot Chat to enable library to be published to Nuget.org

The metadata generated can be found below:

```
<Project Sdk="Microsoft.NET.Sdk">
    <PropertyGroup>
        <TargetFramework>net10.0</TargetFramework>
        <Nullable>enable</Nullable>

        <!-- NuGet Package Metadata -->
        <PackageId>dotNet10Library</PackageId>
        <Version>1.0.0</Version>
        <Authors>Gabriel Lara Baptista</Authors>
        <Company>Software Architecture 5th Edition</Company>
        <Description>A .NET 10 library for managing and calculating evaluations for
various types of content with support for different user types and evaluation
strategies.</Description>
        <PackageTags>evaluation;rating;content;dotnet10</PackageTags>
        <PackageProjectUrl>https://github.com/PacktPublishing/Software-Architecture-
with-.NET-10-and-C-sharp-5E</PackageProjectUrl>
        <RepositoryUrl>https://github.com/PacktPublishing/Software-Architecture-
with-.NET-10-and-C-sharp-5E</RepositoryUrl>
        <RepositoryType>git</RepositoryType>
```

```
        <PackageLicenseExpression>MIT</PackageLicenseExpression>
        <PackageReadmeFile>README.md</PackageReadmeFile>
        <GenerateDocumentationFile>true</GenerateDocumentationFile>
    </PropertyGroup>

    <PropertyGroup Condition="'$(Configuration)|$(Platform)'=='Debug|AnyCPU'">
    <DocumentationFile></DocumentationFile>
  </PropertyGroup>

    <ItemGroup>
        <None Include="README.md" Pack="true" PackagePath="\" />
    </ItemGroup>

</Project>
```

After this, you will only need to build the library and execute the commands below to publish it to Nuget.org:

```
# Build the package
cd [LIBRARY PATH]
dotnet pack --configuration Release

# Publish to NuGet
dotnet nuget push bin/Release/dotNet10Library.1.0.0.nupkg --api-key [YOUR_API_KEY] --
source https://api.nuget.org/v3/index.json
```

It will take up to one hour to have the library published. This is because when you push a package to NuGet.org, it goes through automated checks before it's searchable, including malware/virus scanning. Besides that, the package must be indexed to appear in NuGet.org search results. While it's still being indexed, NuGet.org can show it under **Unlisted Packages** temporarily until indexing completes. After that, you will finally have your library available, as you can see below:

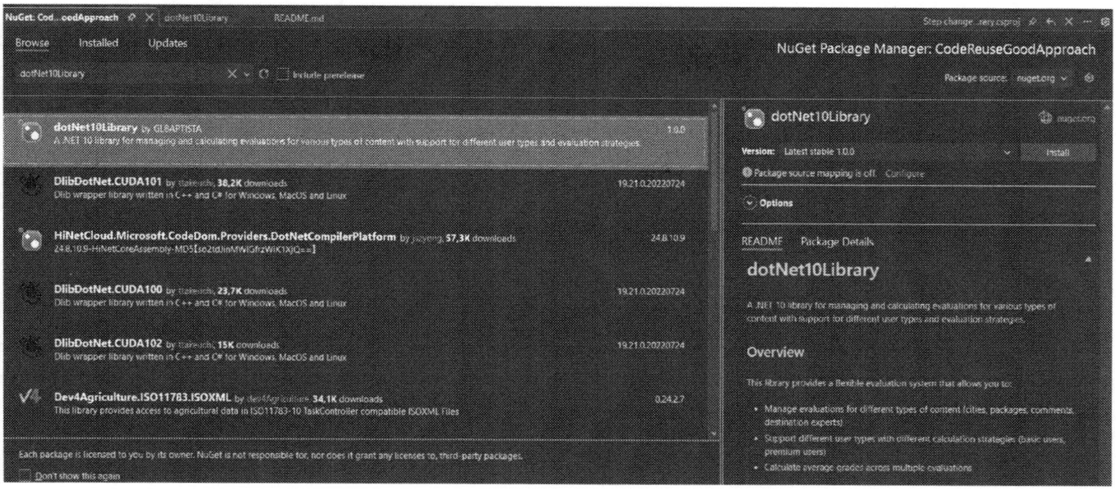

Figure 5.9: Library available at Nuget.org

It is worth noting that this is a manual process and you, as software architect, should define a CI/CD process to publish your libraries. Besides that, the way we have published this code will make it available to anyone, since it was published publicly. Two other actions you may consider in real world scenarios: obfuscation of the code and keys to authorize its usage.

Now that we have covered how to document and publish .NET libraries, it is also important to understand how to document Web APIs. The best-known technique to do so nowadays is by using Swagger. Let's check this out in the next topic.

Documenting a web API using Swagger

There is no doubt that a Web API is one of the technologies that facilitates and promotes code reuse. While a class library is usually the best choice for reusing within the same stack, a Web API becomes more appropriate when the functionality must cross application, platform, or organizational boundaries. In that sense, the architect is balancing ease of integration against scope of reuse. For this reason, ensuring good documentation is good practice. Respecting standards also shows that you are up to date with modern approaches to delivering reusable APIs. To do this, we have **Swagger**, which respects the ***OpenAPI Specification***.

The OpenAPI Specification is known as the standard for describing modern APIs. One of the most widely used tools for documenting APIs in an ***ASP.NET Core Web API*** is `Swashbuckle.AspNetCore`.

The good thing about using the `Swashbuckle.AspNetCore` library is that you can set the ***Swagger UI*** viewer for your Web API, which is a good graphical way to distribute the APIs.

From .NET 9 onward, it is worth noting that ASP.NET Core includes first-party OpenAPI support through packages provided directly by Microsoft. In practice, this means that documenting an API no longer depends exclusively on **Swashbuckle** as the default approach, because the platform itself now supports OpenAPI document generation through the `Microsoft.AspNetCore.OpenApi` package.

This is an important architectural detail because it changes the recommendation, not the validity of Swagger-based tooling. *Swashbuckle* remains a valid and widely known community option, but from .NET 9 onward, it is no longer the default choice included in ASP.NET Core project templates. The Microsoft-supported approach is now the natural baseline, which gives teams a more standardized path that is aligned with the platform itself.

We will learn how to use this library in ASP.NET Core Web APIs in *Chapter 15, Applying Service-Oriented Architectures with .NET*. Until then, it is important to understand that this documentation will help not only your team but also any developer who might use the APIs you are developing.

It is worth mentioning that API reuse depends not only on implementation quality but also on clear, standardized documentation that makes integration easy across teams and systems.

Summary

This chapter aimed at helping you understand the advantages of code reuse. It also gave you an idea about what code is not appropriate for reuse. This chapter also presented approaches for reusing and refactoring code.

Since technology alone doesn't ensure reusability, we presented a systematic process (use-identify-modify-design-build-document) for incorporating reusability into your development lifecycle. This process systematically identifies reuse opportunities from requirements through implementation.

Concluding this chapter, we presented .NET Standard libraries as an approach to reusing code for different C# platforms, indicating that .NET 10 and later versions allow the reuse of code across different platforms. This chapter also reinforced the principles of object-oriented programming when reusing code and presented generics as a sophisticated implementation to simplify the treatment of objects with the same characteristics.

Questions

1. Can copy-and-paste be considered code reuse? What are the impacts of this approach?
2. How can you make use of code reuse without copying and pasting code?
3. Is there a process that can help with code reuse?
4. What is the difference between .NET Standard and .NET?
5. What are the advantages of creating a .NET Standard library?
6. How does object-oriented analysis help with code reuse?
7. How do generics help with code reuse?
8. For new libraries, should you target .NET Standard 2.0 or .NET 10? What factors influence this decision?
9. What are the challenges related to refactoring?
10. How can AI help us evolve the documentation and distribution of .NET libraries?

Further reading

The following are some books and websites where you will find more information about the topics covered in this chapter:

- Clean Code: A Handbook of Agile Software Craftsmanship by Martin, Robert C. Pearson Education, 2012.
- Clean Architecture: A Craftsman's Guide to Software Structure and Design by Martin, Robert C. Pearson Education, 2018

- Design Patterns: Elements of Reusable Object-Oriented Software by Eric Gamma [et al.] Addison-Wesley, 1994.
- Design Principles and Design Patterns by Robert C. Martin, 2000.
- Refactoring by Martin Fowler, 2018.
- If you need more information about .NET Standard:
  - `https://devblogs.microsoft.com/dotnet/introducing-net-standard`
  - `https://github.com/dotnet/standard`
  - `https://devblogs.microsoft.com/dotnet/the-future-of-net-standard`
- A great guide for programming using Generics concept: `https://docs.microsoft.com/dotnet/csharp/programming-guide/generics`
- Some links that may help you with documentation of libraries and APIs:
  - `https://dotnet.github.io/docfx`
  - `https://github.com/domaindrivendev/Swashbuckle.AspNetCore`
  - `https://docs.microsoft.com/en-us/aspnet/core/tutorials/web-api-help-pages-using-swagger`
- If you want to check a bit more about obfuscation, this is a good beginning: `https://learn.microsoft.com/en-us/visualstudio/ide/dotfuscator`

6

Design Patterns and .NET Implementation

Design patterns can be defined as ready-to-use architectural solutions for common problems you encounter during software development. They are essential for understanding the .NET architecture and useful for solving ordinary problems that we face when designing any piece of software. As a software architect, design patterns provide proven standards that improve maintainability and help your team deliver solutions more consistently and efficiently. In this chapter, we will look at the implementation of some design patterns. It is worth mentioning that this book does not explain all the known patterns we can use. The focus here is to explain the importance of studying and applying them.

In this chapter, we will cover the following topics:

- Understanding design patterns and their purpose
- Understanding the design patterns available in .NET
- Recognizing the appropriate contexts and trade-offs for patterns presented

By the end of this chapter, you will have learned about some of the use cases that you can implement with design patterns.

Technical requirements

To complete this chapter, you will need the free Visual Studio 2026 Community Edition or higher. You can find the sample code for this chapter at `https://github.com/PacktPublishing/Software-Architecture-with-.NET-10-and-C-sharp-5E/tree/main/ch06`.

Understanding design patterns and their purposes

Deciding on the design of a system is challenging, and the responsibility associated with this task is enormous. As software architects, we must always keep in mind that features such as great reusability, good performance, and good maintainability are important for delivering a good solution. This is where design patterns help and accelerate the design process.

As we mentioned previously, design patterns are solutions that have already been discussed and defined so that they can solve common software architectural problems. This approach grew in popularity after the release of the book *Design Patterns – Elements of Reusable Object-Oriented Software*, where the **Gang of Four** (GoF) divided these patterns into three types: *creational, structural, and behavioral.*

The reason why you should always consider using design patterns in development is quite simple: as a software architect, you cannot spend time reinventing the wheel. However, there is another great reason for using and understanding them: you will find many of these patterns already implemented on .NET.

But before we start checking some of the well-known design patterns we have in the literature, let's understand how SOLID principles can be used as guardrails for design patterns in the next section.

SOLID principles as guardrails for design patterns

While design patterns help architects and developers apply reusable solution structures, good design also depends on broader principles that guide how classes and components should be organized.

In this context, Uncle Bob introduced the **SOLID principles** to the developer community, offering a practical foundation for organizing functions and data structures more effectively within a system.

The SOLID design principles indicate how the components of software should be designed and connected. It is worth mentioning that, compared to the design patterns presented by GoF, the SOLID principles do not deliver code recipes. Instead, they give you the basic principles to follow when you design your solutions, keeping the software's structure strong and reliable. They can be defined as follows:

Single responsibility

A module or function should be responsible for a single purpose. In .NET, this affects how you split responsibilities across controllers, services, repositories, handlers, and domain classes.

The idea is that a service that validates input, applies business rules, writes to the database, and sends notifications usually carries too many reasons to change. So instead of having, for instance, a large `PaymentService` doing everything, it would be better to design it by splitting responsibility into `PaymentValidator`, `PaymentRepository`, and `NotificationService`.

Open-closed

A software artifact should be open for extension but closed for modification. This shows how architects use extension points to avoid rewriting stable code whenever business rules change.

In .NET, this often appears with the strategy pattern, middleware pipelines, providers, and dependency injection. Think about a payment system where new payment methods are added by implementing an abstraction instead of modifying a single large conditional block.

Liskov substitution principle

The behavior of a program needs to remain unchanged when you substitute one of its components for another component that has been defined by a supertype of the base object.

This matters when inheritance or interface hierarchies are introduced. If one implementation behaves differently from what the contract promises, the architecture becomes fragile.

Just think about a base storage abstraction where one implementation silently rejects operations or throws unsupported exceptions, breaking consumers that relied on the abstraction.

Interface segregation

Depending on the way you create interfaces, you will promote dependencies that are not necessary when you are building their concrete objects, causing harm to the system architecture.

This is one of the reasons interface designs should be treated as an architectural concern, not just a coding detail. When contracts become too broad, they can force implementations to depend on operations that are unrelated to their actual responsibilities, increasing coupling across the solution.

Connect it directly to API and service contract design. In .NET, overly broad interfaces can make services harder to test and harder to evolve.

This happens because large contracts tend to blur responsibilities and make change more expensive over time. A modification introduced for one consumer may affect several other implementations that only rely on a small subset of the interface. From a testing perspective, this also increases the effort required to create mocks, fakes, or stubs, since more members must be implemented even when they are irrelevant to the specific scenario under test.

A concrete example could be replacing a large `IUserManager` with smaller interfaces such as `IUserReader`, `IUserWriter`, and `IUserAuthenticator`.

This kind of separation makes responsibilities more explicit and allows each consuming class to depend only on what it needs. As a result, the design becomes easier to maintain, easier to test, and more adaptable as the system evolves.

Dependency inversion

The most flexible systems are the ones where object dependencies refer only to abstractions.

DI is tied strongly to one of the most important architectural practices in .NET: dependency injection. This principle enables modularity, testability, and replaceable infrastructure.

Consider, as an example, an application service depending on `IEmailSender` instead of a concrete SMTP implementation, allowing the architecture to switch providers or use mocks in tests.

Now that you have checked the SOLID principles and how they can help you, it is important to remember that SOLID defines the qualities that good software structure should preserve. On the other hand, design patterns provide proven ways to realize those qualities in practice. Patterns are therefore not isolated tricks or recipes. They need to be understood as applied solutions that often operate the principles SOLID describes. As you study some of the patterns in the following sections, it is useful to observe not only what problem each one solves, but also which SOLID principle helps reinforce it.

Presenting well-known design patterns

In the next few subsections, we will cover some of the most well-known patterns. The idea of this chapter is just to let you know that they exist and need to be studied so that you can accelerate and simplify your projects. Moreover, each pattern will be presented with a C# code snippet so that you can implement it in your projects, always remembering we are talking about samples, not code ready for production. Let's begin with the Builder pattern.

Builder pattern

There are cases where you will have a complex object with different behaviors due to its configuration. Instead of setting this object up while using it, you may want to decouple its configuration from its usage, using a customized configuration that is already built. This way, you have different representations of the instances you are building. This is where you should use the **Builder pattern**.

The following class diagram shows the pattern that has been implemented for a scenario from this book's use case, presented in *Chapter 22, Case Study: Practical Usage of .NET Aspire*. The idea behind this design choice is to simplify the way rooms from WWTravelClub are described.

The Fluent API implemented in the `Room` class enables us to have the construction of each kind of room defined in each builder (`SimpleRoomBuilder` and `FamilyRoomBuilder`) in a simpler way, as we can see in *Figure 6.1*:

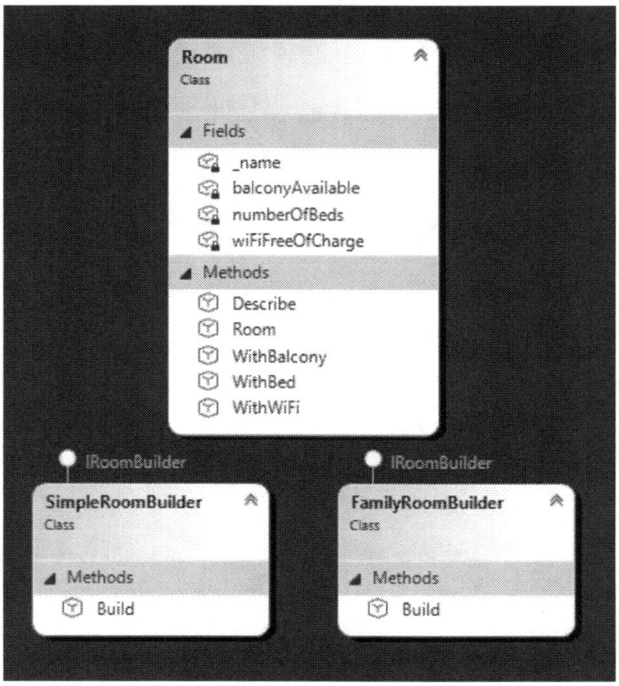

Figure 6.1: Builder pattern

As shown in the following snippet, the code for this is implemented in a way where the configurations of the instances are not set in the main program. Instead, you just build objects using the `Build()` method. This example simulates the creation of different room styles (a single room and a family room) in WWTravelClub:

```
var simpleRoom = new SimpleRoomBuilder().Build();
simpleRoom.Describe();

var familyRoom = new FamilyRoomBuilder().Build();
familyRoom.Describe();
```

The result of this implementation is quite simple but clarifies the reason why you need to implement a pattern:

```
Builder Sample
Simple room
Number of bed(s): 1
There is not a balcony.
This room is not wi-fi Free

Family room
Number of bed(s): 3
There is a balcony.
This room is wi-fi Free
```

As soon as you have the implementation, evolving this code becomes simpler. For example, if you need to build a different style of room, you can just create a new builder for that type of room, and you will be able to use it.

The reason why this implementation becomes quite simple is that the builder also benefits from a fluent interface, where chaining methods in the `Room` class makes the object configuration more expressive and easier to read:

```
public class Room
{
    private readonly string _name;
    private bool wiFiFreeOfCharge;
    private int numberOfBeds;
    private bool balconyAvailable;
    public Room(string name)
    {
        _name = name;
    }
    public Room WithBalcony()
    {
        balconyAvailable = true;
        return this;
```

```
        }
        public Room WithBed(int numberOfBeds)
        {
            this.numberOfBeds = numberOfBeds;
            return this;
        }
        public Room WithWiFi()
        {
            wiFiFreeOfCharge = true;
            return this;
        }
    ...
    }


    class FamilyRoomBuilder : IRoomBuilder
    {
        public Room Build()
        {
            return new Room("Family")
                .WithBalcony()
                .WithWiFi()
                .WithBed(3);
        }
    }
```

Fortunately, if you need to add configuration settings for the product, you can extend the Builder interface to include the new construction step and then update the concrete builders to implement it consistently. This makes the change easier to manage because the construction logic remains centralized and structured.

Although the Builder pattern is useful for complex object construction, it is not a good fit in every scenario. For instance, if an object can be created clearly with a simple constructor or object initializer, introducing a builder may lead to unnecessary abstraction and overengineering. As with any pattern, its value depends on context.

We will see a great implementation of the Builder pattern in .NET in the *Understanding the available design patterns in .NET* section, after covering additional patterns. There, you will be able to understand how Generic Host was implemented using `HostBuilder`. Let's now move to the Factory pattern.

Factory pattern

The **Factory pattern** is useful in situations where you have multiple objects from the same abstraction, and you only know which one needs to be created at runtime. This means you will have to create the instance according to a certain configuration or according to where the software is running now.

For instance, let us check out the WWTravelClub sample. Here, there is a user story that describes that this application will have customers from all over the world paying for their trips. However, in the real world, there are different payment services available for each country. The process of paying is similar for each country, but this system will have more than one payment service available. A good way to simplify this payment implementation is by using the Factory pattern.

The following diagram shows the basic idea of its architectural implementation:

Figure 6.2: Factory pattern

Notice that, since you have an interface that describes what the payment service for the application is, you can use the Factory pattern to change the concrete class according to the services that are available:

```
// In this sample, we will use the Factory Method Pattern
// to create a Payment Service to charge a Brazilian
// customer
ProcessCharging(
    PaymentServiceFactory.ServicesAvailable.Brazilian,
    "gabriel@sample.com",
    178.90m,
    EnumChargingOptions.CreditCard);

// In this sample, we will use the Factory Method Pattern
// to create a Payment Service to charge an Italian
```

```
// customer
ProcessCharging(
    PaymentServiceFactory.ServicesAvailable.Italian,
    "francesco@sample.com",
    188.70m,
    EnumChargingOptions.DebitCard);
```

Once again, the service's usage has been simplified due to the implemented pattern. If you had to use this code in a real-world application, the Factory pattern would allow you to select the appropriate service implementation based on the scenario, while keeping the client code independent from concrete classes. Let's understand the Singleton pattern.

Singleton pattern

When you implement Singleton in your application, you will have a single instance of the object implemented in the entire solution. Historically, this has been one of the most used patterns in every application. The reason is simple—there are many use cases where you need some classes to have just one instance. Singletons solve this by providing a better solution than a global variable does. In modern .NET applications, this intent is often expressed more appropriately through dependency injection lifetimes, where a service can be registered as a singleton without requiring a classic Singleton implementation.

In the **Singleton pattern**, the class is responsible for creating and delivering a single object that will be used by the application. In other words, the Singleton class creates a single instance as shown below:

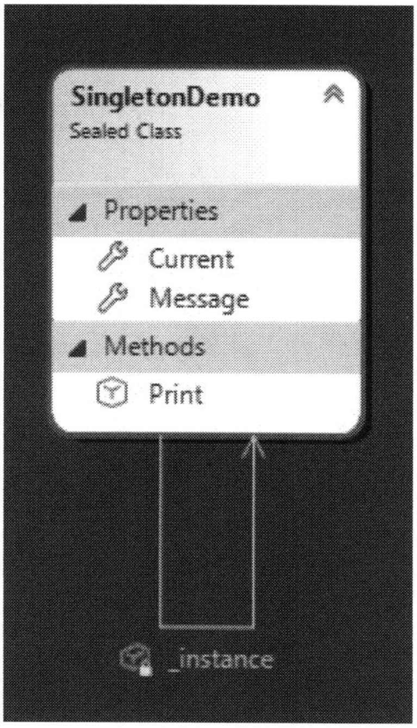

Figure 6.3: Singleton pattern

To do so, the object that is created is `static` and is delivered in a static property or method. The `??=` operator assigns the value of its right operand to its left one if its value is null.

The following code implements the Singleton pattern, which has a `Message` property and a `Print()` method:

```
public sealed class SingletonDemo
{
    #region This is the Singleton definition
    private static SingletonDemo _instance;
    public static SingletonDemo Current => _instance ??= new
        SingletonDemo();
    #endregion
    public string Message { get; set; }
    public void Print()
    {
        Console.WriteLine(Message);
    }
}
```

Its usage is simple – you just need to call the static property every time you need to use the Singleton object:

```
SingletonDemo.Current.Message = "This text will be printed by " +
  "the singleton. Be careful with concurrency.";
SingletonDemo.Current.Print();
```

Note

Be careful because the sample can have concurrency issues according to the usage defined! Please refer to *Chapter 02, Non-Functional Requirements*, to read more about concurrency and multithreading.

One of the places where you may use this pattern is when you need to deliver the app configuration in a way that can be easily accessed from anywhere in the solution. For instance, let us say you have some configuration parameters that are stored in a table that your app needs to query at several decision points. Although we have standard solutions like `appsettings.json` or `web.config`, where caching is out of the box, you may want to have this custom solution. In this case, instead of querying the configuration table directly, you can create a Singleton class to help you, as you can see below:

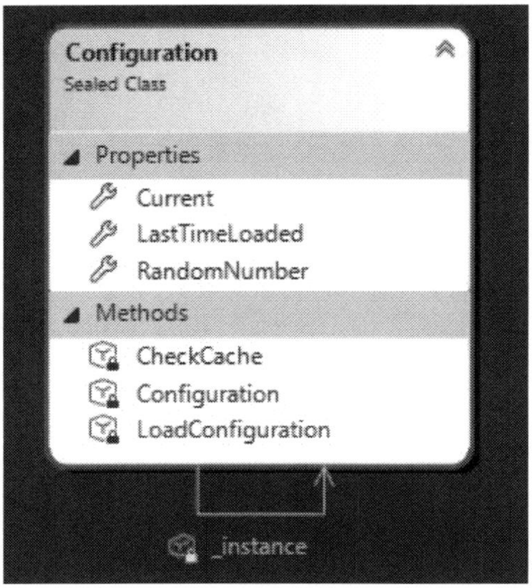

Figure 6.4: Singleton pattern usage

Moreover, you will need to implement a cache in this Singleton, thus improving the performance of the system, since you will be able to decide whether the system will check each configuration in the database every time it needs it or if the cache will be used. The following screenshot shows the implementation of the cache where the configuration is loaded every 5 seconds. The parameter that is being read in this case is just a random number:

```
Singleton Configuration Sample
Loading the configuration
Random Number Parameter: 1005. Last Time Loaded 14/01/2026 21:54:56
Random Number Parameter: 1005. Last Time Loaded 14/01/2026 21:54:56
Loading the configuration
Random Number Parameter: 254. Last Time Loaded 14/01/2026 21:55:01
Random Number Parameter: 254. Last Time Loaded 14/01/2026 21:55:01
Random Number Parameter: 254. Last Time Loaded 14/01/2026 21:55:01
Loading the configuration
Random Number Parameter: 881. Last Time Loaded 14/01/2026 21:55:06
Loading the configuration
Random Number Parameter: 484. Last Time Loaded 14/01/2026 21:55:11
Random Number Parameter: 484. Last Time Loaded 14/01/2026 21:55:11
```

In this example, the `Configuration` class is a sealed singleton that exposes a single global instance through `Configuration.Current`. It creates it lazily the first time it is requested and reuses the same object afterward. It stores two pieces of state, `RandomNumber` and `LastTimeLoaded`, both read-only from outside, and its private constructor immediately loads initial values via `LoadConfiguration()`. On every later access to `Current`, it calls `CheckCache()`, which reloads the configuration only if more than 5 seconds have passed since the last load, so the instance identity stays the same while its cached data can refresh over time. In `LoadConfiguration()`, it logs to the console, generates a pseudo-random number, and updates the timestamp, making this class a simple example of combining the Singleton pattern with time-based cache invalidation.

This is great for the application's performance. Besides, using parameters in several places in your code is simpler since you do not have to create configuration instances everywhere in the code.

It is worth mentioning that due to the dependency injection implementation in .NET, Singleton pattern usage became less common, since you can set dependency injection to handle your Singleton objects. We will cover dependency injection in .NET in later sections of this chapter. Let's check the principles of the Proxy pattern.

Proxy pattern

The **Proxy pattern** is used when you need to provide an object that controls access to another object. One of the biggest reasons why you should do this is related to the cost of creating the object that is being controlled. For instance, if the controlled object takes too long to be created or consumes too much memory, a proxy can be used to guarantee that the largest part of the object will only be created when it is required.

The following class diagram is of a **Proxy pattern** implementation for loading pictures from *Room (see Figure 6.1)*, but only when requested:

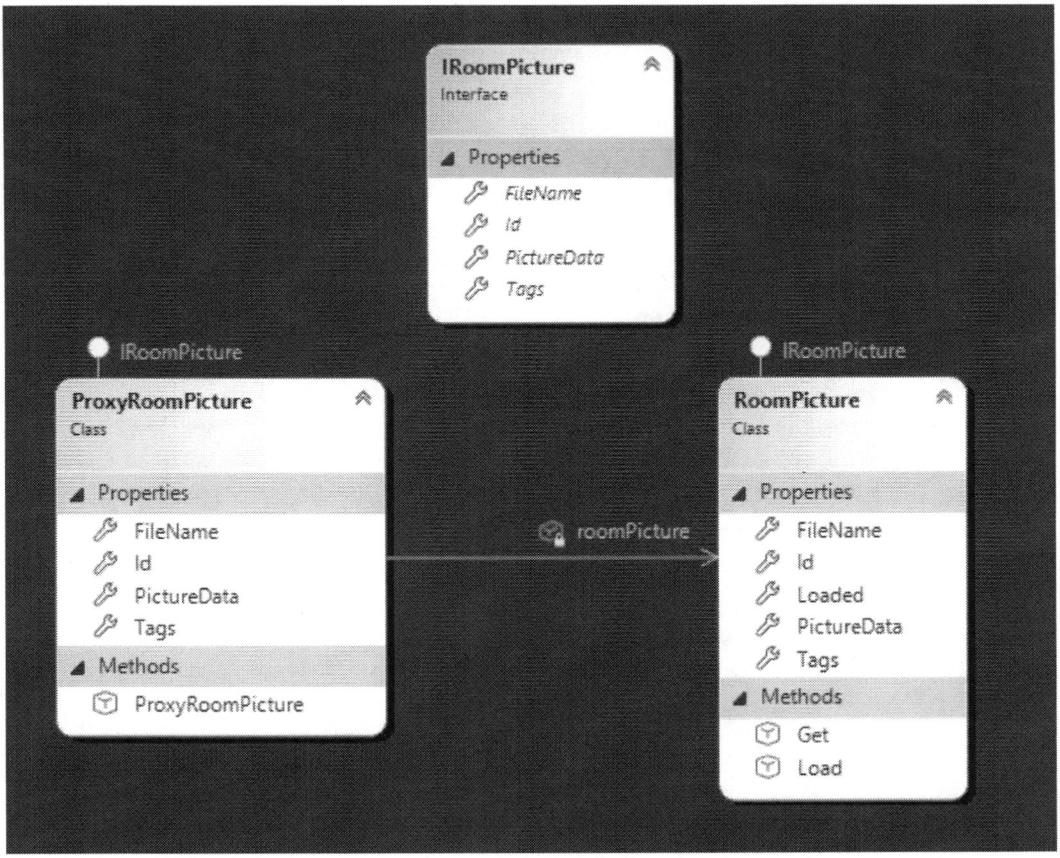

Figure 6.5: Proxy pattern implementation

The client of this proxy will request its creation. Here, the proxy will only gather basic information (`Id`, `FileName`, and `Tags`) from the real object and will not query `PictureData`.

Only when `PictureData` is requested in the first call, the proxy will load it, as we can confirm in the message *"Now the picture is loaded!"*. After that, in the second picture data request, the proxy will not load the `PictureData` again, which causes better performance, as we can see below:

```
class ProxyRoomPicture : IRoomPicture
{
    private RoomPicture roomPicture;

    public Guid Id { get => roomPicture.Id; }
    public string FileName { get => roomPicture.FileName;  }
    public string[] Tags { get => roomPicture.Tags;  }

    public string PictureData
    {
        get
        {
            if (!roomPicture.Loaded)
                roomPicture.Load();
            return roomPicture.PictureData;
        }
    }

    public ProxyRoomPicture()
    {
        roomPicture = new RoomPicture();
        roomPicture.Get();
    }
}

...

static void Main()
{
    Console.WriteLine("Proxy Sample");
    ExecuteProxySample(new ProxyRoomPicture());
}
private static void ExecuteProxySample(IRoomPicture roomPicture)
{
    Console.WriteLine($"Picture Id: {roomPicture.Id}");
    Console.WriteLine($"Picture FileName: {roomPicture.FileName}");
    Console.WriteLine($"Tags: {string.Join(";", roomPicture.Tags)}");
```

```
    Console.WriteLine($"1st call: Picture Data");
    Console.WriteLine($"Image: {roomPicture.PictureData}");
    Console.WriteLine($"2nd call: Picture Data");
    Console.WriteLine($"Image: {roomPicture.PictureData}");
}
```

If `PictureData` is requested again, since image data is already in place, the proxy will guarantee that image reloading will not be repeated. The following screenshot shows the result of running the preceding code:

```
Proxy Sample
Picture Id: 3327f55a-5668-41a9-94c9-93ff797811d4
Picture FileName: picture.jpg
Tags: incredible picture;must seeing!
1st call: Picture Data
Now the picture is loaded!
Image: [DATA FROM PICTURE]
2nd call: Picture Data
Image: [DATA FROM PICTURE]
```

This technique can be referred to by another name: **lazy loading**. In fact, the Proxy pattern is a way of implementing lazy loading. The Proxy pattern can be used to delay the creation or retrieval of an object until it is needed, which helps avoid unnecessary work upfront. In .NET, deferred initialization can also be implemented by using the `Lazy<T>` type. Later in this book, we will see that some frameworks, such as Entity Framework Core, apply similar ideas in more specialized scenarios. In *Chapter 13, Interacting with Data in C# – Entity Framework Core*, you will check that you can turn on lazy loading using proxies. You can find out more about this at `https://docs.microsoft.com/en-us/ef/core/querying/related-data#lazy-loading`. Now let's see how the Command pattern works.

Command pattern

In many software systems, actions such as creating records, sending notifications, or updating data should be handled independently from the code that initiates them. The **Command pattern** supports this by encapsulating a request as an object, which improves decoupling and makes operations easier to organize, queue, log, retry, and, in some scenarios, undo or redo.

> **Note**
>
> There is another design pattern called **Memento** that also has the purpose of implementing undo actions. However, the Command pattern focuses on encapsulating requests as objects, whereas the Memento pattern focuses on capturing and externalizing an object's internal state for the purpose of restoring it later.

For instance, let us imagine that, on the WWTravelClub website, users can evaluate packages by specifying whether they liked, disliked, or even loved their experience.

The following class diagram is an example of what can be implemented to create this rating system with the Command pattern.

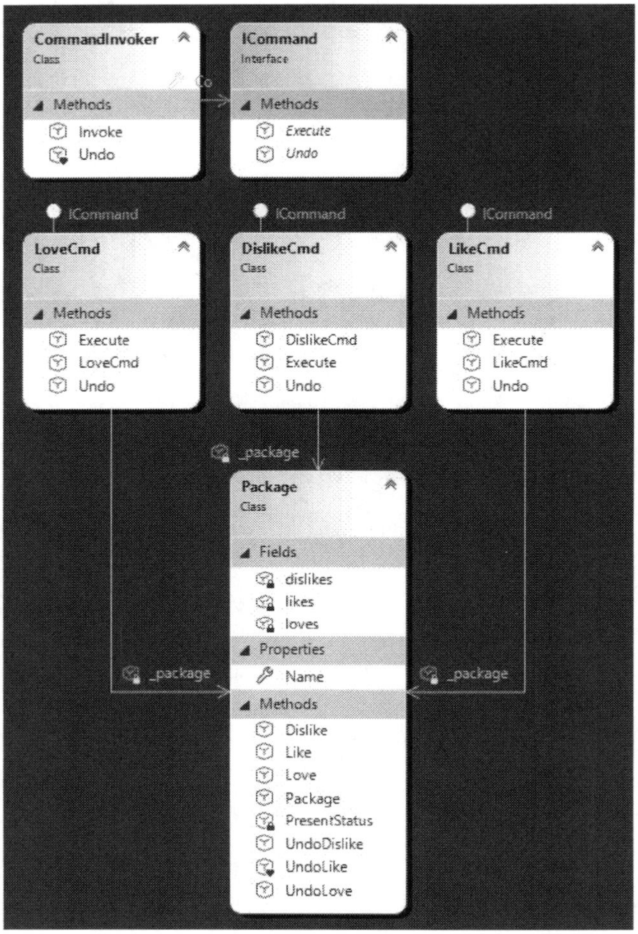

Figure 6.6: Command pattern

Notice the way this pattern works - if you need a different command, such as `Hate`, you will only implement a new class based on the `ICommand` interface. You do not need to change the code from other action classes. The change in the `Package` class will not impact the commands already implemented, which helps preserve the Open-Closed principle. Besides that, if you want to implement the `Redo` method, it can be added in a similar way to the `Undo` method. The full code sample for this is available in this book's GitHub repository.

This approach is especially useful when commands must evolve independently, be queued, logged, reused, or extended with features such as undo and retry. However, if the behavior is simple and unlikely to grow beyond a few direct method calls, introducing separate command classes may add unnecessary complexity.

It might also help to mention that ASP.NET Core MVC uses the Command pattern for its `IActionResult` hierarchy. The business operation described in *Chapter 7, Understanding the Different Domains in Software*

Solutions, will make use of this pattern to execute business rules. Let's now study the Publisher/Subscriber pattern.

Publisher/Subscriber pattern

Providing information from an object to a group of other objects is common in all applications. The **Publisher/ Subscriber** pattern is almost mandatory when there is a large volume of components (subscribers) that will receive a message containing the information that was sent by the object (publisher).

At a conceptual level, this pattern has strong roots in the **Observer pattern**. In both cases, one component produces information and multiple other components react to it. The main difference is architectural scope: while Observer is often applied inside the same process through direct object relationships, Publisher/ Subscriber is typically used in distributed systems, where publishers and subscribers are decoupled through a messaging infrastructure or broker.

The concept here is quite simple to understand and is shown in the following diagram.

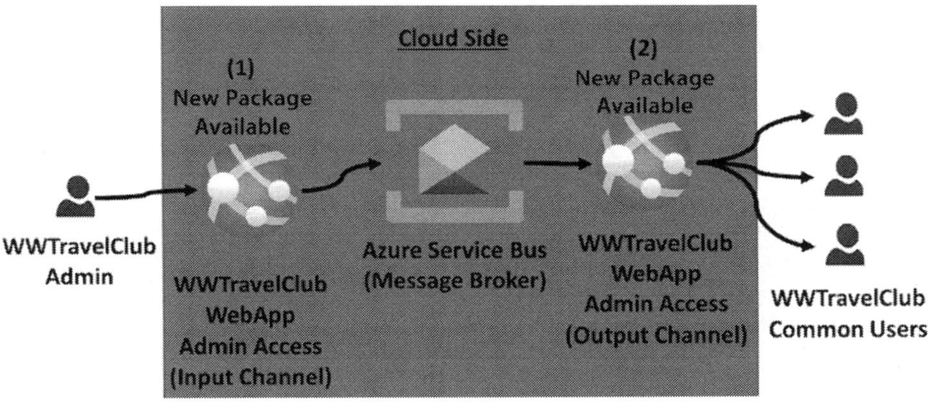

Figure 6.7: Publisher/Subscriber sample case

As you can check, this figure illustrates an event-driven cloud communication flow in WWTravelClub: first, the administrator uses the admin area of the web application as an input channel to publish the event *New Package Available*. That message is then sent to Azure Service Bus, which acts as a message broker in the middle of the architecture. From there, the message is delivered to the output side of the application so it can be propagated to common users, notifying them that a new travel package is available. The main architectural idea is decoupling: the admin side does not communicate directly with users because Azure Service Bus intermediates the exchange, making the solution more scalable, flexible, and easier to evolve.

When you have an indefinite number of different possible subscribers, it is essential to decouple the component that broadcasts information from the components that consume it. The Publisher/Subscriber pattern does this for us.

Implementing this pattern can introduce significant architectural and operational complexity, since distributed environments are not trivial to design. Therefore, it is recommended that you consider pre-existing technologies for implementing the message broker that connects the input channel to the output channels, instead of building it from scratch. Azure Service Bus is a reliable infrastructure component where you can find this pattern provided, so all you need to do is connect to it.

This approach is most appropriate when the system benefits from asynchronous communication, loose coupling, scalability, or support for multiple independent consumers. If the interaction is simple, immediate, and involves only a small number of tightly related components, direct synchronous integration may be a better choice.

RabbitMQ, which we will discuss in *Chapter 11, Applying a Microservice Architecture to Your Enterprise Application* and in *Chapter 14, Implementing Microservices with .NET*, is another service that can be used to implement a message broker, but it is a lower-level infrastructure and requires several manual implementations, such as retries in errors. Let's move to the Dependency Injection pattern.

Dependency injection pattern

The **Dependency injection pattern** is one of the most important ways to implement the SOLID Dependency Inversion principle. In modern .NET development, however, its role goes even further: dependency injection is a foundational architectural mechanism for composing services, managing lifetimes, improving testability, and building maintainable enterprise applications.

The concept is quite simple. Instead of creating instances of the objects that the component depends on, you just need to define their dependencies, declare their interfaces, and enable the reception of the objects by **injection**.

There are three ways to perform dependency injection:

- Use the class constructor to receive the objects, where dependencies are supplied when the object is instantiated
- Tag some class properties to receive the objects, where dependencies are assigned through properties after object creation
- Define an interface with a method to inject all the necessary components, in which dependencies are passed directly to the method that requires them

In practice, constructor injections are usually the best choice because they make mandatory dependencies explicit and keep the object in a valid state from the moment it is created. Property injections are better reserved for optional or framework-managed dependencies, since they can make object configuration less predictable. Method injection is useful when a dependency is required only for a specific action, helping avoid storing it as part of the object's permanent state.

The following diagram shows the implementation of the Dependency Injection pattern using the constructor of the class to receive the objects. In this case, it is receiving `UserAddress` and `DestinationAddress` classes, which can be completely different, but both implement the `IAdddress` Interface, which enables the `DistanceCalculator` to work:

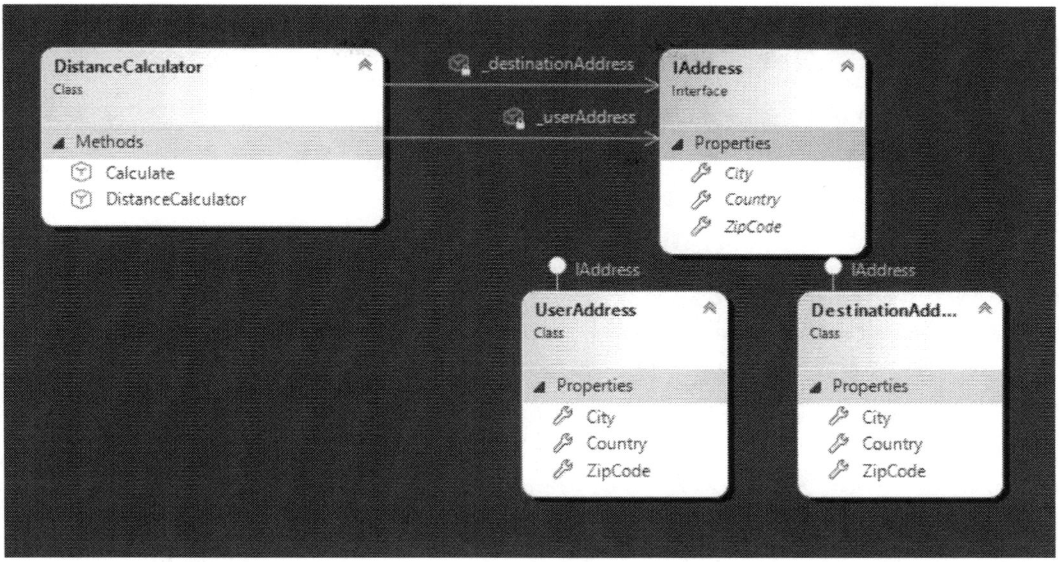

Figure 6.8: Dependency Injection pattern

Apart from these three ways mentioned above, Dependency Injection can be used with an **Inversion of Control** (IoC) container. This container enables the automatic injection of dependencies whenever they are asked for. There are several IoC container frameworks available on the market, but for most cases, there is no need to use third-party software since it contains a set of libraries to solve this in the `Microsoft.Extensions.DependencyInjection` namespace.

This IoC container is responsible for creating and disposing of the objects that are requested. The implementation of Dependency Injection is based on constructor types. There are three options for the injected component's lifetime:

- ***Transient***: The objects are created each time they are requested.
- ***Scoped***: The objects are created for each scope defined in the application. In a web app, a **scope** is identified with a web request, unless you create a custom scope. A good example where a custom scope can be used is in multi-tenant applications. In this case you may want to manage dependencies per tenant.
- ***Singleton***: Each object has the same application lifetime, so a single object is reused to serve all the requests for a given type. If your object contains state, you should not use this one, unless it is thread safe. Remember to check *Chapter 2, Non-Functional Requirements* to learn more about multithreading.

Choosing the right lifetime depends on how dependency is used. Transient is usually a good fit for lightweight, stateless services that do not need to preserve data between operations. Scoped is often the best choice for services that must share context during a single request or unit of work, such as database-related services in web applications. Singleton is appropriate for shared services that are expensive to create or that represent application-wide infrastructure, if they are designed to be safe for concurrent use.

The way you use these options depends on the business rules of the project you are developing. It is also a matter of how you register the services of the application. You need to be careful in deciding on the correct one, since the behavior of the application will change according to the type of object you are injecting. Choosing the wrong lifetime can cause practical problems, such as unnecessary allocations, incorrect sharing of state between requests, or concurrency issues in shared components. For this reason, architects must align the selected lifetime with the responsibilities, state management, and usage context of each service.

Now that you have checked some of the most-known design patterns, let's understand how .NET applies them to facilitate software development.

Understanding the design patterns available in .NET

As we discovered in the previous sections, C# allows us to implement any of the patterns. .NET provides many implementations in its SDK that follow all the patterns we have discussed, such as *Entity Framework Core proxy lazy loading*. Another good example is .NET Generic Host, which does not implement directly a specific pattern, but combines various of them to provide a flexible and extensible host environment for .NET applications.

In .NET, hosting refers to the infrastructure responsible for starting the application, configuring shared services, and managing its lifetime while it runs. In web applications, this includes preparing the HTTP pipeline and the services the app depends on. More broadly, hosting provides the application with a standard way to load configuration, register dependencies, enable logging, and shut down gracefully.

In *Chapter 16, Presenting ASP.NET Core*, we will detail the hosting that's available for web apps on .NET 10. This web host helps us since the startup of the app and lifetime management are set up alongside it. The idea of .NET Generic Host is to enable this way of working for applications that do not need HTTP implementation. With this Generic Host, any .NET program can have a startup class where we can configure the *dependency injection* engine. This can be useful for creating multi-service apps, using *Composite Pattern* as the basis for that.

> **Note**
>
> You can find out more about .NET Generic Host at `https://docs.microsoft.com/en-us/aspnet/core/fundamentals/host/generic-host`, which contains some sample code and is the current recommendation from Microsoft.

The code provided in the GitHub repository is simple, but it focuses on the creation of a console app that can run a service for monitoring. The great thing about this is the way the console app is set up to run, where the *builder configures* the services that will be provided by the application, and the way logging will be managed.

This is shown in the following code:

```
HostApplicationBuilder builder = Host.CreateApplicationBuilder(args);

builder.Services.AddHostedService<HostedService>();
builder.Services.AddHostedService<MonitoringService>();

builder.Logging.ClearProviders();
builder.Logging.AddConsole();
```

```
using IHost host = builder.Build();
host.Run();
```

The preceding code gives us an idea of how .NET uses design patterns. Using the **Builder pattern**, .NET Generic Host allows you to set the classes that will be injected as services. Apart from this, the Builder pattern helps you configure some other features, such as the way logs will be shown/stored. This configuration allows the services to inject `ILogger<out TCategoryName>` objects into any instance.

Other examples of Generic Host usage appear later in this book, in *Chapter 14, Implementing Microservices with .NET*, and Blazor Generic Host is described in *Chapter 18, Client Frameworks: Blazor.* These forward references help show that Generic Host is not limited to one application style but is a recurring foundation across different types of modern .NET solutions.

Since we have checked the impact of design patterns on .NET, let's also check how Cloud computing makes use of these patterns to solve known problems.

Cloud computing design patterns

As technologies and software problems change, more patterns are conceived. The advance of cloud computing has brought a bunch of them, and some can be found at `https://docs.microsoft.com/en-us/azure/architecture/patterns`. The content is organized into three different challenge areas: Data Management, Design and Implementation, and Messaging. Many of them are described in the chapters of this book, as we can see in the list below:

- ***Bulkhead Isolation:*** This pattern is presented while discussing microservices design principles in *Chapter 11, Applying a Microservice Architecture to Your Enterprise Application.*
- ***Cache-Aside:*** Caching was presented in *Chapter 1, Understanding the Importance of Software Architecture.* Its usage with Azure Redis is also presented in *Chapter 12, How to Choose Your Data Storage in the Cloud.*
- ***Circuit-breaker:*** The strategy necessary to implement this is presented in *Chapter 11, Applying a Microservice Architecture to Your Enterprise Application.*
- ***Command Query Responsibility Segregation (CQRS):*** CQRS is described in *Chapter 7, Understanding the Different Domains in Software Solutions*
- ***Publisher/Subscriber:*** The pattern was explained earlier, and it will also be discussed in *Chapter 7, Understanding the Different Domains in Software Solutions.*
- ***Retry:*** The resilient task execution subsection of *Chapter 11, Applying a Microservice Architecture to Your Enterprise Application*, shows how to use Polly, a general framework for applying retries.

The reason why new patterns emerge is related to the challenges we face when new solutions are developed. Today, availability, data management, messaging, monitoring, performance, scalability, resiliency, and security are aspects we must deal with when delivering cloud solutions.

Just as classical and cloud design patterns helped architects to structure object-oriented and distributed systems, the rise of AI is now introducing a new set of patterns for organizing how intelligent agents collaborate, reason, and produce results. The next topic will be about this.

AI agents design patterns

With the advance of AI, new architectural patterns have emerged, especially for orchestrating AI agents. You can find more details about them at `https://learn.microsoft.com/en-us/Azure/architecture/ai-ml/guide/ai-agent-design-patterns`, but basically they discuss how to break down complex problems into specialized units of work or knowledge, calling these different units sequentially, concurrently, or by grouping them.

These patterns became necessary because AI-based solutions often introduce design forces that are less common in traditional software, such as coordinating multiple specialized models or agents, managing limited context windows, selecting tools dynamically, and handling probabilistic outputs that may require validation or refinement. As AI features become more capable, a single model call is not always sufficient, and architects may need to design workflows in which specialized units of work collaborate to produce a reliable outcome.

Many of these new AI patterns parallel ideas that experienced architects already know. For example, sequential orchestration resembles the traditional Pipes and Filters pattern. You can find more details about it at `https://learn.microsoft.com/en-us/azure/architecture/patterns/pipes-and-filters`.

Each stage processes the result of the previous one, but here the stages are specialized AI agents instead of fixed procedural components. This pattern similarity helps explain the opportunity and the challenge: while the structure is familiar, the outputs are not strictly deterministic, so architects must think more carefully about validation, context propagation, latency, and failure handling.

It is worth noting that these patterns should be considered when building features that rely on LLM orchestration rather than a single prompt-response interaction. In practice, architects should begin with the simplest workable option, such as a direct model call or a single agent with tools and adopt multi-agent orchestration only when the problem genuinely requires specialized collaboration, parallel analysis, or stronger separation of responsibilities. Otherwise, the extra coordination overhead, cost, and operational complexity may outweigh the benefits.

Remember that AI agent design patterns extend familiar architectural ideas into AI-driven scenarios, where coordination, validation, and context management become first-class design concerns. The architect's role is to apply these patterns deliberately, adopting orchestration only when the problem justifies the added complexity.

Summary

In this chapter, we have understood why design patterns help with the maintainability and reusability of the parts of the system you are building. We also looked at some typical use cases and code examples that you can consider in your projects, always remembering that they need to evolve to achieve professional delivery.

All this content will help you while architecting new software or even maintaining something existing, since design patterns are already known solutions to some real-life problems in software development.

More importantly, we saw that patterns should not be treated as recipes to be applied mechanically, but as context-dependent choices that support better architectural decisions. For architects, the key skill is not only knowing the patterns themselves, but also recognizing when they are appropriate, what trade-offs they introduce, and how they relate to principles such as SOLID.

We also examined practical examples on .NET, including the .NET Generic Host, to understand how patterns appear in real enterprise platforms. These examples reinforce that design patterns are closely connected to broader architectural concerns such as scalability, extensibility, testability, and long-term maintainability. As your systems evolve, the ability to identify and apply patterns thoughtfully becomes essential both when designing new solutions and when improving existing codebases.

In *Chapter 7, Understanding the Different Domains in Software Solutions*, we will cover the domain-driven design approach. We will also learn how to use the SOLID design principles so that we can map different domains to our software solutions. As you move forward, one useful habit is to start recognizing the patterns already present in the systems you work with, evaluating whether they still fit the problem they were meant to solve, and identifying where a more suitable approach may be needed.

Questions

1. What are design patterns?
2. What is the difference between design patterns and design principles?
3. When is it a good idea to implement the Builder pattern?
4. When is it a good idea to implement the Factory pattern?
5. When is it a good idea to implement the Singleton pattern?
6. When is it a good idea to implement the Proxy pattern?
7. When is it a good idea to implement the Command pattern?
8. When is it a good idea to implement the Publisher/Subscriber pattern?
9. When is it a good idea to implement the Dependency Injection pattern?
10. In a system where object creation involves many optional parameters, validation steps, and different final representations, how would you decide whether the Builder pattern is justified instead of using constructors or object initializers?
11. In a distributed enterprise application, how would you decide whether to use Publisher/Subscriber communication instead of a direct synchronous interaction between services? What trade-offs would influence your decision?

Further reading

The following are some books and websites where you can find out more about what was covered in this chapter:

- Clean Architecture: A Craftsman's Guide to Software Structure and Design, Martin, Robert C., Pearson Education, 2018
- Design Patterns: Elements of Reusable Object-Oriented Software, Erich Gamma et al., Addison-Wesley, 1994
- Design Principles and Design Patterns, Martin, Robert C., 2000

- If you need to get more info about design patterns and architectural principles, please check out the following link:
    - `https://docs.microsoft.com/en-us/dotnet/standard/modern-web-apps-azure-architecture/architectural-principles`
- If you want to check specific cloud design patterns, you can find them at:`https://docs.microsoft.com/en-us/azure/architecture/patterns/`
- If you want to check specific AI design patterns, you can find them at: `https://learn.microsoft.com/en-us/azure/architecture/ai-ml/guide/ai-agent-design-patterns`
- If you want to better understand the idea of Generic Host, follow this link: `https://docs.microsoft.com/en-us/aspnet/core/fundamentals/host/generic-host`
- There is a very good explanation about Service Bus messaging at this link: `https://docs.microsoft.com/en-us/azure/service-bus-messaging/service-bus-dotnet-how-to-use-topics-subscriptions`
- You can learn more about dependency injection by checking out these links:
    - `https://docs.microsoft.com/en-us/aspnet/core/fundamentals/dependency-injection`
    - `https://www.martinfowler.com/articles/injection.html`

7

Understanding the Different Domains in Software Solutions

Modern enterprise software is not dedicated to single separate tasks but is required to embrace the whole enterprise activity. Consequently, smaller independent applications needed to combine into, a unique multidisciplinary bigger, and more complex application developed by a bigger development team. The need to handle such complex applications and to coordinate such big development teams slowed down the evolution of the existing enterprise software until the developers' community moved toward a modern software development technique called **domain-driven design** (DDD), which was first proposed by Eric Evans (see *Domain-Driven Design*: `https://www.amazon.com/exec/obidos/ASIN/0321125215/domainlanguag-20`). While DDD has existed for more than 20 years, it has achieved great success in the last few years because of its ability to cope with two important problems:

1. The first problem is modeling complex systems that involve several domains of knowledge. No single expert has in-depth knowledge of the whole domain; this knowledge is instead split among several people.
2. The second problem is that each expert speaks a language that is specific to their domain of expertise, so for effective communication between the experts and the development team, objects, interfaces, and methods must mimic the language of the domain experts. This means that the different modules that compose an application must use a different vocabulary for each domain of expertise. Consequently, the application must be split into modules that reflect the different domains of knowledge, and the interface between modules that deals with the different domains of knowledge must be carefully designed to carry out the necessary translations.

DDD copes with the first problem by splitting the whole software development and maintenance cycle into independent parts, assigned to different teams. This way, each team can focus on a specific domain of knowledge by interacting only with the experts of that domain.

It is not a coincidence that the evolution of DDD is interleaved with the evolution of microservices. DDD was conceived 20 years before the diffusion of microservices, but became popular only after the appearance of the microservices culture, since microservices furnish a practical way to integrate and maintain software modules developed by completely independent teams.

Thanks to DDD, big projects can be split among several development teams, with each team having a different domain of knowledge. There are many reasons why a project is split among several teams, the most common being the ones below:

- Solving problem 2, that is the problem of different expertise and languages involved in the application by assigning each domain of expertise to a different team
- Experience has proven that teams of more than 6-8 people are not effective and, clearly, different skills and locations prevent tight interaction from occurring

In turn, the importance of the two aforementioned problems has grown in the last few years. Software systems have always taken up a lot of space inside every organization, and they have become more and more complex and geographically distributed.

At the same time, the need for frequent updates has increased so that these complex software systems can be adapted to the needs of a quickly changing market.

In this scenario, it's common to implement complex software systems with associated fast CI/CD cycles that always require more people to evolve and maintain them. In turn, this created a need for technologies that were adequate for high-complexity domains and for the cooperation of several loosely coupled development teams.

In this chapter, we will analyze the basic principles, advantages, and common patterns related to DDD, as well as how to use them in our solutions. More specifically, we will cover the following topics:

- What are software domains?
- Understanding domain-driven design
- Common DDD patterns and architectures

Let's get started.

Technical requirements

This chapter requires Visual Studio 2026 free Community Edition or better, with all the database tools installed.

All the code snippets in this chapter can be found in the GitHub repository associated with this book: `https://github.com/PacktPublishing/Software-Architecture-with-.NET-10-and-C-sharp-5E`.

What are software domains?

As we discussed in *Chapter 2, Non-Functional Requirements*, and *Chapter 3, Documenting Requirements*, the transfer of knowledge from domain experts to the development team plays a fundamental role in software design. Developers try to communicate with experts and describe their solutions in a language that domain experts and stakeholders can also understand. However, often, the same word has a different meaning in various parts of an organization, and what appears to be the same conceptual entities have completely different shapes in different contexts.

For instance, in our WWTravelClub use case, the order-payment and packages-handling subsystems use completely different models for customers. Order-payment characterizes a customer by their payment methods, currency, bank accounts, and credit cards, while packages-handling is more concerned with the locations and packages that have been visited and/or purchased in the past, the user's preferences, and their geographical location. Moreover, while order-payment refers to various concepts with a language that we may roughly define as a **bank language**, that is, the language used by bank employees that process transactions, packages-handling uses the language spoken by the agencies/operators employed that define and propose travel packages.

Summing up, different software modules have quite different views of data and use terms from different domains of knowledge. Traditionally, software architects have addressed these discrepancies using a unified data model approach and data projections.

Thus, in our example, they would use a unique abstract entity called *customer*, which projects into two different views—the order-payment view and the package-handling view. Each projection operation takes some operations and some properties from the *customer* abstract entity and changes their names. Since domain experts only give us the projected views, our main task as system designers is to create a conceptual model that can explain all the views. The following diagram shows how different views are handled:

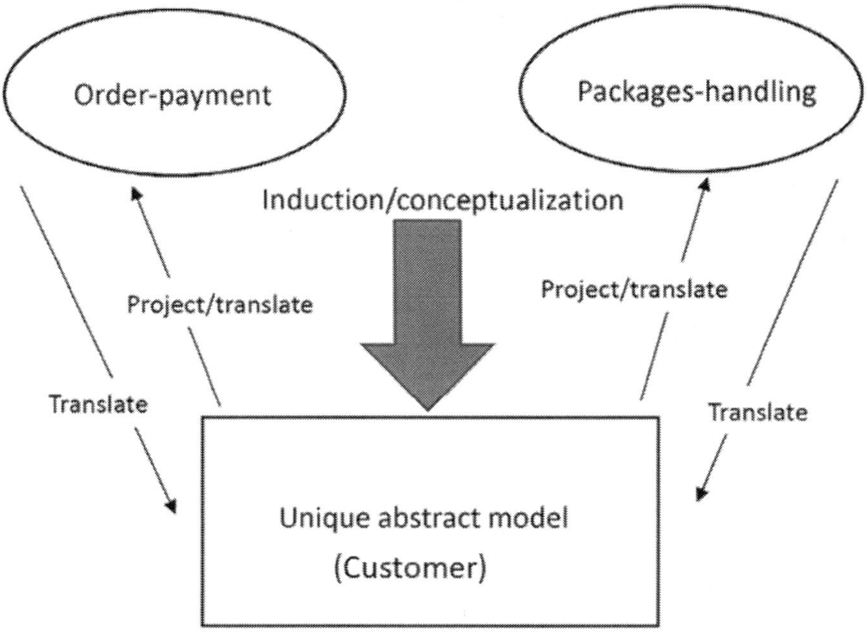

Figure 7.1: Creating a unique model

Please notice how we first integrate the entities behind the order-payment and packages-handling subsystems into a unique data model (translate arrows), and then we get back the separate entities needed by both subsystems through database projections (project/translate arrows).

The main advantage of the classic approach is that we have a unique and coherent representation of the application data. If this conceptual model is built successfully, all the operations will have a formal definition and purpose and the whole abstraction will be a rationalization of the way the whole organization should work, possibly highlighting and correcting errors and simplifying some procedures.

However, what are the downsides of this approach?

Creating a new unified data model or modifying an existing unified data model requires getting all stakeholders to agree on every attribute, every relationship, and every rule, which is a challenging coordination problem. In a small organization with 20 people, you might achieve this consensus in a few meetings. But in an enterprise with 2,000 employees across 10 countries, forcing everyone to adopt a single shared model becomes organizationally impossible.

From one side, big structured companies need to react quickly to market changes, but from the other side, due to the complexity of their organizations, only gradual changes are feasible. Therefore, the changes in their organizations and information systems needed to adapt to the market must be gradual. In turn, a gradual transition is possible only if old data models can coexist with new data models, and if each of the various components of the organization is allowed to change at its own speed; that is, if each component of the organization can evolve independently of the others.

Moreover, as the complexity of a software system grows, several other issues make the unique data model of classical architectures hard to maintain:

- ***Coherency and language issues***: designing and maintaining a unique coherent view of data becomes more and more difficult since we can't retain the complexity when we break these tasks into smaller, loosely coupled tasks. Bugs/errors that are introduced by changes in small subparts of the system may propagate to the whole organization through the uniquely shared model.
- Moreover, a unique data model would mix the different languages used in the various domains of knowledge contained in the model.
- ***Team organization issues***: System modeling must be split among several teams, and only loosely coupled tasks can be given to separate teams; if two tasks are strongly coupled, they need to be given to the same team.
- ***Parallelism issues***: As we will discuss in more detail in *Chapter 11, Applying a Microservice Architecture to Your Enterprise Application*, the need to move to a microservice-based architecture often makes the bottleneck of a unique database unacceptable. In fact, while read parallelism is easily achieved with database replicas, during database updates, some table rows are locked, thus limiting maximum parallelism. Therefore, adopting several different databases instead of a unique database reduces contention on table rows.

As the system grows, it becomes more inefficient to deal with records with hundreds or thousands of fields that project in smaller views. Such inefficiencies originate in database engines that inefficiently handle big records with several fields (memory fragmentation, problems with too many related indices, and so on). However, the main inefficiencies take place in **object-relational mappings** (ORMs) and business layers that are forced to handle these big records in their update operations. In fact, while query operations usually require just a few fields that have been retrieved from the storage engine, updates and business processing involve the whole entity. ORMs are described in detail in *Chapter 13, Interacting with Data in C# – Entity Framework Core.*

As the traffic in the data storage subsystem grows, we need read and update/write parallelism in all the data operations. As we will discover in *Chapter 12, How to Choose Your Data Storage in the Cloud*, while read parallelism is easily achieved with data replication, write parallelism requires sharding, that is, splitting database records among several distributed databases, and it is difficult to shard a uniquely monolithic and tightly connected data model.

These issues are the reason for DDD's success in the last few years because they were characterized by more complex software systems that became the backbones of entire organizations. DDD's basic principles will be discussed in detail in the next section.

Understanding domain-driven design

According to DDD, we should not construct a unique data model that projects into different views in each application subsystem. Instead, the whole application domain is split into smaller domains, each with its own data model. These separate domains are called **Bounded Contexts.** Each Bounded Context is characterized by the language used by the experts and is used to name all the domain concepts and operations.

We define **Ubiquitous Language** as the language used by both the experts and the development team that works on a given Bounded Context. For instance, in our WWTravelClub use case, both order-payment and packages-handling become two different Bounded Contexts. The ubiquitous language of the order-payment Bounded Context is what we call a bank language, and the ubiquitous language of the packages-handling Bounded Context is the language spoken by the agencies/operators.

With this setup, translations are not needed anymore, and if the development team uses C# interfaces as bases for its code, the domain expert is able to understand and validate them since all the operations and properties are expressed in the same language that's used by the expert.

Here, we're getting rid of a cumbersome, unique abstract model, but now we have several separate models that we need to relate to each other somehow. DDD proposes that we handle all these separate models, that is, all the Bounded Contexts, as follows:

- ***We need to add Bounded Context boundaries whenever the meanings of the language terms change.*** In fact, this change of meaning is a signal that the domain of expertise is changing, and since each bounded context must contain a single domain of expertise, a new bounded context must be introduced. For instance, in the WWTravelClub use case, order-payment and packages-handling belong to different Bounded Contexts because they give a different meaning to the word **customer**. This change signals to us that they require different domains of expertise.
- ***We need to explicitly represent relations among Bounded Contexts.*** These relationships represent the interfaces each Bounded Context has with the remainder of the system. Therefore, if we explicitly represent them and if each team working on a Bounded Context takes them as specifications, the overall application coherence can be ensured without continuous coordination among the various teams. In other words, different development teams may independently work on different Bounded Contexts, but each team must have a clear picture of the relationship between the Bounded Context it is working on and all the other models. For this reason, such relationships are represented in a unique document, called **Context Map**, that's shared with every team.
- ***We need to keep all the Bounded Contexts aligned with Continuous Integration***. This is necessary to verify that all Bounded Contexts coherently integrate in the desired application behavior.
- Continuous Integration is achieved by organizing meetings and by building simplified system prototypes in order to verify that all the Bounded Contexts are evolving coherently, that is, that all the Bounded Contexts can be integrated into the desired application behavior. Please refer to *Chapter 8, Understanding DevSecOps Principles and CI/CD*, for more details on Continuous Integration.

The following diagram shows how the WWTravelClub example that we discussed in the previous section changes with the adoption of DDD:

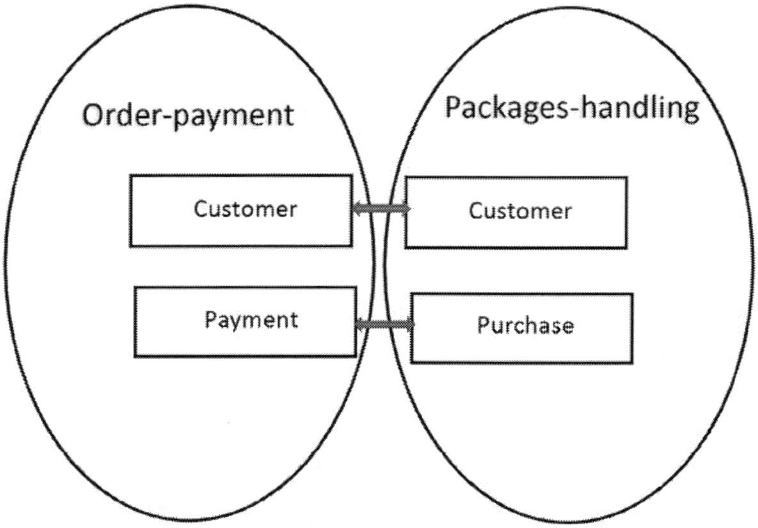

Figure 7.2: Relations between DDD Bounded Contexts

There is a relationship between the Customer entities of each Bounded Context, while the Purchase entity of the packages-handling Bounded Context is related to the Payments. Identifying entities that map to each other in the various Bounded Contexts is the first step of formally defining the interfaces that represent all the possible communications among the contexts.

For instance, in the previous diagram, since payments are done after purchases, we can deduce that the order-payment Bounded Context must have an operation to create a payment for a specific customer. In this domain, new customers are created if they don't already exist.

The payment creation operation is triggered immediately after purchase. Since several more operations are triggered after an item is purchased, we can implement all the communication related to a purchase event with the Publisher/Subscriber pattern we explained in *Chapter 6, Design Patterns and .NET Implementation*. In DDD, these are known as **domain events**. Using events to implement communications between Bounded Contexts is very common since it helps keep Bounded Contexts loosely coupled.

Once an instance of either an event or an operation that's been defined in the Bounded Context's interface crosses the context boundary, it is immediately translated into the Ubiquitous Language of the receiving context. It is important that this translation be performed before the input data starts interacting with the other domain entities to prevent the Ubiquitous Language of the receiving domain from becoming contaminated by extra-contextual terms. An inadequate translation is usually evidenced by the domain expert complaining about words he finds to be "*strange*".

For example, let's suppose that the order-payment Bounded-Context receives a domain event containing information about a purchase being requested by the user:

```
PurchaseOrder
  UserId = 124
  ItemsToBuy = {{Id=12, Price=120}, ….}
```

It is immediately translated into the banking language as:

```
VerifyFundsAvailability
  UserId = 124
  TotalAmount = 550
```

Each Bounded Context implementation must contain a data model completely expressed in terms of the Bounded Context Ubiquitous Language (class and interface names and property and method names), with no contamination from other Bounded Contexts' Ubiquitous Languages, and without contamination from technical programming stuff. This is necessary to ensure good communication with domain experts and to ensure that domain rules are translated correctly into code so that they can be easily validated by domain experts.

> **Note**
>
> When there is a strong mismatch between the communication language and the target Ubiquitous Language, an **anti-corruption layer** is added to the receiving Bounded Context boundary. The only purpose of this anti-corruption layer is to perform a language translation.

Let's analyze in detail how relations among Bounded Contexts are represented.

Relations among bounded contexts

As already hinted, the document that contains a representation of all the Bounded Contexts, along with the Bounded Contexts' mutual relationships and interface definitions, is called a **Context Map**. The relationships between contexts also contain organizational constraints that specify the kind of cooperation required among the teams that are working on the different Bounded Contexts. Such relationships don't constrain the Bounded Context interfaces, but do affect the way they may evolve during the software lifecycle. They represent patterns of team cooperation.

> **Note**
>
> These patterns define how teams collaborate, not just how systems interact.

The most common organizational patterns are as follows:

- ***Partner***: This is the original pattern suggested by Eric Evans, and it is the default organizational pattern because it should be used whenever the conditions for the application of the other patterns are not met. The idea is that the two teams working on the related Bounded Contexts have a mutual dependency on each other for delivery. In other terms, they decide together the Bounded Contexts' mutual communication specifications during the whole software development lifecycle.

- ***Customer/supplier development teams***: In this case, one team acts as a customer and another one acts as a supplier. In a preliminary stage, both teams define the interface of the customer side of the Bounded Context and some automated acceptance tests to validate it. After that, the supplier can work independently. This pattern works when the customer's Bounded Context is the only active part that invokes the interface methods exposed by the other Bounded Context. This is adequate for the interaction between the order-payment and the packages-handling contexts, where order-payment acts as a supplier since its functions are subordinate to the needs of packages-handling. When this pattern can be applied, it decouples both the implementation and the maintenance of the two Bounded Contexts completely.
- ***Conformist***: This is similar to the customer/supplier pattern, but in this case, the customer side accepts an interface that's been imposed by the supplier side with no preliminary negotiation stage. This pattern offers no advantages over the other patterns, but sometimes we are forced into the situation depicted by the pattern since either the supplier's Bounded Context is implemented in a preexisting product that can't be configured/modified too much, or because it is a legacy subsystem that we don't want to modify.

It is worth pointing out that the separation in Bounded Contexts is only effective if the resulting Bounded Contexts are loosely coupled; otherwise, the reduction of complexity that's obtained by breaking a whole system into parts would be overwhelmed by the complexity of the coordination and communication processes.

However, if Bounded Contexts are defined with the language criterion, that is, Bounded Context boundaries are added whenever the Ubiquitous Language changes, this should actually be the case. In fact, different languages may arise as a result of a loose interaction between an organization's subparts since the more each subpart has tight interactions inside of it and loose interactions with other subparts, the more each subpart ends up defining and using its own internal language, which differs from the language used by the other subparts.

Moreover, as all human organizations grow just by evolving into loosely coupled subparts, similarly complex software systems may be implemented just as the cooperation of loosely coupled submodules: this is the only way humans are able to cope with complexity. From this, we can conclude that complex organizations/artificial systems can always be decomposed into loosely coupled subparts. We just need to understand *how*.

Beyond the basic principles we've mentioned so far, DDD provides a few basic primitives to describe each Bounded Context, as well as some implementation patterns. While Bounded Context primitives are an integral part of DDD, the patterns are simply useful heuristics we can use in our implementations, so their usage in some or all Bounded Contexts is not obligatory once we opt for DDD adoption.

In the next section, we describe Bounded Context primitives, while the various patterns are described in the remaining sections of the chapter.

Entities

DDD **entities** represent domain objects that have a well-defined identity, as well as all the operations that are defined on them. They don't differ too much from the entities of other, more classical approaches.

The main difference is that DDD stresses the entities' object-oriented nature, while other approaches use them mainly as **records** whose properties can be written/updated without too many constraints.

That is, in DDD, properties are not modified directly but by calling some entity methods that encode business operations. This way, business rules are automatically encoded inside entity methods, thus ensuring better modularity of the code.

> Note
>
> We may say that DDD enforces better SOLID principles on entities.

For the same reason, *business validation rules that are specific for each entity,* are moved inside of DDD entities. DDD entity validation rules are business-level rules, so they must not be confused with database integrity rules or with user-input validation rules. They contribute to the way entities represent domain objects by encoding the constraints the represented objects must obey.

It is worth pointing out that not all business validation rules can be encoded inside DDD entities. Instead, *business rules that are not specific of single DDD entities,* but involve the interaction of several entities must be encoded in the software module that handles and coordinate the interaction among entities. We will speak more about the software module that coordinates entities interactions later on in this chapter.

The subsection that follows gives more details on entity-level validation rules.

Entity-level validation in .NET

Business validation rules can be implemented in several ways, and are not tied to a specific framework or language. In order to show how to transfer this subject from theory to practice, this section shows possible .NET implementations. Readers can skip these subsections on a first read.

In .NET, business validation can be carried out with one of the following techniques:

- Calling the validation methods in all the class methods that modify the entity
- Hooking the validation methods to all the property setters.
- Decorating the class and/or its properties with custom validation attributes and then invoking the `TryValidateObject` static method of the `System.ComponentModel.DataAnnotations.Validator` class on the entity each time it is modified. The .NET `System.ComponentModel.DataAnnotations` namespace contains predefined validation attributes (see `https://learn.microsoft.com/en-us/aspnet/core/mvc/models/validation?view=aspnetcore-10.0`), but the developer can define also custom validation attributes by inheriting from the `System.ComponentModel.DataAnnotations.ValidationAttribute` abstract class (see `https://makolyte.com/aspnetcore-create-a-custom-model-validation-attribute/`).

> Note
>
> More details on validation attributes will be given both in *Chapter 13, Interacting with Data in C# – Entity Framework Core,* and in *Chapter 16, Presenting ASP.NET Core.*

Once detected, validation errors must be handled somehow; that is, the current operation must be aborted and the error must be reported to an appropriate error handler. The simplest way to handle validation errors is by throwing an exception. This way, both purposes are easily achieved and we can choose where to intercept and handle them. Unfortunately, as we discussed in the *Performance issues that need to be considered while programming in C#* section of *Chapter 2, Non-Functional Requirements*, exceptions imply big performance penalties, and must be used to deal just with "*exceptional circumstances*" so, often, different options are considered. Handling errors in the normal flow of control would break modularity by spreading the code that's needed to handle the error all over the stack of methods that caused the error, with a never-ending set of conditions all over that code. Therefore, more sophisticated options are needed.

A good alternative to exceptions is to notify errors to an error handler that is unique for each processing request. For instance, it can be implemented as a scoped service in the dependency injection engine. Being scoped, the same service instance is returned while each request is being processed so that the handler that controls the execution of the whole call stack can inspect possible errors when the flow of control returns to it, and can handle them appropriately. Unfortunately, this sophisticated technique can't automatically abort the operation's execution and at the same time return immediately to an adequate pre-set error-recovery handler that is in the call stack. Only exceptions can do this!

This is why often exceptions are used for this scenario, notwithstanding their performance issues. The other option is the usage of a **result object** that informs the caller upon the success of the operation in all method calls. However, result objects have their cons: they imply more coupling between the methods involved in the call stack, so during software maintenance, each change might require modifications in several methods.

After this short, after this little parenthesis, let's focus again on entities.

DDD entities in .NET

Since DDD entities must have a well-defined identity, they must have properties that act as primary keys. It is common to override the `Object.Equals` method of all the DDD entities in such a way that two objects are considered equal whenever they have the same primary keys.

Instead of overriding `Object.Equals` in all application entities, it is convenient to factor out this implementation into a unique abstract `Entity` class from which all our entities will inherit. Below is a possible implementation of this `Entity` class:

```
public abstract class Entity<TKey>: IEquatable<Entity<TKey >>
{

    public virtual TKey Id { get; protected set; }
    public bool IsTransient()
    {
        return object.Equals(Id, default(TKey));
    }
    public override bool Equals(object obj)
    {
        return obj is Entity<TKey> entity &&
```

```
            Equals(entity);
    }
    public bool Equals(Entity<TKey>? other)
    {
        if (other == null ||
            other.IsTransient() || this.IsTransient())
            return false;
        return Object.Equals(Id, other.Id);
    }
    int? _requestedHashCode;
    public override int GetHashCode()
    {
        if (!IsTransient())
        {
            if (!_requestedHashCode.HasValue)
                _requestedHashCode = HashCode.Combine(Id);
            return _requestedHashCode.Value;
        }

            return base.GetHashCode();
    }
    public static bool operator ==(Entity<TKey> left, Entity<TKey> right)
    {
        if (object.Equals(left, null))
            return Object.Equals(right, null);
        return left.Equals(right);
    }
    public static bool operator !=(Entity<TKey> left, Entity<TKey> right)
    {
        return !(left == right);
    }
}
```

Note the following things in the code:

- It is worth implementing an `IEntity<K>` interface that defines all the properties/methods of `Entity<K>`. This interface is useful whenever we need to hide data classes behind interfaces.
- The `IsTransient` predicate returns `true` whenever the entity has been recently created and hasn't been recorded in the permanent storage, so its primary key is still undefined.

- In .NET, it is good practice that, whenever you override the `Object.Equals` method of a class, you also override its `Object.GetHashCode` method so that class instances can be efficiently stored in data structures such as dictionaries and sets. That's why the `Entity` class overrides it.
- It is worth pointing out that once we've redefined the `Object.Equals` method in the `Entity` class, we can also override the `==` and `!=` operators.

Entities are not the only data ingredient of DDD. Domain modeling also requires data with no unique identities. That's why Value objects were conceived.

Value objects

Value objects, in contrast to entities, do not represent instances that have an intrinsic identity, but represent just property values. They represent complex types that can't be encoded with numbers, strings, or other primitive types. Therefore, they have no identity and no principal keys. They have no operations defined on them and are immutable; that is, once they've been created, all their fields can be read but cannot be modified. For this reason, they are usually encoded with classes whose properties have protected/private setters.

Two value objects are considered equal when all their independent properties are equal. Some properties are not independent since they just show data that's been encoded by other properties in a different way, as is the case for the ticks of `DateTime` and its representation of the date and time fields.

Value objects are easily implemented with `C# record` types, since all `record types` automatically override the `Equals` method so that it performs a property-by-property comparison. Record types can also be made immutable by adequately defining their properties; once immutable objects are initialized, the only way to change their values is to create a new instance. Here is an example of how to modify a `record`:

```
var modifiedAddress = myAddress with {Street = "new street"}
```

Here is an example of how to define a `record`:

```
public record Address
{
    public string Country {get; init;}
    public string Town {get; init;}
    public string Street {get; init;}
}
```

The `init` keyword is what makes `record` type properties immutable, since it means they can only be initialized.

If we pass all the properties in the constructor instead of using initializers, the preceding definition can be simplified as follows:

```
public record Address(string Country, string Town, string Street) ;
```

Typical value objects include costs represented as a number and a currency symbol, locations represented as longitude and latitude, addresses, and contact information.

> **Note**
>
> The way both entities and value objects typically interact with data storage in .NET applications is explained in *Chapter 13, Interacting with Data in C# – Entity Framework Core.*

Well, you learned that we need two types of building blocks to represent application domains: entities and value objects. However, we need to go more in-depth into the nature of entities to be able to design our application domains.

Aggregates

So far, we have talked about entities as the **units** that are processed by a DDD-based business layer. However, several entities can be manipulated and made into a single entity. An example of this is a purchase order and all of its items. In fact, it makes absolutely no sense to process a single order item independently of the order it belongs to. This happens because order items are actually subparts of an order, not independent entities.

There is no transaction that may affect a single order item without it affecting the order that the item is in. Imagine that two different people in the same company are trying to increase the total quantity of cement, but one increases the quantity of type-1 cement (item 1) while the other increases the quantity of type-2 cement (item 2). If each item is processed as an independent entity, both quantities will be increased, which could cause an incoherent purchase order since the total quantity of cement would be increased twice.

On the other hand, if the whole order, along with all its order items, is loaded and saved with every single transaction by both people, one of the two will overwrite the changes of the other one, so whoever makes the final change will have their requirements set.

A purchase order, along with all its subparts (its order items), is called an **aggregate**.

In general, aggregates are object trees whose tree arcs represent subpart relations. The root of each aggregate object's tree is called the aggregate **root**. Since each aggregate root is the root of the whole object's tree, its pointer is also a pointer to the whole aggregate, so a variable containing the aggregate root also contains the whole object's tree.

Therefore, the aggregate root usually represents the whole aggregate, and all the operations on the aggregate are defined as methods of the aggregate root.

When the aggregate pattern is used, the units of information that are transferred between the business layer and the data layer are called aggregates, queries, and query results. Thus, aggregates replace single entities.

In a few words, aggregates are in-memory representations of storage information that need to be dealt with as a single object. Being an in-memory representation based on an object-oriented paradigm, they take full advantage of all the benefits of object-oriented programming.

Well, so now we understand that our application domain's building blocks are not entities and value objects, but aggregates and value objects.

Let's move to another fundamental DDD key topic: how bounded contexts communicate among them.

Domain events

Domain events are the main communication ingredient of DDD. While DDD doesn't impose constraints on the way communication among bounded contexts is achieved, communication based on the publisher/subscriber pattern described in *Chapter 6, Design Patterns and .NET Implementation*, maximizes independence among bounded contexts. The publisher doesn't need to know about each receiver and how it works, but just publishes the result of its job in a general format. Then, once a publish endpoint receives a message from a sender, it resends it to all subscribers that added themselves to its subscriptions queue. This way, if we add a new Bounded Context, no modification is required for all message senders since they just need to continue sending their messages to the adequate publish endpoints. It is up to the newly added Bounded Context to register itself with the proper publish endpoints.

Practical details on how to trigger these events will be given in the *Command handlers and domain events* subsection of this chapter.

This section ends our trip in the world of DDD basic concepts. Let's move to the descriptions of patterns that are commonly used with DDD:

Common DDD patterns and architectures

Up to now, we have learned the basics of DDD, that is, how to define Bounded Contexts, how to coordinate them, and how to build the data model of each Bounded Context. This final section explains how to organize your code in practice with the help of patterns and architectures that are commonly used with DDD. Some of them can be adopted in all projects, while others can only be used for certain Bounded Contexts.

Before we begin, we need to learn some architectural concepts used in classical architectures that are also used in DDD-based applications, with a few modifications.

Let's start by noticing that, from a conceptual point of view, the functionality of each application can be classified into three groups:

- Handling the interaction with the user
- Performing business-related processing
- Interacting with the storage engine

Each of the above groups uses a different language and different technologies. The first group uses the language of the target users and user interface technologies, the second group uses the language of the domain expert and is focused on application domain modeling, and the third group uses both language and technologies related to databases.

Each of the architectures we will look at organizes these functionalities in different ways. We will start with classic Layers architecture since it is simpler to understand, and then we will describe the more sophisticated Onion architecture.

Classic layered architecture

Classic layers architecture organizes the three groups of functionalities as three loosely coupled sets of classes/interfaces called **layers**, put one after the other:

- The first layer in the sequence is the one that takes care of user interaction, and is called the **Presentation Layer**
- The second layer in the sequence is the one that performs business-related processing, and is called the **Business Layer**
- The third layer is the one dedicated to database interaction, and is called the **Data Layer**

Each layer can communicate directly only with the layer that precedes it and the layer that follows it, as shown in the picture below:

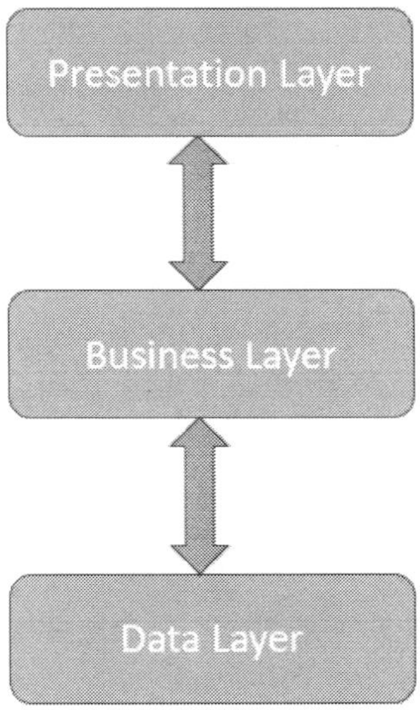

Figure 7.3: Classical layers architecture

In other words, each layer can pass or receive objects only to or from the layers that precede and follow it. This object exchange is performed as follows:

1. A layer, say `A`, calls a public method of an object belonging to the previous layer, say `B`, and passes it some data
2. In turn, the method called at the previous step may recursively call methods of its previous layer to do its job
3. When the method of layer `B` finishes its job, it returns some data to `A`

The Presentation Layer handles not only graphics but also the whole user-machine interaction protocol. During its interaction protocol, the Presentation Layer uses Business Layer methods either to present data to the user or to update the application state.

In turn, the Business Layer uses Data Layer methods to retrieve all data it needs to prepare the user's answer from the data storage and to update the application state.

Each Layer offers a well-defined interface to the layer that precedes it while hiding all implementation details.

Layer architecture promotes modularity since each layer doesn't depend on how the layers that precede it are implemented, and avoids the possibility of the language used by each layer contaminating the language used by the others.

However, data exchanged in the classic Layer architecture are record-type objects with no methods that encode any processing logic, since the whole processing logic is contained in the objects and methods that compose the three layers.

Since record-like objects used by classic Layers architecture are very different from DDD domain objects, which are rich objects that encode most of the business logic in their methods, classic Layers architecture has a poor match with DDD. That's why an improvement on the classic layers architecture, called onion architecture, is usually adopted in all DDD projects.

Onion architecture

In **onion architecture**, layers obey different rules and are defined in a slightly different way. There is:

- An outermost layer that takes care of all interactions with the application environment; that is, the user interface, test software, and interaction with the operating system and data storage
- An application layer
- A domain layer

Here, the domain layer is an abstraction of the classical data layer based on the Ubiquitous Language. It is where DDD entities and value objects are defined, together with abstractions of the operations that retrieve and save them. For better modularity, all or some domain layer classes may be made internal and hidden behind public interfaces.

The application layer, instead, defines operations that use the domain layer public interface (public interfaces and public classes) to get DDD entities and value objects and manipulate them to implement the application business logic. The DDD application layer is called **application services**, since it exposes its functionalities through an API that is completely independent of the outermost layers. This way, for instance, any user interface layer and a test suite both call exactly the same methods to interact with the application logic.

The outermost layer contains the user interface, the functional test suites (if any), and the application interface with the infrastructure that hosts the application.

The infrastructure represents the environment in which the application runs and includes the operating system, any devices, file system services, cloud services, and databases. The infrastructure interface is placed in the outermost level to ensure that no other onion layer depends on it. This maximizes both usability and modifiability.

The infrastructure layer contains all drivers needed to adapt the application to its environment. Infrastructure resources communicate with the application through these drivers, and, in turn, drivers expose the infrastructure resources to all application layers through interfaces that are associated with the drivers implementing them in the dependency injection engine. This way, adapting the application to a different environment just requires changing the drivers.

Here's a sketch of the onion architecture:

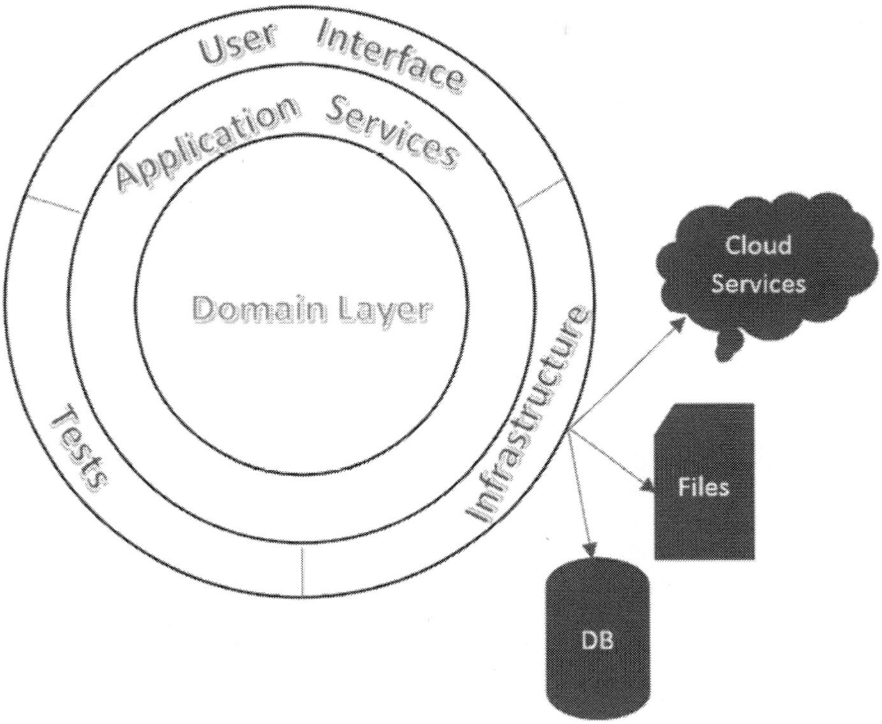

Figure 7.4: Onion architecture

Each ring is a layer. Inward from the outermost layer are the **application services**, and inward from the application services we have the **domain layer**, which contains the data model definition.

Both the application services and the domain layer can be split into sublayers, and all layers/sublayers must conform to the following rule: *Each layer may depend only on inner layers.*

For instance, the domain layer may be split into **Domain Model** and **Domain Services**, where Domain Model is below Domain Services. The **Domain Model** layer contains the classes and interfaces that represent all domain objects, while the **Domain Services** layer contains the so-called repositories that are explained later on in this chapter in the *repository and Unit of Work patterns* section.

The domain layer interacts with the actual database through interfaces that are implemented in an infrastructure library, often called a **DB Driver**. The *DB Driver* is part of the infrastructure part of the outermost layer.

Typically, the whole infrastructure part of the outermost layer is implemented as a set of separate libraries, each responsible for a different infrastructure, so the *DB Driver* is implemented as a separate library.

The whole outermost layer is typically implemented as a library that hosts the dependency injection engine. Here, each infrastructure layer, including the *DB Driver*, is connected with the interfaces it implements through dependency injection engine records.

Thus, the *DB Driver* must have a reference to the Domain Layer containing all interfaces it implements, while the outermost layer is where each domain layer interface is connected with its implementation through a record of the dependency injection engine. More specifically, the only data layer objects referenced by the application layer are these interface implementations that are only referenced in the dependency injection engine.

In turn, Application Services are typically implemented as a separate library that can manipulate both Domain Layer and Domain Services structures, that is: Entities, Value objects, repository interfaces, and other business-related interfaces defined in the Domain Services. Thus, the Application Services Library must have a reference to both the Domain Layer and Domain Services libraries.

Each application layer operation requires the interfaces it needs from the dependency engine, uses them to get DDD entities and value objects, manipulates them, and possibly saves them through the same interfaces.

Here is a diagram that shows the relations among the three layers discussed in this section:

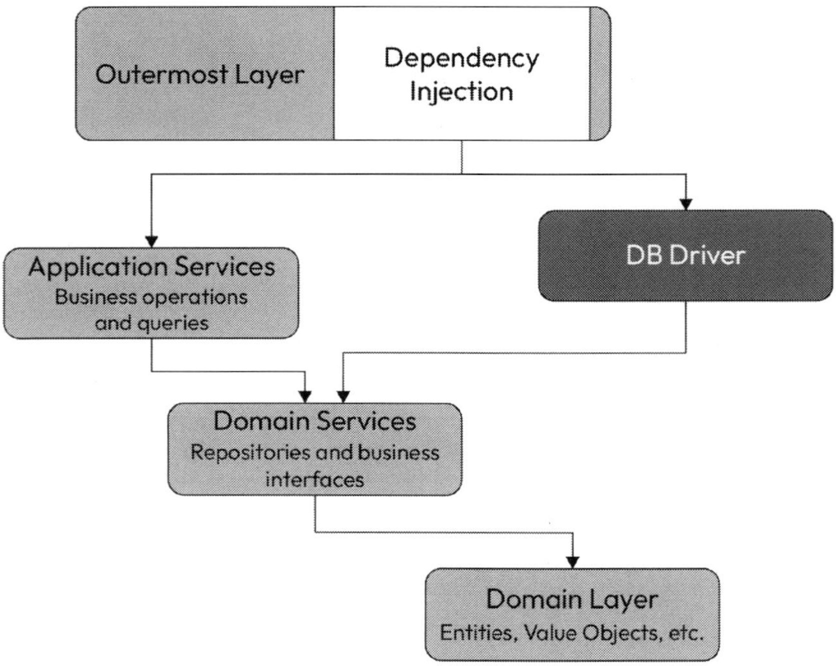

Figure 7.5: Relations among Onion Architecture layers

Each arrow encodes a library reference from the arrow origin to the arrow destination. DB Driver and Application Services don't need to reference the Domain Layer explicitly since they reference Domain Services that, in turn, reference the Domain Layer.

Thus, the domain layer contains the representation of the domain objects, the methods to use on them, validation constraints, and the domain layer's relationship with various entities. To increase modularity and decoupling, communication among entities is usually encoded with events, that is, with the **Publisher/ Subscriber pattern**. This means entity updates can trigger events that have been hooked to business operations, and these events act on other entities.

This layered architecture allows us to change the whole database and/or database engine without affecting the domain layer, which only depends on the domain specifications and language and doesn't depend on the technical details of how the data is handled.

The application layer contains the definitions of all the operations that may potentially affect several entities and the definitions of all the queries that are needed by the applications. Both business operations and queries use the interfaces defined in the Domain Services and the classes defined in the domain layer to interact with the actual data storage.

However, while business operations manipulate and exchange entities with domain services interfaces, queries send query specifications and receive generic **Data Transfer Objects** (DTOs) from them. In fact, the purpose of queries is just to show data to the user, not to act on them; accordingly, query operations don't need whole entities with all their methods, properties, and validation rules, but just property tuples.

Application services operations are invoked by outermost layer classes that handle presentation layer logic, testing, and communication with other Microservices.

Summing up, application services operate on the classes defined in the domain layer instead of interacting directly with their DB Driver implementations, which means that the application layer is decoupled from the DB Driver. More specifically, DB Driver implementations are only mentioned in the dependency injection engine definitions. All the other application layer components refer to the interfaces and classes that are defined in the domain layer, and domain services and the dependency injection engine inject the appropriate implementations.

The outermost layer communicates with other application components through one or more of the following patterns:

- ***It exposes business operations and queries on a communication endpoint***, such as an HTTP Web API (see *Chapter 15, Applying Service-Oriented Architectures with .NET*). In this case, the presentation layer may connect to this endpoint or to other endpoints that, in turn, take information from this and other endpoints. Application components that collect information from several endpoints and expose them in a unique endpoint are called **gateways**. They may be either custom or general-purpose, such as Ocelot.
- ***It implements presentation logic***, such as an ASP.NET Core MVC Web application.
- ***It doesn't expose all the information through endpoints and communicates some of the data it processes/creates to other application components that, in turn, expose endpoints.*** Such communication is often implemented with the Publisher/Subscriber pattern to increase modularity.

It is worth pointing out that there are other architectures similar to the Onion Architecture, namely **Clean Architecture** and **ports and adapters architecture**. Both share the idea of isolating the business code from the specificity of the environment with concepts that are substantially equivalent to the outermost infrastructure layer of Onion Architecture.

For instance, Clean Architecture has a slightly different structure, and names "`Entities`" what in the Onion Architecture is called the Domain Layer. Similarly, it replaces Application Services with "*Use Cases*." However,

"*Use Cases*" operations are more focused on representing a whole Use Case, while Application Services operations represent just atomic business operations, and not necessarily a whole Use Case implementation.

Summing up, you learned two approaches to ensuring application modularity: the classic approach that focuses mainly on the independence of the three parts (presentation, business, and storage), and new approaches like the Onion Architecture, more tied to the DDD methodology, that focus on the independence of the whole business abstraction (business operations + entities).

Having discussed the whole application architecture options, let's move to another important pattern that allows an efficacious implementation of the interaction between business operations and the entity layer.

Repository pattern

The **repository pattern** is an entity-centric approach to the definition of the domain layer interfaces: each entity, or better, each aggregate, has its own repository interface that defines how to retrieve and create it, and that defines all queries that involve entities in the aggregate. The implementation of each repository interface is called a **repository**. Repositories are associated with aggregates instead of entities, since, as discussed in the *Aggregates* subsection, aggregates represent the minimum granularity that makes sense to consider in each data operation.

With the repository pattern, each operation has an easy-to-find place where it must be defined: the interface of the aggregate the operation works on, or, in the case of a query, the aggregate that contains the root entity of the query.

The repository pattern was initially conceived for the classical layer architectures and their record-like objects. Then it was adapted to work with rich DDD entities/aggregates.

Classical repositories contain all methods needed to handle record-like objects, that is, modification, creation, and delete methods, since record-like objects have no modification methods. **DDD-adapted repositories**, instead, only contain create and delete methods since all methods that modify each aggregate are defined as aggregate methods. Moreover, applications based on classic repositories and record-like objects do not have a unique record-like object that represents each domain aggregate, but there are several record-like objects, each containing a different view of the overall domain aggregate. Therefore, classic repositories have modification methods for several different record-like objects.

Both classic and DDD-adapted repositories have methods to retrieve data to be returned to the user. In both cases, these data are represented by record-like objects, since aggregates are built only when domain entities must be modified or created. As already stated before, the choice between classic and DDD-adapted repository is made according to the complexity of business rules: complex business rules benefit from the more sophisticated DDD-adapted pattern, while the simpler classic pattern is better suited for applications with quite simple business rules. More details on the choice between the two patterns are given in the section that follows (*Classic repository pattern versus DDD aggregates*).

The picture below summarizes the differences between the classical and DDD-adapted repository patterns.

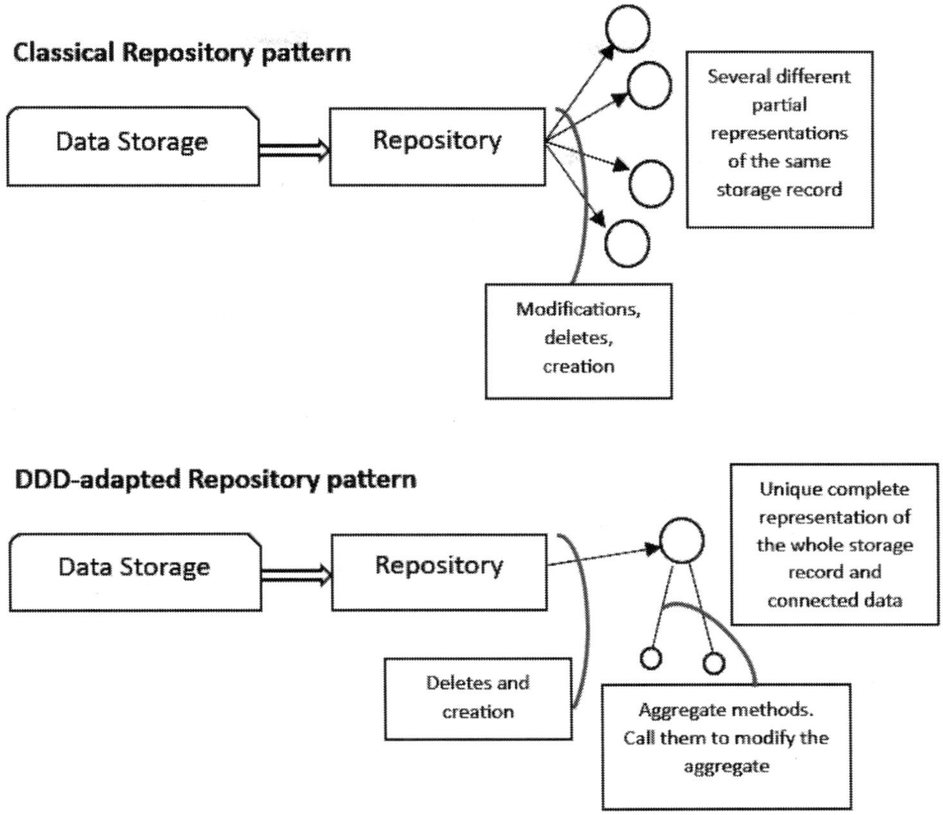

Figure 7.6: Classical and DDD-adapted repository pattern

Summing up, both the classic repository and DDD-adapted repository pattern have the role of connecting business operations with entities that represent the application domain.

Now that we've discussed the basic patterns of DDD, we can discuss some more advanced DDD patterns. We will first discuss how to handle transactions, and then we will introduce the CQRS pattern.

Unit of work pattern

While it is preferable for transactions to be confined within the boundary of a single aggregate design, sometimes application layer transactions might span several aggregates and, accordingly, might use several different repository interfaces.

For instance, buying a travel involves the simultaneous modifications of the following entities:

1. Hotel/travel available places
2. Customer shopping basket

Both operations must be accomplished in a single transaction since either they are both successful or they must both fail. Therefore, we need a way to execute operations on several entities/aggregates in a single transaction, while keeping the methods/code of the involved entities decoupled, according to object-oriented programming best practices.

The **Unit of Work** pattern is a solution that maintains the independence of the domain layer from the underlying domain layer implementation. It states that each repository interface must also contain a reference to a Unit of Work interface that represents the identity of the current transaction. This means that several repositories with the same Unit of Work reference belong to the same transaction.

The Unit of Work pattern can be used with both aggregates and record-like entities.

Both the repository and the Unit of Work patterns can be implemented by defining some seed interfaces:

```
public interface IUnitOfWork
{
    Task<bool> SaveEntitiesAsync();
    Task StartAsync();
    Task CommitAsync();
    Task RollbackAsync();
}
public interface IRepository<T>: IRepository
{
    IUnitOfWork UnitOfWork { get; }
}
```

All repository interfaces inherit from `IRepository<T>` and bind `T` to the aggregate root or entity they are associated with, while Unit of Work simply implements `IUnitOfWork`. When `SaveEntitiesAsync()` is called, all pending modifications, deletes, and creations done on aggregates or on record-like objects are saved in a single transaction in the storage engine. If a wider transaction that starts when some data is retrieved from the storage engine is needed, it must be started and committed/aborted by the application layer handler, which takes care of the whole operation with the help of the `IUnitOfWork` `StartAsync`, `CommitAsync`, and `RollbackAsync` methods. `IRepository<T>` inherits from an empty `IRepository` interface to help automatic repository discovery.

> **Note**
>
> The GitHub repository associated with this book contains a `RepositoryExtensions` class whose `AddAllRepositories` `IServiceCollection` extension method automatically discovers all the repository implementations contained in an assembly and adds them to the dependency injection engine.

As announced, let's move to a pattern that is used substantially in all architectures related to DDD.

Command query responsibility segregation (CQRS) pattern

In its general form, the usage of this pattern is quite easy: *use different structures to store/update and to query data.* Here, the requirements regarding how to store and update data differ from the requirements of queries. This means that both the domain layer and application services of queries and of store/update operations must be designed in completely different ways.

In the case of DDD, the unit of storage is the aggregate, so additions, deletions, and updates involve aggregates, while queries usually involve transformations of properties that have been taken from several aggregates. Moreover, we don't usually perform business operations on query results. We just use them to compute other data (averages, sums, and so on). Therefore, while updates require entities enriched with business logic and constraints (methods, validation rules, encapsulated information, and so on), query results just need sets of property/value pairs, so **Data Transfer Objects** (DTOs) with only public properties and no methods work well.

In its common form, the pattern can be depicted as follows:

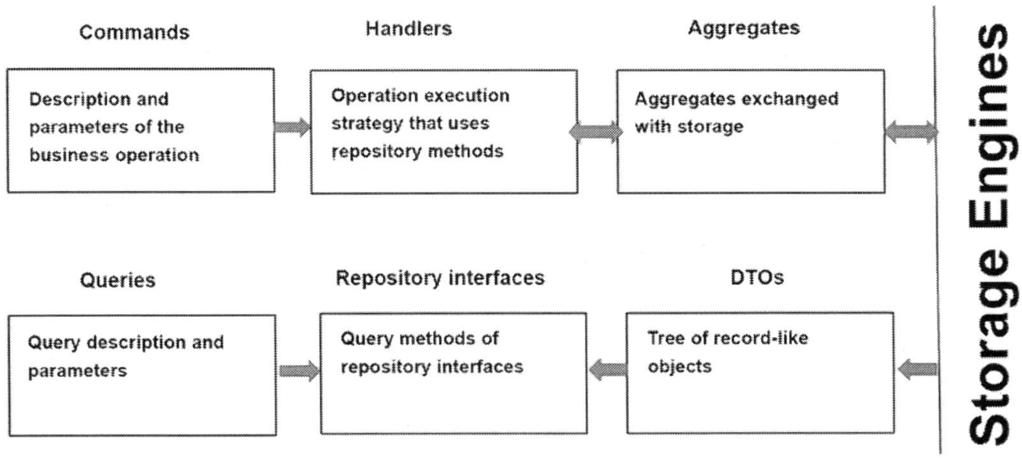

Figure 7.7: Command and query processing

Where:

- The middle boxes (Handlers and Repository interfaces) represent operations
- The leftmost and rightmost boxes represent data
- Arrows simply represent the direction of data

The main takeaway from this is that the extraction of query results doesn't need to pass through the construction of entities and aggregates, but the fields shown in the query must be extracted from the storage engine and projected into ad hoc DTOs.

However, in more complex situations, **CQRS** may be implemented in a stronger form. Namely, we can use different Bounded Contexts to store preprocessed query results.

> **Note**
>
> The strong form of **CQRS** is convenient when the query results must be integrated with data contained in other microservices.

In fact, the other option would be an aggregator microservice that queries all the necessary microservices in order to assemble each query result. However, recursive calls to other microservices to build an answer may result in unacceptable response times. Moreover, factoring out some preprocessing ensures better use of the available resources.

This pattern is implemented as follows:

- Query handling is delegated to separate and specialized components.
- Each query-handling component uses a database table for each query it must handle. There, it stores all fields to be returned by the query. This means that queries are not computed at each request, but pre-computed and stored in specific database tables. Clearly, queries with child collections need additional tables, one for each child collection.
- All components that process updates forward all changes to the interested query-handling components. Records are versioned so the query-handling components that receive the changes can apply them in the right order to their query-handling tables. In fact, since communication is asynchronous to improve performance, changes are not guaranteed to be received in the same order they were sent.
- Changes received by each query-handling microservice are cached while they wait for the changes to be applied. Whenever a change has a version number that immediately follows the last change applied, it is applied to the correct query-handling table.

It is worth noticing that the software "*components*" we mentioned above run as separate processes on possibly different machines and are called microservices. They will be discussed in detail in *Chapter 11, Applying a Microservice Architecture to Your Enterprise Application*.

The usage of this stronger form of the CQRS pattern transforms typical local database transactions into complex, time-consuming distributed transactions, since a failure in a single query preprocessor microservice should invalidate the whole transaction. As we will discuss in *Chapter 11, Applying a Microservice Architecture to Your Enterprise Application*, implementing distributed transactions is usually unacceptable for performance reasons and sometimes is not supported at all, so the common solution is to renounce the idea of a database that is immediately consistent overall and to accept that the overall database will eventually be consistent after each update. Transient failures can be solved with retry policies that we will discuss in *Chapter 11, Applying a Microservice Architecture to Your Enterprise Application*, while permanent failures are handled by performing corrective actions on the already committed local transactions instead of pretending to implement an overall globally distributed transaction.

At this point, you may be asking the following question:

'Why do we need to keep the original data once we have all the preprocessed query results? We will never use it to answer queries!'

Some of the answers to this question are as follows:

- They are the source of truth that we may need to recover from failures.
- We need them to compute new preprocessed results when we add new queries.
- We need them to process new updates. In fact, processing updates usually requires that some of the data be retrieved from the database, possibly shown to the user, and then modified.

For instance, to modify an item in an existing purchase order, we need the whole order so that we can show it to the user and compute the changes so that we can forward it to other microservices. Moreover, whenever we modify or add data to the storage engine, we must verify the coherence of the overall database (unique key constraints, foreign key constraints, and so on).

The next subsection is dedicated to an extreme implementation of the CQRS pattern.

Event sourcing

Event sourcing is a more advanced implementation of the stronger form of CQRS. It is useful when the original Bounded Context is a *source of truth*, that is used for recovering from failures and for software maintenance. In this case, instead of updating data, we simply add events that describe the operation that was performed: *deleted record Id 15*, *changed the name to John in Id 21*, and so on. For instance, in our use case, events triggered by the purchase-order microservice could be something like:

- Added Purchase: `{Id=3456, Items {…}}`
- Deleted Purchase: `{Id=3456}`
- Modified Purchase: `{Id: 3456, NewItems: {…}, RemovedItems: {…}}`

These events are immediately sent to all the dependent Bounded Contexts, and in the case of failures and/or the addition of new queries, all we have to do is reprocess some of them. For performance reasons, together with the events representing all changes, the current state is also maintained; otherwise, each time it is needed, it will need to be recomputed, replaying all events. Moreover, usually, the full state is cached after, say, every `N` changes. This way, if there is a crash or any kind of failure, only a few events must be replayed.

Replaying events can't cause problems if events are *idempotent*, that is, if processing the same event several times has the same effect as processing it once.

As we will discuss in *Chapter 11, Applying a Microservice Architecture to Your Enterprise Application*, idempotency is a standard requirement for microservices that communicate through events.

In the next section, we will describe a common pattern that's used for handling operations that span several aggregates and several Bounded Contexts.

Command handlers and aggregate events

According to the Command pattern each application domain operation is handled by a so-called command handler. Since each command handler encodes a single application domain operation all of its actions must take place in the same transaction, because the operation must succeed or fail as a whole. Command handlers perform their job by calling Aggregates and repository methods. However, some actions might be triggered by state changes inside aggregates, so they can't be called by command handlers, but must rely on some form of direct aggregate to aggregate communication.

To keep aggregates separated, usually, communication among aggregates, and also with other Bounded Contexts, is done through events. We already discussed domain events used to communicate with other bounded contexts in the *Domain events* subsection. However, direct communication among aggregates can also take advantage of the publisher/subscriber pattern to keep the code more modular and easier to modify. It is good practice to store all the events when they are triggered during the processing of each aggregate, instead of executing them immediately, in order to prevent event execution from interfering with the ongoing aggregate processing. This is easily achieved by adding the following code to the abstract `Entity` class defined in the `Entities` subsection of this chapter, as follows:

```
public List<IEventNotification> DomainEvents { get; private set; }
public void AddDomainEvent(IEventNotification evt)
{
    DomainEvents ??= new List<IEventNotification>();
    DomainEvents.Add(evt);
}
public void RemoveDomainEvent(IEventNotification evt)
{
    DomainEvents?.Remove(evt);
}
```

Here, `IEventNotification` is an empty interface that's used to mark classes as events.

Event processing is usually performed immediately before changes are stored in the storage engine. Accordingly, a good place to perform event processing is immediately before the command handler calls the `SaveEntitiesAsync()` method of each `IUnitOfWork` implementation (see the *Repository pattern* subsection). Similarly, if event handlers can create other events, they must process them after they finish processing all their aggregates.

Subscriptions to an event, `T`, can be provided as an implementation of the `IEventHandler<T>` interface:

```
public interface IEventHandler<T>: IEventHandler
    where T: IEventNotification
{
    Task HandleAsync(T ev);
}
```

Analogously, the command pattern is implemented with a `command` object, which contains all the input data of the application domain operation, while the code that implements the actual operation can be provided through a command handler that is an implementation of a `ICommandHandler<T>` interface:

```
public interface ICommandHandler<T>: ICommandHandler
    where T: ICommand
{
    Task HandleAsync(T command);
}
```

Here, `ICommand` is an empty interface that's used to mark classes as commands. `ICommandHandler<T>` and `IEventHandler<T>` are examples of the **Command pattern** we described in *Chapter 6, Design Patterns and .NET Implementation*.

Each ICommandHandler<T> can be registered in the dependency injection engine so that classes that need to execute a command, T, can use ICommandHandler<T> in their constructor. This way, we decouple the abstract definition of a command (the class that implements ICommand) from the way it is executed.

The same construction can't be applied to events, T, and their IEventHandler<T>, because when an event is triggered, we need to retrieve several instances of IEventHandler<T> and not just one. We need to do this since each event may have several subscriptions. However, a few lines of code can easily solve this difficulty. First, we need to define a class that hosts all the handlers for a given event type:

```
public class EventTrigger<T>
    where T: IEventNotification
{
    private IEnumerable<IEventHandler<T>> handlers;
    public EventTrigger(IEnumerable<IEventHandler<T>> handlers)
    {
        this.handlers = handlers;
    }
    public async Task Trigger(T ev)
    {
        foreach (var handler in handlers)
            await handler.HandleAsync(ev);
    }
}
```

Declaring a handlersIEnumerable<IEventHandler<T>> parameter in the EventTrigger<T> constructor lets a .NET dependency injection engine pass all IEventHandler<T> implementations available in the dependency injection container to this handlers parameter.

The idea is that each class that needs to trigger event T requires EventTrigger<T> and then passes the event to be triggered to its Trigger method, which, in turn, invokes all the handlers.

Then, we need to register EventTrigger<T> in the dependency injection engine. A good idea is to define the dependency injection extensions that we can invoke to declare each event, as follows:

```
service.AddEventHandler<MyEventType, MyHandlerType>()
```

This AddEventHandler extension must automatically produce a dependency injection definition for EventTrigger<T> and must process all the handlers that are declared with AddEventHandler for each type, T.

The following extension class does this for us:

```
public static class EventDIExtensions
{
    public static IServiceCollection AddEventHandler<T, H>
        (this IServiceCollection services)
```

```
        where T : IEventNotification
        where H: class, IEventHandler<T>
    {
        services.AddScoped<H>();
        services.TryAddScoped(typeof(EventTrigger<>));
        return services;
    }
    ...
    ...
}
```

The `H` type passed to `AddEventHandler` is recorded in the dependency injection engine, and the first time `AddEventHandler` is called, `EventTrigger<T>` is also added to the dependency injection engine. Then, when an `EventTrigger<T>` instance is required by the dependency injection engine, all `IEventHandler<T>` types added to the dependency injection engine are created, collected, and passed to the `EventTrigger(IEnumerable<IEventHandler<T>> handlers)` constructor.

When the program starts up, all the `ICommandHandler<T>` and `IEventHandler<T>` implementations can be retrieved with reflection and registered automatically. To help with automatic discovery, they inherit from `ICommandHandler` and `IEventHandler`, which are both empty interfaces.

> **Note**
>
> The `EventDIExtensions` class, which is available in this book's GitHub repository, contains methods for the automatic discovery and registration of command handlers and event handlers. The GitHub repository also contains an `IEventMediator` interface and its `EventMediator` implementation, whose `TriggerEvents(IEnumerable<IEventNotification> events)` method retrieves all the handlers associated with the events it receives in its argument from the dependency injection engine and executes them. It is sufficient to have `IEventMediator` injected into a class so that it can trigger events. `EventDIExtensions` also contains an extension method that discovers all the queries that implement the empty `IQuery` interface and adds them to the dependency injection engine.

A more sophisticated implementation is given by the `MediatR` NuGet package.

At this point you also learned the last building block for implementing DDD-based applications: how to implement in practice all business operations contained in the Application Services layer of a business architecture with the help of Commands and Command handlers. This finishes our trip in the world of DDD.

Summary

In this chapter, we learned how to use DDD to build complex enterprise applications and to face the challenges of a quickly changing market. We learned how to identify domains and how to coordinate the teams that work on different domains of the same application with domain maps.

Then, we learned how the usage of aggregates and value objects simplifies the adoption of DDD and how to translate everything in practice with the help of advice and code snippets.

We also learned Onion Architecture and its importance in the implementation of DDD-based applications, when to use it, and when to use more classical, simpler approaches.

We also learned some typical patterns that are used with DDD, that is, the repository and Unit of Work patterns, domain event patterns, CQRS, and event sourcing, when to use them and how to implement them in practice. In particular, we learned how to use and implement domain events to decouple the various Bounded Contexts.

Questions

1. What provides the main hints so that we can discover domain boundaries?
2. What is the main tool that's used for coordinating the development of a separate Bounded Context?
3. Is it true that each entry that composes an aggregate communicates with the remainder of the system with its own methods?
4. Why is there a single aggregate root?
5. How many repositories can manage an aggregate?
6. How does a repository interact with the application layer?
7. Why is the Unit of Work pattern needed?
8. What are the reasons for the light form of CQRS? What about the reasons for its strongest form?
9. What is the main tool that allows us to couple commands/domain events with their handlers?
10. Is it true that event sourcing can be used to implement any Bounded Context?

Further reading

The following are some books and links you may consider reading to gather more information in relation to this chapter:

- Eric Evans, Domain-Driven Design: `https://www.amazon.com/exec/obidos/ASIN/0321125215/domainlanguag-20`
- More resources on DDD can be found here: `https://domainlanguage.com/ddd/`
- A detailed discussion of CQRS design principles can be found here: `http://udidahan.com/2009/12/09/clarified-cqrs/`
- More information on MediatR can be found on MediatR's GitHub repository: `https://github.com/jbogard/MediatR`
- A good description of event sourcing, along with an example of it, can be seen in the following blog post by Martin Fowler: `https://martinfowler.com/eaaDev/EventSourcing.html`

Get this book's PDF version and more

Scan the QR code (or go to `packtpub.com/unlock`). Search for this book by name, confirm the edition, and then follow the steps on the page.

UNLOCK NOW

Note: Keep your invoice handy. Purchases made directly from Packt don't require an invoice.

8

Understanding DevSecOps Principles and CI/CD

In the prior edition of this book, we have presented this chapter as *Understanding DevOps Principles and CI/CD*. However, in today's technology and risk landscape, software delivery cannot be discussed without also considering security. The growth of cyber threats, increasing compliance and regulatory pressure, and the rise of software supply-chain risks have made security an essential concern throughout the delivery lifecycle.

That is why **DevSecOps** is being introduced. Although many people define it as a process, the more you work with it, the better you understand it as a philosophy. While it is frequently presented as a set of practices integrated into delivery pipelines, its real value emerges when it becomes a guiding mindset across the entire software lifecycle. This chapter will cover the main concepts, principles, and tools you need to develop and deliver your software with DevSecOps. The focus is on helping you decide when and how to apply them in the development and delivery of software solutions.

In considering DevSecOps philosophy, this chapter will focus on *service design thinking*, that is, keeping in mind that the software you are designing is a service offered to an organization or part of an organization. This is especially relevant in DevSecOps, because treating software as a service makes feedback loops, operational accountability, and security ownership explicit architectural concerns rather than secondary operational issues.

The main takeaway of this approach is that the highest priority is the value your software gives to the target organization. Moreover, you are not offering just working code and an agreement to fix bugs, but a solution for all the needs that your software was conceived for. In other words, your job includes everything it needs to satisfy those needs, such as monitoring users' satisfaction and quickly adapting the software when the user needs change due to issues or new requirements, always with the commitment of guaranteeing the security aspects needed for the current world.

To do so, **Continuous Integration** (CI) and **Continuous Delivery** (CD) are sometimes stated as prerequisites for DevSecOps. So, the purpose of this chapter is also to discuss how to enable CI/CD in a real scenario, considering the challenges that you, as a software architect, will need to deal with.

The following topics will be covered in this chapter:

- Understanding Service Design Thinking

- Understanding DevSecOps principles: Continuous Integration, Continuous Delivery, Continuous Feedback, and Continuous Security
- Understanding how to implement DevSecOps using Azure DevSecOps and GitHub
- Understanding the risks and challenges when using CI/CD

The *WWTravelClub* project case, presented in *Chapter 22, Case Study: Practical Usage of .NET Aspire*, will be discussed during these topics, giving you the opportunity to understand how DevSecOps can be implemented. All the screenshots exemplifying the DevSecOps principles come from the main use case of the book, so you will be able to understand the DevSecOps principles easily.

By the end of this chapter, you will be able to design software according to service design thinking principles and use Azure Pipelines to deploy your application. You will be able to decide whether to use CI/CD in your project environment. Additionally, you will be able to define the tools needed for the successful use of this approach.

Technical requirements

This chapter requires Visual Studio 2026 Community Edition or better with all the Azure tools installed. You may also need an Azure DevOps Services account, as described in *Chapter 3, Managing Requirements*, but a GitHub account is preferred. It requires a free Azure account too. If you have not already created one, the *Creating an Azure account* subsection of *Chapter 1, Understanding the Importance of Software Architecture*, explains how to do so. The main purpose of the code in this chapter is to detail the CI/CD process. The code for this chapter is available at `https://github.com/PacktPublishing/Software-Architecture-with-.NET-10-and-C-sharp-5E`.

Describing DevSecOps

First, let's understand what DevOps is. This term comes from a union of the words *Development* and *Operations*, and the process simply unifies actions in these two areas. However, when you start to study a little bit more about it, you will realize that just connecting these two areas is not enough to achieve the true goals.

We can also say that DevOps is the process that answers the current needs of people regarding software delivery.

> **Note**
>
> Donovan Brown has a spectacular definition of what DevOps is: *DevOps is the union of people, process, and products to enable continuous delivery of value to our end users* (`https://www.donovanbrown.com/post/what-is-DevOps`).

A way to deliver value continuously to our end users, using process, people, and products: this is the best description of the philosophy. We need to develop and deliver customer-oriented software. As soon as all areas of the company understand that the key point is the end user, your task as a software architect is to present the technology that will facilitate the process of delivery. This is the user approach mentioned by Donovan.

All the content in this book is connected to this approach. It is never a matter of knowing a bunch of tools and technologies. As a software architect, you must understand that there is always a way to bring faster solutions to your end user easily, linked to their real needs.

And then comes the introduction of *DevSecOps*. As software delivery became faster, more distributed, and increasingly dependent on cloud platforms, automation, and third-party components, the industry could no longer treat security as an isolated activity performed only at the end of delivery. At the same time, cybersecurity threats became more frequent and sophisticated, while compliance and privacy requirements also increased. Approaches such as Privacy by Design and Security by Design remain extremely important, but by themselves, they are not enough. *DevSecOps* emerged to make security a continuous concern throughout the DevOps lifecycle, requiring software architects to address it as an ongoing responsibility rather than a final checkpoint. This is the process approach mentioned by the quote.

To finish, the product element mentioned by Donovan will be discussed during the chapter using two incredible tools – Azure DevOps and GitHub. But before going deep through *DevSecOps* principles, however, it is worth first exploring the service-oriented mindset that shapes how these solutions are conceived and delivered. So, let's first understand a bit better about Service Design Thinking.

Service Design Thinking

The simplest way to offer solutions based on web services is to offer their usage as a service, instead of selling the software that implements them.

Service Design Thinking is an approach to solution design that treats software not merely as a technical product, but as a service created to deliver continuous value to users and organizations. Instead of focusing only on features, implementation, or deployment, this perspective emphasizes the full experience of how a solution is consumed, supported, evolved, and improved over time. For software architects, this means designing with the understanding that success is measured not only by whether the system works, but by whether it consistently helps the organization achieve its goals.

A key principle of service design thinking is that software must remain aligned with changing business needs. Organizations evolve, user expectations shift, and operational conditions rarely stay constant for long. As a result, software cannot be treated as something designed once and then left unchanged. It must be continuously observed, evaluated, and refined. This creates a strong connection between architecture, business strategy, and user outcomes, since architectural decisions directly affect the system's ability to adapt over time.

Service design thinking also extends beyond the boundaries of software development. It influences how teams are organized, how responsibilities are assigned, and how collaboration happens across technical and business areas. Because the goal is to maximize the value delivered by the solution, organizations must ensure that product, engineering, operations, and support teams work together rather than in isolation. In this context, the architect is not only concerned with technical structure, but also with enabling a delivery model that supports feedback, responsiveness, and long-term service quality.

From a development perspective, service design thinking encourages practices that keep teams close to users and focused on real outcomes. Agile delivery, continuous integration, continuous deployment, and monitoring become essential because they enable teams to adjust the solution based on evidence rather than assumptions.

In this context, requirements are no longer treated only as functions to implement, but also as contributions to usability, operational efficiency, customer satisfaction, and business value.

At its core, service design thinking reframes software as an evolving service rather than a finished artifact. This broader perspective helps architects connect technical decisions with long-term user and business value.

From a technical standpoint, service design thinking leads to architectures that are observable, scalable, resilient, and easy to change. Systems designed for a service scenario must support monitoring, rapid updates, fault recovery, and demand growth without excessive redesign. This is why service design thinking is closely connected to cloud platforms, automation, modular architectures, and modern operational practices such as DevSecOps. In practice, this means architects must design for change, observability, resilience, and continuous improvement from the start.

It is worth mentioning that service design thinking is strictly tied to the *Software as a Service (SaaS)* model, which is discussed in *Chapter 10, Deciding on the Best Cloud-Based Solution*.

And for this reason, you need to learn the DevSecOps principles, which will be discussed in the next topic of this chapter.

Understanding DevSecOps principles

There are some principles that enable DevSecOps to work well in your team. These principles are *continuous integration (CI), continuous delivery (CD), continuous security (CS), and continuous feedback (CF).*

> **Note**
>
> Microsoft has a specific web page for defining the DevSecOps overview, culture, practices, tools, and its relation to the cloud. Please check this out at `https://www.microsoft.com/en-us/security/business/security-101/what-is-devsecops`.

DevSecOps is represented by the symbol of infinity in many books and technical articles. This represents the necessity for a continuous approach in the software development life cycle. During the cycle, you will need to plan, think about security, build, continuously integrate, deploy, operate, get feedback, and start all over again. The process must be a collaborative one since everybody has the same focus—to deliver value to the end user. Together with these principles, you, as a software architect, will need to decide on the best software development process that fits this approach. We discussed these processes in *Chapter 1, Understanding the Importance of Software Architecture*.

Continuous integration (CI)

When you start building enterprise solutions, collaboration is the key to getting things done faster and to meeting the users' needs. Version control systems, as we discussed in *Chapter 4, Best Practices in Coding C#*, are essential for this process, but these tools do not do the job by themselves, especially if they are not well-configured.

As a software architect, you must know that **continuous integration** (**CI**) will help you to have a concrete approach for software development collaboration. When you implement it, as soon as a developer commits their code, the main code is automatically compiled and tested according to the unit and functional tests available in the project.

The good thing when you start using CI is that you can motivate developers to merge their changes as early as possible to minimize conflicts while merging code. This happens because each integration triggers automated builds and tests, allowing conflicts and defects to be identified quickly. They can also share unit tests, which will improve the quality of the software. As a result, teams avoid long-lived branches, reduce merge complexity, and improve software quality through continuous test execution. This will make your main branch stable and safe after every commit from your team.

The key point of CI is the ability to identify problems faster. You will have this opportunity when you allow the code to be tested and analyzed by others. The only thing the DevSecOps approach helps with is making sure this happens consistently and as early as possible.

In summary, CI strengthens collaboration by ensuring that code is continuously integrated, validated, and kept in a stable state. With this foundation in place, the next step is to understand how continuous delivery carries these validated changes forward into the release process.

Continuous delivery (CD)

Once every single commit of your application is built, and this code is tested with both unit tests and functional tests, you may also want to enable **continuous delivery** (CD). Doing this is not just a matter of configuring the tool. As a software architect, you need to be sure that the team and the process are ready to go to this step.

The CD approach needs to guarantee that the production environment will be kept safe in each new deployment. To do so, a multistage pipeline is a great practice to be adopted.

The following screenshot shows an approach with common stages, using this book's use case, WWTravelClub, as a demonstration:

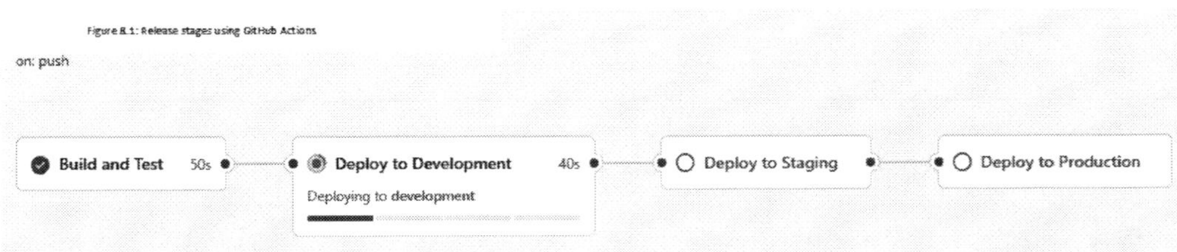

Figure 8.1: Release stages using GitHub Actions

As you can see, these stages were configured using GitHub Actions, which will be explained soon. Each stage has its own purpose, which will affect the quality of the product delivered in the end. Let's look at the stages:

- ***Development:*** This stage is used by developers and testers to build new functionality. This environment will certainly be the one most exposed to bugs and incomplete functions.
- ***Staging:*** This environment gives a preview of new functionalities to areas of the team not related to development and tests. Program managers, marketing, vendors, and others can use it as an area of

study, validation, and even preproduction. Additionally, quality assurance teams can guarantee that the new releases are correctly deployed, considering both functionality and infrastructure.

- ***Production***: This is the stage where customers have their solution running. The goal for a good production environment, according to CD, is to have it updated as quickly as possible. The frequency will vary according to team size, but there are some approaches where this process happens more than once a day.

The adoption of these three stages of deploying your application will positively impact the quality of the solution. It will also enable the team to have a safer deployment process, with fewer risks and better product stability. This approach may look a bit expensive at first sight, since you are maintaining separate environments, automating deployment pipelines, preparing test data, and allocating team time for validation. However, without it, the results of bad deployment will generally be more expensive than this investment. For example, a team may spend additional infrastructure and engineering effort to maintain test and staging environments, but this investment can be far less expensive than resolving a production incident that interrupts users and requires urgent correction.

In summary, continuous delivery creates a safer and more predictable path for moving validated changes toward production. But speed and automation alone are not sufficient, since every stage of this process must also be protected against vulnerabilities, misconfigurations, and supply-chain risks. This is where continuous security becomes essential.

Continuous security (CS)

Now that we have an idea of how useful CI/CD is, it would be nice to think about the risks and challenges you may encounter while implementing it. The goal of this section is to help you, as a software architect, mitigate the risks and find a better way to overcome the challenges using good processes and techniques. Besides that, your role is not only to improve delivery speed, but also to ensure that automation does not introduce security weaknesses, unstable releases, or operational vulnerabilities. For this reason, you must understand that CI/CD provides you with an important opportunity to deliver continuous security to your solution. In this context, CI/CD should be seen as more than a delivery mechanism: it is also an opportunity to apply **continuous security** (**CS**) practices throughout the software lifecycle.

The list of risks and challenges that will be discussed in this section is as follows:

- Unsecure code applied in the repository
- Continuous production deployment
- Incomplete features in production
- Unstable solutions for testing

Taken together, these risks highlight why DevSecOps must address not only delivery speed, but also protection, stability, and release control across the entire pipeline.

Once you have the techniques and the processes defined to deal with them, there is no reason not to use CI/CD.

> **Note**
>
> Remember that DevSecOps does not depend on CI/CD. You can use a process where code integration and software deployment are human-based. However, CI/CD does make DevSecOps work more smoothly.

Now, let us have a look at them.

Insecure code applied in the repository

One of the main risks in a CI/CD scenario is the possibility of insecure code being committed to the repository and then moving quickly through the pipeline. Since CI/CD is designed to accelerate integration, testing, and deployment, any weakness introduced in the codebase may also reach later stages faster if proper controls are not in place. This includes vulnerabilities such as hardcoded secrets, insecure dependencies, weak input validation, broken authentication logic, or incorrect access control rules. For this reason, speed in delivery must always be balanced with security verification.

This risk becomes even more important because modern repositories are not just storage locations for application code. They may also contain infrastructure definitions, pipeline scripts, configuration files, test artifacts, and deployment templates. As a result, insecure code in the repository may compromise not only the application itself, but also the build process, the target environments, and even the credentials used by the delivery pipeline. In a poorly controlled scenario, a single insecure commit may create a chain of problems that affect software integrity, operational stability, and organizational trust.

To mitigate this risk, security must be incorporated directly into the CI/CD process rather than treated as a separate activity performed only at the end. Secure coding standards, peer reviews, branch protection, static application security testing, dependency scanning, secret detection, and policy validation should all be applied as early as possible. From the software architect's perspective, the objective is to ensure that the repository becomes a controlled entry point for trusted changes, so that automation increases delivery efficiency without increasing exposure to vulnerabilities.

Applying continuous production deployment with control

Continuous production deployment is a process where, after a code push and some pipeline steps, the code is deployed to the *production* environment. This is not impossible, but it is hard and expensive to do. Besides, you need to have well-established, sophisticated processes, as well as a team with substantial experience and expertise to enable it. The problem is that most of the demos and samples you will find on the internet presenting CI/CD will show you a fast track to deploying the code. The demonstrations of CI/CD make it look very simple, with a few clicks and voilà! This *simplicity* might suggest that you should implement it as soon as possible. However, direct deployment into production can be dangerous. In a solution that needs to be available 24 hours a day, 7 days a week, this is impractical without many process controls. So, you will need to worry about that and think of different solutions.

The first one is the use of a *multi-stage scenario*, as we described before. The multi-stage scenario can bring more security to the ecosystem of the deployment you are building. In *Figure 8.2*, we can see that GitHub gives us the option to determine different deployment environments just for that. Besides, you will get more options to avoid incorrect deployments into production, such as pre-deployment approvals.

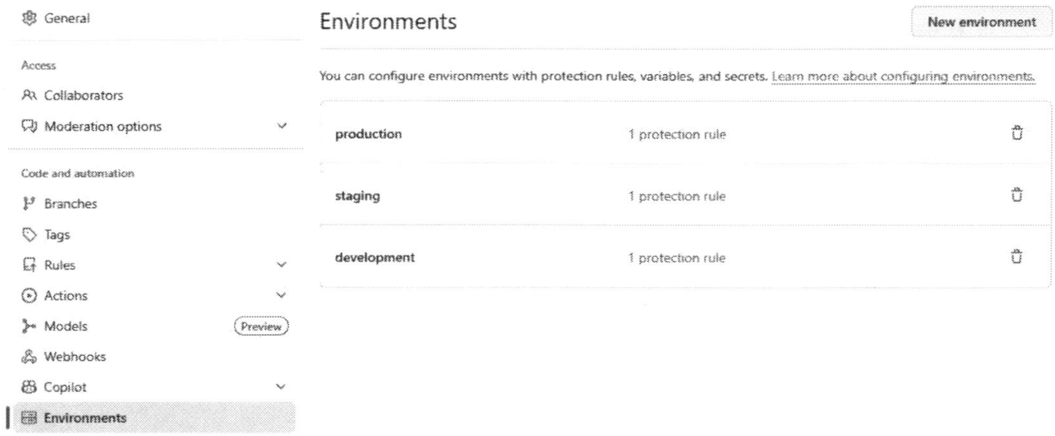

Figure 8.2: Setting multi-staged environments using GitHub

You can build a deployment pipeline where all your code and software structure will be updated by this tool. However, if you have something outside of this scenario, such as database scripts and environment configurations, an incorrect publication into production may cause damage to end users. Besides, the decision of when the production environment will be updated needs to be planned, and in many scenarios, all platform users need to be notified of the upcoming change. That is why we have the possibility to define when the deployment will happen, as we can see in *Figure 8.3*. It is worth mentioning that, in these hard-to-decide cases, it is a good idea to use a *change management* procedure, based *on ITIL (The Information Technology Infrastructure Library)* or ISO 20000.

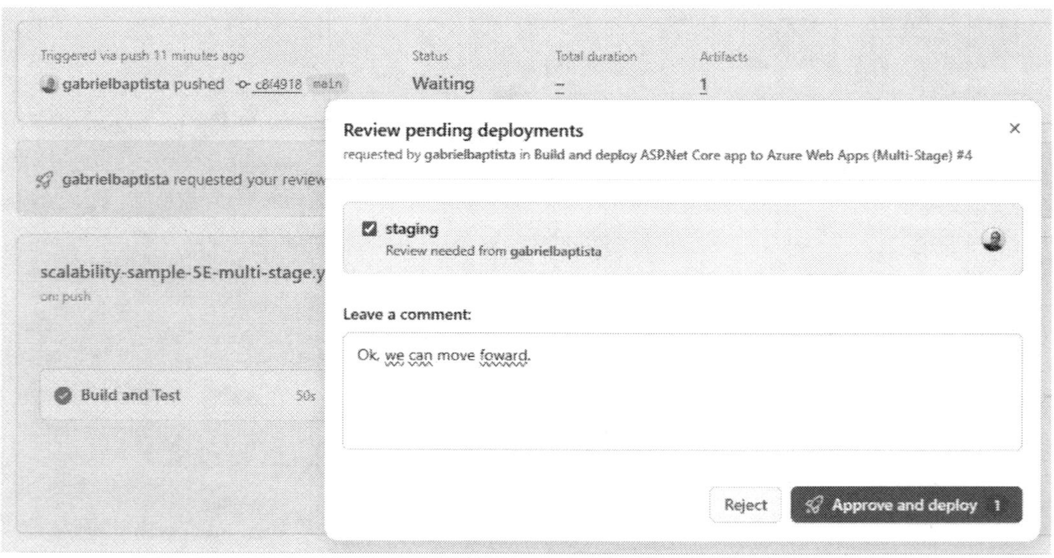

Figure 8.3: Manual approval of deployment

So, the challenge of delivering code to production will make you think about a schedule to do so. It does not matter if your cycle is monthly, daily, or even at each commit. The key point here is that you need to create a process and a pipeline that guarantees that only good and approved software reaches the production stage. It is worth noting, however, that the longer you leave deployments, the scarier they are, because the deviation between the previously deployed version and the new one will be greater, and more changes will be pushed out in one go. The more frequently you can manage this, the better.

Incomplete features

While a developer of your team is creating a new feature or fixing a bug, you will probably consider generating a branch, which means they can avoid the use of the branch designed for CD. A branch can be considered a feature available in code repositories to enable the creation of an independent line of development, since it isolates the code.

As you can see from the following screenshot, creating a branch for WWTravelClub using Visual Studio is quite simple. You just need to go to the **Git Changes** window and click on **New Branch**:

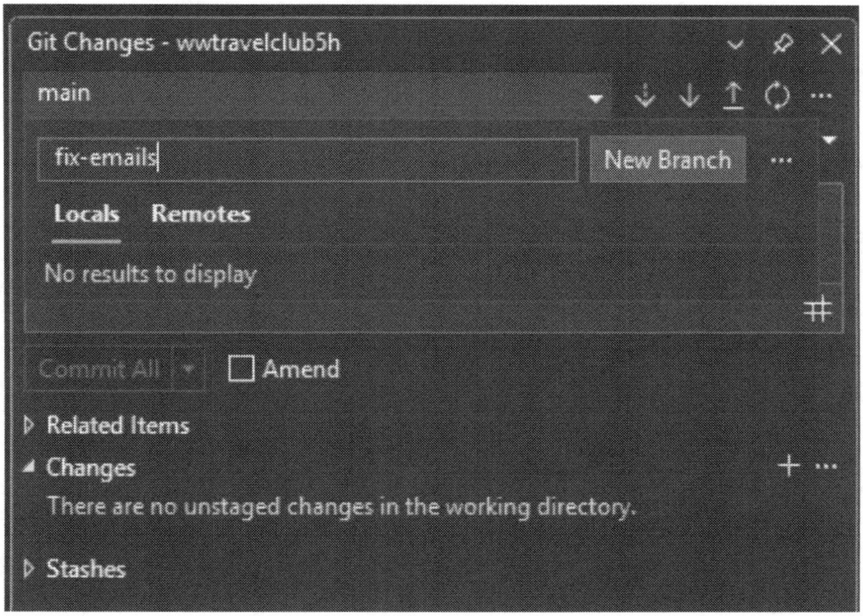

Figure 8.4: Creating a branch in Visual Studio

This seems to be a good approach, but let us suppose that the developer has considered the implementation ready for deployment and has just merged the code into the main branch, although this is also considered bad practice. What if this feature is not ready yet, just because a requirement was omitted? What if the bug has caused incorrect behavior? The result could be a release with an incomplete feature or an incorrect fix.

One of the good practices to avoid broken features and even incorrect fixes in the main branch is the use of **Pull Requests** (PRs). PRs will let other team developers know that the code you developed is ready to be merged. It signals that a change is ready for review and creates an opportunity for other developers to validate the implementation before it is merged. The following screenshot shows how you can use GitHub to **create a pull request** for a change you have made.

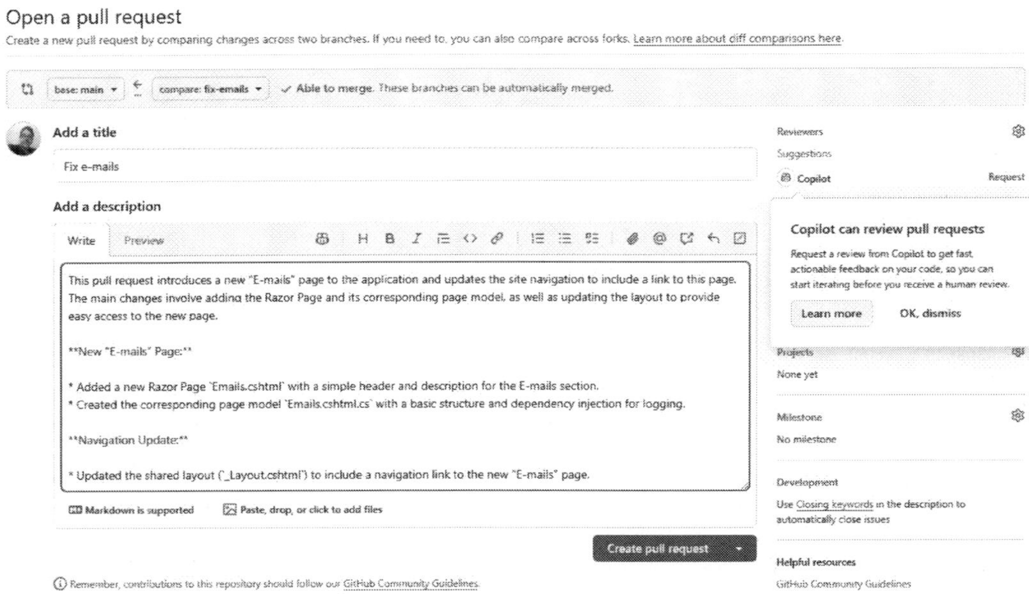

Figure 8.5: Creating a PR

Using GitHub Copilot, it is possible to have the comments from PRs automatically and with a great level of accuracy.

Once the PR is created and the reviewers are defined, each reviewer will be able to analyze the code and decide whether this code is healthy enough to be in the main branch. You can also add GitHub Copilot to evaluate the PR created.

The following screenshot shows the result of the test made by GitHub Copilot for the PR proposed in the WWTravelClub code. It is worth noting that developers keep making the final decision about what to do with the PR.

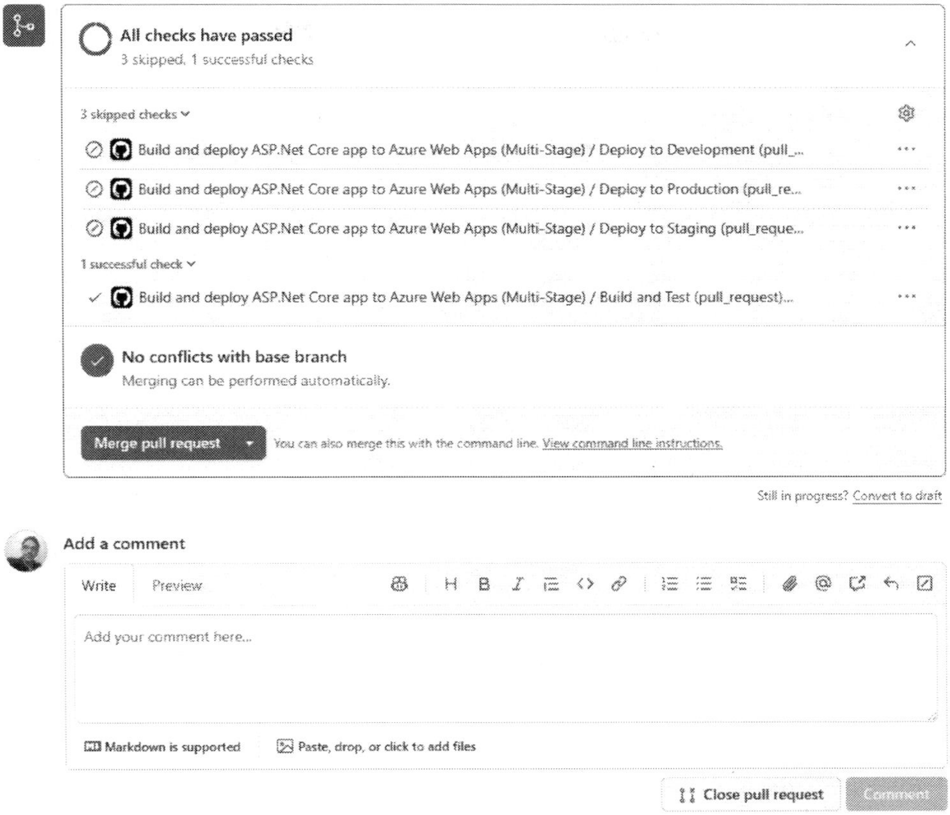

Figure 8.6: Analyzing the PR

Once all approvals are done, you will be able to safely merge the code to the main branch, as you can see in the following screenshot. To merge the code, you will need to click on *Confirm merge*. If the CI trigger is enabled in the WWTravelClub Action, as we will show in this chapter, GitHub will start a build pipeline. It is also important to delete the branches after they are merged.

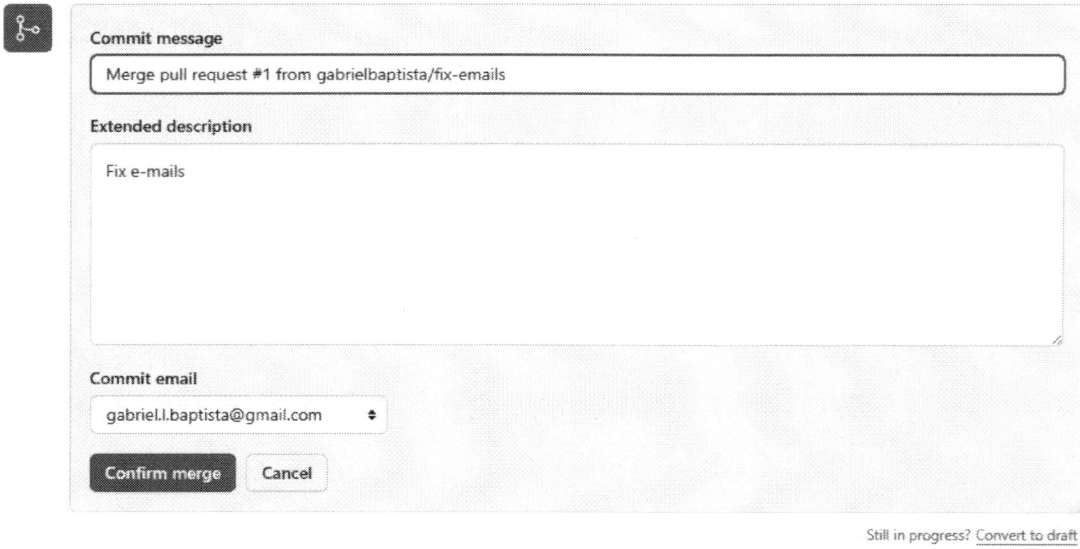

Figure 8.7: Merging the PR

Without a process like this, there is a great chance of having a main branch with a lot of bad code, where this code being deployed, may cause damage together with CD. Code review is an excellent practice in CI/CD scenarios, and it is considered a wonderful practice for creating good quality software in general. Besides that, you may also run static analysis tools, like the ones we have presented in *Chapter 4*, *Best Practices in Coding C#,* to guarantee both *Quality* and *Security*.

After controlling what code can be merged, the next concern is controlling what functionality can be exposed to users. This is another important challenge that you need to focus on here, guaranteeing that only entire features will appear to your end users. You may use the **feature flag** principle to solve this, which is a technique that makes sure only features that are ready are presented to end users.

Feature Flags are runtime controls that enable or disable specific functionality without requiring a new deployment. This allows code to be merged and deployed while keeping incomplete features hidden until they are ready. In this sense, pull requests, that we have discussed before, and feature flags serve different purposes: pull requests help control code quality during CI, while feature flags help control feature availability during CD and production release. Used together, they reduce the risk of both unstable integrations and premature feature exposure.

In the **Feature Flag** or **Feature Toggle** technique, you must create a solution that has in each feature the possibility of testing in a setup to see if it is enabled or not. According to this, all the functionalities will be presented to the user.

Note

It is worth mentioning that for controlling feature availability in an environment, feature flags are much safer than using exclusively branching/PRs. Both have their place, but branching and PRs control code quality before merge, whereas feature flags are for controlling feature availability at the CD stage.

Again, we are not talking about CI/CD as a *tool*, but as a *process* to be defined and used every single time you need to deliver code for production.

An unstable solution for testing

If you have already mitigated the two other risks presented in this section, you may find it uncommon to have bad code after CI/CD. It is true that the worries presented earlier will certainly be lessened if you are working with a multi-stage scenario and PRs before pushing to the final stage. But the risk of having unstable code, especially when it comes to business logic rules, remains even if you apply all the recommendations we have discussed earlier.

But is there a way to accelerate the evaluation of a release while being sure that this new release is ready for your stakeholders' tests? Yes, there is! Technically, the way you can do so is by automating testing in both unit and functional aspects.

Unit tests verify small, isolated parts of the software, such as methods or classes, to ensure they behave correctly under specific conditions. On the other hand, functional tests validate whether complete features work as expected from the user or business perspective, usually by exercising larger parts of the system together. These techniques will be explained in more detail in *Chapter 9*, *Testing Your Enterprise Application*.

However, it is good to say that it is impractical to automate every single part of the software, considering the efforts needed to do so. Besides, the maintenance of automation can be more expensive in scenarios where the user interface or the business rules change a lot. Although this is a tough decision, as a software architect, you must always incentivize the usage of automated testing.

To exemplify it, let us have a look at the following screenshot, which shows the unit and functional test samples for WWTravelClub, created by GitHub Copilot Coding Agent. Both projects make use of xUnit.net libraries. xUnit.net is a free, open source, community-focused unit testing tool for .NET. It supports .NET 8.0 or later, and .NET Framework 4.7.2 or later.

Note

You can check more details about xUnit.net at `https://xunit.net/`.

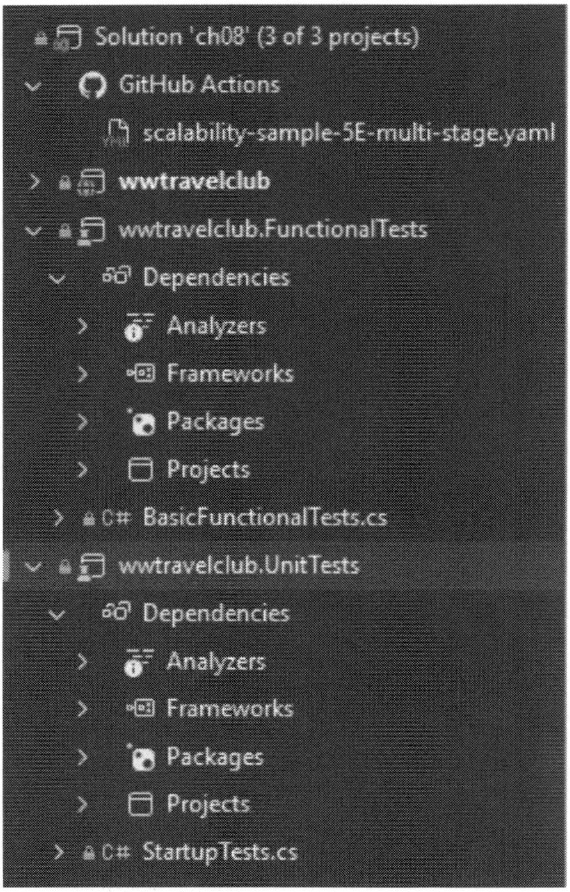

Figure 8.8: Unit and functional test projects

There are some architectural patterns, such as SOLID, presented in *Chapter 6, Design Patterns and .NET Implementation*, and quality assurance approaches, such as peer review, that will give you better results than manual software testing. However, these approaches do not invalidate automation practice, especially considering the power of AI that we have today for creating testing scenarios. The truth is that all of them will be useful for getting a stable solution, especially when you are running a CI scenario. In this environment, the best thing you can do is to detect errors and incorrect behaviors as fast as you can. Both unit and functional tests, as shown earlier, will help you with this.

Unit tests will help you a lot in discovering business logic errors before deployment, during the build pipeline. For instance, in the following screenshot from the WWTravelClub build process, you will find a simulated error that canceled the build since the unit test did not pass.

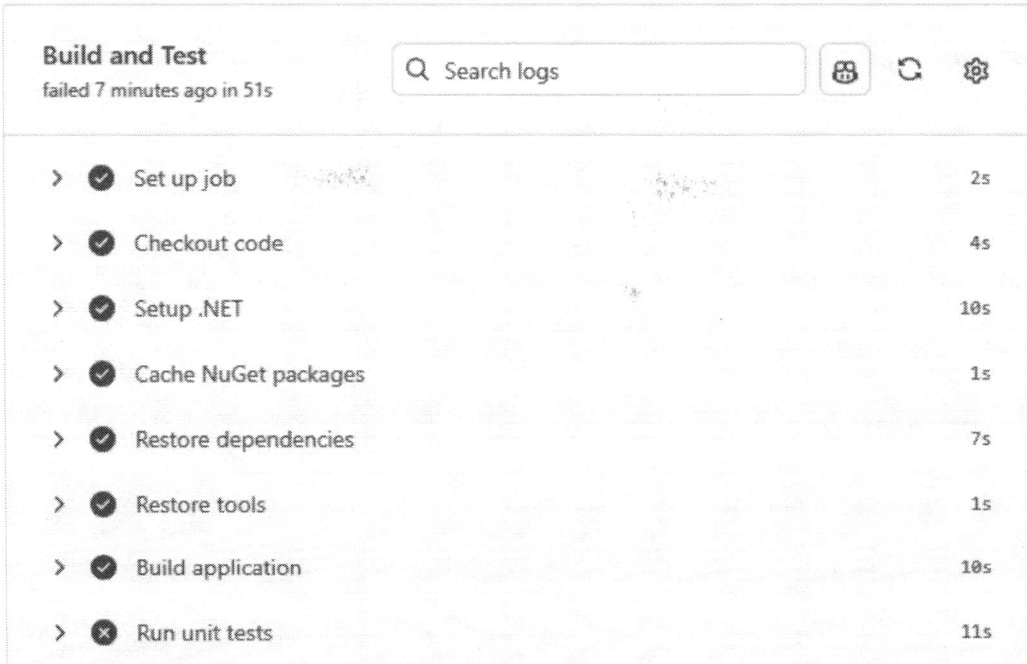

Figure 8.9: Unit test results

The way to get this error is quite simple. You need to code something that does not respond according to what the unit tests are checking. Once you commit it, considering you have the trigger of continuous deployment on, you will have the code building in the pipeline. So, after building the code, the unit tests will run. If the code does not match the tests anymore, you will get an error.

The following screenshot shows an error during the functional tests in the *Development* stage of the WWTravelClub project. At this moment, the *Development* environment has a bug that was rapidly detected by functional tests.

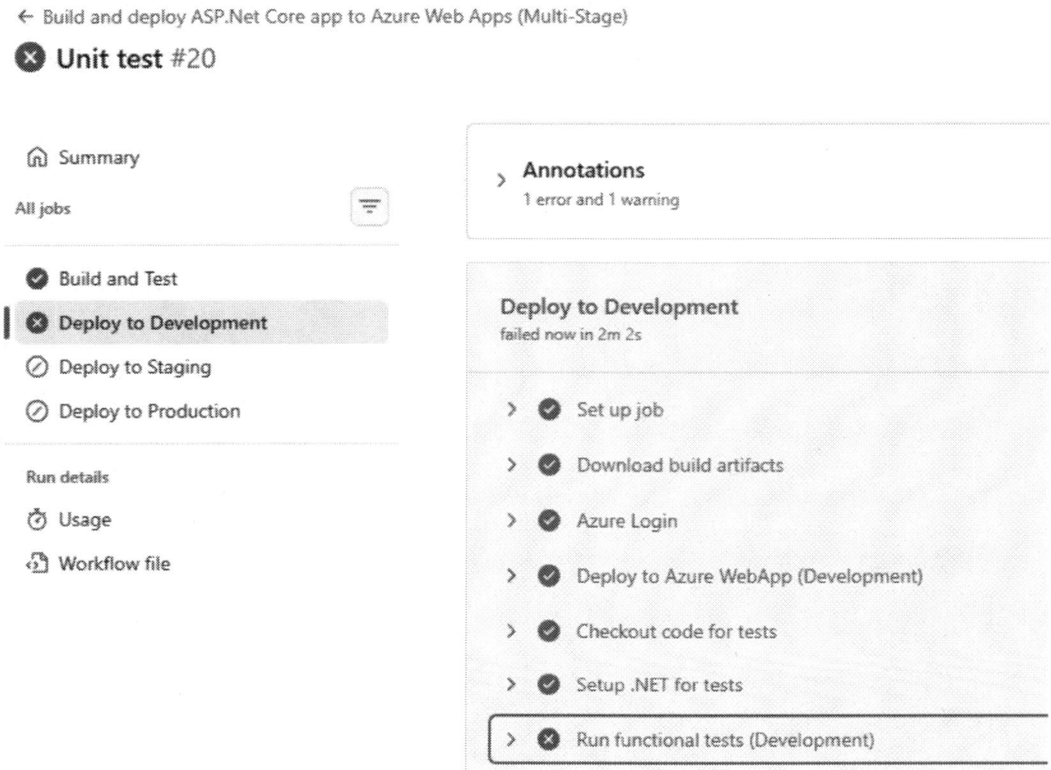

Figure 8.10: Functional tests result

But this is not the only good thing about applying functional tests during CI/CD. Let us look at the following screenshot from the GitHub Actions interface. If you look at this execution, you will realize that all the environments have received this version, since there was the approval of each stage, which guarantees the process will protect other stages from deploying something wrong, especially the WWTravelClub production stage.

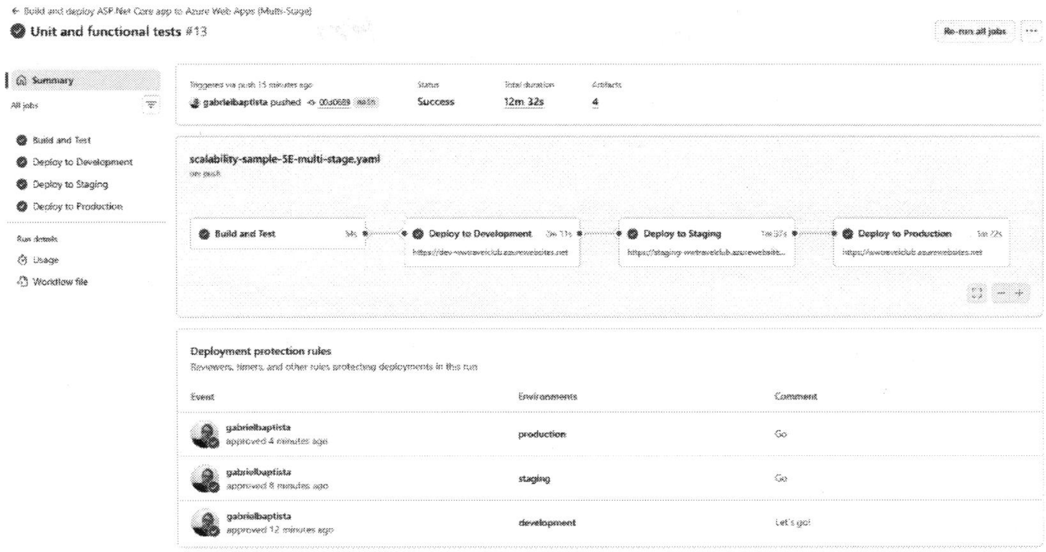

Figure 8.11: Multi-stage environment protection

The key point for success in the CI/CD process is to think about it as a useful tool for accelerating the delivery of software, and not to forget that a team always needs to deliver value to its end users. As we have checked previously, practices such as frequent integration, pull requests, automated validation, and controlled feature exposure, with continuous monitoring of security aspects, work together to reduce integration problems, improve code reliability, and prevent incomplete or unstable changes from reaching users too early.

In summary, the combination of automated tests, staged validation, and controlled approvals helps teams detect problems earlier and deliver changes with greater confidence. When applied delivering value, these techniques help the team build a more stable, predictable, secure, and trustworthy delivery process. This also creates a natural connection to the next topic, where continuous feedback and monitoring will extend these same principles into the operational life of the solution. With this approach, the techniques presented earlier will provide incredible ways to achieve the results that your team aims for.

Continuous feedback (CF)

Once you have a solution that is running perfectly in the deployment scenario described in the last section, feedback will be essential for your team to understand the results of the release and how the version works for the customers. There are some tools that can help both developers and customers, bringing them together to fast-track the feedback process.

The main purpose of **Continuous feedback** (CF) is to enable developers to get information about the application running in production, so that the team can improve the infrastructure of the deployed environment and, at the same time, detect improvements that can be made in the source code and user interface.

In DevSecOps, **Continuous Feedback** closes the loop between delivery and improvement. It helps teams verify whether deployments were successful, whether security and stability were preserved, and whether users are receiving the expected value. Without this feedback loop, teams may deliver quickly, but they will not learn effectively from production.

To support Continuous Feedback, organizations need monitoring tools, logging, tracing, dashboards, alerts, usage analytics, and channels for collecting customer input. However, tools alone are not enough. Teams also need processes to interpret this information, prioritize improvements, and transform operational findings into better architectural, technical, and business decisions.

It is Continuous Feedback that will truly make DevSecOps work, since the feedback results will help operations get the best outcome for the solution delivered, so it should be treated as a core DevSecOps principle.

In summary, Continuous Feedback ensures that delivery does not end at deployment, but continues through observation, learning, and improvement in production. With this principle established, the next section will present the tools that help teams put DevSecOps into practice more effectively.

Tools to facilitate DevSecOps implementation

There are many tools that can be used to help you with DevSecOps implementation. The following topics will present some of the most-used ones in the Microsoft environment.

Azure DevOps

As soon as you start working with a platform such as **Azure DevOps**, enabling CI/CD will be easy when it comes to clicking on the options for doing so. So, technology is not the Achilles' heel for implementing this process.

CI/CD will help you solve some problems. For instance, it will force you to test your code, since you will need to commit the changes faster, so other developers can make use of the code you are programming.

On the other hand, you will not do CI/CD just by enabling a CI build in Azure DevOps. For sure, you will turn on the possibility of starting a build as soon as you get a commit done and the code is done, but this is far from saying you have CI/CD available in your solution.

The reason you as a software architect need to worry a bit more about it is related to a real understanding of what DevSecOps is. The need to deliver value to the end user will always be a good way to decide how the development life cycle will work. So, even if turning on CI/CD is easy, what is the real business impact of this feature being enabled for your end users? Once you have all the answers to this question and you know how to reduce the risks of its implementation, then you will be able to say that you have a CI/CD process implemented.

CI/CD is a principle that will make DevSecOps work better and faster. However, as we have already discussed, DevSecOps can live without a CI/CD process if you are not sure if your team is mature enough to enable code to be continuously delivered.

More than that, if you turn on CI/CD in a team that is not mature enough to deal with its complexity, you will probably cause a bad understanding of DevSecOps, since you will start incurring some risks while deploying your solution. The point is, CI/CD is not a prerequisite for DevSecOps. When you have CI/CD enabled, you can make things faster in DevSecOps. However, you can practice DevSecOps without it.

Deployments and other release-related activities can be managed through **Release Pipelines**, which are responsible for moving already built artifacts into target environments in a controlled and traceable way. The reason they are separated from **Build Pipelines** is that generating an artifact and releasing it are different stages of the delivery process. A build pipeline is concerned with compiling code, running tests, and producing a deployable package, while a release pipeline is concerned with approvals, environment configuration, deployment sequencing, and production governance.

This separation becomes useful when organizations need clearer control over who can deploy, when a deployment can happen, and what checks must be completed before promotion to the next environment. In Azure DevOps, classic Release Pipelines are typically configured through a graphical interface rather than through direct YAML authoring.

GitHub

Since GitHub's acquisition by Microsoft, many features have evolved and new options have been delivered, enhancing the power of this powerful tool. That is the reason why, different from the last editions of this book, we have decided to present this new chapter using GitHub as a basis instead of Azure DevOps. These integrations can be explored using the Azure portal and particularly, using GitHub Actions.

We chose **GitHub** as the basis for this chapter because it combines source control, pull request collaboration, and CI/CD automation in a single platform, making the connection between code changes, review, and delivery easier to understand. GitHub Actions also provides a practical way to demonstrate workflow automation using YAML-based pipelines that integrate naturally with Azure services. For these reasons, GitHub offers a more accessible and cohesive teaching vehicle for the concepts discussed in this chapter than using Azure DevOps alone.

GitHub Actions is a set of tools that helps with the automation of software development. It enables a fast CI/CD service on any platform, using YAML files to define its workflows. You can consider GitHub Actions a new approach presented by Microsoft as an alternative to Azure DevOps Pipelines. You can automate any GitHub event using GitHub Actions, with thousands of actions available on GitHub Marketplace.

> **Note**
>
> Microsoft provides documentation specifically covering Azure and GitHub integration. Check this out at `https://docs.microsoft.com/en-us/azure/developer/github`.

As a software architect, you need to understand which tool best fits your development team. Azure DevOps has a wonderful environment for enabling CI/CD, and so does GitHub. The key point here is that no matter the option you decide upon, there are risks and challenges that you will face once CI/CD is enabled. Let's check them out in the next topic.

Application insights

Application Insights is a feature that any software architect must have for continuous feedback on their solution. Application Insights is part of *Azure Monitor*, a wider suite of monitoring features that also includes alerting, dashboards, and workbooks. As soon as you connect your app to it, you start receiving feedback on each request made to the software. This enables you to monitor not only the requests made but also your database performance, the errors that the application may be suffering from, and the calls that take the most time to process.

Obviously, you will have costs relating to having this tool plugged into your environment, but the facilities that the tool provides will be worth it. It might be worth noting that, for simple applications, it could even be free because you pay for data ingested, for which there is a free quota. Aside from financial cost, you need to understand that there is a very small performance cost since all the requests to store data in *Application Insights* run in a separate thread.

Note

Several services, such as App Services, Functions, and so on, offer an option to add Application Insights as part of the initial creation process, so you may have already created it while following through this book.

The following screenshot shows how easily you can create this resource in your environment:

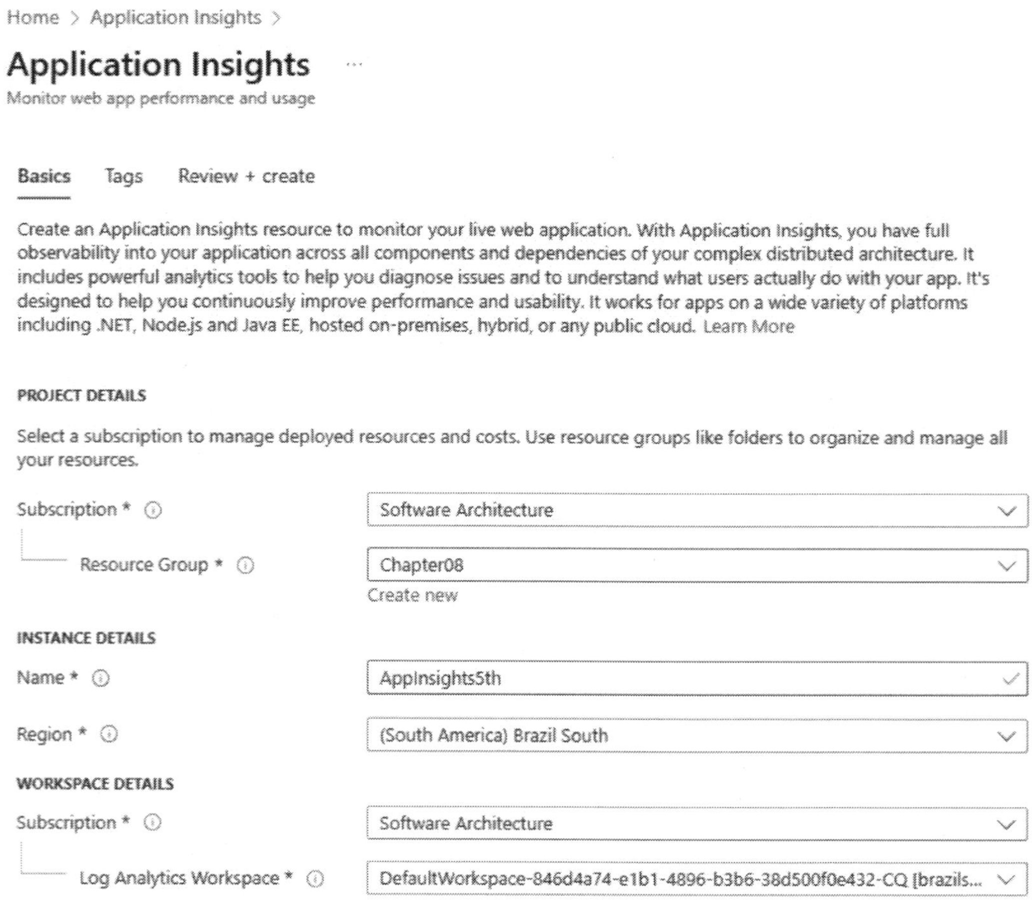

Figure 8.12: Creating Application Insights resources in Azure

Note

If you want to set up Application Insights in your app using Visual Studio, you may find this Microsoft tutorial useful: `https://docs.microsoft.com/en-us/azure/azure-monitor/learn/dotnetcore-quick-start#configure-app-insights-sdk`.

For instance, let's suppose you need to analyze the requests that are taking more time in your application. The process of attaching Application Insights to your web app is quite simple: it can be done as soon as you set it up. If you are not sure whether Application Insights is configured for your web app, you can find out using the Azure portal. Navigate to **App Services** and look at the **Application Insights** settings, as shown in the following screenshot:

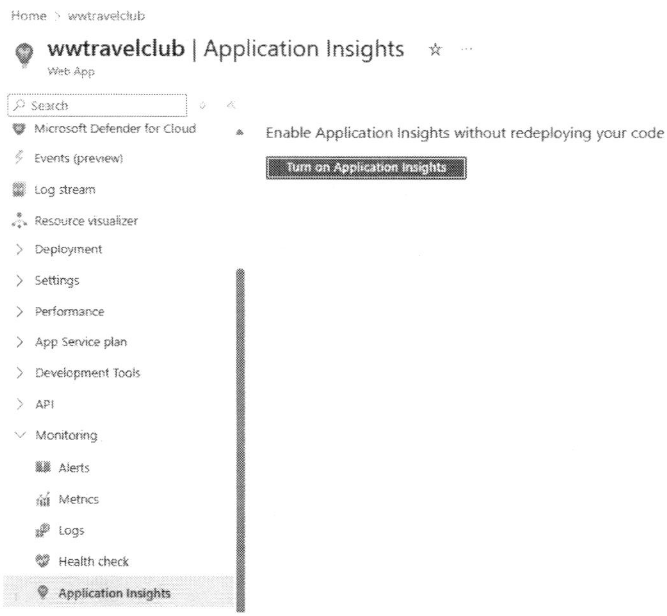

Figure 8.13: Enabling Application Insights in App Services

The interface will give you the opportunity to create or attach an already-created monitor service to your web app. You can connect more than one web app to the same Application Insights component. Once you have Application Insights configured for your web app, you will find the following screen in App Services.

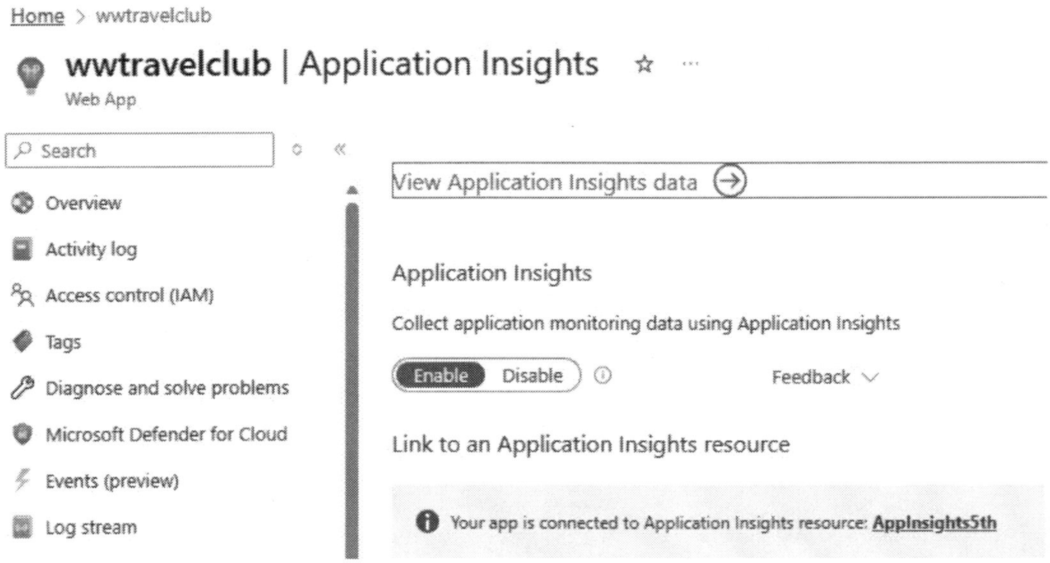

Figure 8.14: App Insights in App Services

Once it is connected to your solution, the data collection will happen continuously, and you will see the results in the dashboard provided by the component. You can find this screen in two places:

- At the same place where you configured Application Insights, inside the web app portal
- In the Azure portal, after navigating through the Application Insights resource, we can check in *Figure 8.15*

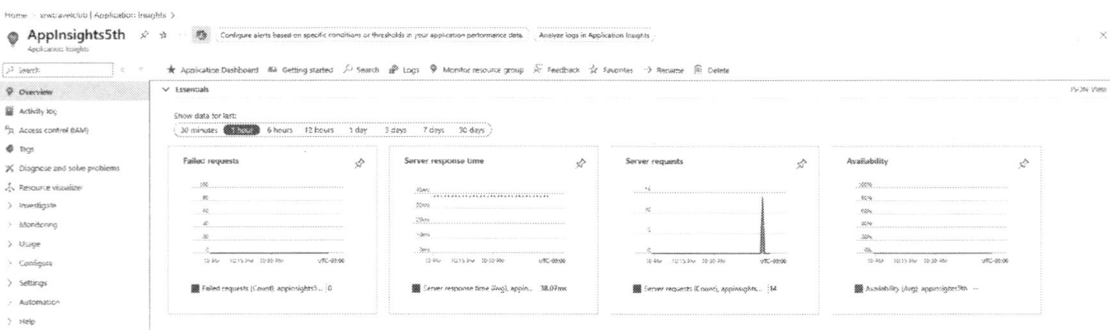

Figure 8.15: Application Insights in action

This dashboard gives you an idea of failed requests, server response time, and server requests. You can also turn on the availability check, which will make requests to your selected URL from any of the Azure data centers.

The beauty of Application Insights lies in how deeply it analyzes your system. In *Figure 8.16*, for example, it shows the number of website requests and allows them to be ranked by processing time or frequency. For DevSecOps, this is particularly valuable because it also highlights failed requests, exceptions, dependency issues, end-to-end transaction behavior, availability test results, and anomaly-based alerts. As a result, teams can use it not only for performance analysis, but also for early detection of instability, incident investigation, and identification of abnormal behavior that may indicate resilience or security concerns.

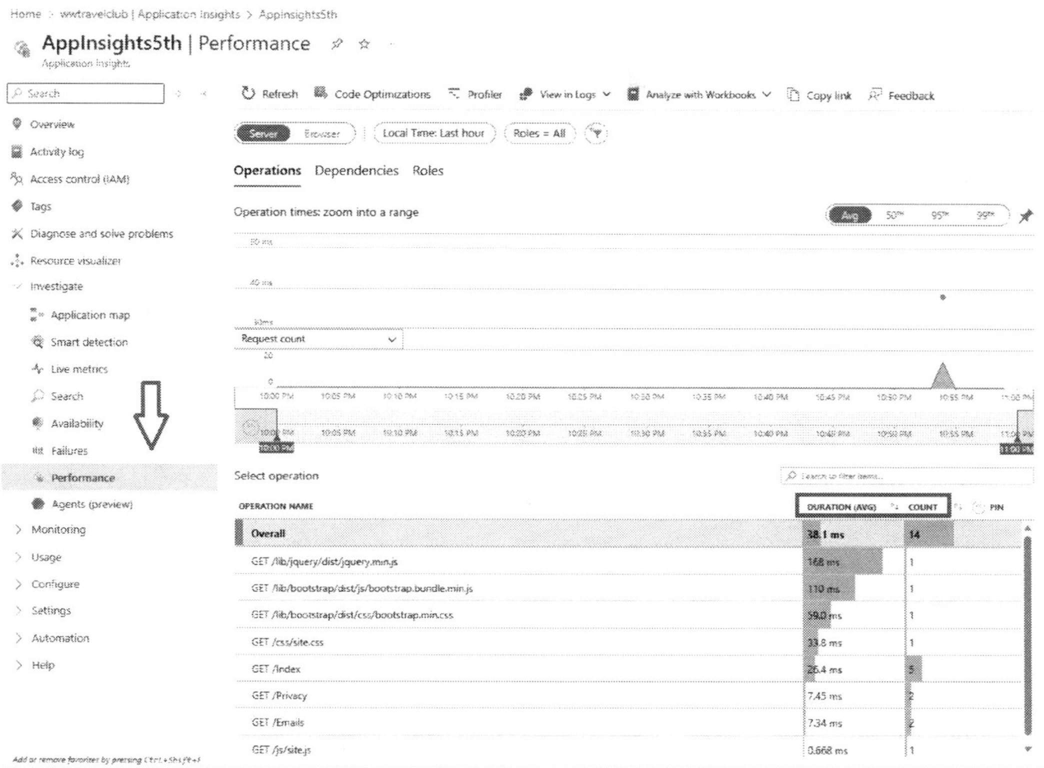

Figure 8.16: Analyzing app performance using Application Insights

Considering that this view can be filtered in different ways and that you receive the information just after it happens in your web app, this is certainly a tool that defines continuous feedback. Real-time feedback allows developers and operators to verify application behavior, identify incidents early, and adjust their response based on actual production evidence. This is one of the best ways you can use DevSecOps principles to achieve exactly what your customer needs.

In summary, Application Insights shows how continuous feedback can be transformed into practical operational and architectural improvement. With this example in mind, we can now close the chapter by reinforcing how DevSecOps principles work together to support secure, reliable, and continuously improving software delivery.

Summary

In this chapter, we have learned that DevSecOps is not only a bunch of techniques and tools used together to deliver software continuously, but a philosophy to enable continuous delivery of value to the end user of the project you are developing, using a structured set of techniques to achieve this goal.

Considering this approach, we saw how CI/CD and continuous feedback are essential to the purpose of DevSecOps. We also saw how Azure, Azure, DevOps, GitHub, and other Microsoft tools help you to achieve your goals.

The chapter has also covered the importance of understanding when you can enable CI/CD in the software development life cycle, considering the risks, and challenges you will take as a software architect, and the security aspects you will need to deal with, once you decide to use it for your solution.

Additionally, the chapter introduced some solutions and concepts that can make this process easier, such as multi-stage environments, PR reviews, feature flags, peer reviews, and automated tests. Understanding these techniques and processes will enable you to guide your project toward safer behavior when it comes to CI/CD in a DevSecOps scenario.

We have also described *service design thinking* principles. Now, you should be able to analyze all the implications of these approaches for an organization, and you should be able to adapt pre-existing software development processes and hardware/software architectures to take advantage of the opportunities they offer.

We also explained the need for, and the techniques involved in, the automation of the software cycle, cloud hardware infrastructure configuration, and application deployment.

Once you have implemented the examples shown, you should be able to use GitHub Actions to automate infrastructure configuration and application deployment. This chapter elucidated this approach using WWTravelClub as an example, enabling CI/CD inside GitHub, and using Application Insights, Unit, and Functional Tests for both technical and functional feedback. In real life, these tools will enable you to understand the current behavior of the system you are developing more quickly, as you will have continuous feedback on it.

In the next chapter, we will see how automation for software testing works.

Questions

1. What is DevSecOps?
2. What is continuous integration (CI)?
3. What is continuous delivery (CD)?
4. What is continuous security (CS)?
5. What is continuous feedback (CF)?
6. Can you have DevSecOps without CI/CD?
7. What are the risks of enabling CI/CD in a non-mature team?
8. How can a multi-stage environment help CI/CD?
9. How can automated tests help CI/CD?
10. How can PRs help CI/CD?
11. Do PRs only work with CI/CD?
12. What is the main purpose of Application Insights in the DevSecOps approach?

13. What is the main goal of service design thinking? When would you choose not to enable continuous production deployment?
14. How would you assess whether your team is ready for CI/CD?

9

Testing Your Enterprise Application

When developing enterprise-level software, it is essential to ensure that an application is as bug-free as possible and that it satisfies all requirements. This can be done by testing all the modules while they are being developed or when the overall application has been either completely or partially implemented.

While most of the key concepts covered by this chapter apply to a wide range of applications and environments, this chapter focuses on essential testing strategies for enterprise-level applications in C# and .NET environments.

Performing all the tests manually is not a feasible option since most of the tests must be executed each time the application is modified, and as explained throughout this book, modern software is being continuously modified to adapt applications to the needs of a fast-changing market. Therefore, automated tests have become indispensable in today's fast-paced environment of continuous development.

This chapter discusses the most common types of tests needed to deliver reliable software and how to organize and automate them. More specifically, this chapter covers the following topics:

- Understanding how to organize tests and the concepts of unit and integration tests, which are the main tools to ensure software reliability and stability.
- Understanding the basics of **Test-Driven Development** (TDD) and how and why it can dramatically reduce the probability of undiscovered bugs
- Functional tests, which are the main tool for enforcing software specifications. As a particular case, we will also analyze modern Behavior Driven Development.
- Defining C# test-specific projects in Visual Studio to take full advantage of the testing tools available in the .NET ecosystem
- Automating functional tests in C#.

At the end of this chapter, you will be able to design an effective testing strategy and apply the techniques learned in the chapter to build robust and reliable enterprise applications that conform to their requirements.

Technical requirements

This chapter requires the Visual Studio 2026 free Community Edition or better, with all database tools installed. The code for this chapter is available at `https://github.com/PacktPublishing/Software-Architecture-with-.NET-10-and-C-sharp-5E`.

Understanding test organization

Testing verifies both that the software is bug free and that it conforms with the agreed specification. Delaying application testing after most of its functionalities have been implemented must be avoided for the following reasons:

- If a class or module has been incorrectly designed or implemented, it might have already influenced the way other modules were implemented. Therefore, at this point, fixing the problem might have a very high cost.
- The possible combination of input that is needed to test all possible paths that execution can take grows exponentially with the number of modules or classes that are tested together. Thus, for instance, if the execution of a class method `A` can take three different paths, while the execution of another method `B` can take four paths, then testing `A` and `B` together would require 3 x 4 different inputs. In general, if we test several modules together, the total number of paths to test is the product of the number of paths to test in each module. If modules are tested separately, instead, the number of inputs required is just the sum of the paths needed to test each module. That's why the so-called **unit tests** verify each class method separately in an exhaustive way as soon as each class is designed. After that, the overall behavior correctness can be verified with an acceptably small number of the so-called **integration tests**, because *integration tests* just need to verify the various classes interaction patterns without analyzing all methods execution paths.
- If a test of an aggregate made of *N* modules fails, then locating the origin of the bug among the *N* modules is usually a very time-consuming activity.
- When *N* modules are tested together, we have to redefine all tests involving the *N* modules, even if just one of the *N* modules changes during the application's lifecycle.

These considerations show that we both need to test each class method separately as soon as possible, but that we also need to test correct module integration.

That is why tests are organized into three stages:

- **Unit tests**: These verify that all or almost all execution paths of each method behave properly. They should be free from external dependencies, such as storage and databases, and should be quite complete; that is, they should cover most of possible paths. This is usually feasible at an acceptable time-cost because there are not too many possible execution paths for each method as compared to the possible execution paths of the whole application.
- **Integration tests**: These are executed once the software passes all its unit tests. Integration tests verify that all modules interact properly to get the expected results. Integration tests do not need to be complete since unit tests will have already verified that all execution paths of each module work

properly. They need to verify as many as possible patterns of interaction, that is, as many as possible the possible ways in which the various modules may cooperate.

- **Acceptance tests**: These are executed at the end of each sprint and/or before releasing the application. They verify that the output of a sprint or the final application satisfies both functional and non-functional requirements. Tests that verify functional requirements are called **functional tests**, while tests that verify performance requirements are called **performance tests**.

The combined application of the three above testing strategies ensures that each module is bug-free, that all modules interact properly, and the application conforms to its specifications. As new bugs are discovered and fixed new tests are added that avoid the solved bugs might reappear. The more the test base is tuned and refined, the more the application stability increases. and the probability that new bugs might occur during the application lifetime and maintenance decreases.

Usually, each interaction pattern has more than one test associated with it: a typical activation of a pattern and some extreme cases of activation. For instance, if a whole pattern of interaction receives an array as input, we will write a test for the typical size of the array, a test with a `null` array, a test with an empty array, and a test with a very big array. This way, we verify that the way the single module was designed is compatible with the needs of the whole interaction pattern. It is worth pointing out that, in our array example, `null`, `0`, `1`, and `many` are equivalence classes that represent in an efficacious way the whole universe of array values.

With the preceding strategy in place, if we modify a single module without changing its public interface, we need to change just the unit tests for that module.

If, instead, the change involves the way some modules interact, then we also have to add new integration tests or modify existing ones. However, usually, this is not a big problem since most of the tests are unit tests, so rewriting a large percentage of all integration tests does not require too much effort. Moreover, if the application was designed according to the *Single Responsibility, Open/Closed, Liskov Substitution, Interface Segregation, and Dependency Inversion SOLID principles, the number of integration tests* that must be changed after a single code modification should be small since the modification should affect just a few classes that interact directly with the modified method or class.

Since tests must be executed each time code changes, it is essential to automate their execution and results presentation. We will analyze this topic in detail in the next subsections.

Automating unit and integration tests

At this point, it should be clear that both unit tests and integration tests must be reused during the entire lifetime of the software. That is why it is worth automating them. The automation of unit and integration tests avoids possible errors of manual test execution and saves time. Reuse of previous tests enables the creation of robust batteries of several thousand automated tests that can verify software integrity following each small modification in a few minutes. In turn, this contains the effect of each software change and helps keep the reliability of the codebase between changes.

> **Note**
>
> As new bugs are found, new tests are added to detect them so that they cannot reappear in future versions of the software. This way, automated tests always become more reliable and protect the software more from bugs introduced as a result of new changes. Thus, the probability of adding new bugs (that are not immediately discovered) is greatly reduced.

The next subsection will give us the basics for organizing and designing automated unit and integration tests, as well as practical details on how to write a test in C# in the *Defining C# test projects in the Visual Studio* section.

Writing automated unit and integration tests

Tests are not written from scratch; all software development platforms have tools that help us to both write tests and launch them (or some of them). Once the selected tests have been executed, these tools usually show a report and give the possibility to debug the code of all failed tests.

More specifically, by and large, all unit and integration test frameworks are composed of three important parts:

1. ***Facilities for defining all tests***: They verify whether the actual results correspond to the expected results. Usually, tests are organized into test classes, where each test class tests either a single application class or a single class method. Each test is split into three stages:
    1. **Test preparation (*Arrange*)**: The general environment needed by one or several tests is prepared. In this stage, we prepare the data to inject into class constructors and simulations of database tables, but we don't prepare the individual inputs for each of the methods we're going to test. Usually, the same preparation procedure is used in several tests, so test preparations are factored out into dedicated modules.
    2. **Test execution (*Act/Assert*)**: The methods to test are invoked with adequate input (*Act*), and all results of their executions are compared with expected results (*Assert*) with constructs such as `Assert.Equal(x,y)` and `Assert.NotNull(x)`.
    3. **Tear-down**: The whole environment is cleaned up to avoid the execution of a test influencing other tests. This step is the converse of step 1. This is just the best way to organize tests, so all testing frameworks conform to it.
2. ***Mock facilities***: In unit tests, the use of other application classes should be avoided because their purpose is to test each isolated method.
    1. Suppose a class under test, say, `A`, uses a method of another application class, `B`, that is injected into its constructor in one of its methods, `M`. In a similar situation, the test of the method `M` should use a mock implementation of `B`, say `B'`, that the test should inject in the constructor of `A` as a replacement for an actual instance of `B`.
    2. Mock frameworks contain facilities to define mock implementations of interfaces and interface methods that return data that can be defined by the test designer. Typically, mock implementations are also able to report information on all mock method calls. Such mock

implementations do not require the definition of actual class files but are done online in the test code by calling methods such as `new Mock<IMyInterface>()`.

3. It is worth pointing out that only classes that do some processing must be replaced by mock implementations, while pure data classes containing no methods can be used without causing problems since they cannot introduce external bugs.

3. ***Execution and reporting tool***: This is a visual configuration-based tool that the developer may use to decide which tests to launch and when to launch them. Moreover, it also shows the final outcome of the tests as a report containing all successful tests, all failed tests, each test's execution time, and other information that depends on the specific tool and how it was configured. Usually, execution and reporting tools that are executed in development IDEs, such as Visual Studio, also give you the possibility of launching a debug session on each failed test.

Since only interfaces allow a complete mock definition of all their methods, we should inject interfaces or pure data classes (that don't need to be mocked) in class constructors and methods if we want to mock all dependencies in our unit tests. Therefore, for each cooperating class that we want to inject into another class and that we want to mock, we must define a corresponding interface.

The subsection that follows focuses on functional and performance tests.

Acceptance tests: writing functional and performance tests

Having discussed how to discover and avoid bugs, let's move on to how to verify that our code actually conforms to the specifications agreed upon with the stakeholders.

Acceptance tests verify that the application behaves as agreed with the project stakeholders, so they define the contract between the stakeholders and the development team.

Acceptance tests verify not only functional specifications but also constraints on the software usability and user interface (UI). Since they also have the purpose of showing how the software appears and behaves on actual computer monitors and displays, they are never completely automatic but consist mainly of lists of recipes and verifications that must be followed by an operator.

A common approach for testing the user interface is the usage of playback tools like **Selenium IDE** (`https://www.selenium.dev/selenium-ide/`) during manual tests so that each manual test can be repeated automatically. It's likely that the code generated automatically by such tools is not robust enough to resist non-trivial changes in the HTML. The Selenium IDE playback code tries to resist HTML changes by attempting several selectors to identify each HTML element, but this only helps with small changes. Therefore, in general, playback code can be reused only for the parts of the application UI that are not affected by changes.

Acceptance tests can also be created programmatically with tools like **Selenium** and **Playwright** (`https://playwright.dev/`). We will describe these tools in more detail in the *Automating functional tests in the C#* section, while functional tests, in general, are discussed in the *Functional tests* section.

Performance tests apply a fake load to an application to see whether it can handle the typical production load, discover its load limits, and locate bottlenecks. The application is deployed in a staging environment that is a copy of the actual production environment in terms of hardware resources.

Then, fake requests are created and applied to the system, and response times and other metrics are collected. Fake request batches should have the same composition as the actual production batches. They can be generated from the actual production request logs if they are available.

If response times are not satisfactory, other metrics are collected to discover possible bottlenecks (low memory, slow storage, or slow software modules). Once located, a software component that is responsible for the problem can be analyzed in the debugger to measure the execution time of the various method calls involved in a typical request.

Failures in the performance tests may lead either to a redefinition of the hardware needed by the application or to the optimization of some software modules, classes, or methods.

In general, while failures of functional tests lead to the redefinition of *what* software modules must do, failures of non-functional tests lead to the redefinition of *how* each software module must accomplish it's *what*. That is why it is so important to distinguish among them.

Summing up, we can say that performance tests verify the performance requirements decided on in the design stage.

Both Azure and Visual Studio offer tools to create fake loads and to report execution metrics. However, they have been declared obsolete and will be discontinued, so we will not describe them. As an alternative, there are both open-source and third-party tools that can be used. Some of them are listed in the *Further Reading* section.

The next section describes a software development methodology that plays a central role in testing.

Understanding test-driven development

Test-driven development (**TDD**) is a software development methodology that gives a central role to unit tests, since TDD considers them a formalization of the specifications of each class because a full unit test battery that covers all code paths univocally defines the code behavior.

It is a specification based on *typical examples* of behavior instead of formal requirements defined in some specification-description language.

The core idea of TDD is that unit tests, being specifications, must be written before the code under test. The ideal way to test software would be to write formal specifications of the whole software behavior and to verify with some wholly automatic tools whether the software that was actually produced conforms to them. In the past, some research effort was spent defining formal languages for describing code specifications, but expressing the behavior the developer has in mind with similar languages was a very difficult and error-prone task. Therefore, these attempts were quickly abandoned in favor of approaches based on examples. At that time, the main purpose was the automatic generation of code.

Nowadays, automatic code generation based on formal specifications has been largely abandoned and survives in small application areas, such as the creation of device drivers. In these areas, the effort of formalizing the behavior in a formal language is worth the time saved in trying to test difficult-to-reproduce behaviors of parallel threads.

Unit tests were initially conceived as a way to encode example-based specifications in a completely independent way as part of a specific agile development methodology called extreme programming. However, since TDD proved to be very efficacious in preventing bugs, nowadays, TDD is used independently of extreme programming and is included as an obligatory prescription in other agile methodologies.

TDD practice proved that well-designed initial unit tests are enough to ensure acceptable software stability, even if, usually, initial tests are not a "*perfect*" specification of the code. However, it is undoubtedly true that unit tests refined after finding hundreds of bugs act as reliable and substantially perfect code specifications.

Well-designed unit tests can't be based on random inputs, since you might need an infinite or at least an immense number of examples to univocally define a code's behavior this way. However, the behavior can be defined with an acceptable number of inputs if you have in mind all possible execution paths. In fact, at this point, it is enough to select a typical example for each execution path.

That's why writing a unit test for a method after that method has been completely coded is easy: it simply requires the selection of a typical instance for each execution path of the already existing code. However, writing unit tests this way does not protect from errors in the design of the execution paths themselves.

> **Note**
>
> Therefore, unit tests must be written before a method has been completely coded, but, while writing unit tests, the developer must somehow forecast all execution paths by looking for extreme cases and by possibly adding more examples than are strictly needed.

In order to exemplify the above concepts, let's put them in practice with a simple self-contained example.

For instance, let's suppose we are writing code that sorts an array. We might start considering all possible extreme cases we are able to forecast before any line of useful method code has been written, that is:

- An empty array
- A null array
- A single-element array
- An array with a few elements
- An array with several elements
- An already ordered array
- A partially ordered array
- An extremely unordered array

After a first version of the algorithm has been written and passes all tests above, other inputs that might cause different execution paths might be discovered by analyzing all execution paths. If this is the case, we add a new unit test for each different execution path discovered.

For instance, in the case of the array sorting method, suppose that we use a divide-and-conquer algorithm, like merge-sort, that recursively splits the array into two halves for recursively reducing the problem to a simpler one. For sure the way arrays with even or odd length are processed will be different, so we must add at least two new tests, one with an even length array and the other with an odd length array.

However, as developers can make mistakes while writing the application code, they can also make mistakes in forecasting all possible execution paths while designing the unit tests!

It seems we have identified a possible drawback of TDD: unit tests themselves may be wrong. That is, not only application code but also its associated TDD unit tests may be inconsistent with the behavior the developer has in mind. Therefore, in the beginning, unit tests can't be considered software specifications but rather a possibly incorrect and incomplete description of the software behavior.

Therefore, we have just two possibly incorrect descriptions of the behavior we have in mind: the application code itself and its TDD unit tests that were written before the application code. However, this is not an issue, because the theory of probability helps us!

> **Note**
>
> What makes TDD work well in practice is the fact that the probability of making exactly the same error while writing the tests and while writing the code is very small. Therefore, whenever a test fails, there is an error either in the tests or in the application code, and conversely, if there is an error either in the application code or in the test, there is a very high probability that a test will fail. That is, notwithstanding that tests might be incorrect themselves, the use of TDD ensures that most of the bugs are found immediately!

Now that we have understood why TDD is efficacious in preventing bugs, and we have learned how to select the inputs for our unit tests, we can move to the description of the TDD-based code-writing process.

Writing a class method or a chunk of code, say for finding the maximum of an array of integers with TDD is a loop composed of three stages:

1. **Red stage**: In this stage, the developer writes an empty method says `MaximumGrade` that throws `NotImplementedException` and new unit tests for them that must necessarily fail because, at this time, no code implements the behavior they describe:

```
int MaximumGrade(int[] grades)
{
    throw new NotImplementedException();
}
```

2. **Green stage**: In this stage, the developer writes the minimum code or makes the minimum modifications to existing code that are necessary to pass all unit tests. Say we test `MaximumGrade` with a `null` array, an array with `0` elements, an array with just one element and an array with several elements. A possible initial code is shown below. In order to pass all tests, the code checks just if the input is `null` because the for loop properly handle both the case of empty and single element arrays.

```
int MaximumGrade(int[] grades)
{
    if(grades == null) return 0;
    int result= 0;
    for(int i = 0; i < grades.Length; i++)
    {
```

```
            if (grades[i]> result) result= grades[i];
        }
        return result;
    }
```

The code example shows that in general not all edge cases we forecast in the test are handled with dedicated if.

3. **Refactoring stage**: Once the test is passed, the code is refactored to ensure good code quality and the application of best practices and patterns. In particular, in this stage, some code can be factored out in other methods or other classes. During this stage, we may also discover the need for other unit tests because new execution paths or new extreme cases are discovered or created. In the case of `MaximumGrade` at this stage we might notice what follows:

    - Instead of returning 0 when the array is `null`, it would be better to define a new exception and throw it.
    - A `foreach` is more efficient and more readable than a `for`.
    - What if all numbers are negative? We must add a new test with an array of negative numbers.

    ```
    int MaximumGrade(int[] grades)
    {
         ArgumentNullException.ThrowIfNull(grades);
        int result= 0;
        foreach(int grade in grades)
        {
            if (grade > result) result= grade;
        }
        return result;
    }
    ```

    `ArgumentNullException.ThrowIfNull` throws a null argument exception if the array is `null`, and a `foreach` replaces the previous `for` statement.

The loop stops as soon as all tests pass without writing new code or modifying the existing code.

In our `MaximumGrade` example, when we repeat the red stage, the newly added test for negative array would fail because of our inadequate initialization:

```
int result=0;
```

So, we need to replace it with:

```
int result= int.MinValue;
```

At this point all tests pass again and we move to the green stage again. There is no need for further refactoring, so the refactoring stage doesn't modify our code, and we can exit the test loop: we are done!

Sometimes, it is very difficult to design the initial unit tests because it is quite difficult to imagine how the code might work and the execution paths it might take. In this case, you can get a better understanding of the specific algorithm to use by writing an initial sketch of the method code. In this initial stage, we need to focus just on the main execution path, completely ignoring extreme cases and input verifications. Once we get a clear picture of the main ideas behind an algorithm that should work, we can enter the standard three-stage TDD loop.

TDD has a fundamental role both in the initial design and in all subsequent changes of each software module since it decreases future bug occurrences by various orders of magnitude. This way, it gives a valuable contribution to both software stability and reliable changes management.

The next section discusses functional tests in detail.

Functional tests

These tests use the same techniques and tools as unit and integration tests but differ from them in that they are run only at the end of each sprint. They have the fundamental role of verifying that the current version of the entire software complies with its specifications.

Since **functional tests** also involves the *user interface (UI)*, it needs further tools to simulate, somehow, how the user acts in the UI. The need for extra tools is not the only challenge the UI brings with it because UIs also see frequent and major changes. Thus, we mustn't design tests that depend on the UI's graphical details, or we might be forced to rewrite all the tests completely at each UI change. We will discuss both the tools and the best practices for optimizing UI tests in the *Automating functional tests in C#* section.

Anyway, it is worth pointing out that sometimes it is better to renounce automated tests for some UI-related features and fall back to manual tests because the time investment is not justified by the short life of the UI code.

Whether automatic or manual, functional testing must be a formal process that is performed for the following purposes:

- Functional tests represent the most important part of the contract between stakeholders and the development team, the other part being the verification of non-functional specifications. The way this contract is formalized depends on the nature of the relationship between the development team and stakeholders:
- In the case of a supplier-customer relationship, the functional tests become part of the supplier-customer business contract for each sprint, and a team that works for the customer writes them. If the tests fail, then the sprint is rejected, and the supplier must run a supplementary sprint to fix all problems.
- If there is no supplier–customer business relationship because the development team and the stakeholder belong to the same company, there is no business contract. In this case, the stakeholder, together with the team, writes an internal document that formalizes the requirements of the sprint. If the tests fail, usually, the sprint is not rejected, but the results of the tests are used to drive the specifications for the next sprints. Of course, if the failure percentage is high, the sprint may be rejected and should be repeated.

- Formalized functional tests that run at the end of each sprint prevent any results achieved in previous sprints from being destroyed by new code.
- When using an agile development methodology, maintaining an updated battery of functional tests is the best way to get a formal representation of the final system specifications since, during agile development, the specifications of the final system are not decided before development starts but are the result of the system's evolution. Agile development and sprints are discussed in detail in *Chapter 1, Understanding the Importance of Software Architecture.*

Since the output of the first sprints may differ a lot from the final system in these early stages, it is not worth spending too much time writing detailed manual tests and/or automated tests. Therefore, you may limit the user stories to just a few examples that will be used both as inputs for software development and as manual tests.

As system functionalities become more stable, it is worth investing time in writing detailed and formal functional tests for them. For each functional specification, we must write tests that verify their operation in extreme cases. For instance, in a cash withdrawal use case, we must write tests that verify all possibilities:

1. Not enough funds
2. Card expired
3. Wrong credentials
4. Repeated wrong credentials

The following diagram sketches the whole process with all possible outcomes:

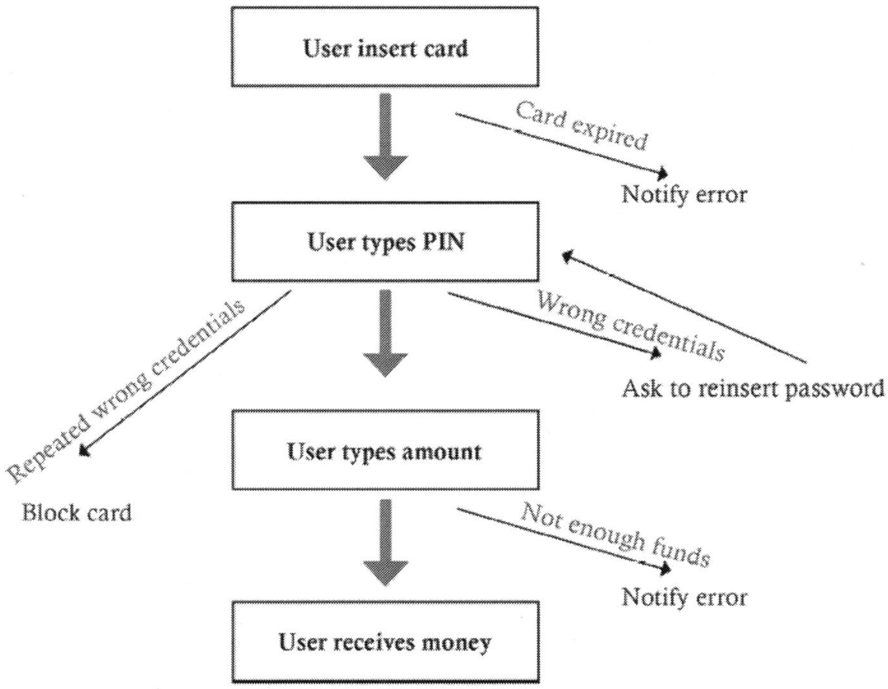

Figure 9.1: Withdrawal example

User inserts card and the card may be rejected because it is expired, or accepted. Then, the user tries their PIN with possible errors, so they might repeat PIN insertion until either they succeed or reach a maximum number of attempts. Finally, the user types the amount and may get their money or a "*Not enough funds*" error.

In the case of manual tests, for each of the preceding scenarios, we must give all the details of all the steps involved in each operation and, for each step, the expected result.

An important decision is whether you want to automate all or a part of the functional tests, since it is very expensive to write automated tests that simulate a human operator interacting with a system's UI. The final decision depends on the cost of the test implementation divided by the expected number of times it will be used.

In the case of CI/CD, the same functional test can be executed several times, but unluckily, functional tests are strictly tied to the way the UI is implemented, and, in modern systems, the UI is changed frequently. Therefore, in this case, a test is executed with exactly the same UI no more than a couple of times.

In order to overcome most of the problems related to the UI, some functional tests can be implemented as **subcutaneous tests**. Subcutaneous tests are a specific type of functional test designed to bypass the user interface (UI) layer of an application. Instead of interacting with the application through its UI, like a user would, these tests directly interact with the application's underlying logic. For example, in an ASP.NET Core application, a subcutaneous test might directly invoke the methods of a controller – the part of the application that handles incoming requests – rather than going through the process of sending these requests via a browser. This approach helps us focus on testing the core functionality of the application without the complexities of the UI.

> **Note**
>
> Subcutaneous tests ensure full control of application input, at the expense of realism. They are the best choice whenever the simplification doesn't affect the result of the test.

Unfortunately, this is not the case for all functional tests since, for example, subcutaneous tests can't detect errors in the UI itself. Moreover, in the case of a web application, subcutaneous tests usually suffer from other limitations because they bypass the whole HTTP protocol.

In particular, in the case of ASP.NET Core applications that will be described in *Chapter 17, Implementing Frontend Microservices in ASP.NET Core*, if we call controller action methods directly, we bypass the whole ASP.NET Core pipeline that processes each request before passing it to the right action method. Therefore, authentication, authorization, CORS, and the behavior of other middleware in the ASP.NET Core pipeline will not be analyzed by the tests.

A complete automated functional test of a web application should do the following things:

1. Start an actual browser on the URL to be tested
2. Wait so that any JavaScript on the page completes its execution
3. Then, send commands to the browser that simulate the behavior of a human operator
4. Finally, after each interaction with the browser, automatic tests should wait so that any JavaScript that was triggered by the interaction completes

Such tests can be executed using browser automatization tools like *Selenium*, which will be discussed in the *Automating functional tests in the C#* section of this chapter.

> **Note**
>
> It is worth pointing out that not all user interface tests can be automated since no automatic test can verify how the user interface appears and how usable it is.

As we've explored the intricacies of functional and subcutaneous testing, it's clear that a comprehensive testing strategy must encompass not only how the tests are performed but also how they are conceptualized and communicated. This brings us to **Behavior Driven Development** (BDD), a methodology that builds upon the principles of functional testing by emphasizing business value and client-side behavior. BDD offers a structured approach to creating tests that are more closely aligned with user requirements and business objectives.

Behavior-Driven development (BDD)

BDD conforms to the rules of TDD we already described but focuses mainly on business value and client-side behavior.

We discussed that the strength of unit tests is as follows: *It is very unlikely that*, when *describing a behavior in two completely different ways—that is, with code and with examples—we might make exactly the same errors, so errors are discovered with a probability that is close to 100%.*

BDD uses the same approach, but the examples used in TDD must not depend on the specific way functionalities might be implemented, since they encode the whole application specifications. That is, examples must be as close as possible to pure specifications expressed in the final user language. This way, we are sure tests can't influence the way functionality is implemented and vice versa; we are not influenced by pure technical facilities or constraints when writing specifications but focus mainly on the user needs.

Moreover, tests should use a vocabulary that can be understood by stakeholders. For these reasons, tests are described by a Given-When-Then syntax. Below is an example:

```
Given the first number is 50
And the second number is 70
When the two numbers are added
Then the result should be 120
```

`Given`, `And`, `When`, and `Then` are keywords, while the remaining text is just natural language containing the example data.

The Given-When-Then formal language is called **Gherkin**. It can be translated into code either manually or with tools that are part of toolsets like Cucumber (`https://cucumber.io/`) or **Reqnroll/SpecFlow** in the case of .NET projects. *Reqnroll/SpecFlow* is a Visual Studio extension that can be installed from the Extensions Visual Studio menu. Once installed, it adds a new kind of test project, a *Reqnroll/SpecFlow* project.

In *Reqnroll/SpecFlow*, `Given-When-Then` tests are defined in `.feature` files, while natural language clauses contained in the description are transformed into code in the so-called step files. Step files are automatically created, but the code inside of them must be written by the developer. Below is the method that is in charge of translating into code the "`Given the first number is 50`" clause:

```
[Given("the first number is (.*)")]
public void GivenTheFirstNumberIs(int number)
{
    _calculator.FirstNumber = number;
}
```

The attribute on top of the method is automatically created by *Reqnroll/SpecFlow*, but the `(.*)` regular expression that extracts the datum from the natural language clause must be written by the developer.

`_calculator` is a variable that must be created by the developer and that contains a class to test:

```
private readonly Calculator _calculator = new();
```

Once completely defined, *Reqnroll/SpecFlow* tests are run by exploiting an underlying test framework supported by .NET. The underlying test framework to use is specified when the *Reqnroll/SpecFlow* project is created.

However, functional tests are where Gherkin and BDD shine for the following reasons:

1. User requirements are not contaminated by possible implementations
2. Tests are expressed in a language that is easy to understand for both stakeholders and users, thus ensuring better interaction with them

A functional test for a user login page might look like this:

```
Given the username inserted by the user is {0}
And the password inserted by the user is {1}
And {0} was registered as user with password {1}
When the user logs in
Then the result is success
```

Where the code associated with "`Then the result is success`" should verify both that a success result is returned by the server and that a valid authentication cookie is emitted as a side effect.

Below is a BDD specification for the banking subsystem:

```
Given that there is a purchase request of user {1} for a total amount {0}
And user {1} credit is greater than {0}
And no purchase restrictions apply to user {1}
When a purchase finalization request is received
Then the result is success.
```

Where the code associated with "`Then the result is success`" should verify both that a success response is returned and that {0} is correctly subtracted from the user credit.

Note

While BDD and the Gherkin syntax can be used in unit, integration, and functional tests, the effort of writing tests in natural language and turning them into code is worth it just for functional tests because functional tests must be easily understood by stakeholders.

When writing unit tests, the BDD rule of independence of tests from implementation improves the tests' quality and lifetime (fewer tests depend on implementation, less they need to be updated). However, keep in mind that the classes that we are unit testing are themselves the result of implementation choices, so an excessive obsession for test independence might result in a waste of time.

Therefore, as far as unit tests are concerned, there is no significant advantage in adopting BDD over the simpler TDD when the class/methods being tested can't be abstracted in general behaviors. On the contrary, BDD might be preferred to TDD for designing implementations of abstract interfaces.

After having described the theory behind testing we are ready to move to practical implementations in C#. In the next section, we will list all test projects available in Visual Studio and describe xUnit in detail.

Defining C# test projects in Visual Studio

In order to exemplify all general concepts learned so far, let's take a look at the testing tools available in the .NET ecosystem. This section is relevant to both software engineers who would like to put into practice the theory exposed so far in their code, and aspiring software architects who would like to reach a more practical understanding of testing.

.NET SDK contains project templates for three types of unit testing frameworks, namely, MSTest, xUnit, and NUnit. Once you start the new project wizard, to visualize the version of all of them that is adequate for .NET C# applications, set the **Project type** as **Test**, **Language** as **C#**, and **Platform** as **Linux** (the last setting just cuts all Aspire projects).

The following screenshot shows the selection that should appear:

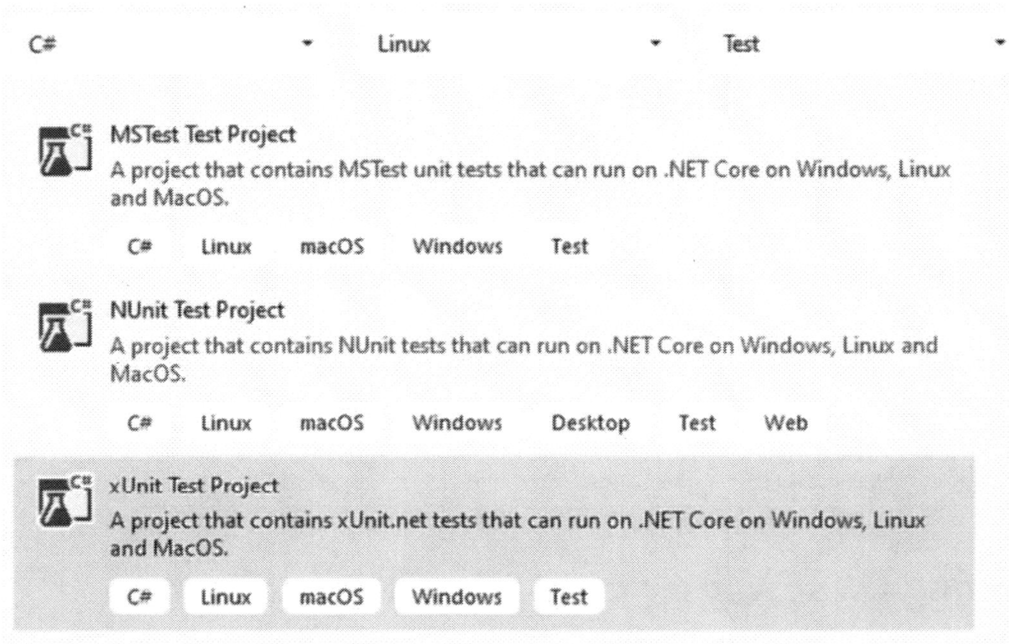

Figure 9.2: Adding a test project

All the preceding projects automatically include the NuGet package for running all the tests in the Visual Studio test user interface (Visual Studio test runner). However, they do not include any facility for mocking interfaces, so you need to add the `Moq` NuGet package, which contains a popular mocking framework.

All these test projects must contain a reference to the project to be tested.

In the next subsection, we will describe xUnit, but all three frameworks are quite similar and differ mainly in the names of the assert methods and in the names of the attributes used to decorate various testing classes and methods.

Using the xUnit test framework

In xUnit, tests are methods decorated with either the `[Fact]` or `[Theory]` attributes. Tests are automatically discovered by the test runner, which lists all of them in the user interface so the user can run either all of them or just a selection of them.

A new instance of the test class is created before running each test, so the *test preparation* code contained in the class constructor is executed before each test of the class. If you also require *tear-down* code, the test class must implement the `IDisposable` interface so that the tear-down code can be included in the `IDisposable.Dispose` method.

The test code invokes the methods to be tested and then tests the results with methods from the `Assert` static class, such as `Assert.NotNull(x)`, `Assert.Equal(x, y)`, and `Assert.NotEmpty(IEnumerable x)`. Some methods verify whether a call throws an exception of a specific type, for instance:

```
Assert.Throws<MyException>(() => {/* test code */ ...}).
```

When an assertion fails, an exception is thrown. A test fails if a non-intercepted exception is thrown either by the test code or by an assertion.

The following is an example of a method that defines a single test:

```
[Fact]
public void Test1()
{
    var myInstanceToTest = new ClassToTest();
    Assert.Equal(5, myInstanceToTest.MethodToTest(1));
}
```

The `[Fact]` attribute is used when a method defines just one test, while the `[Theory]` attribute is used when the same method defines several tests, each on a different tuple of data. Tuples of data can be specified in several ways and are injected into the test as method parameters.

The previous code can be modified to test `MethodToTest` on several inputs as follows:

```
[Theory]
[InlineData(1, 5)]
[InlineData(3, 10)]
[InlineData(5, 20)]
public void Test1(int testInput, int testOutput)
{
    var myInstanceToTest = new ClassToTest();
         Assert.Equal(testOutput,
        myInstanceToTest.MethodToTest(testInput));
}
```

Each `InlineData` attribute specifies a tuple to be injected into the method parameters. Since just simple constant data can be included as attribute arguments, xUnit also gives you the possibility to take all data tuples from a class that implements `IEnumerable`, as shown in the following example:

```
public class Test1Data: IEnumerable<object[]>
{
    public IEnumerator<object[]> GetEnumerator()
    {
        yield return [ 1, 5 ];
```

```
            yield return ] 3, 10 ];
            yield return [ 5, 20 ];
        }
        IEnumerator IEnumerable.GetEnumerator()=>GetEnumerator();
    }
    ...
    [Theory]
    [ClassData(typeof(Test1Data))]
    public void Test1(int testInput, int testOutput)
    {
        var myInstanceToTest = new ClassToTest();
        Assert.Equal(testOutput,
        myInstanceToTest.MethodToTest(testInput));
    }
```

The type of class that provides the test data is specified with the `ClassData` attribute.

It is also possible to take data from a static method of a class that returns an `IEnumerable` with the `MemberData` attribute, as shown in the following example:

```
    [Theory]
    [MemberData(nameof(MyStaticClass.Data),
        MemberType= typeof(MyStaticClass))]
    public void Test1(int testInput, int testOutput)
    {
        ...
```

The `MemberData` attribute is passed the method name as the first parameter, and the class type in the `MemberType` named parameter. If the static method is part of the same test class, the `MemberData` attribute can be omitted.

The next subsection shows how to deal with some advanced preparation and teardown scenarios.

Advanced test preparation and teardown scenarios

Sometimes, the preparation code contains very time-consuming operations, such as opening a connection with a database that doesn't need to be repeated before each test but that can be executed once before all the tests contained in the same class. In xUnit, this kind of test preparation code can't be included in the test class constructor, since a different instance of the test class is created before every single test is executed, so it must be factored out in a separate class called a fixture class.

If we also need a corresponding tear-down code, the fixture class must implement `IDisposable`. In other test frameworks, such as NUnit, the test class instances are created just once instead, so they don't need the fixture code to be factored out in other classes. However, test frameworks such as NUnit, which do not create a new instance before each test, may suffer from bugs because of unwanted interactions between test methods.

The following is an example of an xUnit fixture class that opens and closes a database connection:

```
public class DatabaseFixture : IDisposable
{
    public DatabaseFixture()
    {
        Db = new SqlConnection("MyConnectionString");
    }
    public void Dispose()
    {
        Db.Close()
    }
    public SqlConnection Db { get;  }
}
```

Since a fixture class instance is created just once before all tests associated with the fixture are executed and the same instance is disposed of immediately after the tests, the database connection is created just once when the fixture class is created and is disposed of immediately after the tests when the fixture object is disposed of.

The fixture class is associated with each test class by letting the test class implement the empty `IClassFixture<T>` interface as follows:

```
public class MyTestsClass(DatabaseFixture fixture):
 IClassFixture<DatabaseFixture>
{
    ...
}
```

A fixture class instance is automatically injected into the test class constructor in order to make all data computed in the fixture test preparation available for the tests. This way, for instance, in our previous example, we can get the database connection instance so that all test methods of the class can use it.

If we want to execute some test preparation code on all tests contained in a collection of test classes instead of a single test class, we must associate the fixture class with an empty class that represents the collection of test classes, as follows:

```
[CollectionDefinition("My Database collection")]
public class DatabaseCollection : ICollectionFixture<DatabaseFixture>
{
    // this class is empty, since it is just a placeholder
}
```

The `CollectionDefinition` attribute declares the name of the collection, and the `IClassFixture<T>` interface has been replaced with `ICollectionFixture<T>`.

Then, we declare that a test class belongs to the previously defined collection by applying it to the `Collection` attribute with the name of the collection, as follows:

```
[Collection("My Database collection")]
public class MyTestsClass(DatabaseFixture fixture)
{
    ...
}
```

The `Collection` attribute declares which collection to use, while the `DatabaseFixture` argument in the test class constructor provides an actual fixture class instance, so it can be used in all class tests.

Now that we have seen how to leverage fixture classes to share setup and cleanup code across multiple tests, enhancing our test organization and efficiency, we turn our attention to another powerful technique in our testing arsenal. The following section introduces the use of the `Moq` framework, a tool that allows us to simulate the behavior of complex dependencies in our tests through mocking. This approach is crucial for isolating the component we are testing and verifying its behavior under controlled conditions without the need for the actual implementations of its dependencies.

Mocking interfaces with Moq

Mocking is a technique used in unit testing to isolate classes from dependencies they have on other classes, so we can impute each test failure to the class under test. Classes are isolated from their dependencies by creating a mock, or a fake version, of each dependency.

Mocking capabilities are not included in any of the test frameworks we listed in this section, as they are not included in xUnit, so we must add another library that offers mocking capability. The `Moq` framework, a popular tool in .NET, makes the mocking process super-easy.

Let's explore how to use `Moq` to create mocks and set up our tests effectively. Here we will discuss just how to use `Moq` to create mock classes. A practical and complete example that shows how to use `Moq` in your tests is in the *Testing the WWTravelClub application* section of *Chapter 22, Case Study: Practical Usage of .NET Aspire.*

As a first step, we need to install the `Moq` NuGet package. Then, we need to add a `using Moq` statement to our test files. A mock implementation is easily defined as follows:

```
var myMockDependency = new Mock<IMyInterface>();
```

The behavior of the mock dependency on specific inputs of the specific method can be defined with the `Setup/Return` method pair as follows:

```
myMockDependency.Setup(x=>x.MyMethod(5)).Returns(10);
```

We can add several `Setup/Return` instructions for the same method. This way, we can specify an indefinite number of input/output behaviors.

Instead of specific input values, we may also use wildcards that match a specific type as follows:

```
myMockDependency.Setup(x => x.MyMethod(It.IsAny<int>()))
                  .Returns(10);
```

Where we replaced 5 with its type, `int`.

Once we have configured the mock dependency, we may extract the mocked instance from its `Object` property and use it as if it were an actual implementation, as follows:

```
var myMockedInstance=myMockDependency.Object;
...
myMockedInstance.MyMethod(10);
```

However, mocked methods are usually called by the code under test, so we just need to extract the mocked instance and use it as input in our tests.

We may also mock properties and async methods as follows:

```
myMockDependency.Setup(x => x.MyProperty)
                  .Returns(42);
...
myMockDependency.Setup(x => x.MyMethodAsync(1))
                    .ReturnsAsync("aasas");
var res=await myMockDependency.Object
    .MyMethodAsync(1);
```

With `async` methods, `Returns` must be replaced by `ReturnsAsync`.

Each mocked instance records all calls to its methods and properties, so we may use this information in our tests. The following code shows an example:

```
myMockDependency.Verify(x => x.MyMethod(1), Times.AtLeast(2));
```

The preceding statement asserts that `MyMethod` has been invoked with the given arguments at least twice. There are also `Times.Never` and `Times.Once` (which asserts that the method was called just once), and more.

The `Moq` documentation summarized up to now should cover 99% of the needs that may arise in your tests, but `Moq` also offers more complex options. The *Further reading* section contains the link to the complete documentation.

The *Testing the WWTravelClub application section of Chapter 22, Case study: Practical Usage of .NET Aspire*, shows the practical usage of `Moq` in a complex example.

After exploring the capabilities of Moq and how it enhances our unit testing with effective mock implementations, it is worth mentioning also how Artificial Intelligence tools can be used for the automatic generation of tests. We will focus on the usage of GitHub Copilot.

Automatic generation of tests: GitHub Copilot

If you have a free GitHub subscription and you are logged in to your subscription with Visual Studio, you can use the Visual Studio GitHub Copilot window to automatically generate tests for already existing code.

Requests can be done directly in GitHub Copilot chat in natural language by prefixing them with `@Test`. The object names for which you would like to generate tests can be file, solution, project, class, or method names. You can also specify the testing and mocking frameworks to use.

Below is an example request:

```
@Test class ManagePackageController, targeting 80% code coverage, use xUnit and Moq
```

To avoid ambiguity, the name of the object to test may be preceded by #, like, for instance, `#ManagePackageController`.

Once you send your request, copilot starts an iterative process of analyzing your code that might take some minutes. At the end, it provides the test code based on your selected testing and mocking framework. The window that contains the generated code has a copy icon you can use to copy the code and paste it into your project.

The main drawback of automatic test generators is that they don't know anything about the code's intended behavior, but are based only on the code you already wrote, so they cannot discover all discrepancies between actual and intended behavior. Moreover, we know that tests should be created before actually writing the code as per TDD best practices. These considerations suggest limiting the usage of AI test generators as stated below.

> **Note**
>
> Use automatic test generators just to ensure that the tests you wrote manually during TDD are complete. If not, add the missing tests to the ones you created manually. You can use automatic test generators also for fixing old projects that were created without test suites.

After the exploration of all tools available for performing unit and integration tests in .NET it is time to turn our attention to a different facet of C# application testing – automating functional tests in ASP.NET Core applications. In this next section, we'll dive into how various testing tools and techniques, including some we've just discussed, are applied to ensure our ASP.NET Core applications function as intended, both in isolation and when integrated with other systems and interfaces.

Automating functional tests in C#

Automated functional tests use the same test tools as unit and integration tests. That is, these tests can be embedded in the same xUnit, NUnit, or MSTest projects that we described in the previous section. However, in this case, we must add further tools that can interact with and inspect the UI.

In the remainder of this chapter, we will focus on web applications since they are the main focus of this book. Accordingly, if we are testing web APIs, we just need `HttpClient` instances since they can easily interact with web API endpoints in both XML and JSON.

Organizing functional tests for an application requires that the following decisions are taken for each application subpart to be tested:

1. If the subpart returns HTML or messages. In the first case, the design is more complex since we need tools for parsing and interacting with the HTML to verify its conformance to the specifications. *Selenium* and *Playwright* toolsets are great solutions since they can simulate user interaction with all mainstream browsers and programmatically access the browser DOM. Here we describe Selenium since at the moment it is the most popular and since a final user can also easily record tests with it while interacting with the browser. Usage of Playwright with .NET can be found at `https://playwright.dev/dotnet/docs/intro`.
2. We must decide which tests to execute in a controlled environment, that is, in an environment that is not shared with actual users, and which tests to execute in an environment shared with actual users

Let's analyze in more detail the two kinds of tests defined at point 2:

- **Controlled application**. An `HttpClient` instance connects with a local application that is configured, initialized, and launched before every single test. This scenario is completely analogous to the unit test scenario. Test results are reproducible, the initial state before each test is fixed, tests are easier to design, and the actual database can be replaced by a faster and easier-to-initialize in-memory database. However, in this case, you are far from the actual system's operation.
- **Staging application**. An `HttpClient` instance connects with the actual *staging* web application through the internet/intranet, together with all other humans who are beta-testing the software. The advantage of this approach is that you are testing the *real stuff*, but tests are more difficult to conceive since you can't control the initial state of the application before each test.

A good strategy is to use a **controlled application**, where you have full control of the initial state, for testing the extreme cases and then use a **staging application** for testing random average cases on the *real stuff*. The table below compares the features of staging and controlled applications.

Application type	*Efficacy for edge tests*	*Efficacy for massive average tests*	*Efficacy for testing UI*
Staging	Low	High	High
Controlled	High	Low	Very low

Table 9.1: Comparison between Staging and Controlled Application

The two subsections that follow describe both approaches. The two approaches differ only in the way that you define the fixtures of your tests.

Testing the staging application

In the case of staging applications, your tests need just a class that can issue HTTP requests, which in the case of .NET is the `HttpClient` class. It is enough to define an efficient fixture that supplies the needed `HttpClient` instances, avoiding the risk of running out of operating system connections. Efficient management of the underlying operating system connections can be achieved through the `IHttpClientFactory` interface.

It is enough to add a `HttpClient` management factory to a dependency injection container that will be used by the tests with:

```
services.AddHttpClient(),
```

where the `AddHttpClient` extension belongs to the `Microsoft.Extensions.DependencyInjection` namespace and is defined in the `Microsoft.Extensions.Http` NuGet package. Therefore, our test fixture must create a dependency injection container, call the `AddHttpClient` extension method, and finally build the container. The following fixture class does this job:

```
public class HttpClientFixture
{
    public HttpClientFixture()
    {
        var serviceCollection = new ServiceCollection();
        serviceCollection
            .AddHttpClient();
         ServiceProvider = serviceCollection.BuildServiceProvider();
    }
    public ServiceProvider ServiceProvider { get; }
}
```

After the preceding definition, your tests should look as follows:

```
public class MyUnitTestClass:IClassFixture<HttpClientFixture>
{
    private readonly ServiceProvider _serviceProvider;
    public UnitTest1(HttpClientFixture fixture)
    {
        _serviceProvider = fixture.ServiceProvider;
    }
    [Fact]
    public void MyTest()
    {
        var factory =
            _serviceProvider.GetService<IHttpClientFactory>())
```

```
            HttpClient client = factory.CreateClient();
        }
    }
```

In `Test1`, once you get an HTTP client, you can test the application by issuing an HTTP request and then by analyzing the response returned by the application.

The approach described above is adequate when the HTTP endpoints return data, for instance, in JSON format that can be turned into .NET data by a data serializer/deserializer and then compared with the expected data.

The next subsection describes how to test endpoints that return HTML.

Testing the staging application with Selenium

Most endpoints that return HTML are tested either manually or with playback tools, like Selenium IDE, or Playwright code generator on various browsers. Playback tools record all user actions performed on an actual browser and generate code that repeats the same action sequences with the help of browser drivers.

However, the code generated by playback tools is too sensitive to the DOM structure of each page, so most of the tests must be replaced after each relevant change in the user interface.

Therefore, the code of important and stable UI tests is better created manually in a way that is more robust to DOM changes.

For this purpose, the Selenium toolset contains the `Selenium.WebDriver` NuGet package and a driver for each browser that you would like to adopt, such as, for instance, the `Selenium.WebDriver.ChromeDriver` NuGet package for the Chrome browser.

Manual tests based on Selenium WebDriver look like this:

```
using OpenQA.Selenium;
using OpenQA.Selenium.ChromeDriver;
public class MyUnitTestClass
{
    [Fact]
    public void MyTest()
    {
        using (IWebDriver driver = new ChromeDriver())

        driver.Navigate().GoToUrl("https://localhost:5001/mypage");
        //use driver to interact with the loaded page here
          ...
        var title = driver.Title;
           Assert().Equal("My Application - My Page", title);
           ...
       var submitButton =
        driver.FindElement(By.ClassName("confirm-changes"));
        .submitButton.Clikck();
```

```
        ...


    }
}
```

Once the page to test has been loaded, `driver` is used to explore the page content and to interact with page elements, like buttons, links, and input fields. As shown in the preceding code, the syntax for interacting with the browser is quite simple and intuitive. `driver.FindElement` can find elements by CSS class name, by id, and also through generic CSS selectors.

Adding CSS classes that characterize their role with HTML elements is a good technique for building robust UI tests.

The next subsection explains how to test an application that runs in a controlled environment.

Testing a controlled application

In this case, we create an ASP.NET Core server within the test application and test it with a `HttpClient` instance. The `Microsoft.AspNetCore.Mvc.Testing` NuGet package contains all that we need to create both an HTTP client and the server running the application.

`Microsoft.AspNetCore.Mvc.Testing` contains a fixture class that does the job of launching a local web server and furnishing a client to interact with it. The predefined fixture class is `WebApplicationFactory<T>`. The generic `T` argument must be instantiated with the `Program` class of your web project, that is, with an entry point for the web application.

Tests look like the following class:

```
public class MynitTest
    : IClassFixture<WebApplicationFactory<MyProject.Program>>
{
    private readonly
        WebApplicationFactory<MyProject.Program> _factory;
    public UnitTest1 (WebApplicationFactory<MyProject.Program> factory)
    {
        _factory = factory;
    }
    [Theory]
    [InlineData("/")]
    [InlineData("/Index")]
    [InlineData("/About")]
    ....
    public async Task MustReturnOK(string url)
    {
        var client = _factory.CreateClient();
```

```
        // here both client and server are ready
        var response = await client.GetAsync(url);
        //get the response
        response.EnsureSuccessStatusCode();
        // verify we got a success return code.
    }
    ...
    ---
}
```

The Program class must exist and must be defined as public. Otherwise, WebApplicationFactory has no entry point for starting the application. Therefore, if the code in Program.cs is not enclosed in a public class, as in the default project scaffolded by Visual Studio, you must turn the internal Program class automatically generated by the C# compiler into a public class. This is easily achieved by adding the following code at the end of the Program.cs file:

```
public partial class Program { }
```

If you want to analyze the HTML of the returned pages, you must also reference *Selenium* NuGet packages, as shown in the previous subsection. We will see how to use it in the example in the next section.

The simplest way to cope with databases in this type of test is to replace them with in-memory databases that are faster and automatically cleared whenever the local server is shut down and restarted.

Unlikely, in-memory databases are not 100% compatible with the actual database used, so some tests might fail. Therefore, at least some of the tests might require the actual database.

When performing tests with actual databases, we must also add all the required instructions to clear or recreate from scratch a standard database in the constructor of a custom fixture that inherits from WebApplicationFactory<T>. Note that deleting all database data is not as easy as it might appear, owing to integrity constraints. You have various options, but none is the best for all cases:

1. Delete the whole database and recreate it using SQL scripts or Entity Framework Core migrations that will be analyzed in *Chapter 13, Interacting with Data in C# – Entity Framework Core*. This always works, but it is slow and requires a database user with high privileges.
2. Enclose a test database in a Docker image, and recreate a new container at each new test (Docker will be described throughout *Chapter 11, Applying a Microservice Architecture to Your Enterprise Application*). This is faster than recreating a new database from scratch, but still slow.
3. Disable the database constraints and then clear all tables in any order. This technique sometimes doesn't work and requires a database user with high privileges.
4. Delete all data in the right order, thus without violating all database constraints. This is not difficult if you keep an ordered delete list of all tables while the database grows and you add tables to the database. This delete list is a useful resource that you may also use to fix issues in database update operations and to remove old entries during production database maintenance. Unfortunately, this

method also fails in the rare case of circular dependencies, such as a table that has a foreign key referring to itself.

I prefer method 4 and revert to method 3 only in the rare case of difficulties due to circular dependencies. The reason being that the delete list is a useful resource for fixing database update version when installing a newer version, so the effort of keeping it up to date helps in both keeping the database free of circular dependencies, and in version updates. In contrast preparing a Docker image with all needed initial data requires an effort that can't be reused in other circumstances. Finally, method 1 has the downside of being too slow.

Recording tests with Selenium IDE

Both Playwright and the Selenium toolset give the possibility of recording and replaying browser tests. Here we describe a browser extension based on Selenium called Selenium IDE, since it can also be easily run by final users who are not developers. You can find information about the Playwright recorder at this link, `https://playwright.dev/dotnet/docs/codegen-intro`.

You can download Selenium IDE as an extension for Chrome and Firefox from here: `https://www.selenium.dev/selenium-ide/` while the extension for Microsoft Edge is available on a Microsoft URL: `https://microsoftedge.microsoft.com/addons/detail/selenium-ide/ajdpfmkffanmkhejnopjppegokpogffp`.

In Chrome, once installed, Selenium IDE can be run by clicking the extensions icon and then selecting the Selenium extension from the menu that appears, as shown in the picture below:

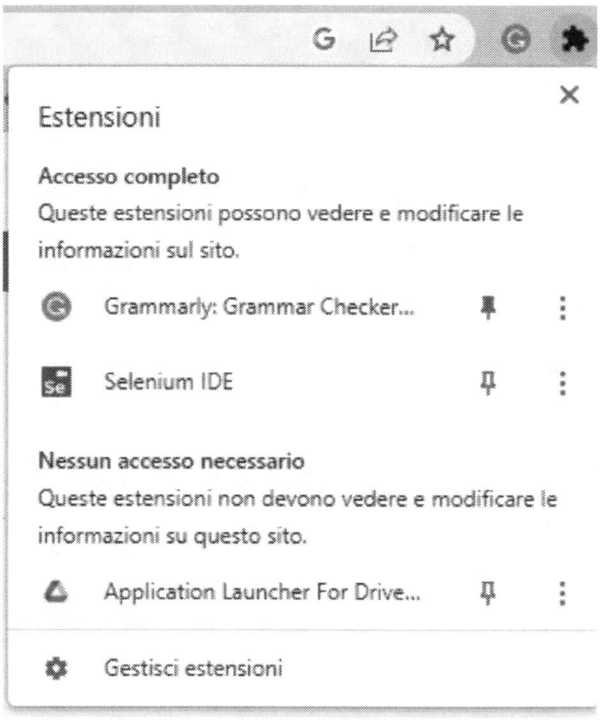

Figure 9.3: Running Selenium IDE

You are prompted for the action you would like to perform, whether to create a new project, access an existing project, etc.

When you create a new project, you are prompted for the project name. At this point, Selenium IDE opens, and you can insert the application URL.

New tests can be created by clicking the plus button next to the tests list.

In order to record a test, select the test name and then click the record icon. A new browser window will open with the application URL. At this point, every action you perform on the application and its results will be recorded.

You can make assertions on the page content by right-clicking on a page element and by selecting the appropriate action from the `Selenium IDE > Assert` submenu. For instance, if you select `the Selenium IDE > Assert > Text` command on a text element, the text value will be stored. When the test is executed, the content of the same text element will be compared with the previously stored value, and the test will fail if the two values are different.

Once all desired actions and assertions have been performed, return to the Selenium IDE window, click the stop recording button, and save the project.

The IDE offers the option to run either a selected test or all tests.

A possible practical approach to automating functional tests can be summarized as follows:

- Use hardcoded Selenium-based code for tests that involve HTML, but that must not depend too much on the specific HTML returned
- Use Selenium IDE to record the remainder of tests that involve HTML
- Test all extreme cases in a controlled environment
- Use a staging application for testing random average cases on the *real stuff*

Summary

In this chapter, we explained why it is worth automating software tests, and then we focused on the importance of unit tests. We explored various types of tests, namely unit tests, integration tests, functional tests, and performance tests, and we learned how each of them contributes to the overall code stability and conformance to the requirements.

We also explored both Test-Driven Development (TDD) and Behavior-Driven Development (BDD) methodologies, learning how each contributes to software quality through slightly different approaches.

Then, this chapter analyzed when it is worth automating some or all functional tests and described how to automate them in ASP.NET Core applications.

Finally, we learned the practical usage of the main test tools available for .NET projects, focusing on the description of `xUnit`, `Moq`, `Microsoft.AspNetCore.Mvc.Testing`, *Selenium*, and showed how to use them in practice with the help of the book's use case.

Chapter 22, Case study: Practical Usage of .NET Aspire applies all test concepts described in this chapter to the book case study.

Questions

1. What is the main reason why TDD is able to discover most bugs immediately?
2. Why is it worth automating unit tests?
3. What is the difference between the `[Theory]` and `[Fact]` attributes of xUnit?
4. Which xUnit static class is used in test assertions?
5. Which methods allow the definition of the `Moq` mocked dependencies?
6. Is it possible to mock `async` methods with `Moq`? If yes, how?
7. Is it always worth automating UI functional tests in the case of quick CI/CD cycles?
8. What is the disadvantage of subcutaneous tests for ASP.NET Core applications?
9. What is the suggested technique for writing ASP.NET Core, code-driven functional tests?
10. What is the suggested way of inspecting the HTML returned by a server?

Further reading

The following are some links you may consider reading to gather more information in relation to this chapter:

- While the documentation on xUnit included in this chapter is quite complete, it doesn't include all configuration options offered by xUnit. The full xUnit documentation is available at `https://xunit.net/`. Documentation for MSTest and NUnit can be found at `https://github.com/microsoft/testfxandhttps://docs.nunit.org/`, respectively.
- For more information on BDD and SpecFlow, refer respectively to the Cucumber official Web Site `https://cucumber.io/`, and to the SpecFlow documentation `https://www.specflow.com/`.
- Full `Moq` documentation is available at `https://github.com/moq/moq4/wiki/Quickstart`.
- Here are some links to performance test frameworks for web applications:
  - `https://jmeter.apache.org/` (free and open source)
  - `https://www.neotys.com/neoload/overview`
  - `https://www.microfocus.com/en-us/products/silk-performer/overview`
- More details on the `Microsoft.AspNetCore.Mvc.Testing` NuGet package can be found in the official documentation at`https://docs.microsoft.com/en-US/aspnet/core/test/integration-tests`.
- More information on Playwright can be found at: `https://playwright.dev/`
- Practical usage of Playwright with .NET is explained here: `https://playwright.dev/dotnet/docs/intro`

- More information on Selenium IDE can be found on the official website: `https://www.selenium.dev/selenium-ide/`.
- More information on Selenium WebDriver can be found on the official website: `https://www.selenium.dev/documentation/webdriver/`.

Get this book's PDF version and more

10

Deciding on the Best Cloud-Based Solution

When designing your application to make it cloud-based, you must understand different architectural designs – from the simplest to the most sophisticated. In fact, cloud technology offers the possibility to optimize costs, to decrease the time-to-market, and to make your solution fault-tolerant and easily scalable. However, each optimization has its cons, so you must choose the right compromise for your needs. For instance, adopting an out-of-the-box application already available in the cloud, like Microsoft 365, reduces both development costs and time-to-market, but it lacks the flexibility of a custom application.

In this chapter, we'll explore different software architecture models and examine the various cloud service types —IaaS, PaaS, SaaS, and Serverless—discussing ideal scenarios for each and how to leverage cloud opportunities in your solutions. By the end, you'll be able to choose the right model for your scenario.

The following topics will be covered in this chapter:

- Infrastructure as a Service solutions
- Platform as a Service solutions
- Software as a Service solutions
- Serverless solutions
- How to use hybrid solutions and why they are so useful

It is worth mentioning that the choice to be made between these options depends on different aspects of the project scenario, such as the need for flexibility and/or highly customized solutions versus simplicity, low maintenance costs, and low time-to-market. These trade-offs will be discussed throughout the whole chapter.

Technical requirements

For the practical content in this chapter, you must create or use an Azure account. We can find the detailed procedure for creating an Azure account in *Chapter 1, Understanding the Importance of Software Architecture*, in the *Creating an Azure account* section.

Different software deployment models

Cloud solutions can be classified into three main categories:

- **Infrastructure as a Service** (**IaaS**), which offers just the bare hardware as a service.
- **Platform as a Service** (**PaaS**), that offers an out-of-the-box platform based on a standard architecture, where the developer needs just to upload its application code and data.
- **Software as a Service** (**SaaS**), offers out-of-the-box applications like Office 365 that the developer just needs to configure.
- **Serverless** (also known as **FaaS),** Offers a billing model based on actual computation time and automatically scale to zero when there is no computation.

Summing up, IAAS offers the bare infrastructure, PaaS pre-organized frameworks, SaaS already working applications that need just to be configured, while FaaS is similar to PaaS but offers a billing model based on just computation time.

Let's begin our exploration with IaaS, the foundational layer of cloud computing. IaaS offers a flexible and scalable infrastructure, which is crucial for businesses with specific hardware requirements or those transitioning from on-premises solutions to the cloud.

> **Note**
>
> Organizations with strong infrastructure engineering teams typically gravitate toward IaaS, which leverages their existing expertise. Conversely, companies where IT isn't the core business often prefer SaaS systems. Developers frequently choose PaaS or Serverless options when infrastructure delivery isn't their responsibility.

As a software architect, you must architect and configure Cloud solutions that optimize cost and work factors, not only during the initial application development but also during its maintenance. Also, as an architect, you must understand the needs of your system and work hard to connect those needs to best-in-class peripheral solutions to speed up delivery and keep the solution as close as possible to the customer's specifications.

Let's start by analyzing in detail IaaS solutions, then we will also move on to PaaS and SaaS detailed features.

IaaS and Azure opportunities

Infrastructure as a Service was the first service offered by all Cloud providers and can be summarized as *your hardware infrastructure delivered on the internet and managed by the Cloud operator.*

Usually, IaaS offers you virtualized components, such as virtual servers, storage, virtual networks, and firewalls managed by the Cloud operator. In a few words, all the hardware you need is hosted in the cloud and maintained by the cloud provider instead of being hosted in your private datacenter. This includes servers delivered as virtual machines, possibly connected in private networks, disk storage, and firewalls. You don't buy the hardware but pay for its usage, and you can scale to a more powerful configuration at 0 cost.

You can access your cloud hardware as if it were hosted in your private datacenter, but hardware maintenance is taken care of by the cloud provider. Moreover, you can scale your hardware gradually as your application traffic increases without installation and purchase costs, and without migrating data to new hardware. Scaling is performed with simple configuration instructions.

Among the various cloud providers, Azure is the one with the most complete and sophisticated offer, so you can easily find a perfect match with any hardware need. Most of Azure **IaaS** solutions have no free plans, so you should pay attention to this when it comes to testing. It is worth mentioning that this book does not set out to describe all IaaS services that Azure provides in detail. However, as a software architect, you just need to understand that you will find services such as the following:

- ***Virtual machines***: Windows Server, Linux, Oracle, data science, and machine learning
- ***Network***: Virtual networks, load balancers, and DNS zones
- ***Storage***: Files, tables, databases, and Redis
- ***Message brokers***: Advanced communication solutions that support various communication patterns such as the Publisher-subscriber pattern described in *Chapter 6, Design Patterns and .NET Implementation*

Obviously, these are not the only ones available as IaaS models, so the first step is to look at the service options available in Azure. To create any service in Azure, you must find the service that best fits your needs and then create a resource. All resources must be added to an Azure subscription and organized in groups called **Resource groups**. Then you have the option to select between various service levels, that is, between resources with different performances and different costs by setting various options. Each option contains explanations, descriptions, and possible links to further documentation. As an example, let's take a look at the configuration wizard of a Windows VM in the following screenshot:

Figure 10.1: Creating a virtual machine in Azure

After the general subscription/resource group options, we have resource-specific options. Following the wizard, you will be able to connect to it by using **Remote Desktop Protocol** (RDP). Among the various options, it is worth pointing out that you may choose among different types of servers, with a different number of cores, memory size, and other hardware features. These are some of the hardware options you have for deploying a virtual machine. You can show them by clicking on the size dropdown and then selecting the **show all sizes** option, as shown below:

VM Size	Type	vCPUs	RAM (GiB)	Data disks	Max IOPS
Most used by Azure users	The most used sizes by users in Azure				
D2ls_v5	General purpose	2	4	4	3750
D2as_v5	General purpose	2	8	4	3750
D2ads_v5	General purpose	2	8	4	3750
D2s_v5	General purpose	2	8	4	3750
D4as_v5	General purpose	4	16	8	6400
D8as_v5	General purpose	8	32	16	12800
B2as_v2	General purpose	2	8	4	3750
B4as_v2	General purpose	4	16	8	6400
B-Series v2	Ideal for workloads that do not need continuous full CPU performance				

Figure 10.2: Virtual machine sizes available in Azure

The cloud's elasticity particularly shines in scenarios that would be impractical on-premises. For instance, there are machines with 64 CPUs, 256 GB of RAM, and temporary storage of 512 GB. This is something you probably will not find in an on-premises data center, for instance, if you have a temporary workload, or it will take you a lot to deliver if you have a brand-new business idea that needs this computing power. Besides, in the temporary workload scenario, this machine will be underutilized, so it would be impossible to justify its purchase in an on-premises scenario.

Note

The main takeaway is that IaaS can be adopted whenever you would like to keep some advantages of cloud computing, namely, redundancy and scalability, but full control over your infrastructure has priority on the time-to-market of your solution.

In fact, while IaaS improves the time-to-market of on-premises solutions, this improvement is not so drastic. That's why sometimes other PaaS and SaaS options that offer shorter time-to-market are preferred during the initial application deployment. Then, once the application and its load stabilize, it might be worth moving to IaaS.

Before we pass to the description of other cloud solutions, it is worth pointing out what the Cloud Provider's security responsibilities are in the case of IaaS.

Security responsibilities in IaaS

Security responsibility is another important thing to know about an IaaS platform. Many people think that once you decide to go to the cloud, all the security is done by the provider. However, this is not true, as you can see in the following screenshot:

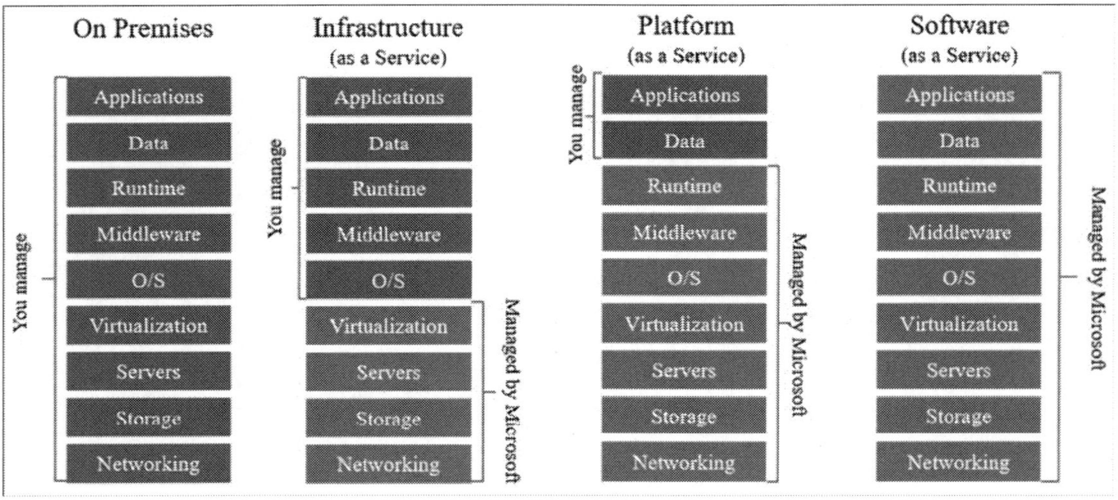

Figure 10.3: Managing security in cloud computing

IaaS will force you to take care of security from the operating system to the application. In some cases, this is inevitable, but you must understand that this will increase your system cost. Thus, for instance, you need to define manually all Windows users and their privileges, while in a PaaS solution, one needs just to care for the application user, that is, the application login and related application user permissions.

IaaS can be a good option if you just want to move an already existing on-premises structure to the cloud (known as lift and shift). This enables scalability, due to the tools that Cloud providers offer you, along with several other services.

However, if you are planning to develop an application from scratch, you should also compare the advantages offered by IaaS solutions with the lower maintenance costs and shorter time-to-market offered by other solutions like PaaS.

PaaS – a world of opportunities for developers

As we already discussed, **Platform as a Service** (**PaaS**) is the best choice when rapid development and deployment capabilities have priority over full resource control.

As you can see in *figure 10.3*, PaaS allows you to worry about security only in terms of aspects that are closer to your business: your data and applications. For developers, this represents freedom from having to implement a bunch of configurations that make your solution work safely.

Security handling is not the only advantage of PaaS. As a software architect, you can introduce these services as an opportunity to deliver richer solutions faster. Time-to-market can surely justify the cost of many applications that run on a PaaS basis.

PaaS solutions free you from managing all details involved in your solution deployment without creating an excessive dependency on the PaaS supplier. In fact, your software need not depend too much on the chosen PaaS, and small dependencies can be isolated in adequately designed drivers. In other words, it is always easy to move to a different PaaS solution or to an IaaS solution if the software is designed with driver-based architecture like the Onion architecture we described in the *Layers and the Onion architecture* section of *Chapter 7, Understanding the Different Domains in Software Solutions*. Therefore, PaaS may be a good choice to reduce the time to market, especially when one plans to move to IaaS in the long run.

Delving deeper into PaaS, let's examine how Azure implements this model through its diverse range of services. Azure's PaaS offerings are designed to cater to various development needs, from web applications to complex data processing.

There are lots of services delivered as PaaS nowadays in Azure, and the array of available services is continuously expanding, reflecting the evolving needs of developers and businesses.

Again, it is not the purpose of this book to list all of them. However, some do need to be mentioned. The list keeps growing, and the recommendation here is: use and test these services as much as you can! Make sure that you deliver better-designed solutions with this thought in mind.

On the other hand, it is worth mentioning that, with PaaS solutions, you will not have full control of the operating system. In fact, in many situations, you do not even have a way to connect to it. This is good most of the time, but in some debugging situations, you may miss this feature. The good thing is that PaaS components are evolving every single day, and one of the biggest concerns from Microsoft is making them widely visible.

The following subsections introduce the most common PaaS components delivered by Microsoft for .NET web apps, that is, Azure Web Apps and Azure SQL Server.

Of the many PaaS services, web apps stand out for their versatility and ease of use. Azure's web app service simplifies the deployment of various types of applications, demonstrating the practicality and accessibility of PaaS solutions.

Web apps

A web app is a PaaS option you can use to deploy your web app. You can deploy different types of applications, such as .NET, .NET Core, Java, PHP, Node.js, and Python. An example of this was presented in *Chapter 1, Understanding the Importance of Software Architecture*.

The good thing is that creating a web app does not require any structure and/or IIS web server setup. In some cases, where you are using Linux to host your .NET application, you do not have IIS at all. Web apps' flexibility in hosting options, such as not requiring IIS for Linux-based deployments, underscores their adaptability to various development and deployment environments.

Moreover, web apps have a plan option where you do not need to pay for usage. Of course, there are limitations, such as only running 32-bit apps and failing to enable scalability. This free tier is ideal for learning and for initial application prototyping, offering essential features without the financial commitment.

Web apps should be chosen whenever we would like to deploy a Web application as PaaS, that is, without the overhead of architecting and maintaining the needed hardware infrastructure.

SQL databases

Imagine how quickly you can deploy a solution if you have the complete power of a SQL server without needing to pay for a big server to deploy this database. This applies to SQL databases. With them, you can use Microsoft

SQL Server for what you need the most – storage and data processing. In this scenario, Azure assumes responsibility for backing up the database.

Here we will discuss shortly just the advantages of having your databases in the cloud. Databases are discussed in detail in both *Chapter 12, How to Choose Your Data Storage in the Cloud*, and *Chapter 13, Interacting with Data in C# - Entity Framework Core*.

Say, you are starting a new business application, and say, initially, your data storage and traffic requirements are quite low, but you need advanced features such as data replication to safeguard your data and to offer high performance to geographically distributed users. Without Azure SQL databases, you would be forced to buy several SQL licenses since SQL Server free edition doesn't cover similar scenarios.

With Azure SQL databases, instead, you can have the top features of an SQL Server Enterprise edition without paying for an expensive license, but paying just for your initially small storage and traffic needs.

The SQL database even gives you the option to manage performance by itself. This is called automatic tuning. That is, your traffic requirements are automatically scaled to keep response time acceptable as requests increase. This also means that your costs might automatically increase, but you can define maximum expense limits.

Again, with PaaS components, you will be able to focus on what is important to your business: a very fast time-to-market.

The steps for creating a SQL database for testing are quite simple, like what we have seen with other components. However, there are two things you need to pay attention to: the creation of the server and how you will be charged. In fact, understanding the various configurations and their costs is essential for finding the best trade-off between your application and maximum cost requirements.

When you create a resource, you can search for *SQL Database*, and you will find this wizard to help you as shown in the following screenshot:

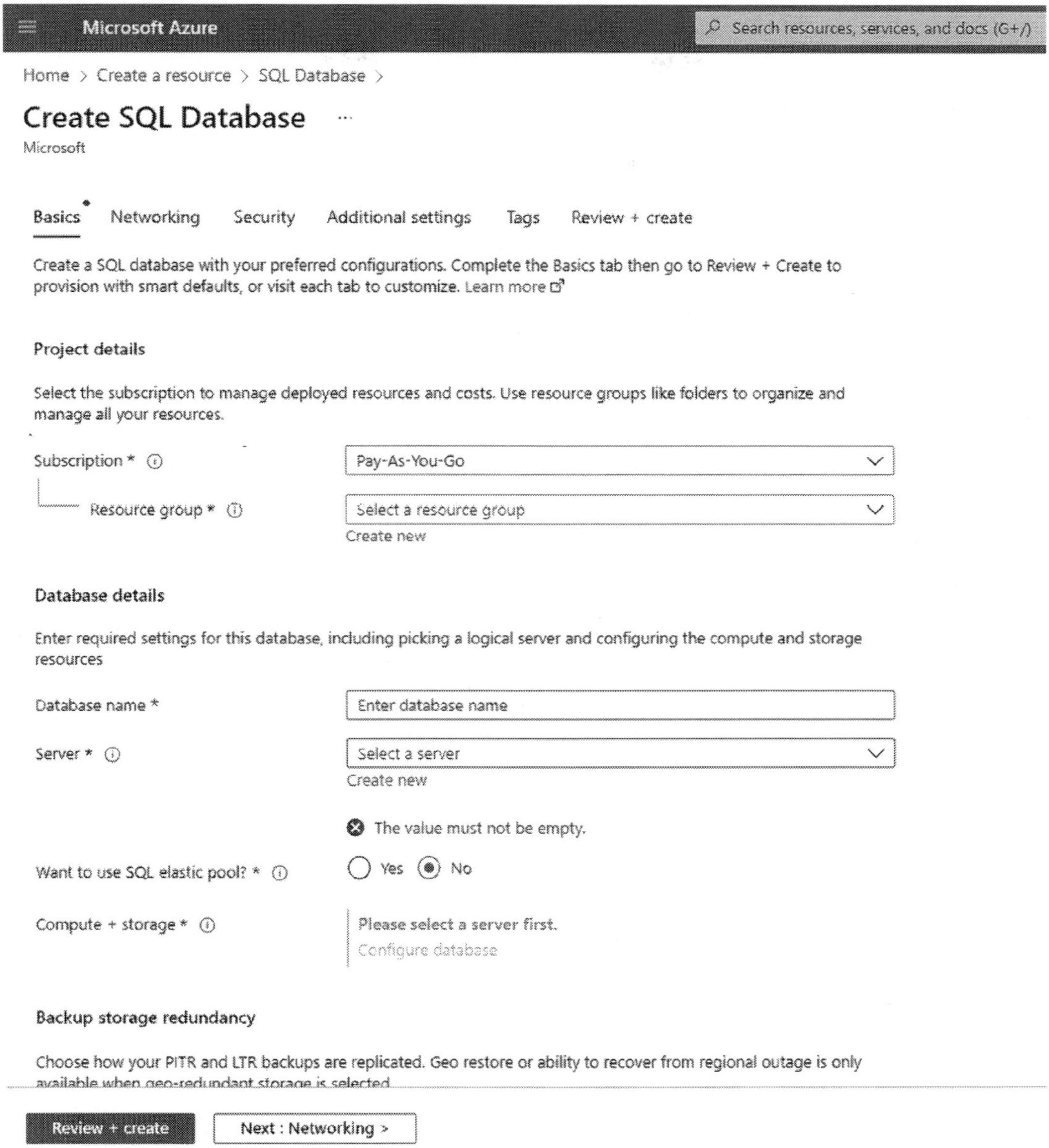

Figure 10.4: Creating a SQL database in Azure

The SQL database depends on an SQL server to host it. For this reason, as you can see, you must create (at least for the first database) a `database.windows.net` server, where your databases will be hosted. This server will provide all the parameters you need to access the SQL server database using current tools, such as Visual Studio, and SQL Server Management Studio. It is worth mentioning that you have a bunch of features regarding security, such as Transparent Data Encryption and IP firewalls.

As soon as you decide on the name of your database server, you will be able to choose the pricing tier on which your system will be charged. Especially in SQL databases, there are several different pricing options. You should study each of them carefully because, depending on your scenario, you may save money by optimizing a pricing tier.

You should select the cheapest option that satisfies the application performance requirements, in terms of operations per unit of time, and available storage. The choice must be based on the current time requirements without worrying about future expansions, because you can move toward more performant solutions as soon as your requirements change.

> **Note**
>
> Summing up, we can say that the decision on the right price tier to adopt should be based mainly on your throughput and storage size requirements.

For more information about SQL configuration, you can use this link:`https://azure.microsoft.com/en-us/services/sql-database/`.

More details on database solutions are discussed in *Chapter 12, How to Choose Your Data Storage in the Cloud*, and *Chapter 13, Interacting with Data in C# - Entity Framework Core.*

Once you have completed the configuration, you will be able to connect to this server database in the same way you do when your SQL server is installed on-premises. The only detail that you must pay attention to is the configuration of the Azure SQL Server firewall, but this is quite simple to set up and a good demonstration of how safe the PaaS service is.

Having also explored PaaS peculiarities and offers, it is time to move to another kind of solution: SaaS.

SaaS – just sign in and get started!

SaaS is probably the easiest way to use cloud-based services. The application you need is already available on the cloud, and you just need to configure and use it! Cloud players provide many good options that solve common problems in a company for their end users. From email services to comprehensive business management tools, SaaS offers a wide array of applications that you can tailor to your various business needs.

A good example of this type of service is Office 365. The key point with these platforms is that you do not need to worry about application maintenance. This is particularly convenient in scenarios where your team is totally focused on developing the core business of the application. For example, if your solution needs to deliver good reports, maybe you can design them using Power BI (which is included in Office 365). Thus, integrating Office 365 in your solution allows for seamless data analysis and reporting, immediately enhancing the overall efficiency and productivity of your business operations.

SaaS solutions can be customized in various ways, the most powerful technique being the addition of custom plugins. For instance, you can customize your Office 365 tenant by adding various kinds of plugins that are available in public repositories and/or by developing your own custom plugins.

It is worth pointing out that even if you decide to invest in custom plugins, you already have, say, 90% of the application already running and stable, so both the initial investment and the time to market are incredibly reduced.

Summing up, on one side, SaaS offers immediately sophisticated and proven solutions, but on the other side, SaaS offers very limited customization options. So, how to decide when to use a SaaS solution?

1. ***Evaluate Existing Solutions***: First of all, you need to verify if a SaaS that matches your needs already exists
2. ***Consider Customization and Integration***: Then, you need to verify if the selected options can be adapted to your needs, and the investment required to adapt them
3. ***Analyze Cost Implications***: At this point, you must analyze the impact of the inevitable compromises you will be forced to accept, and the overall cost implied by each candidate's SaaS adoption, which includes the overall cost of the impact it has on your organization
4. ***Review Security and Compliance***: you need to verify that the users/security model used by the SaaS is compatible with your needs, and that, in general, the application fulfills all constraints required by your organization
5. ***Assess Vendor Reliability and Support***: The impact of having a strong dependency on the SaaS supplier is a key factor in your final decision. Keep in mind that once you incorporate a SaaS solution into your business, it might be very difficult to move to a different solution. That is, the contractual power of your supplier might rise over time to unacceptable levels. For the same reason, an unreliable supplier (for instance, a young startup) or a supplier that can't offer adequate product support might cause unacceptable damage.
6. ***Plan for Scalability and Future Growth***: You must also consider the future of your organization. Thus, you must also verify if the candidate options are scalable and can be adapted to your growing needs and traffic.
7. ***Test the Solution***: finally, you need to test in practice the chosen solution in a staging environment, to verify that your overall analysis and predictions are correct

Another pretty good example of a SaaS platform is Azure DevOps. As a software architect, before Azure DevOps, you needed to install and configure **Team Foundation Server** (TFS) (or even older tools like Microsoft Visual SourceSafe) to have your team working with a common repository and an application life cycle management tool.

We used to spend a lot of time just working either on preparing the server for TFS installation or on upgrading and continuously maintaining the TFS already installed. This is no longer needed due to the simplicity of SaaS Azure DevOps.

Having learned how to decide also the adoption of SaaS, you need to learn just about the last kind of Cloud solution: serverless.

Understanding what Serverless means

Serverless computing addresses a fundamental inefficiency in traditional cloud models: paying for idle resources. By charging only for actual execution time and automatically scaling to zero when unused, serverless can dramatically reduce costs for event-driven workloads—but at the cost of cold start latency and vendor-specific APIs.

However, there are also other advantages. For instance, in a serverless solution, you have a very fast, simple, and agile application life cycle since almost all serverless code is stateless and loosely coupled with the remainder of the system. Some authors refer to this as **Function as a Service** (FaaS).

Of course, the server runs somewhere. The key point here is that you do not need to worry about this or even scalability. This will enable you to focus completely on your app's business logic. Again, the world needs fast development and good customer experiences at the same time. The more you focus on customer needs, the better!

FaaS offers the shortest time-to-market and the lowest cost threshold, together with large scalability possibilities. So, they are convenient in situations where it is extremely difficult to forecast the application workload, or when the application workload has a high and difficult to forecast variance. Suppose, for instance, you are looking for a solution for email mass-sending to connect to your application. If your applications also handle marketing campaigns, there would be traffic peaks that might also be 100 times your average traffic. A Faas solution might be able to cover easily these huge peaks without impacting the average costs you have outside of them.

On the contrary, in a similar situation, PaaS or IaaS would force you to move to a higher price tier even if you don't need it during your average periods, but just during your marketing campaign peaks.

If the workload becomes more and more stable, and it is easier to draw reliable lower and higher bounds, FaaS becomes less convenient due to the higher cost of FaaS on higher workloads. As an example, recently, Amazon Prime publicized its savings from switching from FaaS to IaaS.

Unluckily, moving from FaaS to PaaS or IaaS is not easy, since FaaS code is strictly tied to the chosen FaaS solution.

This issue can be partially mitigated by avoiding too fragmented FaaS code made of small functions, and, instead, using a few functions that trigger the execution of bigger conventional software modules enclosed inside the FaaS solution. This way, moving to a different FaaS, or to IaaS / PaaS, would require just rewriting a few FaaS mains, while keeping the bigger software modules unchanged.

In my experience, FaaS proves to be useful either in the early stages of a presumably high-traffic but low-complexity application, or for low-complexity applications like our previous email-sending application that are specifically designed for handling high and difficult to forecast peaks. In fact, in these applications, almost complete code-rewrites are acceptable since the investment for the code development is low as compared with the savings implied by an almost immediate time-to-market and by an efficacious handling of big and hard to forecast traffic peaks.

Next, the subsections compare IaaS, PaaS, SaaS and FaaS along several axes.

Comparing IaaS, PaaS, SaaS, and FaaS

In the previous sections, we described various types of solutions offered by all main Cloud providers with advantages and disadvantages. The table below briefly summarizes the main advantages offered by each of them, assigning a note between 1 (less good) and 4 (very good) to five axes. You should prefer solutions that score 3 or 4 on priority dimensions and should avoid using solutions that score 1 along priority dimensions.

	Time-To-Market	Customization possibility	Maintenance effort	Scalability	Cost
IaaS	1	4	1	1	4
PaaS	2	3	2	2	3
SaaS	4	1	4	Depends on the application	1
FaaS	3	2	3	4	2

Table 10.1: Comparison among the four different types of cloud solutions

The table above can be used to decide the best solution for your application as follows:

1. Remove the Cloud solutions that, for some reason, are not available from the possible candidates. Thus, for instance, if no SaaS solution is available from a reliable supplier, remove it.
2. Rate the importance of each of the 5 dimensions (table columns) with a percentage. The sum of all percentages must be 100. Thus, for instance, if our priorities are time-to-market and scalability but we are still interested in acceptable maintenance effort, cost, and customizability, we might assign these column percentages: (35, 10, 10, 35, 10).
3. Rate each row that was not removed in step 1 by multiplying each column percentage by the score in the intersection between the row and the column percentage. Then, sum all products obtained this way. In our example, we would obtain:
    1. IaaS: `35+40+10+35+40 = 160`
    2. Paas: `140+30+20+70+30 = 290`
    3. SaaS: Not Available
    4. FaaS: `105+20+30+140+20 = 315`
4. Select the Cloud technology with the highest score, in our example FaaS. If two technologies have quite close scores, you can make a more detailed comparison between them. In our example, we might decide to perform a close comparison between FaaS and PaaS.

There are cases where, for some reasons, not all computing can be moved to the Cloud; in this case, we speak of hybrid solutions. Let's analyze where and how to use them.

Why are hybrid applications so useful in many cases?

In the case of the Cloud, the word *hybrid* refers to solutions that mix cloud subsystems with on-premises subsystems.

Due to the number of services Azure can provide and the number of design architectures that can be implemented, hybrid applications are probably the best answer to the main question addressed in this chapter: how to use the opportunities offered by the cloud in your projects.

Nowadays, many current projects are moving from an on-premises solution to a cloud architecture and, depending on where you are going to deliver these projects, you will still find many bad preconceptions regarding moving to the cloud. Most of them are related to cost, security, and service availability.

Unluckily, some concerns about security are somehow justified, since one must trust the Cloud provider. For sure, you as a software architect cannot ignore them. Especially when you develop a critical system, you must decide whether everything can go on the cloud or whether it is better to deliver part of the system on the edge. Therefore, understanding these factors is key to navigating the hybrid landscape, which ensures that you balance cost, security, and availability according to your specific needs.

With reference to security concerns, it is worth mentioning a real-life example that might clarify the need for hybrid solutions. Recently, some customers of a SaaS solution we offer objected that they can't move reserved and business-critical documents to the cloud. Our solution was to equip our SaaS with file-handling drivers capable of retrieving files from an in-house document server located in the customer's private intranet. In a few words, we satisfied the customer's need by adding an on-premise subsystem to our cloud solution.

Summary

This chapter covered the various options for delivering an application in the Cloud, and how to choose among them. We also pointed out how Cloud operators continuously add new options, so that customers can find solutions that fits always better their needs. As a software architect, you need to analyze your environment and your team, and then decide on the best cloud architecture to implement in your solution.

The next chapter is dedicated to building a flexible architecture comprising small scalable software modules called microservices.

Questions

1. What kind of solution to choose to move quickly a pre-existing solution to the Cloud, IaaS, PaaS, FaaS, or SaaS?
2. What is the fastest way to deliver on Azure: a recently implemented web application, IaaS, PaaS, FaaS, or SaaS?
3. Why should you use SaaS in your solution?
4. What kind of solution to choose for a Cloud application that is used just a few days in the year but has high traffic peaks, IaaS, PaaS, FaaS, or SaaS?
5. What is the advantage of using an Azure SQL Server database?
6. How can hybrid architectures help you to design a better solution?

Further reading

You can check out these web links to study the topics covered in this chapter in greater depth:

- https://learn.microsoft.com/en-us/azure/azure-functions/
- https://azure.microsoft.com/overview/what-is-iaas/
- https://docs.microsoft.com/en-us/azure/security/azure-security-iaas
- https://azure.microsoft.com/services/app-service/web/
- https://azure.microsoft.com/services/sql-database/
- https://azure.microsoft.com/en-us/services/virtual-machines/data-science-virtual-machines/
- https://docs.microsoft.com/azure/sql-database/sql-database-automatic-tuning
- https://azure.microsoft.com/en-us/services/cognitive-services/
- https://docs.microsoft.com/en-us/azure/architecture/
- https://powerbi.microsoft.com/
- https://office.com
- https://azure.microsoft.com/en-us/overview/what-is-serverless-computing/
- https://azure.microsoft.com/en-us/pricing/details/sql-database/

11

Applying a Microservice Architecture to Your Enterprise Application

This chapter is dedicated to describing highly scalable architectures based on small modules called microservices. The microservice architecture allows for fine-grained scaling operations where every single module can be scaled as required without affecting the remainder of the system. Moreover, they allow for better Continuous Integration/Continuous Deployment (CI/CD) by permitting every system subpart to evolve and be deployed independently of the others. The chapter also explains how to balance these advantages with the greater development cost of a Microservices-based architecture when deciding on the adoption and configuration of a Microservice architecture.

In this chapter, we will cover the following topics:

- What are microservices?
- How does .NET deal with microservices?
- Which tools are needed to manage microservices?

By the end of this chapter, you will understand the principles of microservice design with a focus on .NET Microservices. *Chapter 19, Orchestrators and .NET Aspire*, also explains how to debug and manage a whole microservices-based application. *Chapter 14, Implementing microservices with .NET*, and *Chapter 17, Implementing Front-end Microservices with ASP.NET Core*, are step-by-step guides to the practical implementation of microservices with .NET.

Technical requirements

The code for this chapter is available at `https://github.com/PacktPublishing/Software-Architecture-with-.NET-10-and-C-sharp-5E`.

In this chapter, you will need the following:

- Visual Studio 2026 free Community Edition or better, with all the database tools installed.

- A free Azure account. The *Creating an Azure account* section in *Chapter 1, Understanding the Importance of Software Architecture*, explains how to create one.
- ***Docker Desktop for Windows*** if you want to debug Docker containerized microservices in Visual Studio (`https://www.docker.com/products/docker-desktop`).
- In turn, ***Docker Desktop for Windows*** requires at least Windows 10 with either **WSL** (Windows Subsystem for Linux).

WSL enables Docker containers to run on a Linux virtual machine and can be installed as follows (see also `https://learn.microsoft.com/en-us/windows/wsl/install`):

- Type `powershell` in the Windows 10/11 search bar
- When ***Windows PowerShell*** is proposed as a search result, click on **Run as an administrator**
- In the Windows PowerShell administrative console that appears, run the command `wsl --install`

What are microservices?

Microservices are essentially small units that make up a larger software application and that may be implemented, maintained, and scaled independently of each other, each with its specific role and functionality. Splitting a software application into independent microservices allows each module that makes up a solution to be scaled independently from the others to achieve the maximum throughput with minimal cost. Fine-grained control of subsystem scaling has a considerable impact on the system's overall cost because scaling the whole system instead of its current bottlenecks inevitably results in a remarkable waste of resources.

However, microservices are more than scalable components – they are software building blocks that can be developed, maintained, and deployed independently of each other. Splitting development and maintenance among modules that can be independently developed, maintained, and deployed improves the overall system's **CI/CD cycle** (CI/CD was described in detail in *Chapter 8, Understanding DevSecOps Principles and CI/CD*).

Both mentioned benefits will be analyzed in more detail later on in this chapter and stated as fundamental microservices design principles.

The CI/CD improvement is due to microservice *independence* because it enables the following:

- Scaling and distributing microservices on different types of hardware.
- Since each microservice is deployed independently from the others, there can't be binary compatibility or database structure compatibility constraints. Therefore, there is no need to align the versions of the different microservices that compose the system. This means that each of them can evolve as needed without being constrained by the others.
- However, attention must be paid to the choice of communication protocols and messages and to their versions, which must be supported by all involved microservices. Protocols that are widely supported and that facilitate backward compatibility with previous versions of messages should be preferred.
- Assigning their development to completely separate smaller teams, thus simplifying job organization and reducing all the inevitable coordination inefficiencies that arise when handling large teams
- Implementing each microservice with more adequate technologies and in a more adequate environment since each microservice is an independent deployment unit. This means choosing tools

that best fit your requirements and an environment that minimizes development efforts and/or maximizes performance.

- Since each microservice can be implemented with different technologies, programming languages, tools, and operating systems, enterprises can use all available human resources by matching environments with developers' competencies. For instance, all available Java and .NET developers can cooperate in the same application, thus exploiting all available resources.
- Legacy subsystems can be embedded in independent microservices, thus enabling them to cooperate with newer subsystems. This way, companies may reduce the time to market of new system versions. Moreover, in this way, legacy systems can evolve slowly toward more modern systems with an acceptable impact on costs and the organization.

Summing up, splitting an application into independent microservices improves team organization, design optimization, and application maintenance.

As an example, suppose a big company, let's call it `tires.com`, that produces and sells tires, decides to build a unified company information system. Each office has its own development team specialized in some frameworks, say Java and .NET. Moreover, each office has different needs, and commercial offices are the ones that must respond more quickly to market changes.

The adoption of a microservices architecture would bring the following advantages:

- Each team can continue using its preferred framework, since integrating different technologies is not a problem. Therefore, we would maximize human resource utilization.
- Each team can continue working in its remote office since one can assign a different microservice to each team, and teams working on different microservices do not need tight interaction. Therefore, there would be no catastrophic organizational change.
- Teams working on microservices related to commercial activities can release new versions more frequently than other teams, since each microservice is versioned independently of the others. Therefore, development effort would be concentrated on the microservices that need to evolve more quickly.
- Useful legacy software can be reused by embedding each useful module in a separate microservice at a cost of architecting just the communication interface with the remainder of the application. Therefore, the impact of the change would be gradual.

Once we have understood the basic ideas behind microservices, we can dive into the details. Let's start with a historical perspective. The next subsection explains how the concept of microservices was conceived. Then, we will continue this introductory section by exploring basic microservice design principles and analyzing why microservices are often designed as Docker containers.

Microservices and the evolution of the concept of modules

For a better understanding of the advantages of microservices, as well as their design techniques, we must keep the two-fold nature of software modularity and software modules in mind:

- **Code modularity** refers to code organization that makes it easy for us to modify a chunk of code without affecting the remainder of the application. It is usually enforced with object-oriented design, where modules can be identified with classes.
- **Deployment modularity** depends on what your deployment units are and which properties they have. The simplest deployment units are executable files and libraries. Thus, for instance, **dynamic link libraries** (DLLs) are, for sure, more modular than static libraries since they must not be linked with the main executable before being deployed.

> **Note**
>
> While the fundamental concepts of code modularity have reached stasis, the concept of deployment modularity is still evolving, and microservices are currently state-of-the-art along this evolutionary path.

As a short review of the main milestones on the path that led to microservices, we can say that, first, monolithic executables were broken into static libraries. Later on, DLLs replaced static libraries, so that the same DLL can be used by several applications, thus simplifying installations and software updates.

Then, .NET (and other analogous frameworks, such as Java) enabled libraries to be deployed on different hardware and on different operating systems since they are distributed in an intermediary language that is compiled when the library is executed for the first time. Moreover, .NET libraries overcome further versioning issues since any executable can bring with it a DLL with a version that differs from the version of the same DLL that is installed on the operating system.

However, .NET can't accept two referenced DLLs – let's say, `A` and `B` – using two different versions of a common dependency – let's say, `C`. For instance, suppose there is a newer version of `A` with many new features we would like to use that, in turn, relies on a newer version of `C` that is not supported by `B`. In this situation, we should renounce the newer version of `A` because of the incompatibility of `C` with `B`. The situation is depicted in *Figure 11.1*.

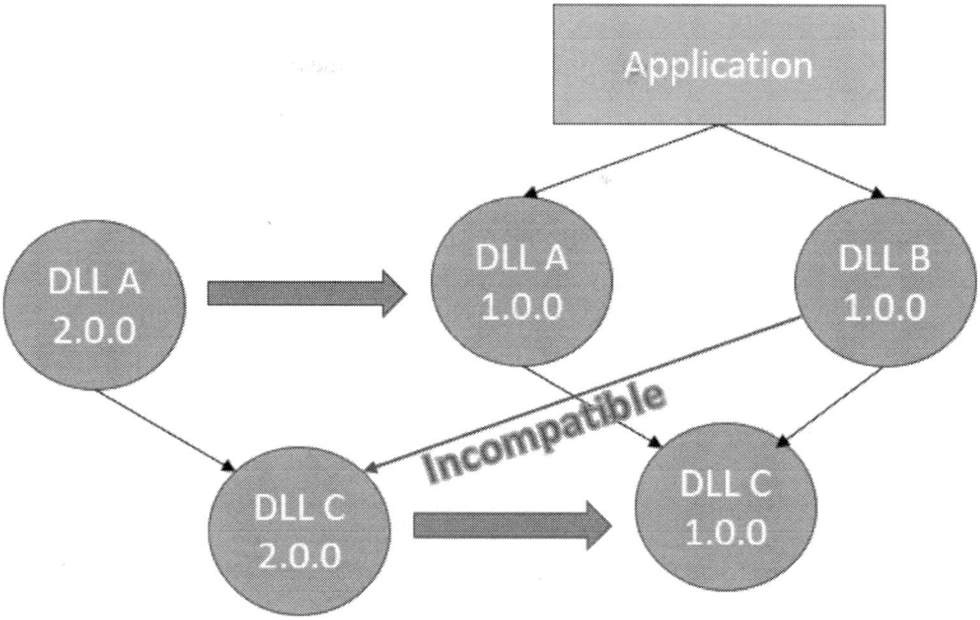

Figure 11.1: Incompatibility of DLL B version 1.00 with DLL C version 2.0.0 prevents adoption of the new 2.00 version of DLL A

This difficulty has led to two important changes:

- The development world moved from using single DLLs and/or single files as deployment units to using **packages** composed of both DLLs and metadata as deployment units, where packages are handled by **package management systems** such as *NuGet* and *npm*, which use package metadata to automatically check version compatibility with the help of semantic versioning.
- **Service-Oriented Architecture** (SOA). Deployment units started being implemented as **SOAP** and then as **REST** web services. This solves the version compatibility problem since each web service runs in a different process and can use the most adequate version of each library with no risk of causing incompatibilities with other web services.

Moreover, the interface that is exposed by each web service is platform-agnostic; that is, web services can connect with applications using any framework and run on any operating system since web service protocols are based on universally accepted standards. SOAs and protocols will be discussed in more detail in *Chapter 14, Implementing Microservices with .NET*, and *Chapter 15, Applying Service-Oriented Architectures with .NET*.

Tip

Microservices are an evolution of ***SOA*** and add more features and more constraints that improve the scalability and modularity of services to improve the overall CI/CD cycle. It's sometimes said that *microservices are SOA done well*. Moreover, as we will see in the next section, microservices are strictly tied to the ***DDD*** methodology described in *Chapter 7, Understanding the Different Domains in Software Solutions*.

To sum things up, the microservice architecture is an SOA that maximizes independence and fine-grained scaling.

Now that we've clarified all the advantages of microservice independence and fine-grained scaling, as well as the very nature of independence, we are in a position to look more formally at microservice design principles.

Microservices design principles

This section covers the basic design principles that form the foundation for designing both individual microservice architectures and overall application structure.

Let's start with principles that arise from the independence constraint. We will discuss each in a separate subsection.

The independence of design choices

A fundamental design principle is the *independence of design choices*, which can be stated as follows:

> *The design of each microservice must not depend on the design choices that were made in the implementation of other microservices.*

This principle enables the full independence of each microservice CI/CD cycle and leaves us with more technological choices on how to implement each microservice. This way, we can choose the best available technology to implement each microservice.

Another consequence of this principle is that different microservices can't connect to the same shared storage (database or filesystem) since sharing the same storage also means sharing all the design choices that determine the structure of the storage subsystem (database table design, database engine, and so on). Thus, either a microservice has its own data storage, or it has no storage at all and communicates with other microservices that take care of handling storage.

In order to better understand the need for separated storage, let's suppose that microservices `A` and `B` share the same products database `P`. Then, changes made to `P` for new requirements of `A` would cause code changes in `B`, too. Moreover, in turn, these changes might cause an exponential wave of changes all over the application.

Summing up, our previous design principle immediately implies a new design principle:

> *Each microservice must have its dedicated database.*

Dedicated data storage can be implemented either by physically including the database service within the boundary of the Microservice or with an external database that the Microservice has exclusive access to. Both are acceptable design choices. However, external databases are usually adopted because, for performance reasons, database engines are better run on dedicated hardware and with OS and hardware features that are optimized for their storage functionalities.

Usually, the *independence of design choices* is interpreted in a lighter form by distinguishing between logical and physical microservices. More specifically, logical microservices are the result of splitting the application into logically independent modules. If the application is designed with a domain-driven design methodology, logical microservices correspond to DDD **bounded contexts**, which we discussed in detail in *Chapter 7, Understanding the Different Domains in Software Solutions*.

In turn, each logical microservice may be split into various physical microservices that use the same data storage but are load-balanced independently to achieve a better load balance.

For instance, in the book case study, travel payments are handled by the Payments bounded context described in the *Understanding the domains of the WWTravelClub application section of Chapter 22, Case Study: Practical Usage of .NET Aspire*, which gives rise to a unique logical microservice. However, its practical implementation requires two main submodules:

1. A customer credit card verification and authorization module that takes care of all credit card verifications
2. A user credits management module that handles both credits the user has already purchased, card information already loaded in the platform, and new credit card info loading

Since the process of credit card verification and authorization might be very time-consuming, it is convenient to implement the two submodules above as independent physical microservices, so they can be load balanced separately.

Together with independence of design choice, independence from the deployment environment also plays a fundamental role. Let's analyze it in detail.

Independence from the deployment environment

During load balance, a microservice can be moved from very busy hardware nodes to more idle nodes. However, dependencies of each microservice on other software/files of the destination hardware nodes constrain the possible destination nodes.

Therefore, the more we reduce microservice dependencies, the more freedom we have to move them from busy nodes to idle nodes, the better the load balance, and the more we exploit the available hardware nodes.

Accordingly, we can state the following design principle:

> *Microservices architectures must minimize the dependency of each microservice from the execution environment.*

This is the reason microservices are often containerized and use Docker. Containers will be discussed in more detail in the *Containers and Docker* subsection of this chapter, but basically, containerization is a technique that allows each microservice to bring its dependencies with it so that it can run anywhere. However, this is not a must because in some applications, one might verify that all dependency requirements of all microservices can be easily satisfied by all available nodes.

As we explore how microservices operate within their containerized environments, another key architectural principle comes into play: the concept of loose coupling.

Loose coupling

Another important principle comes from both SOLID and performance constraints:

> *Microservices architectures must minimize communication among microservices, that is microservices must be loosely coupled.*

Each microservice must be loosely coupled with all the other microservices. This principle has a two-fold nature. On the one hand, this means that, according to object-oriented programming principles, the interface that's exposed by each microservice must not be too specific but as general as possible. However, it also means that communications among microservices must be minimized in order to reduce communication costs since microservices don't share the same address space and run on different hardware nodes.

Loose coupling can be achieved with the following techniques:

- Using Design Driven Design to discover each microservice's boundaries. In fact, if we implement each DDD bounded context with a different microservice, communications between microservices should be automatically minimized as explained in *Chapter 7, Understanding the Different Domains in Software Solutions*.
- Together with communications minimization, we must also avoid that changes applied to a microservice might propagate to other microservices. For instance, adding a new microservice to our application must not cause changes in existing microservices that must communicate with it. The adoption of the publisher-subscriber pattern for all communication is the best way to prevent change propagation.

Minimizing inter-service communications is not enough to get good performance. We must also minimize the time lost waiting for responses. The first step toward this target is the avoidance of long chained requests/responses that will be analyzed in the next section.

No chained requests/responses

When a request reaches a microservice, it must not cause a recursive chain of nested requests/responses to other microservices since a similar chain would result in an unacceptable response time.

For instance, suppose that a microservice `A` issues a request to a microservice `B`, and then waits for `B` to answer, and `B` does the same with `C`, and `C` does the same with `D`, and so on. As a result, `A` remains blocked waiting for its answer for the whole time the request propagates from `A` to `D`, and then all answers propagate back.

Similar request/response propagations may have an unacceptable impact on the response time seen by the users, they must be avoided.

Chained requests/responses can be avoided if the private data models of all the microservices synchronize with push events each time they change. In other words, as soon as the data that are handled by a microservice change, those changes are sent to all the microservices that may need them to serve their requests. This way, each microservice has all the data it needs to serve all its incoming requests in its private data storage, with no need to ask other microservices for the data that it lacks.

Figure 11.2 shows how updates are sent to all interested microservices as soon as they are produced and how each microservice combines all received updates in a local database. Each arrow represents paths followed by messages. This way, each query microservice has all the data it needs to answer queries in its local database.

Please notice that messages propagate through a maximum of 2 microservices, so long chains are avoided. Moreover, no microservice remains frozen waiting for a response, because each sender doesn't need a response to continue its processing.

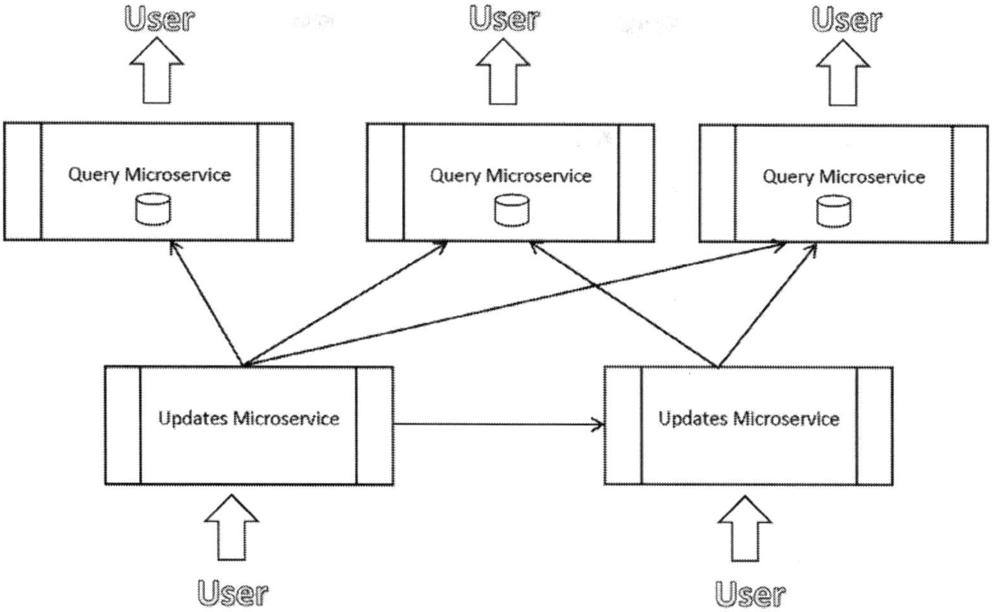

Figure 11.2: Push events

In conclusion, every microservice must contain all the data it needs to serve incoming requests and ensure fast responses. To keep their data models up to date and ready for incoming requests, microservices must communicate their data changes as soon as they take place. These data changes should be communicated through asynchronous messages since synchronous nested messages cause unacceptable performance because they block all the threads involved in the call tree until a result is returned.

Tip

It is worth pointing out that the Independence of design choices principle is substantially the bounded context principle of domain-driven design, which we discussed in detail in *Chapter 7, Understanding the Different Domains in Software Solutions*. In this chapter, we have seen that, often, a full domain-driven design approach is useful for the update subsystem of each microservice.

It's not trivial that, in general, all systems that have been developed according to the bounded context principle are better implemented with a microservice architecture. In fact, once a system has been decomposed into several completely independent and loosely coupled parts, it is very likely that these different parts will need to be scaled independently because of different traffic and different resource requirements.

Fine-grained scaling is a key aspect of microservices architecture, involving several critical software and infrastructure requirements:

1. First of all, microservices must be small enough to isolate well-defined functionalities

2. We also need a complex infrastructure that takes care of automatically instantiating microservices and allocating instances on various hardware computational resources, commonly called **nodes**
3. The same infrastructure must take care of scaling microservices and load balancing them on the available nodes

These kinds of structures will be introduced in the *Which tools are needed to manage microservices?* section of this chapter, and discussed in detail in *Chapter 19, Orchestrators and .NET Aspire.*

Moreover, fine-grained scaling of distributed microservices that communicate through asynchronous communication requires each microservice to be resilient. In fact, communication that's directed to a specific microservice instance may fail due to a hardware fault or for the simple reason that the target instance was killed or moved to another node during a load-balancing operation.

Temporary failures can be overcome with exponential retries. This is where we retry the same operation after each failure with a delay that increases exponentially until a maximum number of attempts is reached. For instance, first, we would retry after 10 milliseconds, and if this retry operation results in a failure, a new attempt is made after 20 milliseconds, then after 40 milliseconds, and so on.

On the other hand, long-term failures often cause an explosion of retry operations that may saturate all system resources in a way that is similar to a denial-of-service attack. Therefore, usually, exponential retries are used together with a circuit break strategy: after a given number of failures, a long-term failure is assumed, and access to the resource is prevented for a given time by returning an immediate failure without attempting the communication operation.

It is also fundamental that the congestion of some subsystems, due to either failure or a request peak, does not propagate to other system parts in order to prevent overall system congestion. **Bulkhead isolation** avoids congestion propagation with strategies like the one described below:

- Only a maximum number of similar simultaneous outbound requests are allowed; let's say, 10. This is similar to putting an upper bound on thread creation.
- Requests exceeding the previous bound are queued.
- If the maximum queue length is reached, any further requests result in exceptions being thrown to abort them.

The practical .NET implementation of exponential retries, circuit break, and bulkhead isolation is described in the *Resilient task execution subsection* of this chapter.

Retry policies may make it so that the same message is received and processed several times because the sender has received no confirmation that the message has been received or simply because it has timed out the operation while the receiver actually received the message. The only possible solution to this problem is designing all messages so that they're idempotent, that is, designing messages in such a way that processing the same message several times has the same effect as processing it once. Some operations, such as updates to a new value are idempotent since repeating them once or twice has exactly the same effect, but others, such as increments or additions of new entities are not.

Microservice designers should make an effort to design the overall application with as many idempotent messages as possible. The remaining non-idempotent messages must be transformed into idempotent with the techniques depicted in *Figure 11.3* and explained in the points below, or with other similar techniques:

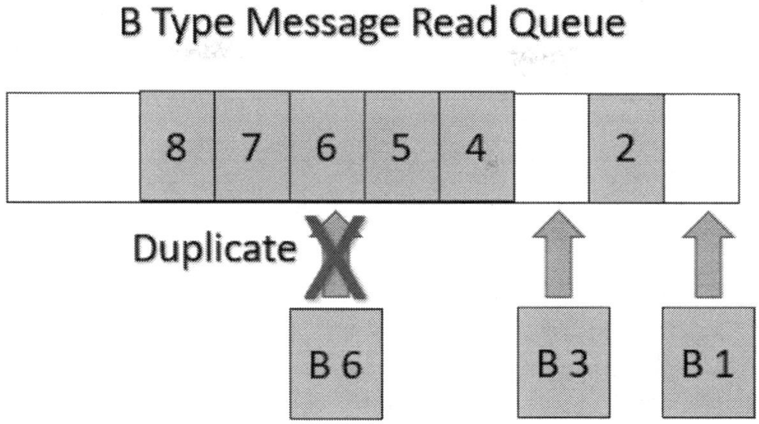

Figure 11.3: Recognizing duplicates

- Attach both a time and an identifier that uniquely identifies each message.
- Store all the messages that have been received in a dictionary that's indexed by the unique identifier attached to the message mentioned in the previous point.
- Reject old messages.
- When a message that may be a duplicate is received, verify whether it's contained in the dictionary. If it is, then it has already been processed, so reject it.
- Since old messages are rejected, they can be periodically removed from the dictionary to prevent it from growing exponentially.

In *Chapter 14*, *Implementing Microservices with .NET*, we will use this technique in practice and discuss communication and coordination problems in more detail.

It is worth pointing out that some message brokers, such as Azure Service Bus, offer facilities for implementing the technique described previously. However, the receiver must always be able to recognize duplicate messages since, due to time-outs in the reception of acknowledgments, messages might be resent. Azure Service Bus is discussed in the *.NET communication facilities* subsection.

Now that we have understood what microservices are, what problems they can solve, and their basic design principles, we are ready to analyze when and how to use them in our system architecture. The next section analyzes when we should use them.

When do microservices help?

The answer to this question requires us to understand the roles microservices play in modern software architectures. We will look at this in the following two subsections:

- Layered architectures and microservices
- When is it worth considering microservice architectures?

Let's start with a detailed look at layered architectures and microservices.

Layered architectures and microservices

As discussed in *Chapter 7, Understanding the Different Domains in Software Solutions*, enterprise systems are usually organized in logically independent layers.

In the case of onion architectures, each layer takes data by interacting with previous layers, processes them, and possibly passes some results back to previous layers. Thrown exceptions can't jump layers as they are—each layer must take care of intercepting all the exceptions and either *solve them* somehow or transform them into other exceptions that are expressed in the language of the calling layer. The layered architecture ensures the complete independence of the functionalities of inner layers from the functionalities of outer layers.

That being said, how do microservices fit into a layered architecture? Are they adequate for the functionalities of all the layers or just some layers? Can a single microservice span several layers?

The last question is the easiest to answer: yes! In fact, we've already stated that microservices should store the data they need within their logical boundaries. Therefore, for sure there are microservices that span all layers.

However, since we said that each logical microservice can be implemented with several physical microservices for pure load balancing reasons, some microservices that take care of encapsulating data used by another microservice might remain confined in the domain layer.

Moreover, we also said that while each microservice must have its exclusive storage, it can also use external storage engines. Therefore, we have the following three possibilities:

1. The storage engine is part of the microservice itself. This solution is adequate for simple microservices that don't need to be replicated and that don't have stringent performance requirements.
2. The storage engine is implemented by other microservices. This solution is adequate when there are more serious performance requirements, but we need full control of the storage engine and database replications.
3. External engine. The storage engine is not part of the microservices architecture and is implemented with other technologies. This solution is adequate when the database runs on dedicated machines and/or we would like to share it with other microservices and applications.

The diagram below depicts the difference between the external storage engine and the other two options.

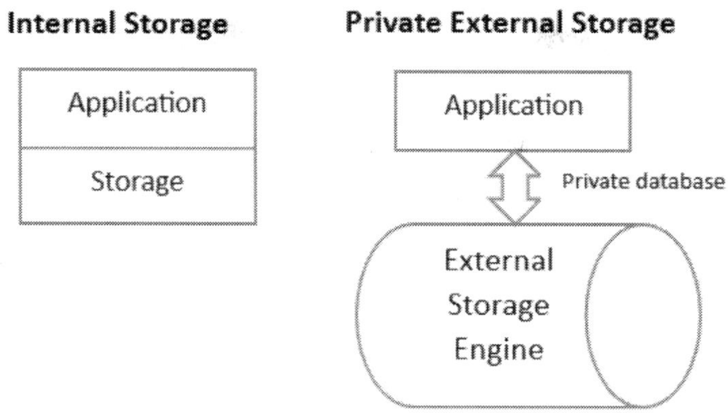

Figure 11.4: External or internal storage

It is worth pointing out that option 2 consists of implementing the storage engine itself as a set of physical microservices that are associated with no logical microservice, since they may be considered part of the infrastructure.

This is the case, for instance, for storage engines based on the distributed REDIS in-memory storage, where we use microservices facilities offered by our infrastructure to implement a scalable 1-primary/many-read-only-replicas, or a sophisticated many-primaries/many-read-only-replicas distributed in-memory storage, as shown in *Figure 11.5*.

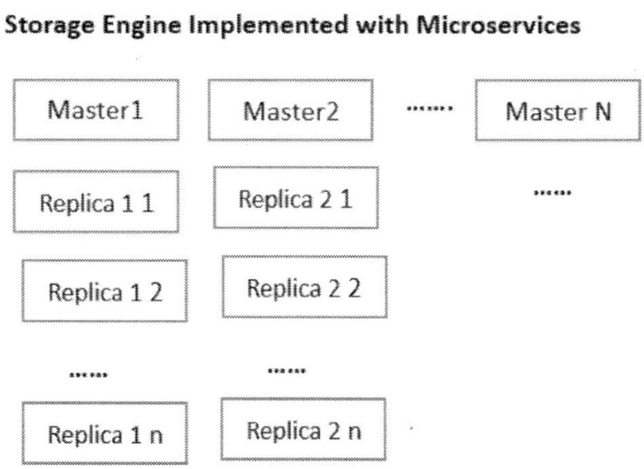

Figure 11.5: Many-master/many-read-only-replicas storage engine

Each master has its associated read-only replicas. Storage updates can be passed just to masters that replicate their data to all their associated read-only replicas.

Each master takes care of a portion of the storage space, for instance, all products whose name starts with "A", and so on. This way, the load is balanced between all masters.

Thus, we may have data layer only microservices, and microservices that implement a physical storage. What about the **User Interface**?

The user interface

The user interface fits into the outermost layer of an Onion architecture if it is implemented on the server side, that is, if the whole graphics that interact with the user are built on the server side and not on the user client machine (mobile device, desktop, etc.).

When there are microservices that interact directly with the user, we speak of server-side implementation of the user interface, since the HTML and/or all elements of the user interface are created by the frontend that sends the response to the user.

This kind of microservice is called frontend microservices. While microservices that do back-office work without interacting with the user are called worker microservices. The diagram below summarizes the frontend/worker organization.

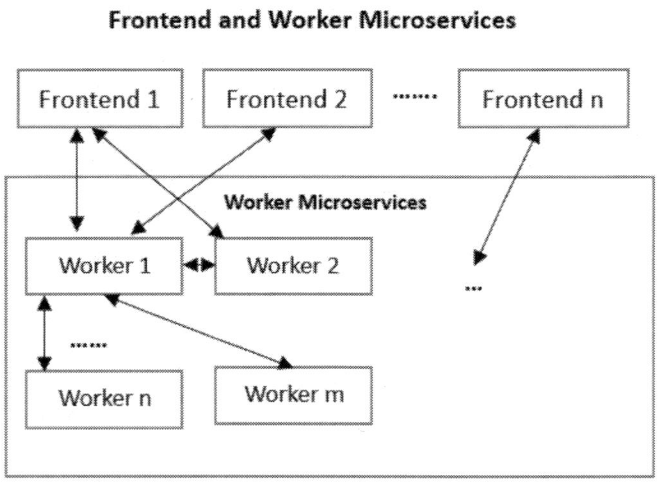

Figure 11.6: Frontend and Worker microservices

When, instead, the HTML and/or all elements of the user interface are generated on the user machine, we speak of client-side implementation of the user interface. The so-called Single-page applications and mobile applications run the user interface on the client machine and interact with the application through communication interfaces exposed by dedicated microservices. These dedicated microservices are completely analogous to the frontend microservices depicted in *Figure 11.6*, and often are called frontend microservices themselves, too. Actually, they are just microservices that expose externally reachable APIs. These APIs receive external traffic through a common load-balanced service which is called **API gateway** to underline its role of exposing a public API for connecting client devices with the whole microservices infrastructure. The picture below exemplifies the way API Gateways work.

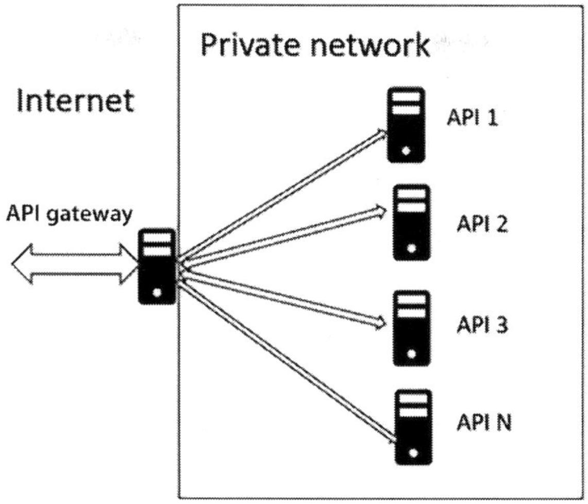

Figure 11.7: API Gateway that interfaces with externally reachable Microservices

Together with exposing a unique entry point, an API gateway takes care of authenticating and translating external requests into requests for externally reachable Microservices. This includes address translations and possible protocol translation (such as from https to http). API gateway services are offered by all major Cloud providers, and are also implemented by various open-source projects. More details on API gateway can be found in *Chapter 17, Implementing Frontend Microservices with ASP.NET Core.*

In turn, an externally reachable Microservice interacts with the remainder of the application in exactly the same way as HTML-based frontend Microservices.

Single page applications and mobile/desktop client applications are discussed in *Chapter 18, Client Frameworks: Blazor.*

In a microservice architecture, when the user interface is a website, it can be implemented with a set of several physical microservices. However, if it requires heavy web servers and/or heavy frameworks, containerizing them may not be convenient. This decision must also consider the loss of performance that happens when containerizing the web server and the possible need for hardware firewalls between the web server and the remainder of the system.

ASP.NET Core is a lightweight framework that runs on the light Kestrel web server, so it can be containerized efficiently and used as-is in the worker microservices. The usage of ASP.NET Core in the implementation of worker microservices is described in great detail in *Chapter 14, Implementing Microservices with .NET.*

Instead, frontend and/or high-traffic websites have more compelling security and load-balancing requirements that can be satisfied just with fully-featured web servers. Accordingly, architectures based on microservices usually offer specialized components that take care of interfacing with the outside world made up of web servers organized in a *Web Server Farm*. External requests are split among the servers composing the *Web Server Farm* by hardware-software modules called **Load Balancers**.

Monolithic websites can be easily broken into load-balanced, smaller subsites without microservice-specific technologies, but a microservice architecture can bring all the advantages of microservices into the construction of a single HTML page. More specifically, different microservices may take care of different areas of each HTML page. Microservices that cooperate in the construction of the HTML of application pages, and in general in the construction of any kind of user interface, are named **Micro-Frontends**. We will speak in more detail about micro-frontends in *Chapter 17, Implementing Front-end Microservices with ASP.NET Core.*

When the HTML is created on the server side, the various micro-frontends create HTML chunks that are combined either on the server side or directly in the browser.

When, instead, the HTML is created directly on the client, each micro-frontend provides a different chunk of code to the client. These code chunks are run on the client machine, and each of them takes care of different pages/page areas.

Now that we've clarified which parts of a system can benefit from the adoption of microservices, we are ready to state the rules when it comes to deciding how they're adopted.

When is it worth considering microservices architectures?

Microservices can improve the implementation of both the business and data layers, but their adoption has some costs:

- Allocating instances to nodes and scaling them has a cost in terms of cloud fees or internal infrastructure and licenses.
- Splitting a unique process into smaller communication processes increases communication costs and hardware needs, especially if the microservices are containerized.
- Designing and testing software for a microservice requires more time and increases engineering costs, both in time and complexity. In particular, making microservices resilient and ensuring that they adequately handle all possible failures, as well as verifying these features with integration tests, can increase the development time by more than one order of magnitude (that is, about 4-5 times)

So, when are microservices worth the cost of using them? Are there functionalities that must be implemented as microservices?

A rough answer to the second question is yes when the application is big enough in terms of traffic and/or software complexity. In fact, as an application grows in complexity and its traffic increases, it's recommended that we pay the costs associated with scaling it since this allows for more scaling optimization and easier and more efficient application maintenance when it comes to the development team. The costs we pay for these would soon exceed the cost of microservice adoption.

Thus, if fine-grained scaling makes sense for our application, and if we are able to estimate the savings that fine-grained scaling and development give us, we can easily compute an overall application throughput limit that makes the adoption of microservices convenient.

Microservice costs can also be justified by an increase in the market value of our products/services. Since the microservice architecture allows us to implement each microservice with a technology that has been optimized for its use, the quality that's added to our software may justify all or part of the microservice costs.

However, scaling and technology optimizations are not the only parameters to consider. Sometimes, we are forced to adopt a microservice architecture without being able to perform a detailed cost analysis.

If the size of the team that takes care of the CI/CD of the overall system grows too much, the organization and coordination of this big team cause difficulties and inefficiencies. In this type of situation, it is desirable to move to an architecture that breaks the whole CI/CD cycle into independent parts that can be taken care of by smaller teams.

Moreover, since these development costs are only justified by a high volume of requests, we probably have high traffic being processed by independent modules that have been developed by different teams. Therefore, scaling optimizations and the need to reduce interaction between development teams make the adoption of a microservice architecture very convenient.

From this, we may conclude that if the system and the development team grow too much, it is necessary to split the development team into smaller teams, each working on an efficient bounded context subsystem. It is very likely that, in a similar situation, a microservice architecture is the only possible option.

Another situation that forces the adoption of a microservice architecture is the integration of newer subparts with legacy subsystems based on different technologies, since containerized microservices are the only way to implement an efficient interaction between the legacy system and the new subparts in order to gradually replace the legacy subparts with newer ones. Similarly, if our team is composed of developers with experience in different development stacks, an architecture based on containerized microservices may become a *must*.

Summing up, microservices adoption is justified only when the required development team exceeds 10 people, or when the load generated by all users requires several servers. In extreme cases, such as a 100-person development team or a load that would require more than 20 powerful servers, the decision is immediate, but intermediate cases might need a detailed cost analysis of both adopting and not adopting the microservice architecture.

In the next subsection, we will talk about microservice containerization based on Docker.

Containers and Docker

We've already discussed the advantages of having microservices that don't depend on the environment where they run: microservices can be moved from busy nodes to idle nodes without constraints, thus achieving a better load balance and consequently a better usage of the available hardware.

However, if we need to mix legacy software with newer modules, the ability to mix several development stacks in order to use the best stack for each module implementation, and so on, we are faced with the problem that the various microservices have different hardware/software prerequisites. In these cases, independence of each microservice from the hosting environment can be restored by deploying each microservice with all its dependencies on a private virtual machine.

However, starting a virtual machine with its private copy of the operating system takes some minutes, which is an unacceptable time, since microservices must be started and stopped in a few seconds to reduce load balancing and fault recovery costs. In fact, new microservices may be started either to replace faulty ones or because they were moved from one hardware node to another to perform load balancing. Moreover, adding a whole copy of the operating system to each microservice instance would be an excessive overhead.

Luckily, microservices can rely on a lighter form of technology: **Containers**. Containers may be considered a kind of light virtual machine. They don't need to launch an operating system since they use the operating system of the underlying machine, so they can be launched quickly because they avoid the costly operating-system launching operation.

In fact, they virtualize just the filesystem that sits on top of the host machine's OS kernel. They use the OS of the hosting machine (kernel, DLLs, and drivers) and rely on the OS's native features to isolate processes and resources to ensure an isolated environment for the images they run.

As a consequence, containers are tied to a specific operating system, but they don't suffer the overhead of copying and starting a whole OS in each container instance.

> **Tip**
>
> On each host machine, containers are handled by a runtime that takes care of creating them from *Images* and creating an isolated environment for each of them. The most popular container image format is Docker, which is a *de facto* standard for container images.

Images contain files needed to create each container and specify which container resources, such as communication ports, to expose outside of the container. However, they need not explicitly contain all involved files since they can be layered. This way, each image is built by adding new files and configuration information on top of another existing image that is referenced from inside the newly defined image, as shown by the picture below:

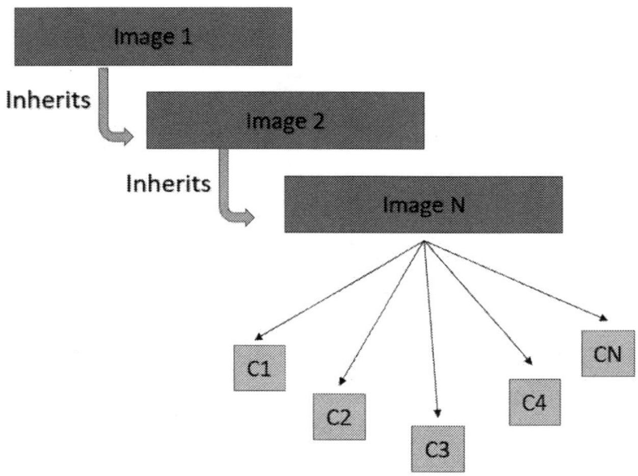

Figure 11.8: Image hierarchy and containers

For instance, if you want to deploy a .NET application as a Docker image, it is enough to just add your software and files to your Docker image and then reference an already existing .NET Docker image.

To allow for easy image referencing, images are grouped into registries that may be either public or private. They are similar to `NuGet` or `npm` registries. Docker offers a public registry (`https://hub.docker.com`) where you can find most of the public images you may need to reference in your own images. However, each company can define private registries. For instance, Microsoft offers Azure Container Registry, where you can define your private container registry service: `https://azure.microsoft.com/en-us/services/container-registry/`. There, you can also find most of the .NET-related images you might need to reference in your code.

Before instantiating each container, the Docker runtime must solve all the recursive references. This cumbersome job is not performed each time a new container is created since the Docker runtime has a cache where it stores the fully assembled images that correspond to each input image and that it has already processed.

We will analyze in more detail Docker and Docker images in the *How does .NET deal with microservices?* section of this chapter.

Image names have the following format:

```
<classification>/<subclassification>/…./<actual name>: version
```

Where version is a string that specifies the code version such as `v1.1.1`. When no version is specified, the `latest` version is assumed, which represents the latest version.

For instance, `mcr.microsoft.com/mssql/server:2022-CU16-ubuntu-22.04` is the version 22.04 of SQL-server 2022 for Ubuntu. The domain is Microsoft registry domain, while the image is classified as `mssql`, that is as a SQL-server image. Both version and target operating system are specified in the version part of the image name.

The Docker runtime handles images and containers on a single machine, but usually, containerized microservices are deployed and load-balanced on clusters that are composed of several machines. Clusters are handled by pieces of software called **Orchestrators**. Orchestrators will be introduced in the *Which tools are needed to manage microservices?* section of this chapter, and described in detail in *Chapter 19*, *Orchestrators and .NET Aspire*.

Having discussed in detail the theory behind microservices, it's time to shift to the tools needed for their practical implementation and maintenance. In the next section, we will analyze building blocks and tools that are available for the implementation of .NET-based microservices.

How does .NET deal with microservices?

The new .NET, which evolved from .NET Core, was conceived as a multi-platform framework that was light and fast enough to implement efficient microservices. In particular, ASP.NET Core is the ideal tool for implementing text-REST and binary gRPC APIs to communicate with a microservice since it can run efficiently with light web servers such as Kestrel and is itself light and modular.

The whole .NET stack evolved with microservices as a strategic deployment platform in mind and has facilities and packages for building efficient and light HTTP and gRPC communication to ensure service resiliency and to handle long-running tasks. The following subsections describe some of the different tools or solutions that we can use to implement a .NET-based microservice architecture.

.NET communication facilities

Microservices need two kinds of communication channels:

- The first communication channel receives external requests, either directly or through an API gateway. HTTP is the usual protocol for external communication due to available web service standards and tools. .NET's main HTTP/gRPC communication facility is ASP.NET Core since it's a lightweight HTTP/gRPC framework, which makes it ideal for implementing web APIs in small microservices. We will describe ASP.NET REST API apps in detail in *Chapter 15, Applying Service-Oriented Architectures with .NET*, and we will describe gRPC services in Chapter *14, Implementing Microservices with .NET*. .NET also offers an efficient and modular HTTP client solution that is able to pool and reuse heavy connection objects.
- The second one is a different type of communication channel to push updates to other microservices. In fact, we have already mentioned that intra-microservice communication cannot be triggered by an ongoing request since a complex tree of blocking calls to other microservices would increase request latency to an unacceptable level. As a consequence, updates must not be requested immediately before they're used and should be pushed whenever state changes take place. Ideally, this kind of communication should be asynchronous to achieve acceptable performance. In fact, synchronous calls would block the sender while they are waiting for the result, thus increasing the idle time of each microservice. However, synchronous communication that just puts the request in a processing queue and then returns confirmation of the successful communication instead of the final result is acceptable if communication is fast enough (low communication latency and high bandwidth). A publisher/subscriber communication would be preferable since, in this case, the sender and receiver don't need to know each other, thus increasing the microservices' independence. In fact, all the receivers that are interested in a certain type of communication merely need to register to receive a specific *event*, while senders just need to publish those events. All the wiring is performed by a service that takes care of queuing events and dispatching them to all the subscribers. The publisher/subscriber pattern has been described in *Chapter 6, Design Patterns and .NET Implementation*, along with other useful patterns.

While .NET doesn't directly offer tools that may help in asynchronous communication or client/server tools that implement publisher/subscriber communication, Azure offers a similar service with **Azure Service Bus** (`https://docs.microsoft.com/en-us/azure/service-bus-messaging/`). Azure Service Bus handles both queued asynchronous communication through Azure Service Bus *queues* and publisher/subscriber communication through Azure Service Bus *topics*.

Once you've configured the Azure Service Bus on the Azure portal, you can connect to it in order to send messages/events and receive messages/events through a client contained in the `Azure.Messaging.ServiceBus` NuGet package.

Azure Service Bus has two types of communication: queue-based and topic-based. In queue-based communication, each message that's placed in the queue by a sender is removed from the queue by the first receiver that pulls it from the queue. Topic-based communication, on the other hand, is an implementation of the publisher/subscriber pattern. Each topic has several subscriptions, and a different copy of each message sent to a topic can be pulled from each topic subscription.

The design flow is as follows:

1. Define an Azure Service Bus private namespace
2. Get the root connection strings that were created by the Azure portal and/or define new connection strings with fewer privileges
3. Define queues and/or topics where the sender will send their messages in binary format
4. For each topic, define names for all the required subscriptions
5. In the case of queue-based communication, the sender sends messages to a queue, and the receivers pull messages from the same queue. Each message is delivered to one receiver. That is, once a receiver gains access to the queue, it reads and removes one or more messages.
6. In the case of topic-based communication, each sender sends messages to a topic while each receiver pulls messages from its private subscription associated with that topic

There are also other commercial and free open-source alternatives to direct interaction with Azure Service Bus, such as **NServiceBus** (`https://particular.net/nservicebus`), **MassTransit** (`https://masstransit-project.com/`), and **Brighter** (`https://www.goparamore.io/`). **NServiceBus** and **MassTransit** enhance existing brokers (like Azure Service Bus itself) with higher-level functionalities, while *Brighter* is just a library that enables you to code your custom messaging solution.

There is also a free, completely independent option that can be used on on-premises platforms: **RabbitMQ**. It is free and open source and can be installed locally, on a virtual machine, or in a Docker container. Then, you can connect with it through the client contained in the `RabbitMQ.Client` NuGet package.

The functionalities of RabbitMQ are similar to the ones offered by Azure Service Bus, but you have to take care of more implementation details, like serialization, reliable messages, and error handling, while Azure Service Bus takes care of all the low-level operations and offers you a simpler interface. However, there are clients that build a more powerful abstraction on top of RabbitMQ, like, for instance, EasyNetQ. The choice between an open-source message broker like RabbitMQ and message brokers offered by the Cloud provider like Azure Service Bus is mainly based on the possible requirement that the application must not depend on a specific Cloud Provider since the cost of the Cloud message broker service is substantially negligible.

The publisher/subscriber-based communication pattern used by both Azure Service Bus and RabbitMQ has been described in *Chapter 6*, *Design Patterns and .NET Implementation*. RabbitMQ will be described in more detail in *Chapter 14*, *Implementing Microservices with .NET*.

Reliable communication is strictly tied with the more general topic of resilient task execution. Let's analyze which tools the .NET ecosystem provides to handle resiliency.

Resilient task execution

Resilient communication and, in general, resilient task execution can be implemented easily with the help of a .NET library called Polly, whose project is a member of the .NET Foundation. Polly is available through the `Polly.Core` NuGet package.

In Polly, you define a resiliency pipeline, then add resiliency strategies to this pipeline and finally execute tasks in the context of all added strategies, as follows:

```
var pipeline = new ResiliencePipelineBuilder()
 .AddStrategy1(<strategy options>)
 .AddStrategy2(<strategy options>)
 ...
 ...
 .Build();
...
await pipeline.ExecuteAsync(static async token =>
 {
  /* Your resilient tasks goes here */
 },
 cancellationToken);
```

Where `AddStrategy1` and `AddStrategy2` are placeholders for methods that add specific strategies. The code you would like to protect with your resiliency strategies goes in the lambda function body, and is passed the same cancellation token you pass as the second argument to `ExecuteAsync`. Each time your code throws an exception, all strategies you defined are triggered.

Below is the definition of an exponential retry strategy:

```
.AddRetry(
  new RetryStrategyOptions
  {
      ShouldHandle =
        new PredicateBuilder().Handle<SomeExceptionType>(),
      BackoffType = DelayBackoffType.Exponential,
      UseJitter = true,  // Adds a random factor to the delay
      MaxRetryAttempts = 4,
      Delay = TimeSpan.FromSeconds(3),
  };
)
```

Where `ShouldHandle` specifies all exceptions that must be handled by this strategy (all exceptions if no exception is specified), `Delay` is the initial delay that is then increased exponentially, `MaxRetryAttempts` is the maximum number of retries that must be done. When this limit is reached, the exception is passed outside of the `ExecuteAsync` call, if the same exception is not handled by another strategy. `BackoffType` specifies the strategy that in our case is exponential. Other parameters allow the complete customization of the overall delay generator and of the exponent used by the strategy, which defaults to 2.

Below is the definition of a circuit breaker strategy:

```
. AddCircuitBreaker (
  new CircuitBreakerStrategyOptions
  {
      FailureRatio = 0.5,
      SamplingDuration = TimeSpan.FromSeconds(10),
      MinimumThroughput = 8,
      BreakDuration = TimeSpan.FromSeconds(30),
      ShouldHandle = new PredicateBuilder().Handle<SomeExceptionType>()
  };
)
```

As in the previous strategy, `ShouldHandle` specifies the exceptions handled by the strategy. The strategy is applied whenever a percentage of `FailureRatio` of the attempts done in the time specified by `SamplingDuration` fail. Moreover, the strategy is applied only after `MinimumThroughput` attempts are done. When the strategy applies, it blocks any further attempt and any other call to the `pipeline.ExecuteAsync` method for a time of `BreakDuration`.

Note

Further calls to the `pipeline.ExecuteAsync` method are blocked by the circuit breaker strategy only if they are done through the same `ResiliencePipeline` instance, since the state of all resiliency strategies is maintained there.

Below is the definition of a rate limiter strategy:

```
.AddRateLimiter(new SlidingWindowRateLimiter(
        new SlidingWindowRateLimiterOptions
        {
            PermitLimit = 100,
            SegmentsPerWindow = 4,
            Window = TimeSpan.FromMinutes(1)
        }));
```

It limits the maximum number `pipeline.ExecuteAsync` can be called in a time defined by `Window` to `PermitLimit`. If this limit is exceeded, it throws an `RateLimiterRejectedException` exception. The time window is split into `SegmentsPerWindow` time slots. When a new time slot is passed, it replaces the oldest time slot in the time window, then `PermitLimit` is checked.

Polly offers several more options, such as generic methods for tasks that return a specific type, timeout policies, task result caching, the ability to define custom policies, and so on. It is also possible to configure Polly as part of an `HttpClient` definition in the dependency injection section of any ASP.NET Core and .NET application. This way, it is quite immediate to define resilient clients.

Finally, below is a timeout strategy:

```
.AddTimeout(TimeSpan.FromSeconds(3))
```

When the timeout expires, the `token` passed to the lambda `pipeline.ExecuteAsync(token => {…})` is signaled, thus informing the protected code it must terminate execution.

Polly's official documentation can be found in its GitHub repository here: `https://github.com/App-vNext/Polly`.

Practical usage of Polly is explained in the *A worker microservices with ASP.NET core* section of *Chapter 22, Case Study: Practical Usage of .NET Aspire.*

The resilience and robustness provided by tools like Polly are crucial components of microservice architecture, particularly when managing complex tasks and processes.

This brings us to another fundamental aspect of microservices: the implementation of generic hosts.

Using hosts in .NET

Each microservice may need to run several independent threads, each performing a different operation on requests received. Such threads need several resources, such as database connections, communication channels, specialized modules that perform complex operations, and so on. Moreover, all processing threads must be adequately initialized when the microservice is started and gracefully stopped when the microservice is stopped as a consequence of either load balancing or errors.

All the above operations may be facilitated by software that offers facilities for handling tasks, resources, and dependency injection services, called **hosts**.

Accordingly, .NET offers various kinds of hosts and the so-called **hosted services**. A .NET host creates an adequate environment for running several tasks, known as **hosted services**, and provides them with resources, common settings, and graceful start/stop.

The simplest way to discuss .NET Host features is to select a **Service** -> **Worker Service** project.

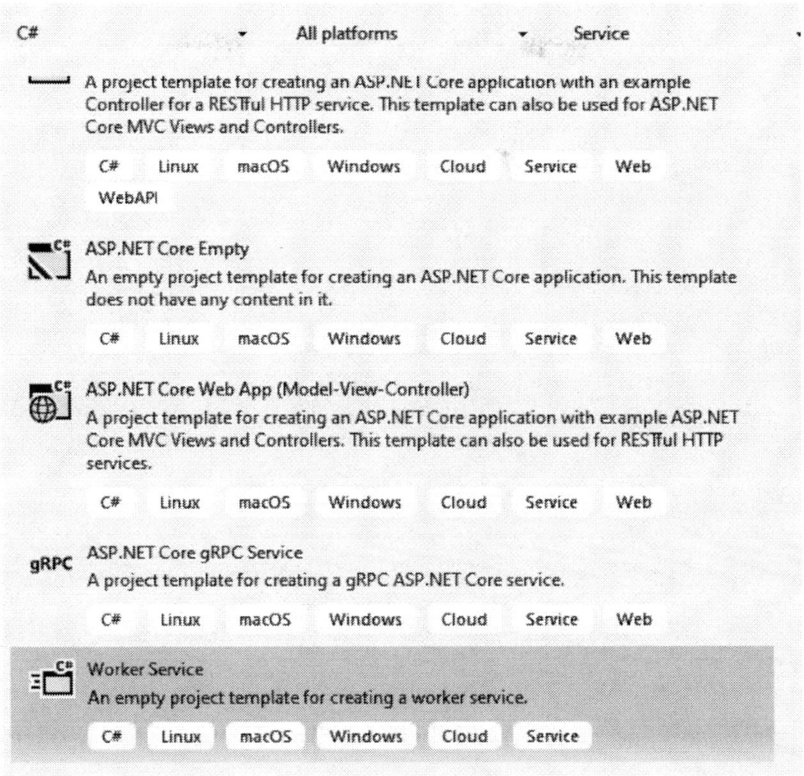

Figure 11.9: Creating a Worker Service project in Visual Studio

All features related to the concept of a `Host` are contained in the `Microsoft.Extensions.Hosting` NuGet package.

A host is configured by specifying all hosted services and resources that must be handled in the application, and then it is built according to the **builder pattern** described in *Chapter 6, Design Patterns and .NET implementation.*

In all .NET SDK project templates, `Program.cs` contains some skeleton code for configuring the host with a fluent interface, starting with the `CreateApplicationBuilder` method of the `Host` class that creates a partially preconfigured builder object. Then, there is the actual host configuration. The final step of this configuration is calling the `Build` method, which assembles the actual host with all the configuration information we provided to the builder object:

```
var builder = Host.CreateApplicationBuilder(args);
...//
...
var app = builder.Build();
...
```

Host configuration includes defining the common resources, defining the default folder for files, loading the configuration parameters from several sources (JSON files, environment variables, and any arguments that are passed to the application), and declaring all the hosted services.

It is worth pointing out that ASP.NET Core and Blazor projects use methods that perform pre-configuration of the `Host`, including several of the tasks listed previously.

Then, the `host` is started, which causes all the hosted services to be started:

```
host.Run();
```

Also possible:

```
await host.RunAsync();
```

The program remains blocked on the preceding instruction until the host is shut down. The host is automatically shut down when the operating system kills the process. However, the host can also be shut down manually either by one of the hosted services or externally by calling `await host.StopAsync(timeout)`. Here, `timeout` is a time span defining the maximum time to wait for the hosted services to stop gracefully. After this time, all the hosted services are aborted if they haven't been terminated. We will explain how a hosted service can shut down the host later on in this subsection.

When the thread contains a `host.RunAsync`, it is launched from within another thread instead of `Program.cs`. The fact that the host thread is being shut down can be signaled by a `cancellationToken` passed to `RunAsync`:

```
await host.RunAsync(cancellationToken);
```

This way of shutting down is triggered as soon as the `cancellationToken` enters a canceled state by another thread.

By default, the host has a 5-second timeout for shutting down; that is, it waits 5 seconds before exiting once a shutdown has been requested. This time can be changed within the `builder.Services.Configure` method, which is used to define host options:

```
var builder = Host.CreateApplicationBuilder(args);
...
builder.Services.Configure<HostOptions>(options =>
{
    options.ShutdownTimeout = TimeSpan.FromSeconds(10);
});
...
```

However, increasing the host timeout doesn't increase the orchestrator timeout, so if the host waits too long, the whole microservice is killed by the orchestrator.

If no cancellation token is explicitly passed to Run or RunAsync, a cancellation token is automatically generated and is automatically signaled when the operating system informs the application it is going to kill it. This cancellation token is passed to all hosted services to give them the opportunity to stop gracefully.

Hosted services are implementations of the IHostedService interface, whose only methods are StartAsync(cancellationToken) and StopAsync(cancellationToken).

Both methods are passed a cancellationToken. The cancellationToken in the StartAsync method signals that a shutdown was requested. The StartAsync method periodically checks this cancellationToken while performing all operations needed to start the host, and if it is signaled, the host start process is aborted. On the other hand, the cancellationToken in the StopAsync method signals that the shutdown timeout expired.

Hosted services can be declared in the same ConfigureServices method that's used to define host options, as follows:

```
builder.Services.AddHostedService<MyHostedService>();
```

Most declarations performed with builder.Services require the addition of the following namespace:

```
using Microsoft.Extensions.DependencyInjection;
```

Usually, the IHostedService interface isn't implemented directly but can be inherited from the BackgroundService abstract class, which exposes the easier-to-implement ExecuteAsync(CancellationToken) method, which is where we can place the whole logic of the service. A shutdown is signaled by passing cancellationToken as an argument, which is easier to handle. We will look in more detail at an implementation of IHostedService in *Chapter 14, Implementing Microservices with .NET.*

To allow a hosted service to shut down the whole host, we need to declare an IApplicationLifetime interface as its constructor parameter:

```
public class MyHostedService(IHostApplicationLifetime applicationLifetime):
BackgroundService
{

    protected override async Task ExecuteAsync(CancellationToken token)
    {
        ...
        applicationLifetime.StopApplication();
        ...
    }
}
```

When the hosted service is created, it is automatically passed an implementation of IHostApplicationLifetime, whose StopApplication method will trigger the host shutdown. This implementation is handled automatically, but we can also declare custom resources whose instances will be automatically passed to all the host service constructors that declare them as parameters. Therefore, say we define a constructor like this one:

```
Public MyClass(MyResource x, IResourceInterface1 y)
{
    ...
}
```

There are several ways to define the resources needed by the preceding constructor:

```
builder.Services.AddTransient<MyResource>();
builder.Services.AddTransient<IResourceInterface1, MyResource1>();
builder.Services.AddSingleton<MyResource>();
builder.Services.AddSingleton<IResourceInterface1, MyResource1>();
```

When we use `AddTransient`, a different instance is created and passed to all the constructors that require an instance of that type. On the other hand, with `AddSingleton`, a unique instance is created and passed to all the constructors that require the declared type. The overload with two generic types allows you to pass an interface and a type that implements that interface. This way, a constructor requires the interface and is decoupled from the specific implementation of that interface.

If resource constructors contain parameters, they will be automatically instantiated with the types declared with `builder.Services` in a recursive fashion. This pattern of interaction, called **dependency injection** (DI), has already been discussed in detail in *Chapter 6, Design Patterns and .NET Implementation*.

`IHostBuilder` also has a method we can use to define the default folder, that is, the folder used to resolve all relative paths mentioned in all .NET methods:

```
.UseContentRoot("c:\\<deault path>")
```

It also has methods that we can use to add logging targets:

```
.ConfigureLogging((hostContext, configLogging) =>
    {
        configLogging.AddConsole();
        configLogging.AddDebug();
    })
```

The previous example shows a console-based logging source, but we can also log into Azure targets with adequate providers. Once you've configured logging, you can enable your hosted services and log custom messages by adding an `ILogger<T>` parameter in their constructors. `ILogger<T>` has methods for logging messages with several severity levels: Trace, Debug (lowest), Information, Warning, Error, Critical, None (highest). In turn, the application configuration specifies the minimum severity level needed to actually output log messages. All messages that pass the severity filter are simultaneously sent to all configured targets.

The only purpose of the type `T` is used to classify the message through its full name.

The developer can specify the minimum severity level in a configuration file. We may have different severity levels for each type of `T`.

For instance:

```
{
  "Logging": {
    "LogLevel": {
      "Default": "Information",
      "Microsoft.AspNetCore": "Warning"
    }
  }
}
```

In the above configuration file, the default severity level is "*Information*," but all types whose names start with "`Microsoft.AspNetCore`" have a "*Warning*" severity level.

Finally, `IHostBuilder` has methods we can use to read configuration parameters from various sources:

```
.ConfigureAppConfiguration(configHost =>
    {
        configHost.AddJsonFile("settings.json", optional: true);
        configHost.AddEnvironmentVariables(prefix: "PREFIX_");
        configHost.AddCommandLine(args);
    })
```

The way parameters defined in configuration streams can be used from inside the application will be explained in more detail in *Chapter 16*, *Presenting ASP.NET Core*, which is dedicated to ASP.NET.

As we transition from the specificities of ASP.NET Core to the broader realm of application deployment and environment setup, an important tool comes into play: Visual Studio Docker support.

Visual Studio support for Docker

Visual Studio offers support for creating, debugging, and deploying Docker images. Docker deployment requires us to install **Docker Desktop for Windows** on our development machine so that we can run Docker images. The download link can be found in the *Technical requirements* section at the beginning of this chapter. Before we start any development activity, we must ensure it is installed and running (you should see a Docker icon in the window notification bar when the Docker runtime is running).

Docker support will be described with a simple ASP.NET Core MVC project. Let's create one. To do so, follow these steps:

1. Name the project `MvcDockerTest`
2. For simplicity, disable authentication if it is not already disabled
3. You are given the option to add Docker support when you create the project, but please don't check the **Docker support** checkbox. You can test how Docker support can be added to any project after it has been created.

Once you have your ASP.NET MVC application scaffolded and running, right-click on its project icon in **Solution Explorer**, select **Add**, and then select **Container Support**. If you installed both WSL and Windows Containers, a dialog for choosing between Linux and Windows will appear. Otherwise, Linux will be automatically chosen if you installed just WSL.

Please select Linux, since it is the default used by the Docker server when WSL is available.

If your Docker runtime has been installed properly and is running, you should be able to run the Docker image from Visual Studio. Please try it!

Now that we have explored how to configure and run Docker images, let's delve deeper into the structure and composition of these images. Understanding the Docker file created by Visual Studio is key to grasping how it orchestrates the creation and management of these images.

Analyzing the Docker file

Let's analyze the Docker file that was created by Visual Studio. It is a sequence of image creation steps. Each step enriches an existing image with something else with the help of the `From` instruction, which is a reference to an already existing image. The following is the first step:

```
FROM mcr.microsoft.com/dotnet/aspnet:x.x AS base
...
WORKDIR /app
EXPOSE 8080
EXPOSE 8081
```

The first step uses the `mcr.microsoft.com/dotnet/aspnet:x.x` ASP.NET (Core) runtime that was published by Microsoft in the Docker public repository (where `x.x` is the ASP.NET (Core) version that was selected in your project).

The `WORKDIR` command creates the directory that follows the command within the image that is going to be created. The two `EXPOSE` commands declare which ports will be exposed outside the image and mapped to ports of the actual hosting machine. Mapped ports are decided in the deployment stage as command-line arguments of a Docker command. In our case, there are two ports: one for HTTP (8080) and another for HTTPS (8081).

This intermediate image is cached by Docker, which doesn't need to be recomputed since it doesn't depend on the code we write but only on the selected version of the ASP.NET (Core) runtime.

The second step produces a different image that will not be used to deploy. Instead, it will be used to create application-specific files that will be deployed:

```
FROM mcr.microsoft.com/dotnet/sdk:10.0 AS build
ARG BUILD_CONFIGURATION=Release
WORKDIR /src
COPY ["MvcDockerTest/MvcDockerTest.csproj", "MvcDockerTest/"]
RUN dotnet restore "./MvcDockerTest/MvcDockerTest.csproj"
COPY . .
WORKDIR "/src/MvcDockerTest "
RUN dotnet build "./MvcDockerTest.csproj" -c $BUILD_CONFIGURATION -o /app/build
FROM build AS publish
ARG BUILD_CONFIGURATION=Release
RUN dotnet publish "./MvcDockerTest.csproj" -c $BUILD_CONFIGURATION -o /app/publish /
p:UseAppHost=false
```

This step starts from the ASP.NET SDK image, which contains parts we don't need to add for deployment; these are needed to process the project code. The new `src` directory is created in the `build` image and made the current image directory. Then, the project file is copied into `/src/MvcDockerTest`.

The `RUN` command executes an operating system command on the image. In this case, it calls the `dotnet` runtime, asking it to restore the NuGet packages that were referenced by the previously copied project file.

Then, the `COPY..` command copies the whole project file tree into the `src` image directory. Finally, the project directory is made the current directory, and the `dotnet` runtime is asked to build the project in release mode and copy all the output files into the new `/app/build` directory. Finally, the `dotnet publish` task is executed in a new image called `publish`, outputting the published binaries into `/app/publish`.

The final step starts from the image that we created in the first step, which contains the ASP.NET (Core) runtime and adds all the files that were published in the previous step:

```
FROM base AS final
WORKDIR /app
COPY --from=publish /app/publish .
ENTRYPOINT ["dotnet", "WebApplication1.dll"]
```

The `ENTRYPOINT` command specifies the operating system command that's needed to execute the image. It accepts an array of strings. In our case, it accepts the `dotnet` command and its first command-line argument, that is, the DLL we need to execute. With that out of the way, let's now publish our little project!

Publishing the project

If we right-click on our project and click **Publish**, we are presented with several options:

1. Publish the image to an existing or new web app (automatically created by Visual Studio)

2. Publish to one of several Docker registries, including a private Azure Container Registry that, if it doesn't already exist, can be created from within Visual Studio
3. Right click on the Dockerfile icon in Solution Explorer and select the option to build it. This will build the Dockerfile in release mode and will add an image tagged with the `latest` tag after its name. You can see it in your Docker Desktop user interface. This image can be manually loaded in any containers registry or launched from within the Docker Desktop user interface. Please notice that also launching the application in Visual Studio creates an image marked with `dev` after the application name, but this image can be used only from within Visual Studio since it is built in debug mode and contains the code for communicating with the debugger.

A Docker file can also be built with the console command below:

```
docker build <path to the folder containing the docker file> -t <desired image
name>:<image version>
```

Thus, if you opened a console in the same folder that contains the Dockerfile, the above command becomes:

```
docker build ./ -t <image name>:<image version>
```

Once you have an image on your Docker Desktop, you can create a container with:

```
docker run --name <name of the container to create> <image name>:<image version>
```

As soon as the container is created it is also launched.

If the image listens to some ports in its file system, when you create the container, you can map these ports on your machine ports with the `-p` option:

```
  docker run --name mycontainer -p <host port>:<container port> mayimage:latest
```

A launched container can be stopped without destroying it with:

```
docker stop mycontainer
```

Then it can be destroyed with:

```
docker rm mycontainer
```

It can also be restarted with:

```
docker restart mycontainer
```

Once all containers based on a given image have been destroyed, you can also destroy the image itself with:

```
docker rmi myimage:latest
```

The list of all images in your Docker Container is available in Docker Desktop UI, but can also be obtained with:

```
docker images
```

The list of all containers is available in Docker Desktop UI, too. However, all running containers can be obtained with:

```
docker ps
```

While the list of all containers is returned by:

```
docker ps --all
```

More information on Docker, on how to use command-line Docker commands and on how to create running containers from images, stop them, and restart them can be found in the official Docker documentation: `https://docs.docker.com/`. A good and self-contained description of both Docker and Kubernetes can be found in this book dedicated to distributed computing: *Practical Serverless and Microservices with C#* (`https://www.amazon.com/dp/B0DNSLZRB1`).

Which tools are needed to manage microservices?

Effectively handling microservices in your CI/CD cycles requires both a private Container image registry and a state-of-the-art microservice orchestrator that's capable of doing the following:

- Allocating and load-balancing microservices on available hardware nodes
- Monitoring the health state of services and replacing faulty services if hardware or software failures occur
- Logging and presenting analytics
- Allowing the designer to dynamically change requirements such as hardware nodes allocated to a cluster, the number of service instances, and so on

Microservices orchestrators are described in *Chapter 19*, *Orchestrators and .NET Aspire*. Here we describe just how to interact with a container image registry with Docker.

Interacting with a container registry

A private **Container registry** can be easily created in all main Clouds like Azure, AWS and Google Cloud. However, it can also be easily implemented On-Premise in your private data center with the help of open-source software that conforms to the **OCI** (Open Container Initiative) distribution specification. Among them, it is worth mentioning **Docker Registry** (`https://hub.docker.com/_/registry`) that is available as a Docker image.

Before interacting with a private registry, you need to authenticate with the Docker `login` command:

```
docker login -u <username> -p <user-password> <registry url>
```

Where user-password is either the main user registry password or a temporary password (token) created somehow by the registry. Needless to say, a temporary password is preferable for security reasons.

Once logged in, you can download images in your local Docker repository with the pull command:

```
docker pull my.registry.com/<image name>
```

Where the image name has the format of a Web path, path/subpath/name.

Using the following command, you should see myimage within the list of local images:

```
docker images
```

Instead, if we would like to upload a local image on our private registry, we must first tag it with the name it will have on the registry, which must include the registry domain with the tag command:

```
docker tag <local image name> my.registry.com/<image target name>
```

At this point, we can upload it with the push command by using the newly created tag:

```
docker push my.registry.com/<image target name>
```

Summary

In this chapter, we described what microservices are and how they have evolved from the concept of a module. In this chapter we learned the advantages of microservices and when it is worth using them, as well as general criteria for their design. We also learned why and how Docker containers are useful in microservice architectures. A historical perspective helped the understanding of all fundamentals of microservice architecture.

Then, we learned also about practical implementations based on all tools that are available in .NET and what kind of infrastructures are needed to run microservices.

This chapter was just a general introduction to microservices; further chapters will discuss in more detail most of the subjects introduced here, while showing practical implementation techniques and code examples.

This ends the first part of the book dedicated to fundamentals. The next chapter, *How to Choose Your Data Storage in the Cloud*, starts the second part of the book, which is dedicated to specific technologies.

Questions

1. What is the two-fold nature of the module concept?
2. Is scaling optimization the only advantage of microservices? If not, list some further advantages.
3. How would you face, unreliable communication in a .NET microservice?
4. What kind of Docker support is offered by Visual Studio?
5. What is an orchestrator?

6. How would you protect a microservice application where new microservices are often added from an exponential chain of changes?
7. What is RabbitMQ?
8. In case of unreliable communication, how do you protect your microservices from erroneously processing replicas of already processed messages?
9. If your application must minimize its dependency from the running environment what is the best choice between Azure Service Bus and RabbitMQ?

Further reading

The following are links to the official documentation for Azure Service Bus, RabbitMQ, and other event bus technologies:

- Azure Service Bus: `https://docs.microsoft.com/en-us/azure/service-bus-messaging/`
- NServiceBus:`https://particular.net/nservicebus`
- MassTransit: `https://masstransit-project.com/`
- Brighter: `https://www.goparamore.io/`
- RabbitMQ: `https://www.rabbitmq.com/getstarted.html`
- EasyNetQ: `https://easynetq.com/`
- Official Docker documentation: `https://docs.docker.com/`.

A good and self-contained description of both Docker and Kubernetes can be found in this book dedicated to distributed computing: *Practical Serverless and Microservices with C#* (`https://www.amazon.com/dp/B0DNSLZRB1`).

Below are also links for Polly, Docker, and Docker Registry:

- The documentation for Polly, a tool for reliable communication/tasks, can be found here: `https://github.com/App-vNext/Polly`
- More information on Docker can be found on Docker's official web site: `https://docs.docker.com/`
- Docker Registry is available as a Docker image on Docker Hub at: `https://hub.docker.com/_/registry`

Get this book's PDF version and more

Scan the QR code (or go to `packtpub.com/unlock`). Search for this book by name, confirm the edition, and then follow the steps on the page.

UNLOCK NOW

Note: Keep your invoice handy. Purchases made directly from Packt don't require an invoice.

Part 2

Technologies and Programming Solutions

This second part of the book is dedicated to technologies that are particularly well-suited for enterprise applications. While some technologies, like Kubernetes, are not tied to a specific technology stack, we focus primarily on .NET and its related ecosystem. By the end of this part, you will be able to develop and secure enterprise applications using .NET, as well as work with advanced microservices technologies such as Kubernetes and .NET Aspire. The last chapter presents a detailed case study that exemplifies the practical application of everything you learned throughout the book.

This part of the book includes the following chapters:

- *Chapter 12, How to Choose Your Data Storage in the Cloud*
- *Chapter 13, Interacting with Data in C# – Entity Framework Core*
- *Chapter 14, Implementing Microservices with .NET*
- *Chapter 15, Applying Service-Oriented Architectures with .NET*
- *Chapter 16, Presenting ASP.NET Core*
- *Chapter 17, Implementing Frontend Microservices with ASP.NET Core*
- *Chapter 18, Client Frameworks: Blazor*
- *Chapter 19, Orchestrators and .NET Aspire*
- *Chapter 20, Securing Data and Applications*
- *Chapter 21, Hardening Cloud-based Solution*
- *Chapter 22, Case Study: Practical Usage of .NET Aspire*

12

How to Choose Your Data Storage in the Cloud

What happens when a global application must process massive volumes of data with low latency, high availability, and room to scale? In Azure, as in other cloud platforms, storage design is one of the first architectural decisions that shapes that outcome. One possible approach is to define a scalable set of cloud-hosted virtual machines (IaaS) and implement custom storage solutions on top of them. For example, you could deploy a SQL Server cluster on Azure virtual machines to increase reliability and computational capacity. However, while this approach is sometimes valid, it often does not fully benefit from the elasticity, operational simplicity, and managed capabilities that cloud platforms provide. For this reason, this chapter focuses on **Platform as a Service** (PaaS) storage offerings that make fuller use of cloud capabilities.

Therefore, this chapter will not discuss such custom architectures but will focus mainly on the various **Platform as a Service** (PaaS) storage offerings that are available in the cloud and on Azure. These offerings include scalable solutions based on plain disk space, relational databases, NoSQL databases, and in-memory data stores such as Redis.

Choosing a more adequate storage type is based not only on the application's functional requirements, but also on performance and scaling-out requirements. In fact, while scaling out when processing resources causes a linear increase in performance, scaling out storage resources does not necessarily imply an acceptable increase in performance. In short, no matter how much you duplicate your data storage devices, if several requests affect the same chunk of data, they will always queue for the same amount of time to access it!

> **Note**
>
> Scaling computing usually adds power. Scaling storage does not automatically remove contention, so storage does not scale like computing.

Scaling out data causes linear increases in read operations since each copy can serve a different request, but it doesn't imply the same increase in throughput for write operations since all copies of the same chunk of data must be updated! Accordingly, more sophisticated techniques are required to scale out storage devices, and not all storage engines scale equally well.

Relational databases do not scale well in all scenarios. Therefore, scaling needs and the need to distribute data geographically play a fundamental role in the choice of a storage engine, as well as in the choice of a SaaS offering.

For architects, the practical takeaway is that storage decisions must be evaluated not only by capacity, but by how contention, distribution, and scale will affect the application under real load.

In this chapter, we will cover the following topics:

- Understanding the different repositories for different purposes
- Choosing between SQL or NoSQL document-oriented databases
- Azure Cosmos DB – an opportunity to manage a multi-continental database

Let's get started!

Technical requirements

This chapter requires that you have the following:

- Visual Studio 2026 free Community edition or better, with all the database tools components installed.
- A free Azure account. The Creating an Azure account subsection in *Chapter 1, Understanding the Importance of Software Architecture*, explains how to create one.
- For a better development experience, we advise that you also install the local emulator of Cosmos DB, which can be found at `https://aka.ms/cosmosdb-emulator`.
- You can find the sample code for the chapter at `https://github.com/PacktPublishing/Software-Architecture-with-.NET-10-and-C-sharp-5E/`.

Repository options for different purposes

This section describes the functionalities that are offered by the most popular data storage techniques. Mainly, we will focus on the functional requirements they are able to satisfy. Performance and scaling-out features will be analyzed in the next section, which is dedicated to comparing relational and NoSQL databases.

In Azure, the various offerings can be found by typing product names into the search bar at the top of all Azure portal pages.

The following subsections describe the main storage options we can use in C# projects and, more importantly, the kinds of architectural problems each one is best suited to solve.

Relational databases

For many enterprise systems, **relational databases** are still the default choice when the solution depends on transactional consistency, structured schemas, and strong relationships between data entities. In Azure, this usually leads architects to consider services such as Azure SQL Database, Azure SQL Managed Instance, or SQL Server on Azure Virtual Machines. These options support workloads such as financial systems, online stores, manufacturing applications, and corporate back-office platforms. In all of them, the design starts with the same principle: identifying the entities to be stored, defining their attributes, and modeling the relationships that preserve the integrity and usability of the data.

For decades, relational databases were the standard choice for enterprise applications. Many big companies in the world have built their own database management systems. Oracle, MySQL, and MS SQL Server would be listed by many as the ones you can trust to store your data.

Usually, clouds offer several database engines. Azure offers a variety of popular database engines, such as Oracle, MySQL, PostgreSQL, and SQL Server (Azure SQL).

For Oracle database workloads, Azure provides Oracle-published virtual machine images through Azure Marketplace. In practice, when you browse Oracle VM offers in the Marketplace or in the virtual machine creation flow, you will find Oracle-based images intended for deploying Oracle workloads on Azure. Microsoft documents these offers as bring-your-own-license (BYOL): Azure charges for the virtual machine infrastructure, storage, and networking, but Oracle licenses are not included, so you must provide the appropriate Oracle licenses and support agreement.

When it comes to MySQL on Azure, you pay to use a private instance. The fees you incur depend on the number of cores you have, how much memory must be allocated, and backup retention time.

MySQL instances are redundant, and you can choose between local or geographically distributed redundancy. *Figure 12.1* shows the redundancy options available when creating a MySQL server. Note the choice between local and geo-distributed redundancy, which we discussed in *Chapter 2, Non-Functional Requirements.*

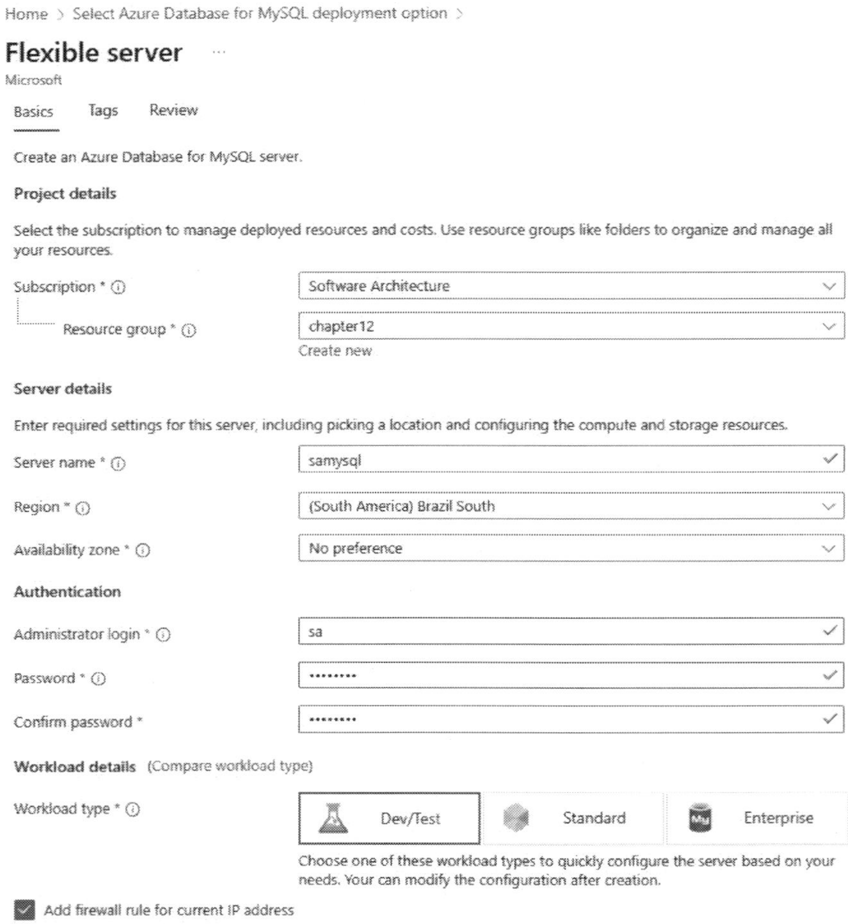

Figure 12.1: Creating a MySQL server on Azure

Azure SQL is the most flexible offer and offers even a serverless pricing model. Here, you can configure resources that are used by every single database. When you create a database, you have the option to place it on an existing server instance or create a new instance. There are several pricing options that you may choose while defining your solution and Azure keeps incrementing them to make sure you will be able to handle your data in the cloud. Basically, they vary due to the computing capacity you need.

Remember that Azure SQL pricing models mainly reflect the level of compute and performance isolation a workload needs, so the choice should be driven by expected demand rather than storage alone.

For instance, in the **Database Transaction Units** (DTUs) model, pricing is based on the reserved database storage and on a combined measure of I/O, CPU, and memory consumption derived from a reference workload.

Note

Roughly, maximal database performance increases linearly when you increase DTUs. You can find detailed information about the options you have for purchasing Azure SQL Database at `https://learn.microsoft.com/en-us/azure/azure-sql/database/purchasing-models?view=azuresql`.

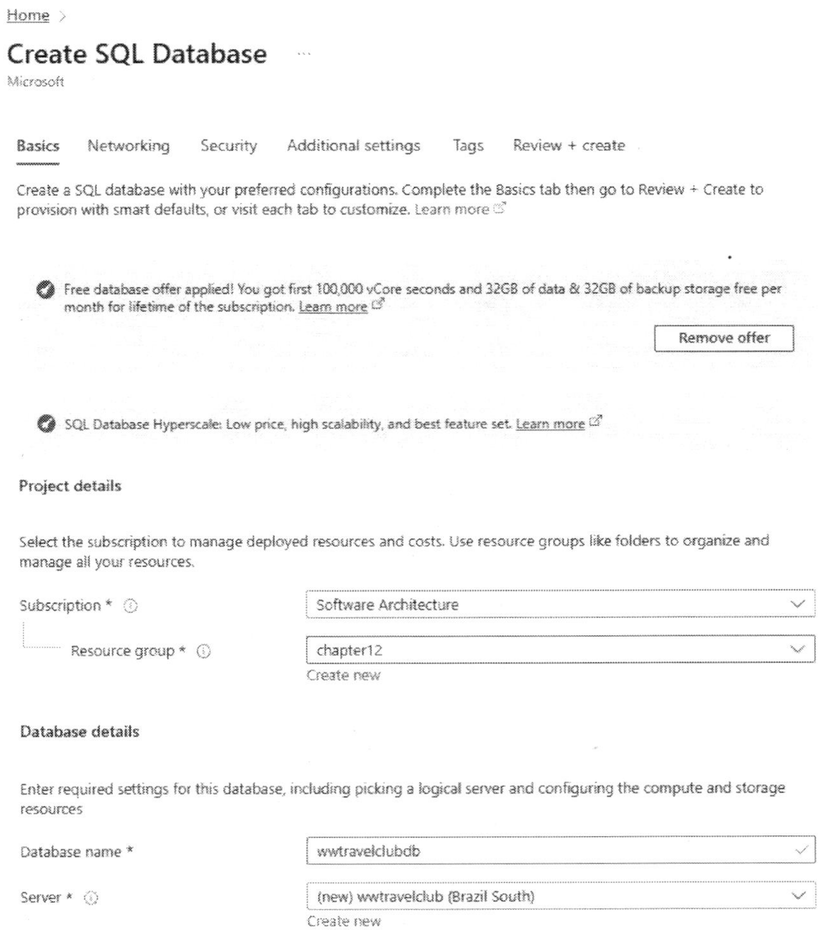

Figure 12.2: Creating an Azure SQL Database

Figure 12.2 shows the interface used to create a SQL database in Azure SQL Database. Notice that you must also define a logical server to host and process the database you want to create.

You can also configure data replication by enabling read scale-out. This way, you can improve the performance of read operations. This feature routes read-only workloads to secondary replicas instead of the primary replica, which is especially useful for reporting, analytics, dashboards, and other read-intensive scenarios.

By isolating these queries from transactional workloads, read scale-out can improve overall performance and reduce contention on the primary database. However, because reads from replicas are asynchronous relative to the primary, recently committed changes might not be visible immediately. Backup retention is fixed for each offering level (basic, standard, and premium).

If you select ***Yes*** for "*Want to use SQL elastic pool?*", the database will be added to an elastic pool. Databases that are added to the same elastic pool will share their resources, so resources that are not used by a database can be used during the CPU usage peaks of other databases. Elastic pools are especially useful when multiple databases have different usage patterns, because they share a pool of compute resources on the same server and reduce overprovisioning. All databases in an elastic pool, however, must be hosted on the same server. This approach is particularly effective when databases balance resource consumption and cost reduction.

> **Note**
>
> Azure has released a free offer of Azure SQL Database, which can enable a lot of studies and, more importantly, can help you understand the usage of a new application. There is a limit on the usage of this offer, and you may choose between auto-pausing the database until next month or continuing to use the database for additional charges. Please check more details at `https://learn.microsoft.com/en-us/azure/azure-sql/database/free-offer`.

While relational databases excel in many scenarios, they can be less effective when applications demand greater schema flexibility or need to process large volumes of semi-structured or unstructured data. For these situations, non-relational databases often provide a more suitable alternative.

When schema flexibility and distributed scaling become more important than rigid structure, the discussion naturally moves from relational systems to NoSQL options. Let's check this out now.

NoSQL databases

One of the biggest challenges that relational databases have caused software architects is related to how we deal with database structural schema changes. The agility of changes needed at the beginning of this century brought the opportunity to use a new database style, called NoSQL. There are several types of NoSQL databases, as we can see here. These categories are best understood through the access pattern they optimize: documents for flexible application data, graphs for relationships, key-value stores for very fast lookups or caching, and wide-column stores for large, sparse datasets.

- ***Document-Oriented Database:*** The most common one, where you have the key and complex data called a document. In Azure, this model is supported by *Azure Cosmos DB for NoSQL* and *Azure Cosmos DB for MongoDB*
- ***Graph Database:*** Social media tend to use this kind of database since the data is stored as graphs. Azure, this model is supported by *Azure Cosmos DB for Apache Gremlin*.

- ***Key-Value Database:*** A useful database for implementing caches since you have the opportunity of storing key-value pairs. In Azure, this model can be implemented with *Azure Cosmos DB for Table*, while low-latency caching scenarios are commonly handled by *Azure Managed Redis or Azure Cache for Redis*.
- ***Wide-Column Store Database:*** A database where the same column in each row can store different data. In Azure, this model is supported by *Azure Cosmos DB for Apache Cassandra*, and Azure also provides *Managed Cassandra* as a dedicated option for Cassandra workloads.

For instance, in NoSQL document-oriented databases, relational tables are replaced with more general collections that can contain heterogeneous JSON objects. That is, collections have no predefined structure and no predefined fields with length constraints (in the case of strings), but can contain any type of object. The only structural constraint associated with each collection is the name of the property that acts as a primary key.

More specifically, each collection entry can contain nested objects and object collections nested in object properties, that is, related entities that, in relational databases, are contained in different tables and connected through external keys. In NoSQL, databases can be nested in their parent entities. Since collection entries contain complex nested objects instead of simple property/value pairs, as is the case with relational databases, entries are not called tuples or rows, but *documents*.

No relations and/or external key constraints can be defined between documents that belong to the same collection or to different collections. If a document contains the primary key of another document in one of its properties, it does so at its own risk. This is an important architectural trade-off: the application layer becomes responsible for maintaining the consistency of these references and for handling cases such as orphaned, invalid, or outdated links between documents, so the developer has the responsibility of maintaining and keeping these references coherent.

Finally, NoSQL storage is quite cheap. You can store a great amount of data as Base64 string properties. The developer can define rules to decide what properties to index in a collection. Since documents are nested objects, properties are tree paths. It is worth saying that you can specify which collection of paths and subpaths is indexed.

Almost all NoSQL databases are queried either with a subset of SQL or with a JSON-based language where queries are JSON objects whose paths represent the properties to query and whose values represent the query constraints that have been applied to them.

The possibility of nesting children's objects inside documents can be simulated in relational databases with the help of one-to-many relationships. However, with relational databases, we are forced to redefine the exact structure of all the related tables, while NoSQL collections do not impose any predefined structure on the objects they contain. The only constraint is that each document must provide a unique value for the primary key property.

Modern relational databases such as Azure SQL support JSON columns, enabling hybrid approaches that combine structured relational schemas with flexibility for semi-structured data. This can be useful when part of the data model must remain stable and strongly governed, while other parts need to evolve more dynamically. Even so, NoSQL databases remain the more appropriate choice when object structures are highly variable, evolve frequently, or are better represented without rigid relational constraints.

However, often they are chosen for the way they scale out read and write operations and, more generally, for their performance advantages in distributed environments. Their performance features will be discussed in the next section, which compares them to relational databases.

The graph data model is an extreme case of a completely unstructured document. The whole database is a graph where queries can add, change, and delete graph documents.

In this case, we have two kinds of documents: nodes and relationships. While relationships have a well-defined structure (the primary key of the nodes connected by the relationship, plus the relationship's name), nodes have no structure at all since properties and their values are added together during node update operations.

Graph data models were conceived to represent the features of people and the objects they manipulate (media, posts, and so on), along with their relationships in *social applications*. The Gremlin language was conceived specifically to query graph data models.

We will not discuss this in this chapter, but references are available in the *Further Reading* section.

NoSQL databases will be analyzed in detail in the remaining sections of this chapter, which are dedicated to describing Azure Cosmos DB and comparing it with relational databases. But now let's check how Redis can help us in a good variety of scenarios.

Redis

Redis is a distributed in-memory storage based on key-value pairs and supports distributed queuing. It can be used as permanent, in-memory storage and as a web application cache for database data. Alternatively, it can be used as a cache for pre-rendered content.

Redis can also be used to store a web application's user session data. In fact, ASP.NET Core supports session data to overcome the fact that the HTTP protocol is stateless. More specifically, user data that is kept between page changes is maintained in server-side stores such as Redis and indexed by a session key stored in cookies.

Interaction with the Redis server in the cloud is typically based on a client implementation that offers an easy-to-use interface. The client for .NET is available through the `StackExchange.Redis` NuGet package. The basic operations of the `StackExchange.Redis` client have been documented in `https://stackexchange.github.io/StackExchange.Redis/Basics`, while the full documentation can be found at `https://stackexchange.github.io/StackExchange.Redis`.

> **Note**
>
> Microsoft has announced Azure Managed Redis in November 2024. This is a great alternative for those who need the enterprise stack from this solution. Before it, the resource available was Azure Cache for Redis, which is now entering retirement.

There are several details to be set while configuring Azure Managed Redis. They primarily depend on the kind of application you will run over it, where you will select the amount of data, where this data will be stored, and the CPU to process it. It is also possible to configure geo-redundancy, which is very important to guarantee the reliability of the application, as we discussed in *Chapter 2, Non-Functional Requirements*.

Redis is no longer used only as a cache. In AI-oriented architectures, it can also support semantic cache and low-latency vector similarity search over embeddings, which makes it useful in retrieval-augmented generation (RAG) and recommendation scenarios. This is relevant here because it shows that Redis is no longer only a traditional cache choice. It can also support newer low-latency AI workloads that influence storage architecture decisions.

In these cases, application content is often divided into smaller chunks, embeddings are generated for each chunk, and vector search is used to retrieve the most semantically relevant content for a user query. This approach can accelerate access to relevant information, although architects must still decide where vectors and chunks should reside.

Redis is attractive when very low latency is required, while services such as Azure AI Search are often more appropriate when the solution also needs richer indexing, document retrieval, and search-oriented capabilities.

> **Note**
>
> A quick start guide that explains how to use Azure Redis credentials and the URI with the `StackExchange.Redis` .NET client can be found at `https://docs.microsoft.com/en-us/azure/azure-cache-for-redis/cache-dotnet-core-quickstart`.

If Redis addresses ultra-low-latency access patterns, the next storage option to consider is Azure Storage Accounts, which are better suited to durable, general-purpose object and file storage.

Azure storage accounts

Storage accounts are usually the strongest fit when the main requirement is durable and scalable storage for files, blobs, backups, logs, or queues rather than rich relationships or query-heavy application data. Depending on the scenario, other storage services may offer additional features or specialized capabilities, but blob storage remains a strong and widely used option. Depending on the scenario you have, Azure NoSQL databases are a better option than tables, and Azure Redis turns into a better option than Azure storage queues.

In practice, choose storage accounts for durable file and object storage, NoSQL databases for flexibility in querying application data, and Redis when ultra-low latency is more important than long-term persistence.

Figure 12.3 shows the storage account creation screen, where readers can identify the main configuration choices related to redundancy, performance tier, and deployment settings.

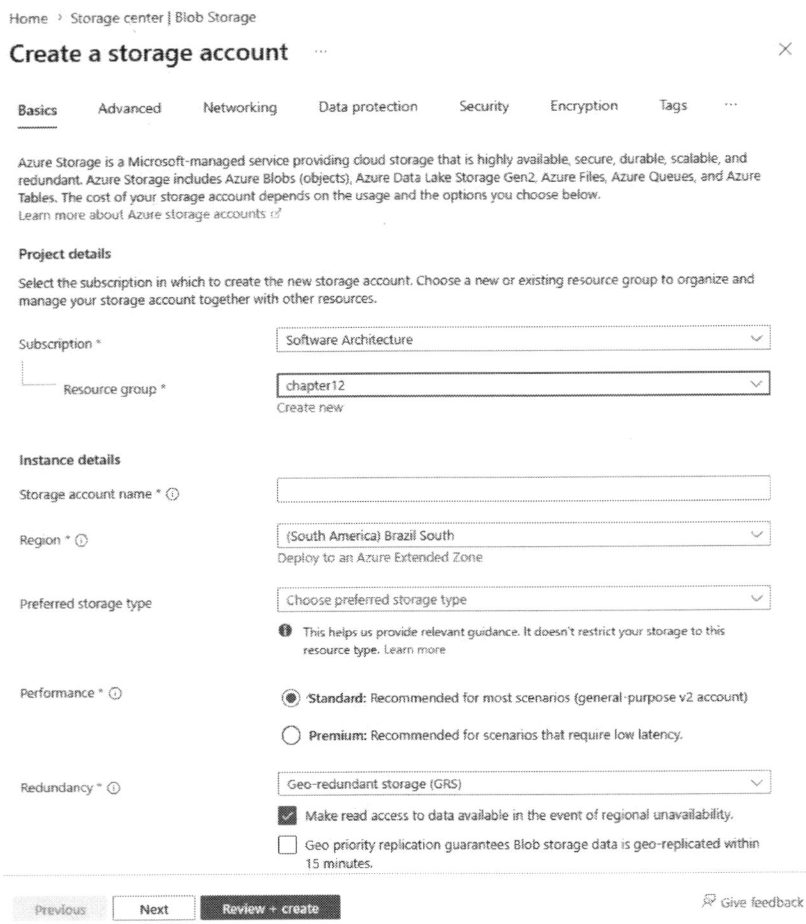

Figure 12.3: Creating a storage account

Up to here, we have checked some repository options for attending different purposes. In the rest of this chapter, we will focus on NoSQL databases and how they differ from relational databases. Next, we will look at how to choose one over the other.

Choosing between SQL and NoSQL document-oriented databases

As a software architect, you may consider some aspects of SQL and NoSQL databases to decide the best storage option for you. At a high level, the trade-off is simple: relational databases favor stable schemas and strong constraints, whereas document databases favor flexible schemas and locality of related data.

> **Note**
>
> In many cases, both SQL and NoSQL databases will be needed. The key point here will surely be how organized your data is and how big the database will become.

In the previous section, we stated that NoSQL document-oriented databases should be preferred when data has almost no predefined structure. They not only keep variable attributes close to their owners, but they also keep some related objects close since they allow related objects to be nested inside properties and collections.

Unstructured data can be represented in relational databases if variable properties of a tuple (t) can be placed in a connected table containing the property name, property value, and the external key of t.

For instance, a `Customer` table might contain fixed attributes such as `CustomerId` and `Name`, while a separate table stores variable properties such as `PreferredLanguage`, `LoyaltyLevel`, or `FavoriteCategory` using columns like `CustomerId`, `PropertyName`, and `PropertyValue`.

The drawback of this approach is performance: instead of keeping the data for one object together, the database spreads these properties across multiple rows, which increases query complexity and the effort required to reconstruct the object.

In a small database, *all over the available memory space* means far away but on the same disk; in a bigger database, it means far away but in different disk units; in a distributed cloud environment, it means far away but in different—and possibly geographically distributed—servers.

On the other hand, in NoSQL document-oriented database design, we always try to put all related objects that are likely to be processed together into a single entry. Related objects that are accessed less frequently are placed in different entries. Since external key constraints are not enforced automatically and NoSQL transactions are very flexible, the developer can choose the best compromise between performance and coherence.

It is important to mention that today we can store unstructured data as columns with JSON (or XML) types in relational databases. This approach allows the use of patterns typically implemented in document databases to also be achievable in relational databases, like avoiding `joins` by inserting complete objects in a JSON column. However, the NoSQL document-oriented database adoption can be considered the best option since it was designed for this purpose.

Therefore, we can conclude that relational databases perform well when tables that are usually accessed together can be stored close together. NoSQL document-oriented databases, on the other hand, automatically ensure that related data is kept close together since each entry keeps most of the data it is related to inside it as nested objects. Therefore, NoSQL document-oriented databases perform better when they are distributed across different memory and to different geographically distributed servers.

Unfortunately, the only way to scale out storage write operations is to split collection entries across several servers according to the values of `shard keys`. For instance, we can place all the records containing usernames that start with `A` on a server, the records containing usernames that start with `B` on another server, and so on. This way, write operations for usernames with different start letters may be executed in parallel, ensuring that the write throughput increases linearly with the number of servers.

In short, writing scale-out becomes possible only when data is partitioned so that independent writing can be processed in parallel.

Figure 12.4 illustrates how the partition key groups data into logical partitions and how those partitions are then mapped to the underlying physical infrastructure for scale-out.

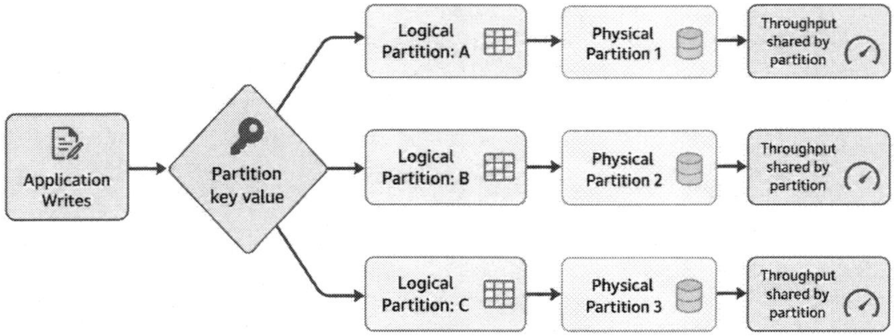

Figure 12.4: Partition-key-based data distribution across logical and physical partitions

However, when related collections are distributed across different servers, write gains do not remove the cost of multi-server reads and updates on data that are usually processed together.

This issue significantly degrades performance in relational databases if access to related distributed objects must be transactional and/or must ensure structural constraints (such as external key constraints) are not violated. In this case, all related objects must be blocked during the transaction, preventing other requests from accessing them during the whole lifetime of a time-consuming distributed operation.

Document-oriented NoSQL databases usually handle sharding and horizontal write scaling more naturally than relational databases because related data is often modeled as a single self-contained document instead of being distributed across multiple tables. This makes partitioning more efficient and reduces the cost of distributed operations. However, this advantage comes with an important trade-off: transactional guarantees are usually limited to a single document or logical partition. In Azure Cosmos DB, ACID transactions are supported within one logical partition key, but operations that span multiple partitions require application-level consistency strategies. For this reason, architects often redesign aggregates, collocate related data, and use patterns such as Transactional Batches, Change feed, Outbox, or SAGA when broader consistency is required.

It is worth mentioning that there are situations where relational databases perform well with sharding. A typical example is a multi-tenant application, that is, an application in which a single software solution serves multiple customers, organizations, or groups, called tenants, while keeping their data logically separated. In a multi-tenant application, all entry collections can be partitioned into non-overlapping sets called **tenants**. Only entries belonging to the same tenant can refer to each other, so if all the collections are sharded in the same way according to their object tenants, all related records end up in the same shard, that is, in the same server, and can be navigated efficiently.

Multi-tenant applications are not rare in the cloud since all applications that offer the same services to several different users are often implemented as multi-tenant applications, where each tenant corresponds to a user subscription. Accordingly, relational databases are conceived to work in the cloud, such as Azure SQL Server, and usually offer sharding options for multi-tenant applications. Typically, sharding is not a cloud service and must be defined with database engine commands. Here, we will not describe how to define shards with Azure SQL Server, but the *Further reading* section contains a link to the official Microsoft documentation. The following table presents the pros and cons for each database approach, considering subjects like schema, performance, language, consistency, transactions, and scale. Please use this as a fast tool for deciding the best data solution for your scenario:

Subject	SQL	NoSQL document-oriented DB
Schema	Easy to deal with in well-structured schemas. Today, it is possible to design hybrid solutions with JSON/XML columns, storing unstructured data.	Preferred when data has almost no predefined structure.
Performance	In general, bad performance in distributed environments.	In general, good performance for reading and writing distributed data.
Language	Declarative to query and update data.	Procedural to query and update operations.
Consistency	Strong use of foreign keys.	All related objects that are likely to be processed together into a single entry.
Transactions	Supported	By default, not supported.
Scale	Vertically upgrading hardware.	Horizontally with data sharding.

Table 12.1: Pros and cons of each database approach

As you can see in *Table 12.1*, SQL remains the safer default for strongly structured and transactional workloads, while document-oriented NoSQL becomes more attractive when flexibility and horizontal scale dominate the design.

In conclusion, relational databases provide a logical view of data that is independent of how the data is physically stored. They also use a declarative language for queries and updates, which simplifies development and maintenance. However, this model can lead to performance challenges in distributed environments that require write scale-out. Document-oriented NoSQL databases, in contrast, require developers to handle more details about data storage and about how queries and updates are performed. This increases design responsibility, but it also allows better optimization for distributed environments that need both read and write scale-out.

In the next section, we will look at Azure Cosmos DB, the main Azure NoSQL offering.

Azure Cosmos DB – an opportunity to manage a multi-continental database

Azure Cosmos DB is Azure's main NoSQL offering. Azure Cosmos DB has its own interface that is a subset of SQL, but it can be configured with a MongoDB interface, a Table API, or a Cassandra API. It can also be configured as a graph data model that can be queried with Gremlin. Cosmos DB allows replication for fault tolerance and for reading scale-out. Replicas are maintained within each configured region, and the database account can be deployed in one or more Azure regions, depending on whether the goal is local high availability only or geographic distribution as well. Moreover, you can specify which data center all the replicas are placed in. The user also has the option to write-enable all the replicas so that writes are immediately available in the geographical area where they are done. Writing scale-out is achieved with sharding, which the user can configure by defining which properties to use as shard keys.

To make these choices concrete, the next subsections move from account creation to container modeling, to application access, and finally to consistency and indexing decisions. These initial configuration choices matter because they shape cost, regional behavior, availability, and the operational model of the application from the beginning.

Creating an Azure Cosmos DB account

You can define a Cosmos DB account by typing Cosmos DB into the Azure portal search bar and clicking + *Create*. The following page will appear:

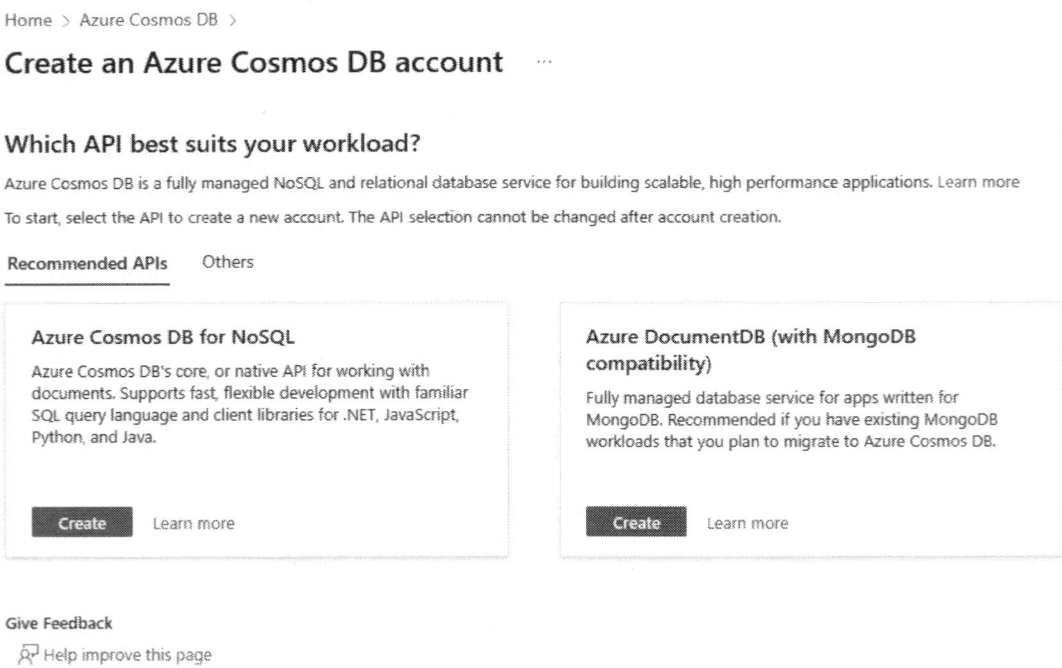

Figure 12.5: Creating an Azure Cosmos DB account

Figure 12.5 shows the first Cosmos DB account-creation screen, where the key design choices include the API model, account name, region, and capacity mode.

For instance, if you select the *Azure Cosmos DB for NoSQL* option, the account name you choose is used in the resource URI as `{account_name}.documents.azure.com`. Then, you can decide which *Location* the main database will be placed in and the *Capacity mode*. You can check more information about the capacity modes available at `https://docs.microsoft.com/en-us/azure/cosmos-db/throughput-serverless`. For example, we will choose *Serverless* because it's cost-effective for learning and development environments.

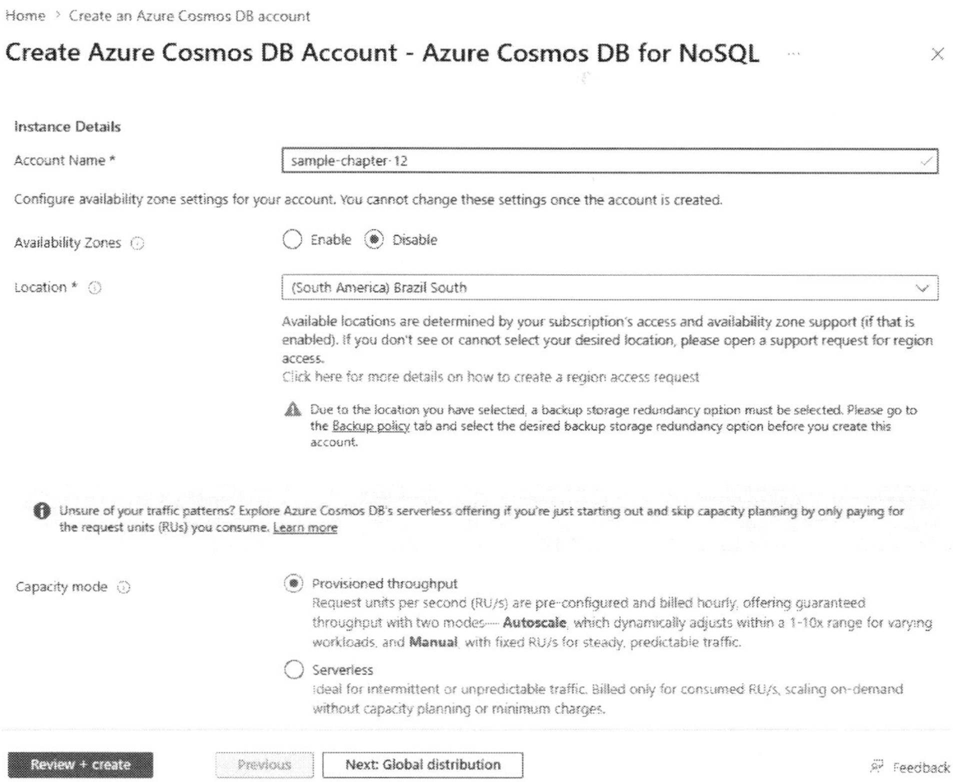

Figure 12.6: Creating an Azure Cosmos DB account

Note

Microsoft keeps improving many of its Azure services. The best way to keep updated about new features of any Azure component is by checking its documentation from time to time.

In the *Global Distribution* tab, the *Multi-region Writes* toggle enables active-active writes across the configured Azure regions. If you leave it disabled, the account operates with a single write region, and all writes are directed there. This option is available only if you decide to use *Provisioned throughput* capacity mode. Finally, you may also define *Network connectivity*, ***Backup policies***, and ***Security*** during the creation process.

Creating an Azure Cosmos container

Once your Azure Cosmos DB for NoSQL account is ready, you can create databases and containers. However, this step should be approached as a modeling decision rather than only as a configuration task. In Azure Cosmos DB, the container is the main unit for scaling storage and throughput, which means its design directly influences performance, cost, and growth strategy. Throughput can be provisioned for an individual container or shared across a database, so the choice depends on whether your workload needs isolated performance guarantees or can share capacity with other containers. Since data is distributed according to the partition key, container design and partitioning strategy must be considered together from the beginning.

Since databases just have a name and no configuration, you can create a **New Container** directly and then place the database where you wish as shown below:

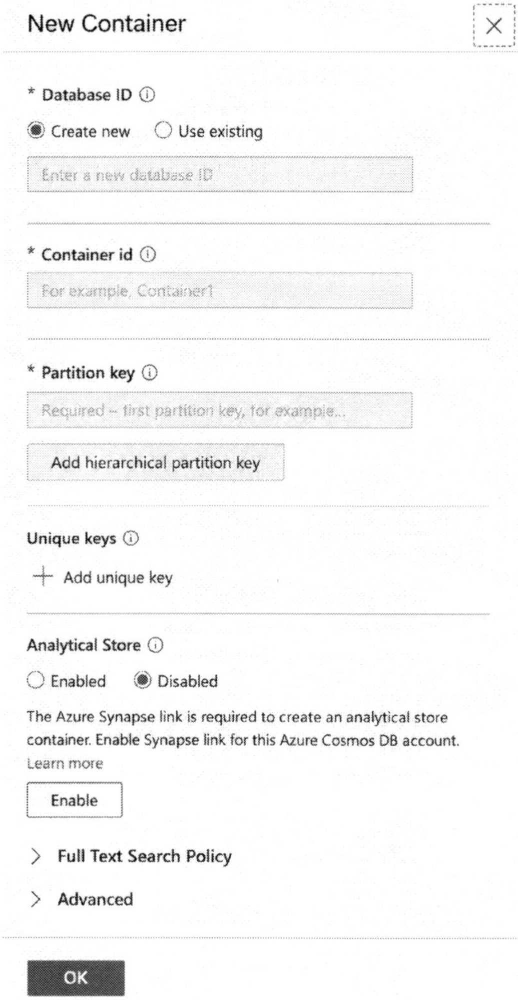

Figure 12.7: Adding a container in Azure Cosmos DB

Here, you define the database and container names, choose the partition key, and optionally configure unique key constraints. In Azure Cosmos DB, the partition key is the property whose value determines how items are grouped into logical partitions and distributed across the underlying infrastructure for horizontal scaling. Because document data is stored as JSON, this property is specified by using a path such as `/customerId` or `/tenantId`. You can also define unique keys to ensure that one or more property values remain unique within a logical partition.

Choosing a partition key is one of the most important modeling decisions in Cosmos DB. A good partition key should have high cardinality, distribute requests and data evenly, and align with the most common access patterns so that many reads and queries can be resolved within a single partition. Poor choices can create hot partitions, increase cross-partition queries, reduce throughput efficiency, and raise cost. If no single natural property distributes data well enough, one common option is to create a synthetic partition key; for more advanced scenarios, Cosmos DB also supports hierarchical partition keys.

It is also important to note that uniqueness is enforced only within a logical partition. In Azure Cosmos DB, the combination of the partition key value and the ID uniquely identify an item, and unique key constraints also apply only within that same partition scope. This means that the same ID or unique-key value can appear in different partitions without conflict. For example, in a multi-tenant system partitioned by `/tenantId`, two tenants may each have an item with the same `id` or the same business identifier, because each tenant's data is stored in a separate logical partition. The unique rule applies only within that tenant's partition. This behavior is often useful in SaaS systems, where each tenant should have isolated data while still allowing familiar identifiers to be reused across tenants.

Once the container model and uniqueness rules are clear, the next step is understanding how applications securely connect to and use the data.

Accessing Azure Cosmos data

After creating the Azure Cosmos container, you will be able to access data. To get connection information, you can select the **Keys** menu. There, you will see all the information you need to connect with your Cosmos DB account from your application. The connection information page will provide you with the account URI and two connection keys, which can be used interchangeably to connect with the account.

Figure 12.8 shows the connection information page, where the account URI and access keys needed by the client application can be retrieved.

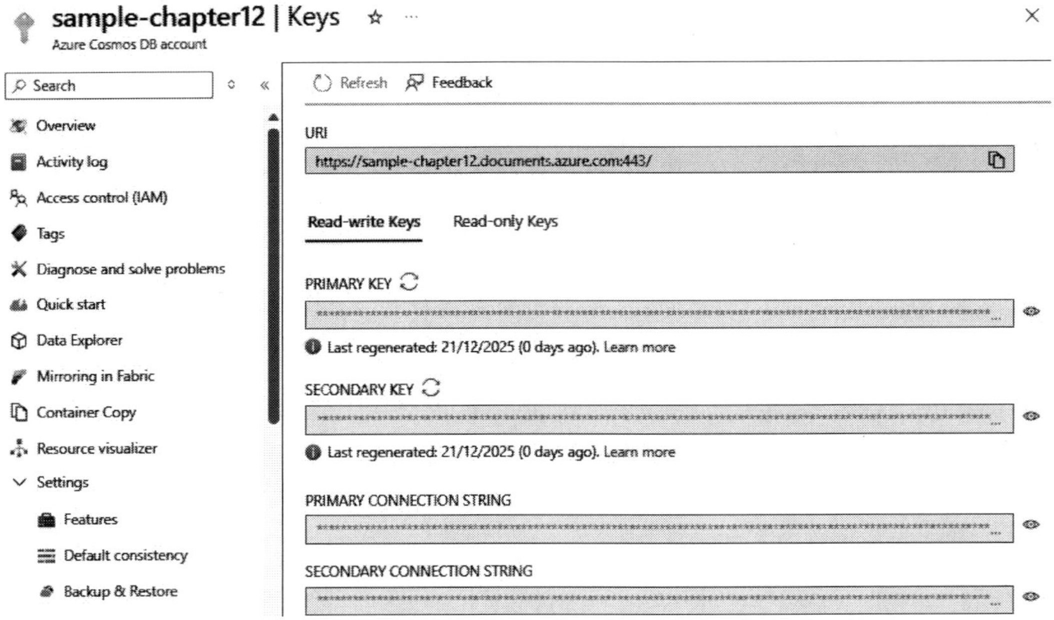

Figure 12.8: Connection information page

There are also keys with read-only privileges. Every key can be regenerated, and each account has two equivalent keys, like many other Azure components. The reason Azure provides paired keys is to support *key rotation without downtime*: an application can be switched from the primary key to the secondary key, the old key can then be regenerated, and the process can be repeated later in the opposite direction. This approach enables operations to be handled efficiently; that is, when a key is changed, the other one is kept. Therefore, existing applications can continue using the other key before upgrading to the new key, enabling safer secret rotation, staged deployments, and incident response without forcing all clients offline at the same time.

Defining database consistency

Because Azure Cosmos DB is a globally distributed database built on replication, you, as a software architect, must choose how fresh reads need to be and how much latency, availability trade-off, and throughput cost the application can tolerate. Azure Cosmos DB exposes five consistency levels so that this choice is explicit rather than hidden. The default consistency is configured at the account level and applies to all databases and containers in that account. When needed, the client can relax that setting for individual reads through the SDK, but not strengthen it beyond the account default.

So this default can be overridden in each container, either from Data Explorer or programmatically. Consistency problems in read/write operations are a consequence of data replication. More specifically, the results of various read operations may be incoherent if the read operations are executed on different replicas that have received different partial updates.

It is worth noting that, in practice, this is not just a database setting. It is an application design decision. A financial workflow, a shopping cart, a social feed, and an analytics dashboard may all use the same database engine, but they do not need the same freshness guarantees. Azure Cosmos DB, therefore, lets you place each workload at a different point on the spectrum between strict correctness and lower-latency, higher-throughput reads.

The following are the available consistency levels. These have been ordered from the strongest to the weakest. In practice, choose Strong or Bounded Staleness when stale reads would break the business flow, Session for most user-facing transactional experiences, Consistent Prefix when order matters more than immediate freshness, and Eventual when scale and latency matter more than recency.

- ***Strong:*** This means every read returns the latest committed value. Readers never observe stale, partial, or out-of-order committed data. Choose it when correctness is more important than latency, such as account balances, inventory decrements for scarce items, or workflow steps that must never act on stale state. The trade-off is that reads and especially cross-region writes are more expensive from a latency perspective, and strong consistency also reduces read throughput compared with weaker levels.
- ***Bounded Staleness:*** This is associated either with a delay time, Delta, or with a number of operations, N. Each reader sees the results of all the write operations that were performed before Delta (or before the last N operations). That is, its reads converge with the result of all the writes with a maximum time delay of Delta (or a maximum operations delay of N). Choose it when "*slightly old data is acceptable, but arbitrarily old is not*," such as globally distributed product catalogs, reporting portals, or near-real-time dashboards.
- ***Session:*** This is the same as the consistency prefix but also guarantees that each writer sees the result of their own writes in all subsequent read operations and that subsequent readers of each reader are coherent (either the same database or a more updated version of it). For instance, let's imagine a vacation package that currently costs US$900.00. If user A updates its price to US$1,000.00 and reads it again, the price will be US$1,000.00. But if User B reads it at the same time, the price may still be US$900.00 briefly.
- ***Consistent Prefix:*** All the writes are executed in the same order on all the replicas. So, if there are n write operations, each read is consistent with the result of applying the first m writes for some m less than or equal to n. Choose it when order matters more than freshness, such as append-only event displays, activity timelines, or sequential status updates where seeing "*A then B*" is acceptable even if "*C*" has not arrived yet, but seeing "*B before A*" would be wrong.
- ***Eventual consistency:*** After enough time has passed, if no further writing operations are done, all the reads converge and apply all the writes. The order of writes is also not guaranteed, so while writing is being processed, you could also end up reading an earlier version than the one you have previously read. Choose this level only when approximate freshness is acceptable, such as likes, retweet counts, or other high-scale signals where absolute recency is not critical.

The strongest consistency can be obtained at the detriment of performance. By default, the consistency is set to *Session*, which is a good compromise between coherence and performance. A lower level of consistency is difficult to handle in applications and is only usually acceptable if sessions are either read-only or write-only. The reason that Session is the default is that it keeps the application model natural for most interactive systems. Users expect to see their own changes immediately, while Cosmos DB can still serve reads using the cheaper, weaker-consistency path instead of the more expensive quorum-style reads used by Strong and Bounded Staleness. Microsoft explicitly says the weaker levels deliver about *2x read throughput* compared with Strong and Bounded Staleness.

If you select the **Settings** option in the Data Explorer menu of the container of your database, you can configure which paths to index and which kind of index to apply to each data type of each path. The configuration consists of a JSON object. Let us analyze its various properties:

```
{
    "indexingMode": "consistent",
    "automatic": true,
    ...
```

Note

Most teams should begin with the default indexing policy. Azure Cosmos DB automatically indexes every property in every item and applies range indexes to strings and numbers, which gives strong query performance without manual tuning. You should customize indexing only when you have a clear reason: for example, a write-heavy workload, large properties that are never queried, bulk ingestion scenarios, or multi-property queries that need composite indexes.

If you set `indexingMode` to none instead of consistent, no index is generated, and the collection can be used as a key-value dictionary that is indexed by the collection's primary key. In this scenario, no secondary indexes are generated, so the primary key cannot efficiently be searched on.

Before looking at the indexing policy details, it is worth reinforcing that the default indexing configuration is appropriate for most applications and should be customized only for clear performance or cost reasons.

When `automatic` is set to `true`, all document properties are automatically indexed:

```
{
    ...
    "includedPaths": [
        {
            "path": "/*",
            "indexes": [
                {
                    "kind": "Range",
                    "dataType": "Number",
                    "precision": -1
                },
                {
                    "kind": "Range",
                    "dataType": "String",
                    "precision": -1
                },
                {
                    "kind": "Spatial",
                    "dataType": "Point"
```

```
                }
            ]
        }
    ]
},
...
```

Each entry in the `includedPaths` specifies a path pattern such as `/subpath1/subpath2/?` (settings apply just to the `/subpath1/subpath2/property`) or `/subpath1/subpath2/*` (settings apply to all the paths starting with `/subpath1/subpath2/`).

Patterns contain the [] symbol when settings must be applied to child objects contained in collection properties; for example, `/subpath1/subpath2/[]/?`, `/subpath1/subpath2/[]/childpath1/?`, and so on. Settings specify the index type to apply to each data type (string, number, geographic point, and so on). Range indexes are needed for comparison operations, while hash indexes are more efficient if we need equality comparisons.

It is possible to specify a precision, that is, the maximum number of characters or digits to use in all the index keys. `-1` means the maximum precision and is always recommended:

```
    ...
    "excludedPaths": [
   {
          "path": "/\"_etag\"/?"
      }
    ]
```

Paths contained in `excludedPaths` are not indexed at all. Index settings can also be specified programmatically. Excluding paths reduces index size, write latency, and RU consumption because fewer properties need to be maintained in the index on each write. This is especially useful for large JSON fields that you store but never filter or sort on. Conversely, if you rely on queries with multi-property `ORDER BY` clauses or combined equality-and-range filters, you may need composite indexes to avoid unnecessary RU cost. Here, you have two options to connect to Cosmos DB: use a version of its official client for your preferred programming language or use Cosmos DB's Entity Framework Core provider.

Use the *Azure Cosmos DB SDK* when you want first-class access to Cosmos-specific features such as partition-aware operations, request-level consistency control, session-token handling, detailed diagnostics, and the full performance-tuning surface. Use *Entity Framework Core* when your team already works comfortably with `DbContext`, LINQ, and EF mapping patterns and wants a more familiar programming model for a document database.

In the following subsections, we will have a look at both options. Then, we will describe how to use Cosmos DB's Entity Framework Core provider with a practical example.

The Cosmos DB client

The Cosmos DB client for .NET 10 is available through the `Microsoft.Azure.Cosmos` NuGet package. It offers full control of all Cosmos DB features, while the Cosmos DB Entity Framework provider is easier to use but hides some Cosmos DB peculiarities. Follow these steps to interact with Cosmos DB through the official Cosmos DB client for .NET 10.

The following example creates the database if it does not already exist, creates a container partitioned by /`DestinationName`, and then inserts sample items. The endpoint is the URI of your Azure Cosmos DB account, and the key is one of the account keys shown in the *Keys* section of the Azure portal.

Do not forget that the client must be disposed of by calling its Dispose method (or by enclosing the code that references it in a using statement) when you do not need it anymore:

```
// These values come from your Azure Cosmos DB account in the Azure portal.
// - endpoint: the account URI / endpoint
// - key: one of the account keys shown in the Keys section
private const string endpoint = "<your-cosmos-account-endpoint>";
private const string key = "<your-cosmos-account-key>";
private const string databaseId = "WWTravelClub";
private const string containerId = "Destination";

public static async Task CreateCosmosDbAsync()
{
    // CosmosClient is thread-safe and is typically kept as a single
    // application-wide instance. It is shown inline here for
    // simplicity.
    using var cosmosClient = new CosmosClient(endpoint, key);
    Database database =
        await cosmosClient.CreateDatabaseIfNotExistsAsync(databaseId);

    // /DestinationName is the partition key path.
    ContainerProperties containerProperties =
        new ContainerProperties(containerId, "/DestinationName");

    Container container =
      await
    database.CreateContainerIfNotExistsAsync(containerProperties);

    await AddItemsToContainerAsync(container);
}
```

During collection creation, you can pass a `ContainerProperties` object, where you can specify the consistency level, how to index properties, and all the other collection features.

Then, you must define the .NET classes that correspond to the structure of the JSON document you need to manipulate in your collections, in this case, a structure from the WWTravelClub case study.

```
public class Destination
{
    public string id { get; set; }
    public string DestinationName { get; set; }
    public string Country { get; set; }
    public string Description { get; set; }
    public Package[] Packages { get; set; }
}
```

Once you have all the necessary classes, you can use client methods to `ReadItemAsync`, `CreateItemAsync`, and `DeleteItemAsync`. You can also query data using a `QueryDefinition` object that accepts SQL commands. You can find a complete introduction to this library at `https://docs.microsoft.com/en-us/azure/cosmos-db/sql-api-get-started`.

Now that you have checked how to use the *Azure Cosmos DB SDK*, let's move to *Entity Framework Core*, which will be useful if your team already works comfortably with `DbContext`, LINQ, and EF mapping patterns.

The Cosmos DB Entity Framework Core provider

The Cosmos DB provider for Entity Framework Core is contained in the `Microsoft.EntityFrameworkCore.Cosmos` NuGet package. Once you've added this to your project, you can proceed similarly to when you used the SQL Server provider in *Chapter 13, Interacting with Data in C# – Entity Framework Core*, but with a few differences. Let us look:

- Cosmos DB databases only support Async operations. This is not just a coding style preference. Cosmos DB operations are remote network calls to a distributed service, and the underlying SDK is designed around asynchronous I/O. Because of that, EF Core's Cosmos provider expects methods such as `ToListAsync`, `FirstOrDefaultAsync`, and `SaveChangesAsync` rather than their synchronous counterparts. Blocking on these operations wastes threads under load and can even introduce deadlocks, which is why recent EF Core versions now reject synchronous Cosmos access by default.
- There are no migrations since Cosmos DB databases have no structure to update. Instead, the method `EnsureCreatedAsync()` ensures that the database, along with all the necessary collections, is created. This changes the development workflow. In a relational database, a model change usually leads to a migration script that alters tables, columns, constraints, or indexes. In Cosmos DB, model evolution is typically handled in the application layer: new documents may be written in a new shape, while the application remains capable of reading older shapes during a transition period. In other words, compatibility with older documents becomes part of software design instead of database administration tasks.
- By default, the EF Core Cosmos provider maps all entity types in a `DbContext` to the same container. This is not only a cost optimization; it is also often a good architectural default in document databases. Collocating related entity types in a smaller number of containers can improve query efficiency, reduce

network round trips, and enable transactional operations within a shared logical partition. When needed, you can override this behavior and map a specific entity type to a different container.

```
builder.Entity<MyEntity>()
      .ToContainer("collection-name");
```

- One of the few commonly needed annotations on entity classes [Key]. It is particularly useful when the primary-key property is not named Id or <TypeName>Id, since those are the names EF Core recognizes as keys by convention. Otherwise, the key should be configured explicitly.
- Primary keys in Cosmos DB should be generated explicitly by the application rather than auto-incremented by the database. So primary keys must be strings and cannot be auto-incremented to avoid synchronization issues in a distributed environment. The uniqueness of primary keys can be ensured by generating GUIDs and transforming them into strings: `Guid.NewGuid().ToString()`.
- When defining relationships between entities, you can specify that an entity or a collection of entities is owned by another entity, in which case it is stored together with the parent entity.

Keep in mind that using EF Core with Cosmos DB does not make Cosmos DB behave like a relational database. The provider gives you a familiar programming model, but the architectural mindset remains document-oriented, where operations are asynchronous, schema evolution is handled through application compatibility, containers and partitioning influence design decisions, and identifiers must be generated in a way that works well in a distributed environment. With these differences in mind, we will look at the usage of Cosmos DB's Entity Framework provider in the next chapter.

Summary

In this chapter, we looked at the main storage options available in Azure and learned when to use them. Then, we compared relational and NoSQL databases. We pointed out that relational databases offer automatic consistency checking and transaction isolation, but NoSQL databases are cheaper and offer better performance, especially when distributed writes form a high percentage of the average workload.

Then, we described Azure's main NoSQL option, Cosmos DB, and explained how to configure it and how to connect with a client.

Finally, we learned how to interact with Cosmos DB with Entity Framework Core and looked at a practical example based on the WWTravelClubDB use case. Here, we learned how to decide between relational and NoSQL databases for all families of data involved in an application. This way, you can choose the kind of data storage that ensures the best compromise between data coherence, speed, and parallel access to data in each of your applications.

In the next chapter, we will learn all about how to interact with Data in C# - Entity Framework Core.

Questions

1. Is Redis a valid alternative to relational databases?
2. Are NoSQL databases a valid alternative to relational databases?

3. What operation is more difficult to scale out in relational databases?
4. What is the main weakness of NoSQL databases? What is their main advantage?
5. Can you list all Cosmos DB consistency levels?
6. Can we use auto-increment integer keys with Cosmos DB?
7. Which Entity Framework configuration method is used to store an entity inside its related parent document?
8. Can nested collections be searched efficiently with Cosmos DB?
9. You are designing an e-commerce system in which each user must immediately see updates to their own shopping cart, but other users do not need to see those updates instantly. Which Cosmos DB consistency level would you choose, and why?
10. A social media application stores posts, likes, and counters for millions of users across regions. Which consistency level would likely be sufficient for showing like counts, and what trade-off would this decision involve?
11. A SaaS platform stores tenant data in Cosmos DB. How would you choose a partition key if the system must scale across many tenants while still allowing efficient tenant-level queries?
12. Your application currently stores documents with one JSON structure, but a new release requires a different structure. Without relational migrations, how would you evolve the data model while keeping the system running?

Further reading

Here, you have some links you may consider using to gather more information about this chapter:

- In this chapter, we did not talk about how to define sharding with Azure SQL. Here is the link to the official documentation if you want to find out more: `https://docs.microsoft.com/en-us/azure/sql-database/sql-database-elastic-scale-introduction`.
- Cosmos DB was described in detail in this chapter, but further details can be found in the official documentation: `https://docs.microsoft.com/en-us/azure/cosmos-db/`.
- The following is a reference to the Gremlin language, which is supported by Cosmos DB: `http://tinkerpop.apache.org/docs/current/reference/#graph-traversal-steps`.
- The following is a general description of the Cosmos DB Graph Data Model: `https://docs.microsoft.com/en-us/azure/cosmos-db/graph-introduction`.
- Details on how to use Cosmos DB's official .NET client can be found at `https://docs.microsoft.com/en-us/azure/cosmos-db/sql-api-dotnetcore-get-started`.

Subscribe to Deep Engineering

Join thousands of developers and architects who want to understand how software is changing, deepen their expertise, and build systems that last.

Deep Engineering is a weekly expert-led newsletter for experienced practitioners, featuring original analysis, technical interviews, and curated insights on architecture, system design, and modern programming practice.

Scan the QR or visit the link to subscribe for free.

`https://packt.link/deep-engineering-newsletter`

13

Interacting with Data in C# – Entity Framework Core

All microservice and enterprise applications rely on storage engines to represent and store domain data. In order to avoid having the whole software depends on a specific storage engine, dependency on the selected storage engine is factored out in database drivers, as we discussed in the *Onion architecture* section of *Chapter 7, Understanding the Different Domains in Software Solutions.*

Notwithstanding the differences between the various database engines, it turns out that the functionalities of a database driver are quite standard: it has the main purpose of mapping data from a data storage subsystem into objects called aggregates and vice versa.

This led to the conception of general-purpose frameworks for implementing database drivers in a substantially declarative way. In simple terms, the purpose of these tools is the transformation of database table rows into objects of an object-oriented language, and vice versa.

These tools are called **Object-Relational Mapping** (ORM) tools since they were initially conceived for interfacing **relational** databases, then their scope was extended to include also modern **non-relational** storage classified as **NoSQL databases** (NoSQL databases are discussed in *Chapter 12, How to choose your data storage in the Cloud*).

ORMs improve and simplify the whole development process since they factor out and take the burden of mapping data into objects and vice versa, so developers can focus just on the peculiarity of the business being handled by the application.

In this chapter, we will cover the following topics:

- Understanding ORM basics
- Configuring Entity Framework Core
- Entity Framework Core migrations
- Compiled models
- Querying and updating data with Entity Framework Core
- Deploying your data layer

- Entity Framework Core and NoSQL databases: the Cosmos DB provider
- Understanding Entity Framework Core advanced features

This chapter describes ORMs and how to configure them, and then focuses on Entity Framework Core, the ORM included in .NET 10.

Before delving into ORM basics, let's look at the technical requirements needed to follow the practical examples in this chapter.

Technical requirements

This chapter requires the free Visual Studio 2026 Community Edition or better with all the database tools installed.

All the concepts in this chapter will be clarified with practical examples. You will find the code for this chapter at `https://github.com/PacktPublishing/Software-Architecture-with-.NET-10-and-C-sharp-5E`.

Understanding ORM basics

ORMs' main purpose is the translation of the data model used by databases, which is based on tuples and relations, into the data model of modern object-oriented languages based on classes and their mutual relations.

ORMs perform this translation by mapping relational DB tables into in-memory collections of objects where object properties correspond to DB table columns. During this mapping, some types are easily translated since they have a substantially equivalent definition in both data models. This is the case for Booleans, numeric types, and strings.

The translation of other types is a little bit more complex and depends on the target object language. For instance, in the case of C#, all database date and time types could be mapped into different C# types, such as: `DateTime`, `DateTimeOffset`, `DateOnly`, `TimeOnly`, etc. Therefore, further configuration information is needed to define their language-specific target types.

GUIDS have great importance in distributed applications and databases, since they replace classic auto-increment integer fields that do not perform well in distributed environments. However, notwithstanding their importance, not all databases have a GUID type, so when interfacing with these databases, ORMs translate GUIDs into some of their equivalent string formats.

Since the string properties of most object-oriented languages have no length limits associated with them (while DB string fields usually have length limits), the DB limits are taken into account in the DB mapping configuration. In general, when the mapping between DB types and object-oriented language types needs options to be specified, these options are declared in the mapping configuration.

The way the whole configuration is defined depends on the specific ORM. Entity Framework Core offers three options:

- Data annotations: C# attributes are added to the class properties mapped to table fields.

- Name conventions, such as a field named `Id`, are interpreted as a principal key.
- A so-called **fluent configuration interface**. Each object to be mapped to a database table has an associated configuration class whose methods are used to specify configuration settings.

While the fluent interface can be used to specify any configuration option, the data annotations and name conventions can be used for a smaller subset of them.

> **Tip**
>
> Relying on name conventions for complex settings is very dangerous, since there are no compile-time checks on name conventions, so a re-engineering operation might erroneously change or destroy some ORM settings.

Personally, I use name conventions only for specifying the principal key with an ID property name since that name has become a de facto standard, and the probability of misspelling it is very low.

The choice between data annotations and a fluent interface is mainly a matter of code readability and modularity. On one side, fluent configurations can be defined in separate files, so they are modular, but on the other side, the direct application of configuration data on the classes mapped to data tables increases code readability.

> **Tip**
>
> Personally, I try to take the best of the two techniques by using data annotations whenever they increase code readability, and the fluent interface for all other configurations. More specifically, I use data annotations mainly for specifying constraints on the possible values of properties, such as the maximum length of a string value, or the fact that a property is obligatory and can't be null. In fact, these constraints restrict the type specified in each property, so placing them next to the properties they are applied to increases the code's readability.

All other settings are better grouped and organized by using the fluent interface in order to increase code readability and maintainability.

Each ORM adapts to a specific DB type (Oracle, MySQL, SQL Server, and so on) with DB-specific adapters called **providers** or **connectors**. Entity Framework Core has providers for most of the available DB engines.

A complete list of providers can be found at `https://docs.microsoft.com/en-US/ef/core/providers/`. Providers are available as NuGet packages, so once you select your database type, you just need to add the NuGet package that implements its adapter to your data processing library.

Adapters are necessary for the differences in DB types, for the way transactions are handled, and for all other features that are not standardized by the SQL language.

Relations among tables are represented with object pointers. For instance, in a *one-to-many* relationship, like the relation between a customer and its purchase orders, the class that's mapped to the *one* side of the relationship (say, `Customer`) contains a collection that is populated with the related objects on the *many* side of the relationship (say, `MyPurchaseOrders`). On the other hand, the class mapped to the *many* sides of the relationship (say, `PurchaseOrder`) has a simple property that is populated with a uniquely related object on the *one* side of the relationship (say, `MyAssociatedCustomer`).

In a *one-to-one* relation, each class has a simple property that is populated with the uniquely related object on the other side of the relationship.

In many-to-many relations, both classes contain a collection that is populated with all related objects on the other side of the relationship. Thus, for instance, in a `Student-Course` relation, the `Student` class has a collection (say `MyCourses`) containing all related `Course` instances, while the `Course` class contains a collection (say `CourseStudents`) containing all `Student` instances related to the `Course`.

The whole database (or just a part of it) is represented by an in-memory cache class containing a collection for each mapped DB table, which in Entity Framework Core is called `DbContext`. Developers inherit from `DbContext` and add their database-mapping instructions inside overridden methods. While the application runs, instances of these customized `DbContext` subclasses are created to store partial snapshots of the DB that are synchronized with the database to get/update the actual data. DB queries are performed with a query language made of method calls on the collections of the in-memory cache class. The actual SQL is created and executed during the synchronization stage. For instance, Entity Framework Core performs **Language Integrated Query** (LINQ) queries on the collections mapped to the DB tables.

In general, LINQ queries produce instances of the `IQueryable` interface that inherits from `IEnumerable`. An `IQueryable` contains all the information that's needed to issue a query to the database, but the actual SQL is produced and executed when the first element of the `IQueryable` is retrieved. This is called lazy evaluation or deferred execution. It works as follows:

- LINQ queries that start from a mapped collection of a `DbContext` that is itself an `IQueryable`, say `ctx.Packages`. Where `ctx` is a `DBContext` instance.
- Query instructions are added to filter and transform the data, such as `ctx.Packages.Where(m => m.StartValidityDate>today)`. Where `today` is a variable containing today's date.
- Typically, each Entity Framework query ends with a `ToListAsync` or `ToArrayAsync` operation that transforms the `IQueryable` into a list or array, thereby causing the actual execution of the query on the database. Thus, in our example, we have:

  ```
  var result = await ctx.Packages.Where(m => m.StartValidityDate>today)
      .ToListAsync();
  ```

Queries that don't return collections are handled as follows:

- If the query is expected to return just a single element or no element at all, we typically execute a `FirstOrDefaultAsync` operation that returns a single element, if any, or `null`. This operation may also be used when several results are expected, but we need just one. In this case, we might also use `LastOrDefaultAsync`.
- If we need just to count the total results, for instance, for adequately organizing paging information, we can use `CountAsync()`.

Thus, for instance, packages can be counted as follows:

```
var result = await ctx.Packages.Where(m => m.StartValidityDate>today)
    .CountAsync();
```

Also, updates, deletions, and the addition of new entities to a DB table are performed by mimicking these operations on a `DbContext` collection property that represents the database table. However, entities may only be updated or deleted this way after they have been loaded in that memory collection by means of a query. Typically, an update query requires the in-memory representation of the entity to be modified as needed, while a delete query requires the in-memory representation of the entity to be removed from its in-memory mapped collection. In Entity Framework Core, the removal operation is performed by calling the `Remove(entity)` method of the collection.

The addition of a new entity has no further requirements. It is enough to add the new entity to the in-memory collection. Updates, deletions, and additions that are performed on various in-memory collections are actually passed to the database with an explicit call to a DB synchronization method.

For instance, Entity Framework Core passes all the changes that are performed on a `DbContext` instance to the database when you call the `DbContext.SaveChangesAsync()` method.

> **Note**
>
> Possible database errors are returned when `SaveChangesAsync()` is executed. Therefore, it is best practice to enclose this statement within a `try-catch` block.

Changes that are passed to the database during a synchronization operation are executed in a single transaction. Moreover, for ORMs, such as Entity Framework Core, that have an explicit representation of transactions, if a synchronization operation is executed in the scope of a transaction, it uses that transaction instead of creating a new one.

This section ends what can be said on ORMS in general. The remainder of the chapter is dedicated to the description and practical usage of Entity Framework Core. The next section explains the initial configuration of the object-database mapping.

Configuring Entity Framework Core

Since, as detailed in *Chapter 7, Understanding the Different Domains in Software Solutions*, database handling is confined within a dedicated database driver, it is good practice to define your Entity Framework Core (`DbContext`) in a separate library. Accordingly, we need to define a .NET class library project.

We have two different kinds of library projects: **.NET Standard** and **.NET (Core)**. Please refer to *Chapter 5, Implementing Code Reusability in C#*, for a discussion on the various kinds of libraries.

Our .NET 10 library project can be created by right-clicking on our Visual Studio solution and selecting **Add new project**, then selecting **Class Library**, and .NET 10 as the .NET version.

After that, you must add the Entity Framework DB provider NuGet package for your chosen database. It will carry with it all other needed Entity Framework Core NuGet packages as dependencies. Thus, for instance, in the case of SQL Server, you must add the `Microsoft.EntityFrameworkCore.SqlServer` NuGet package.

Note

If you plan to use several database engines, you can also add other providers since they can work side by side. Later in this chapter, we will install other NuGet packages that contain tools that we need to process our Entity Framework Core configuration.

Once you have your project ready, as a first step, you must define your custom DbContext by inheriting from `DbContext` and overriding its `OnModelCreating` method, as shown below:

```
using System;
using Microsoft.EntityFrameworkCore;
namespace WWTravelClubDB
{
    public class MainDbContext(DbContextOptions options): DbContext(options)
    {
        protected override void OnModelCreating(ModelBuilder
        builder)
        {
        }
    }
}
```

Our constructor must accept a `DbContextOptions` parameter that we must pass to the `DbContext` base constructor. This parameter contains creation options, such as the database connection string, which depends on the target DB engine. All the collections that have been mapped to database tables will be added as properties of `MainDbContext`. The mapping configuration will be defined inside the overridden `OnModelCreating` method with the help of the `ModelBuilder` object passed as a parameter.

The next step is the creation of all the classes that represent the database tables. These are called entities. We need an entity class for each DB table we want to map. Let's create a `Models` folder in the project root where we can place all entities. The definition and configuration of all entities are explained in detail in the next subsection.

Defining DB entities

Let's suppose that, in some iteration of our application development, we need a prototype with two database tables: one for all the travel packages and another one for all the locations referenced by the packages. Each package covers just one location, while a single location may be covered by several packages, so the two tables are connected by a one-to-many relationship.

So, let's start with the location database table. As we mentioned at the end of the previous section, we need an entity class to represent the rows of this table. Let's call the entity class `Destination`:

```
namespace WWTravelClubDB.Models
{
    public class Destination
    {
        public int Id { get; set; }
        public required string Name { get; set; }
        public required string Country { get; set; }
        public string? Description { get; set; }
    }
}
```

All the DB fields must be represented by read/write C# properties. Since both the `Name` and `Country` properties are obligatory, but we are not going to define a constructor, we added the `required` keyword to inform the compiler that these two properties will be provided with a not-null value in the **object initializer**, as shown below:

```
new Destination() {
  Name=…,
  Country=…
}
```

Suppose that each destination is something like a town or a region that can be defined by just its name and the country it is in, and that all the relevant information is contained in its `Description`. In future application iterations, we will probably add several more fields. `Id` is an auto-generated key.

Once we have defined our entities, we must specify how to map them to database tables.

As a first step, we must configure how all fields are mapped to DB fields. In Entity Framework Core, all the primitive types are mapped automatically to DB types by the DB engine-specific provider that's used (in our case, the SQL Server provider), so we must focus just on the following configurations:

- ***Length limits on the string***: They can be taken into account by applying adequate `MaxLength` and `MinLength` attributes to each string property. All the attributes that are useful for the entity's configuration are contained in the `System.ComponentModel.DataAnnotations` and `System.ComponentModel.DataAnnotations.Schema` namespaces. Therefore, it's good practice to add both of them to all the entity definitions.
- ***Specifying which fields are obligatory and which ones are optional***: If the project is not using the **Nullable Reference Type** feature, by default, all the reference types (such as all the strings) are assumed to be optional, while all the value types (numbers and GUIDs, for instance) are assumed to be obligatory. If we want a reference type to be obligatory, then we must decorate it with the `Required` attribute. On the other side, if we want a `T` type property to be optional, and `T` is a value type or the

Nullable Reference Type feature is on, then we must replace `T` with `T?`. As a default, .NET 10 projects have the Nullable Reference Type feature set. Therefore, in the remainder of the chapter, we will assume that the Nullable Reference Type feature is on.

- ***Specifying which property represents the primary key***: The key may be specified by decorating a property with the `Key` attribute. However, if no `Key` attribute is found, a property named `Id` (if there is one) is taken as the primary key. In our case, there is no need for the `Key` attribute.

Since each destination is on the *one* side of a one-to-many relationship, it must contain a collection for the related package entities; otherwise, it will be difficult to refer to the related entities in the clauses of our LINQ queries. This collection will have a fundamental role in our LINQ queries and will be populated by Entity Framework Core. However, as we will see later on in this chapter, it must be ignored in most of the database update operations; therefore, the best option to avoid compiler warnings is to assign them the null-forgiving fake default value: `null!`.

Putting everything together, the final version of the `Destination` class is as follows:

```
using System.Collections.Generic;
using System.ComponentModel.DataAnnotations;
using System.ComponentModel.DataAnnotations.Schema;
namespace WWTravelClubDB.Models
{
    public class Destination
    {
        public int Id { get; set; }
        [MaxLength(128)]
        Public required string Name { get; set; }
        [MaxLength(128)]
        Public required string Country { get; set; }
        public string? Description { get; set; }
        public ICollection<Package> Packages { get; set; } = null!
    }
}
```

Since the `Description` property has no length limits, it will be implemented with a SQL Server `nvarchar(MAX)` field of indefinite length. We can write the code for the `Package` class in a similar way:

```
using System;
using System.ComponentModel.DataAnnotations;
using System.ComponentModel.DataAnnotations.Schema;
namespace WWTravelClubDB.Models
{
    public class Package
    {
        public int Id { get; set; }
```

```
        [MaxLength(128)]
        Public required string Name { get; set; }
        [MaxLength(128)]
        public string? Description { get; set; }
        public decimal Price { get; set; }
        public int DurationInDays { get; set; }
        public DateTime? StartValidityDate { get; set; }
        public DateTime? EndValidityDate { get; set; }
        public Destination MyDestination { get; set; } = null!

        public int DestinationId { get; set; }
    }
}
```

Each package has a duration in days, as well as optional start and stop dates, during which the package offer is valid. `MyDestination` connects packages with their destinations in the many-to-one relationship that they have with the `Destination` entity, while `DestinationId` is the external key of the same relation.

While it is not obligatory to specify the external key, it is good practice to do so for the following reasons:

- The obligatoriness of the relation is connected to the nullability of the external key. For instance, in our case, since `DestinationId` is an `int` (not a nullable type), it is obligatory. Therefore, the relationship here is one-to-many and not (0, 1)-to-many. Defining `DestinationId` as `int?`, instead of `int`, would turn the one-to-many relationship into a (0, 1)-to-many relationship.
- By having the external key explicitly represented in our entity, we can assign it a value, and as we will see later on in this chapter, this simplifies a lot some update operations.

In the next section, we will explain how to define the in-memory collection that represents the database tables.

Defining the mapped collections

Once we have defined all the entities that are object-oriented representations of the database rows, we need to define the in-memory collections that represent the database tables themselves. As we mentioned in the *Understanding ORM basics* section, all the database operations are mapped to the operations on these collections (the *Querying and updating data with Entity Framework Core* section of this chapter explains how). It is enough to add a `DbSet<T>` collection property to our `DbContext` for each entity, `T`. Usually, the name of each of these properties is obtained by pluralizing the entity name. Thus, we need to add the following two properties to our `MainDbContext`:

```
public DbSet<Package> Packages { get; set; }
public DbSet<Destination> Destinations { get; set; }
```

Up until now, we've translated database stuff into properties, classes, and data annotations. However, Entity Framework needs further information to interact with a database. The next subsection explains how to provide it.

Completing the mapping configuration

The mapping configuration information that we couldn't specify in the entity definitions must be added with configuration code based on a fluent interface. The simplest way to add this configuration information is to add it using the `OnModelCreating DbContext` method. Each configuration information relative to an entity, `T`, starts with `builder.Entity<T>()` and continues with a call to a method that specifies that kind of constraint. Further nested calls specify further properties of the constraint. For instance, our one-to-many relationship may be configured as follows:

```
builder.Entity<Destination>()
    .HasMany(m => m.Packages)
    .WithOne(m => m.MyDestination)
    .HasForeignKey(m => m.DestinationId)
    .OnDelete(DeleteBehavior.Cascade);
```

The two sides of the relationship are specified through the navigation properties that we added to our entities. `HasForeignKey` specifies the external key. Finally, `OnDelete` specifies what to do with packages when a destination is deleted. In our case, it performs a cascade delete of all the packages related to that destination.

The same configuration can be defined by starting from the other side of the relationship, that is, starting with `builder.Entity<Package>()`. Clearly, the developer must choose just one of the options:

```
builder.Entity<Package>()
    .HasOne(m => m.MyDestination)
    .WithMany(m => m.Packages)
    .HasForeignKey(m => m.DestinationId)
    .OnDelete(DeleteBehavior.Cascade);
```

The only difference is that the previous statement's `HasMany-WithOne` methods are replaced by the `HasOne-WithMany` methods since we started from the other side of the relationship. Here, we can also choose the precision with which each decimal property is represented in its mapped database field. By default, decimals are represented by 18 digits and 2 decimals. You can change this setting for each property with something like:

```
...
.Property(m => m.Price)
        .HasPrecision(10, 3);
```

The `ModelBuilder builder` object allows us to specify database indexes with something such as the following:

```
builder.Entity<T>()
   .HasIndex(m => m.PropertyName);
```

Multi-property indexes are defined as follows:

```
builder.Entity<T>()
    .HasIndex("propertyName1", "propertyName2", ...);
```

Indexes can also be defined with attributes applied to the class. The following is the case of a single-property index:

```
[Index(nameof(Property), IsUnique = true)]
public class MyClass
{
    public int Id { get; set; }
    [MaxLength(128)]
    public string Property { get; set; }
}
```

The following is the case of a multi-property index:

```
[Index(nameof(Property1), nameof(Property2), IsUnique = false)]
public class MyComplexIndexClass
{
    public int Id { get; set; }
    [MaxLength(64)]
    public string Property1 { get; set; }
    [MaxLength(64)]
    public string Property2 { get; set; }
}
```

Configuration options that are specific to an entity can also be grouped in separate configuration classes, one for each entity:

```
internal class DestinationConfiguration :
    IEntityTypeConfiguration<Destination>
{
    public void Configure(EntityTypeBuilder<Destination> builder)
    {
        builder
            .HasIndex(m => m.Country);
        builder
            .HasIndex(m => m.Name);
        ...
    }
}
```

Each of these classes must implement the `IEntityTypeConfiguration<>` interface, whose unique method is `Configure`. Then, the configuration class can be declared with a class-level attribute:

```
[EntityTypeConfiguration(typeof(DestinationConfiguration))]
public class Destination
{
   ...
```

The configuration class can also be recalled from within the `OnModelCreating` method of the context class:

```
new DestinationConfiguration()
         .Configure(builder.Entity<Destination>());
```

However, in most cases, the best option is adding all configuration information defined in the assembly with:

```
builder.ApplyConfigurationsFromAssembly(typeof(MainDbContext).Assembly);
```

If we add all the necessary configuration information, then our `OnModelCreating` method will look as follows:

```
protected override void OnModelCreating(ModelBuilder builder)
{
   builder.Entity<Destination>()
        .HasMany(m => m.Packages)
        .WithOne(m => m.MyDestination)
        .HasForeignKey(m => m.DestinationId)
        .OnDelete(DeleteBehavior.Cascade);
builder.ApplyConfigurationsFromAssembly(
typeof(MainDbContext).Assembly);
}
```

Together with the two configuration classes:

```
using Microsoft.EntityFrameworkCore;
using Microsoft.EntityFrameworkCore.Metadata.Builders;
namespace WWTravelClubDB.Models
{
    internal class DestinationConfiguration :
        IEntityTypeConfiguration<Destination>
    {
        public void Configure(EntityTypeBuilder<Destination> builder)
        {
            builder
                .HasIndex(m => m.Country);
            builder
```

```
                .HasIndex(m => m.Name);
        }
    }
}
using Microsoft.EntityFrameworkCore;
using Microsoft.EntityFrameworkCore.Metadata.Builders;
namespace WWTravelClubDB.Models
{
internal class PackageConfiguration:
IEntityTypeConfiguration<Package>
    {
        public void Configure(EntityTypeBuilder<Package> builder)
        {
            builder
                .HasIndex(m => m.Name);
            builder
                .HasIndex(nameof(Package.StartValidityDate),
                 nameof(Package.EndValidityDate));
        }
    }
}
```

I prefer to define just the general configuration and relations in the context class. It is also convenient to use data annotation just for restricting property values (maximum and minimum length, required fields, and so on) since this enhances code readability. The best place for other entity-specific configuration is the configuration class.

The previous example shows a one-to-many relation, but Entity Framework Core 10 also supports many-to-many relations:

```
modelBuilder
  .Entity<Teacher>()
  .HasMany(e => e.Classrooms)
  .WithMany(e => e.Teachers)
```

In the preceding case, the join entity and the database join table are created automatically, but you can also specify an existing entity as the join entity. In the previous example, the join entity might be the course that the teacher teaches in each classroom:

```
modelBuilder
  .Entity<Teacher>()
  .HasMany(e => e.Classrooms)
  .WithMany(e => e.Teachers)
      .UsingEntity<Course>(
           b => b.HasOne(e => e.Teacher).WithMany()
```

```
            .HasForeignKey(e => e.TeacherId),
            b => b.HasOne(e => e.Classroom).WithMany()
            .HasForeignKey(e => e.ClassroomId));
```

Once you've configured Entity Framework Core, we can use all the configuration information we have to create the actual database and put all the tools we need in place in order to update the database's structure as the application evolves. The next section explains how.

Entity Framework Core migrations

Now that we've configured Entity Framework and defined our application-specific `DbContext` subclass, we can use the Entity Framework Core design tools to generate the physical database and create the database structure snapshot that's needed by Entity Framework Core to interact with the database.

Entity Framework Core design tools must be installed in each project that needs them as NuGet packages. There are two equivalent options:

- ***Tools that work in any operating system console***: These are available through the `Microsoft.EntityFrameworkCore.Design` NuGet package. All Entity Framework Core commands are in the `dotnet ef .....` format since they are contained in the `ef` command line's .NET Core application.
- ***Tools that are specific to the Visual Studio Package Manager Console***: These are contained in the `Microsoft.EntityFrameworkCore.Tools` NuGet package. They don't need the `dotnet ef` prefix since they can only be launched from the **Package Manager Console** inside of Visual Studio.

Entity Framework Core's design tools are used within the design/update procedure. This procedure is as follows:

1. We modify `DbContext` and the entities' definitions as needed
2. We launch the design tools to ask Entity Framework Core to detect and process all the changes we made
3. Once launched, the design tools update the database structure snapshot and generate a new *migration*, that is, a file containing all the instructions we need in order to modify the physical database to reflect all the changes we made
4. We launch another tool to update the database with the newly created migration
5. We test the newly configured DB driver. If new changes are necessary, we go back to step 1.
6. When the DB driver is ready, it is deployed in staging or production, where all the migrations are applied once more to the actual staging/production database

This procedure is repeated several times in the various software project iterations and during the lifetime of the application: each time we need to change the database structure, we code the needed changes in both configuration and entities, and then generate a new migration and apply it to the database.

If we operate on an already existing database, we need to configure `DbContext` and its models to reflect the existing structure of all the tables we want to map. This can be done automatically with the `Scaffold-DbContext` command (see `https://learn.microsoft.com/en-us/ef/core/managing-schemas/scaffolding/?tabs=vs` for more details).

All classes generated by .NET are partial classes so the user can enrich them with further methods without modifying the scaffolded code by adding the new methods to partial classes with the same names.

Then, if we want to start using migration instead of continuing with direct database changes, we can call the design tools with the `-IgnoreChanges` option so that they generate an empty migration. Also, this empty migration must be passed to the physical database so that it can synchronize a database structure version associated with the physical database with the version that's been recorded in the database snapshot. This version is important because it determines which migrations must be applied to a database and which ones have already been applied.

However, developers may also choose to continue modifying the database manually and repeating the scaffold operation after each change.

The whole design process needs a test/design database and, if we operate on an existing database, the structure of this test/design database must reflect the actual database – at least in terms of the tables we want to map. To enable design tools so that we can interact with the database, we must define the `DbContextOptions` options that they pass to the `DbContext` constructor. These options are important at design time since they contain the connection string of the test/design database. The design tools can be informed about our `DbContextOptions` options if we create a class that implements the `IDesignTimeDbContextFactory<T>` interface, where `T` is our `DbContext` subclass:

```
using Microsoft.EntityFrameworkCore;
using Microsoft.EntityFrameworkCore.Design;
namespace WWTravelClubDB
{
    public class LibraryDesignTimeDbContextFactory
        : IDesignTimeDbContextFactory<MainDbContext>
    {
        private const string connectionString =
            @"Server=(localdb)\mssqllocaldb;Database=wwtravelclub;
                Trusted_Connection=True;MultipleActiveResultSets=true";
        public MainDbContext CreateDbContext(params string[] args)
        {
            var builder = new DbContextOptionsBuilder<MainDbContext>();

            builder.UseSqlServer(connectionString);
            return new MainDbContext(builder.Options);
        }
    }
}
```

`connectionString` will be used by Entity Framework to create a new database in the local SQL Server instance that's been installed on the development machine and connects with Windows credentials. You are free to change it to reflect your needs.

Now, we are ready to create our first migration! Let's get started:

1. Let's go to the **Package Manager Console** and ensure that *WWTravelClubDB* is selected as our default project
2. Now, type `Add-Migration initial` and press `Enter` to issue this command. Verify that you added the `Microsoft.EntityFrameworkCore.Tools` NuGet package before issuing this command, otherwise you might get an "`unrecognized command`" error:

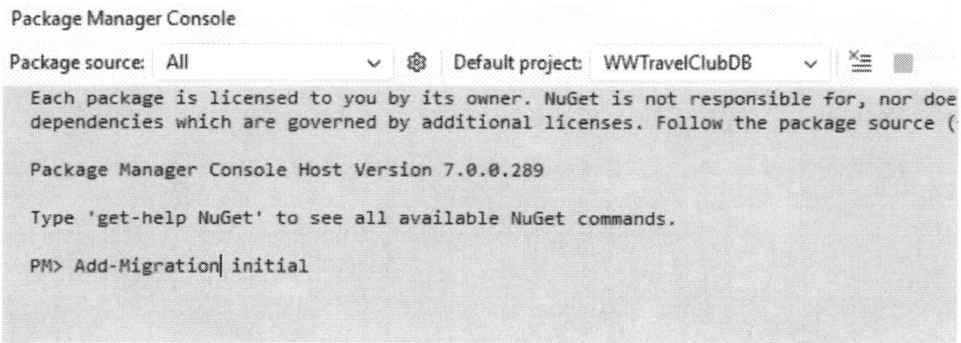

Figure 13.1: Adding the first migration

3. `initial` is the name we gave our first migration. So, in general, the command is `Add-Migration <migration name>`. When we operate on an existing database, we must add the `-IgnoreChanges` option to the first migration (and just to that) so that an empty migration is created. References to the whole set of commands can be found in the *Further reading* section.
4. If, after having created the migration, but before having applied the migration to the database, we realize we made some errors, we can undo our action with the `Remove-Migration` command. If the migration has already been applied to the database, the simplest way to correct our error is to make all the necessary changes to the code and then apply another migration.
5. As soon as the `Add-Migration` command is executed, a new folder appears in our project:

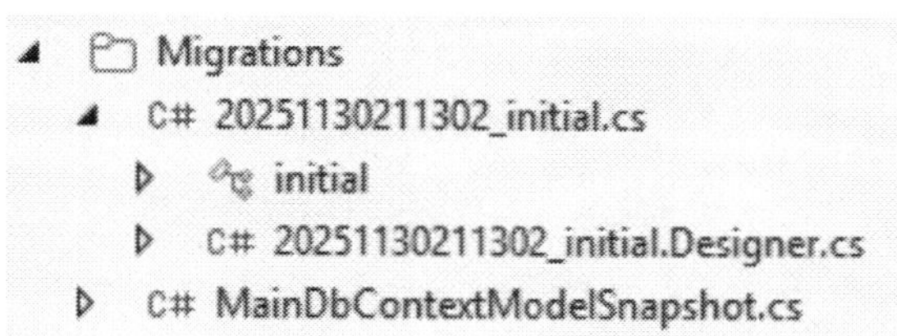

Figure 13.2: Files created by the Add-Migration command

`20251130211302_initial.cs` is our migration expressed in easy-to-understand language.

You may review the code to verify that everything is okay; you may also modify the migration content (only if you are enough of an expert to do it reliably), or simply undo the migration with the `Remove-Migration`, which *is the advised way to proceed when we discover errors.*

Each migration contains an `Up` method and a `Down` method.

The `Up` method applies the migration, while the `Down` method undoes its changes. Accordingly, the `Down` method contains the reverse actions of all the actions included in the `Up` method in reverse order.

`20251130211302_initial.Designer.cs` is the Visual Studio designer code, which you must not modify, while `MainDbContextModelSnapshot.cs` is the overall database structure snapshot. If you add further migrations, new migration files and their designer counterparts will appear and the unique `MainDbContextModelSnapshot.cs` database structure snapshot will be updated to reflect the database's overall structure.

The same command can be issued in an operating system console by typing `dotnet ef migrations add initial`. This command must be issued from within the project's root folder (not from within the solution's root folder).

However, if `Microsoft.EntityFrameworkCore.Design` is installed globally with `dotnet tool install --global dotnet-ef`, then we can use it in a project after adding it to that project by typing `dotnet add package --project <project path> Microsoft.EntityFrameworkCore.Design`. In this case, commands can be issued from any folder by specifying the `--project <project path>` option.

Migrations can be applied to the database by typing `Update-Database` in the Package Manager Console. The equivalent console command is `dotnet ef database update`. Let's try using this command to create the physical database!

The next subsection explains how to create database stuff that Entity Framework is unable to create automatically. After that, in the next section, we will use Entity Framework's configuration and the database we generated with `dotnet ef database update` to create, query, and update data.

Understanding stored procedures and direct SQL commands

Some database structures, like, for instance, stored procedures, can't be generated automatically by the Entity Framework Core commands and declarations we described previously. Stored procedures, such as generic SQL strings, can be included manually in the `Up` and `Down` methods through the `migrationBuilder.Sql("<sql command>")` method.

The safest way to do this is by adding a migration without performing any configuration changes so that the migration is empty when it's created. Then, we can add the necessary SQL commands to the empty `Up` method of this migration and their converse commands in the empty `Down` method. It is good practice to put all the SQL strings in the properties of resource files (`.resx` files).

> **Note**
>
> Stored procedure should replace EF commands in the following circumstances:
>
> - When we need to perform manual SQL optimizations to increase the performance of some operations.
> - When EF doesn't support the SQL operation we need to perform. A typical example is the increment or decrement of a numeric field, which occurs in all booking operations (air travel, hotels, and so on). Actually, we might replace the increment/decrement operation with a

database read, an in-memory increment/decrement, and finally a database update, all enclosed in the same transaction scope. However, this might be overkill for performance.

Before starting to interact with our database, we can perform a further optional step: model optimization.

Compiled models

Starting from version 6, Entity Framework Core introduces the possibility to create precompiled data structures that improve Entity Framework Core performance by about 10 times in the case of models with hundreds of entities (see the reference in the *Further reading* section for more details). This step is accomplished by generating some code that, once compiled together with the data layer project, creates data structures that our context classes can use to improve performance.

The usage of pre-compilation is advised just after one verifies that the system experiences slow-downs, also on very simple queries. In other words, it is better to start without pre-compilation and then possibly add it in case of slowdowns caused by the EF infrastructure.

Code is generated with the `Optimize-DbContext` command provided by the `Microsoft.EntityFrameworkCore.Tool` NuGet package that we already installed. The command accepts the folder name to place the code and the namespace to place all classes. In our case, let's choose the `Optimization` folder and the `WWTravelClubDB.Optimization` namespace:

```
Optimize-DbContext -Context MainDBContext -OutputDir Optimization -Namespace
WWTravelClubDB.Optimization
```

Where the `-Context` parameter must be passed the name of our context class. The `Optimization` folder is automatically created and filled with classes.

The optimization code depends on the ORM configuration, so the `Optimize-DbContext` command must be repeated each time a new migration is created.

Optimizations are enabled by passing the root of our optimization model as an option when an instance of the context class is created. Let's open the `LibraryDesignTimeDbContextFactory.cs` file and add the line below:

```
builder.UseSqlServer(connectionString);
//Line to add. Add it after that the optimization model has been created
builder.UseModel(Optimization.MainDbContextModel.Instance);
return new MainDbContext(builder.Options);
```

We have finished all relevant aspects of Entity Framework configuration and performance optimization, so we can move on to how to use it in our application code for querying and updating data.

Querying and updating data with Entity Framework Core

To test our DB layer, we need to add a console project based on the same .NET Core version as our library to the solution. Let's get started:

1. Let's call the new console project `WWTravelClubDBTest`
2. Now, we need to add our database driver as a dependency of the console project by right-clicking on the **Dependencies** node of the console project and selecting **Add Project Reference**
3. Remove the content of the `Program.cs` file and start by writing the following:

```
Console.WriteLine("program start: populate database, press a key to continue");
Console.ReadKey();
```

4. Then, add the following namespaces at the top of the file:

```
using WWTravelClubDB;
using WWTravelClubDB.Models;
using Microsoft.EntityFrameworkCore;
using WWTravelClubDBTest;
```

Now that we have finished preparing our test project, we can experiment with queries and data updates. Let's start by creating some database objects, that is, some destinations and packages. Follow these steps to do so:

1. First, we must create an instance of our `DbContext` subclass with an appropriate connection string. We can use the same `LibraryDesignTimeDbContextFactory` class that's used by the design tools to get it:

```
var context = new LibraryDesignTimeDbContextFactory()
    .CreateDbContext();
```

2. New rows can be created by simply adding class instances to the mapped collections of our `DbContext` subclass. If a `Destination` instance has packages associated with it, we can simply add them to its `Packages` property:

```
var firstDestination= new Destination
{
    Name = "Florence",
    Country = "Italy",
    Packages = new List<Package>()
    {
        new Package
        {
            Name = "Summer in Florence",
            StartValidityDate = new DateTime(2019, 6, 1),
```

```
                EndValidityDate = new DateTime(2019, 10, 1),
                DurationInDays=7,
                Price=1000
            },
            new Package
            {
                Name = "Winter in Florence",
                StartValidityDate = new DateTime(2019, 12, 1),
                EndValidityDate = new DateTime(2020, 2, 1),
                DurationInDays=7,
                Price=500
            }
        }
};
context.Destinations.Add(firstDestination);
await context.SaveChangesAsync();
Console.WriteLine(
 $"DB populated: first destination id is {firstDestination.Id}");
Console.ReadKey();
```

There is no need to specify primary keys since they are auto-generated and will be filled in by the database. In fact, after the `SaveChangesAsync()` operation synchronizes our context with the actual DB, the `firstDestination.Id` property has a non-zero value. The same is true for the primary keys of `Package`. Key auto-generation is the default behavior for all integer types.

> **Note**
>
> The `SaveChangesAsync()` synchronization instruction is the main tool for implementing the unit-of-work pattern described in *Chapter 7, Understanding the Different Domains in Software Solutions*, because when it is called, independent changes made to various aggregates are applied in a single transaction.

When we declare that an entity (in our case, `Package`) is a child of another entity (in our case, `Destination`) by inserting it in a parent entity collection (in our case, the `Packages` collection), there is no need to explicitly set its external key (in our case, `DestinationId`) since it is inferred automatically by Entity Framework Core. Once we have created `firstDestination` and synchronized it with the database, we can add further packages in two different ways:

- Create a `Package` class instance, set its `DestinationId` external key to `firstDestination.Id`, and add it to `context.Packages`
- Create a `Package` class instance, with no need to set its external key, and then add it to the `Packages` collection of its parent `Destination` instance

The latter approach should be preferred when the two entities do not belong to the same *aggregate*, as in the case of a purchase order entity with its connected detail items, since in this case the whole aggregate must be loaded in memory before operating on it to be sure all business rules are correctly applied and to prevent incoherences caused by simultaneous operations on different parts of the same aggregate (see the *Aggregates* subsection of *Chapter 7*, *Understanding the Different Domains in Software Solutions*).

If, instead, the entity belongs to different aggregates the first approach should be preferred since it simplifies and decouples the code that processes different aggregates.

Moreover, the latter option is the only possibility when a child entity (`Package`) is added with its parent entity (`Destination`) and the parent entity has an auto-generated principal key, since in this case, the external key isn't available at the time we perform the additions.

In most of the other circumstances, the former option is simpler since the second option requires the parent `Destination` entity to be loaded in memory, along with its `Packages` collection, that is, together with all the packages associated with the `Destination` object (by default, connected entities aren't loaded by queries).

Now, let's say we want to modify the `Florence` destination and give a 10% increment to all `Florence` package prices. How do we proceed? Follow these steps to find out how:

1. First, comment out all previous instructions for populating the database while keeping the `DbContext` creation instruction:

```
Console.WriteLine("program start: populate database, press a key to continue");
Console.ReadKey();
var context = new LibraryDesignTimeDbContextFactory()
    .CreateDbContext();
//var firstDestination = new Destination
//{
//    Name = "Florence",
//    Country = "Italy",
//    Packages = new List<Package>()
//    {
//        new Package
//        {
//            Name = "Summer in Florence",
//            StartValidityDate = new DateTime(2026, 6, 1),
//            EndValidityDate = new DateTime(2026, 10, 1),
//            DurationInDays=7,
//            Price=1000
//        },
//        new Package
//        {
//            Name = "Winter in Florence",
//            StartValidityDate = new DateTime(2026, 12, 1),
//            EndValidityDate = new DateTime(2027, 2, 1),
//            DurationInDays=7,
//            Price=500
```

```
//          }
//      }
//};
//context.Destinations.Add(firstDestination);
//await context.SaveChangesAsync();
//Console.WriteLine(
//      $"DB populated: first destination id is {firstDestination.Id}");
//Console.ReadKey();
```

2. Then, we need to load the entity into memory with a query, modify it, and call `await SaveChangesAsync()` to synchronize our changes with the database
3. If we want to modify, say, just its description, a query such as the following is enough:

```
var toModify = await context.Destinations
    .Where(m => m.Name == "Florence").FirstOrDefaultAsync();
```

4. Instead, if we would like to change all destination package prices, we need to load all the related destination packages that are not loaded by default. This can be done with the `Include` clause, as follows:

```
var toModify = await context.Destinations
    .Where(m => m.Name == "Florence")
    .Include(m => m.Packages)
    .FirstOrDefaultAsync();
```

5. After that, we can modify the description and package prices, as follows:

```
toModify.Description =
  "Florence is a famous historical Italian town";
foreach (var package in toModify.Packages)
   package.Price = package.Price * 1.1m;
await context.SaveChangesAsync();
var verifyChanges= await context.Destinations
    .Where(m => m.Name == "Florence")
    .FirstOrDefaultAsync();
Console.WriteLine(
    $"New Florence description: {verifyChanges.Description}");
Console.ReadKey();
```

If entities included with the `Include` method themselves contain a nested collection we would like to include, we can use `ThenInclude`, as shown here:

```
.Include(m => m.NestedCollection)
.ThenInclude(m => m.NestedNestedCollection)
```

Since Entity Framework always tries to translate each LINQ into a single SQL query, sometimes the resulting query might be too complex and slow. In such cases, starting from version 5, we can give Entity Framework permission to split the LINQ query into several SQL queries, as shown here:

```
.AsSplitQuery().Include(m => m.NestedCollection)
.ThenInclude(m => m.NestedNestedCollection)
```

Performance issues can be addressed by inspecting the SQL generated by a LINQ query with the help of the `ToQueryString` method:

```
var mySQL = myLinQQuery.ToQueryString ();
```

Starting from version 5, included nested collections can also be filtered with `Where`, as shown here:

```
.Include(m => m.Packages.Where(l-> l.Price < x))
```

So far, we've performed queries whose unique purpose is to perform an immediate update of the retrieved entities. Moreover, we have not applied the prescriptions of the Onion Architecture. In the subsections that follow we will show how the DB driver passes read-only queries and aggregates to the domain layer and application services.

Let's start with read-only queries.

Returning query results to the outer layer

To keep the layers separated and to adapt queries to the data that's actually needed by the application services entities aren't sent as they are to the application services and to the domain layer.

In the case of read-only queries, results are projected into smaller classes that contain the aggregated data we must show to the user. Objects like read-only query results that move data from one layer to another are called **Data Transfer Objects** (DTOs).

As an example, let's create a DTO containing the summary information that is worth showing when returning a list of packages to the user (we suppose that, if needed, the user can get more details by clicking the package they are interested in):

1. Let's add a DTO to our *WWTravelClubDBTest* project that contains all the information that needs to be shown in a list of packages:

```
namespace WWTravelClubDBTest
{
```

```
    public record PackagesListDTO
    {
        public int Id { get; init; }
        public required string Name { get; init; }
        public decimal Price { get; init; }
        public int DurationInDays { get; init; }
        public DateTime? StartValidityDate { get; init; }
        public DateTime? EndValidityDate { get; init; }
        public required string DestinationName { get; init; }
        public int DestinationId { get; init; }
        public override string ToString()
        {
         return string.Format("{0}. {1} days in {2}, price: {3}",
                Name, DurationInDays, DestinationName, Price);
        }
    }
}
```

2. We don't need to load entities in memory and then copy their data into the DTO, but database data can be projected directly into the DTO, thanks to the `LINQ Select` clause. This minimizes how much data is exchanged with the database.
3. As an example, we can populate our DTOs with a query that checks all the packages that are available around August 10:

```
var period = new DateTime(2026, 8, 10);
var list = await context.Packages
    .Where(m => period >= m.StartValidityDate
&.<= m.EndValidityDate)
    .Select(m => new PackagesListDTO
    {
        StartValidityDate=m.StartValidityDate,
        EndValidityDate=m.EndValidityDate,
        Name=m.Name,
        DurationInDays=m.DurationInDays,
        Id=m.Id,
        Price=m.Price,
        DestinationName=m.MyDestination.Name,
        DestinationId = m.DestinationId
    })
    .ToListAsync();
foreach (var result in list)
    Console.WriteLine(result.ToString());
Console.ReadKey();
```

4. In the `Select` clause, we can also navigate to any related entities to get the data we need. For instance, the preceding query navigates to the related `Destination` entity to get the `Package` destination name.
5. The programs stop at each `Console.ReadKey()` method, waiting for you to hit any key. This way, you have time to analyze the output that's produced by all the code snippets that we added to the `Main` method.
6. Now, right-click on the `WWTravelClubDBTest` project in Solution Explorer and set it as the start project. Then, run the solution.

In the Onion architecture, database updates are performed by manipulating aggregates that are quite different from the entities returned by Entity Framework Core or by other ORMS. The next subsection explains how to build domain layer aggregates from entities returned by an ORM like Entity Framework Core.

How to turn Entity Framework Core entities into aggregates

As discussed in *Chapter 7, Understanding the Different Domains in Software Solutions*, classical layer architectures use plain objects and repositories to communicate with the other layers.

Therefore, the entities that define Entity Framework Core configuration themselves can be used as they are to communicate with other layers, since they are just record-like lists of public properties, as prescribed for plain objects.

The case of domain layers and onion architectures is slightly more complex, since, in this case, the domain layer communicates with the application layer through aggregates that are rich objects whose methods represent application domain rules. Accordingly, in general, the remainder of the application can't access all aggregate properties but is forced to modify them through their own methods in order to enforce domain rules.

In other words, Entity Framework entities are record-like lists of public properties with almost no methods, while aggregates should have methods that encode domain logic, more sophisticated validation logic, and read-only properties. While further validation logic and methods can be added without breaking Entity Framework's operations, adding read-only properties that must not be mapped to database properties can create problems that must be handled adequately. Preventing properties from being mapped to the database is quite easy—all we need to do is decorate them with the `NotMapped` attribute, or use the fluent API as: `.Ignore(e => e.PropertyName)`.

However, restricting access to some entity properties and adding aggregate methods directly to Entity Framework Entities is a more complex problem.

First of all, if we decide to use Entity Framework entities directly as aggregates, we must define them directly in the domain layer DLL, so we must remove any ORM-specific code from them since the ORM is a DB driver and the domain layer can't have any reference to the DB Driver DLL.

Last but not least, we must restrict access to the entity properties to reflect business constraints without breaking the entity-database mapping.

Note

Deciding how to implement aggregates with ORMS entities is the key architectural decision when integrating EF with Onion architecture and must be made with care.

Summing up, we are left with the following two options:

- ***Map Entity Framework entities to different classes***: Define the aggregates as different classes and copy data to/from them when entities are returned/passed to repository methods. However, this is not enough, because all changes done on the aggregates must be reflected back to Entity Framework entities, because database updates are generated by detecting all changes performed on all Entity Framework entities and transforming them into SQL instructions when the SaveChangesAsync() is called. This can be done by hiding the Entity Framework entity behind an interface that represents the aggregate state, and passing it in the aggregate constructor. This way, the aggregate may store all its changes into this state interface, thus automatically updating the Entity Framework core entity. We will give more details on this technique in this section and will adopt it throughout the whole book.
- ***Map table fields to private properties***: In this case Entity Framework entities are turned into aggregates by letting Entity Framework Core map table fields to private class fields so that you can decide how to expose them through properties with custom getters and/or setters, or through complex business methods. For exposing them with properties it is enough to give either the _<property name> name or the _<property name in camel or case> name to these private fields, and Entity Framework will use them instead of their associated properties. Otherwise, the mapping can be defined through the Entity Framework fluent interface. If we opt for this approach, we can't use data annotations to configure each property because aggregates can't depend on how the underlying DB driver is implemented. Therefore, we must configure all database mapping in the OnModelCreating DbContext method, or in configuration classes associated with each. Renouncing to annotations is a minor problem. The main issue of this approach is that once the mapping properties are decided, they cannot be changed to adapt the code to database changes because entities are defined in the domain layer DLL, and the domain layer can't be influenced by changes in the DB driver.

Summing up, the second approach is simpler, but has a negative impact on code modifiability and modularity, so it should be used just with very simple database tables.

Let's suppose that we would like to define a state interface called IDestinationState to store the whole state of the DestinationAggregate that represents destinations in the domain layer. Both DestinationAggregate and IDestinationState must be defined in the domain layer, while the Entity Framework Destination entity is defined in the DB driver and implements IDestinationState.

This way the DB Driver DLL has a dependency on the domain layer DLL but the domain layer has no dependency on the DB driver, as prescribed by the Onion architecture constraints.

The IDestinationState interface has basically the same properties as the Destination entity, but this doesn't create a dependency of IDestinationState on the entity Destination because we are free to modify Destination to adapt it to database changes without affecting IDestinationState: we change Destination as needed, and then we implement properly all properties prescribed by IDestinationState. Below is a possible definition of IDestinationState:

```
public interface IDestinationState
{
    int Id { get; set;}
```

```
    string Name { get; set;}
    string Country { get; set;}
    string? Description { get; set;}
}
```

While DestinationAggregate is defined in the domain layer, all its instances must be created by DB driver methods since they must be injected with the actual Destination implementation of IDestinationState in their constructors. Below, a skeleton of the DestinationAggregate class:

```
public class DestinationAggregate(IDestinationState state)
{
   ....
}
```

All operations on a DestinationAggregate cause changes in its state, that is, in the Destination entity that implements IDestinationState and that is mapped to a database table.

A complete example of this technique is described in upcoming chapters , which also shows a complete implementation of all Onion architecture layers.

> **Note**
>
> The aggregate-state approach we described in detail has no drawbacks but requires more time to be implemented. Accordingly, the other approach should be preferred only when aggregates are very simple and contain almost no business logic so that it is not worth spending too much time with the implementation of the status interface technique.

Now, we will learn how Entity Framework Core handles operations that can't be effectively mapped to the immediate operations in the in-memory collections that represent the database tables.

Issuing direct SQL commands

Unluckily, the ORM model is not adequate for all situations. For instance, incrementing the reserved seats in a reservation system would require the loading of the whole aggregate that represents a flight, incrementing the reserved seats, and then re-synchronization with the database. This operation must be handled within a transaction to avoid errors if another user performs the same operation on the same flight. However, most databases offer direct increment operations that simplify the whole procedure a lot. Analogous situations can be handled in a very simple way with database stored procedures.

Thus, in some cases breaking the ORM model by issuing direct SQL commands to the database might be useful to simplify the overall application architecture. Therefore, it is worth analyzing the tools offered by Entity Framework Core for bypassing the ORM model and issuing direct SQL commands to the database.

There are two possibilities: SQL statements that perform database operations but do not return entities, and SQL statements that do return entities.

SQL commands that don't return entities can be executed with the `DbContext` method as follows:

```
Task<int> DbContext.Database.ExecuteSqlRawAsync(string sql, params object[] parameters)
```

Parameters can be referenced in the string as `{0}, {1}, ..., {n}`. Each `{m}` is filled with the object contained at the `m` index of the `parameters` array, which is converted from a .NET type into the corresponding SQL type. The method returns the number of affected rows.

SQL commands that return collections of entities must be issued through the `FromSqlRaw` method of the mapped collection associated with those entities:

```
context.<mapped collection>.FromSqlRaw(string sql, params object[] parameters)
```

Thus, for instance, a command that returns `Package` instances would look something like this:

```
var results = await context.Packages.FromSqlRaw("<some sql>", par1,
par2, ...).ToListAsync();
```

SQL strings and parameters work like the ones in the `ExecuteSqlRaw` method. The following is a simple example:

```
var allPackages = await context.Packages.FromSqlRaw(
    "SELECT * FROM Products WHERE Name = {0}",
    myPackageName).ToListAsync();
```

We can also use string interpolation:

```
var allPackages = await context.Packages.FromSqlRaw(
  $"SELECT * FROM Products WHERE Name = {myPackageName}").ToListAsync();
```

In case the objects to be returned by the SQL query are not mapped objects represented by collections added to the DB context like `context.Packages`, we can use a new method added in .NET 7:

```
IQueryable<TResult> DbContext.Database.SqlQueryRaw<TResult> (string sql, params object[]
parameters)
```

`SqlQueryRaw` is a method of the `Database` property of the DB context object, and it accepts the class of the objects to return as a generic parameter (`TResult`). However, in this case Entity Framework Core is able to transform the SQL tuples returned by the database into objects only if the column names in the tuples are equal to the property names in `TResult`. Name mismatches in some properties can be overcome by decorating these properties with the names of the columns they must be mapped from with the `[Column("<column name")]` attribute. Also possible using fluent API configuration: `.HasColumnName(<column name")`.

It is good practice to put all the SQL strings in resource files and encapsulate all the `ExecuteSqlRawAsync` and `FromSqlRaw` calls inside the public methods that you defined in your `DbContext` subclasses, in order to keep the dependence on a specific database inside of your Entity Framework Core-based DB driver.

At this point, you have learned how to configure and interact with an ORM and in particular, with Entity Framework Core. However, you still need to learn how to handle both queries and updates in a single transaction.

Handling transactions

All the changes that are made to a `DbContext` instance are passed in a single transaction at the first `SaveChangesAsync` call. However, sometimes it is necessary to include queries and updates in the same transaction. In these cases, we must handle the transaction explicitly. This is the case, for instance, of reservation: we need to verify if a seat is available (query) and reserve it (update), avoiding interferences from other SQL operations. Several Entity Framework Core commands can be included in a transaction if we put them inside a `using` block associated with a transaction object:

```
using var dbContextTransaction = context.Database.BeginTransaction();
try{
    ...
    ...
    dbContextTransaction.Commit();
}
catch
{
    dbContextTransaction.Rollback();
}
```

In the preceding code, `context` is an instance of our `DbContext` subclass. Inside of the `using block`, the transaction can be aborted and committed by calling its `Rollback` and `Commit` methods. Any `SaveChangesAsync` call that is included in the transaction block uses the transaction they are already in, instead of creating a new one.

At this point you should have learned how to build a DB driver and a database structure with the help of Entity Framework Core, so it is time to learn how to deploy your database solution in production.

Deploying your data layer

When your database driver is deployed in production or in staging, usually, an empty database already exists, so you must apply all the migrations in order to create all the database objects. This can be done by calling `context.Database.Migrate()`. The `Migrate` method applies the migrations that haven't been applied to the database yet, so it may be called safely several times during the application's lifetime.

`context` is an instance of our `DbContext` class that must be passed through a connection string with enough privileges to create tables and to perform all the operations included in our migrations. Thus, typically, this connection string is different from the string we will use during normal application operations.

During the deployment of a web application on Azure, we are given the opportunity to check migrations with a connection string we provide. We can also check migrations manually by calling the `context.Database.Migrate()` method when the application starts. This will be discussed in detail in *Chapter 17, Implementing Frontend Microservices with ASP.NET Core*, which is dedicated to frontend applications based on ASP.NET Core MVC.

In some production environments it is not possible to apply migrations during the application deployment because the person in charge of the deployment does not have enough privileges to create a new database and/or to create and modify tables. In this case, we must transform migrations into SQL commands and pass them to the database administrator who, after having verified they will not damage the existing database and data, applies them.

We can transform all migrations in a given interval into SQL with the `Script-Migration` command (see `https://learn.microsoft.com/en-us/ef/core/cli/powershell`):

```
Script-Migration -From <initial migration> -To <final migration> -Output <name of output
file>
```

For desktop applications, we can apply migrations during the installation of the application and its subsequent updates.

At the first application installation and/or in subsequent application updates, we may need to populate some tables with initial data. For web applications, this operation can be performed at application start, while for desktop applications, this operation can be included in the installation.

Database tables can be populated with Entity Framework Core commands. First, though, we need to verify whether the table is empty in order to avoid adding the same table rows several times. This can be done with the `Any()` LINQ method, as shown in the following code:

```
if(!context.Destinations.Any())
{
    //populate here the Destinations table
}
```

Summing up, you must always keep in mind that you must deploy just the database changes in production. If your application has the permissions needed to modify the database, this can be done automatically with the `context.Database.Migrate()`. Otherwise, you must generate SQL scripts containing all changes to apply to the database with the `Script-Migration` command, and pass them to a database administrator.

Up to now we implicitly assumed that our database is relational, but Entity Framework Core has providers for interfacing also with NoSQL databases. Let's analyze what changes in what we described so far when we operate with a NoSQL database.

Entity Framework Core and NoSQL databases: the Cosmos DB provider

As a final step in your learning path on ORMs and Entity Framework Core, let's learn what changes if our database is a NoSQL database. The way Entity Framework Core handles all NoSQL databases is quite the same, but for the sake of simplicity we will use the Cosmos DB provider as a typical NoSQL example.

The Cosmos DB provider for Entity Framework Core is contained in the `Microsoft.EntityFrameworkCore.Cosmos` NuGet package. Once you've added it to your project, you can proceed as you would with a classical relational database but with the key differences below:

- There are no migrations since Cosmos DB databases have no structure to update. Instead, they have a method that ensures that the database, along with all the necessary collections is created:

```
context.Database.EnsureCreated();
```

- By default, the `DbSet<T>` properties from `DBContext` are mapped to a unique container (Cosmos DB table) since this is the cheapest option. You can override this default and map several entities to the same container by explicitly specifying which container you want to map some entities with the following configuration instruction:

```
builder.Entity<MyEntity>()
    .ToContainer("collection-name");
```

- The only meaningful annotation on entity classes is the `Key` attribute, which becomes obligatory when the primary keys are not called `Id`.
- Primary keys must be strings and cannot be auto-incremented to avoid synchronization issues in a distributed environment. The uniqueness of primary keys can be ensured by generating GUIDs and transforming them into strings.
- When defining relationships between entities, you can specify that an entity or a collection of entities is owned by another entity, in which case it is stored together with the parent entity. This can be done with the configuration below:

```
builder.Entity<Destination>()
    .OwnsMany(m =>m.Packages);
```

It is also worth pointing out that while all connection features of a typical relational database are specified with a unique connection string, in the case of Cosmos DB and other NoSQL databases we must handle several separate parameters.

More specifically, in the case of a typical relational database, the options parameters of the `DbContext` class can be created with:

```
var builder = new DbContextOptionsBuilder<MainDbContext>();
            builder.UseSqlServer(dbconnectionString);
```

In the case of Cosmos DB, we have:

```
var builder = new DbContextOptionsBuilder<MainDBContext>();
   builder.UseCosmos(endpoint, key, databaseName);
```

Where, `endpoint` is the URL of your Cosmos DB instance, `key` is a credential for accessing its services, and `databaseName` is the name of the specific database you would like to connect with.

At this point you finished your learning path on ORMs and Entity Framework Core. Before moving on to another topic, let's take a look at a few Entity Framework Core advanced features that might simplify your architectural choices in complex situations.

Understanding Entity Framework Core advanced features

This section contains selected advanced capabilities that might simplify architectural design decisions and simplify your overall architecture.

Let's start with global filters, which were introduced at the end of 2017. They enable techniques such as soft delete and multi-tenant tables that are shared by several users, where each user just *sees* its records.

Global filters are defined with the `modelBuilder` object, which is available in the `DbContext OnModelCreating` method. The syntax for this method is as follows:

```
modelBuilder.Entity<MyEntity>().HasQueryFilter(m => <define filter condition here>);
```

For instance, if we add an `IsDeleted` property to our `Package` class, we may soft delete a `Package` without removing it from the database by defining the following filter:

```
modelBuilder.Entity<Package>().HasQueryFilter(m => !m.IsDeleted);
```

However, filters contain `DbContext` properties. Thus, for instance, if we add a `CurrentUserID` property to our `DbContext` subclass (whose value is set as soon as a `DbContext` instance is created), then we can add a filter like the following one to all the entities that refer to a user ID:

```
modelBuilder.Entity<Document>().HasQueryFilter(m => m.UserId == CurrentUserId);
```

With the preceding filter in place, the currently logged-in user can only access the documents they own (the ones that have their `UserId`). Similar techniques are very useful in the implementation of multi-tenant applications.

Another interesting feature that is worth mentioning is mapping entities to un-updatable database queries, which was introduced in version 5.

When you define an entity, you can define explicitly either the name of the mapped database table or the name of a mapped updatable view:

```
modelBuilder.Entity<MyEntity1>().ToTable("MyTable");
modelBuilder.Entity<MyEntity2>().ToView("MyView");
```

When an entity is mapped to a view, no table is generated by database migration, so the database view must be defined manually by the developer.

If the view we would like to map our entity in is not updatable, LINQ cannot use it to pass updates to the database. In this case, we can map the same entity simultaneously to a view and a table:

```
modelBuilder.Entity<MyEntity>().ToTable("MyTable").ToView("MyView")
```

Entity Framework will use the view for the queries and the table for the updates. This is useful when we create a newer version of a database table but we want to also take data from the old version of the table in all queries. In this case, we may define a view that takes data from both the old and the new tables, but pass all updates only to the new table.

The option to set property defaults is also interesting. This can be done by specifying an override for the `ConfigureConventions DbContext` method. For instance, we can set a default precision for all decimal properties:

```
protected override void ConfigureConventions(
    ModelConfigurationBuilder configurationBuilder)
{
     configurationBuilder.Properties<decimal>()
         .HavePrecision(10, 3);
         ...
}
```

Specifying a default maximum length for all string properties is also useful:

```
protected override void ConfigureConventions(
    ModelConfigurationBuilder configurationBuilder)
{
     configurationBuilder.Properties<decimal>()
         .HavePrecision(10, 3);
     configurationBuilder.Properties<string>()
```

```
            .HaveMaxLength(128);
        ...
}
```

Another interesting feature that was gradually introduced in the last versions of Entity Framework Core is the mapping of JSON database Columns. In particular JSON data contained in a single JSON column can be queried, and their JSON objects mapped to .NET Types.

Suppose that an `Author` class that must be mapped to a database table has a `Contact` property containing a complex object, and suppose we would like to store this object in a database JSON column of the `Author` table. We can do it with the help of the `OwnsOne` configuration method, as follows:

```
modelBuilder.Entity<Author>().OwnsOne(
     author => author.Contact, ownedNavigationBuilder =>
     {
       ownedNavigationBuilder.ToJson();
     });
```

After this configuration, the `Contact` object can be queried as a standard navigation property:

```
 context.Authors
  .Where(m => m.Contact.Email == searchEmail).FirstOrDefaultAsync();
```

We can recursively map also sub-objects contained in the contact object, such as a collection of addresses, but in this case, we must use `OwnsMany`:

```
modelBuilder.Entity<Author>().OwnsOne(
    author => author.Contact, ownedNavigationBuilder =>
    {
         ownedNavigationBuilder.ToJson();
          ownedNavigationBuilder.OwnsMany(
                 contactDetails => contactDetails.Addresses);
    });
```

After that, the nested Addresses JSON collection can also be queried with the usual LINQ syntax:

```
context.Authors
  .Where(m => m.Contact.Addresses.Any()).FirstOrDefaultAsync();
```

The above query returns all authors with a nonempty addresses list.

Summing up, Entity Framework Core has tools for accessing just a database projection (global filters), handling database Views efficiently, defining global configuration defaults, and storing and querying complex JSON data.

Summary

In this chapter, you learned the essentials of ORM basics, why they are so useful, and their architectural implications and learned the peculiarity of Entity Framework Core. In particular, you learned how to configure database mappings and which important choices must be made during this configuration.

Then, you learned how to create data structures for improving ORM performance and how to automatically create and update the physical database with the help of migrations, as well as how to query and pass updates to the database through Entity Framework Core.

Moreover, you also learned how to integrate an ORM in the Onion architecture, that is, how to place all the ORM's mappings and entities in the DB driver and how to interface it with the domain layer. More specifically, you learned how to face all design choices involved in the implementation of aggregates with ORM entities.

Finally, you learned how to simplify your design by passing direct SQL commands to the database and how to handle complex situations with transactions, as well as how to deploy a DB driver based on an ORM and in particular based on Entity Framework Core.

This chapter also reviewed some advanced features that were introduced in the latest Entity Framework Core releases that may simplify important design choices.

In the next chapter, we move to the practical design of worker microservices.

Questions

1. How does Entity Framework Core adapt to several different database engines?
2. How are primary keys declared in Entity Framework Core?
3. How is a string field's length declared in Entity Framework Core?
4. How are indexes declared in Entity Framework Core?
5. How are relations declared in Entity Framework Core?
6. What are the two most important migration commands?
7. By default, are related entities loaded by LINQ queries?
8. Is it possible to return database data in a class instance that isn't a database entity? If yes, how?
9. How are migrations applied in production and staging?

Further reading

Here, you have some links you may consider using to gather more information about this chapter:

- More details about migration commands can be found at `https://docs.microsoft.com/en-US/ef/core/miscellaneous/cli/index` and the other links contained there
- More details about Entity Framework Core compiled models can be found in the official Microsoft documentation: `https://docs.microsoft.com/en-us/ef/core/what-is-new/ef-core-6.0/whatsnew#compiled-models`

- More details about Entity Framework Core can be found in the official Microsoft documentation: `https://docs.microsoft.com/en-us/ef/core/`
- More details on LINQ queries can be found here: `https://learn.microsoft.com/en-us/dotnet/csharp/linq/`

Get this book's PDF version and more

Scan the QR code (or go to `packtpub.com/unlock`). Search for this book by name, confirm the edition, and then follow the steps on the page.

14

Implementing Microservices with .NET

In *Chapter 11, Applying a Microservice Architecture to Your Enterprise Application*, you learned the theory and basic concepts of microservices. In this chapter, you will learn how to put into practice those general concepts and tools to implement microservices in .NET. This way, you will have a practical understanding of how high-level architectural decisions translate into concrete .NET code. More specifically, you will learn the internal organization of a microservice and how to design the communication with other microservices.

The focus of this chapter is on worker microservices, that is, microservices that are not part of the public interface of your application; other kinds of microservices will be focused on in other chapters. Worker microservices process jobs that are not connected to a specific user. Each worker microservice transforms available data into the data needed for assembling the responses of several other frontend microservices. They are the assembly line of each application, so their design priorities are efficiency in both communication and local processing, together with protocols that ensure data coherence and fault tolerance. Their architecture differs significantly from that of frontend microservices, which work with a classic request/response pattern and are user-scoped. However, it is worth pointing out that frontend microservices are initial and/or final stations of the same assembly line of worker microservices, so some of their modules are implemented with the same worker microservices techniques that are described in this chapter.

The implementation of frontend services, presentation layers, and public APIs is covered in *Chapters 16, 17*, and *18*.

This chapter explains the structure of a .NET microservice and discusses the options for exchanging messages and serializing .NET data structures. In particular, we will put into practice a lot of concepts analyzed in *Chapter 11, Applying a Microservice Architecture to Your Enterprise Application*, such as the concept of Host, the techniques for ensuring reliable communication (exponential retry, etc.), forward communication, and message idempotency.

More specifically, in this chapter, you will learn about the following subjects:

- Communication and data serialization

- Implementing worker microservices with ASP.NET Core
- Implementing microservices with .NET worker services and message brokers

Together, these three areas form a complete picture of how to design a worker microservice. In fact, a worker microservice does its job by extracting messages from some message queues, filtering them to remove duplicates, putting them in the right order, and then passing them to the actual business logic that processes them.

Each point will be discussed in depth, and the reader can find further practical details in the section *A worker microservices with ASP.NET Core* section of *Chapter 22, Case Study: Practical Usage of .NET Aspire,* which describes in detail 2 complete implementations of Worker microservices.

The first section of the chapter discusses the main coordination and queuing problems that arise in microservices communication and how to solve them with either message brokers or custom permanent queues. These topics are fundamental in the design of efficient and fault-tolerant communication, which, in turn, are essential requirements for ensuring coherent behavior and low response times of the overall application.

The remaining sections explain how to implement a worker microservice with two different techniques. The techniques in the second section are based on the ASP.NET Core implementation of **gRPC**, and on an SQL Server-based permanent queue. It is worth pointing out that this technique requires *HTTP/2*. The example in the third section, instead, shows how to use message brokers. Message brokers are fundamental for three main reasons:

1. They take care of most of the communication overhead,
2. They support the publisher/subscriber pattern that promotes independence of communicating microservices,
3. All main Cloud providers offer message broker services. Our code uses **RabbitMQ**, but **RabbitMQ** can be replaced by **Azure Service Bus,** the message broker offered by Azure.

The chapter also explains the pros and cons of different serialization techniques.

Technical requirements

This chapter requires the free Visual Studio 2026 Community Edition or better with all database tools installed. The code for this chapter is available at at `https://github.com/PacktPublishing/Software-Architecture-with-.NET-10-and-C-sharp-5E`.

Experimenting with message brokers also requires the installation of the **RabbitMQ** message broker version 3.9 or higher, which in turn requires the previous installation of a 64-bit version of Erlang. An adequate Erlang version for **RabbitMQ** 4.2.1 can be downloaded from `https://www.erlang.org/patches/otp-27.3.4.6`. The **RabbitMQ** Windows installer can be downloaded from `https://github.com/rabbitmq/rabbitmq-server/releases/download/v4.2.1/rabbitmq-server-4.2.1.exe`. We recommend you launch both installations from an administrative account.

Two complete examples of a worker microservice are in the *A worker microservice with ASP.NET Core,* and *A worker microservice based on RabbitMQ* sections of *Chapter 22, Case Study: Practical Usage of .NET Aspire*. Each of them exemplifies a technique described in this chapter and shows an alternative way of collecting travel statistics in the case study application.

Communication and data serialization

In order to ensure acceptable response times, user requests to a frontend microservice can't cause communication with too many other microservices to assemble the final response.

In particular, as explained in the *Microservices design principles subsection of Chapter 11, Applying a Microservice Architecture to Your Enterprise Application*, requests to a microservices-based application can't cause long chains of recursive microservices calls. In fact, each call adds both a wait time and a communication time to the actual processing time, thus leading to unacceptable levels of overall response time, as shown in the figure below.

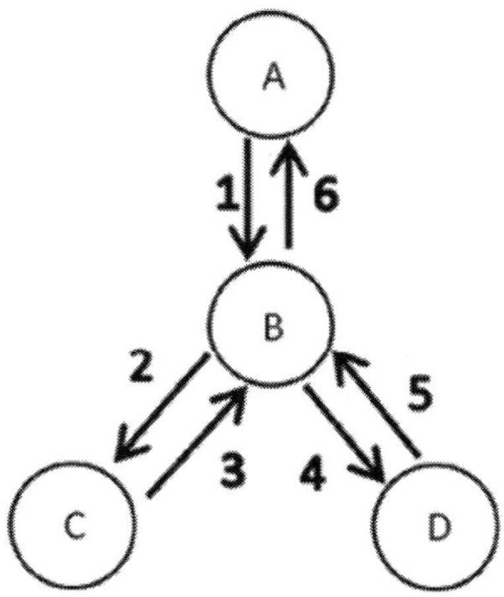

Figure 14.1: Tree of blocking RPC calls

Messages `1`-`6` are triggered by a request to the `A` microservice and are sent in sequence, so their processing times sum up to the response time. So, if, for instance, each communication takes half a second, the whole communication tree adds 3 more seconds to the response time. Moreover, once sent, message `1` from microservice `A` remains blocked until it receives the last message (`6`); that is, it waits for the whole lifetime of the overall recursive communication process. In turn, microservice `B` waits for two responses, one from `C` and the other from `D`.

> **Note**
>
> Summing up, **Remote Procedure Calls** (RPC) involve high response times and a waste of microservices computation time.

That's why microservices avoid blocking recursive RPC and prefer a data-driven approach that starts from the leaves of the above tree, that is, from the microservices that contain the data needed to assemble the response. Put simply, tree nodes, instead of waiting for requests from their parent nodes, send pre-processed data to all their possible callers each time their private data changes, as shown in the figure below.

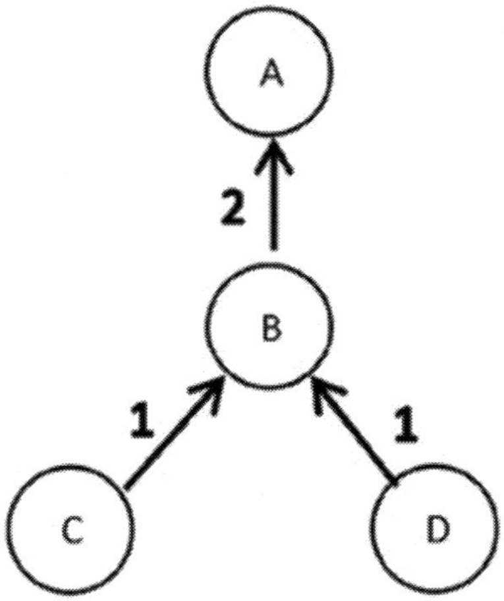

Figure 14.2: Data-driven asynchronous communication

Both communications labeled `1` are triggered when the data of the `C/D` microservices changes, and they may occur in parallel. Moreover, once a communication is sent, each microservice can return to its job without waiting for a response. Finally, when a request arrives at microservice `A`, `A` already has all the data it needs to build the response with no need to interact with other microservices.

In general, microservices based on the data-driven approach pre-process data and send it to whichever other service might be interested. This way, each microservice already contains pre-computed data it can use to respond immediately to user requests with no need for further request-specific communications.

More specifically, as new data becomes available, each microservice does its job and then sends the results to all interested microservices with asynchronous communications; that is, a microservice doesn't wait for any acknowledgment from its recipients. Asynchronous communication is a must, since each communication act usually triggers other communication acts recursively for the recipient, so we can't block the whole tree of microservices until the final acknowledgment arrives from all the tree leaves, as in the case of RPC.

However, here's the catch. The 'fire and forget' approach of asynchronous communication eliminates blocking, but it introduces new challenges: How do you know if the message was received? How do you ensure processing happened exactly once? How do you maintain consistency across services when there's no immediate confirmation? These questions of coordination, idempotency, and fault tolerance drive the design patterns explored in the rest of this section.

Here, it is just worth stating the following thumb rule:

> **Tip**
>
> Use the data-driven approach for all high-traffic worker microservices, but use RPC when there are short request-response chains together with low or medium traffic.

Therefore, actual applications mix efficient short-path RPC calls with the data-driven approach.

The choice between data-driven and RPC communication is the most important decision in the design of internal communications between the application microservices. Another important decision is whether to secure or not internal communications and how to secure them. The following rule of thumb is quite popular.

> **Tip**
>
> In the absence of strict 0-trust requirements, when all microservices are part of the same private network, it is common to secure just communication in/out of this private network and not secure all the intranet communications, both to simplify the design of the overall communication strategy and to save the performance cost of encryption.

Anyway, when security is needed, and communication relies on an underlying TCP/IP connection, we can simply use TLS/SSL (the same protocol used by HTTPS connections). However, in this case, since we are speaking of communications among servers, so there is no actual human user, it is common to use the mTLS (mutual TLS) protocol, where both communicating microservices authenticate each other with private key certificates and then agree on a cryptographic protocol and key to secure their mTLS/SSL communication. .NET furnishes all tools for negotiating an mTLS/SSL connection based on reciprocal authentication between servers.

In inter-application communications, compatibility requirements have a lower priority than performance requirements, so efficient protocols might be preferred even when they are not an official standard.

Therefore, when communications involve a large quantity of data, we may choose protocols based on binary serialization, which produce shorter messages and require less bandwidth and less processing time. In fact, for instance, representing an integer within an object with a binary serialization costs about 4 bytes, that is, basically the same number of bytes needed to store it in the computer memory (there is a small overhead for protocol-handling metadata), while representing the same integer as text requires a byte for each digit, plus the bytes needed for the field name.

Binary serialization is discussed in detail in the next subsection. Then, RPC- and data-driven asynchronous communication will also be analyzed in dedicated subsections.

Efficient and flexible binary serialization

As already hinted at in inter-application communication, the trade-off between performance and compatibility is more in favor of efficiency, at least when a big amount of data is involved. Therefore, non-standard binary protocols must also be considered among the design choices.

The process of transforming data in a way that they can be sent on a communication channel, or stored in a file, is called **Serialization**. Therefore, the adoption of binary communication protocols reduces to the choice of an adequate serialization technique.

The .NET ecosystem contains several fast, platform-specific binary serializers that are able to produce compact, short messages with very low computational costs. Unfortunately, efficient binary serializers suffer from a couple of well-known problems:

- Since the most performant binary serializers are tied to a specific platform, they are not interoperable. Thus, for instance, the Java binary format is not compatible with the .NET binary format. This constraint creates problems when your application microservices are heterogeneous and use different technologies.

- If one uses the same platform-specific, in-memory binary format, adding/removing properties to/from an object breaks compatibility. Thus, a microservice that uses an old version of a class is not able to deserialize data created with a newer version of the same class. This constraint creates dependencies between the microservices' CI/CD cycles, because when a microservice changes to meet new requirements, it causes recursive changes in all other microservices that communicate with it.

In *Chapter 15, Applying Service-Oriented Architectures with .NET*, we will see that the *JSON* format was widely adopted because it avoids these two problems since it is not tied to any specific language/runtime, and added properties can be simply ignored, while removed properties are handled by assigning default values.

The **Protocol Buffer (Protobuf)** binary format was conceived to ensure the same JSON serialization/deserialization advantages for binary formats.

Protobuf achieves interoperability by defining abstract elementary types and their binary representations. Then, each framework takes care of converting its native types to/from them. Elementary types are combined into complex structures called messages, which represent classes.

In order to ensure compatibility with newer versions of the messages, which may contain further properties, each property is assigned a unique integer name. This way, receivers compatible with older versions can identify each property they know of through its unique integer name and ignore all newly added properties. When a property number is not found in the serialized data, the default value is taken for the associated property. This way, Protobuf messages have the same serialization/deserialization advantages as JSON objects.

Summing up, we can state the following property of the Protobuf binary format:

> **Note**
>
> Compatibility among different versions is ensured if the developer doesn't change the number associated with each property. He can also remove properties, but without assigning their numbers to new properties, because these numbers have the purpose of naming (with very short names) all fields. The receiver uses these integer names to restore the messages.

There are also other serialization proposals similar to Protobuf. Some of them also ensure better performance, but at the moment, Protobuf, which was created by Google, is the de facto standard for interoperable binary communication.

Protobuf messages are defined in `.proto` files and are then compiled into code in the target language by language-specific tools. The section that follows describes the Protobuf data description language.

Each .proto file starts with a declaration of the version of Protobuf. At the moment, the highest available version is proto3:

```
syntax = "proto3";
```

Since .NET SDK will generate classes out of Protobuf definitions, if the target language is .NET, you can specify the namespace where you generate all the .NET classes corresponding to the Protobuf types defined in the file:

```
option csharp_namespace = "MyCSharpNamespace";
```

Then, you can import definitions contained in other `.proto` files, with one or more import declarations:

```
import "google/protobuf/timestamp.proto";
```

The above definition imports the definition of the `TimeStamp` type, which encodes both the `DateTime` and `DateTimeOffset` .NET types. `TimeStamp` is not a Protobuf simple type but is defined in a standard Protobuf types library.

Finally, we can scope all message definitions to a package to avoid name collisions. Protobuf packages have the same role as a .NET namespace, but are not automatically converted into .NET namespaces during .NET code generation, since .NET namespaces are specified with the option C# declaration:

```
package purchase;
```

Each `.proto` file can contain several message definitions. Below is an example message:

```
message PurchaseMessage {
  string id = 1;
  google.protobuf.Timestamp time = 2;
  string location = 3;
  int32 cost =4;
  google.protobuf.Timestamp purchaseTime = 5;
}
```

Each property is specified by the property type, followed by the property name, and then by the unique integer associated with that property. Property names must be in camel case, but they are converted to Pascal case during .NET code generation.

If a new version of `PurchaseMessage` is created, compatibility with the past version can be maintained by not reusing the integers assigned to the properties of the old version and by removing just unused properties, as in the example shown below:

```
message PurchaseMessage {
  string id = 1;
  int32 cost =4;
  google.protobuf.Timestamp purchaseTime = 5;
  Reseller reseller = 7;
}
```

The new version of `PurchaseMessage` doesn't contain properties 2 and 3, but it contains the new `reseller` property, marked with the new 7 integer. The `Reseller` type is defined by another message that can be contained either in the same `.proto` file or in an imported file.

Clearly, compatibility is maintained only with clients that don't use the removed properties, while clients directly affected by the changes must be updated.

Collections are represented by prefixing the name of the collection element type with the repeated keyword:

```
message PurchaseMessage {
  ...
  repeated Product products = 3;
  ...
}
```

Repeated data is translated into the `Google.Protobuf.Collections.RepeatedField<T>` .NET type, which implements `IList<T>`.

Dictionaries are represented with the `map<T1, T2>` type:

```
message PurchaseMessage {
  ...
  map<string, int> attributes = 3;
  ...
}
```

Messages can be nested into other messages, in which case they generate classes defined in other .NET classes during code generation:

```
message PurchaseMessage {
  message Product {
    int32 id = 1;
    string name = 2;
    uint32 cost = 3;
    uint32 quantity = 4;
  }
  ...
  repeated Product products = 3;
  ...
}
```

We can also define enum types that translate directly to .NET enum types:

```
enum ColorType {
    RED = 0;
    GREEN = 1;
    ...
  }
```

It is also possible to define messages with conditional content. This is useful for sending either a response or error information:

```
message Payload {
    ...
}
message Error {
    ...
}
message ResponseMessage {
  one of result {
    Error error = 1;
    Person payload = 2;
  }
}
```

Once a microservice receives a .NET object of the ResponseMessage type, it can process it as follows:

```
ResponseMessage  response = ...;
switch (response.ResultCase)
{
    case ResponseMessage.ResultOneofCase.Payload:
        HandlePayload(response.Payload);
        break;
    case ResponseMessage.ResultOneofCase.Error:
        HandleError(response.Error);
        break;
    default:
        throw new ArgumentException();
}
```

Compatibility between the .NET types used in your code and your Protobuf definitions can be ensured with the help of the table below that summarizes the correspondence between all the `ProtoBuf` simple types and .NET types:

.NET types	Protobuf types
double	double
float	float
string	string
bool	bool
ByteString	bytes
int	int32, sint32, sfixed32
uint	uint32, fixed32
long	Int64, sint64, sfixed64
ulong	uint64, fixed64

Table 14.1: .NET – Protobuf type conversion

The `ByteString` .NET type is defined in the `Google.Protobuf` namespace contained in the `Google.Protobuf` NuGet package. It can be converted to `byte[]` with its `.ToByteArray()` method. A `byte[]` object can be converted into a `ByteString` with the `ByteString.CopyFrom(byte[] data)` static method.

`int32`, `sint32`, and `sfixed32` encode .NET `int`. Now, `sint32` is convenient when the integer is more likely to be negative, while the `sfixed32` type is convenient when the integer is likely to contain more than 28 bits. The same considerations apply to `uint32` and `fixed32`.

The same criteria apply to 64-bit integers, but in this case, the threshold for the convenience of `sfixed64` and `fixed64` is 56 bits.

Protobuf simple types are not nullable. This means that they can't have a `null` value, and if no value is assigned to them, they take a default value. The default value of a string is an empty string, while the default value of a `ByteString` is an empty `ByteString`.

If you need nullable types, you must include a predefined `.proto` file:

```
import "google/protobuf/wrappers.proto"
```

Below is a table that details the correspondence between .NET nullable simple types and Protobuf nullable wrappers:

.NET types	Protobuf types
double?	google.protobuf.DoubleValue
float?	google.protobuf.FloatValue
string?	google.protobuf.StringValue
bool?	google.protobuf.BoolValue
ByteString?	google.protobuf.BytesValue
int?	google.protobuf.Int32Value
uint?	google.protobuf.UInt32Value
long?	google.protobuf.Int64Value
ulong?	google.protobuf.UInt64Value

Table 14.2: Nullable types .NET – Protobuf conversion

`DateTime`, `DateTimeOffset`, and `TimeSpan` have no direct equivalent in Protobuf, but the `Google.Protobuf.WellKnownTypes` namespace contained in the `Google.Protobuf` NuGet package contains the `Timestamp` type, which maps from/to `DateTime` and `DateTimeOffset`, and the `Duration` type, which maps from/to `TimeSpan`. The mapping is completely analogous to that of `ByteString`. Thus, for instance, a `Duration` is obtained from a `TimeSpan` with the `Duration.FromTimeSpan` static method, while a `Duration` is transformed into a `TimeSpan` by calling its `.ToTimeSpan` instance method.

The usage of `Duration` and `Timestamp` in `.proto` files is shown below:

```
syntax = "proto3"
import "google/protobuf/duration.proto";
import "google/protobuf/timestamp.proto";
message PurchaseMessage {
  string id = 1;
  google.protobuf.Timestamp time = 2;
  string location = 3;
  int32 cost =4;
  google.protobuf.Timestamp purchaseTime = 5;
  google.protobuf.Duration travelDuration = 6;
}
```

Please note that usage requires the import of predefined `.proto` files.

At the moment, there is no equivalent to the .NET decimal type. However, you can encode decimals with two integers, one for the integer part and the other for the decimal part, with a message like the one below:

```
message ProtoDecimal {
    // Whole units part of the decimal
    int64 units = 1;
    // Nano units of the decimal (10^-9)
    // Must be same sign as units
    sfixed32 nanos = 2;
}
```

We can add implicit conversion to the .NET decimal with a partial class that combines with another partial class, which is automatically generated from the `.proto` file:

```
public partial class DecimalValue
{
    private const decimal nanoFactor = 1000000000m;

    public static implicit operator decimal(ProtoDecimal pDecimal)
    {
        return pDecimal.Units + pDecimal.Nanos / nanoFactor;
    }
    public static implicit operator ProtoDecimal (decimal value)
    {
        return new ProtoDecimal
          {
              Units = decimal.ToInt32(value),
              Nanos= decimal.ToInt32((value - Units) * nanoFactor),
          };
    }
}
```

We have described almost completely the Protobuf data description language. The only missing subject is the representation of variable/unknown types, which are rarely used. However, the *Further Reading* section contains a link to the official documentation. Now, let's briefly see how this translates into practice by furnishing code snippets for performing both serialization and deserialization.

Protobuf serialization

An object tree can be serialized as shown below:

```
using Google.Protobuf;
...
PurchaseMessage purchase = ....
byte[]? body = null;
```

```
using (var stream = new MemoryStream())
{
    purchase.WriteTo(stream);
    stream.Flush();
    body = stream.ToArray();
}
```

The `WriteTo` method needs a stream, so create an in-memory stream. After, we create a byte array from the stream with `ToArray`. `stream.Flush()` ensures that the stream buffer is actually written into the stream before attempting the extraction of the byte array.

Deserialization, instead, is performed as follows:

```
Byte[] body = ...
PurchaseMessage? message = null;
using (var stream = new MemoryStream(body))
{
    message = PurchaseMessage.Parser.ParseFrom(stream);
}
```

Here, since ParseFrom also needs a `stream`, we generate a stream from the message bytes.

The next subsection describes the usage of RPC in microservices.

Efficient and flexible RPC

The RPC approach can be adopted in some intra-application communication with good results, only if some conditions are met to avoid time-consuming chained calls:

- Use RPC when the chain of recursive calls is very short, usually just one call without recursive calls. Avoid it when there are long nested calls.
- Avoid RPC whenever the request processing time is not very low.
- Avoid RPC when either the communication latency is high or the channel bandwidth is low. Luckily, intranet communications usually take place on high-speed Ethernet within the same data center.
- Avoid RPC if data is not serialized quickly and in a very size-efficient format. Luckily, an efficient binary serializer overcomes these problems.

The above constraints are satisfied if we use efficient communication channels with efficient serialization, and if RPC is used just to queue a request without waiting for the result of the processing; the response contains just the confirmation that the request has been correctly queued. This way, RPC is used to simulate an asynchronous communication with reception confirmation.

On the contrary, when the communicating microservices are geographically distributed and are part of a WAN instead of a LAN, waiting for confirmation of reception of an RPC message might be unacceptable for high-traffic microservices. In these cases, it is better to rely on message brokers that support completely asynchronous communications.

The **gRPC** protocol brings all the advantages of Protobuf to RPC since, by default, it is based on Protobuf. gRPC/Protobuf is a binary protocol that works over an HTTP/2 connection. It is worth pointing out that gRPC can't work with HTTP versions less than 2. In the remainder of the chapter, we will always assume that gRPC uses Protobuf.

gRPC uses `.proto` files, but together with data, gRPC `.proto` files also define services with their RPC methods. Below is a service definition:

```
service Counter {
  // Accepts a counting request
  rpc Count (CountingRequest) returns (CountingReply);
 //Get current count for a given time slot
  rpc GetCount (TimeSlotRequest) returns (TimeSlotDataReply);
}
```

Each service is introduced by the `service` keyword, while each method is introduced by the `rpc` keyword. Each service specifies an input message and an output message. If either of these two messages is empty, we can use the predefined `google.protobuf.Empty` message, as shown below:

```
...
import "google/protobuf/empty.proto";
...
service Counter {
  ...
  rpc AllSlots(google.protobuf.Empty) return (AllDataReply);
}
```

`.proto` files can be used to generate both server code and client code. In client code, each service is translated into a proxy class with the same methods declared in the service. Each of the proxy methods automatically invokes the remote service method and returns its result.

The server code, instead, translates each service into an abstract class, whose virtual methods correspond to methods declared in the service. The developer is responsible for inheriting from this abstract class and providing implementations for all service methods.

Below is an example of how to inherit from a similar class:

```
public class CounterService: Counter.CounterBase
{
    ...
    public override async  Task<CountingReply> Count(
          CountingRequest request, ServerCallContext context)
    {
        CountingReply reply =...
          return reply;
```

```
    }
}
```

Each method receives both the input message and a context object. Since gRPC services use ASP.NET Core infrastructure, the context object furnishes access to the request `HttpContext` through `context.GetHttpContext()`.

An ASP.NET Core application is enabled to gRPC with `builder.Services.AddGrpc()` and by declaring each service with something like `app.MapGrpcService<CounterService>()`.

More details on both gRPC servers and clients will be given while discussing the example in the *A worker microservices with ASP.NET Core* section of *Chapter 22, Case Study: Practical Usage of .NET Aspire*.

Services can receive as input and return continuous streams of data, where a long-term connection between client and server is established. However, the usage of streams in microservices is not common since microservices are ephemeral processes that are frequently shut down and moved from one processing node to another by orchestrators, so long-term connections are not easy to maintain.

Below is a service that accepts and returns a stream:

```
service StreamExample {
  rpc Echo (stream MyMessage) returns (stream MyMessage);
}
```

Each input stream is passed as an argument to the .NET implementation of the method. If the method returns a stream, the .NET implementation of the method must return a Task, and the output stream is also passed as an argument to the method:

```
public override async Task Echo(
      IAsyncStreamReader<MyMessage> requestStream
       IServerStreamWriter<MyMessage> responseStream,
       ServerCallContext context){
      ...
           While(...)
           {
               bool inputFinished =  !await requestStream.MoveNext();
               var current = requestStream.Current;
               ...
               await responseStream.WriteAsync(result);
           }
}
```

On the client side, both input and output streams are available in the call object that is returned when the proxy method is called without awaiting it, as shown below:

```
var call = client.Echo();
...
await call.RequestStream.WriteAsync(...);
...
bool inputFinished =  ! await call.ResponseStream.MoveNext();
var current = call.ResponseS.Current;
...
Await call.RequestStream.CompleteAsync();
```

The `CompleteAsync()` method closes the request stream, declaring that the input is finished.

More practical details on the client usage are given in the example in the *A worker microservices with ASP.NET core* section of *Chapter 22, Case Study: Practical Usage of .NET Aspire*, while the *Further reading* section contains a link to the .NET gRPC official documentation.

The next subsection describes how to implement data-driven asynchronous communication.

Reliable data-driven asynchronous communication

Non-blocking communication must necessarily rely on non-volatile queues to decouple the sender thread from the receiving thread, since each message must wait for an available thread that processes it. There are two main options:

1. A unique queue handled by a third actor called the **Message Broker** that handles the message till the receiver successfully receives and processes it, possibly resending it if no receipt confirmation is received
2. A queue in the sender and a queue in the receiver. The queue in the sender is needed for resending messages that do not receive confirmation of receipt, while the queue in the receiver is needed for waiting for an available thread that processes them.

In essence the message broker of the first approach, being in the middle between sender and receiver, is able to play the role of both the sender and receiver queues of the second approach with just one queue.

Azure Service Bus, which we described in the *.NET communication facilities subsection of Chapter 11, Applying a Microservice Architecture to Your Enterprise Application*, is a message broker that, like most message brokers, offers queuing services and publisher/subscriber communication. In this chapter, we will also describe **RabbitMQ**, which offers queuing services and publisher/subscriber communication that is broadly similar to Azure Service Bus topics. Since it is easier to debug code that uses a local instance of RabbitMQ, often it is convenient to use RabbitMQ during development and then move to Azure Service Bus.

Queues decouple the sender and receiver but do not ensure that messages are not lost. In the *Resilient task execution* section of *Chapter 11, Applying a Microservice Architecture to Your Enterprise Application,* we already discussed strategies for achieving reliable communication. Below, we give more practical details for preventing message losses with confirmations and timeouts:

- Queues must be stored on permanent storage; otherwise, their content can be lost if the processes controlling them either crash or are shut down.
- If a confirmation that the message was successfully inserted in the queue doesn't arrive within a timeout period, the source assumes that the message was lost and retries the operation.
- When a message is extracted from a queue, it remains blocked and inaccessible to other consumers. If a confirmation that the message has been successfully processed arrives within a timeout period, the message is removed from the queue; otherwise, it is unblocked and becomes available again to other consumers.

All confirmations can be handled asynchronously with the exception of the insertion in the first queue of a communication path. In fact, if the sending code doesn't remain blocked waiting for the confirmation but moves to further processing and the message is lost, there is no way to resend the message, since the message cannot be taken from any other queue.

For this reason, sometimes microservices that use a message broker also have an internal queue. More specifically, the main microservice thread produces all messages and stores them in a local queue that can be implemented with a database table. Another thread takes care of extracting messages from this queue and sending them to the message broker. Messages that are removed from the local queue are blocked and removed only when an asynchronous confirmation arrives from the message broker. This technique is used in the example of *Chapter 17, Implementing Frontend Microservices with ASP.NET Core*. The main advantage of the local queue is that confirmation from a local queue usually arrives faster because of there being less concurrency with other threads/processes (don't forget that each microservice should have its private database/permanent storage), so the blocking time is more acceptable.

Using a queue inside each receiver is a viable alternative to message brokers. The main advantage of private queues is that the process that handles the queue is not shared among several microservices, so all queue operations are faster. In particular, the confirmation of each insertion is immediate, so the sender can use a blocking RPC call to send the message. However, this simple solution has the following disadvantages:

- There is no way to implement the publisher/subscriber pattern.
- Just one microservice instance can extract messages from the queue. Therefore, microservices can't be scaled horizontally. Limited vertical scaling can be achieved by increasing the number of processor cores and by processing queue messages with parallel threads.

A similar approach can be efficiently implemented with gRPC and ASP.NET Core as follows:

1. The sender sends the message to a gRPC method
2. The gRPC method just enqueues the message and immediately returns a confirmation to the sender
3. An ASP.NET Core-hosted process takes care of extracting the messages from the queue and passing them to several parallel threads
4. When a message is passed to a thread, it remains blocked and inaccessible. It is removed only after the thread confirms that the message has been successfully processed. If, instead, a thread reports a failure, the corresponding message is unblocked so it can be passed to another thread.

ASP.NET Core threads take care of the necessary input parallelism. Some horizontal parallelism can be achieved by using load balancers and several web servers. However, in this case, either all the web servers use the same database, thus increasing the concurrency on the queue, or we use several sharded databases.

This approach is described in more detail in the example in the *Implementing worker microservices with ASP.NET Core* section. As we will see, it is simple to implement and ensures good response time, but due to its limited scalability, it is adequate just for small or medium-sized applications with low to medium traffic.

If, for some reason, either an insertion in a queue or the processing of a message extracted by a queue requires more time than the timeout time, the operation is repeated so that the same message is processed twice. Therefore, messages must be idempotent, meaning processing them once or several times must have the same effect. Record updates and deletes are intrinsically idempotent since repeating an update or a delete several times doesn't change the result, but record additions are not.

Idempotency can always be forced by assigning a unique identifier to messages and then storing the identifiers of the already processed messages. This way, each incoming message can be discarded when its identifier is found among the identifiers of the already processed messages. We will use this technique in all examples in this chapter.

Queues, confirmations, and message resends ensure that requests to a single microservice are safely processed, but how can we handle requests that involve several cooperating microservices? We will discover that in the next subsection. There, we will explain how distributed microservices can coordinate and reach agreements to yield a coherent behavior with only the help of asynchronous communication.

Distributed transactions

Everyone knows what a database transaction is: several records are modified one after the other, but if a single action fails, all previous modifications are also undone before aborting the transaction. That is, either all operations succeed or they fail simultaneously.

A distributed transaction does the same job, but in this case the records are not part of a single database, but are distributed among the databases associated with several cooperating microservices.

The reliable data-driven communication techniques described so far are the building blocks for solving more complex cooperation problems.

Let's suppose that a user operation triggers processing and storage in several related microservices. The user operation can be considered successfully completed only if all involved processing/storage operations succeed.

Moreover, if a single processing/storage operation also fails for some fundamental reason, retrying the failed operation doesn't help. Think, for instance, of a purchase that fails because the user has not got enough funds to complete the payment: the only way out is to undo all the operations that have already been performed.

In general, similar situations must be handled in a transactional way; either all operations are performed, or no operation is performed. Transactions that span several microservices are known as distributed transactions. In theory, distributed transactions can be handled with the following two-stages protocol:

1. In the first stage, all operations are executed, each one in the scope of a local transaction (for instance, within the scope of each microservice database transaction). The success or failure of each operation is then returned to a transaction coordinator.
2. In the second stage, the transaction coordinator informs all microservices of the success or failure of the overall operation. In the case of failure, all local transactions are rolled back; otherwise, they are committed.

When using asynchronous messages, confirmations may arrive after quite a large amount of time and may interleave with other transactions performed on the same resources. Therefore, having all local resources blocked by a local transaction during a possibly time-consuming distributed transaction is not acceptable.

For this reason, microservices transactions use the **saga pattern**: all local operations are performed without opening a local transaction, and in the case of failure, they are compensated by other operations that undo the initial operations.

Undoing a database insertion is quite easy, since it is enough to remove the added item, but undoing modifications and deletes is quite difficult and requires the storage of additional information. The general solution to this problem is storing records that represent all database changes in a table. These records can be used to compute a compensation operation or to restore the previous database state starting from a reference database state. We already discussed this storage technique, which is called **event sourcing**, in the *Event Sourcing section of Chapter 7, Understanding the Different Domains in Software Solutions.* Just to recap, and in a few words, each database stores not only the actual state, but also the history of all changes up to a certain previous time.

When a saga transaction is undone, if other saga transactions depend on the undone changes, we must also undo them. For instance, suppose that an accepted purchase order depends on the funds uploaded by a user on an e-commerce platform. Then, if the funds upload transaction is undone, the purchase must also be undone.

In order to avoid similar chain reactions when a saga transaction is undone, often new transactions are accepted only if they depend on changes that took place before a certain safety interval. Thus, for instance, uploaded funds are made available only after, say, 5-10 minutes, because it is very unlikely that a transaction will be undone after more than 5-10 minutes.

Figure 14.3 shows a failed SAGA with a compensation action.

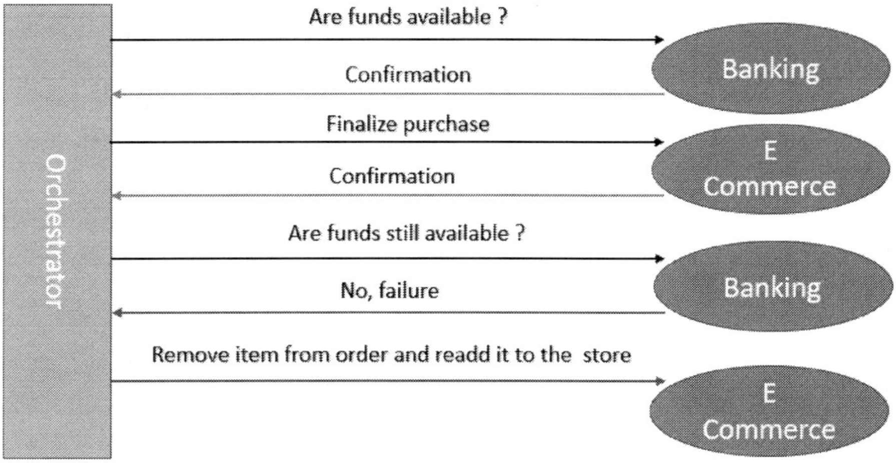

Figure 14.3: Failed E-Commerce SAGA with compensation action

The E-Commerce SAGA fails because of a lack of funds. However, it is worth noticing that availability of funds was verified at the start of SAGA, so failure was caused by an interference that took place during the short time of the SAGA execution. All well-designed SAGAs should include similar verifications, so that they might fail only for interferences that take place during the short time of the SAGA execution. This ensures that failures are rare events.

Saga transactions may use two fundamental techniques:

- **Orchestration**: When the transaction starts, an orchestrator component is created that takes care of sending the necessary messages to all involved microservices and receiving their success/failure messages. This technique is easy to implement but creates dependencies between the software lifetimes of the involved microservices since the orchestrator must depend on the details of all microservices involved in the saga. Moreover, this technique may have poor performance since the orchestrator becomes a bottleneck.
- **Choreography**: There is no centralized control of the transaction but each microservice is invoked by a different sending microservice and forward the success/failure messages it receives to other communication neighbors. Choreography overcomes the disadvantages of orchestration but it is more difficult to implement and test.

The table below summarizes the pros and cons of the two techniques:

	Code maintainability	***Difficulties in designing and debugging***
Choreography	Good	Quite high
Orchestration	Low	No particular difficulty

Table 14.3: Comparison between Choreography and Orchestration

Therefore, the choice between the two techniques should be based on a trade-off between maintainability needs and the difficulties implied by a Choreography-based algorithm.

The next section explains how to organize in practice the processing of a worker microservice that does not use a message broker.

Implementing worker microservices with ASP.NET Core

In this section, we explain how to code a worker microservice that receives its input through ASP.NET Core gRPC.

As previously discussed, if we don't use a message broker, but opt in for synchronous communication, we must implement an internal queue where to store all received messages. This way, when a message is received, it is immediately enqueued without processing it, so that a "*received*" confirmation response can be immediately returned.

In order to clarify how to implement in practice a solution based on gRPC, we describe in detail a possible .NET code implementation.

First of all, the application level needs a repository interface that handles the input queue. Below is a possible definition of this interface:

```
public interface IMessageQueue
{
    Task<IList<QueueItem>> Top(int n);
    Task Dequeue(IEnumerable<QueueItem> items);
    Task Enqueue(QueueItem item);
}
```

Where:

- `QueueItem` is a class that contains all request information
- `Enqueue` adds a new message to the queue
- `Top` returns the first `n` queue items without removing them from the queue
- `Dequeue` removes some messages from the queue

The actual implementation of the above interface can be based on a database table, or an any other storage media. Since databases already have all tools for handling efficaciously concurrency and transactions they are the preferred choice.

The application level can be implemented with an ASP.NET Core gRPC project that organizes all gRPC stuff for you:

Figure 14.4: Creating a gRPC Server project

The project template contains a `proto` folder where all `.proto` files should be placed. Definitions placed here automatically generate C# classes. More specifically, messages generate flat classes with no methods, while services generate abstract classes and service methods generate abstract methods. Actual implementations of service methods are provided by inheriting from the service classes generated by the .NET SDK and overriding all their abstract methods. gRPC functionalities are provided by the `Grpc.AspNetCore` NuGet package that is automatically added to the project and by its dependencies.

There is no specific project template for gRPC service clients, so client gRPC functionalities are provided by manually adding these NuGet packages: `Google.Protobuf`, `Grpc.NET.Client`, and `Grpc.Tools`.

The project template contains a `Services` folder where to place all service implementations. The template also contains a `GreeterService` service example to show how the whole service definition process works in practice.

The actual request processing is performed by a worker-hosted service that runs in parallel with the ASP.NET Core pipeline. It is implemented with the hosted services we discussed in the *Using generic hosts section of Chapter 11, Applying a Microservice Architecture to Your Enterprise Application*. It is worth recalling that hosted services are implementations of the `IHostedService` interface defined in the dependency injection engine as follows:

```
builder.Services.AddHostedService<MyHostedService>();
```

Being defined in the dependency injection engine, they are automatically injected services in their constructors. Hosted services are used to execute parallel threads that run independently of the remainder of the application. Usually, they are not defined by directly implementing the `IHostedService` interface, but by inheriting from the abstract `BackgroundService` class and overriding its Task `ExecuteAsync(CancellationToken token)` abstract method.

The `ExecuteAsync` method usually contains an endless loop that exits only when the application is shut down. This endless loop defines the behavior of a worker-hosted service that repeats a certain task. In our case, the task to repeat is the continuous extraction and processing of `N` items from the queue.

Below is a possible organization of our hosted service:

```
public class ProcessPurchases(IServiceProvider services)
 BackgroundService
{
```

```
    protected override async Task ExecuteAsync(
  CancellationToken stoppingToken)
    {
        bool queueEmpty = false;
        while (!stoppingToken.IsCancellationRequested)
        {
            while (!queueEmpty &&
        !stoppingToken.IsCancellationRequested)
            {
                ...
            }
             await Task.Delay(100, stoppingToken);
             queueEmpty = false;
        }
    }
}
```

The class constructor is not injected with the specific services it needs, but instead has the `IServiceProvider` that can be used to get any service defined in the dependency injection engine. The reason for this choice is that it will launch several threads (one for each of the N messages extracted from the queue), and, in general, different threads can't share the same service instance.

The problem is caused by services with a session scope. Usually, these services are not designed to be thread-safe since the single session-scoped instance used throughout a whole ASP.NET Core request is never shared among parallel threads. However, we are not going to use our services from within the usual ASP.NET Core pipeline but from within parallel threads launched by our hosted service. Therefore, we need a different session scope for each parallel thread. Thus, the right way to process is to use `IServiceProvider` to create each necessary scope and then use each scope to get a different instance for each parallel thread, as shown in the figure below:

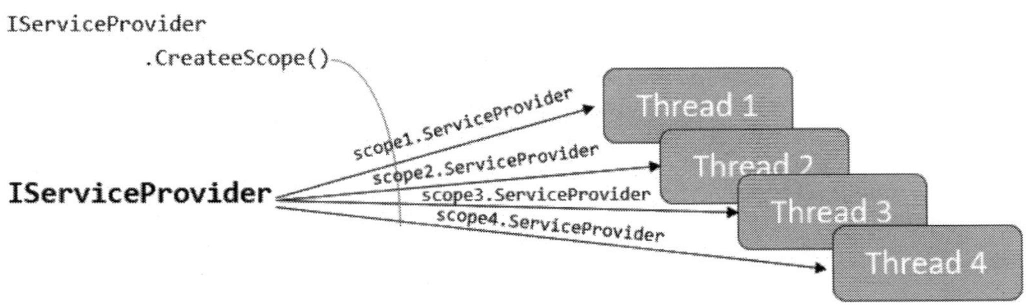

Figure 14.5: Each thread needs a different session-scoped service provider

This way, session-scoped service instances will never be shared between threads, because each thread has a different session scope. Be patient, the full code that handles all threads will be shown shortly!

The inner `while` loop runs until the queue is empty, then the worker thread sleeps for 100 milliseconds and then tries the inner loop again to see if, in the meantime, some new message reached the queue.

When the application is shut down, the `stoppingToken CancellationToken` is signaled and both loops exit, so that the whole `ExecuteAsync` method exits and the worker thread dies.

Below is the content of the inner `while`:

```
using var scope = services.CreateScope();

IMessageQueue queue =
 scope.ServiceProvider.GetRequiredService<IMessageQueue>();

var toProcess = await queue.Top(10);
if (toProcess.Count > 0)
{
    Task<QueueItem?>[] tasks = new
       Task<QueueItem?>[toProcess.Count];
    for (int i = 0; i < tasks.Length; i++)
    {
        tasks[i] = toExecute();
    }
    await Task.WhenAll(tasks);
    await queue.Dequeue(tasks.Select(m => m.Result)
       .Where(m => m != null).OfType<QueueItem>());
}
else queueEmpty = true;
```

As already hinted, we create a new session scope. This session scope surrounds the whole code since we need a unique instance of `IMessageQueue` to manipulate the queue.

The code tries to extract `N` messages from the queue. If no message is found, `queueEmpty` is set to `true` so that the inner loop exits; otherwise, a for loop creates a separate task for each extracted request and inserts it in the `tasks` array.

Then, `Task.WhenAll` awaits all tasks. Finally, `queue.Dequeue` removes from the queue all not-null requests returned from the tasks. Since a not-null request is returned only in the case of successful processing, `queue.Dequeue` removes just the successfully processed requests.

The `toExecute` method performs the actual request processing that depends on the specific application.

Readers looking for more practical details are encouraged to jump to the *A worker microservice with ASP.NET core* section of *Chapter 22, Case Study: Practical Usage of .NET Aspire*. The complete source code of the example is contained in the folder associated with this chapter of the GitHub book.

After having explored an implementation based on synchronous communication and internal queues, we complete the exposition of the possible design choices by describing also how to implement a microservice that receives its input from a message broker. More specifically, the next section shows you how to modify the code of this section to use communication based on the RabbitMQ message broker.

Implementing microservices with .NET worker services and message brokers

This section explains the modifications needed to use a message broker instead of gRPC communication with an internal queue. This kind of solution is usually more difficult to test and design, but allows for better horizontal scaling.

The message broker used in code is **RabbitMQ**. However, we could also replace it with **Azure Service Bus** using the code available in the GitHub repository associated with the book. The next subsection explains how to install RabbitMQ on your development machine. We used RabbitMQ to give the reader the opportunity to install and study it, since Azure Service Bus needs less configuration and is immediately ready to use. In an actual production system, one might choose RabbitMQ just for not being tied to a specific Cloud provider, because while Azure Service Bus is available just on Azure, RabbitMQ can be installed in any Cloud or on-premises environment.

Installing RabbitMQ

This subsection explains how to install RabbitMQ, You need to read it just if you would like to install it on your machine to test our code examples, and/or the book use-case. Therefore, you can jump it in a first read of the chapter.

Before installing RabbitMQ, you need to install **Erlang** from the link given in the *Technical requirements* section. Just download and execute the installer from an administrative account. After that, you can download and install RabbitMQ from the link in the *Technical requirements* section.

If installation is successful, you should find a service called RabbitMQ among your machine's Windows services. If you don't find it or it is not running, restart your computer.

Administrative commands can be issued to RabbitMQ from the command prompt, which you can find in the RabbitMQ Server Windows menu folder.

You can also enable a web-based administrative UI. Let's open the RabbitMQ command prompt and issue the following command:

```
rabbitmq-plugins enable rabbitmq_management
```

Then, browse to `http://localhost:15672`. If you are not able to reach the web application, please restart your computer. Once in the application, you will be prompted for a username and password. Initially, they are both set to `guest`. From there, you may inspect all active connections and channels and all communication queues that have been created. The queues page contains all queues that have been defined. By clicking on each of them, you move to a queue-specific page where you can inspect the queue content and perform various operations on the specific queue.

The next subsection contains a short survey of RabbitMQ features.

RabbitMQ basics

Natively, RabbitMQ supports the **AMQP** asynchronous message protocol, which is one of the most used asynchronous protocols, the other being **MQTT**, which has a specific syntax for the publisher/subscriber pattern. Support for MQTT can be added with a plugin, but RabbitMQ has facilities for easily implementing a publisher/subscriber pattern on top of AMQP. Moreover, RabbitMQ offers several tools to support scalability, disaster recovery, and redundancy, so it fulfills all requirements to be a first-class actor in Cloud and microservices environments. More specifically, it supports data replication like most SQL and NoSQL databases, and also supports cooperation among several servers based on sophisticated and flexible techniques. For lack of space, in this section we will describe just RabbitMQ basic operation, but the reader can find more details in the tutorials and documentation of RabbitMQ official Website `https://www.rabbitmq.com/`.

RabbitMQ messages must be prepared in binary format, since RabbitMQ messages must be just an array of bytes. Therefore, we need to serialize .NET objects with a binary formatter before sending them. In all examples in this book, we will use the Protobuf serializer. It might also be possible to use a JSON serializer to ensure better compatibility if there are compatibility issues among microservices implemented with different frameworks by different teams, and/or if there are legacy microservices. It is worth recalling that JSON is usually more compatible but less efficient, while binary formats are less compatible. Protobuf tries to solve the binary compatibility issue by defining a universal binary language, but it is not an official standard but a de facto standard.

As *Figure 14.6* shows, messages are not sent directly to queues, but to other entities called `exchanges` that route them to queues. Exchanges are AMQP-specific concepts, and are RabbitMQ's way to configure complex communication protocols like the publishing/subscriber protocol.

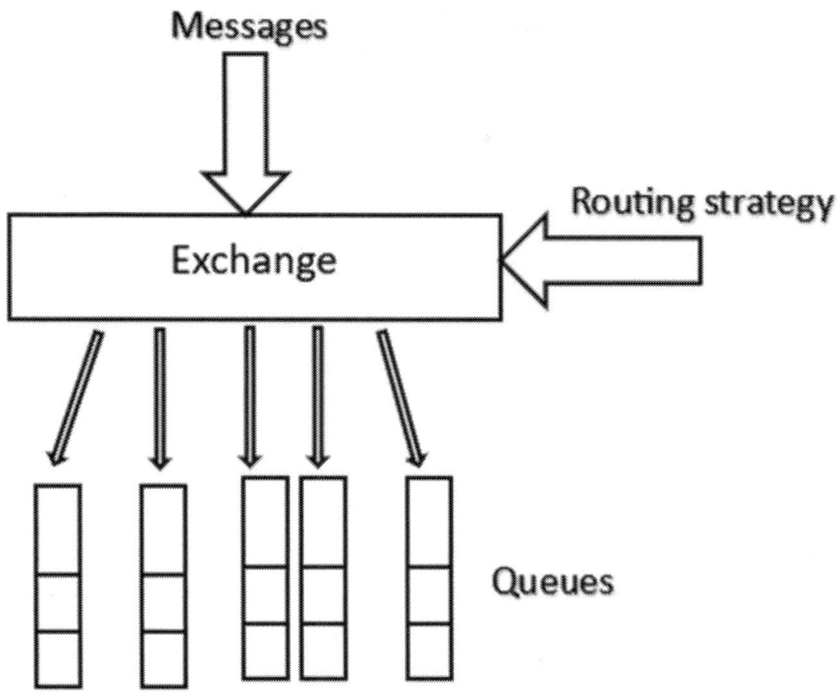

Figure 14.6: RabbitMQ Exchanges

Adequately defining the exchange routing strategy, we can implement several patterns. More specifically:

- When we use a `default` exchange, the message is sent to a single queue and we can implement asynchronous direct calls.
- When we use a `fanout` exchange, the exchange will send the messages to all queues that subscribe to that exchange. This way, we can implement the publisher/subscriber pattern. There is also a topic exchange that enhances the publisher/subscriber pattern by enabling the matching of several events with wildcard characters. However, it is not usually needed in microservices for enterprise applications.

It is worth remembering that the usage of the publisher/subscriber pattern enhances microservices decoupling.

Our examples will describe just direct calls, but the *Further reading* section contains a link to RabbitMQ tutorials that show examples of publisher/subscriber implementations.

The next section explains how to modify the code in the previous section to use RabbitMQ-based direct communication.

Replacing internal queues with RabbitMQ

As previously discussed, in high traffic WAN networks, also receiving a synchronous received-message acknowledgment has an unacceptable performance impact, so no RPC protocol can be used. Moreover, often microservices use the publisher/subscriber pattern to achieve best decoupling. In these cases, using a message broker is a MUST. Finally, having all queues handled by a unique scalable broker enables independent and easy scaling of the communication resources. This capability is fundamental for optimizing the performance of applications made of hundreds or thousands of microservices.

Summing up, there are cases where message brokers are a MUST or are at least the best choice. Therefore, in this section, we will show how to use them by transforming the previous project so that it uses RabbitMQ instead of gRPC and internal queues.

Unluckily, this transformation requires a complete restructuring of the microservice project. We can save the business and data layer, but we need to move from an ASP.NET Core project to a different project template called **Worker Service**.

Therefore, let's replace the ASP.NET Core project with a Worker Service project. It is enough to select **Service** in the Visual Studio project type dropdown to find it as shown below:

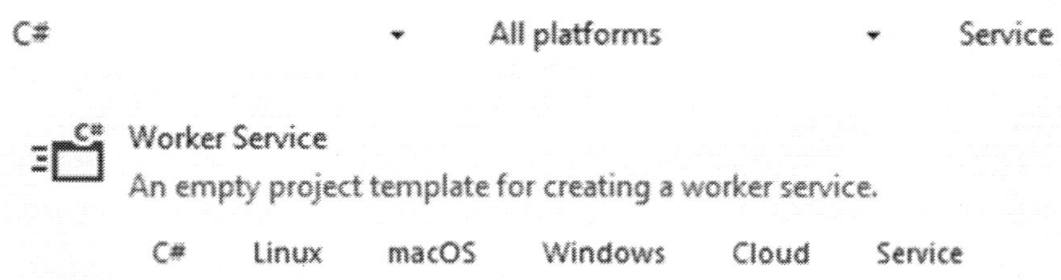

Figure 14.7: Worker Service project template

We don't need the gRPC services anymore, but we need Protobuf because RabbitMQ works with binary messages. All Protobuf functionalities are provided by the `Google.Protobuf` and `Grpc.NET.Client` NuGet packages, which must be added manually.

The Worker Service project automatically scaffolds a hosted service (Hosted Service was discussed in detail in the *Using generic hosts section of Chapter 11, Applying a Microservice Architecture to Your Enterprise Application*). However, the `ExecuteAsync` method of this hosted service must be a little bit different:

```
protected override async Task ExecuteAsync(CancellationToken stoppingToken)
{
    while (!stoppingToken.IsCancellationRequested)
    {
        try
        {
            var factory =
        new ConnectionFactory() { HostName = "localhost" };
            using var connection = factory.CreateConnection();
            using var channel = connection.CreateModel();
                channel.QueueDeclare(queue: "purchase_queue",
                                     durable: true,
                                     exclusive: false,
                                     autoDelete: false,
                                     arguments: null);
```

```
                channel.BasicQos(prefetchSize: 0,
                     prefetchCount: 1, global: false);
                var consumer = new EventingBasicConsumer(channel);
                consumer.Received += async (sender, ea) =>
                {
                    // Message received even handler
                    ...
                };
                channel.BasicConsume(queue: "purchase_queue",
                            autoAck: false,
                            consumer: consumer);
                 await Task.Delay(1000, stoppingToken);
            }
        catch { }
    }
}
```

Inside the main loop, if an exception is thrown, it is intercepted by the empty catch. Since the two using statements are left, both the connection and channel are disposed of. Therefore, after the exception, a new loop is executed that creates a new fresh connection and a new channel.

Intercepting exceptions is fundamental for several reasons:

1. First of all, it avoids the microservice crash
2. It enables a complete reset of all client objects involved in the communication with the RabbitMQ server that might be damaged by the error
3. It allows error logging that, in an actual production environment, is the basic monitoring tool. For simplicity, error logging is not shown in the code snippets.
4. In the `using` statement body, we ensure that our queue exists, and then set prefetch to 1

Ensuring the queue exists and creating them if they don't exist is better than relying on a single microservice for creating them, since this would introduce hard-to-trace and maintain constraints on the order microservices must be started.

Setting prefetch to 1 causes each server to extract just one message at a time, which ensures a fair distribution of the load among all servers. However, setting `prefetchCount` to `1` might not be convenient when each server runs several equal parallel threads to process the incoming messages, since it sacrifices thread usage optimization in favor of fair distribution of messages among servers. As a consequence, threads that could successfully process further messages (after the first) might remain idle, thus possibly wasting processor cores available on each server machine.

Then, we define a message received event handler. `BasicConsume` starts the actual message reception. With `autoAck` set to `false`, when a message is read from the queue, it is not removed but just blocked, so it is not available to other servers that read from the same queue. The message is actually removed when a confirmation that it has been successfully processed is sent to RabbitMQ. We can also send a failure confirmation, in which case the message is unblocked and becomes available for processing again.

If no confirmation is received, the message remains blocked until the connection and channel are disposed of.

Since `BasicConsume` is non-blocking, the `Task.Delay` after it blocks until the cancellation token is signaled. In any case, after 1 second `Task.Delay` unblocks, and both the connection and the channel are replaced with fresh ones. This avoids that non-confirmed messages might remain blocked forever.

Making instructions like `BasicConsume` non-blocking avoids having a thread waste processor cores by remaining blocked while it waits for an event. Instead, the thread is put in sleeping mode by instructions like `Task.Delay`, thus freeing up all its resources and its assigned processor core, which can then be assigned to another parallel thread that was waiting for a free core for its execution.

Let's move on to the code inside the 'message received' event. This is the place where the actual message processing takes place.

As a first step, the code verifies if the application is being shut down, in which case it disposes of the channel and connection and returns without performing any further operations:

```
if (stoppingToken.IsCancellationRequested)
{
    channel.Close();
    connection.Close();
    return;
}
```

Then, a session scope is created to access all session-scoped dependency injection services:

```
using (var scope = services.CreateScope())
{
  try
  {
  // actual application dependent message processing
  ...
  }
  catch {
    ((EventingBasicConsumer)sender).Model.BasicNack(ea.DeliveryTag, false, true);
  }
}
```

In the case that an exception is thrown during the message processing, a `Nack` message is sent to RabbitMQ to inform it that the message processing failed. `ea.DeliveryTag` is a tag that uniquely identifies the message. The second argument set to `false` informs RabbitMQ that the `Nack` is just for the message identified by ea.DeliveryTag and that it doesn't also involve all other messages waiting for confirmation from this server. Finally, the last argument set to true asks RabbitMQ to requeue the message whose processing failed.

Inside the try block, there is the actual message processing. Its first step is the message deserialization:

```
var body = ea.Body.ToArray();
MyMessageClass? message = null;
using (var stream = new MemoryStream(body))
{
    message = PurchaseMessage.Parser.ParseFrom(stream);
}
```

After that there is the actual application dependent message processing. If this processing fails, we must send a Nack; otherwise, we must send an Ack:

```
if(success)
    ((EventingBasicConsumer)sender).Model
        .BasicAck(ea.DeliveryTag, false);
else
    ((EventingBasicConsumer)sender).Model
        .BasicNack(ea.DeliveryTag, false, true);
```

The full code of a complete example is in the GrpcMicroServiceRabbitProto subfolder of the ch14 folder in the GitHub repository of this book. A detailed description of this example is in the *A worker microservice based on RabbitMQ* section of *Chapter 22, Case Study: Practical Usage of .NET Aspire.*

Summing up, we analyzed how to design a worker microservice that relies on a message broker for its communication and described in detail how to install and handle the RabbitMQ message broker.

The next chapter describes Service-Oriented architecture and how to implement it with ASP.NET Core.

Summary

In this chapter, we analyzed various options for efficient internal microservices communication. We explained the importance of a binary serialization that is interoperable and ensures compatibility with previous message versions, and we described in detail Protobuf.

We analyzed the limits of RPC communication and why data-driven communication must be preferred. Then, we focused on how to achieve reliable asynchronous communication and efficient distributed transactions.

After having described the conceptual problems and techniques of reliable asynchronous communication, we looked at two architectures. The first one was based on gRPC, ASP.NET Core, and internal queues, and the second one was based on message brokers like RabbitMQ and .NET worker services.

The chapter explained, using practical examples, how to implement all the communication protocols that have been discussed and the architectural options for implementing worker microservices that are available in .NET.

Questions

1. Why are queues so important in microservices communication?
2. How do we recall another `.proto` file?
3. How can we represent a `TimeSpan` in the ProtoBuf language?
4. What are the advantages of Protobuf and gRPC over other binary options?
5. What are the advantages of using message brokers instead of internal queues?
6. Why is it acceptable to use a blocking gRPC call to enqueue a message in a recipient queue?
7. How do we enable `.proto` file code generation in a .NET project file?
8. How to send a message on a RabbitMQ channel with the official .NET client?
9. How to wait until a message sent on a RabbitMQ channel is safely saved on disk with the official .NET client?

Further reading

Here, you have some links you may consider using to gather more information about this chapter.

- The official .NET documentation on Protobuf can be found here: `https://learn.microsoft.com/it-it/aspnet/core/grpc/protobuf?view=aspnetcore-10.0`.
- The .NET documentation on gRPC is here: `https://learn.microsoft.com/it-it/aspnet/core/grpc/?view=aspnetcore-10`.
- Finally, the official Google documentation on the whole Protobuf language is here: `https://developers.google.com/protocol-buffers/docs/proto3`.
- Complete tutorials on RabbitMQ can be found here: `https://www.rabbitmq.com/tutorials/tutorial-two-dotnet.html`.
- The complete documentation for RabbitMQ is here: `https://www.rabbitmq.com/`.

15

Applying Service-Oriented Architectures with .NET

Service-Oriented Architecture (SOA) is a modular architecture where interaction between system components is achieved through communication, instead of memory-pointer sharing. Its main purpose is to overcome any kind of binary compatibility problems between the modules. This approach has evolved for years and is now the basis of all communication between systems over the Internet. SOA allows applications from different organizations to exchange data and transactions automatically. Besides that, it allows organizations to offer services on the Internet. For instance, in a banking application, SOA can allow separate services for account management, transaction processing, and customer support to communicate seamlessly.

SOA overcomes binary compatibility problems between modules simply because each module runs in a different memory space and communication is achieved through messages.

With SOA and its pattern of communication, you do not need to deploy different copies of the same component in the various systems/subsystems that use it – each component only needs to be deployed in one place. Moreover, modules can be written in different programming languages and using different frameworks, thus simplifying the overall cycle of Continuous Integration/Continuous Delivery (CI/CD).

If a newer version conforms to the communication interface that is declared to the clients, no incompatibilities can occur. For instance, if you have a backend service that calculates tax based on a specific rule and the entry of selling data, if the specific rule changes, but the selling data doesn't, you will be able to update the service without changing the application in the clients. On the other hand, with DLLs/packages, when the same interface is maintained, incompatibilities may arise because of possible version mismatches in terms of the dependencies of other DLLs/packages that the library module might have in common with its clients.

Organizing clusters/networks of cooperating services was discussed in *Chapter 11, Applying a Microservice Architecture to Your Enterprise Application*. In this chapter, we will focus on the SOAP and REST communication interfaces used all over the world. More specifically, we will discuss the following topics:

- Understanding the principles of the SOA approach
- SOAP and REST web services
- How does .NET 10 deal with SOA?

By the end of this chapter, you will know how to publicly expose data from an application through an ASP.NET Core service.

Technical requirements

This chapter requires the Visual Studio 2026 free Community edition or better with all the database tools installed. All concepts in this chapter are clarified with practical examples based on the WWTravelClub book use case, located in *Chapter 22, Case Study: Practical Usage of .NET Aspire*. You will find the code for this chapter at `https://github.com/PacktPublishing/Software-Architecture-with-.NET-10-and-C-sharp-5E`.

Understanding the principles of the SOA approach

Like classes in an object-oriented architecture, services are implementations of interfaces that, in turn, come from a system's functional specifications. Therefore, the first step in service design is the definition of its abstract interface. During this initial stage, you might have two approaches:

1. Define all the service operations as interface methods that operate on the types of your favourite language (C#, Java, C++, JavaScript, and so on) and decide which operations to implement with synchronous communication and which ones to implement with asynchronous communication.
2. Create the contract first in an interoperable format. In this approach, you can use definition files using patterns like OpenAPI, Protobuf, WSDL, and AsyncAPI without touching the programming language with which the services will be developed, using some tools to help.

As we will see later on in the chapter, the two approaches are basically equivalent since definitions based on specific programming interfaces can be converted into definitions expressed in interoperable formats and vice versa.

The interfaces that are defined in this initial stage will not necessarily be used in the actual service implementation and are just useful design tools. Once we have decided on the architecture of the services, these interfaces are usually redefined so that we can adapt them to the peculiarity of the architecture.

It is worth pointing out that SOA messages must keep the same kind of semantics as method calls/answers.

> **Note**
>
> Besides, a key principle here is statelessness; that is, the reaction to a message must not depend on any previously received messages because the server does not save information from prior requests, which means the messages must be independent of each other.

For instance, if we send a message containing a new customer to store, then we cannot send another message that simply list the customer purchase orders without mentioning the customer, since the server doesn't remember that the previous message contain a customer, so there is no context for guessing the ownership of the purchase orders.

In particular, if the purpose of a messages is to create a new database entry, this semantic must not change with the context of other messages, and the way the database entry is created must depend just on the content of the current message and not on other previously received messages. Consequently, a client cannot create sessions and cannot log in to a service, perform some operations, and then log out. An authentication token must be repeated in each message.

The reasons for this constraint are modularity, testability, and maintainability, that are good practices for implementing any kind of software modules. In fact, a session-based service would be very hard to test and modify due to the interactions that are hidden in the session data.

Once you have decided on the interface that is going to be implemented by a service, you must decide which communication stack/SOA to adopt. The communication stack must be part of some official or de facto standard to ensure the interoperability of the service.

> **Tip**
>
> Interoperability is the main constraint prescribed by SOA: services must offer a communication interface that does not depend on a specific library used, implementation language, or deployment platform.

Once you have decided on the communication stack/architecture, you need to adapt your previous interfaces to the peculiarities of the architecture (see the *REST web services* subsection of this chapter for more details). Then, you must translate these interfaces into the chosen communication language. This means that you must map all the programming language types into types that are available in the chosen communication language.

The actual translation of data is usually performed automatically by the SOA libraries that are used by your development environment. However, some configuration might be needed, and, in any case, we must be aware of how our programming language types are transformed before each communication.

> **Note**
>
> For instance, some numeric types might be transformed into types with less precision or with different ranges of values. In .NET 10, for instance, you should be aware that floating-point numeric types vary between float (~6-9 digits), double (~15-17 digits), and decimal (~28-29 digits). You may consider the alternative of using string variables to reduce the risk of imprecision while transferring numeric types.

The interoperability constraint can be interpreted in a lighter form in the case of microservices that are not accessible outside of their clusters, since they need to communicate with other microservices that belong to the same cluster. In this case, this means that the communication stack might be platform-specific so that it can increase performance, but it must be standard to avoid compatibility problems with other microservices that might be added to the cluster as the application evolves.

We have spoken of the communication stack and not of the communication protocol because SOA communication standards usually define the format of the message's content and provide different possibilities for the specific protocol that is used to embed those messages. For instance, REST services usually run over HTTP/HTTPS based on JSON messages, while the SOAP protocol just defines an XML-based format for the various kinds of messages, but SOAP messages can be conveyed by various protocols.

Usually, the most common protocol that is used for SOAP is also HTTP, but you may decide to jump to the HTTP level and send SOAP messages directly over TCP/IP for better performance.

When choosing a communication stack, please, use the following checklist:

- ***Compatibility constraints***: If your service must be publicly available on the Internet to business clients, then you must conform to the most common choices, which means using *either SOAP over HTTP or REST* services. The most common choices are different if your clients are not business clients but Internet of Things (IoT) clients. Also, within IoT, the protocols that are used in different application areas can be different. For instance, marine vehicle status data is typically exchanged with Signal K. Although this protocol is too specific and is presented here just as an example, as a software architect, you must understand that you may face this kind of standard in a specific area.
- ***Development/deployment platform:*** Not all communication stacks are available on all development frameworks and on all deployment platforms, but luckily, all the most common communication stacks used in public business services, such as SOAP- and JSON-based REST communication, are available on all main development/deployment platforms.
- ***Performance:*** If your system is not exposed to the outside world and is a private part of your microservice cluster, performance considerations have a higher priority. In this scenario, gRPC, which was discussed in *Chapter 14, Implementing Microservices with .NET*, can be a better option since gRPC is a more compact binary format that requires less bandwidth.
- ***Availability of tools and knowledge in your team:*** Knowing about the availability of tools in your team/organization is important when it comes to choosing between acceptable communication stacks. However, this kind of constraint always has less priority than compatibility constraints since it makes no sense to conceive a system that is easy to implement for your team but that almost nobody can use.
- ***Simplicity versus available features:*** Some communication solutions, while less complete, are easier to implement and version, while other solutions, though more complete, impose too many formal constraints that complicate the design and the API versioning. The simplification of the formal steps needed to define a service and the need for improved compatibility among different versions of the same API started a movement from SOAP-based services to the less formal REST services in the last few years. This point will be discussed in more detail when we describe SOAP and REST services in the remainder of this section.
- ***Service description:*** When services must be exposed on the Internet, client applications need a publicly available description of the service specifications to enable the design of compatible communication clients. Some communication stacks include languages and conventions to describe service specifications. Formal service specifications that are exposed this way enable the automatic creation of communication clients. SOAP goes further and allows service discoverability by means of a public XML-based directory containing information about the tasks each web service can carry out.

Once you have chosen the communication stack you wish to use, you must use the tools that are available in your development environment to implement the service in a way that conforms to the chosen communication stack. Sometimes, communication stack compliance is automatically ensured by the development tools, but sometimes, it may require some development effort. For instance, in the .NET world, the compliance of SOAP services is automatically ensured by development tools if you use WCF (Windows Communication Foundation), while the compliance of REST services falls under the developer's responsibility, although you have, since .NET 5, automatic support for the OpenAPI. Some of the fundamental features of SOA solutions are as follows:

- **Authentication**: Allows the client to authenticate to access service operations.

- **Authorization**: Handles the client's permissions.
- **Security**: This is how communication is kept safe, that is, how to prevent unauthorized systems from reading and/or modifying the content of the communication. Typically, encryption prevents both unauthorized modifications and reading, while electronic signature algorithms prevent just modifications.
- **Exceptions**: Returns exceptions to the client.
- **Message reliability**: Ensures that messages reliably reach their destination in case of possible infrastructure faults.

Though sometimes desirable, the following features are not always necessary:

- ***Distributed transactions:*** The capability to handle distributed transactions, thus undoing all the changes you have made whenever the distributed transactions fail or are aborted.
- ***Support for the Publisher/Subscriber pattern:*** If and how events and notifications are supported.
- ***Addressing:*** If and how references to other services and/or methods are supported.
- ***Routing:*** If and how messages can be routed through a network of services.

The remainder of this section will describe SOAP services a little bit. However, the focus will be on REST services since today they are the de facto standard for business services that are exposed outside of their clusters/servers. For performance reasons, microservices use other protocols, discussed in *Chapter 11, Applying a Microservice Architecture to Your Enterprise Application*, and *Chapter 14, Implementing Microservices with .NET*. In particular, for inter-cluster communication, **Advanced Message Queuing Protocol** (AMQP) is often used (see *Chapter 14*).

SOAP and REST Web services

In order to understand modern systems, you need to know the main Web services communication stacks, SOAP and OpenApi. Let's start with SOAP.

SOAP Web services

While SOAP Web services are becoming always less diffuse, they are still the standard in some enterprise environments, such as banking, so a minimal knowledge of SOAP is necessary. We will describe them shortly before moving to the more widespread REST services.

The **Simple Object Access Protocol** (SOAP) allows both one-way messages and request/reply messages. Communication can be both synchronous and asynchronous, as explained in *Chapter 1, Understanding the Importance of Software Architecture*, and *Chapter 2, Non-Functional Requirements*, but if the underlying protocol is synchronous, such as in the case of HTTP, the sender receives an acknowledgment saying that the message was received (but not necessarily processed). When asynchronous communication is used, the sender must listen for incoming communications. Often, asynchronous communication is implemented with the Publisher/Subscriber pattern, which we described in *Chapter 6, Design Patterns and .NET Implementation*, and detailed in *Chapter 14, Implementing Microservices with .NET*.

Messages are represented as XML documents called **envelopes.** Each **envelope** contains a header, body, and fault elements. The body is where the actual content of the message is placed. The **fault element** contains possible errors, so it is the way exceptions are exchanged when communication occurs. Finally, the header contains any auxiliary information that enriches the protocol but does not contain domain data. For example, the header may contain an authentication token and/or a signature if the message is signed.

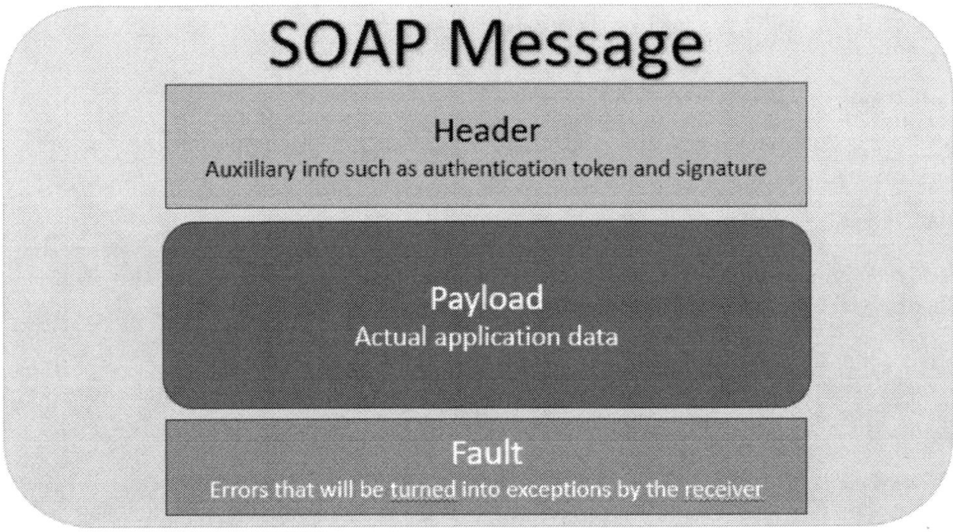

Figure 15.1: SOAP message

> **Note**
>
> You can find the default XML namespace for the SOAP envelope at `https://www.w3.org/2003/05/soap-envelope/`.

The underlying protocol that is used to send the XML envelopes is usually HTTP, since this is the protocol of the Internet, but the SOAP specification allows any protocol, such as TCP/IP or SMTP. In practice, HTTP has become a de facto standard for the underlying, so if you do not have a specific reason to choose another protocol, you should use HTTP to maximize the interoperability of the service. SOAP has constraining specifications for all aspects of communications, from authentication to distributed transactions. Let us describe shortly how such specifications are organized.

SOAP specifications

SOAP specifications contain the basics of message exchange, while other auxiliary features are described in separate specification documents called `WS- *` and are usually handled by adding extra information in the SOAP header. `WS-*` specifications handle all the fundamental and desirable features of SOA we listed previously. We have some of them below:

WS-*	Main objective
`WS-Security`	Takes care of security, including authentication, authorization, and encryption/signatures
`WS-Eventing / WS-Notification`	Two alternative ways of implementing the Publisher/ Subscriber pattern
`WS-ReliableMessaging`	Concerned with the reliable delivery of messages in case of possible faults
`WS-Transaction`	Concerned with distributed transactions

Table 15.1: Main SOAP specifications

In essence, most of practical application just need the above features also if the previous list is in no way exhaustive. As a matter of facts, actual implementations in various environments (such as Java and .NET) furnish the more relevant `WS- *` services, but no implementation supports all the `WS- *` specifications. Therefore, the remaining specifications that are not listed in the previous table are rarely used. As a rule of thumb, one should use just the specifications supported by all main stacks, such as .NET and Java.

All the XML documents/document parts involved in the SOAP protocol are formally defined in XSD documents, like in the example below, which are special XML documents whose content provides a description of XML structures.

```
<?xml version="1.0"?>
<xs:schema id="sample" targetNamespace="http://tempuri.org/sample.xsd"
elementFormDefault="qualified" xmlns="http://tempuri.org/sample.xsd"
xmlns:xs="http://www.w3.org/2001/XMLSchema">
  <xs:element name='mySample'>
    <xs:complexType>
      <xs:simpleContent>
        <xs:extension base='xs:decimal'>
          <xs:attribute name='sizing' type='xs:string' />
        </xs:extension>
      </xs:simpleContent>
    </xs:complexType>
  </xs:element>
</xs:schema>
```

Also, all your custom data structures (classes and interfaces in an object-oriented language) must be translated into XSD if they are going to be part of a SOAP envelope. Each XSD specification has an associated namespace that identifies the specification and a physical location where it can be found. Both the namespace and the physical location are URIs. The location URI does not need to be publicly accessible if the web service is accessible just from within an intranet.

The whole definition of a service is an XSD specification that may contain references to other namespaces, that is, to other XSD documents. Simply put, all the messages via SOAP communication must be defined in an XSD specification. Then, a server and a client can communicate if they refer to the same XSD specifications. This means, for instance, that you need to create a new XSD specification each time you add another field to a message. After that, you need to update all the XSD files that reference the old message definition to the new message definition by creating a new version of them. In turn, these modifications require the creation of other versions for other XSD files, and so on. Therefore, simple modifications that maintain compatibility with the previous behaviour (clients could simply ignore the field that was added) may cause an exponential chain of version changes.

After discussing, SOAP and its specifications briefly, we can analyse why it is better to prefer REST services whenever we don't need features that are supported only by SOAP.

The turning point toward the new REST standard

In the last few years, the difficulty in handling modifications, along with the complexity of handling the configuration of all the `WS- *` specifications and performance problems, caused a gradual move toward the simpler REST services that we will describe in the upcoming subsections. This move started with services that were called from JavaScript due to the difficulty of implementing complete SOAP clients that were able to run efficiently in a web browser. Moreover, the complex SOAP machinery was oversized for the simple needs of the typical clients running in a browser and may have caused a complete waste of development time.

Finally, as hinted in the previous subsections, SOAP services don't handle API versioning effectively.

For this reason, services aimed at non-JavaScript clients started a massive move toward REST services, and nowadays, the preferred choice is REST services, with SOAP being used either for compatibility with legacy systems or when features that are not supported by REST services are needed.

Today, we can consider REST services that transfer data with JSON, the most-used approach all over the world. Security aspects, design patterns for enabling transactional support, performance, and even documentation have improved all over the years, so this is certainly the best alternative for applying SOAs nowadays. Let's have a look at REST web services in the next topic.

REST web services

REST services were initially conceived to avoid the complex machinery of SOAP in simple cases, such as calls to a service from the JavaScript code of a web page. Then, they gradually became the preferred choice for complex systems. REST services use HTTP to exchange data in JSON or, less commonly, in XML format. Simply put, they replace the SOAP body with the HTTP body, the SOAP header with the HTTP header, and the HTTP response code replaces the fault element and furnishes further auxiliary information on the operation that was performed. That is, REST replaces complex SOAP structures built on top of HTTP with native HTTP features, as exemplified in the table below.

SOAP message part	***Corresponding REST message part***
SOAP body	HTTP body
SOAP header	HTTP header
SOAP fault	HTTP response code and response message

Table 15.2: How REST Simplifies SOAP over HTTP

As you can see, HTTP already offers most of the SOAP features natively, which means we can avoid building a SOAP layer on top of HTTP. *This was the main reason behind the success of the REST protocol.*

Moreover, the whole HTTP machinery is simpler than SOAP: simpler to program, simpler to configure, and simpler to implement efficiently.

Finally, REST services impose fewer constraints on the clients. Type compatibility between servers and clients conforms to the more flexible JavaScript type compatibility model because JSON is a subset of JavaScript. Moreover, when XML is used in place of JSON, it maintains the same JavaScript type compatibility rules. No XML namespaces need to be specified.

When using JSON and XML, if the server adds some more fields to the response while keeping the same semantics of all the other fields compatible with the previous client, they can simply ignore the new fields. Accordingly, changes that are made to a REST service definition only need to be propagated to previous clients in the case of breaking changes that cause actual incompatible behaviour in the server.

Moreover, it is likely that changes will be self-limited and won't result in an exponential chain of changes because type compatibility does not require the reference to a specific type to be defined in a unique shared place and simply requires that the shape of types is compatible.

Service type compatibility rules

Let's clarify the REST service type compatibility rules with an example. Imagine that several services use a `Person` object that contains `Name`, `Surname`, and `Address` string fields. This object is served by S1:

```
{
  Name: string,
  Surname: string,
  Address: string
}
```

Type compatibility is ensured if the service and client refer to different copies of the preceding definition. It is also acceptable for the client to use a definition with fewer fields since it can simply ignore all the other fields:

```
{
  Name: string,
```

```
    Surname: string,
}
```

You can only use a definition with fewer fields within your "*own*" code. Attempting to send information back to the server without the expected fields may cause problems.

Now, imagine the scenario where you have an S2 service that takes `Person` objects from S1 and adds them to the responses it returns on some of its methods. Suppose the S1 service that handles the `Person` object replaces the Address string with a complex object:

```
{
  Name: string,
  Surname: string,
  Address:
  {
    Country: string,
   Town: string,
   Location: string
  }
}
```

After the breaking change, the S2 service will have to adapt its communication client that calls the S1 service to the new format. Then, it can convert the new `Person` format into the older one before using `Person` objects in its responses. This way, the S2 service avoids propagating the breaking change of S1.

In general, basing type compatibility on the object shape (tree of nested properties) instead of a reference to the same formal type definition increases flexibility and modifiability. The price we pay for this increased flexibility is that type compatibility cannot be computed automatically by comparing the formal definition of server and client interfaces. In fact, in the absence of a univocal specification, each time a new version of the service is released, the developer must verify that the semantics of all the fields that the client and server have in common remain unchanged from the previous version.

The basic idea behind REST services is to give up the severity checks and complex protocols for greater flexibility and simplicity, while SOAP does exactly the opposite.

REST and native HTTP features

The REST services manifesto states that REST uses native HTTP features to implement all the required service features. So, for instance, authentication will be performed directly with the HTTP `Authorization` field, encryption will be achieved with HTTPS, exceptions will be handled with an HTTP error status code, and routing and reliable messaging will be handled by the machinery the HTTP protocol relies on. Addressing is achieved by using URLs to refer to services, their methods, and other resources.

There is no native support for asynchronous communication since HTTP is a synchronous protocol.

There is also no native support for the Publisher/Subscriber pattern, but two services can interact with the Publisher/Subscriber pattern by each exposing an endpoint to the other, as shown in *Figure 15.2*.

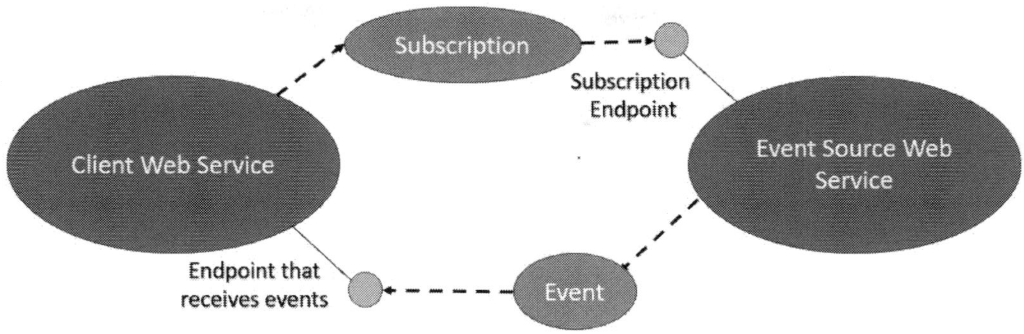

Figure 15.2: REST implementation of the Publisher/Subscriber pattern

The event source exposes a subscription endpoint, while its client exposes an endpoint where it receives its notifications, which are authorized through a common secret that is exchanged during the subscription. This pattern is quite common. GitHub also allows us to send repository events to our REST services.

REST services offer no easy options when it comes to implementing distributed transactions, since HTTP is stateless. However, one can use the SAGA pattern, described in *Chapter 14, Implementing Microservices with .NET*.

The REST manifesto not only prescribes the usage of the predefined solutions that are already available in HTTP, but also the usage of a web-like semantics. In general, service operations can be conceived as CRUD operations, but not limited to them, on resources that are identified by URLs (the same resource may be identified by several URLs). In fact, REST is an acronym for Representational State Transfer, meaning that each URL is the representation of some sort of entity. As a best practice, each kind of service request needs to adopt the appropriate HTTP verb and return the status. You should use a different verb for each of the possible actions you perform on a resource (read, creation, deletion, or modification):

- ***GET (read operation)***: The URL represents the resource that must be returned by the read operation. Thus, GET operations mimic pointer dereferencing. In the case of a successful operation, a 200 (OK) status code is returned.
- ***POST (creation operation)***: The JSON/XML object that is contained in the request body is added as a new resource to the object represented by the operation URL. If the new resource is successfully created immediately, a 201 (created) status code is returned, along with an optional custom object. The response must also contain a `Location` header whose value is the most specific URL that identifies the created resource. If creation is deferred to a later time, a 202 (accepted) status code is returned.
- ***DELETE***: The resource referenced by the request URL is removed. In the case of a successful operation, a 200 (OK) status code is returned.
- ***PUT (edit operation)***: The JSON/XML object contained in the request body replaces the object referenced by the request URL. In the case of a successful operation, a 200 (OK) status code is returned. This operation is idempotent, meaning that repeating the same request twice causes the same modification. 204 (No Content) is also a possible return value.
- ***PATCH***: The JSON/XML object contained in the request body contains instructions on how to modify the object referenced by the request URL. This operation is not idempotent since the modification may

be an increment of a numeric field. In the case of a successful operation, a 200 (OK) status code is returned

If the resource has been moved from the request URL to another URL, a redirect code is returned:

- **301 (moved permanently)**, plus the new URL where we can find the resource
- **307 (moved temporarily)**, plus the new URL where we can find the resource

If the operation fails, a status code that depends on the kind of failure is returned. Some examples of failure codes are as follows:

- **400 (bad request)**: The request that was sent to the server is ill formed.
- **404 (not found)**: When the request URL does not refer to any known object.
- **405 (method not allowed)**: When the request verb is not supported by the resource referenced by the URL.
- **401 (unauthorized)**: The operation requires authentication, but the client has not furnished any valid authorization header.
- **403 (forbidden)**: The client is correctly authenticated but has no right to perform the operation.
- **409 (conflict)**: The operation failed due to some conflict with the current state of the server. For instance, the resource you tried to update is being modified by another request.
- **412 (precondition failed)**: The operation failed due to some failed precondition.
- **422 (unprocessable content)**: The request was well formatted, but there are semantic errors in it.

The previous list of status codes is not exhaustive. A reference to an exhaustive list will be provided in the *Further Reading* section. It is fundamental to point out that *POST/PUT/PATCH/DELETE* operations may have – and usually have – side effects on other resources. Otherwise, it would be impossible to code operations that act simultaneously on several resources. In other words, the HTTP verb must conform with the operation that is performed on the resource and referenced by the request URL, but the operation might affect other resources. The same operation might be performed with a different HTTP verb on one of the other involved resources. It is the developer's responsibility to choose which way to perform the same operation to implement it in the service interface.

Thanks to the side effects of HTTP verbs, REST services can encode all these operations as CRUD operations on resources represented by URLs.

The adoption of full REST semantics has the advantage that services can be extended with or without small modifications being made to the preexisting operation definitions. In fact, extensions should mainly manifest as additional properties of some objects and as additional resource URLs with some associated operations. Therefore, preexisting clients can simply ignore them.

Often, moving an existing service to REST requires us to split the various inputs between the request URL and the request body. More specifically, we extract the input fields that univocally define one of the objects involved in the method's execution and use them to create a URL that univocally identifies that object. Then, we decide on which HTTP verb to use based on the operation that is performed on the selected object. Finally, we place the remainder of the input in the request body.

If our services were designed with an object-oriented architecture focused on the business domain objects (such as DDD, as described in *Chapter 7, Understanding the Different Domains in Software Solutions*), the REST translation of all the service methods should be quite immediate since services should already be organized around domain resources. Otherwise, moving to REST might require some service interface redefinitions.

Example of methods in the REST language

Now, let us learn how methods can be expressed in the REST language with a simple example of an intra-bank money transfer. We will present here two approaches. In the first one, a bank account can be represented by a URL as follows: `https://mybank.com/accounts/{bank account number}`

If we imagine a bank transfer, we may represent it as a PATCH request, whose body contains an object with properties representing the amount of money, the time of transfer, description, and the account receiving the money.

The operation modifies the account mentioned in the URL but also the receiving account as a side effect. If the account doesn't have enough money, a 422 (unprocessable content) status code is returned, along with an object with all the error details (an error description, the available funds, and so on).

However, since all bank operations are recorded in the account statement, the creation and addition of a new transfer object for a bank account operations collection associated with the bank account is a better way to represent the transfer. In this second approach, the URL might be something like

the following:

```
https://mybank.com/accounts/{bank account number}/transactions
```

Here, the HTTP verb is POST since we are creating a new object. The body content is the same, and a 422 status code is returned if there is a lack of funds.

Both representations of the transfer cause the same changes in the database. Moreover, once the inputs are extracted from the different URLs and from the possibly different request bodies, the subsequent processing is the same. In both cases, we have the same inputs and the same processing – it is just the exterior appearance of the two requests that are different.

However, the introduction of the virtual transactions collection allows us to extend the service with several more transaction collection-specific methods. It is worth pointing out that the transaction collection does not need to relate to a database table or any physical object: it lives in the world of URLs and creates a convenient way for us to model the transfer.

The increased usage of REST services leads to a description of REST service interfaces to be created like the ones developed for SOAP. This standard is called **OpenAPI**. We will talk about this in the following subsection.

The OpenAPI standard

OpenAPI is a specification that is used worldwide for describing the REST APIs. *It was conceived to improve interoperability, and to enable the automatic creation of clients.*

The OpenAPI Initiative was founded in November 2015, as an open-source project under the Linux Foundation, with the help of companies like SmartBear, Google, IBM, and Microsoft. The specification is currently versioned as 3.1.

The whole service is described by a JSON or YAML endpoint, that is, an endpoint that describes the service with a JSON object. This JSON object has a general section that applies to the whole service and contains the general features of the service, such as its version and description, as well as shared definitions.

> **Note**
>
> You can find OpenAPI specification and examples at `https://github.com/OAI/OpenAPI-Specification/`.

Then, each service endpoint has a specific section that describes the endpoint URL or URL format (in case some inputs are included in the URL), all its inputs, all the possible output types and status codes, and all the authorization protocols. Each endpoint-specific section can reference the definitions contained in the general section.

A complete description of the OpenAPI syntax is out of the scope of this book, but you will find visual editors on the Internet that can help you clarify the specification mentioned before. A great example is provided by SmartBear, one of the companies that founded the initiative, and it is called Swagger Editor. In the beta version of the online tool, you can load an example using OpenAPI version 3.1.0. This helps companies to create API contracts even before deciding the programming language of the API.

Various development frameworks automatically generate OpenAPI documentation by processing the REST API code, and further information is provided by the developer, so your team does not need to have in-depth knowledge of OpenAPI syntax. An example of this is the `Microsoft.AspNetCore.OpenApi` NuGet package that we will describe in this chapter.

The *"How does .NET 10 deal with SOA?"* section explains how we can automatically generate OpenAPI documentation in ASP.NET Core REST API projects, while the use case presented in *Chapter 22, Case Study: Practical Usage of .NET Aspire*, will provide a practical example of its usage.

We will end this subsection by talking about how to handle authentication and authorization in REST services.

REST services authentication and authorization

Since the HTTP protocol is stateless, when authentication is required, the client must send an authentication token in every single request. According to the HTTP protocol that token must be placed in the HTTP `Authorization` header. The simplest way to authenticate is through the explicit transmission of a shared secret. This can be done with the following code:

```
Authorization: Api-Key <string known by both server and client>
```

It is worth mentioning that API-key-based authentication needs HTTPS to stop shared secrets from being stolen. API keys are very simple to use, but they do not convey information about user authorizations, so they can be adopted when the operations allowed by the client are quite standard, and there are no complex authorization patterns. Moreover, since API-keys have no expiration they are quite vulnerable.

Safer techniques use shared secrets that are valid for a long period of time, just by the user logging in. Then, the login returns a short-life token that is used as a shared secret in all the subsequent requests.

When the short-lived secret is going to expire, it can be renewed with a call to a renew endpoint. The whole logic is completely decoupled from the short-life token-based authorization logic. The login is usually based on login endpoints that receive long-term credentials and return short-life tokens. Login credentials are either usual username-password pairs that are passed as input to the login method or other kinds of authorization tokens that are converted into short-life tokens that are served by the login endpoint. Login can also be achieved with various authentication protocols based on X.509 certificates. We will discuss certificate-based authentication in *Chapter 20, Securing Data and Applications.*

The most widespread short-life token type is the so-called bearer token. Each bearer token encodes information about how long it lasts and a list of assertions, called claims, that can be used for authorization purposes. Bearer tokens are returned by either login operations or renewal operations. Their characteristic feature is that they are not tied to the client that receives them or to any other specific client, but they identify the client, which can simply use them in its invocations.

No matter how a client gets a bearer token, this is all a client needs to be granted, including all the rights implied by its claims. It is enough to transfer a bearer token to another client to empower that client with all the rights implied by all the bearer token claims since no proof of identity is required by bearer-token-based authorization.

Therefore, once a client gets a bearer token, it can delegate some operations to third parties by transferring its bearer token to them. Typically, when a bearer token must be used for delegation, during the login phase, the client specifies the claims to include to restrict what operations can be authorized by the token.

Compared to API key authentication, bearer-token-based authentication is disciplined by standards. They must use the following Authorization header:

```
Authorization: Bearer <bearer token string>
```

Bearer tokens can be implemented in several ways. REST services typically use JWTs that are strings with a Base64 URL encoding of JSON objects. More specifically, JWT creation starts with a JSON header, as well as a JSON payload. The JSON header specifies the kind of token and how it is signed, while the payload consists of a JSON object that contains all the claims as property/value pairs.

More details on JWT tokens will be given in *Chapter 20, Securing Data and Applications.*

Another important topic is how REST API supports several versions simultaneously, let discuss it in the next subsection.

API versioning

Considering a natural scenario where the number of APIs will increase in your application, and, more than that, the business logic will obviously evolve, as a software architect, you must decide how you are going to version the APIs, guaranteeing the compatibility between your services and the clients that consume these services.

It is important to mention that there are several versioning options for doing so:

- ***URI***: It consists of defining the version of the API in its URI, for example, `https://wwtravelclub.com/v1/trips`.
- ***Parameter***: You can define a parameter in the request that defines the version, for instance, `https://wwtravelclub.com/trips?version=2`.
- ***Media type***: In this case, the desired version of the API will be presented in the HTTP Accept header.
- ***Custom request header***: Like the media type versioning technique, but in this case, the HTTP header is completely custom.

The first two alternatives are the most commonly used, but the important point here is that you must consider the crucial implementation of a versioning technique, so that several versions can be accessed simultaneously.

The next section is more practical and discusses the .NET facilities for defining and communicating with REST and SOAP services.

How does .NET 10 deal with SOA?

Now that we've explored the main concepts behind both SOAP and REST, let's move to their practical implementation and to the support offered by .NET.

WCF technology has not been ported to .NET 5+, and there are no plans to perform a complete port of it. Part of the source code was donated, and an open-source project started out of it. You can find information about this project at https://github.com/CoreWCF/CoreWCF. Instead, Microsoft is investing in gRPC, Google's open-source technology. Besides, .NET 10 has excellent support for REST services through ASP.NET Core.

The main reasons behind the decision to abandon WCF are as follows:

- As we have already discussed, SOAP technology has been overtaken by REST technology in most application areas.
- WCF technology is strictly tied to Windows, so it would be very expensive to reimplement all its features from scratch in .NET 5+. Since support for full .NET will continue, users who need WCF can still rely on it.
- As a general strategy, with .NET 5+, Microsoft prefers investing in open-source technologies that can be shared with other competitors. That is why, instead of investing in WCF, Microsoft provided a gRPC implementation starting from .NET Core 3.0.

The next subsections will cover the support provided inside Visual Studio for each technology we have mentioned.

SOAP client support

In WCF, service specifications are defined through .NET interfaces, and the actual service code is supplied in classes that implement those interfaces. Endpoints, underlying protocols (HTTP and TCP/IP), and any other features are defined in a configuration file. In turn, the configuration file can be edited with an easy-to-use configuration tool. Therefore, the developer is responsible for providing just the service behaviour as a standard .NET class and for configuring all the service features in a declarative way. This way, the service configuration is completely decoupled from the actual service behaviour, and each service can be reconfigured so that it can be adapted to a different environment without the need to modify its code.

While .NET 10 does not support SOAP technology for creating new services, it does support the usage of SOAP clients when there are many legacy SOAP services. More specifically, it is quite easy to create a SOAP service proxy for an existing SOAP service in Visual Studio (please refer to *Chapter 6, Design Patterns and .NET Implementation*, for a discussion of what a proxy is and of the Proxy pattern).

In the case of services, a proxy is a class that implements the service interface and whose methods perform their jobs by calling the analogous methods of the remote service. To create a service proxy, in Solution Explorer click on **Connected Service**. Then, In the page that appears, click on the **Add a service reference** link, select **WCF Web service,** and click **Next**.

In the form that appears, you can specify the URL of the service (where the WSDL service description is contained), the namespace where you wish to add the proxy class, and much more. At the end of the wizard, Visual Studio automatically adds all the necessary NuGet packages and scaffolds the proxy class. This is enough to create an instance of this class and to call its methods so that we can interact with the remote SOAP service.

There are also third parties, such as NuGet packages, that provide limited support for SOAP services, but currently, they aren't very useful since such limited support does not include features that aren't available in REST services, too.

.NET also support a the gRPC protocol conceived by Google that was discussed in more detail in *Chapter 14, Implementing Microservices with .NET*. It is worth recalling here its main features, and how it compares with the REST protocol.

gRPC support

The .NET SDK supports the gRPC project template, which scaffolds both a gRPC server and a gRPC client. gRPC implements a remote procedure call pattern that offers both synchronous and asynchronous calls, reducing the traffic of messages between the client and server. Using gRPC is super easy since Visual Studio's gRPC project template scaffolds everything so that the gRPC service and its clients are working. The developer just needs to define the application-specific C# service interface and a class that implements it.

For configuring it, services are defined through interfaces written in a Protobuf file, and their code is provided in C# classes that implement those interfaces, while clients interact with those services through proxies that implement the same service interfaces.

gRPC is a good option for internal communications within a microservices cluster. Since there are gRPC libraries for all the main languages and development frameworks, it can be used in Kubernetes-based clusters. Besides, gRPC is more efficient than the REST services protocol due to its more compact representation of data and its being easier to use since everything to do with the protocol is taken care of by the development framework.

For this reason, we have added a chapter dedicated to discussing this how to use both message brokers and gRPC in the implementation of worker microservices: *Chapter 14, Implementing Microservices with .NET*. There, you may find a good description of gRPC, and all the needed practical details to adopt it in .NET projects.

The remainder of the section is dedicated to .NET support for REST services from both the server and client sides.

REST services and ASP.NET Core

.NET supports REST services through ASP.NET Core, so we gives a short preview of ASP.NET Core features in these subsections before describing REST services in more detail in the next subsection.

ASP.NET Core applications are .NET applications based on the Host concept we described in the Using generic hosts subsection of *Chapter 11, Applying a Microservice Architecture to Your Enterprise Application.*

The `Program.cs` file of each ASP.NET application now creates a host, adds services, builds it, and runs it:

```
var builder = WebApplication.CreateBuilder(args);
// Add services to the container.
builder.Services.AddControllers();
// Learn more about configuring OpenAPI at //https://aka.ms/aspnet/openapi
builder.Services.AddOpenApi();
var app = builder.Build();
// Configure the HTTP request pipeline.
if (app.Environment.IsDevelopment())
{
   //defines an OpenAPI documentation endpoint at /openapi/v1.json
   //but v1 can be changed with a custom name
   app.MapOpenApi();
}
app.UseHttpsRedirection();
app.UseAuthorization();
app.MapControllers();
app.Run();
```

`Environment` is taken from the `ASPNETCORE_ENVIRONMENT` environment variable. In turn, it is defined in the `Properties\launchSettings.json` file when the application runs in Visual Studio over Solution Explorer. In this file, you can define several running profiles that can be selected with the dropdown next to Visual Studio's run button. By default, the file contains an `http` and an `https` profile, and both of them set `ASPNETCORE_ENVIRONMENT` to `Development`. The following is a typical `launchSettings.json` file:

```
{
  "$schema": "https://json.schemastore.org/launchsettings.json",
  "profiles": {
    "http": {
      "commandName": "Project",
      "dotnetRunMessages": true,
      "launchBrowser": false,
      "applicationUrl": "http://localhost:5153",
      "environmentVariables": {
        "ASPNETCORE_ENVIRONMENT": "Development"
```

```
        }
      },
      "https": {
        "commandName": "Project",
        "dotnetRunMessages": true,
        "launchBrowser": false,
        "applicationUrl": "https://localhost:7160;http://localhost:5153",
        "environmentVariables": {
          "ASPNETCORE_ENVIRONMENT": "Development"
        }
      }
    }
  }
```

The value to use for ASPNETCORE_ENVIRONMENT when the application is published can be added to the published XML file after it has been created by Visual Studio. This value is `<EnvironmentName>Staging</EnvironmentName>`. It can also be specified in your Visual Studio ASP.NET Core project file (.csproj):

```
<PropertyGroup>
<EnvironmentName>Staging</EnvironmentName>
</PropertyGroup>
```

Each middleware in the pipeline is defined by an `app.Use<something>` method, which often accepts some options. Each of them processes the requests and then either forwards the modified request to the next one in the pipeline or returns an HTTP response. When an HTTP response is returned, it is processed by all the previous ones in reverse order.

Modules are inserted in the pipeline in the order they are defined by the `app.Use<something>` method calls.

The previous code adds an OpenAPI documentation endpoint only if `ASPNETCORE_ENVIRONMENT` is `Development`. This documentation endpoint can also be added when the application is released but before publishing it the developer must decide if protecting it with authorization, and should also cache the documentation file to avoid it is recomputed at each request. More details on OpenAPI support will be given in the *ASP.NET Core support for OpenAPI* section.

A complete description of the ASP.NET Core pipeline will be given in *Chapter 16*, *Presenting ASP.NET Core*. In the next subsection, we will explain how ASP.NET Core lets you implement REST services.

Implementing REST services with ASP.NET Core

Today, we can guarantee that the use of MVC and a web API is consolidated. In the MVC framework, HTTP requests are processed by classes called controllers. Each request is mapped to the call of a controller's public method. The selected controller and controller methods depend on the shape of the request path, and they are defined by routing rules, which, for the REST API, are usually provided through attributes associated with both the Controller class and its methods.

ASP.NET Core also supports implementing APIs with its so-called minimal APIs. You can find a good explanation of it at `https://docs.microsoft.com/en-us/aspnet/core/fundamentals/minimal-apis`.Controller methods that process HTTP requests are called **action methods**. When the controller and action methods are selected, the ASP.NET Core framework creates a controller instance to serve the request.

All parameters of the controller constructors are resolved with dependency injection.

> **Note**
>
> Please refer to the *Using generic hosts* subsection of *Chapter 11, Applying a Microservice Architecture to Your Enterprise Application*, for a description of how to use dependency injection with a .NET host and to the *Dependency injection pattern* subsection of *Chapter 6, Design Patterns and .NET Implementation*, for a general discussion of dependency injection.

The following is a typical REST API controller and its controller method definitions:

```
[Route("api/[controller]")]
[ApiController]
public class ValuesController : ControllerBase
{
    // GET api/values/5
   [HttpGet("{id}")]
   public ActionResult<string> Get(int id)
  {
     ...
```

The `[ApiController]` attribute declares that the controller is a REST API controller. `[Route("api/[controller]")]` declares that the controller must be selected on paths that start with `api/<controllername>`. The controller's name is the name of the controller class without the `Controller` postfix. This is preferred over hardcoding a controller name to save time on refactoring. Thus, in the case of our example, the controller is selected for paths that start with `api/values`.

`[HttpGet("{id}")]` declares that the method must be invoked on `GET` requests of the `api/values/<id>` type, where `id` must be a number that's passed as an argument to the method invocation. This can be done with `Get(int id)`. There are also `Http<verb>` attributes for all other HTTP verbs such as `HttpPost`, `HttpPatch` and `HttpDelete`.

We may also have another method defined like so:

```
[HttpGet]
public ... Get()
```

This method is invoked on GET requests of the `api/values` type, that is, on GET requests without `id` after the controller's name.

In general, several action methods can have the same name, but only one should be compatible with each request path; otherwise, an exception is thrown. In other words, routing rules and `Http<verb>` attributes must univocally determine which controller and which of its action methods to select for each request.

By default, parameters are passed to the action methods of API controllers according to the following rules. Simple types (integers, floats, DateTimes, strings, etc.) are taken from the request path if routing rules specify them as parameters, as in the case of the previous example's `[HttpGet("{id}")]` attribute. If they are not found in the routing rules, the ASP.NET Core framework looks for query string parameters with the same name. Thus, for instance, if we replace `[HttpGet("{id}")]` with `[HttpGet]`, the ASP.NET Core framework will look for something like `api/values?id=<id type>`.

Complex types are extracted from the request body by formatters. The right formatter is chosen according to the value of the request's Content-Type header. If no Content-Type header is specified, the JSON formatter is taken. The JSON formatter tries to parse the request body as a JSON object and then tries to transform this JSON object into an instance of the .NET complex type. If either the JSON extraction or the subsequent conversion fails, an exception is thrown. As described in *Chapter 2, Non-Functional Requirements*, be careful with exceptions since their computational costs are much higher than a normal code flow.

If an exception is inevitable, consider using the recommendations for logging described in *Chapter 4, Best Practices in Coding C#*. By default, just the JSON input formatter is supported, but you can also add an XML formatter that can be used when Content-Type specifies XML content.

You can customize the source that is used to fill an action method parameter by prefixing the parameter with an adequate attribute. The following code shows some examples of this:

```
...MyActionMethod(....[FromHeader] string myHeader....)
// x is taken from a request header named myHeader
...MyActionMethod(....[FromServices] MyType x....)
// x is filled with an instance of MyType through dependency injection
```

The return type of an action method can be an `IActionResult` interface, a type that implements that interface, or a DTO directly. In turn, `IActionResult` has just the following method: `Task ExecuteResultAsync(ActionContext context);`

This method is called by the ASP.NET Core framework at the right time to create the actual response and response headers. The `ActionContext` object, when passed to the method, contains the whole context of the HTTP request, which includes a request object with all the necessary information about the original HTTP request (headers, body, and cookies), as well as a response object that collects all the pieces of the response that is being built.

You do not have to create an implementation of `IActionResult` manually since `ControllerBase` already has methods to create `IActionResult` implementations so that all the necessary HTTP responses are generated. Some of these methods are as follows:

- `OK`: This returns a 200 status code, as well as an optional result object. It is used as either return `OK()` or `OK(myResult)`.

- `BadRequest`: This returns a 400 status code, as well as an optional response object.
- `Created(string uri, object o)`: This returns a 201 status code, as well as a result object and the URI of the created resource.
- `Accepted`: This returns a 202 status result, as well as an optional result object and resource URI.
- `NoTFound`: This returns a 404 status code.
- `Unauthorized`: This returns a 401 status result, as well as an optional result object.
- `Forbid`: This returns a 403 status code, as well as an optional list of failed permissions.
- `StatusCode(int statusCode, object o = null)`: This returns a custom status code, as wellas an optional result object.

An action method can return a result object directly with something like `return myObject`. This is equivalent to returning `OK(myObject)`.

By default, result objects are serialized in JSON in the response body. However, if an XML formatter has been added to the ASP.NET Core framework processing pipeline, the way the result is serialized depends on the Accept header of the HTTP request. More specifically, if the client explicitly requires XML format with the Accept header, the object will be serialized in XML; otherwise, it will be serialized in JSON.

Complex objects that are passed as input to action methods can be validated with validation attributesas follows:

```
public record MyType
{
[Required]
public string Name{get; set;}
...
[MaxLength(64)]
public string Description{get; set;}
}
```

If the controller has been decorated with the [ApiController] attribute and if validation fails, the ASP.NET Core framework automatically creates a `BadRequest` response containing a dictionary with all the validation errors detected, without executing the action method. Therefore, you do not need to add further code to handle validation errors.

Action methods can also be declared as async methods, as follows:

```
public async Task<IActionResult>MyMethod(......)
{
    await MyBusinessObject.MyBusinessMethod();
...
}
public async Task<ActionResult<MyType>>MyMethod(......)
```

```
{
...
```

Practical examples of controllers/action methods will be shown in Use case – *Exposing WWTravelClub packages using Web APIs*, presented in *Chapter 22, Case Study: Practical Usage of .NET Aspire*. In the next subsection, we will explain how to handle authorization and authentication with JWTs.

ASP.NET Core service authorization

ASP.NET Core authorization is based on claims contained in an authorization token that can be conveyed by a Cookie, a Bearer token or any other technique. All user claims can be accessed in any action method through the `User.Claims` controller property. Since `User.Claims` is an `IEnumerable<Claim>`, it can be processed with LINQ to verify complex conditions on claims.

If authorization is based on role claims, you can simply use the `User.IsInRole` function, as shown in the following code:

```
If(User.IsInRole("Administrators") || User.IsInRole("SuperUsers"))
{
    ...
}
else return Forbid();
```

However, permissions are not usually checked from within action methods and are automatically checked by the ASP.NET Core through authorization attributes that decorate either the whole controller or a single action method. If an action method or the whole controller is decorated with `[Authorize]`, then access to the action method is possible only if the request has a valid authentication token, which means we don't have to perform a check on the token claims. It is also possible to check whether the token contains a set of roles using the following code:

```
[Authorize(Roles = "Administrators,SuperUsers")]
```

More complex conditions on claims require that authorization policies be defined while building the application in `Program.cs`, as shown in the following code:

```
var builder = WebApplication.CreateBuilder(args);
// Add services to the container.
builder.Services.AddControllers();
...
builder.Services.AddAuthorizationBuilder()
  .AddPolicy("CanDrive", policy =>
    policy.RequireAssertion(context =>
    context.User.HasClaim(c => c.Type == "HasDrivingLicense")));
```

After that, you can decorate the action methods or controllers with `[Authorize(Policy = " CanDrive ")]`.

Before using authorization, you must configure it in `Program.cs`. First, you must add the middleware that processes authentication tokens in ASP.NET Core, as shown here:

```
var app = builder.Build();
  ...
app.UseAuthorization();
app.MapControllers();
app.Run();
```

Then, you must configure the authentication services. There, you define the authentication options that will be injected through dependency injection into the authentication middleware:

```
var builder = WebApplication.CreateBuilder(args);
// Add services to the container.
builder.Services.AddControllers();
...
builder.Services.AddAuthentication(
  JwtBearerDefaults.AuthenticationScheme)
    .AddJwtBearer(options => {
      options.TokenValidationParameters =
       new TokenValidationParameters
        {
         ValidateIssuer = true,
         ValidateAudience = true,
         ValidateLifetime = true,
         ValidateIssuerSigningKey = true,
         ValidIssuer = "My.Issuer",
         ValidAudience = "This.Website.Audience",
         IssuerSigningKey = new
         SymmetricSecurityKey(Encoding.ASCII.GetBytes("MySecret"))
       };
 });
```

The above code provides a name to the authentication scheme, that is, a default name for JWT-based authentication. Then, it specifies JWT authentication options. The `AddJwtBearer` extension method is available after we add the `Microsoft.AspNetCore.Authentication.JwtBearer` NuGet package.

Usually, we require that the authentication middleware verifies that the JWT is not expired (`ValidateLifetime = true`), that it has the right issuer and audience (see *Chapter 20, Securing Data and Applications*), and that its signature is valid.

The preceding example uses a symmetric signing key generated from a string. This means that the same key is used to sign and verify the signature. This is an acceptable choice if JWTs are created by the same website that uses them, but it is not an acceptable choice if there is a unique JWT issuer that controls access to several web API sites.

More details on JWT generation and handling will be given in *Chapter 20, Securing Data and Applications.*

In the next subsection, we will learn how to empower our web API with an OpenAPI documentation endpoint so that proxy classes for communicating with our services can be generated automatically.

ASP.NET Core support for OpenAPI

OpenApi support is quite easy to add, it is enough to add a reference to the `Microsoft.AspNetCore.OpenApi` NuGet package and then adding the `buider.Services.AddOpenApi()` and `app.MapOpenApi()` calls in `Programs.cs` as shown below:

```
var builder = WebApplication.CreateBuilder(args);
builder.Services.AddControllers();
builder.Services.AddOpenApi();
...
var app = builder.Build();
app.MapOpenApi();
```

With just this in place ASP.NET Core use reflection to add a documentation endpoint at `"/openapi/v1.json"`.

When you create a new ASP.NET Core WEB API project you can require the addition of OpenAPI support by simply checking a checkbox, so you don't need to manually add NuGet packages and the code shown above.

As a default a 3.1 OpenApi document is generated, but you can change this version as you can change also the `v1` document name by passing an option object to `AddOpenApi` as shown below:

```
builder.Services.AddOpenApi(
    "myapyv1", o =>
{
    o.OpenApiVersion = OpenApiSpecVersion.OpenApi3_0;
    o.ShouldInclude = (x) => x.GroupName == "Version1";
});
```

`ShouldInclude` specifies which action methods to include in the document. It is useful to generate several documents based, for instance, on version. It is called for each action method and is passed very detailed information on each action method you can use to decide if to include the action method or not in the document. In our example we based our decision on the action method `GroupName`. controllers and action methods can be assigned to groups by decorating them with the `[EndpointGroupName("mygroup")]` attribute.

We can specify several endpoints, for instance, one for each API version, with the help of `ShouldInclude` and by adding several `AddOpenApi` calls with different options, as shown below:

```
builder.Services.AddOpenApi(
    "v1", o =>
{
    o.ShouldInclude = (x) => x.GroupName == "Version1";
});
builder.Services.AddOpenApi(
    "v2", o =>
{
    o.ShouldInclude = (x) => x.GroupName == "Version2";
});
```

Authorization may be added to the document endpoints as shown below:

```
app.MapOpenApi()
    .RequireAuthorization("MyAuthorizationrPolicy");
```

Where `RequireAuthorization` is passed an authorization policy name.

The document is recomputed at each request. Therefore, if the documentation endpoint must be deployed in production the document must be cached using caching features available in ASP.NET Core:

```
var builder = WebApplication.CreateBuilder();
builder.Services.AddOutputCache(options =>
{
    options.AddBasePolicy(policy => policy.Expire(TimeSpan.FromMinutes(30)));
});
….
app.UseOutputCache();

if (app.Environment.IsDevelopment())
{
    app.MapOpenApi();
}
else
{
   app.MapOpenApi()
        .CacheOutput();
}
```

The API documentation can be enriched with the help of attributes:

- `[EndpointName]`, `[EndpointSummary]`, and `[EndpointDescription]` can be applied to each action method to provide respectively an endpoint unique name, and endpoint summary and an endpoint description. If no unique name is provided a unique name is generated automatically.
- Possible also adding tags to each endpoint by applying the `TagsAttribute` to each action method as shown below:

```
[Tags(["tag1", "tag2"])]
```

- Possible also providing a description to object properties and action method parameter with `[Description("…")]`.
- Possible also to specify the features of all possible action method responses with the `ProducesResponseType<T>`, (used when an object of type `T` is returned) and `ProducesResponseType` (used when no object is returned) attribues:

```
[ProducesResponseType<Package>(StatusCodes.Status200OK,
    "application/json", Description = "Returns the requested Package.")]
[ProducesResponseType(StatusCodes.Status404NotFound,
    Description = "Requested Package not found.")]
```

In the next subsection, you will learn how to invoke a REST API from another REST API or from a .NET client.

.NET HTTP clients

The `HttpClient` class in the `System.Net.Http` namespace and is implemented in the `System.Net.Http` NuGet package. While it could be used directly whenever we need to interact with a REST service, there are some problems in creating and releasing `HttpClient` instances repeatedly, as follows:

- Their creation is expensive.
- When an `HttpClient` is released, for instance, in a using statement, the underlying connection is not closed immediately but at the first garbage collection session. Therefore, repeated creations and release operations quickly exhaust the maximum number of connections the operating system can handle.
- Each time we create an instance we must configure it to add credentials to hit the right domain, and so on

Therefore, either a single `HttpClient` instance is reused, such as a Singleton, or `HttpClient` instances are somehow pooled. The `HttpClientFactory` class was introduced to pool HTTP clients. More specifically, whenever a new `HttpClient` instance is required from an `HttpClientFactory` object, a new `HttpClient` is created. However, the underlying

`HttpClientMessageHandler` instances, which are expensive to create, are pooled until their maximum lifetime expires.

`HttpClientMessageHandler` instances must have a finite duration since they cache DNS resolution information that may change over time. The default lifetime of `HttpClientMessageHandler` is 2 minutes, but it can be redefined by the developer. Using `HttpClientFactory` allows us to automatically pipeline all the HTTP operations with other operations. For instance, we can add a Polly retry strategy to handle all the failures of all our HTTP operations automatically. For an introduction to Polly, please refer to the *Resilient task execution* subsection of *Chapter 11, Applying a Microservice Architecture to Your Enterprise Application.*

The simplest way to exploit the advantages offered by the `HttpClientFactory` class is to add the `Microsoft.Extensions.Http` NuGet package and then follow these steps:

- Define a proxy class, say, `MyProxy`, to interact with the desired REST service.
- Let `MyProxy` accept an `HttpClient` instance in its constructor.
- Use the `HttpClient` that was injected into the constructor to implement all the necessary operations.
- Declare your proxy in the services configuration method of your host, which, in the case of an ASP.NET Core application, is in the `Program.cs` class. In the simplest case, the declaration is something similar to `builder.Services.AddHttpClient<MyProxy>(myHttpClient => {…})`.

This will automatically add `MyProxy` to the services that are available for dependency injection, so you can easily inject it, for instance, in your controller's constructors. Moreover, each time an instance of `MyProxy` is created, an `HttpClient` is returned by an `HttpClientFactory` and is automatically injected into its constructor. The client is configured with the action passed as argument to the `AddHttpClient` call.

In the constructors of the classes that need to interact with a REST service, we may also need an interface instead of a specific proxy implementation with a declaration of the type:

```
builder.Services.AddHttpClient<IMyProxy, MyProxy>( myHttpClient => {
  myHttpClient.BaseAddess=new Uri("https://www.myapi.com");
  …
});
```

Thanks to the action passed as `AddHttpClient` argument each client that is passed to the proxy can be preconfigured with the server base address, and other server-specific options. Once the base address has been defined, each HTTP request needs to specify just the relative path of the service method to call. The following code shows how to perform a POST to a service. This requires an extra package, `System.Net.Http.Json`, because of the usage of `PostAsJsonAsync`. Here, we are stating that the `HttpClient` that was injected into the proxy constructor has been stored in the `webClient` private field:

```
//Add a bearer token to authenticate the call
webClient.DefaultRequestHeaders.Add("Authorization",
   "Bearer " + token);
...
//Call service method with a POST verb and get response
var response = await webClient.PostAsJsonAsync<MyPostModel>("my/method/relative/path",
```

```
new MyPostModel
{
//fill model here
...
});
//extract response status code
var status = response.StatusCode;
...
//extract body content from response
string stringResult = await response.Content.ReadAsStringAsync();
```

Once received the response, first, you need to verify the status code to decide what to do next. Then, if there are not errors that invalidate the response content, you can parse the JSON string contained in the response body to get a .NET instance of a type that, in general, depends on the status code. The code to perform the parsing is based on the `System.Text.Json` NuGet package's `JsonSerializer` class and is as follows:

```
var result =
    JsonSerializer.Deserialize<MyResultClass>(stringResult);
```

Performing a GET request is similar, but instead of calling `PostAsJsonAsync`, you need to call `GetAsync`, as shown here. The use of other HTTP verbs is completely analogous:

```
var response =
   await webClient.GetAsync("my/getmethod/relative/path");
```

There are also untyped overloads of `AddHttpClient` that can be used to get named `HttpClient` instances:

```
builder.Services.AddHttpClient("myHttpClientName", myHttpClient => {
   myHttpClient.BaseAddess=new Uri("https://www.myapi.com");
   …
});
```

You can have several named `HttpClient` prototypes defined this way. In order to get a specific named `HttpClient` you first require an `IHttpClientFactory` instance and then require it the `HttpClient` with the desired name:

```
…(IHttpClientFactory httpClientFactory, …)
{
    …
    myClient =  httpClientFactory.CreateClient("myHttpClientName");
}
```

All AddHttpClient overloads return an IHttpClientBuilder instance that can be used to continue the HttpClient configuration. More specifically, we may use this instance to add service discovery and preconfigured Polly-based resiliency policies:

```
var httpBuilder= builder.Services.AddHttpClient(.....);
httpBuilder.AddStandardResilienceHandler(o => {
  ...
  ...
  o.Retry =...
  ...
});
httpBuilder.AddServiceDiscovery();
```

If no option is passed to AddStandardResilienceHandler default resiliency policies are applied. The usage of AddStandardResilienceHandler requires a reference to the Microsoft.Extensions.Http.Resilience NuGet package, while the usage of AddServiceDiscovery requires a reference to the Microsoft.Extensions.ServiceDiscovery NuGet package, plus the addition of service discovery to the dependency injection engine:

```
builder.Services.AddServiceDiscovery();
```

In a few words service discovery enables the replacement of HttpClient base addresses with symbolic environment-independent strings. The actual addresses are then obtained from the application configuration. Service discovery will be discussed in detail in *Chapter 19, Orchestrators and .NET Aspire*.

One can use a specific named HttpClient also in gRPC-based communication. The HttpClient must be passed in an option object when creating the gRPC channel, as shown in the example below:

```
using var channel = GrpcChannel.ForAddress("http://localhost:5071",
    new GrpcChannelOptions
   {
        HttpClient=myNamedHttpClient
   });
```

Finally, we can use an IHttpClientBuilder to define default settings for all named and typed clients with the ConfigureHttpClientDefaults extension method as shown in the example below:

```
builder.Services.ConfigureHttpClientDefaults(http =>
{
   http.AddStandardResilienceHandler(o => {
  ...
  ...
  o.Retry =...
```

```
    ...
  });

});
```

Where `AddStandardResilienceHandler()` applies a default resilience policy that can be configured with the option object o to all named and typed clients.

Summing up, in the previous subsection you learned how to define an ASP.NET Core REST service, while in this this section we you learned how to use and configure in .NET HTTP clients for communicating with REST services.

Summary

In this chapter, we introduced SOA, its design principles, and its constraints. Among them, interoperability is worth remembering.

Then, we focused on well-established standards for business applications that achieve the interoperability that is needed for publicly exposed services. Therefore, SOAP and REST services were discussed in detail, along with the transition from SOAP services to REST services that has taken place in most application areas in the last few years. Then, REST service principles, authentication/authorization, and documentation were described in greater detail.

Finally, we looked at the tools that are available in .NET 10 that we can use to implement and interact with services. We looked at a variety of frameworks for intra-cluster communication, such as .NET remoting and gRPC, and tools for SOAP- and REST-based public services.

Here, we mainly focused on REST services. Their ASP.NET Core implementations were described in detail, along with the techniques we can use to authenticate/authorize them and their documentation.

We also focused on how to implement efficient .NET proxies so that we can interact with REST services. In the next chapter, we will learn how to use .NET 10 to implement microservices with ASP.NET Core.

Questions

1. Can services use cookie-based sessions?
2. Is it good practice to implement a service with a custom communication protocol? Why or why not?
3. Can a POST request to a REST service cause a deletion?
4. By default, where are the complex type parameters of a REST service's action methods taken from?
5. How is a controller declared as a REST service?
6. How are ASP.NET Core REST service routing rules declared?
7. How should a proxy be declared so that we can take advantage of the .NET `HttpClientFactory` class features?

Further reading

Here, you have some links you may consider using to gather more information about this chapter.

- This chapter mainly focused on the more commonly used REST service. If you are interested in SOAP services, a good place to start is the Wikipedia page regarding SOAP specifications: `https://en.wikipedia.org/wiki/List_of_web_service_specifications`. On the other hand, if you are interested in the Microsoft .NET WCF technology for implementing SOAP services, you can refer to WCF's official documentation here: `https://docs.microsoft.com/en-us/dotnet/framework/wcf/`.
- This chapter mentioned the AMQP protocol as an option for intra-cluster communication without describing it. Detailed information on this protocol is available on AMQP's official site: `https://www.amqp.org/`.
- More details on ASP.NET Core services are available in the official documentation: `https://docs.microsoft.com/en-US/aspnet/core/web-api/`. More information on the .NET HTTP client is available here: `https://docs.microsoft.com/en-US/aspnet/core/fundamentals/http-requests`.
- Minimal APIs are described at `https://docs.microsoft.com/en-us/aspnet/core/fundamentals/minimal-apis`.
- More information on JWT authentication is available here: `https://jwt.io/`. If you would like to generate JWTs with IdentityServer, you may refer to its official documentation page: `https://docs.duendesoftware.com/identityserver/`.
- More information on OpenAPI is available at `https://swagger.io/docs/specification/about/`.

16

Presenting ASP.NET Core

This chapter introduces ASP.NET Core from the perspective of server-rendered web applications. It first explains the hosting, middleware, configuration, and pipeline concepts that MVC depends on, and then shows how controllers, ViewModels, Razor views, tag helpers, layouts, partial views, and view components work together to create maintainable presentation layers.

In this chapter, you will learn how to implement a Web application and a Web-based presentation layer. More specifically, you will learn ASP.NET Core and how to implement a web application presentation layer based on ASP.NET Core MVC.

ASP.NET Core is a .NET framework for building web applications. ASP.NET Core Web API has been partially described in previous chapters, so this chapter focuses on the broader ASP.NET Core ecosystem, with particular emphasis on ASP.NET Core MVC. More specifically, this chapter will cover the following topics:

- Understanding the presentation layers of web applications
- Understanding the basics of ASP.NET Core
- Understanding how ASP.NET Core MVC creates the response HTML
- Understanding the connection between ASP.NET Core MVC and design principles

We will review and give further details on the structure of the ASP.NET Core framework, which, in part, is discussed in *Chapter 10, Deciding on the Best Cloud-Based Solution*, and *Chapter 15, Applying Service-Oriented Architectures with .NET*. Here, the focus is on how to implement web-based presentation layers based on the so-called **Model View Controller** (MVC) architectural pattern.

We will also understand how server-side HTML is created with ASP.NET Core **MVC Razor** template language.

This chapter introduces each concept with focused code examples and shows how these concepts prepare the ground for a complete ASP.NET Core MVC frontend. *Chapter 17, Implementing Frontend Microservices with ASP.NET Core*, then brings these ideas together in the structure of a complete frontend microservice. For readers who want to see the concepts integrated into a production application, the *A Frontend Microservice* section of *Chapter 22, Case Study: Practical Usage of .NET Aspire*, demonstrates real-world usage patterns.

Technical requirements

This chapter requires the free Visual Studio 2026 Community Edition or better with all database tools installed.

Understanding the presentation layers of web applications

This chapter discusses the architecture for implementing the presentation layers of web-based applications based on the ASP.NET Core framework. The presentation layers of web applications are based on three techniques:

- ***Mobile or desktop native applications that exchange data with servers through REST or SOAP services:*** we will discuss desktop applications in *Chapter 18, Client Frameworks: Blazor*.
- ***Single-Page Applications (SPAs):*** These are HTML-based applications whose dynamic HTML is created on the client either in JavaScript or with the help of WebAssembly (a kind of cross-browser assembly that can be used as a high-performance alternative to JavaScript). Like native applications, **Single-Page Applications (SPAs)**exchange data with the server through HTTP-based APIs, but they have the advantage of being independent of the device and its operating system since they run in a browser. *Chapter 18, Client Frameworks: Blazor,* describes the Blazor SPA framework, which is based on WebAssembly, since it is based on a .NET runtime compiled in WebAssembly.
- ***HTML pages created by the server whose content depends on the data to be shown to the user:*** The ASP.NET Core MVC framework, which will be discussed in this chapter, is a framework for creating such dynamic HTML pages.

It is worth noting that each approach has its pros and cons. The table below presents important information for you, as a software architect, to decide when to choose each of them.

Approach	Best choice when	Main strengths	Main trade-offs
Native mobile or desktop application	The solution requires deep device or operating system integration, offline support, or platform-specific user experience.	High performance, rich access to device capabilities, strong platform integration.	Higher development and maintenance effort across platforms, installation required.
Single-Page Application (SPA)	The application requires a highly interactive browser-based user interface with rich client-side behavior.	Responsive user experience, cross-platform access through the browser, no installation required.	Greater client-side complexity, more JavaScript / Web Assembly concerns, SEO and initial load may require extra attention.

Server-rendered HTML pages (ASP.NET Core MVC)	The application is mainly form-based, content-driven, or benefits from simpler architecture and server-side rendering.	Simpler delivery model, strong server control, good fit for many business applications, easier SEO.	Less dynamic user experience than a SPA, more page reloads, less client-side interactivity.

Table 16.1: Presentation layers techniques

Now that you have understood the advantages and disadvantages of each technique, the remainder of this chapter focuses on the server-rendered HTML approach and, more specifically, on ASP.NET Core MVC, because it provides the controller, view, and routing mechanisms needed to implement this type of presentation layer.

Understanding the basics of ASP.NET Core

ASP.NET Core is based on the concept of the generic host, as explained in the *Using generic hosts* subsection of *Chapter 11, Applying a Microservice Architecture to Your Enterprise Application*. The generic host provides the shared infrastructure for concerns such as configuration, dependency injection, logging, and lifetime management. The basic architecture of ASP.NET Core was outlined in the subsection *A short introduction to ASP.NET Core* at *Chapter 15, Applying Service-Oriented Architectures with .NET*.

It is worth remembering that the host configuration consists mainly of adding services to the Dependency Injection (DI) application through the Services property of a host builder instance whose type implements the `IServiceCollection` interface. The code below represents the main execution of an ASP.NET Core app:

```
var builder = WebApplication.CreateBuilder(args);

// Add services to the container.
builder.Services.AddRazorPages();

var app = builder.Build();

// Configure the HTTP request pipeline.
if (!app.Environment.IsDevelopment())
{
    app.UseExceptionHandler("/Error");
    // The default HSTS value is 30 days. You may want to change this for production
scenarios, see https://aka.ms/aspnetcore-hsts.
    app.UseHsts();
}

app.UseHttpsRedirection();

app.UseRouting();

app.UseAuthorization();
```

```
app.MapStaticAssets();
app.MapRazorPages()
   .WithStaticAssets();

app.Run();
```

The `IServiceCollection` interface implemented by `builder.Services` defines all services that can be injected into object constructors through DI. DI was described in detail in the subsection *Using generic hosts* in *Chapter 11, Applying a Microservice Architecture to Your Enterprise Application*. Services are also explained in this subsection and can be defined either by calling the various overloads of `AddTransient`, and `AddSingleton` directly in `Program.cs`, or by grouping these calls in `IServiceCollection` extension methods that are then called in `Program.cs`.

Here, it is worth pointing out that together with singleton and transient services ASP.NET Core supports also another kind of service lifetime: session lifetime, that is the lifetime of a single web request served by the ASP.NET Core application. Session-scoped services are declared with `AddScoped` overloads that are completely analogous to the overloads of `AddTransient`, and `AddSingleton`.

Session-scoped services are useful for storing data that is specific for a single request that must be used throughout the whole request by several application components. Typical .NET session-scoped services are Entity Framework Core `DBContexts`. In fact, all operations performed on the various aggregates involved in the request must use the same request-specific `DBContext`, so that all changes can be saved to the database in a single transaction with a unique `SaveChanges` operation.

Practical applications of session-scoped `DBContexts` and other services are described in more details in *Chapter 17, Implementing Frontend Microservices with ASP.NET Core.*

Usually, all applications define most of the application configuration through the host builder so that, after the host is built with `var app = builder.Build()`, the application can be launched with `app.Run()` or `await app.RunAsync()`.

ASP.NET Core host configuration, however, does not end when the host is built. After `builder.Build()`, the application still needs to define the *HTTP request processing pipeline*, which determines how each incoming request is handled and how the final response is produced. The key takeaway is that the host prepares the application services, while the pipeline defines the behavior of the web application at runtime.

ASP.NET Core middleware

ASP.NET Core middleware is important in this chapter mainly because it explains how requests reach MVC and how MVC participates in the overall request-processing flow. Therefore, the following discussion focuses on the middleware concepts that directly affect routing, authorization, static files, endpoint execution, and controller invocation.

To understand how ASP.NET Core applications are hosted, it is important to look at the web server responsible for receiving HTTP requests. ASP.NET Core includes an internal web server called **Kestrel**, which provides core web server functionality. So, in simple applications such as IOT applications, or worker microservices, we can avoid the overhead of a full-optional complex webserver like IIS, Apache, or NGINX.

In case ASP.Net Core is used to implement the application layer of a frontend microservice/application or a classic website, Kestrel can be interfaced with all major Webservers that proxy their request to Kestrel.

Since version 8, Kestrel supports all protocols up to and including version Http /3.

In turn, Kestrel passes all requests to a set of configurable modules you can assemble according to your needs. Each module takes care of the functionality that you may or may not need. Examples of such functionalities include authorization, authentication, static file processing, protocol negotiation, and CORS handling. Since most of the modules apply transformations to the incoming request and to the final response, these modules are usually referred to as **middleware**.

You can put together all the *middleware* modules you need by inserting them into a common processing framework called the **ASP.NET Core pipeline**.

More specifically, ASP.NET Core requests are processed by pushing a context object through a pipeline of ASP.NET Core modules, as shown in the following diagram:

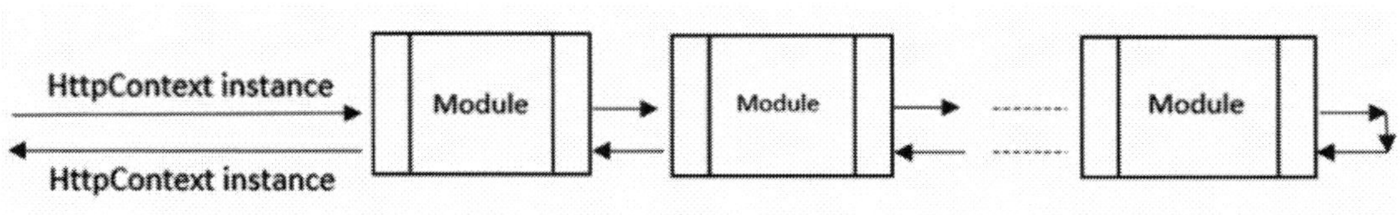

Figure 16.1: ASP.NET Core pipeline

The object that is inserted into the pipeline is an `HttpContext` instance that contains the data of the incoming request. More specifically, the Request property of `HttpContext` contains an `HttpRequest` object whose properties represent the incoming request in a structured way. There are properties for headers, cookies, the request path, parameters, form fields, and the request body.

The various modules can contribute to the construction of the final response that is written in an `HttpResponse` object contained in the Response property of the `HttpContext` instance. The `HttpResponse` class is like the `HttpRequest` class, but its properties refer to the response being built.

Some modules can build an intermediate data structure that is then used by other modules in the pipeline. In general, such intermediary data can be stored in custom entries of `IDictionary<object, object>`, which is contained in the Items property of the `HttpContext` object. However, there is a predefined property, `User`, that contains information about the currently logged-in user. The logged-in user is not computed automatically, so it must be computed by an authentication module. The *ASP.NET Core service authorization* subsection of *Chapter 15, Applying Service-Oriented Architectures with .NET*, explained how to add the standard module that performs JWT-based authentication to the ASP.NET Core pipeline.

`HttpContext` also has a Connection property that contains information on the underlying connection established with the client, as well as a `WebSockets` property that contains information on possible WebSocket-based connections established with the clients.

HttpContext also has a Features property that contains IDictionary<Type, object>, which specifies the features supported by the web server that hosts the web application and by the pipeline. Features can be set using the .Set<TFeature>(TFeature o) method and retrieved using the .Get<TFeature>() method.

Web server features are automatically added by the framework, while all other features are added by pipeline modules when they process HttpContext.

HttpContext also gives us access to the DI engine through its RequestServices property. You can get an instance of a type managed by the dependency engine by calling the .RequestServices.GetService(Type t) method or, even better, the .GetRequiredService<TService>() extension method that is built on top of it. However, as we will see in the remainder of this chapter, all types managed by the DI engine are usually automatically injected into constructors, so these methods are only used when we're building custom *middleware* or other customizations of the ASP.NET Core engine.

The HttpContext instance that is created for processing a web request is not only available to modules, but also to the application code through DI. It is enough to insert an IHttpContextAccessor parameter into the constructor of a class that is automatically dependency injected and then access its HttpContext property. All controllers that inherit from Controller or ControllerBase (see later in this section) expose an HttpContext property that contains the request HttpContext.

A middleware module is any class with the following structure:

```
public class CoreMiddleware
{
    private readonly RequestDelegate _next;
    public CoreMiddleware(RequestDelegate next, ILoggerFactory
    loggerFactory)
    {
        ...
        _next = next;
        ...
    }
    public async Task InvokeAsync(HttpContext context)
    {
        /*
            Insert here the module specific code that processes the
            HttpContext instance before it is passed to the next
            module.

        */

        await _next.Invoke(context);
        /*
            Insert here other module specific code that processes the
            HttpContext instance, after all modules that follow this
```

```
            module finished their processing.
        */
    }
}
```

It is also possible to pass InvokeAsync directly as a lambda to app.Use, as shown here:

```
app.Use(async (context, next) =>
{
    ...
    await next(context);
});
```

In general, each middleware processes the HttpContext instance that was passed by the previous module in the pipeline and then calls await _next.Invoke(context) to invoke the modules in the remainder of the pipeline. When the other modules have finished their processing and the response for the client has been prepared, each module can perform further post-processing of the response in the code that follows the _next.Invoke(context) call.

Modules are registered in the ASP.NET Core pipeline by calling the UseMiddleware<T> method of the built host, as shown here:

```
    var app = builder.Build();
    ...
    app.UseMiddleware<MyCustomModule>
    ...
    app.Run();
```

Middleware modules are inserted into the pipeline in the same order when UseMiddleware is called. Since each functionality that's added to an application might require several modules and might require operations other than adding modules, you usually define an IApplicationBuilder extension such as UseMyFunctionality, as shown in the following code:

```
public static class MyMiddlewareExtensions
{
    public static IApplicationBuilder UseMyFunctionality(this
    IApplicationBuilder builder,...)
    {
        //other code
        ...
        builder.UseMiddleware<MyModule1>();
        builder.UseMiddleware<MyModule2>();
        ...
        //Other code
```

```
            ...
            return builder;
        }
    }
```

After that, the whole functionality can be added to the application by calling `app.UseMyFunctionality(...)`. In modern ASP.NET Core applications, MVC endpoint execution is typically configured through endpoint mapping calls such as `app.MapControllerRoute(...)` or `app.MapControllers(...)`, depending on the routing style used by the application.

Often, functionalities that are added to each `app.Use...` require that some .NET types are added to the application DI engine. In these cases, we also define an `IServiceCollection` extension named `AddMyFunctionality`, which must be called by `builder.Services` in `Program.cs`.

For instance, ASP.NET Core MVC requires a call such as the following:

```
builder.Services.AddControllersWithViews(o =>
{
    //set here MVC options by modifying the o option parameter
}
```

If you don't need to change the default MVC options, you can simply call `builder.Services.AddControllersWithViews()`.

The next subsection describes another important feature of the ASP.NET Core framework, namely, how to handle application configuration data.

Loading configuration data and using it with the options framework

Before examining MVC itself, we need to understand how ASP.NET Core loads and exposes configuration data, because controllers, services, and infrastructure components often depend on settings that change across environments.

We briefly look at configuration, because presentation-layer behavior often depends on environment-specific settings such as connection strings, logging levels, URLs, and external service parameters. In practice, configuration in ASP.NET Core can be understood in two steps: first, the application loads settings from one or more configuration providers; then, these settings are accessed directly or mapped to strongly typed .NET objects through the options framework.

Default configuration files

In the default .NET template where an ASP.NET Core application starts, it reads configuration information (such as a database connection string) from the `appsettings.json` and `appsettings.[EnvironmentName].json` files, where `EnvironmentName` is a string value that depends on where the application is deployed.

Typical values for `EnvironmentName` string are as follows. To understand better the multi-environment concept, please refer to *Chapter 8, Understanding DevSecOps Principles and CI/CD.*

- `Development` is used during development
- `Staging` is used when the application is tested in staging
- `Production` is used for production deployment

The two JSON trees that were extracted from the `appsettings.json` and `appsettings.[EnvironmentName].json` files are merged into a unique tree, where the values contained in `[EnvironmentName].json` override the values contained in the corresponding paths of `appsettings.json`. This way, the application can be run with different configurations in different deployment environments. You may use a different database connection string, and hence, a different database instance in each different environment. You can check an example of how app settings files merge in *Figure 16.2*.

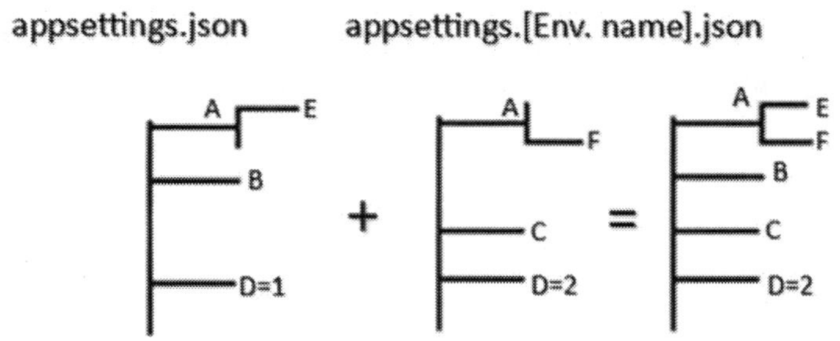

Figure 16.2: Configuration files merging

The previous example showed how environment-specific JSON files override shared configuration values. ASP.NET Core can also load configuration from other sources, which is useful when values must come from deployment platforms, command-line arguments, or runtime systems instead of files.

Other configuration sources

Configuration information can also be passed on from other sources. Given a lack of space, we list here all the other possibilities without discussing them:

- XML files
- .ini files
- Operating system environment variables. The variable name is the name of the setting prefixed by the `ASPNETCORE_` string, while the variable value is the setting value.
- Command-line arguments of a dotnet command that invokes the application.
- An in-memory collection of key-value pairs

The JSON format can be considered the most practical and readable option, but JSON, XML, and INI files are substantially equivalent, and choosing among them is just a matter of preferences in this scenario.

In memory collections of key-value pairs offer the possibility of taking data from a database, so they are a useful option for those parameters that need to be changed by an administrator while the application is running.

Finally, command lines arguments and environment variable are a good options when the application can't easily access disk storage, as for instance in the case of Deployments running in a Kubernetes cluster. In fact, environment variables can be passed as parameters in the Kubernetes .YAML files. They are also an acceptable choice for passing sensitive data that it is not adequate to store in files in plain format.

From version 8 onwards, ASP.NET Core allows Kestrel HTTP and HTTPS listening ports as configuration variables. More specifically, HTTP_PORTS contains the semicolon-separated list of all Kestrel Http listening ports whose defaults are the usual Http and Https ports, that is 80, and 443.

After seeing where configuration values can come from, we now need to understand how ASP.NET Core chooses the current environment, because that value determines which environment-specific configuration file is loaded and which runtime behavior is applied.

Setting the environment name

The `[EnvironmentName]` string itself is taken from the `ENVIRONMENT` configuration setting. Clearly, since it is needed to decide which configuration files to use, it cannot be contained in a configuration file, so it must be taken from the `ASPNETCORE_ENVIRONMENT` operating system environment variable, or from the arguments of the dotnet command used to launch the application.

> **Note**
>
> When the application is deployed to IIS instead of being launched as a standalone program, `ASPNETCORE_ENVIRONMENT` can't be passed on the dotnet command line.

In this case, it can be set in the IIS application settings. This can be done after the applications has been deployed by clicking on the Configuration Editor and then selecting the `system.webServer/aspNetCore` section. In the window that opens, then select `environmentVariables`, and there add the `ASPNETCORE_ENVIRONMENT` variable with its value. As you can see in *Figure 16.3*, the current value of `ASPNETCORE_ENVIRONMENT` in IIS application settings is `Staging`.

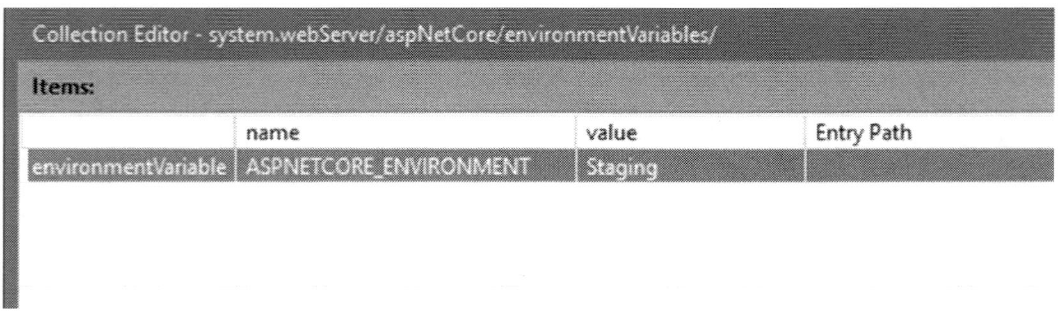

Figure 16.3: Changing ASPNETCORE_ENVIRONMENT in IIS

However, when the application is modified and deployed again the setting is reset to its default value which is `Production` and must be set again.

Using publish profiles and project files

A better choice is to modify the *publish profile* in Visual Studio as follows

- During Visual Studio deployment, *Visual Studio's Publish wizard* creates an XML publish profile. Once the preferred deployment type (Azure, Web Deploy, folder, and so on) has been chosen, and before publishing, you can edit the publish settings by choosing **Edit** from the **More actions** dropdown in the window that appears.
- Once you have your publish file properly set, in *Visual Studio Solution Explorer*, open the profile that you just prepared with Visual Studio wizard. Profiles are saved in the `Properties/PublishProfiles/<profile name>.pubxml` path of the project folder.
- Then, edit the profile with a text editor and add an XML property such as `<EnvironmentName>Staging</EnvironmentName>`. Since all the already defined publish profiles can be selected during the application's publication, you may define a different publish profile for each of your environments and then you may select the one you need during each publication.

The value you must set `ASPNETCORE_ENVIRONMENT` to during deployment can also be specified in the Visual Studio ASP.NET Core project file (.csproj) of your application by adding the following code:

```
<PropertyGroup>
    <EnvironmentName>Staging</EnvironmentName>
</PropertyGroup>
```

This is the simplest way to do `ASPNETCORE_ENVIRONMENT`, but not the more modular, since we are forced to change the application code before publishing to a different environment.

Specifying the environment either in the publish profile or in the project file works only for deployment types based on direct communication between Visual Studio and the web server, because in other deployment types Visual Studio cannot inform the web server on how to set `ASPNETCORE_ENVIRONMENT` or on how to pass the environment when the application is launched. Now, the techniques described work just for Web Deploy or when publishing on Azure.

During development in Visual Studio, the value to give to `ASPNETCORE_ENVIRONMENT` when the application is run can be specified in the `Properties\launchSettings.json` file of the ASP.NET Core project. The `launchSettings.json` file contains several named groups of settings. These settings configure how to launch the web application when it is run from Visual Studio. You may choose to apply all the settings of a group by selecting the group name with the drop-down list next to Visual Studio's run button:

Figure 16.4: Choice of launch settings group

Your selection from this drop-down list will be shown in the run button, with the default selection being IIS Express.

Consider a development environment setup, as illustrated in this typical `launchSettings.json` file:

```
{
  "iisSettings": {
    "windowsAuthentication": false,
    "anonymousAuthentication": true,
    "iisExpress": {
      "applicationUrl": "http://localhost:2575",
      "sslPort": 44393
    }
  },
  "profiles": {
    "IIS Express": {
      "commandName": "IISExpress",
      "launchBrowser": true,
      "environmentVariables": {
        "ASPNETCORE_ENVIRONMENT": "Development"
      }
    },
    ...
    ...
    }
  }
}
```

Accessing the environment at runtime

The named groups of settings are under the profile's properties. There, you may choose where to host the application (***IISExpress***), where to launch the browser, and the values of some environment variables.

The current environment that's been loaded from the `ASPNETCORE_ENVIRONMENT` operating system environment variable is available in the `app.Environment` property during the ASP.NET Core pipeline definition.

`app.Environment.IsEnvironment(string environmentName)` checks whether the current value of `ASPNETCORE_ENVIRONMENT` is `environmentName`. There are also specific shortcuts for testing development (`.IsDevelopment()`), production (`.IsProduction()`), and staging (`.IsStaging()`). `app.Environment` also contains the current root directory of the ASP.NET Core application (`.WebRootPath`) and the directory reserved for the static files (`.ContentRootPath`) that are served as-is by the web server (CSS, JavaScript, images, and so on).

Both `launchSettings.json` and all publish profiles can be accessed as children of the *Properties* node in Visual Studio Explorer, as shown in the following screenshot:

Figure 16.5: Launch settings file

Mapping configuration to .NET objects

As we can check, understanding how to map the merged configuration settings to .NET objects is key for effective data management in ASP.NET Core applications.

Once `appsettings.json` and `appsettings.[EnvironmentName].json` have been loaded, the configuration tree resulting from their merge can be mapped to the properties of .NET objects. For example, let's suppose we have an Email section of the `appsettings` file that contains all the information needed to connect to an email server, as shown here:

```
{
    "ConnectionStrings": {
        "DefaultConnection": "...."
    },
    "Logging": {
        "LogLevel": {
            "Default": "Warning"
        }
    },
    "Email": {
        "FromName": "MyName",
        "FromAddress": "info@MyDomain.com",
        "LocalDomain": "smtps.MyDomain.com",
        "MailServerAddress": "smtps.MyDomain.com",
        "MailServerPort": "465",
        "UserId": "info@MyDomain.com",
        "UserPassword": "mypassword"
    }
```

Then, the whole `Email` section can be mapped to an instance of the following class:

```
    public class EmailConfig
    {
        public String FromName { get; set; }
        public String FromAddress { get; set; }
        public String LocalDomain { get; set; }
        public String MailServerAddress { get; set; }
        public String MailServerPort { get; set; }
```

```
        public String UserId { get; set; }
        public String UserPassword { get; set; }
    }
```

The code that performs the mapping must be inserted in the host building stage since the `EmailConfig` instance will be available through DI. The code we need is shown here:

```
Var builder = WebApplication.CreateBuilder(args);
....
builder.Services.Configure<EmailConfig>(Configuration.GetSection("Email"));
...
```

Once we've configured the preceding settings, classes that need `EmailConfig` data must declare an `IOptions<EmailConfig>` options parameter that will be provided by the DI engine. An `EmailConfig` instance is contained in `options.Value`.

It is worth mentioning that the option classes' properties can be applied to the same validation attributes we will use for ViewModels (see the *Server-side and client-side validation* subsection).

The next subsection describes the basic ASP.NET Core pipeline modules needed by an ASP.NET Core MVC application.

Defining the ASP.NET Core pipeline

This section now narrows the pipeline discussion to the steps that matter most for ASP.NET Core MVC applications. Rather than revisiting middleware in general, it focuses on how routing, authorization, static assets, and endpoint mapping cooperate to select and execute MVC handlers.

Understanding the ASP.NET Core pipeline is key for customizing application behavior. When you create a new ASP.NET Core MVC project in Visual Studio, a standard pipeline is created in the `Program.cs` file. There, if needed, you may add further middleware or change the configuration of the existing middleware.

Middleware order is important because each component depends on work performed by the previous ones. For example, authorization can only be evaluated after routing has identified the target endpoint and authentication has populated `HttpContext.User`. A simplified request flow is as follows:

1. `UseRouting` analyzes the request URL and selects the matching endpoint.
2. `UseAuthentication` identifies the current user and populates HttpContext.User.
3. `UseAuthorization` checks whether that user is allowed to access the selected endpoint.
4. An MVC endpoint-mapping middleware executes the selected controller action.

If `UseAuthorization` is placed before `UseRouting` or `UseAuthentication`, it does not yet have the endpoint metadata or the authenticated user information it needs to evaluate access correctly.

Note

Reordering these calls may cause middleware to run without the context it requires, leading to incorrect behavior or failed authorization checks.

Each new version of .NET has a simpler initial pipeline, but in general the main concept and each command keep working.

Note

To get the best of the middleware available, please check out at `https://learn.microsoft.com/en-us/aspnet/core/fundamentals/middleware/`

The initial pipeline definition code handles errors and performs basic HTTPS configuration:

```
// Configure the HTTP request pipeline.
if (!app.Environment.IsDevelopment())
{
    app.UseExceptionHandler("/Error");
    // The default HSTS value is 30 days. You may want to change this for production
scenarios, see https://aka.ms/aspnetcore-hsts.
    app.UseHsts();
}

app.UseHttpsRedirection();
```

If the application is in a development environment, you can add the module installed by `UseDeveloperExceptionPage` adds a detailed error report to the response. This module is a valuable debugging tool.

```
// Configure the HTTP request pipeline.
if (!app.Environment.IsDevelopment())
{
    app.UseExceptionHandler("/Error");
    // The default HSTS value is 30 days. You may want to change this for production
scenarios, see https://aka.ms/aspnetcore-hsts.
    app.UseHsts();
}
```

If an error occurs when the application is not in development mode, `UseExceptionHandler` restores the request processing from the path it receives as an argument; that is, from `/Home/Error`. In other words, it simulates a new request with the `/Home/Error` path. This request is pushed into the standard MVC processing until it reaches the endpoint associated with the /Home/Error path, where the developer is expected to place the custom code that handles the error.

When the application is not in development, UseHsts adds the Strict-Transport-Security header to the response, which informs the browser that the application must only be accessed with HTTPS. After this declaration, compliant browsers should automatically convert any HTTP request of the application into an HTTPS request for the time specified in the Strict-Transport-Security header. By default, UseHsts specifies 30 days as the time in the header, but you may specify a different time and other header parameters by adding in the builder.Services a AddHsts that configures an options object:

```
builder.Services.AddHsts(options =>
{
    options.Preload = true;
    options.IncludeSubDomains = true;
    options.MaxAge = TimeSpan.FromDays(60);
});
```

UseHttpsRedirection causes an automatic redirection to an HTTPS URL when an HTTP URL is received, in a way that forces a secure connection. Once the first HTTPS secure connection is established, the Strict-Transport-Security header prevents future redirections that might be used to perform man-in-the-middle attacks.

The following code shows the remainder of the default pipeline:

```
app.UseRouting();

app.UseAuthorization();

app.MapStaticAssets();
app.MapRazorPages()
   .WithStaticAssets();
...
```

UseRouting handles the so-called ASP.NET Core endpoints. An endpoint is an abstraction of a handler that serves specific classes of URLs. These URLs are transformed into an Endpoint instance with patterns. When a pattern matches a URL, an Endpoint instance is created and filled with both the pattern's name and the data that was extracted from the URL. This is a consequence of matching URL parts with named parts of the pattern. This can be seen in the following snippet code:

```
Request path: /UnitedStates/NewYork
Pattern: Name="location", match="/{Country}/{Town}"
Endpoint: DisplayName="Location", Country="UnitedStates", Town="NewYork"
```

UseRouting adds a module that processes the request path to get the request Endpoint instance and adds it to the HttpContext.Features dictionary under the IEndpointFeature type. The actual Endpoint instance is contained in the Endpoint property of `IEndpointFeature`. Each pattern also contains the handler that should process all the requests that match the pattern. This handler is passed to Endpoint when it is created.

`UseAuthorization` enables authorization based on the Authorize attribute. Options can be configured by adding `builder.Services.AddAuthorization` to the host building stage. These options allow you to define the policies for claims-based authorization.

For more information on authorization, please refer to the *ASP.NET Core service authorization* subsection of *Chapter 15, Applying Service-Oriented Architectures with .NET.*

`UseAuthorization` must always be placed after both `UseAuthentication` and `UseRouting` because it needs both the `HttpContext.User` that is filled by `UseAuthentication` and the handler selected by `UseRouting` to verify whether a user is authorized to access the selected request handler.

It is also worth mentioning also the `.UseCors()` middleware that enables the application to handle CORS policies. We will discuss it in the *Communication with the server* section of *Chapter 18, Client Frameworks: Blazor.*

`MapStaticAssets` maps static asset endpoints for optimized static file serving. Static assets, also called static files, are files that aren't dynamically generated, such as HTML, CSS, image, and JavaScript files. On the other hand, `MapRazorPages` enables Razor processing of MVC.

Having described the basic structure of the ASP.NET Core framework, we can now move toward more MVC-specific features. The next subsection describes controllers and explains how they interact with the UI components known as Views through ViewModels.

Defining controllers and ViewModels

In ASP.NET Core MVC, the presentation layer is organized around a collaboration between controllers, ViewModels, and views. Controllers receive incoming requests, coordinate the application logic needed to answer them, and select the response to return. When the response involves rendering HTML, controllers typically pass data to the view through ViewModels, which are classes designed to carry only the data needed by the user interface. With this overall picture in mind, let's start by understanding how requests issued at specific PATHs are passed to controllers.

The calls associate URL patterns with controllers and with the methods of these controllers, where controllers are classes that inherit from the `Microsoft.AspNetCore.Mvc.Controller` class. Controllers are discovered by inspecting all the application's .dll files and are added to the DI engine. This job is performed by the call to `builder.Services.AddControllersWithViews` in the `Program.cs` file.

The pipeline module that's added by `UseEndpoints` takes the controller's name from the controller pattern variable, and the name of the controller method to invoke from the action pattern variable. Since, by convention, all controller names are expected to end with the Controller suffix, the actual controller type name is obtained from the name found in the controller variable by adding this suffix. Hence, for instance, if the name found in controller is Home, then the `UseEndpoints` module tries to get an instance of the `HomeController` type from the DI engine. All Controller public methods can be selected by the routing rules. The use of a controller public method can be prevented by decorating it with the `[NonAction]` attribute. All controller methods available to the routing rules are called action methods.

MVC controllers work like the API controllers that we described in the *Implementing REST services with ASP.NET Core* subsection of *Chapter 15, Applying Service-Oriented Architectures with .NET*. The only difference is that API controllers are expected to produce JSON or XML, while MVC controllers are expected to produce HTML. For this reason, while API controllers inherit from the `ControllerBase` class, MVC controllers inherit from the Controller class, which, in turn, inherits from the `ControllerBase` class and adds its methods that are useful for HTML generation, such as invoking views, which are described in the next subsection, and creating a redirect response.

MVC controllers may also use a routing technique like one of the API controllers; that is, routing based on controllers and controller method attributes. This behavior is enabled by calling the `app.MapControllers()` method in the pipeline definition code in `Program.cs`. If this call is placed before all other `app.MapControllerRoute` calls, then the controller routes have priority over `MapControllerRoute` patterns; otherwise, the opposite is true.

`MapControllerRoute` has the advantage of deciding in a single place the whole paths used by the whole application. This way, one may optimize all application paths for search engine, or simply for better user navigation by changing a few lines of code in a single place. For these reasons, `MapControllerRoute` is almost always used in MVC `application`. However, `MapControllerRoute` is rarely used with REST API because the priority of REST API is to avoid changes in the associations between paths and controllers since they might prevent existing clients from working properly.

All the attributes we have seen for API controllers can also be used with MVC controllers and action methods (HttpGet, HttpPost, ..., Authorize, and so on). Developers can write their own custom attributes by inheriting from the `ActionFilter` class or other derived classes. We will not give details on this right now, but these details can be found in the official documentation, which is referred to in the *Further reading section*.

When the `UseEndpoints` module invokes a controller, all its constructor parameters are filled by the DI engine since the controller instance itself is returned by the DI engine, and since DI automatically fills constructor parameters with DI in a recursive fashion.

Action methods take both their input and services they from their parameters, so it crucial to understand how these parameters are filled by ASP.NET Core. They are taken from the following sources:

- Request headers
- Variables in the pattern matched by the current request
- Query string parameters
- Form parameters (in the case of POST requests)
- Request body
- Dependency injection (DI), in case of services needed to process the request.

While the parameters filled with DI are matched by type, all other parameters are matched by *name* while ignoring the letter casing. That is, the action method parameter name must match the header, query string, form, or pattern variable. In turn, pattern variables are filled by matching the pattern with the request path.

When the parameter is a complex type, the behavior depends on the source.

If the source is the request body, a **formatter** adequate for the `Content-Type` request is selected. **Formatters** are software modules capable of building complex entities starting from a text representation of them. As a default, the request body is taken as a source for selected Content-Types, such as `application/json` and binary MIME types, because each of such MIME types requires a different deserialization algorithm that is specific for it.

If the source is not the request body, instead, an algorithm called model binding is used to fill all complex object public properties.

The model binding algorithm searches for a match in each property (remember just properties are mapped, fields are not mapped), using the property name for the match. In the case of nested complex types, a match is searched for each nested property's path, and the name associated with the path is obtained by chaining all the property names in the path and separating them with dots. For instance, a parameter whose name is `Property1.Property2.Property3...Propertyn` is mapped with the `Propertyn` property that is in the following path of nested object properties: `Property1`, `Property2`, ..., `Propertyn`.

The name that's obtained this way must match a header name, pattern variable name, query string parameter name, and so on. For instance, an `OfficeAddress` property containing a complex Address object would generate names like `OfficeAddress.Country` and `OfficeAddress.Town`.

The model binding algorithm can also fill collections and dictionaries, but for lack of space, we can't describe these cases. However, the *Further reading* section contains a link to an excellent Phil Haack post that explains them in detail.

By default, simple type parameters are matched with pattern variables and query string variables, while complex type parameters are matched with form parameters or with the request body (depending on their MIME types). However, the preceding defaults can be changed by prefixing the parameters with attributes, as detailed here:

- `[FromForm]` forces a match with form parameters
- `[FromBody]` forces the extraction of data from the request body
- `[FromHeader]` forces a match with a request header
- `[FromRoute]` forces a match with pattern variables
- `[FromQuery]` forces a match with a query string variable
- `[FromServices]` forces the use of DI

It is worth pointing out that version 8 of ASP.NET Core enhanced Minimal API to support basically the same parameter bindings of controller's action methods, and all the above parameter attributes.

During the match, the string that was extracted from the selected source is converted into the type of action method parameter using the current thread culture. If either a conversion fails or no match is found for an obligatory action method parameter, then the whole action method invocation process fails, and a 404 response is automatically returned. For instance, in the following example, the `id` parameter is matched with query string parameters or pattern variables since it is a simple type, while `myclass` properties and nested properties are matched with form parameters since `MyClass` is a complex type. Finally, `myservice` is taken from DI since it is prefixed with the `[FromServices]` attribute:

```
public class HomeController : Controller
{
    public IActionResult MyMethod(
        int id,
        MyClass myclass,
        MyService myservice)
    {
        ...
```

If no match is found for the id parameter and if the id parameter is declared as obligatory in the `MapControllerRoute` pattern, a 404 response is automatically returned since pattern matching fails. It is common to declare parameters as not optional when they match not nullable single types. If, instead, no `MyService` instance is found in the DI container, an exception is thrown away because in this case, the failure doesn't depend on a wrong request but on a design error.

MVC controllers return an `IActionResult` interface or a `Task<IActionResult>` result if they are declared as `async`. `IActionResult` defines the unique method with the `ExecuteResultAsync(ActionContext)` signature, which, when invoked by the framework, produces the actual response.

For each different `IActionResult`, MVC controllers have methods that return them. The most used `IActionResult` is `ViewResult`, which is returned by a View method:

```
public IActionResult MyMethod(...)
{
    ...
    return View("myviewName", MyViewModel)
}
```

`ViewResult` is a very common way for a controller to create an HTML response. More specifically, the controller interacts with business/data layers to produce an abstraction of the data that will be shown on the HTML page. This abstraction is an object called a **ViewModel**. The ViewModel is passed as a second argument to the View method, while the first argument is the name of an HTML template, called View, that is instantiated with the data contained in the ViewModel.

Summing this up, the MVC controllers' processing sequence is as follows:

1. The controllers perform some processing to create the ViewModel, which is an abstraction of the data to show on the HTML page.
2. Then, the controllers create `ViewResult` by passing a View name and ViewModel to the View method.

3. The MVC framework invokes `ViewResult` and causes the template contained in the View to be instantiated with the data contained in the ViewModel.
4. The result of the template's instantiation is written in the response with adequate headers.

This way, the controller performs the conceptual job of HTML generation by building a ViewModel, while the View – that is, the template – takes care of all the presentation details.

Views will be described in greater detail in the next subsection, while the Model (ViewModel) View Controller pattern will be discussed in more detail in the *Understanding the connection between ASP.NET Core MVC and design principles* section of this chapter. Finally, a practical example will be provided in *Chapter 17, Implementing Frontend Microservices with ASP.NET Core*.

Another common `IActionResult` is `RedirectResult`, which creates a redirect response, hence forcing the browser to move to a specific URL. Redirects are often used once the user has successfully submitted a form that completes a previous operation. In this case, it is common to redirect the user to a page where they can select another operation.

The simplest way to return `RedirectResult` is by passing a URL to the Redirect method. This is the advised way to perform a redirect to a URL that is outside the web application. On the other hand, when the URL is within the web application, it is advisable to use the `RedirectToAction` method, which accepts the controller's name, the action method name, and the desired parameters for the target action method. This method has several overloads, where each overload omits some of the above parameters. In particular, the controller name can be omitted if the URL we define is handled by the same controller.

The framework uses this data to compute a URL that causes the desired action method to be invoked with the parameters provided. This way, if the routing rules are changed during the application's development or maintenance, the new URL is automatically updated by the framework with no need to modify all occurrences of the old URL in the code.

The following code shows how to call RedirectToAction:

```
return RedirectToAction("MyActionName", "MyControllerName",
        new {par1Name=par1Value,..parNName=parNValue});
```

Another useful `IActionResult` is `ContentResult`, which can be created by calling the Content method. `ContentResult` allows you to write any string to the response and specify its MIME type, as shown in the following example:

```
return Content("this is plain text", "text/plain");
```

Finally, the File method returns `FileResult`, which writes binary data in the response. There are several overloads of this method that allow the specification of a byte array, a stream, or the path of a file, plus the MIME type of the binary data.

Now, let's move on to describing how actual HTML is generated in Views.

Understanding how ASP.NET Core MVC creates the response HTML

When a browser sends a request to an ASP.NET Core MVC application, the request is routed to a controller action. If that action returns a view, ASP.NET Core MVC selects the corresponding Razor view, combines it with the data provided by the controller—typically through a ViewModel—and renders the final HTML that is sent back to the browser. In other words, the response HTML is produced through a sequence involving routing, controller execution, view selection, and Razor rendering. With this overall flow in mind, we can now examine the role of Razor views in more detail.

Razor Views

ASP.NET Core MVC uses a language called **Razor** to define the HTML templates contained in the Views. Razor views are files that are compiled into .NET classes when they're first used, when the application has been built, or when the application has been published. By default, both pre-compilation on build and on publish are enabled, but you can also enable runtime compilation so that the Views can be modified once they have been deployed. This option can be enabled by checking the *Enable Razor runtime compilation* checkbox when the project is created in Visual Studio. You can also disable compilation on build and on publish by adding the following code to the web application project file:

```
<PropertyGroup>
  <TargetFramework> net10.0 </TargetFramework>
  <!-- add code below -->
  <RazorCompileOnBuild>false</RazorCompileOnBuild>
  <RazorCompileOnPublish>false</RazorCompileOnPublish>
  <!-- end of code to add -->
    ...
</PropertyGroup>
```

Views can also be precompiled into Views libraries if you choose a Razor view library project in the window that appears once you have chosen an ASP.NET Core project.

Also, following the compilation, Views remain associated with their paths, which become their full names. Each controller has an associated folder under the **Views** folder with the same name as the controller, which is expected to contain all the Views used by that controller.

The following screenshot shows the folder associated with a possible `HomeController` and its Views:

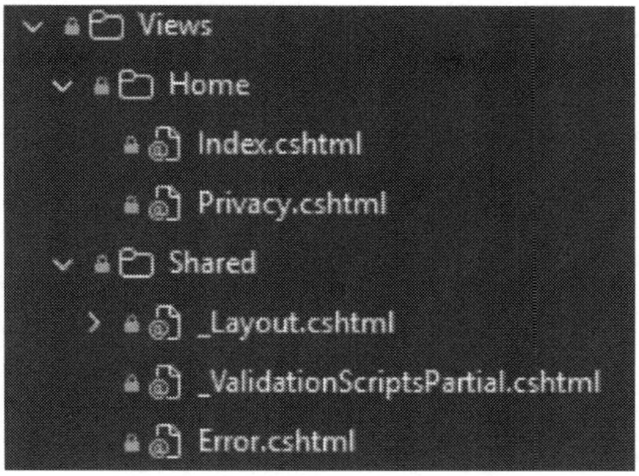

Figure 16.6: View folders associated with controllers and the shared folder

The preceding screenshot also shows the **Shared** folder, which is expected to contain all the Views or partial views used by several controllers. The controller refers to views in the View method through their paths without the `cshtml` extension. If the path starts with /, the path is interpreted as relative to the application root. Otherwise, as a first attempt, the path is interpreted as relative to the folder associated with the controller. If no View is found there, the View is searched for in the **Shared** folder.

Hence, for instance, the `Privacy.cshtml` View file in the preceding screenshot can be referred to from within `HomeController` as `View("Privacy", MyViewModel)`. If the name of the View is the same as the name of the action method, we can simply write `View(MyViewModel)`.

Razor views are a mix of HTML code with C# code, plus some Razor-specific statements. They usually begin with a header that contains the type of ViewModel that the View is expected to receive.

```
@model MyViewModel
```

This declaration may be omitted, but in this case, the view will not be specific to a specific type, and we will not be able to use the model property names in the Razor code.

Each view may also contain some `using` statements whose effect is the same as the using statements of standard code files:

```
@model MyViewModel
@using MyApplication.Models
```

`@using` statements declared in the special `_ViewImports.cshtml` file – that is, in the root of the `Views` folder – are automatically applied to all views.

Each view can also require instances of types from the DI engine in its header with the syntax shown here:

```
@model MyViewModel
@using MyApplication.Models
@inject IViewLocalizer Localizer
```

The preceding code requires an instance of the `IViewLocalizer` interface and places it in the Localizer variable.

The remainder of the View is a mix of C# code, HTML, and Razor control flow statements. Each area of a view can be either in HTML mode or C# mode. The code in a View area that is in HTML mode is interpreted as HTML, while the code in a View area that is in C# mode is interpreted as C#.

The topic that follows explains the Razor flow of control statements.

Learning the Razor flow of control statements

A significant benefit of the Razor flow of control statements is that it enables the HTML returned to the client to vary according to the application data, while preserving a clear connection between the rendered markup and the conditions that govern it. This approach simplifies the implementation of dynamic views and improves maintainability by keeping presentation logic close to the corresponding user interface elements.

For instance, a product page may show an availability warning only when an item is no longer in stock, a restricted section of the UI may be rendered only for authorized users, and a monitoring page may emphasize overdue operations when deadlines have been exceeded. As a result, Razor offers a practical and elegant way to create views whose behavior is driven by the current execution context. Below you have some code snippets to help you understand the possibilities.

If you want to write some C# code in an HTML area, you can create a C# area with the `@{..}` Razor flow of control statement, as shown here:

```
@{
    //place C# code here
    var myVar = 5;
    ...
    <div>
        <!-- here you are in HTML mode again -->
        ...
    </div>
    //after the HTML block you are still in C# mode
    var x = "my string";
}
```

The preceding example shows that it is enough to write an HTML tag to create an HTML area inside the C# area and so on recursively. As soon as the HTML tag closes, you are in C# mode again.

If we need to create an HTML area but we don't want to enclose it in a HTML tag, we may use the fake `<text>` tag provided by Razor syntax:

```
<text>
<!-- here you entered HTML mode without adding an enclosing
    HTML tag -->
        ...
</text>
```

C# code produces no HTML, while HTML code is added to the response in the same order in which it appears. You can add text computed with C# code while in HTML mode by prefixing any C# expression with @. If the expression is complex in that it is composed of a chain of properties and method calls, it must be enclosed by parentheses. The following code shows some examples:

```
<span>Current date is: </span>
<span>@DateTime.Today.ToString("d")</span>
...
<p>
  User name is: @($"{myName} {mySurname}")
</p>
...
<input type="submit" value="@myUserMessage" />
```

The "@" itself can be escaped by repeating it twice @@.

Types are converted into strings using the current culture settings (see the *Understanding the connection between ASP.NET Core MVC and design principles* section for details on how to set the culture of each request). Moreover, strings are automatically HTML-encoded to avoid the < and > symbols, which might interfere with the view HTML.

HTML encoding can be prevented with the `@HTML.Raw` function, as shown here:

```
@HTML.Raw(myDynamicHtml)
```

In an HTML area, alternative HTML can be selected with the `@if` Razor statement:

```
@if(myUser.IsRegistered)
{
    //this is a C# code area
    var x=5;
    ...
    <p>
     <!-- This is an HTML area -->
    </p>
    //this is a C# code area again
}
else if(myUser.IsNew)
{
    ...
}
else
{
```

```
..
}
```

As shown in the preceding code, the beginning of each block of a Razor control flow statement is in C# mode and remains in C# mode until the first HTML open tag is encountered, and then HTML mode starts. C# mode is resumed after the corresponding HTML close tag.

An HTML template can be instantiated several times with the `@for`, `@foreach`, `@while`, and `@do` Razor statements, as shown in the following examples:

```
@for(int i=0; i< 10; i++)
{
//your code here
}

@foreach(var x in myIEnumerable)
{
//your code here
}

@while(true)
{
//your code here
}

@do
{
//your code here

}
while(true)
```

Razor views can contain comments that do not generate any code. Any text included within `@*...*@` is considered a comment and is removed when the page is compiled. With a good understanding of controllers and their operational mechanics, let's now turn to how ASP.NET Core MVC generates HTML responses using Razor views.

Understanding Razor View properties

Some standard variables are predefined in each view. The most important variable is `Model`, which contains the ViewModel that was passed to the view. For instance, if we pass a Person model to a view, then `<span>@Model.Name</span>` displays the name of the Person model that was passed to the view.

The `ViewData` variable contains `IDictionary<string, object>`, which is shared with the controller that invoked the view. That is, all controllers also have a `ViewData` property containing `IDictionary<string,`

`object>`, and every entry that is set in the controller is also available in the `ViewData` variable of the invoked `view.ViewData` is an alternative to the `ViewModel` for a controller for passing information to its invoked view. It is worth mentioning that the `ViewData` dictionary can also be accessed as a dynamic object through the `ViewBag` property. This means that dynamic `ViewBag` properties are mapped to `ViewData` string indices and that their values are mapped to the `ViewData` entries corresponding to those indices. Using `ViewData` or `ViewBag` is just a matter of preference; neither of them has advantages over the other.

Often, `ViewData` is used to store collateral data, such as the value-string pairs used to populate an HTML Select. For instance, let suppose the ViewModel model contains `TownId` and `TownName` properties, that the user can change by selecting a different town from an HTML-select. In this case the action method might fill the `"AllTowns"` entry of ViewData with all possible `town id` and `town name` pairs:

```
ViewData[=["AllTowns"]= await townsRepo.GetAll();
...
return View(new AddressViewModel{...});
```

Note

Both controllers and Views contain also a `TempData` dictionary whose entries are remembered between two successive requests. For lack of space, we can't discuss its properties and its usage, but the interested reader can refer to the official Microsoft documentation at `https://learn.microsoft.com/en-us/aspnet/core/fundamentals/app-state`

The `User` view variable contains the currently logged user; that is, the same instance contained in the current request's `Http.Context.User` property. The `Url` variable contains an instance of the `IUrlHelper` interface whose methods are utilities for computing the URLs of application pages. For instance, `Url.Action("action", "controller", new {par1=valueOfPar1,...})` computes the URL that causes the action method, action, of controller to be invoked with all the parameters specified in the anonymous object passed as its parameters.

The `Context` variable contains the whole request's `HttpContext`. The `ViewContext` variable contains data about the context of the view invocation, including metadata about the action method that invoked the view.

The next topic describes how Razor views enhance HTML tag syntax.

Using Razor tag helpers

Tag helpers simplify common MVC patterns such as generating URLs from routes, binding form fields to ViewModel properties, displaying validation messages, selecting environment-specific resources, and managing static file versions. Instead of writing this behavior manually in plain HTML, developers express it through HTML-like attributes that are processed on the server when the Razor view is rendered.

When building views, developers often need HTML elements that are connected to ASP.NET Core MVC features such as routing, model binding, validation, and form handling. Writing all this behavior manually with plain HTML can be repetitive and error-prone. Tag helpers address this problem by allowing server-side behavior to be expressed directly in HTML-like syntax, making views easier to read and closer to standard markup.

Tag helpers in ASP.NET Core MVC are powerful tools for enhancing HTML tags with additional functionalities. More specifically, a tag helper, either enhances existing HTML tags with new tag attributes or defines completely new tags.

While Razor views are compiled, any tag is matched against existing tag helpers. When a match is found, the source tag is replaced with HTML created by the tag helpers. Several tag helpers may be defined for the same tag. They are all executed in an order that can be configured with a priority attribute associated with each tag helper.

All tag helpers defined for the same tag may cooperate while each tag instance is being processed. This is because they are passed a shared data structure where each of them may apply a contribution. Usually, the final tag helper that is invoked processes this shared data structure to produce the output HTML.

Tag helpers are classes that inherit from the `TagHelper` class. This topic doesn't discuss how to create new tag helpers but introduces the main predefined tag helpers that come with ASP.NET Core MVC. A complete guide on how to define tag helpers is available in the official documentation, which is referenced in the *Further reading* section.

To use a tag helper, you must declare the `.dll` file containing it with a declaration like the following:

```
@addTagHelper *, Dll.Complete.Name
```

If you would like to use just one of the tag helpers defined in the `.dll` file, you must replace * with the tag name.

The preceding declaration can be placed either in each view that uses the tag helpers defined in the library or, once and for all, in the `_ViewImports.cshtml` file in the root of the Views folder. By default, `_ViewImports.cshtml` adds all predefined ASP.NET Core MVC tag helpers with the following declaration:

```
@addTagHelper *, Microsoft.AspNetCore.Mvc.TagHelpers
```

The anchor tag is enhanced with attributes that automatically compute the URL and that invoke a specific action method with given parameters, as shown here:

```
<a asp-controller="{controller name}"
asp-action="{action method name}"
asp-route-{action method parameter1}="value1"
...
asp-route-{action method parametern}="valuen">
    put anchor text here
</a>
```

Below is an example of usage:

```
<a asp-controller="Home" asp-action="Index">
 Back Homen
</a>
```

The HTML created is:

```
<a href="Home/Index">
 Back Homen
</a>
```

It might appear that there is almost no advantage in using the tag helper. However, this is false! The advantage is that whenever the routing rules change, the tag helper automatically updates the `href` it generates to conform to the new routing rules.

A similar syntax is added to the form tags:

```
<form asp-controller="{controller name}"
asp-action="{action method name}"
asp-route-{action method parameter1}="value1"
...
asp-route-{action method parametern}="valuen"
...
>
...
```

The `script` tag is enhanced with attributes that allow us to fall back to a different source if the download fails. Typical usage is to download scripts from some cloud service to optimize the browser cache and to fall back to a local copy of the script in case of failure. The following code uses the fallback technique to download the Bootstrap JavaScript file:

```
<script src="https://stackpath.bootstrapcdn.com/
 bootstrap/4.3.1/js/bootstrap.bundle.min.js"
 asp-fallback-src="~/lib/bootstrap/dist/js/bootstrap.bundle.min.js"
 asp-fallback-test="window.jQuery && window.jQuery.fn && window.jQuery.fn.modal"
 crossorigin="anonymous"
 integrity="sha384-xrRywqdh3PHs8keKZN+8zzc5TX0GRTLCcmivcbNJWm2rs5C8PRhcEn3czEjhAO9o">
</script>
```

`asp-fallback-test` contains a JavaScript test that verifies whether the download succeeded. In the preceding example, the test verifies whether a JavaScript object has been created.

All HTML tags that admit a `src` attribute, that is, the `img` and the script tags, can be added as an `asp-append-version` attribute set to true. The `asp-append-version` attribute set to `true` doesn't change the syntax of the `img` and `script` tags but adds just a hash to the `src` query string to prevent caching each time the image or script file changes. Here is an example:

```
<img src="~/images/myImage.png" asp-append-version="true">
```

Which is rendered as:

```
<img src="/images/myImage.png?v=kM_dqr9NVtnMdsM2MUgdskVVFD">
```

The hash passed in the v query parameter is computed from the content of the image file, so it changes whenever the image changes, thereby preventing the browser from rendering an old, cached copy of the image.

The `~/ symbol` is not a feature specific to the `img` tag helper, but a Razor native feature you can use in all links contained in any tag of a Razor file. It stands for the application root. It is not equivalent to the HTML / symbol that stands for the root of the domain, because ASP.NET Core applications may also be placed in subfolders of the domain. So `~/ translates` to / only when the application is placed in the domain root, otherwise it translates to `/{application subfolder name}/`.

The `environment` tag can be used to select different HTML for different environments (development, staging, and production). Its typical usage is selecting the debug versions of JavaScript files during development, as shown in this example:

```
<environment include="Development">
        @*development version of JavaScript files*@
</environment>
<environment exclude="Development">
        @*development version of JavaScript files *@
</environment>
```

There is also a `cache` tag, which caches its content in memory to optimize rendering speed:

```
<cache>
    @* heavy to compute content to cache *@
</cache>
```

By default, content is cached for 20 minutes, but the tag has attributes that must be defined when the cache expires, such as `expires-on="{datetime}"`, `expires-after="{timespan}"`, and `expires-sliding="{timespan}"`. Here, the difference between `expires-sliding` and `expires-after` is that, in the second attribute, the expiration time count is reset each time the content is requested. The vary-by attribute causes the creation of a different cache entry for each different value passed to `vary-by`. There are also attributes such as `vary-by-header`, which creates a different entry for each different value assumed by the request header specified in the `vary-by-cookie` attribute, and so on.

All input tags – that is, `textarea`, `input`, and `select` – have an `asp-for` attribute that accepts a properties path rooted in the view's ViewModel as their value. For instance, if the view has a `Person` ViewModel, we may have something like this:

```
<input type="text" asp-for"Address.Town"/>
```

The first thing the preceding code does is assign the value of the Town nested property to the value attribute of the input tag. In general, if the value is not a string, it is converted into a string using the current request culture.

However, it also sets the name of the input field to Address.Town and the id of the input field to Address_Town. This is because dots are not allowed in tag ids.

A prefix can be added to these standard names by specifying it in ViewData.TemplateInfo.HtmlFieldPrefix. For instance, if the previous property is set to MyPerson, the name becomes MyPerson.Address.Town.

If the form is submitted to an action method that has the same Person class as one of its parameters, the name of Address.Town that's given to the input field will cause the Town property of this parameter to be filled with the input field. In general, the string contained in the input field is converted into the type of property it has been matched with using the current request culture. Summing this up, the names of input fields are created in such a way that a complete Person model can be recovered in the action method when the HTML page is posted.

The same asp-for attribute can be used in a label tag to cause the label to refer to the input field with the same asp-for value.

The following code is an example of an input/label pair:

```
<label asp-for="Address.Town"></label
<input type="text" asp-for="Address.Town"/>
```

When no text is inserted into the label, the text shown in the label is taken from a Display attribute that decorates the property (Town, in this example), if any; otherwise, the name of the property is used.

If span or div contains an asp-validation-for ="Address.Town" error attribute, then validation messages concerning the Address.Town input will be inserted automatically inside that tag. The validation framework will be described in the *Understanding the connection between ASP.NET Core MVC and design principles* section.

It is also possible to automatically create a validation error summary by adding the attribute that follows a div or a span:

```
asp-validation-summary="ValidationSummary.{All, ModelOnly}"
```

If the attribute is set to ValidationSummary.ModelOnly, only messages that are not associated with specific input fields will be shown in the summary, while if the value is ValidationSummary.All, all error messages will be shown.

The asp-items attribute can be applied to any select tag to automatically generate all the select options. It must be passed an IEnumerable<SelectListItem>, where each SelectListItem contains both the text and value of an option. SelectListItem also contains an optional Group property you can use to organize the options shown in select into groups.

Here is an example of how to use `asp-items`:

```
...
@{
 var choices = new List<SelectListItem>
 {
   new SelectListItem {Value="value1", Text="text1", Group="group1"},
   new SelectListItem {Value="value2", Text="text2", Group="group1"}
   ...
   new SelectListItem {..., Group="group2"}
   ...
 }
}
<select asp-for="MyProperty"  asp-items="choices">
 <option value="">Select a value</option>
</select>
...
```

When added, option tags are placed before the ones generated by `asp-items`.

So far, we have seen how ASP.NET Core MVC generates response HTML by selecting Razor views, binding them to ViewModels, and combining HTML markup with C# code and Razor control flow statements. We also examined the main view properties that allow the view to access model data, controller-provided values, user information, and URL-generation utilities. Having established how views are structured and how they produce dynamic output, we then examined how ASP.NET Core MVC enriches standard HTML through tag helpers. These helpers make views easier to write and maintain by connecting markup more directly with routing, validation, model binding, and form processing features. The next topic shows how to reuse view code.

Reusing view code

The following reuse techniques build on one another. Layouts define the shared structure of full pages, partial views extract reusable HTML fragments, and view components add reusable UI elements that also contain their own processing logic.

ASP.NET Core MVC includes several techniques for reusing view code. Layouts are best for shared page structure, partial views are best for repeated markup that does not require much logic, and view components are best when the reusable UI fragment needs its own data loading or processing. Together, these techniques keep the view layer consistent without duplicating code. Let's check them.

Layouts – Shared page structure

In each web application, several pages share the same structure; for instance, the same main menu or the same left or right bar. In ASP.NET Core, this common structure is factored out in views called layout pages/views as shown below:

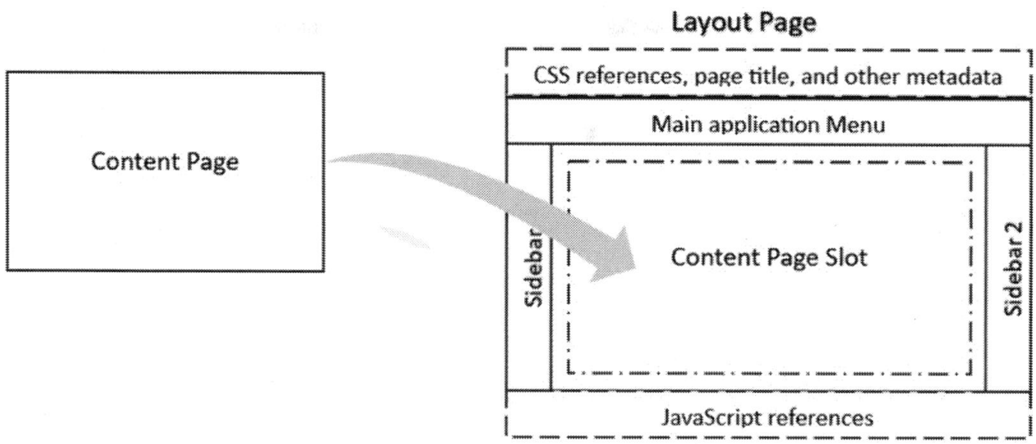

Figure 16.7: Using Layout pages

Each view can specify the view to be used as its layout page with the following code:

```
@{
    Layout = "_MyLayout";
}
```

If no layout page is specified, a default layout page, defined in a `_ViewStart.cshtml` file located in the Views folder, is used. The default content of `_ViewStart.cshtml` is as follows:

```
@{
    Layout = "_Layout";
}
```

Therefore, the default layout page in the files scaffolded by Visual Studio is `_Layout.cshtml`, which is contained in the Shared folder.

The layout page contains the HTML that's shared with all its children pages, the HTML page headers, and the page references to CSS and JavaScript files. The HTML produced by each view is placed inside its layout place, where the layout page calls the `@RenderBody()` method, as shown in the following example:

```
...
<main role="main" class="pb-3">
    ...
    @RenderBody()
    ...
</main>
...
```

`ViewData` of each `View` is copied into `ViewData` of its layout page, so `ViewData` can be used to pass information to the view layout page. Typically, it is used to pass the view title to the layout page, which then uses it to compose the page's title header, as shown here:

```
@*In the view *@
@{
    ViewData["Title"] = "Home Page";
}
@*In the layout view*@
<head>
    <meta charset="utf-8" />
    ...
    <title>@ViewData["Title"] - My web application</title>
    ...
```

While the main content produced by each view is placed in a single area of its layout page, each layout page can also define several sections placed in different areas where each view can place further secondary content.

For instance, suppose a layout page defines a Scripts section, as shown here:

```
...
<script src="~/js/site.js" asp-append-version="true"></script>
@RenderSection("Scripts", required: false)
...
```

Then, the view can use the previously defined section to pass some view-specific JavaScript references, as shown here:

```
.....
@section scripts{
    <script src="~/js/pages/pageSpecificJavaScript.min.js"></script>
}
.....
```

If an action method is expected to return HTML to an AJAX call, it must produce an HTML fragment instead of a whole HTML page. Therefore, in this case, no layout page must be used. This is achieved by calling the `PartialView` method instead of the View method in the controller action method. `PartialView` and `View` have the same overloads and parameters.

Partial Views – Reusable HTML fragments

Another way to reuse view code is to factor out a view fragment that's common to several views into another view that is called by all previous views. A view can call another view with the partial tag, as shown here:

```
<partial name="_viewname" for="ModelProperty.NestedProperty"/>
```

The preceding code invokes _viewname and passes it to the object contained in Model.ModelProperty.NestedProperty as its ViewModel. When a view is invoked by the partial tag, no layout page is used since the view is expected to return an HTML fragment.

The ViewData.TemplateInfo.HtmlFieldPrefix property of the called view is set to the ModelProperty.NestedProperty string. This way, possible input fields rendered in _viewname.cshtml will have the same name as if they had been rendered directly by the calling view.

Instead of specifying the ViewModel of _viewname through a property of the caller view (ViewModel), you can also directly pass an object that is contained in a variable or returned by a C# expression by replacing for with model, as shown in this example:

```
<partial name="_viewname" model="new MyModel{...})" />
```

In this case, the ViewData.TemplateInfo.HtmlFieldPrefix property of the called view keeps its default value; that is, the empty string.

View Components – Reusable components with logic

A view can also call something more complex than another view; that is, another controller method that, in turn, renders a view. Controllers that are designed to be invoked by views are called **view components**. The following code is an example of component invocation:

```
<vc:[view-component-name] par1="par1 value" par2="parameter2 value"> </vc:[view-
component-name]>
```

Parameter names must match the ones used in the view component method. However, both the component's name and parameter names must be translated into kebab case; that is, all the characters must be transformed into lowercase if all the characters that in the original name were in uppercase, though the first one word must be preceded by a -. For instance, MyParam must be transformed into my-param.

View components are either classes that derive from the ViewComponent class, classes decorated with the [ViewComponent] attribute, or classes whose names end with the ViewComponent suffix. When a component is invoked, the framework looks for either an Invoke method or an InvokeAsync method and passes it all the parameters that were defined in the component's invocation. InvokeAsync must be used if the method is defined as async; otherwise, we must use Invoke.

The following code is an example of a view component definition:

```
public class MyTestViewComponent : ViewComponent
    {

        public async Task<IViewComponentResult> InvokeAsync(
        int par1, bool par2)
        {
            var model= ....
```

```
            return View("ViewName", model);
        }

    }
```

The previously defined component must be invoked with a call such as the following:

```
<vc:my-test par1="10" par2="true"></vc:y-test>
```

If the component is invoked by a view of a controller called `MyController`, `ViewName` is searched for in the following paths:

- /Views/MyController/Components/MyTest/ViewName
- /Views/Shared/Components/MyTest/ViewName

So far, we have seen that ASP.NET Core MVC offers several levels of reuse in the view layer. Layouts make it possible to share the overall page structure across multiple views, partial views allow common HTML fragments to be factored out and reused, and view components support the creation of reusable UI elements that also include their own processing logic. Together, these mechanisms help keep views more modular, consistent, and maintainable. With this foundation in place, we can now examine how ASP.NET Core MVC reflects broader design principles in the way controllers, views, ViewModels, and supporting framework features are organized.

Understanding the connection between ASP.NET Core MVC and design principles

ASP.NET Core MVC reflects several design principles discussed earlier in this book. Its pipeline separates request-processing responsibilities into middleware. Its DI model keeps framework services replaceable and testable. Its validation and globalization features move cross-cutting concerns out of controllers and views. Finally, the MVC pattern separates user interaction logic from presentation details. Together, these choices help architects design presentation layers that are modular, maintainable, and easier to evolve.

Up to this point, we have examined how ASP.NET Core MVC handles requests, generates HTML responses, and supports reuse in the view layer through layouts, partial views, and view components. These mechanisms already show that the framework is not just a collection of technical features, but an architecture shaped by explicit design choices. In this subsection, we move from how ASP.NET Core MVC works to why it is organized this way, examining how its pipeline, validation system, globalization support, and MVC structure reflect broader software design principles.

The whole ASP.NET Core framework is built on top of the design principles and patterns that we analyzed in the following chapters:

- *Chapter 5, Implementing Code Reusability in C#,*
- *Chapter 6, Design Patterns and .NET Implementation,*
- *Chapter 7, Understanding the Different Domains in Software Solutions,*

- *Chapter 11, Applying a Microservice Architecture to Your Enterprise Application*, and
- *Chapter 13, Interacting with Data in C# – Entity Framework Core.*

Moreover, all framework functionalities are provided through DI so that each of them can be replaced by a customized counterpart without it affecting the remainder of the code. Moreover, these providers are not added individually to the DI engine; instead, they are grouped into collection properties of option objects (see the *Loading configuration data and using it with the options framework* subsection) for improved maintainability, and to conform to the Separation of Concerns principle, which is a generalization of the Single Responsibility Principle. In fact, the order in which providers are added to their collection does matter, since they are processed in the same order as they are in the collection. Moreover, the effect of a provider also depends on the other providers that belong to the same collection, so sometimes it is not enough to replace a provider or to add a new provider, but it is necessary to also remove/replace other providers to remove their side effects.

Examples of providers grouped in collections include all model binders, validation providers, and data annotation providers.

Moreover, configuration data, instead of being available from a unique dictionary created from a configuration file, is organized into option objects thanks to the options framework we described in the first section of this chapter. This is also an application of the SOLID Interface Segregation Principle.

More specifically, the discussion that follows shows how ASP.NET Core separates responsibilities across middleware modules, how its validation infrastructure improves extensibility and maintainability, how globalization is delegated to dedicated framework services, and how the MVC pattern itself supports modularity, testability, and clearer interaction between presentation and application logic.

However, ASP.NET Core also applies other patterns that are specific instances of the general Separation of Concerns principle, which is a generalization of the Single Responsibility Principle. They are as follows:

- The middleware modules architecture (ASP.NET Core pipeline)
- Factoring out validation and globalization from the application code
- The MVC pattern itself

We will analyze each of these in the various subsections that follow.

Advantages of ASP.NET Core pipeline

ASP.NET Core pipeline architecture has two important advantages:

- All the different operations that are performed at the initial request are factored out into different modules, according to the Single Responsibility Principle.
- The modules that perform these different operations don't need to call each other because each module is invoked once and for all by the ASP.NET Core framework. This way, the code for each module is not required to perform any action that is connected to responsibilities that have been assigned to other modules.

This ensures maximum independence of functionalities and simpler code. For instance, once the authorization and authentication modules are on, no other module needs to worry about authorization anymore. Each controller code can focus on application-specific business stuff.

One important consequence of this architectural style is that recurring concerns are removed from controllers and views and delegated to specialized framework mechanisms. Validation is a clear example of this approach. Instead of scattering input checks throughout the application code, ASP.NET Core MVC centralizes validation in a dedicated infrastructure that can be applied consistently across requests and user interfaces. Let's check this out.

Server-side and client-side validation

For architects, validation and globalization are not only implementation details. Validation protects the consistency of the application boundary by ensuring that user input is checked before it reaches business logic. Globalization makes the presentation layer adaptable to different cultures without duplicating pages or controllers. Both features support cleaner separation of concerns and make the application easier to extend across users, regions, and deployment contexts.

Validation deserves special attention because checking user input in only one place is not enough for real applications. Client-side validation improves usability by showing errors before a form is submitted, reducing unnecessary roundtrips and giving faster feedback to the user. Server-side validation, however, remains indispensable because all input arriving at the server must still be treated as untrusted. Requests may bypass browser checks entirely, or malicious users may tamper with them, so validation must always be enforced again on the server. ASP.NET Core MVC supports both concerns in a coordinated way, combining better user experience with reliable enforcement of business constraints.

Validation logic has been completely factored out from the application code and has been confined to the definition of validation attributes. The developer just needs to specify the validation rule to apply to each model property by decorating the property with an adequate validation attribute.

Validation rules are checked automatically when action method parameters are instantiated. Both errors and paths in the model (where they occurred) are then recorded in a dictionary that is contained in the `ModelState` controller property. The developer has the responsibility for verifying whether there are errors by checking `ModelState.IsValid`, in which case the developer must return the same `ViewModel` to the same view so that the user can correct any errors.

Error messages are automatically shown in the view with no action required from the developer. The developer is only required to do the following:

- Add `span` or `div` with an `asp-validation-for attribute` next to each input field, which will be automatically filled with the possible error.
- Add `div` with an `asp-validation-summary` attribute that will be automatically filled with the validation error summary. See the *Using Razor tag helpers section for more details.*

It is enough to add some JavaScript references by invoking the `_ValidationScriptsPartial.cshtml` view with the partial tag to enable the same validation rules on the client side so that errors are shown to the user before the form is posted to the server. Some predefined validation attributes are contained in the

`System.ComponentModel.DataAnnotations` and `Microsoft.AspNetCore.Mvc` namespaces and include the following attributes:

- The `Required` attribute requires the user to specify a value for the property that it decorates. An implicit `Required` attribute is automatically applied to all non-nullable properties, such as all floats, integers, and decimals, since they can't have a null value.
- The `Range` attribute constrains numeric quantities within a range.
- They also include attributes that constrain string lengths.

Custom error messages can be inserted directly into the attributes, or attributes can refer to the property of resource types containing them.

> **Note**
>
> The developer can define their custom attributes by providing the validation code both in C# and in JavaScript for client-side validation. The definition of custom validation attributes is discussed in this article: `https://learn.microsoft.com/pt-br/archive/blogs/mvpawardprogram/asp-net-core-mvc`.

Attribute-based validation can be replaced by other validation providers, such as the **FluentValidation** library that defines validation rules for each type using a fluent interface. It is enough to change a provider in a collection contained in the MVC options object. This can be configured through an action passed to the `builder.Services.AddControllersWithViews` method.

MVC options can be configured as follows:

```
builder.Services.AddControllersWithViews(o => {
    ...
    // code that modifies o properties
});
```

The validation framework automatically checks whether numeric and date inputs are well-formatted according to the selected culture.

Validation is not the only cross-cutting concern that ASP.NET Core factors out of application code. Another important example is globalization, which affects how applications present content and interpret user input in different linguistic and cultural contexts. For this reason, ASP.NET Core provides dedicated mechanisms for selecting cultures, formatting values, and localizing content in a consistent way across the whole request pipeline.

ASP.NET Core globalization

Globalization should not be seen as an optional refinement added near the end of development. In production systems, applications often serve users with different languages, regional conventions, and formatting expectations, and failures in this area can easily compromise both usability and correctness. Dates, decimal separators, currencies, localized strings, and validation messages all influence how users understand and interact with the system. For this reason, ASP.NET Core treats globalization as a first-class architectural concern and provides dedicated mechanisms to configure and apply culture-specific behavior consistently across requests.

In multicultural applications, pages must be served according to the language and cultural preferences of each user. Typically, multicultural applications can serve their content in a few languages, and they can handle dates and numeric formats in several more languages. In fact, while the content in all supported languages must be produced manually, .NET has the native capability of formatting and parsing dates and numbers in all cultures.

For instance, a web application might not support unique content for all English-based cultures (en) but might support all known English-based cultures regarding number and date formats (en-US, en-GB, en-CA, and so on).

The culture used for numbers and dates in a .NET thread is contained in the `Thread.CurrentThread.CurrentCulture` property. Hence, by setting this property to new `CultureInfo("en-CA")`, numbers and dates will be formatted/parsed according to the Canadian culture. `Thread.CurrentThread.CurrentUICulture`, instead, decides on the culture of the resource files; that is, it selects a culture-specific version of each resource file or view. Accordingly, a multicultural application is required to set the two cultures associated with the request thread and organize multilingual content into language-dependent resource files and/or views.

According to the **Separation of Concerns principle**, the whole logic used to set the request culture according to the user's preferences is factored out into a specific module of the ASP.NET Core pipeline. To configure this module, as a first step, we set the supported date/number cultures, as in the following example:

```
var supportedCultures = new[]
{
    new CultureInfo("en-AU"),
    new CultureInfo("en-GB"),
    new CultureInfo("en"),
    new CultureInfo("es-MX"),
    new CultureInfo("es"),
    new CultureInfo("fr-CA"),
    new CultureInfo("fr"),
    new CultureInfo("it-CH"),
    new CultureInfo("it")
};
```

Then, we set the languages supported for the content. Usually, a version of the language that is not specific for any country is selected to keep the number of translations small enough, as shown here:

```
var supportedUICultures = new[]
{
    new CultureInfo("en"),
    new CultureInfo("es"),
```

```
        new CultureInfo("fr"),
        new CultureInfo("it")
};
```

Then, we add the culture middleware to the pipeline, as shown here:

```
app.UseRequestLocalization(new RequestLocalizationOptions
{
    DefaultRequestCulture = new RequestCulture("en", "en"),
    // Formatting numbers, dates, etc.
    SupportedCultures = supportedCultures,
    // UI strings that we have localized.
    SupportedUICultures = supportedUICultures,
    FallBackToParentCultures = true,
    FallBackToParentUICultures = true
});
```

If the culture requested by the user is explicitly found among the ones listed in `supportedCultures` or `supportedUICultures`, it is used without modifications. Otherwise, since `FallBackToParentCultures` and `FallBackToParentUICultures` are true, the parent culture is tried; that is, for instance, if the required `fr-FR` culture is not found among those listed, then the framework searches for its generic version, `fr`. If this attempt also fails, the framework uses the cultures specified in `DefaultRequestCulture`.

By default, the `culture` middleware searches the culture selected for the current user with three providers that are tried in the order shown here:

1. The middleware looks for the `culture` and `ui-culture` query string parameters
2. If the previous step fails, the middleware looks for a cookie named `.AspNetCore.Culture`, the value of which is expected to be as in this example: `c=en-US|uic=en`
3. If both previous steps fail, the middleware looks for the `Accept-Language` request header sent by the browser, which can be changed in the browser settings, and which is initially set to the operating system culture

With the preceding strategy, the first time a user requests an application page, the browser culture is taken (the provider listed in *step 3*). Then, if the user clicks a language-change link with the right query string parameters, a new culture is selected by provider 1. Usually, once a language link has been clicked, the server also generates a language cookie to remember the user's choice through provider 2.

The simplest way to provide content localization is to provide a different view for each language. Hence, if we would like to localize the `Home.cshtml` view for different languages, we must provide views named `Home.en.cshtml`, `Home.es.cshtml`, and so on. If no view specific to the `ui-culture` thread is found, the non-localized `Home.cshtml` version of the view is chosen.

View localization must be enabled by calling the AddViewLocalization method, as shown here:

```
builder.Services.AddControllersWithViews()
    .AddViewLocalization(LanguageViewLocationExpanderFormat.Suffix)
```

Another option is to store simple strings or HTML fragments in resource files specific to all supported languages. The usage of resource files must be enabled by calling the `AddLocalization` method in the configure services section, as shown here:

```
builder.Services.AddLocalization(options =>
    options.ResourcesPath = "Resources");
```

`ResourcesPath` is the root folder where all resource files will be placed. If it is not specified, an empty string is assumed, and the resource files will be placed in the web application root. Resource files for a specific view, say, the `/Views/Home/Index.cshtml` view, must have a path like this:

```
<ResourcesPath >/Views/Home/Index.<culture name>.resx
```

Hence, if `ResourcesPath` is empty, resources must have the `/Views/Home/Index.<culture name>.resx` path; that is, they must be placed in the same folder as the view.

Once the key-value pairs for all the resource files associated with a view have been added, localized HTML fragments can be added to the view, as follows:

- Inject `IViewLocalizer` into the view with `@injectIViewLocalizer` Localizer
- Where needed, replace the text in the View with access to the `Localizer` dictionary, such as `Localizer["myKey"]`, where "myKey" is a key used in the resource files.

The following code shows an example of the IViewLocalizer dictionary:

```
@{
    ViewData["Title"] = Localizer["HomePageTitle"];
}
<h2>@ViewData["MyTitle"]</h2>
```

If localization fails because the key is not found in the resource file, the key itself is returned. Strings used in data annotation, such as validation attributes, are used as keys in resource files if data annotation localization is enabled, as shown here:

```
builder.Services.AddControllersWithViews()
    .AddViewLocalization(LanguageViewLocationExpanderFormat.Suffix)
    .AddDataAnnotationsLocalization();
```

Resource files for data annotations applied to a class whose full name is, say, `MyWebApplication.ViewModels.Account.RegisterViewModel`, must have the following path:

```
{ResourcesPath}/ViewModels/Account/RegisterViewModel.{culture name}.resx
```

It is worth pointing out that the first segment of the namespace that corresponds to the `.dll` application name is replaced with `ResourcesPath`. If `ResourcesPath` is empty and if you use the default namespaces created by Visual Studio, then the resource files must be placed in the same folder that contains the classes they are associated with.

It is possible to localize strings and HTML fragments in controllers, or wherever dependencies can be injected, by associating each group of resource files with a type, such as `MyType`, and then injecting either `IHtmlLocalizer<MyType>` for HTML fragments or `IStringLocalizer<MyType>` for strings that need to be HTML-encoded.

Their usage is identical to the usage of `IViewLocalizer`. The path of the resource files associated with `MyType` is computed, as in the case of data annotations. If you would like to use a unique group of resource files for the whole application, a common choice is to use the Startup class as the reference type (`IStringLocalizer<Startup> and IHtmlLocalizer<Startup>`). Another common choice is to create various empty classes to use as reference types for various groups of resource files.

Now that we've learned how to manage globalization in your ASP.NET Core projects, in the next subsection, we will describe the more important pattern used by ASP.NET Core MVC in enforcing a *Separation of Concerns: the MVC pattern itself.*

The MVC pattern

As we have checked since the starting point of this chapter, ASP.NET Core MVC is not only a way to generate HTML on the server, but also a structured approach to organizing the presentation layer. Controllers coordinate user interactions, ViewModels describe what must be shown, and views decide how that information appears in HTML. This separation is what makes MVC a practical architectural choice for many server-rendered web applications.

MVC is a pattern used to implement the presentation layers of a web application. The basic idea is to apply a **Separation of Concerns** between the logic of the presentation layer and its graphics. Logic is taken care of by controllers, while graphics are factored out into views. Controllers and views communicate through the model, which is often called the **ViewModel** to distinguish it from the models of the business and data layers. It is worth pointing out that the original definition of the MVC pattern proposes directly the use of domain models instead of ViewModels, but then, most of the MVC web frameworks started using the concept of ViewModel because specifying the information to render in a view requires just a projection of the original domain model (just some model data possibly organized in different way) and often also additional data, such as, for instance, the items-per-page of a pager, and the items required by the type input selected.

However, what is the logic of a presentation layer? In *Chapter 1, Understanding the Importance of Software Architecture*, we saw that software requirements can be documented with use cases that describe the interaction between the user and the system.

Roughly speaking, the logic of the presentation layer consists of the management of use cases; hence, roughly, use cases are mapped to controllers, and every single operation of a use case is mapped to an action method of those controllers. Hence, controllers take care of managing the protocol of interaction with the user and rely on the business layer for any business processing involved during each operation.

Each action method receives data from the user, performs some business processing, and, depending on the results of this processing, decides what to show to the user and encodes it in the ViewModel. Views receive ViewModels that describe what to show to the user and decide the graphics to use; that is, the HTML to use.

For example, in an e-commerce application, a `ProductsController` might manage the use case of browsing and purchasing products. One action method could display the details of a selected product, another could add the product to the shopping cart, and a third could complete the checkout step. The business rules involved in pricing, availability, discounts, or order creation would belong to the business layer, while the controller would coordinate the interaction and prepare an appropriate ViewModel. The corresponding view would then decide how to present the product data, the cart summary, or possible validation messages to the user. In the same way, in an administration module, a controller action might receive user input for account creation, rely on the business layer to apply policies, and then return a view showing either the created account or the errors that must be corrected.

What are the advantages of separating the logic and user interface into two different components? The main advantages are listed here:

- Changes in graphics do not affect the remainder of the code, so you can experiment with various user interface elements to optimize the interaction with the user without putting the reliability of the remainder of the code at risk.
- The application can be tested by instantiating controllers and passing the parameters, with no need to use testing tools that operate on the browser pages. In this way, tests are easier to implement. Moreover, they do not depend on the way graphics are implemented, so they do not need to be updated each time the graphics change.
- It is easier to split the job between developers who implement controllers and graphic designers who implement views. Often, graphic designers have difficulties with Razor, so they might just furnish an example HTML page that developers transform into Razor views that operate on the actual data.

The key takeaway is that ASP.NET Core MVC does not apply design principles only at the level of abstract architecture diagrams – it embeds them directly into the framework mechanisms used in everyday development. Middleware promotes separation of responsibilities in request processing, validation and globalization are factored out into dedicated infrastructure, and the MVC pattern separates interaction logic from presentation concerns. As a result, the framework encourages applications that are easier to evolve, test, and maintain over time.

For an example of how to put into practice the general principles discussed above please refer to the *A Frontend Microservice* section of *Chapter 22, Case study: Practical Usage of .NET Aspire*, but it is better to read the next *Chapter 17, Implementing Frontend Microservices with ASP.Net Core* before. There, we'll look at how to create a front-end microservice with ASP.NET Core MVC.

Summary

In this chapter, we analyzed the ASP.NET Core pipeline and various modules that comprise an ASP.NET Core MVC application in detail, such as authentication/authorization, the options framework, and routing. Then, we described how controllers and Views map requests to response HTML. We also analyzed all the design patterns implemented in the ASP.NET Core MVC framework and the importance of the Separation of Concerns principle and how ASP.NET Core MVC implements it in the ASP.NET Core pipeline, as well as in its validation and globalization modules. We focused in more detail on the importance of Separation of Concerns between the presentation layer logic and graphics, as well as how the MVC pattern ensures it.

You can find a full example of how to use ASP.NET Core MVC in the next chapter, which deals with frontend microservices and describes a complete frontend microservice whose presentation layer uses ASP.NET Core MVC.

Questions

1. Can you list all the middleware modules scaffolded by Visual Studio in an ASP.NET Core project?
2. Does the ASP.NET Core pipeline module need to inherit from a base class or implement some interface?
3. Is it true that a tag must have just one tag helper defined for it, otherwise an exception is thrown?
4. Do you remember how to test if validation errors have occurred in a controller?
5. What is the instruction in a layout view for including the output of the main view?
6. How are secondary sections of the main view invoked in a layout view?
7. How does a controller invoke a view?
8. By default, how many providers are installed in the globalization module?
9. Are ViewModels the only way for controllers to communicate with their invoked views?

Further reading

Here, you have some links you may consider using to gather more information about this chapter:

- More details on the ASP.NET Core and ASP.NET Core MVC framework are available in its official documentation at `https://docs.microsoft.com/en-US/aspnet/core/`.
- More details on the Razor syntax can be found at `https://docs.microsoft.com/en-us/aspnet/core/razor-pages`.
- How to model bind collections and dictionaries is explained in this excellent Phil Haack post: `https://haacked.com/archive/2008/10/23/model-binding-to-a-list.aspx`.
- Documentation on the creation of custom tag helpers that were not discussed in this chapter can be found at `https://docs.microsoft.com/en-US/aspnet/core/mvc/views/tag-helpers/authoring`.

- Documentation on the creation of custom controller attributes can be found at `https://docs.microsoft.com/en-US/aspnet/core/mvc/controllers/filters`.
- The definition of custom validation attributes is discussed in this article: `https://blogs.msdn.microsoft.com/mvpawardprogram/2017/01/03/asp-net-core-mvc`.

17

Implementing Frontend Microservices with ASP.NET Core

This chapter explains how to put together techniques analyzed in other chapters in the overall organization of microservices that communicate with the world outside of the application, that is, of microservices that play the role of frontends within a microservices-based application.

Microservices that communicate with the external world act according to a user-based request-response pattern, so they differ a lot from the worker microservice studied in *Chapter 14, Implementing Microservices with .NET*, which are organized as stations of an assembly line. As a consequence, they add new problems and need different techniques.

You will learn how to implement a frontend microservice with the coherent organization of techniques studied in previous chapters, namely, the techniques of *Chapter 16, Presenting ASP.NET Core,* for interacting with the user according to a request-response pattern, some DDD-related techniques and Onion Architecture studied in *Chapter 7, Understanding the Different Domains in Software Solutions*, and some general microservices techniques studied in *Chapter 11, Applying a Microservice Architecture to Your Enterprise Application.*

It is worth pointing out that microservices that communicate with a human user must implement a presentation module or must expose APIs that conform to well-established standards. Moreover, web APIs that target **single-page applications** (SPAs) must conform to browser policies; that is, either they are exposed on a single domain that is the same domain from which the SPA was downloaded, or they must configure **Cross-Origin Resource Sharing** (CORS) policies. We will see how to address both CORS and issues due to browser policies in *Chapter 18, Client Frameworks: Blazor.*

It's worth mentioning also all challenges brought by any presentation layer, that is, ensuring a fast and effective interaction with the user, and managing the state of the interaction with the user with maintainable code without falling into spaghetti code. General usability problems and solutions were discussed in the *Usability – why inserting data takes too much time* section of *Chapter 2, Non-Functional Requirements.* We will discuss more technology-specific usability and status management problems in this chapter and in *Chapter 18, Client Frameworks: Blazor.*

Finally, all frontend microservices must put in place solid security policies to defend the application from hackers. Some techniques are common to both frontends and web APIs, and are automatically handled by all major web servers, such as countermeasures against path traversal attacks and denial of service. Some of these techniques will be discussed in *Chapter 20, Securing Data and Applications*.

We will discuss various implementation options and how to architect the whole layer structure of a frontend microservice. A complete example that shows how all layers of a frontend microservice work together, in practice, is described in the *A Frontend Microservice* section of *Chapter 22, Case Study: Practical Usage of ASP.NET Aspire*.

More specifically, this chapter covers the following topics:

- Frontends and micro-frontends
- Defining the microservice architecture
- Defining the domain layer
- Defining the DB driver
- Defining the application services
- Defining the authentication strategy
- Defining controllers

We will use the onion architecture and the patterns described in *Chapter 7, Understanding the Different Domains in Software Solutions*. It is worth recalling that the onion architecture has the purpose of decoupling the business-specific code, which is the one with the highest value for the company, from details of the deployment environment, such as operating system, chosen database, and user interface.

Technical requirements

This chapter requires the free Visual Studio 2026 Community edition or better, with all database tools installed.

The code samples necessary to clarify the concepts in this chapter will be taken from a practical example application based on the WWTravelClub book use case. The full example application is described in detail in the A Frontend Microservice section of *Chapter 22, Case Study: Practical Usage of ASP.NET Aspire*. While its code is available at `https://github.com/PacktPublishing/Software-Architecture-with-.NET-10-and-C-sharp-5E`.

Frontends and micro-frontends

The main peculiarity of frontend microservices is that they need a robust web server that is able to optimize the whole request/response handling and ensure the needed level of security. Moreover, high-traffic applications also need a load balancer.

For a better understanding of why a web server is a MUST, and which of its services must be enabled, let's list some of the services offered by robust web servers like IIS, Apache, and NGINX:

- Limiting access to just some file types and directories, to prevent access to private files and to prevent remote file execution, that is, execution of server commands/scripts through Web requests.

- Blocking dangerous requests that might cause access to unwanted files or directories (path-traversal attacks).
- Blocking requests that exceed a customizable length since they might cause a denial of service
- Logging and IP address blocking to discover and contrast hacker attacks.
- Redirecting requests to the frontend associated with each URL.
- Queueing requests and assigning them to available threads. This capability is fundamental for performance optimization, since executing too many requests compared to the available processor cores might cause unacceptable performance.
- Ensuring isolation of applications running in the same process but in different threads.

Together, these responsibilities highlight that frontend microservices MUST be placed behind a robust web server. As we will see in *Chapter 19, Orchestrators and .NET Aspire*, all orchestrators offer this option. You may also use the above list as a checklist for the services to enable on your web servers.

Architectures based on several cooperating front-end microservices are called micro-frontend architectures. The reasons for using micro-frontends are the same as the ones for using other microservices. We discussed them in detail in *Chapter 11, Applying a Microservice Architecture to Your Enterprise Application*, but it is worth repeating here the more important ones:

- Optimizing the usage of hardware resources by scaling just the microservices that need more resources
- Having independent software lifecycles for each microservice, so each microservice can evolve independently from the others to match user needs, and so that each microservice's developer team can work independently from the others

Micro-frontend architectures use quite different techniques for HTML websites, like the ASP.NET Core MVC websites, and for web APIs. Actually, the word 'micro-frontend' is used just with HTML websites/SPAs, while web APIs exposed to the outside world are referred to as public web APIs. We will describe public web APIs and HTML micro-frontends, and the techniques they use, in two dedicated subsections, starting with public web APIs.

Public web APIs

Even **public Web APIs** play a fundamental role in exposing the application to the external world when the HTML is not generated on the server side, but the user interface runs completely on the client. In fact, in this case, they are the bridge between the client UX and the server application.

In the case of web APIs, all microservices are accessible through a unique load-balanced piece of software called an API gateway that sits in between the clients and the various API services. The basic role of an API gateway is to make the whole API accessible from a unique domain to both avoid problems with the browsers' unique domain policy and to make simpler the usage of all API services. *Figure 17.1* shows an API gateway–based architecture.

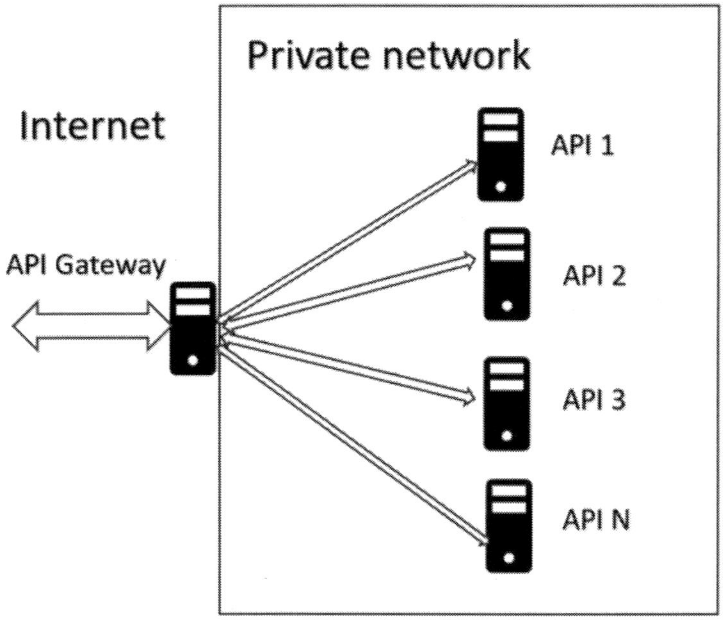

Figure 17.1: API Gateway

However, the API gateway offers the opportunity to centralize other functions that are common to all API services, such as:

- **Authentication**, that is, validating and decoding the authentication token that comes with each request (please do not confuse authentication with login).
- **Caching**, that is, caching responses according to configurable caching policies.
- **Translation**, that is, adapting the interface, as seen by the client, to the actual signature of the various API methods. This way, each API can change its interface without affecting existing clients.
- **Versioning**, that is, directing each request toward a compatible version of each API service.
- **Documentation**, that is, offering a unique documentation endpoint.

The above are just the main services offered by API gateways, but API gateways are in continuous evolution, absorbing and offering more and more functions, giving rise to the so-called **API management systems** that now automate and take care of most of the burden of handling public web APIs.

It is worth mentioning that API Management and API gateway need not be implemented from scratch, but are available both as services and products.

For instance, Azure, like all clouds, offers a good API management service. You can find more information about it here: `https://azure.microsoft.com/en-gb/products/api-management/`.

Among the products, it is also worth mentioning **Ocelot** (`https://docs.microsoft.com/en-us/dotnet/architecture/microservices/multi-container-microservice-net-applications/implement-api-gateways-`

`with-ocelot`), a library for easily creating custom API gateways. You can either use it to fill in configuration files or as a base for a completely custom API gateway.

Now we are ready to discuss HTML micro-frontends, which also add the challenge of combining several HTML fragments into a unique HTML page.

HTML micro-frontends

Usually, in microservices applications, several HTML frontends cooperate in the same application by furnishing each a different set of web pages. In this case, coordinating them requires just a web server that chooses the frontend to which to forward each request according to the request URL (this service is called **virtual hosting**). This is the classical and more common pattern of frontend cooperation.

We reserve the micro-frontend term for the more complex cases where several frontends cooperate in the construction of *every single page*. This is necessary when an HTML page that combines information from various sources can't be built efficiently by a single frontend since the information conveyed by the page falls within the boundaries of several microservices. In similar situations, several micro-frontends cooperate in the construction of the same page by supplying various page areas. In these cases, a software component must take the burden of assembling the various parts into a unique page.

The main difficulty of combining several HTML fragments into a single HTML page is offering a coherent experience to the user, thus avoiding assembling all page areas in a way that is hard to understand for the user. Another problem is avoiding the continuous page flipping and reorganization each time new content reaches the browser. In what follows, we will discuss how these problems are solved by different technologies.

Figure 17.2 shows a classic web application that builds the HTML on the server side. There, an interface frontend furnishes the page layout and then calls various micro-frontends to fill various layout areas.

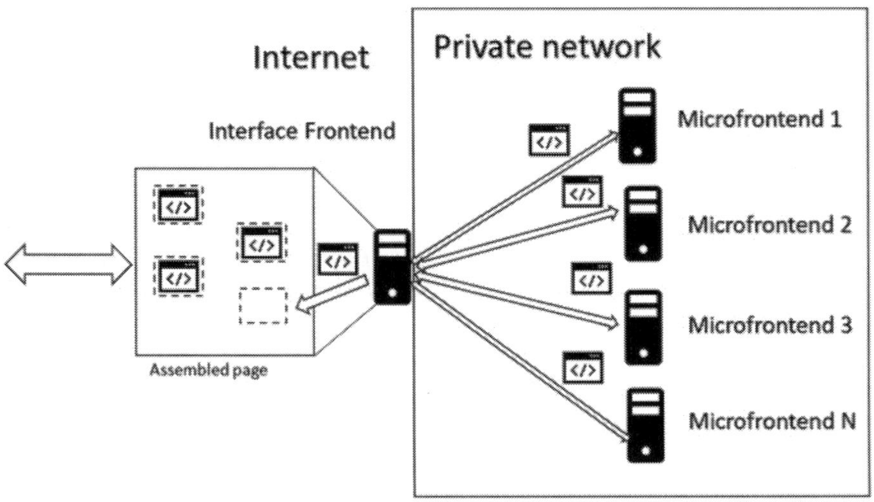

Figure 17.2: Server-side Microfrontend

In this case, there are no browser page flipping and reorganization issues since the whole HTML page is assembled on the server side and sent to the browser only when it is ready. However, we pay for this advantage with memory consumption for the whole time needed to assemble the whole page before sending it to the browser.

Both the layout to use and which calls to make to the involved micro-frontends are obtained by processing the request URL according to rules that are either hardwired in the code or, better, stored in one or more configuration sources (in the simplest case, a unique configuration file). Using predefined page patterns ensures coherence and a good user experience, but we pay a cost in maintainability because we need to update and test the interface application at each non-trivial change of any single micro-frontend that furnishes page areas.

In the case of SPAs, the assembling process takes place on the client, that is, in the browser:

1. A master application furnishes the initial HTML page
2. The master application downloads a JavaScript file from each micro-frontend. Each of these JavaScript files is a micro-SPA that creates page areas.

The master application, based on the current URL, decides which URL to pass to each micro-SPA and then puts the HTML produced by each micro-SPA in the right place. *Figure 17.3* shows how a master application creates the initial page with all micro-SPAs (App1, App2, App3, AppN). Then each micro-SPA exchanges data with an API (API 1, API 2, API 3, API N) through an API Gateway.

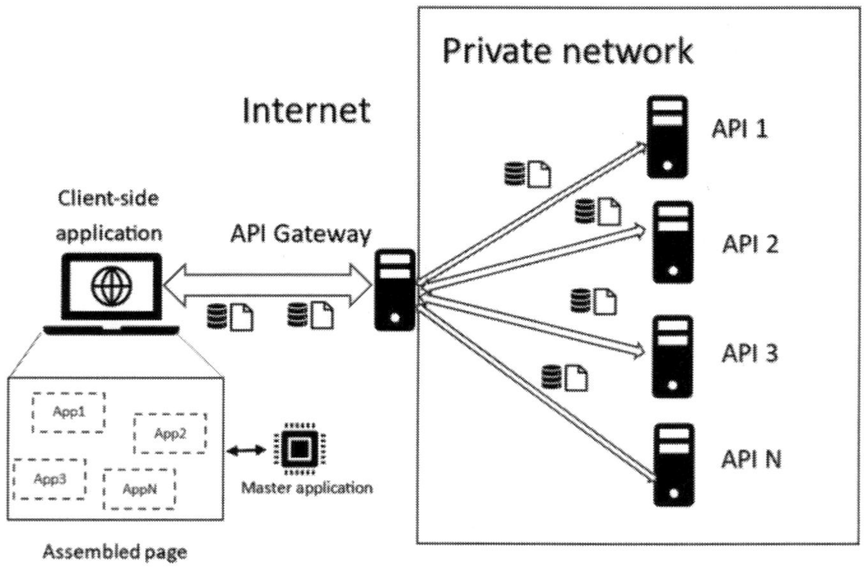

Figure 17.3: Client-side Micro Frontend

The various micro-SPAs do not interfere with each other because each of them runs in a separate JavaScript scope. Therefore, for instance, we can mix micro-SPAs implemented with different and incompatible versions of Angular and/or React.

Micro-frontends can also be implemented using WebAssembly frameworks, like Blazor (see *Chapter 18, Client Frameworks: Blazor*), that run .NET code. However, in this case, the various micro-SPAs do not run in separate environments, so they must be based on compatible .NET versions.

SPAs' micro-frontends have the same maintainability costs as server-based micro-frontends and also have the browser page flipping and reorganization issue, since the page is created dynamically as new content and/or data reach the browser. This problem can be solved by pre-allocating each content area in the browser page with fixed-size HTML tags. Thus, for instance, we may pre-allocate a 300px x 300px area to show weather forecasts, and show some picture or animation while the actual content is loading.

When several pages combine information from several sources, the alternative to micro-frontends is integration frontends that aggregate information from all needed sources. However, the design of these aggregators is strictly tied to the design of the microservices that furnish the information to aggregate, thus violating the rule of microservice design independence and causing modularity and maintainability issues.

Micro-frontends overcome these issues by adopting general-purpose pattern-based aggregation techniques that do not depend on the way the source microservices are designed. However, while specific-purpose aggregators can be easily designed to optimize the user experience, it is not easy to design general-purpose pattern-based aggregations that offer coherent and efficacious user interfaces.

> **Note**
>
> Therefore, in similar situations, we have a trade-off between difficult-to-design and coordinate micro-frontends that ensure strong modularity and maintainability, and easier-to-design aggregators that suffer from modularity and maintainability issues.

In the next section, we will introduce the architectural schema for building a frontend microservice based on ASP.NET Core MVC.

Defining the microservice architecture

Designing the internal organization of a .NET frontend microservice requires the simultaneous adoption of best practices for implementing microservices and an efficacious implementation of the use cases with ASP.NET Core controllers.

The adoption of microservices best practices is ensured by the usage of the **Domain-Driven Design** (DDD) approach and associated patterns described in *Chapter 7, Understanding the Different Domains in Software Solutions,* and already used in *Chapter 14, Implementing Microservices with .NET,* so having a good understanding of these chapters is a fundamental prerequisite to reading this chapter.

While an efficacious implementation of the application user cases can be enforced with the usage of ASP.NET Core MVC, other approaches based on client frameworks will be shown in *Chapter 18, Client Frameworks: Blazor.*

As per microservices best practices, we will use the Onion Architecture described in *Chapter 7, Understanding the Different Domains in Software Solutions,* based on four layers: domain layer, domain services, application services, and an outermost layer that contains both the user interface and the DB driver.

Let's summarize what these four layers become in our case (each of the listed items is implemented as a separate DLL):

- There's a DB Driver, based on Entity Framework Core, which contains all repository implementations and the database entities. It is a .NET library project. It is part of the onion architecture's outermost layer and is implemented as a separate DLL.
- The domain models layer contains DDD aggregates. According to the best practices described in the *How to turn Entity Framework Core entities into aggregates* section of *Chapter 13, Interacting with Data in C# – Entity Framework Core*, we implemented aggregates as independent classes that store information in a state object. Each state object implements an interface that is defined in the domain models, and that is implemented by a DB Driver entity. Hence, for instance, the `PackageAggregate` aggregate stores its state in a corresponding `IPackage` interface defined in the domain model layer. In turn, `IPackage` is implemented by the Entity Framework Core `Package` entity defined in the DB Driver. The domain model layer also contains the definitions of all the domain events, while the event handlers that will subscribe to these events are defined in the application layer.
- The domain services layer contains repository specifications; that is, interfaces that describe repositories. These repository interfaces are then implemented in the DB driver library.
- The application services layer that contains all commands and query definitions together with their handlers, and together with all event handlers.
- Finally, the presentation logic that is part of the outermost layer is an ASP.NET Core MVC application. Controllers fill query objects and execute them to get `ViewModels` they can pass to Views. They update storage by filling command objects and executing their associated command handlers. In turn, command handlers use repository interfaces and `IUnitOfWork` instances coming from the domain layer to manage and coordinate transactions. The outermost layer takes the burden of connecting all abstract interfaces (repository interfaces, aggregate state interfaces, etc.) with their implementations.

As for common microservices best practices, the application uses the *Command Query Responsibility Segregation (CQRS)* pattern; therefore, it uses command objects to modify the storage and query objects to query it. CQRS was described in the *Command Query Responsibility Segregation (CQRS) pattern* subsection of *Chapter 7, Understanding the Different Domains in Software Solution.*

The chain of objects and calls involved in the execution of commands is quite involved. This is because it requires the construction and modification of aggregates, as well as a definition of the interaction between several aggregates and between aggregates and other applications through domain events to be provided.

For a better understanding of how the whole architecture works, *Figure 17.4* gives a sketch of how storage update operations are performed. The circles are data being exchanged between the various layers, while rectangles are the procedures that process them. Moreover, dotted arrows connect implementations with either the interfaces they implement or with types that require them in their constructors:

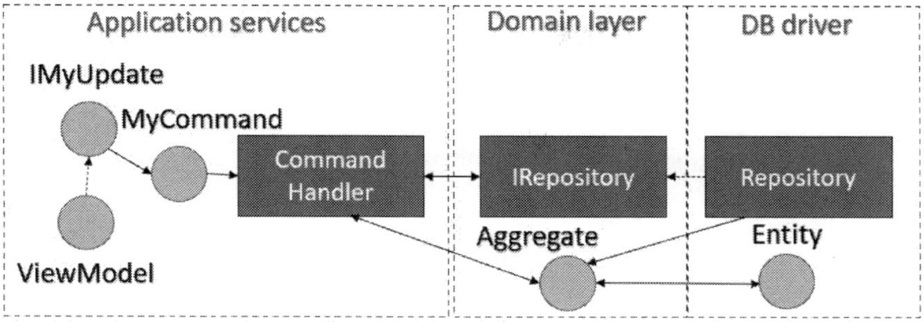

Figure 17.4: Diagram of command execution

Here's the flow of action through *Figure 17.4* as a list of steps:

1. A controller's action method receives a ViewModel and performs validation. The figure shows just the ViewModel entering the application layer.
2. The ViewModel containing changes to apply is hidden behind an interface (`IMyUpdate`). Since `IMyUpdate` is defined in the domain models layer, changes described in this interface can be passed to inner layers. As a first step, the controller action method passes `IMyUpdate` to the `MyCommand` command to start the application services layer processing.
3. At this point, the application services layer comes into play. A command handler matching the command `MyCommand` filled with `IMyUpdate` is retrieved via Dependency Injection (DI) in the controller action method. Then, the command handler is executed. During its execution, the handler interacts with various repository interface methods and with the aggregates they return (`IRepository` and `Aggregate` in the figure).
4. When creating the command handler in step 3, the ASP.NET Core DI engine automatically injects all parameters declared in its constructor. In particular, it injects all repository interface implementations needed to perform all command handler transactions. The command handler performs its job by calling the methods of the repository implementations received in its constructor to build aggregates and by modifying the built aggregates. Aggregates either represent already-existing entities or newly created ones.

   Command handlers use the `IUnitOfWork` interface, as well as the concurrency exceptions returned by the domain layer, to organize their operations as transactions. It is worth recalling that each aggregate has its own associated repository interface, and that the whole logic for updating each aggregate is defined in the aggregate itself, not in its associated repository interface, to keep the code more modular.
5. Behind the scenes, in the DB driver, repository implementations use Entity Framework to perform their job. Aggregates are created by passing Entity Framework entities that implement their state interfaces in their constructors. `IUnitOfWork` methods, which handle transactions and pass changes to the database, are implemented with `DbContext` methods. In other words, `IUnitOfWork` is implemented with the application's Entity Framework Core `DbContext`.

6. Domain events are generated during each aggregate processing and are added to the aggregates themselves by us calling the aggregate `AddDomainEvent` methods (see the *Command Handlers and Aggregate events* subsection of *Chapter 7, Understanding the Different Domains in Software Solutions*). However, domain events are not triggered immediately. Usually, they are triggered at the end of all the aggregates' processing and before changes are passed to the database; however, this is not a general rule.
7. The application handles errors by throwing exceptions. A more efficient approach would be to define a request-scoped object in the dependency engine, where each application subpart may add its errors as domain events. However, while this approach is more efficient, it increases the complexity of the code and the application development time.

Summing up, a Visual Studio solution based on an onion architecture and suitable for an ASP.NET Core MVC frontend microservices should be composed of 5 projects:

- A project containing the domain model, which is a .NET library.
- A project containing the domain services, which is a .NET library.
- A project containing the application services, which is a .NET library.
- A project containing the DB Driver, which is a .NET library based on Entity Framework Core.
- Finally, an ASP.NET Core MVC project that contains the onion architecture outermost layer. When you define this project, select **No Authentication**; otherwise, the user database will be added directly to the ASP.NET Core MVC project instead of to the database layer. Authentication must be added manually in the proper way. See *Chapter 20, Securing Data and Applications*, for adequate options for adding authentication.

In the remaining sections, we will describe the implementation of each layer that composes the architecture described so far, starting with the domain layer.

Defining the Domain Layer

The **domain layer** is composed of two libraries: domain models, which contain aggregate definitions, and domain services, which contain the repository interface definitions. The domain services library needs a reference to the domain model library.

Below is an example of an aggregate definition:

```
public class DestinationAggregate(IDestination state): Entity<int>
{
    public override int Id => state.Id;
    public string Name => state.Name;
    public string Country => state.Country;
    public string? Description => state.Description;
    public void ChangeDescription(string newText) =>
       state.Description=newText;
}
```

Where, `Entity<int>` is the base class for all aggregates discussed in the *DDD Entities in .NET* subsection of *Chapter 7, Understanding the Different Domains in Software Solutions*. It is worth recalling that aggregates are DDD building blocks for modeling all business objects.

We also have an `Event` folder containing all domain event definitions. Events are triggered whenever a change in an aggregate has consequences either on other aggregates or on other microservices. They are a way to implement weak interactions between aggregates and microservices while keeping the code of aggregates independent of each other.

By using events, we may keep the code of each aggregate substantially independent of the code of other aggregates that are involved in the same database transactions: each aggregate generates events that might interest other aggregates, such as a price change in a touristic package aggregate, and all other aggregates that depend on this price subscribe to that event, so they can update their data coherently. This way, when a new aggregate that depends on the touristic package price is added during system maintenance, we don't need to modify the touristic package aggregate.

When the event might interest other microservices, the event is also passed to a message broker that makes the event available for subscription to code in other microservices. Message brokers were discussed in *Chapter 14, Implementing Microservices with .NET*.

Below is an example event definition:

```
public record PackagePriceChangedEvent(int PackageId, decimal NewPrice,
        long OldVersion, long NewVersion): IEventNotification;
```

When an aggregate sends all its changes to another microservice, it should have a version property. The microservice that receives the changes uses this version property to apply all changes in the right order. An explicit version number is necessary because changes are sent asynchronously, so the order they are received in may differ from the order they were sent in. For this purpose, events that are used to publish changes outside of the application have both `OldVersion` (the version before the change) and `NewVersion` (the version after the change) properties. Events associated with delete events have no `NewVersion` since, after being deleted, an entity can't store any versions.

In the domain services library, an `IRepositories` folder contains all repository interfaces; below is an example repository interface:

```
public interface IPackageRepository: IRepository
{
    Task<IList<PackageInfosDTO>> GetAllInfo();
    Task<IPackage?> GetAsync(int id);
    PackageAggregate New(string name, string description, decimal price,
        int durationInDays, DateTime? startValidityDate,
        DateTime? endValidityDate, int DestinationId);
    Task<PackageAggregate?> Delete(int id);
}
```

`PackageInfosDTO` is a DTO defined in the domain services. In fact, domain services also contain DTOs used to return query results instead of aggregates. These query results are returned by repository methods called by application services' **query objects**.

Repositories always contain just a few methods since all business logic should be represented as aggregate methods – in the above example, just the methods to create a new package, to retrieve an existing package, and to delete an existing package. The logic to modify an existing package is included in the package aggregate.

The next section explains how the DB driver implements both repositories and aggregate state interfaces.

Defining the DB driver

An Entity Framework core DB Driver library project contains references to the Entity Framework Core driver NuGet packages for the chosen database, and to `Microsoft.EntityFrameworkCore.Tools`, which are needed to generate database migrations as explained in the Entity Framework Core migrations section of *Chapter 13, Interacting with Data in C# – Entity Framework Core.*

It also needs a reference to the domain services library in order to access all aggregates, their state interface, and all repository interfaces. Moreover, the ASP.NET Core-based outermost layer must have a reference to it in order to connect all interfaces with their implementations.

The DB driver contains all entity definitions in a `Model` folder. When needed, each entity has an associated `IEntityTypeConfiguration`-based configuration class. Entity definitions are similar to the ones in *Chapter 13, Interacting with Data in C# – Entity Framework Core.* However, some entities might have an `EntityVersion` property decorated with the `[ConcurrencyCheck]` attribute. It contains the entity version that is needed for sending changes to other microservices. The `ConcurrencyCheck` attribute is needed to prevent concurrency errors while updating the entity version. This prevents suffering the performance penalty implied by a transaction.

More specifically, when saving entity changes, if the value of a field marked with the `ConcurrencyCheck` attribute is different from the one that was read when the entity was loaded in memory, a concurrency exception is thrown to inform the calling method that someone else modified this value after the entity was read, but before we attempted to save its changes. This way, the calling method can repeat the whole operation with the hope that this time, no one will write the same entity in the database during its execution. For more information and practical usage of `EntityVersion` and `[ConcurrencyCheck]`, please refer to the *A Frontend Microservice* section of *Chapter 22, Case Study: Practical Usage of .NET Aspire* that contains a full example of a frontend microservice.

Below is the code of an example Package entity that uses `EntityVersion` and `[ConcurrencyCheck]`:

```
public class Package : IPackage
{
    public int Id { get; set; }
    [MaxLength(128)]
    public required string Name { get; set; }
    [MaxLength(128)]
```

```
    public string? Description { get; set; }
    public decimal Price { get; set; }
    public int DurationInDays { get; set; }
    public DateTime? StartValidityDate { get; set; }
    public DateTime? EndValidityDate { get; set; }
    public Destination MyDestination { get; set; } = null!;
    [ConcurrencyCheck]
    public long EntityVersion { get; set; }

    public int DestinationId { get; set; }
}
```

`MainDBContext` implements `IUnitOfWork`. The following code shows the implementation of all methods that start, roll back, and commit a transaction:

```
public async Task StartAsync(IsolationLevel isolationLevel =
IsolationLevel.ReadCommitted)
{
    await Database.BeginTransactionAsync(isolationLevel);
}
public async Task CommitAsync()
{
    await Database.CommitTransactionAsync();
}
public async Task RollbackAsync()
{
    await Database.RollbackTransactionAsync();
}
```

However, they are rarely used by command classes in a distributed environment. In fact, like distributed transactions, local database blocking transactions are also avoided because they might block database resources for too much time, which is incompatible with the maximization of traffic typical of microservices-based applications.

Likely, as already mentioned, all databases support tagging some row fields as **Concurrency Checks**. In Entity Framework Core, this is done by decorating the entity property corresponding to the field with the `ConcurrencyCheck` attribute.

Concurrency Checks detect interference of another transaction B on a record while performing a transaction `A`. This way, we can perform transaction A without blocking any database record or table, and if we detect an interference, we abort transaction `A` and retry it until it succeeds without interferences. This technique works well if transactions are very quick and consequently, interferences are rare.

More specifically, if during transaction `A` the value of the Concurrency Checks specified by an update operation differs from the one stored in the record being updated, the update is aborted, and a concurrency exception is thrown. The rationale is that another transaction B modified the Concurrency Check, thus interfering with the operation being performed by A.

Accordingly, the method that passes all changes applied to DbContext to the database performs a check for concurrency exceptions:

```
public async Task<bool> SaveEntitiesAsync()
{
    try
    {
        return await SaveChangesAsync() > 0;
    }
    catch (DbUpdateConcurrencyException ex)
    {
        foreach (var entry in ex.Entries) await entry.ReloadAsync();
        throw new ConcurrencyException(ex);
    }
    catch (DbUpdateException ex)
    {
        throw new ConstraintViolationException(ex);
    }
}
```

The preceding implementation just calls the SaveChangesAsync DbContext context method, which saves all changes to the database, but then it intercepts all concurrency exceptions and reloads all the entities involved in the concurrency error from the context. This way, the next time a command retries the whole failed operation, their updated versions will be used.

In other words, when the update fails because of the interference of a transaction B, we let the interfering transaction B finish its job. Then, EF reloads all entities modified by B that contain the value of the concurrency check modified by B. This way, when the operation is retried, if no other transaction interferes, there will be no conflict on the concurrency check.

The practical usage of concurrency checks is detailed in the *A Frontend Microservice* section of *Chapter 22, Case Study: Practical Usage of ASP.NET Aspire*.

All repository implementations are defined in a Repositories folder, to ensure better maintainability. It is worth pointing out that we don't need to add manually all repositories to the dependency injection engine since all repositories are automatically discovered and added to the application DI engine, calling the AddAllRepositories method, which is defined in the DDD tools we added to the domain layer project. More details on how to ensure this method is called when the application starts are given in the example detailed description in the *A Frontend Microservice* section of *Chapter 22, Case Study: Practical Usage of ASP.NET Aspire.*

Defining the application services

The **application layer** contains the definition of all business operations. Each of the business operations defined in this layer is then called by an MVC or API controller as a consequence of its interaction with the user. More specifically, each action method reacts to the user request that activated it by calling one or more application services business operations. Each business operation is handled as a single database transaction, so if an action method calls several business operations, then each of them is an independent transaction that may succeed or not.

These business operations use data provided by the user to modify domain layer abstraction aggregates, such as touristic packages. When an application service's business operation is finalized, a `IUnitOfWork.SaveEntitiesAsync()` operation is performed to save all changes to the database.

Business operations that create or modify aggregates are encoded by **Commands** that contain all operation input, and are executed by command handlers associated with these commands. Operations whose only purpose is to show data to the user are executed by **Query** objects. For more details on Commands and Query, please refer to *Chapter 7, Understanding the Different Domains in Software Solutions*.

The application services layer can take advantage of the utilities contained in the GitHub `ch07/OnionArchitecture/ApplicationServices` folder in the root of our `PackagesManagementApplicationServices` project. The `Tools` folder contains:

- The `IQuery` and `ICommand` are empty interfaces that mark all commands so that they can be easily found with reflection and added with their handlers to the dependency injection engine.
- The `IEventHandler<Event>` interface that marks all event handlers associated with the same event `Event` so that they can be easily found with reflection and added to the dependency injection engine.
- The `ICommandHandler<Command>` interface that marks all command handlers associated with the same command `Command` so that they can be easily found with reflection and added to the dependency injection engine.
- The `EventMediator` class is added to the dependency injection engine and used by all command handlers to trigger all events added to any aggregate. It uses the `EventTrigger` to retrieve all event handlers associated with the same event from the dependency injection engine.

The `Extensions` folder contains the extension methods that add command handlers, event handlers, queries and `EventMediator` to the dependency injection engine. They must be called by `Program.cs` in the `PackagesManagement` project, as shown below:

```
...
builder.Services.AddDbDriver(...)
builder.Services.AddApplicationServices();
...
```

A `Queries` folder contains all queries and their associated interfaces. Below is an example of a Query class:

```
public class PackagesListQuery(IPackageRepository repo):
    IPackagesListQuery
{
    public async Task<IList<PackageInfosDTO>> GetAllPackages()
    {
        return await repo.GetAllInfo();
    }
}
```

The simple query class above just calls a method of the repository that is automatically injected in its constructor without further processing. However, in general, more than one repository call is needed, followed by processing of all results.

All commands can be placed in a `Command` folder. Below is an example command:

```
public class UpdatePackageCommand : ICommand
{
    public int Id { get; init; }
    public required string Name { get; init; }
    public required string Description { get; init; }
    public decimal Price { get; init; }
    public int DurationInDays { get; init; }
    public DateTime? StartValidityDate { get; init; }
    public DateTime? EndValidityDate { get; init; }
}
```

Both command handler and event handler may be placed in a `Handler` folder. Below is the command handler associated with the previous command. It updates touristic packages:

```
public class UpdatePackageCommandHandler(IPackageRepository repo,
    IEventMediator mediator)
```

Its principal constructor has automatically injected the `IPackageRepository` repository and an `EventMediator` instance needed to trigger event handlers. The following code also shows the implementation of the standard `HandleAsync` command handler method:

```
public async Task HandleAsync(UpdatePackageCommand command)
{
    bool done = false;
    PackageAggregate? model;
    while (!done)
    {
```

```
            try
            {
                model = await repo.GetAsync(command.Id);
                if (model is null) return;
                model.Name= command.Name;
                model.Description = command.Description;
                model.DurationInDays = command.DurationInDays;
                model.Price = command.Price;
                model.StartValidityDate = command.StartValidityDate;
                model.EndValidityDate = command.EndValidityDate;

                await mediator.TriggerEvents(model.DomainEvents);
                await repo.UnitOfWork.SaveEntitiesAsync();
                done = true;
            }
            catch (ConcurrencyException)
            {
                //add here some logging
            }
        }
    }
```

`HandleAsync` uses the repository to get an instance of the aggregate to modify. If the aggregate is not found (it has been deleted), the command stops its execution. Otherwise, all changes are passed to the retrieved aggregate. Immediately after the update, all events contained in the aggregate are triggered. In particular, if the price has changed, the event handler associated with the price change is executed.

The while loop repeats the operation in case it has been aborted because of a `ConcurrencyException` caused by the violation of a `[ConcurrencyCheck]`.

Up to now we discussed how business operations are implemented and executed, but how can we verify if the current user has the right to perform each specific business operation?

Let's discuss authentication and authorization techniques in the next section.

Defining the authentication strategy

In a microservice application containing several frontend microservices, both login and authentication must be defined by a unique module working as an authentication server.

If each HTML-based frontend is directly accessible to the users, then the best solution is the adoption of an authentication server together with an OAuth protocol that transforms the authentication token provided by the authentication server into a cookie-based authentication token suitable for the frontend that needs user authentication. Then, each frontend uses that token to decide user authorizations on the various operations.

If, on the other side, all frontends are behind a unique microservice that takes care of interfacing all requests, then that microservice can take care of handling login, authenticating each request, and authorizing or not the operation contained in the request. However, also in this case, an authorization token must be forwarded to each destination frontend for the following reasons:

- The interface microservice can base its operation authorization just on the URL format, but sometimes authorization may depend also on the values of parameters contained in the URL
- When an operation is authorized to a user, the result of the operation may depend on the user and on its claims. For instance, in a customer's listing the actual customers listed might depend on the user: a manager might see all customers, while other employees might see just the customers assigned to them

In this case, the interface microservice might add a bearer token to each request to enable each frontend to fine-tune authorization.

The authorization and authentication middleware must be added to ASP.NET Core to properly handle both authentication and authorization, as shown below:

```
...
app.UseAuthentication();
app.UseRouting();
app.UseAuthorization();
...
```

All authentication options, including the type of authentication chosen, are specified in the services definition area of `Program.cs`:

```
builder.Services.AddAuthentication(
    <default authentication schema name>)
    .Add<authettication type 1>(o =>
    {
        ...
    })
    .Add<authettication type 2>(o =>
    {
        ...
    })
    ...
    .;
```

Where, `Add<authetication type 1>` and `Add<authetication type 2>` stand for different kinds of authentication techniques supported, since each application may support several authentication mechanisms. There are `Add...` methods for cookie-based authentication, for bearer-token-based authentication, and for OAuth-based authentication. Each authentication schema has an associated option object the developer can use to fine-tune its features. For more information on authentication in ASP.NET Core please refer to the Defining the ASP.NET Core pipeline section of *Chapter 20, Securing Data and Applications*.

At this point, we need just the last piece of our architecture: how action methods invoke Commands and Queries.

Defining controllers

Each controller takes care of handling a use case that emerged in the analysis stage with its action methods. Action methods do their job by requiring command handlers and query interfaces from the dependency injection engine.

Below is an example of how query objects are required and used. The action method requires the `IPackagesListQuery` query interface with the `[Fromservices]` attribute. Then it invokes one of its methods, and uses the data returned to fill the ViewModel that is returned to the View.

```
[HttpGet]
public async Task<IActionResult> Index([FromServices] IPackagesListQuery query)
{
    var results = await query.GetAllPackages();
    var vm = new PackagesListViewModel
       { Items = new ReadOnlyCollection<PackageInfosDTO>(results) };
    return View(vm);
}
```

Below, instead the usage of command handlers:

```
[HttpPost]
public async Task<IActionResult> Edit(
    PackageFullEditViewModel vm,
    [FromServices] ICommandHandler<UpdatePackageCommand> command)
{
    if (ModelState.IsValid)
    {
        await command.HandleAsync(new UpdatePackageCommand {
            Id = vm.Id,
            Name = vm.Name,
            Description = vm.Description,
            Price = vm.Price,
            DurationInDays=vm.DurationInDays,
            StartValidityDate=vm.StartValidityDate,
            EndValidityDate=vm.EndValidityDate
        });
        return RedirectToAction(
            nameof(ManagePackagesController.Index));
    }
    else
```

```
        return View(vm);
}
```

ICommandHandler<UpdatePackageCommand> retrieves the command handler associated with the `UpdatePackageCommand` command from DI.

If `ModelState` is valid, `UpdatePackageCommand` is created and its associated handler is invoked; otherwise, the View is displayed again to the user to enable them to correct all the errors.

Summing up, the job of controllers is quite easy; they just perform input validation and take care of organizing the interaction with the user. Actual operations are performed by calling adequate command handlers defined in the application services layer that take care of executing the appropriate business operations as transactions.

Summary

In this chapter, we analyzed the peculiarities of frontend microservices and the techniques used to implement them.

Then, we put together the techniques learned in this chapter and in previous chapters in the complete implementation of a frontend microservice.

We used an onion architecture with a DB Driver and a domain model, domain services, application services, and an ASP.NET Core MVC application as the outermost layer. We implemented each layer as a separate project.

The microservice used the CQRS pattern and used a queue implemented with a database table to store the events to send to other microservices.

The next chapter explains how to implement a presentation layer with client-based techniques. We will use Blazor as an example client framework.

Questions

1. What is the difference between a Frontend and an API Gateway?
2. Why all frontends and API Gateway should use a robust web server?
3. Why should complex blocking database transactions be avoided?
4. When does the concurrency technique ensure better performance?
5. What is the advantage of using domain events to implement interactions between different aggregates?

Further reading

The following are some links you may consider reading to gather more information in relation to this chapter:

- Ocelot GitHub repository: `https://github.com/ThreeMammals/Ocelot`
- How to implement your API gateway with Ocelot: `https://docs.microsoft.com/en-us/dotnet/architecture/microservices/multi-container-microservice-net-applications/implement-api-gateways-with-ocelot`

- Azure API Management: `https://azure.microsoft.com/en-gb/products/api-management/`
- Azure App Service: `https://azure.microsoft.com/en-us/services/app-service/`
- More information on MediatR can be found on MediatR's GitHub repository: `https://github.com/jbogard/MediatR`

Get this book's PDF version and more

Scan the QR code (or go to `packtpub.com/unlock`). Search for this book by name, confirm the edition, and then follow the steps on the page.

UNLOCK NOW

Note: Keep your invoice handy. Purchases made directly from Packt don't require an invoice.

18

Client Frameworks: Blazor

In this chapter, you will learn how to implement presentation layers based on client technologies. They run the whole presentation logic on the client machine (mobile device, desktop computer, laptop, etc.) and interact with a server just to exchange data with the Web API.

In other words, in applications based on client technology, the whole UI is created by code that runs on the user's device, which also controls the whole user-application interaction. Both the business logic and domain layer, instead, run on server machines to prevent users from violating business rules and authorization policies by hacking the code that runs on their devices.

In turn, applications based on client technologies can be classified as single-page applications, which benefit from Web standards, or as native applications, which are tied to specific operating systems and take advantage of specific device peculiarities.

Single-page applications are based on JavaScript or WebAssembly and run in any browser; they heavily rely on Web technologies. Accordingly, this chapter uses many technologies we already analyzed in *Chapter 16, Presenting ASP.NET Core,* such as dependency injection and Razor. Therefore, we strongly recommend studying *Chapter 16, Presenting ASP.NET Core,* and *Chapter 17, Implementing Frontend Microservices with ASP.NET Core,* before reading this chapter.

As an example of a single-page application, we will analyze the Blazor WebAssembly framework that relies on a .NET implementation that runs in WebAssembly. Accordingly, Blazor WebAssembly applications are developed in C#.

As an example of native technologies, we will analyze native .NET MAUI Blazor, which is completely analogous to Blazor WebAssembly, but instead of using browser WebAssembly, it uses .NET that is compiled just in time into the assembly of the target device. Not being limited by browser restrictions, .NET MAUI Blazor can access all device features through adequate .NET libraries.

More specifically, in this chapter, you will learn about the following subjects:

- Comparison of the various types of client technologies
- Blazor WebAssembly architecture
- Blazor pages and components

- Blazor forms and validation
- Modifying HTML <head> content from Blazor components
- Blazor advanced features, such as globalization, authentication, and JavaScript interoperability
- .NET MAUI Blazor
- Developing native applications with Blazor

While there is also server-side Blazor, which runs on the server like ASP.NET Core MVC, this chapter discusses just Blazor WebAssembly and .NET MAUI Blazor, since the main focus of the chapter is client-side technology. Moreover, server-side Blazor wastes significantly more server resources than other server-side technologies, like ASP.NET Core MVC, which we analyzed in *Chapter 16, Presenting ASP.NET Core.*

Anyway, server-side Blazor is based on the same principles and primitives as Blazor WebAssembly, but UI code is executed both on the client and on the server thanks to a continuous message exchange between the browser and server. The continuous message exchange overloads the server, so server-side Blazor can support just hundreds of users, but the application starts immediately because it can start before the whole framework (5-10 megabytes) is downloaded in the browser.

The first section summarizes and compares the various kinds of client technologies, while the remainder of the chapter discusses in detail Blazor WebAssembly and .NET MAUI Blazor.

Technical requirements

This chapter requires the free Visual Studio 2026 Community edition or better, with all the database tools installed.

> **Note**
>
> All concepts are clarified with simple example applications based on the WWtravelClub book use case that you can find in the *Using Client Technologies* section of *Chapter 22, Case Study: Practical Usage of .NET Aspire.*

The code for this chapter is available at `https://github.com/PacktPublishing/Software-Architecture-with-.NET-10-and-C-sharp-5E`.

Comparison of the various types of client technology

Client technologies offer a better UI than server-side technology because the application reacts immediately to any input, since they don't need to send a request to the server to react to user actions. Therefore, they must be preferred whenever a rich UI is a priority, while server-side technology should be preferred when on each screen there is a very limited set of actions that the user can take.

However, what are all the available client technologies, and how does one choose among them? This section will guide the choice of all available client technologies, namely:

1. Single Page Applications that run in the browser with all browser restrictions

2. A progressive web application that runs in the browser but can be installed like a usual application, and that can overcome some browser restrictions (after user permission is granted)
3. Native applications that are tied to a specific device/operating system, but can take full advantage of all device/operating system features
4. Cross-platform technologies that, like native applications, can take full advantage of all device features but that are compatible with several devices/operating systems

Each of the above technologies will be discussed in dedicated sections where we will analyze their features and when it's worth using them. After that, in a further section, we will present a few rules of thumb for deciding which technology to use. Let's start with a discussion of single-page applications.

Single-Page Applications

At the moment, most SPA frameworks are JavaScript-based. Among them, it is worth mentioning Angular, Vue.js, and React, which are the most popular. Blazor, which will be discussed in detail in this chapter, is the only popular SPA framework based on WebAssembly.

The situation changes if we move to frameworks for implementing Web games, where WebAssembly is a common choice due to its performance peculiarities. Among the WebAssembly-based game engines, it is worth mentioning Unity and Unreal.

The main reason to adopt a web-based client technology is the ability to deploy to many users at the same time any new version of the application, regardless of the kind of device and operating system they use, since they run in any browser. Moreover, the security policies that are automatically enforced by all browsers also encourage the usage and diffusion of web applications.

So, a good question here would be, why are SPAs not always the preferred choice for a client's technology? The best answer might be a lack of connectivity, and, as a software architect, you need to be alert to this, as we discussed in *Chapter 2, Non-Functional Requirements*.

For instance, in the WWTravelClub case, there is a first user story that says: "*As a common user, I want to view promotional packages on the home page, so that I can easily find my next vacation.*" At first sight, you may determine that a web app is the only option, especially because there is also a system requirement that says: "*The system will run on the Windows, Linux, iOS, and Android platforms.*"

However, imagine that a user browses a lot of destinations and packages to find their perfect vacation, and that they are going to reserve it when suddenly the WEB application crashes because of a lack of web connectivity. In a similar situation, the user would lose all their browsing effort and would be forced to start searching for their package from scratch once Web connectivity is restored. The issue can be overcome by an application that is able to save its state instead of crashing when there are WEB connectivity issues. This way, the user can complete their task as soon as Web connectivity is restored, without wasting whatever they have already done before the WEB connectivity issue.

> **Note**
>
> Another issue with SPAs is that they must download the application code each time the user enters the application with the browser.

So maybe, for some parts of the solution, a native application with some data already downloaded would be a better option. However, the issue can also be solved by a particular kind of modern WEB application, Progressive Applications, that we will analyze in the next subsection.

Progressive Applications

Progressive web applications are single-page applications that run in the browser but can be installed like native applications. Moreover, they can run offline. Therefore, they solve the problem of keeping the application state once the browser is offline. Moreover, installation avoids the application code from being downloaded at each application access, without renouncing the automatic version update, because each time the version changes, the browser automatically downloads the new code.

However, it is worth mentioning that progressive web applications can't replace native applications. In fact, native applications still remain the best choice when performance is a priority requirement and when we need to take full advantage of device hardware peculiarities.

Progressive applications are a new web standard that is supported by all mainstream browsers, so they keep all the advantages of standard SPA but overcome some of its disadvantages.

Blazor WebAssembly, which we will describe in the next sections of this chapter, supports Progressive Web Applications: it is enough to check the Progressive Web Application checkbox that appears when you create a Blazor WebAssembly project. This is all you need to do to create a Blazor progressive web application.

If you ship your Blazor application as a progressive application, you overcome the problem of the initial download time (4-8 seconds) due to the need to download the whole .NET framework, which is the main disadvantage of Blazor.

However, notwithstanding that Progressive Web Applications are installed applications, they automatically update to the latest available version because each time they are launched, they verify if a more recent version is available, and if there is one, they automatically download it before running. That is, they keep the advantage of automatically running the most recent available version that characterizes all classical Web applications.

The option to install the Blazor progressive web application is not available during development because this would interfere with the usual modification-test cycle. Therefore, you need to publish your application to test its progressive application peculiarities.

It is worth pointing out that progressive applications must be organized to take full advantage of their ability to work offline. Therefore, following repeated communication errors, the application should save all the data to be sent to the server in the browser's local storage, where it can remain saved while waiting for a connection to be established successfully.

It is also possible to maintain the whole application state in a centralized service so that the user can serialize and save it to local storage before quitting the application. This way, when the application is offline, data to be sent to the server is not lost because it remains in the application state that is saved to disk.

When a progressive web application doesn't fulfill your requirements because it is not able to use device peculiarity you need, but you must support several different devices. You should consider cross-platform Native Applications, which have full access to all device features, but can still support several hardware/software platforms. We will discuss them in the last subsection.

Native Applications

Native development can be considered the beginning of UI development. There was no concept of sharing code between machines with different hardware/operating systems when the idea of assigning software production to another person or company originally emerged.

The situation changed with the need to deploy the same applications to different platforms, and with the importance of evergreen applications that automatically update as soon as a new version is available.

Considering this scenario, the big question is – when do I have to use a native app? There are cases where they still remain the best option:

- There is no need to deploy on different platforms
- There is a huge connection to the hardware
- The performance provided by a Web client is not acceptable
- The application needs device resources that can't be accessed through a browser because of a browser's security policies

The decision between developing native or not can be difficult to make without a proof of concept (POC). As a software architect, you should be the one to recommend this kind of POC. The constraint of being tied to a specific platform can be removed with a small performance penalty by cross-platform applications that will be analyzed in the next subsection.

Cross-platform Applications

In some scenarios, we need all the advantages of native applications but can pay a small performance penalty. In these scenarios, cross-platform technologies make total sense. Among them, it is worth mentioning .NET MAUI and the UNO platform, which can be published on Android, iOS, and Windows.

The advised choice for a cross-platform application is .NET MAUI. However, at themoment, MAUI supports Windows and all main mobile platforms, but not Linux. The UNO platform (`https://platform.uno/`) and the Avalonia platform (`https://avaloniaui.net/`) support Linux together with all main mobile platforms, but they are not Microsoft products maintained by Microsoft. Anyway, they can be downloaded as a Visual Studio extension.

In this chapter, we will not analyze either UNO, Avalonia, or all options offered by .NET MAUI, but just .NET MAUI Blazor, since it is very similar to Blazor WebAssembly. Learning Blazor enables you to develop Single Page Applications, Progressive Applications, and Cross-platform applications. .NET MAUI Blazor is described in the *.NET MAUI Blazor* section of this chapter.

How to choose the Client Technology for your Application.

This section explains how to organize the choice of the client technology that is most adequate for your application.

The first choice you must make is whether it is adequate to implement your application with a Web technology, that is, as a possibly progressive SPA. You can do it with the following criteria, which are listed in order of importance:

1. Browser security limitations are an advantage or a disadvantage for your application. If security is your main issue, browser limitations increase the security of your application, so implementing it as an SPA may be convenient. On the contrary, if simple access to all hardware resources of the device is a priority, you should avoid implementing it as an SPA.
2. If exploiting all features of a specific device is a priority, you should avoid implementing it as a SPA
3. If immediate deployment through a browser is a priority or if accepting all rules imposed to publish an application in various stores with the associated waste of time is unacceptable for your application, you should choose an SPA
4. Finally, if achieving maximum performance is a priority, you should not select a SPA

Other features of native applications are not relevant to the choice between SPA, native and cross-platform technologies, since they can also be met by progressive SPA.

Once you opt in for a SPA, you can implement it as a progressive application if your target user doesn't mind installing your application and if you need some of the opportunities offered by progressive applications, such as working offline and avoiding the application download time at each application access.

On the contrary, if you reject SPAs, the choice between a native application and a cross-platform application should be based on the following criteria:

1. Cost of implementing N separate native applications instead of a unique cross-platform application versus maximal usage of each device's specific features. For instance, native iOS applications have a very peculiar user interface that can't be achieved with cross-platform applications. Therefore, if having a "*typical iOS user interface*" is a priority, you can't choose a cross-platform application.
2. If the performance penalty implied by a cross-platform application is not acceptable for your application, you should choose a native application

Summing up, the first choice is between SPA and native application, then if you select a SPA, you need to verify if it must be progressive, while if you select a native application, you must choose between N different applications, one for each device type, or a single multi-platform application.

This finishes our comparison of client technologies. The remainder of the chapter will be dedicated to the description of two specific technologies, namely: Blazor WebAssembly, which is .NET's preferred choice for SPA and progressive applications, and .NET MAUI. Let's start with Blazor.

Blazor WebAssembly architecture

Blazor WebAssembly uses the new WebAssembly browser feature to execute the .NET runtime in the browser. This way, it enables all developers to use the whole .NET code base and ecosystem in the implementation of applications capable of running in any WebAssembly-compliant browser. WebAssembly was conceived as a high-performance alternative to JavaScript. It is an assembly capable of running in a browser and obeying the same limitations as JavaScript code. This means that WebAssembly code, like JavaScript code, runs in an isolated execution environment that has very limited access to all machine resources.

At the moment, Blazor is one of the few frameworks for implementing WebAssembly-based SPA enterprise applications, since most of the SPA frameworks are still JavaScript-based. Blazor pros with respect to other SPA frameworks based on JavaScript are:

- It relies on the more efficient WebAssembly
- It is based on .NET, which is a framework conceived for building big, maintainable codebases
- It benefits from all development tools available for .NET, thus offering a fast development experience

WebAssembly differs from similar options of the past, like Flash and Silverlight, since it is an official **W3C** standard. More specifically, it became an official standard on December 5, 2019, so it is expected to have a long life, because no browser will stop supporting it, as was the case with Flash and Silverlight. As a matter of fact, at the moment, all mainstream browsers support it.

However, WebAssembly doesn't bring just performance with it; it also creates the opportunity to run whole code bases associated with modern and advanced object-oriented languages such as C++ (direct compilation), Java (bytecode), and C# (.NET) in browsers.

Before WebAssembly, presentation logic running in a browser could only be implemented in JavaScript, with all the problems associated with the maintenance of big code bases implemented in a language that is not strictly typed. However, we must consider that on one hand, the usage of TypeScript in part solves JavaScript's lack of strict typing, and on the other hand, .NET brings with it the problem of the binary compatibility of modules implemented with different .NET versions.

Anyway, with Blazor, C# developers can now implement complex applications in their favorite language, with all the comforts offered to this language by the C# compiler and Visual Studio.

Moreover, with Blazor, all .NET developers can use the full power of the .NET framework, with the only limitations imposed by the browser security policies, for the implementation of presentation logic that runs in the browser and that shares libraries and classes with all other libraries that run on the server side.

The subsections that follow describe the overall Blazor architectures. The first subsection explores the general concept of a single-page application, describing Blazor's peculiarities.

Blazor and single-page applications

A **single-page application** (SPA) is an HTML-based application, where the HTML is changed by code that runs in the browser instead of issuing a new request to the server and rendering a new HTML page from scratch. SPAs can simulate a multi-page experience by replacing complete page areas with new HTML.

SPA frameworks are frameworks explicitly designed for implementing SPAs. Before WebAssembly, all SPA frameworks were based on JavaScript. The most popular JavaScript-based SPA frameworks are Angular, React.js, and Vue.js.

All SPA frameworks provide ways to transform data into HTML to show to the user and rely on a module called **router** to simulate page changes. Typically, data fills in the placeholders of HTML templates, selects which parts of a template to render (if-like constructs), and how many times to render it (for-like constructs).

The Blazor template language is Razor, which we described in *Chapter 16, Presenting ASP.NET Core*.

In order to increase modularity, code is organized into components that are a kind of virtual HTML tags that, once rendered, generate actual HTML markup. Like HTML tags, components have attributes, which are usually called parameters, and custom events. It is up to the developer to ensure that each component uses its parameters to create proper HTML and to ensure that it generates adequate events. Components can be used inside other components in a hierarchical fashion.

Components can be associated with URLs in the application Web domain, in which case they are called pages. These URLs can be used in usual HTML links, and following them causes the upload of the page into an application area thanks to framework services called **Routers**.

Some SPA frameworks also provide a predefined dependency injection engine in order to ensure better separation between components on one side and general-purpose services plus business code that runs in the browser on the other. Among the frameworks listed in this subsection, only Blazor and Angular have an out-of-the-box dependency injection engine.

In order to reduce the overall application file size, SPA frameworks based on JavaScript usually compile all JavaScript code into a few JavaScript files and then perform so-called tree-shaking, that is, the removal of all unused code. This technique sensibly reduces the application load time.

At the moment, instead, Blazor keeps all DLLs (Dynamic Link Libraries) referenced by the main application separate and performs tree-shaking on each of them separately.

The next subsection starts to describe the Blazor architecture. We challenge you to create a Blazor WebAssembly project called `BlazorReview` so you can inspect the code and the constructs explained throughout the chapter.

Select **Blazor WebAssembly Standalone Application**, then select **Individual Accounts** as the authentication type, and ensure that the **Include sample pages** checkbox is checked, as shown in the picture below.

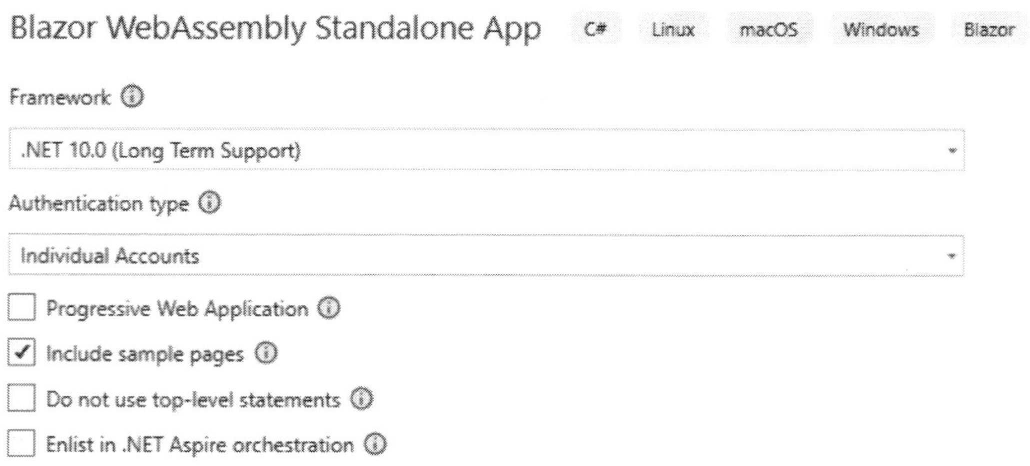

Figure 18.1: Creating the BlazorReview application

This way, Visual Studio will create all components and logic to handle both authentication and authorization on the Blazor pages.

If you start the application, the application works properly, but if you try to log in, the following error message will appear: "*There was an error trying to log you in: 'Network Error'.*" This is because you need to configure an identity provider to authenticate users. By default, the application is configured to use an OAuth-based identity provider. You just need to add the provider configuration data to a configuration file. We will discuss this in more detail in the *Authentication and authorization* section.

The next subsection is an overview of the Blazor project organization.

Loading and starting the application

The folder structure of a Blazor WebAssembly application always includes an `index.html` static HTML page. In our BlazorReview project, `index.html` is in `BlazorReview->wwwroot->index.html`. This page is the container where the Blazor application will create its HTML. It contains an HTML header with a viewport meta declaration, title, and the overall application's CSS. The Visual Studio default project template adds an application-specific CSS file and **Bootstrap** CSS, with a neutral style. You can replace the default Bootstrap CSS either with a customized style or with a completely different CSS framework.

The body contains the code that follows:

```
<body>
    <div id="app">
        <svg class="loading-progress">
            <circle r="40%" cx="50%" cy="50%" />
            <circle r="40%" cx="50%" cy="50%" />
        </svg>
        <div class="loading-progress-text"></div>
    </div>

    <div id="blazor-error-ui">
        An unhandled error has occurred.
        <a href="." class="reload">Reload</a>
        <span class="dismiss"> ✕ </span>
    </div>
    <script src="_content/Microsoft.AspNetCore.Components.WebAssembly.Authentication/
AuthenticationService.js"></script>
    <script src="_framework/blazor.webassembly#[.{fingerprint}].js"></script>
</body>
```

The initial `div` with the `app id` is where the application will place the code it generates. Any markup placed inside this `div` will appear just while the Blazor application is loading and starting, then it will be replaced by the application-generated HTML. By default, it contains a `svg` image and text that show the loading progress, both controlled by the JavaScript code that takes care of loading the framework. The loading animation is based on a CSS animation contained in the "css/app.css" main application CSS file. However, you can replace both the default content and the CSS animation.

The second div is normally invisible and appears only when Blazor intercepts an unhandled exception.

blazor.webassembly.js contains the JavaScript part of the Blazor framework. Among other things, it takes care of downloading the .NET runtime, together with all application DLLs. More specifically, blazor.webassembly.js downloads the blazor.boot.json file that lists all application files with their hashes. Then, blazor.webassembly.js downloads all resources listed in this file and verifies their hashes. All resources downloaded by blazor.webassembly.js are created when the application is built or published. While loading, blazor.webassembly.js periodically updates the --blazor-load-percentage and --blazor-load-percentage-text CSS variables with the loading percentage, respectively in numeric and text formats.

AuthenticationService.js is added only when the project enables authentication and takes care of the **OpenID Connect** protocol used by Blazor to exploit other identity providers to get bearer tokens, which are the preferred authentication credentials for clients that interact with a server through web APIs.

Authentication is discussed in more detail in the *Authentication and authorization* subsection later on in this chapter, while bearer tokens are discussed *in Chapter 20, Securing Data and Applications.*

The Blazor application entry point is in the BlazorReview ->Program.cs file. This file doesn't contain a class but just the code that must be executed when the application is launched:

```
var builder = WebAssemblyHostBuilder.CreateDefault(args);
builder.RootComponents.Add<App>("#app");
builder.RootComponents.Add<HeadOutlet>("head::after");
// Services added to the application
// Dependency Injection engine declared with statements like:
// builder.Services.Add...
await builder.Build().RunAsync();
```

WebAssemblyHostBuilder is a builder for creating a WebAssemblyHost, which is a WebAssembly-specific implementation of the generic host discussed in the *Using generic hosts* subsection of *Chapter 11, Applying a Microservice Architecture to Your Enterprise Application* (you are encouraged to review that subsection). The first builder configuration instruction declares the Blazor root component (App), which will contain the whole component tree, and specifies in which HTML tag of the index.html page to place it (#app). More specifically, RootComponents.Add adds a hosted service that takes care of handling the whole Blazor component tree. We can run several Blazor WebAssembly user interfaces on the same HTML page by calling RootComponents.Add several times, each time with a different HTML tag reference.

As a default, just another root component is added, HeadOutlet, and is placed immediately after the HTML Head tag. It is used for dynamically changing the index.html title (the text shown in the browser tab). For more information on the HeadOutlet component, see the *Modifying HTML <head> content from Blazor components* subsection.

builder.Services contain all the usual methods and extension methods to add services to the Blazor application dependency engine: AddScoped, AddTransient, AddSingleton, and so on. Like in ASP.NET Core MVC applications (*Chapter 16, Presenting ASP.NET Core*, and *Chapter 17, Implementing Frontend Microservices with ASP.NET Core*), services are the preferred places to implement business logic and to store shared state. While in ASP.NET Core MVC, services were usually passed to controllers, in Blazor WebAssembly, they are injected into components.

The default project scaffolded by Visual Studio contains just two services, one for communicating with the server and the other for handling OAuth-based authentication. We will discuss both of them later on in this chapter.

The next subsection is about Blazor's implementation of SPA routing, that is, it explains how Blazor implements page changes on the client side.

Routing

The root `App` class referenced by the host building code is defined in the `BlazorReview ->App.razor` file. `App` is a Blazor component, and like all Blazor components, it is defined in a file with a `.razor` extension and uses Razor syntax enriched with component notation, that is, with HTML-like tags that represent other Blazor components. It contains the whole logic for handling application pages:

```
<CascadingAuthenticationState>
    <Router AppAssembly="@typeof(App).Assembly"
        NotFoundPage="typeof(Pages.NotFound)" >
        <Found Context="routeData">
            <AuthorizeRouteView RouteData="@routeData"
                    DefaultLayout="@typeof(MainLayout)">
                <NotAuthorized>
                  @if (context.User.Identity?.IsAuthenticated != true)
                  {
                        <RedirectToLogin />
                  }
                  else
                  {
                      <p role="alert">
                       You are not authorized to access this resource.
                      </p>
                  }
                </NotAuthorized>
            </AuthorizeRouteView>
            <FocusOnNavigate RouteData="@routeData" Selector="h1" />
        </Found>
    </Router>
</CascadingAuthenticationState>
```

All tags in the preceding code represent either components or particular component parameters, called **templates**. Components will be discussed in detail throughout the chapter. For the moment, imagine them as a kind of custom HTML tag that we can define somehow with C# and Razor code. Templates, instead, are parameters that accept Razor markup as values. Templates are discussed in the *Templates and cascading parameters* subsection later on in this section.

The `CascadingAuthenticationState` component only has the function of passing authentication and authorization information to all components of the component tree that are inside of it. The Blazor project template generates it only if one chooses to add authorization during project creation.

> **Note**
>
> Blazor router logic takes on the burden of providing authorization services to all pages.

The `Router` component is the actual application router. It scans the assembly passed in the `AppAssembly` parameter, looking for components containing routing information, that is, for components that can work as pages. In the Blazor project template, the `Router` component is passed the assembly that contains the class of the App component, that is, the main application. Pages contained in other assemblies can be added through the `AdditionalAssemblies` parameter, which accepts an `IEnumerable` of assemblies.

> **Note**
>
> Blazor router logic automatically discovers pages by inspecting application assemblies.

After that, the router intercepts all page changes performed either by code or through the usual `<a>` HTML tags that point to an address inside the application base address. Navigation can be handled by code by requiring a `NavigationManager` instance from dependency injection.

> **Note**
>
> Blazor routing works by intercepting browser URL changes and using URLs that point inside the application to load pages.

The `Router` component has a template for the case where a page for the requested URI is found (`Found`), and the `NotFoundPage` parameter that specifies which page to load when the requested URI is not found.

> **Note**
>
> Blazor routing automatically handles all edge cases: page not found, unauthorized pages, user not logged in, etc.

When the application uses authorization, the `Found` template consists of the `AuthorizeRouteView` component, which further distinguishes whether the user is authorized to access the selected page or not. When the application doesn't use authorization, the `Found` template consists of the `RouteView` component:

```
<RouteView RouteData="@routeData" DefaultLayout="@typeof(MainLayout)" />
```

`RouteView` takes the selected page and renders it inside the layout page specified by the `DefaultLayout` parameter. This specification acts as a default since each page can override it by specifying a different layout page. In the Blazor project template, the default layout page is in the `BlazorReview->Layout->MainLayout.razor` file.

Blazor layout pages work similarly to ASP.NET Core MVC layout pages described in the *Reusing view code* subsection of *Chapter 16, Presenting ASP.NET Core*, the only difference being that the place to add the page markup is specified with `@Body`, as shown below:

```
<article class="content px-4">
      @Body
</article>
```

If the application uses authorization, `AuthorizeRouteView` works like `RouteView`, but it also allows the specification of a template for a case where the user is not authorized:

```
<NotAuthorized>
@if (!context.User.Identity.IsAuthenticated)
{
  <RedirectToLogin />
}
else
{
  <p role ="alert">You are not authorized to access this resource.</p>
}
</NotAuthorized>
```

If the user is not authenticated, the `RedirectToLogin` component uses a `NavigationManager` instance to move to the login logic page; otherwise, it informs the users that they do not have enough privileges to access the selected page.

Blazor WebAssembly also allows the lazy loading of assemblies to reduce the initial application loading time, but we will not discuss it here due to a lack of space. The *Further reading* section contains references to the official Blazor documentation.

As we will discuss in more detail later on in this chapter, the `PageTitle` component, used in all project example pages, enables the developer to set the page title that appears in the browser tabs. The `FocusOnNavigate` component near the end of `App.razor`, instead, sets the HTML focus on the first HTML element that satisfies the CSS selector passed in its `Selector` parameter, immediately after a page is navigated.

The next section delves deeper into the Blazor implementation of SPA components.

Blazor pages and components

SPA Components are a kind of virtual HTML tags that, once rendered, generate actual HTML markup. Components are the main SPA tool for enforcing modularity. Like HTML tags, components have attributes, which are usually called parameters, and custom events. Component code ensures that each component uses its parameters to create proper HTML and generates adequate events. Components can be used inside other components in a hierarchical fashion.

In this section, you will learn the fundamentals of Blazor components, including how to construct a component, its structure, how to attach events to HTML tags, how to specify their characteristics, and how to use other components within your components. We have divided the content into several sub-sections:

1. Component structure
2. Templates and cascading parameters
3. Error handling
4. Events
5. Bindings
6. How Blazor updates HTML
7. Component lifecycle

The next subsection explains the basic structure of components and how to code them.

Component structure

Components are the core of all main client frameworks. They are the key ingredient to building a modular UI, whose parts are easily modifiable and reusable. In a few words, they are the graphical counterpart of classes. In fact, just like classes, they allow encapsulation and code organization. Moreover, the component architecture allows the formal definition of efficacious UI update algorithms, as we will see in the *How Blazor updates HTML* subsection.

Components are defined in files with a `.razor` extension. Once compiled, they become classes that inherit from `ComponentBase`.

Like all other Visual Studio project elements, Blazor components are available through the **Add New Item** menu. Usually, components to be used as pages are defined in the `Pages` folder, or in its subfolders, while other components are organized in different folders. Default Blazor projects add all their non-page components inside the `Layout` folder, but you can organize them differently.

The component that plays the role of pages must specify the page URL, and a possible custom layout page to use. Moreover, since all components will be compiled into classes, they must specify all typical properties of classes, such as namespace, `using` declarations, classes they inherit from, interfaces they implement, generic parameters if any, and services to be injected in the class constructors.

By default, pages are assigned a namespace that corresponds to the path of the folder they are in. Thus, for instance, in our example project, all pages that are in the `BlazorReview->Pages` path are assigned to the

`BlazorReview.Pages` namespace. However, you can change this default namespace with a `@namespace` declaration placed in the declaration area that is at the top of the component file.

> **Note**
>
> All component class-related and page-related features are specified with further declarations placed at the beginning of the component code.

The following example shows all declarations:

```
@page "/counter"
@layout MyCustomLayout
@namespace BlazorReview.Pages
@using Microsoft.AspNetCore.Authorization
@implements MyInterface
@inherits MyParentComponent
@typeparam T
@attribute [Authorize]
@inject NavigationManager navigation
```

The first two directives make sense only for components that must work as pages, while all others may appear in any component. Below is a detailed explanation of each declaration:

- The `@layout` directive, when specified, overrides the default layout page with another component.
- The `@page` directive defines the path of the page (route) within the application base URL. Thus, for instance, if our application runs at https://localhost:5001, then the URL of this page will be https://localhost:5001/counter.
- `@namespace` overrides the default namespace of the component, while `@using` is equivalent to the usual C# `using`. All `@using` declared in the special `{project folder}->_Imports.razor` folder are automatically applied to all components.
- `@inherits` declares that the component is a subclass of another component, while `@implements` declares that it implements an interface.
- `@typeparam` is used if the component is a generic class, and declares the name of the generic parameter. `@typeparam` also allows the specification of generic constraints with the same syntax used in classes: `@typeparam T where T: class`.
- `@attribute` declares any attribute applied to the component class. Property-level attributes are applied directly to properties defined in the code area, so they don't need special notation. The `[Authorize]` attribute, applied to a component class used as a page, prevents unauthorized users from accessing the page. It works exactly in the same way as when it is applied to a controller or to an action method in ASP.NET Core MVC.
- Finally, the `@inject` directive requires a type instance to the dependency injection engine and inserts it in the field declared after the type name; in the previous example, in the navigation parameter.

Page routes can also contain parameters, like in this example: `/orderitem/{customer}/{order}`. Parameter names must match public properties defined as parameters by the components. The match is case-insensitive, and parameters will be explained later on in this subsection. The string that instantiates each parameter is converted into the parameter type, and if this conversion fails, an exception is thrown. This behavior can be prevented by associating a type with each parameter, in which case, if the conversion to the specified type fails, the match with the page URL fails. Only elementary types are supported: `/orderitem/{customer:int}/{order:int}`. As a default, parameters are obligatory; that is, if they are not found, the match fails, and the router tries other pages. However, you can make parameters optional by post-fixing them with a question mark: `/orderitem/{customer?:int}/{order?:int}`. If an optional parameter is not specified, the default for its type is used. Parameters can also be extracted from the query string: `/orderitem/{customer:int}?order=123`.

The middle part of the component file contains the HTML that will be rendered by the component with Razor markup, enriched with the possible invocation of child components.

The bottom part of the file is enclosed by an @code construct and contains fields, properties, and methods of the class that implements the component:

```
@code{
  ...
  private string myField="0";
  [Parameter]
  public int Quantity {get; set;}=0;
  private void IncrementQuantity ()
  {
          Quantity++;
  }
  private void DecrementQuantity ()
  {
         Quantity--;
         if (Quantity<0) Quantity=0;
  }
  ...
}
```

Public properties decorated with the `[Parameter]` attribute work as component parameters; that is, when the component is instantiated into another component, they are used to pass values to the decorated properties, and those values are passed to HTML elements in HTML markup:

```
<OrderItem Quantity ="2" Id="123"/>
```

Values can also be passed to component parameters by page route parameters or query string parameters that match the property name in a case-invariant match:

```
OrderItem/{id}/{quantity}
OrderItem/{id}?quantity = 123
```

However, the match with query string parameters is enabled only if the property is also decorated with the `SupplyParameterFromQuery` attribute:

```
[Parameter]
[SupplyParameterFromQuery]
public int Quantity {get; set;}=0;
```

Component parameters can also accept complex types and functions:

```
<modal title='() => "Test title" ' ...../>
```

If components are generic, when called, they must be passed type values for each generic parameter declared with `@typeparam`:

```
<myGeneric T= "string"...../>
```

However, often, the compiler is able to infer generic types from the types of other parameters.

Finally, the code enclosed in the @code directive can also be declared in a partial class with the same name and namespace as the component:

```
public partial class Counter
{
  [Parameter]
  public int CurrentCounter {get; set;}=0;
  ...
  ...
}
```

Usually, these partial classes are declared in the same folder as the component and with a filename equal to the component's filename with a .cs postfix added. Thus, for instance, the partial class is associated with the `counter.razor` component will be `counter.razor.cs`.

Each component may also have an associated CSS file, whose name must be the name of the component file plus the `.css` postfix. Thus, for instance, the CSS file is associated with the `counter.razor` component will be `counter.razor.css`. The CSS contained in this file is applied only to the component and has no effect on the remainder of the page. This is called CSS isolation, and at the moment, it is implemented by adding a unique attribute to all component HTML roots. Then, all selectors of the component CSS file are scoped to this attribute so that they can't affect other HTML.

Of course, we can also use global application CSS, and in fact, the Blazor template creates the `wwwroot/css/app.css` file for this purpose.

When the Blazor application is packaged either during a build or during its publication, all isolated CSS is processed and placed in a unique CSS file called: `<assembly name>.Client.styles.css`. That's why the `index.html` page of our BlazorReview application contains the following CSS reference:

```
<head>
    ...
    <link href="BlazorReview.Client.styles.css" rel="stylesheet" />
</head>
```

It is worth mentioning that isolated CSS can also be obtained with pure CSS techniques or by using the **Sass** language, which compiles to CSS.

Whenever a component decorates an `IDictionary<string, object>` parameter with `[Parameter(CaptureUnmatchedValues = true)]`, then all unmatched parameters are inserted into that dictionary; that is, all parameters without a matching component property are added to the `IDictionary` as key-value pairs.

This feature provides an easy way to forward parameters to HTML elements or other child components contained in the component markup. For instance, if we have a `Detail` component that displays a detail view of the object passed in its `Value` parameter, we can use this feature to forward all usual HTML attributes to the root HTML tag of the component, as shown in the following example:

```
<div  @attributes="AdditionalAttributes">
...
</div>
@code{
 [Parameter(CaptureUnmatchedValues = true)]
 public Dictionary<string, object>
 AdditionalAttributes { get; set; }
 [Parameter]
 Public T Value {get; set;}
}
```

This way, usual HTML attributes added to the component tag such as, for instance, class, are forwarded to the root div of the components and somehow used to style the component:

```
<Detail Value="myObject" class="my-css-class"/>
```

Once we have learned how to code and use components, we can move to more advanced concepts. The next subsection explains how to pass markup-generating functions to components.

Templates and cascading parameters

Blazor works by building a data structure called a render tree, which is updated as the UI changes. At each change, Blazor locates the part of the HTML that must be rendered and uses the information contained in the render tree to update it.

The `RenderFragment` delegate defines a function that is able to add further markup to a specific position of the render tree. There is also `RenderFragment<T>`, which accepts a further argument you can use to drive the markup generation. For instance, you can pass a `Customer` object to `RenderFragment<Customer>` so that it can render all the data for that specific customer.

You can define `RenderFragment` or `RenderFragment<T>` with C# code, but the simplest way is to define them in your components with Razor markup. The Razor compiler will take care of generating the proper C# code for you:

```
RenderFragment myRenderFragment = @<p>The time is @DateTime.Now.</p>;
RenderFragment<Customer> customerRenderFragment =
    (item) => @<p>Customer name is @item.Name.</p>;
```

The information on the location to add the markup is passed in the `RenderTreeBuilder` argument `RenderFragment` receives as an argument. You can use `RenderFragment` in your component Razor markup by simply invoking it as shown in the following example:

```
RenderFragment myRenderFragment = ...
  ...
<div>
  ...
  @myRenderFragment
  ...
</div>
  ...
```

The position where you invoke `RenderFragment` defines the location where it will add its markup, since the component compiler is able to generate the right `RenderTreeBuilder` argument to pass to it. `RenderFragment<T>` delegates are invoked as shown here:

```
Customer myCustomer = ...
  ...
<div>
  ...
  @myRenderFragment(myCustomer)
  ...
```

```
</div>
  ...
```

Note

Use `RenderFragment` and `RenderFragment<T>` to define functions that render HTML with the help of the powerful Razor syntax.

`RenderFragment` is the base for modifying dynamically the way components render content by passing them **templates** that specify how to render component areas.

In fact, being functions, render fragments can be passed to component parameters like all other types. However, Blazor has a specific syntax to make it easier to simultaneously define and pass render fragments to components: the **template syntax**. First, you define the parameters in your component (we suppose the component name is `Detail`):

```
[Parameter]
Public RenderFragment<Customer> CustomerTemplate {get; set;}
[Parameter]
Public RenderFragment Title {get; set;}
```

Then, when you call the `Detail` component, you can do the following:

```
<Detail>
  <Title>
    <h5>This is a title</h5>
  </Title>
  <CustomerTemplate Context=customer>
    <p>Customer name is @customer.Name.</p>
  </CustomerTemplate >
</Detail>
```

Each `RenderFragment` parameter is represented by a tag with the same name as the parameter. You can place the markup that defines `RenderFragment` inside of it. For the `CustomerTemplate` that has a parameter, the `Context` keyword defines the parameter name inside the markup. In our example, the chosen parameter name is `customer`.

When a component has just one render fragment parameter, if it is named `ChildContent`, the template markup can be enclosed directly between the open and end tag of the component:

```
[Parameter]
Public RenderFragment<Customer> ChildContent {get; set;}
...............
...............
```

```
<IHaveJustOneRenderFragment Context=customer>
  <p>Customer name is @customer.Name.</p>
</IHaveJustOneRenderFragment>
```

In order to familiarize ourselves with component templates, let's modify the `Pages->Weather.razor` page so that, instead of using `foreach`, it uses a `Repeater` component.

Let's right-click on the `Layout` folder, select Add, then Razor Component, and add a new `Repeater.razor` component. Then, replace the existing code with this:

```
@typeparam T
@foreach(var item in Values)
{
  @ChildContent(item)
}
@code {
    [Parameter]
    public RenderFragment<T> ChildContent { get; set; }
    [Parameter]
    public IEnumerable<T> Values { get; set; }
}
```

The component is defined with a generic parameter so that it can be used with any `IEnumerable`. Now let's replace the markup in the `tbody` of the `Weather.razor` component with this:

```
<Repeater Values="forecasts" Context="forecast">
  <tr>
    <td>@forecast.Date.ToShortDateString()</td>
    <td>@forecast.TemperatureC</td>
    <td>@forecast.TemperatureF</td>
    <td>@forecast.Summary</td>
  </tr>
</Repeater>
```

Since the `Repeater` component has just one template, and since we named it `ChildContent`, we can place our template markup directly within the component's open and close tags. Run it and verify that the page works properly. You have learned how to use templates, and that markup placed inside a component defines a template.

Note

Templates and generics together increase the component modularity by enabling the component to render a wide range of content. In fact, together with the instantiation of a generic with a concrete type, the developer can also specify how to render this concrete type with a template.

However, the usage of templated components is not limited to the customization of graphics. As an example, let's consider an important predefined templated Blazor component, the `CascadingValue` component. *It renders the content placed inside it with no changes, but passes a type instance to all its descendant components*:

```
<CascadingValue  Value="new MyOptionsInstance{...}">
......
</CascadingValue >
```

All components placed inside the `CascadingValue` tag and all their descendant components can now capture the instance of `MyOptionsInstance` passed in the `CascadingValue` parameter. It is enough that the component declares a public or private property with a type that is compatible with `MyOptionsInstance` and that decorates it with the `CascadingParameter` attribute:

```
[CascadingParameter]
private MyOptionsInstance options {get; set;}
```

Matching is performed by type compatibility. If there's ambiguity with other cascaded parameters with compatible types, we can specify the `Name` optional parameter of the `CascadingValue` component and pass the same name to the `CascadingParameter` attribute: `[CascadingParameter("myUnique name")]`.

The `CascadingValue` tag also has an `IsFixed` parameter that should be set to `true` whenever possible for performance reasons. In fact, propagating cascading values is very useful for passing options and settings, but it has a very high computational cost.

When `IsFixed` is set to true, propagation is performed just once, the first time that each piece of involved content is rendered, and then no attempt is made to update the cascaded value during the content's lifetime. Thus, `IsFixed` can be used whenever the pointer of the cascaded object is not changed during the content's lifetime.

An example of a cascading value is the `CascadingAuthenticationState` component we encountered in the Routing subsection, which cascades authentication and authorization information to all rendered components.

We discussed components and how they receive input from parameters and cascading parameters, but what about exceptions? What happens if an exception is raised in the code of a component?

The next subsection explains how Blazor handles exceptions.

Error handling

As a default, when an error in a component occurs, the exception is intercepted by the .NET runtime, which automatically makes visible the error code contained in index.html:

```
<div id="blazor-error-ui">
        An unhandled error has occurred.
    <a href="" class="reload">Reload</a>
```

```
    <a class="dismiss">   </a>
</div>
```

> **Note**
>
> However, it is desirable that SPA components intercept and handle exceptions in the adequate places, similarly to how class methods do it with the `try` and `catch` pattern.

In Blazor, exceptions can be intercepted and handled locally by enclosing the Razor code inside a `ErrorBoundary` component. Below, the code of the `Repeater` example in the previous subsection has been modified to locally handle errors that might occur in each row:

```
<Repeater Values="forecasts" Context="forecast">
  <tr>
   <ErrorBoundary>
    <ChildContent>
    <td>@forecast.Date.ToShortDateString()</td>
    <td>@forecast.TemperatureC</td>
    <td>@forecast.TemperatureF</td>
    <td>@forecast.Summary</td>
    </ChildContent>
    <ErrorContent>
     <td colspan="4" class="my-error">Nothing to see here. Sorry!</td>
    </ErrorContent>
   </ErrorBoundary>
  </tr>
</Repeater>
```

The standard code is placed in the `ChildContent` template, while the `ErrorContent` template is shown if there's an error.

We need one last tile to understand how Blazor components work, how they return output. The next subsection explains how components return output through events.

Events

Both HTML tags and Blazor components use attributes/parameters to get input. HTML tags provide output to the remainder of the page through events, and Blazor allows C# functions to be attached to HTML `on{event name} attributes`. The syntax is shown in the `Pages->Counter.razor` component:

```
<p role="status">Current count: @currentCount</p>
<button class="btn btn-primary" @onclick="IncrementCount">Click me</button>
@code {
private int currentCount = 0;
private void IncrementCount()
```

```
        {
            currentCount++;
        }
    }
```

The function can also be passed inline as a lambda. Moreover, it accepts the C# equivalent of the usual event argument. The *Further reading* section contains a link to the Blazor official documentation page that lists all supported events and their arguments.

Note

Since the idea behind SPA framework components is to define a kind of power-HTML-elements, SPA framework components, like HTML elements, can also have events, but in this case, both event features and implementation are defined by the developer.

In Blazor components, events are defined as parameters whose type is either `EventCallBack` or `EventCallBack<T>`. `EventCallBack` is the type of component event with no arguments while `EventCallBack<T>` is the type of component event with an argument of type `T`. In order to trigger an event, say MyEvent, the component calls:

```
await MyEvent.InvokeAsync()
```

or

```
await MyIntEvent.InvokeAsync(arg)
```

These calls execute the handlers bound to the events or do nothing if no handler is bound.

Once defined, component events can be used exactly in the same way as HTML element events, the only difference being that there is no need to prefix the event name with an `@`, since `@` in HTML events is needed to distinguish between the HTML attribute and the Blazor-added parameter with the same name:

```
[Parameter]
Public EventCallback MyEvent {get; set;}
[Parameter]
Public EventCallback<int> MyIntEvent {get; set;}
...
...
<ExampleComponent
MyEvent="() => ..."
MyIntEvent = "(i) =>..." />
```

Actually, HTML element events are also `EventCallBack<T>` events. That is why both event types behave in exactly the same way. `EventCallBack` and `EventCallBack<T>` are structs, not delegates, since they contain a delegate, together with a pointer to the entity that must be notified that the event has been triggered. Formally, the entity to be notified is represented by a `Microsoft.AspNetCore.Components.IHandleEvent` interface. Needless to say, all components implement this interface. The notification informs `IHandleEvent` that a state change took place. State changes play a fundamental role in the way Blazor updates the page HTML. We will analyze them in detail in the next subsection.

For HTML elements, Blazor also provides the possibility to stop the event's default action and the event bubbling by adding the `:preventDefault` and `:stopPropagation` directives to the attribute that specifies the event, like in these examples:

```
@onkeypress="KeyHandler" @onkeypress:preventDefault="true"
@onkeypress:stopPropagation ="true"
```

`:preventDefault` and `:stopPropagation` are prefixed with the event name to get new attributes. Then preventing default or propagation is just a matter of setting `true` these attributes.

While events, parameters, cascading parameters, and error handling are everything a component needs to work efficaciously, Blazor has another feature that simplifies a lot the usage of components: bindings, which are explored in the next subsection.

Bindings

Often, a component parameter value must be kept synchronized with an external variable, property, or field. The typical application of this kind of synchronization is an object property being edited in an input component or HTML tag. Whenever the user changes the input value, the object property must be updated coherently, and vice versa. The object property value must be copied into the component as soon as the component is rendered so that the user can edit it.

Similar scenarios are handled by parameter-event pairs. More specifically, on one side, the property is copied into the input component parameter. From the other side, each time the input changes value, a component event that updates the property is triggered. This way, property and input values are kept synchronized.

This scenario is so common and useful that Blazor has a specific syntax for simultaneously defining the event and copying the property value into the parameter. This simplified syntax requires that the event has the same name as the parameter involved in the interaction, but with a `Changed` postfix.

Suppose, for instance, that a component has a `Value` parameter. Then, the corresponding event must be `ValueChanged`. Moreover, each time the user changes the component value, the component must invoke the `ValueChanged` event by calling `await ValueChanged.InvokeAsync(arg)`. With this in place, a property called `MyObject.MyProperty` can be synchronized with the `Value` property with the syntax shown here:

```
<MyComponent @bind-Value="MyObject.MyProperty"/>
```

The preceding syntax is called **binding**. Blazor takes care of automatically attaching an event handler that updates the `MyObject.MyProperty` property to the `ValueChanged` event.

Bindings of HTML elements work in a similar way, but since the developer can't decide the names of parameters and events, a slightly different convention must be used. First of all, there is no need to specify the parameter name in the binding, since it is always the HTML input value attribute. Therefore, the binding is written simply as `@bind="object.MyProperty"`. By default, the object property is updated on the change event, but you can specify a different event by adding `@bind-event` attribute as shown here: `@bind-event="oninput"`.

Moreover, bindings of HTML inputs try to automatically convert the input string into the target type. If the conversion fails, the input reverts to its initial value. This behavior is quite primitive since, in the event of errors, no error message is provided to the user, and the culture settings are not taken into account properly (HTML5 inputs use invariant culture, but text input must use the current culture). We advise binding inputs only to string target types. Blazor has specific components for handling dates and numbers that should be used whenever the target type is not a string. We will describe these components in the Blazor forms and validation section.

In order to familiarize ourselves with events, let's write a component that synchronizes the content of an input type text when the user clicks a confirmation button. Let's right-click on the `Layout` folder and add a new `ConfirmedText.razor` component. Then replace its code with this:

```
<input type="text" @bind="Value" @attributes="AdditionalAttributes"/>
<button class="btn btn-secondary"
  @onclick="Confirmed">@ButtonText</button>

@code {
   [Parameter(CaptureUnmatchedValues = true)]
   public Dictionary<string, object> AdditionalAttributes { get; set; }
   [Parameter]
   public string Value {get; set;}
   [Parameter]
   public EventCallback<string> ValueChanged { get; set; }
   [Parameter]
   public string ButtonText { get; set; }
   async Task Confirmed()
     {
         await ValueChanged.InvokeAsync(Value);
     }
}
```

The `ConfirmedText` component exploits the button-click event to trigger the `ValueChanged` event. Moreover, the component uses `@bind` to synchronize its `Value` parameter with the HTML input. It is worth pointing out that the component uses `CaptureUnmatchedValues` to forward all HTML attributes applied to its tag to the HTML input. This way, users of the `ConfirmedText` component can style the input field by simply adding class and/or style attributes to the component tag.

Now, let's use this component in the `Pages->Index.razor` page by placing the following code at the bottom of `Home.razor`:

```
<ConfirmedText @bind-Value="textValue" ButtonText="Confirm" />
<p>
    Confirmed value is: @textValue
</p>
@code{
private string textValue = null;
}
```

If you run the project and play with the input and its Confirm button, you will see that each time the Confirm button is clicked, not only are the input values copied in the `textValue` page property, but also the content of the paragraph that is behind the component is coherently updated.

We explicitly synchronized `textValue` with the component with `@bind-Value`, but what takes care of keeping `textValue` synchronized with the content of the paragraph? The answer is in the next subsection.

How Blazor updates HTML

When we write the content of a variable, property, or field in Razor markup with something like `@model.property`, Blazor not only renders the actual value of the variable, property, or field when the component is rendered, but tries also to update the HTML each time that this value changes, with a process called **change detection**. Change detection is a feature of all the main SPA frameworks, but the way Blazor implements it is very simple and elegant.

The basic idea is that, once all HTML has been rendered, changes may occur only because of code executed inside events. That is why `EventCallBack` and `EventCallBack<T>` contain a reference to an `IHandleEvent`. When a component binds a handler to an event, the Razor compiler creates an `EventCallBack` or `EventCallBack<T>`, passing its struct constructor the function bound to the event and the component where the function was defined (`IHandleEvent`).

Once the code of the handler has been executed, the Blazor runtime is notified that the `IHandleEvent` might have changed. In fact, the handler code can only change the values of variables, properties, or fields of the component where the handler was defined. In turn, this triggers a change detection process rooted in the component. Blazor verifies which variables, properties, or fields are used in the component Razor markup and updates the associated HTML.

If a changed variable, property, or field is an input parameter of another component, then the HTML generated by that component might also need updates. Accordingly, another change-detection process rooted in that component is recursively triggered.

The algorithm sketched previously discovers all relevant changes only if the following conditions are met:

- No component references data structures belonging to other components in an event handler
- All inputs to a component arrive through its parameters and not through method calls or other public members

When there is a change that is not detected because of the failure of one of the preceding conditions, the developer must manually declare the possible change of the component. This can be done by calling the `StateHasChanged()` component method. Since this call might result in changes to the page's HTML, its execution cannot take place asynchronously but must be queued in the HTML page's UI thread. This is done by passing the function to be executed to the `InvokeAsync` component method.

Summing up, the instruction to execute is `await InvokeAsync(StateHasChanged)`.

The next subsection concludes the description of components with an analysis of their lifecycle and the associated lifecycle methods.

Component lifecycle

Each component lifecycle event has an associated method. Some methods have both synchronous and asynchronous versions, some have just an asynchronous version, and some others have just a synchronous version.

The component lifecycle starts with parameters passed to the component being copied into the associated component properties. You can customize this step by overriding the following method:

```
public override async Task SetParametersAsync(ParameterView parameters)
{
  await ...
  await base.SetParametersAsync(parameters);
}
```

Typically, customization consists of the modification of additional data structures, so the base method is called to also perform the default action of copying parameters into the associated properties.

After that, there is the component initialization that is associated with the two methods:

```
protected override void OnInitialized()
{
    ...
}
protected override async Task OnInitializedAsync()
{
  await ...
}
```

They are called once in the component lifetime, immediately after the component has been created and added to the render tree. Please place any initialization code there, and not in the component constructor, because this will improve component testability, because there, you have all parameters set, and because future Blazor versions might pool and reuse component instances.

If the initialization code subscribes to some events or performs actions that need a cleanup when the component is destroyed, implement `IDisposable` and place all cleanup code in its Dispose method. In fact, whenever a component implements `IDisposable`, Blazor calls its `Dispose` method before destroying it.

After the component has been initialized and each time a component parameter changes, the following two methods are called:

```
protected override async Task OnParametersSetAsync()
{
  await ...
}
protected override void OnParametersSet()
{
    ...
}
```

They are the right place to update data structures that depend on the values of the component parameters.

After that, the component is rendered or re-rendered. You can prevent component re-rendering after an update by overriding the ShouldRender method:

```
protected override bool ShouldRender()
{
...
}
```

Letting a component re-render only if you are sure its HTML code will change is an advanced optimization technique used in the implementation of component libraries.

The component rendering stage also involves the invocation of its children components. Therefore, component rendering is considered complete only after all its descendant components have completed their rendering, too. When rendering is complete, the following methods are called:

```
protected override void OnAfterRender(bool firstRender)
{
    if (firstRender)
    {
    }
...
}
protected override async Task OnAfterRenderAsync(bool firstRender)
{
    if (firstRender)
    {
        await...
```

```
            ...
        }
        await ...
    }
```

Since when the preceding methods are called, all component HTML has been updated, and all child components have executed all their lifetime methods, the preceding methods are the right places for performing the following operations:

- Calling JavaScript functions that manipulate the generated HTML. JavaScript calls are described in the *JavaScript interoperability* subsection.
- Processing information attached to parameters or cascaded parameters by descendant components. In fact, tab-like components and other components might need to register some of their subparts in the root component, so the root component typically cascades a data structure where some child components can register. Code written in `AfterRender` and `AfterRenderAsync` can rely on the fact that all the parts have completed their registration.

Table 18.1 summarizes the lifecycle events sequence:

Lifecycle event	Description	When it is fired
OnParametersSet() OnParametersSetAsync	Parameters change handling	Whenever a component parameter changes
OnInitialized OnInitializedAsync	Component initialization	Just at component creation, after parameters have been passed to it
ShouldRender	Confirmation that the component must be rendered	Immediately before component rendering
OnAfterRender OnAfterRenderAsync	Running customization code after the component was rendered	Whenever the component is rendered

Table 18.1: Blazor: Lifecycle events

We explored all secrets of components, but we still need a final piece to be able to implement a Blazor application: how to collect and validate related user inputs. We explore this in the next subsection.

Blazor forms and validation

Similar to all major SPA frameworks, Blazor offers specific tools for processing user input while providing valid feedback to the user with error messages and immediate visual cues.

In classic HTML websites, HTML forms are used to collect input, to validate it, and to send it to the server. In client frameworks, data is not sent to the server by submitting forms, but forms keep their validation purpose.

More specifically, they act as validation units, that is, as a container for inputs that must be validated together because they are the input of a unique task. Accordingly, when a submit button is clicked, an overall validation is performed, and the result is notified via events. This way, the developer can define what to do in case of errors and what to do when the user has successfully completed their input.

It is worth pointing out that validation performed on the client side doesn't ensure data integrity because a malicious user might easily hack all client validation rules because they have full access to the client-side code in the browser. The purpose of client-side validation is just to furnish immediate feedback to the user.

Accordingly, the validation step must be repeated on the server side to enforce data integrity.

Both server-side and client-side validation can be performed with the same code shared between the Blazor client and the server. In fact, both ASP.NET Core REST API and Blazor support validation based on validation attributes, so it is enough to share the same ViewModels equipped with validation attributes between the Blazor and the Server projects by putting them in a library that is referenced by both projects. ASP.NET Core validation is discussed in the *Server-side and client-side validation* section of *Chapter 16*, *Presenting ASP.NET Core*.

The whole toolset is known as **Blazor Forms** and consists of a form component called `EditForm`, various input components, a data annotation validator, a validation error summary, and validation error labels.

`EditForm` takes care of orchestrating the state of all input components through an instance of the `EditContext` class that is cascaded inside the form. The orchestration comes from the interaction of both input components and the data annotation validator with this `EditContext` instance. A validation summary and error message labels don't take part in the orchestration but register for some `EditContext` events to be informed about errors.

`EditForm` must be passed the object whose properties must be rendered in its `Model` parameter. It is worth pointing out that input components bound to nested properties are not validated, so `EditForm` must be passed a flattened ViewModel. `EditForm` creates a new `EditContext` instance, passes the object received in its `Model` parameter in its constructor, and cascades it so it can interact with the form content.

You can also directly pass an `EditContext` custom instance in the `EditContext` parameter of `EditForm` instead of passing the object in its `Model` parameter, in which case `EditForm` will use your custom copy instead of creating a new instance. Typically, you do this when you need to subscribe to the `EditContext` `OnValidationStateChanged` and `OnFieldChanged` events.

When an `EditForm` is submitted with a `Submit` button, and there are no errors, the form invokes its `OnValidSubmit` callback, where you can place the code that uses and processes the user input. If, instead, there are validation errors, they are displayed, and the form invokes its `OnInvalidSubmit` callback.

The state of each input is reflected in some CSS classes that are automatically added to them, namely `valid`, `invalid`, and `modified`. You can use these classes to provide adequate visual feedback to the user. The default Blazor template already provides some CSS for them.

Here is a typical form:

```
<EditForm Model="FixedInteger"OnValidSubmit="@HandleValidSubmit" >
  <DataAnnotationsValidator />
```

```
    <ValidationSummary />
    <div class="form-group">
      <label for="integerfixed">Integer value</label>
      <InputNumber @bind-Value="FixedInteger.Value"
           id="integerfixed" class="form-control" />
      <ValidationMessage For="@(() => FixedInteger.Value)" />
    </div>
    <button type="submit" class="btn btn-primary"> Submit</button>
</EditForm>
```

The label is a standard HTML label, while `InputNumber` is a Blazor-specific component for number properties. `ValidationMessage` is the error label that appears only in the event of a validation error. By default, it is rendered with a `validation-message` CSS class. The property associated with the error message is passed in the `for` parameter with a `parameterless` lambda, as shown in the example.

The `DataAnnotationsValidator` component adds a validation based on the usual .NET validation attributes, such as `RangeAttribute`, `RequiredAttribute`, and so on. You can also write your custom validation attributes by inheriting from the `ValidationAttribute` class. ASP.NET Core validation is discussed in the *Server-side and client-side validation* section of *Chapter 16, Presenting ASP.NET Core.*

You can provide custom error messages in the validation attributes. If they contain a `{0}` placeholder, this will be filled with the property display name declared in a `DisplayAttribute` if one is found, otherwise with the property name.

Together with the `InputNumber` component, Blazor also supports an `InputText` component for string properties, an `InputTextArea` component for string properties to be edited in an HTML `textarea`, an `InputCheckbox` component for bool properties, and an `InputDate` component that renders `DateTime` and `DateTimeOffset`, `DateOnly`, and `Time` types. They all work in exactly the same way as the `InputNumber` component, but as an InputDateType Type parameter for specifying the desired HTML5 input to render (date, datetime-local, month, or time). No component is available for other HTML5 input types. In particular, no component is available for rendering numbers with a range widget, or colors.

In case you need an HTML5 input that is not available as a Blazor input-forms component, you are left with the option of implementing it yourself or using a third-party library that supports it.

You can implement rendering time or date and time by inheriting from the `InputBase<TValue>` class and overriding the `BuildRenderTree`, `FormatValueAsString`, and `TryParseValueFromString` methods. The sources of the InputNumber component show how to do it: `https://github.com/dotnet/aspnetcore/blob/main/src/Components/Web/src/Forms/InputNumber.cs`. You can also use the third-party libraries described in the *Third-party tools for Blazor WebAssembly* section.

Blazor also has a specific component for rendering a select, which works as in the following example:

```
<InputSelect @bind-Value="order.ProductColor">
  <option value="">Select a color ...</option>
```

```
    <option value="Red">Red</option>
    <option value="Blue">Blue</option>
    <option value="White">White</option>
</InputSelect>
```

Starting from .NET 6, `InputSelect` can also be bound to `IEnnumerable<T>` properties, in which case it is rendered as a multi-select.

One can also render enumerations with a radio group thanks to the `InputRadioGroup` and `InputRadio` components, as shown in the following example:

```
<InputRadioGroup Name="color" @bind-Value="order.Color">
    <InputRadio Name="color" Value="AllColors.Red" /> Red<br>
    <InputRadio Name="color" Value="AllColors.Blue" /> Blue<br>
    <InputRadio Name="color" Value="AllColors.White" /> White<br>
</InputRadioGroup>
```

Finally, Blazor also offers an `InputFile` component together with all the tools for processing and uploading the file. We will not cover this here, but the *Further reading* section contains links to the official documentation.

The next section describes Blazor tools for modifying the host page `<head>` tag.

Modifying HTML <head> content from Blazor components

Since the whole component tree is placed inside the body of the `index.html` host page, components' markup has no direct access{XE"Blazorcomponents:HTML<head> content, modifying from" } to the index.html host page `<head>` tag. Modifying the content of the `<head>` tag is necessary when the developer would like to adapt the title shown in the browser tab to the actual Blazor page that is being displayed. In fact, this title is contained within the `<head>` tag:

```
<head>
    <title>This is the title shown in the browser tab</title>
    ...
</head>
```

For this reason, starting from the .NET 6 version of Blazor, there are specific constructs for modifying the host page `<head>` tag from inside Blazor components.

First of all, we must inform the Blazor application about how to reach the tag content. This is done in `Program.cs` with the same technique used to specify the Blazor application root:

```
var builder = WebAssemblyHostBuilder.CreateDefault(args);
builder.RootComponents.Add<App>("#app");
```

```
// The line below adds support for modifying
// the <head> tag content
builder.RootComponents.Add<HeadOutlet>("head::after");
...
```

After that, each component can replace the HTML title by specifying the new string inside a `PageTitle` component instance:

```
<PageTitle>This string replaces the page title</PageTitle>
```

Moreover, each component can append other HTML content to the `<head>` tag by placing it inside a `HeadContent` instance:

```
<HeadContent>
    <meta name="description" content="This is a page description">
</HeadContent>
```

Up to now you learned all that is needed to write a simple Blazor application that doesn't exchange data with a server. The next section analyses some advanced features and will enable you to interact with a server, handle authentication and authorization and more.

Blazor advanced features

Up to now, we have described just Blazor basic features, needed to implement a simple Blazor application. However, Blazor offers further advanced features that help to fulfill specific needs. We describe them in this section. At first read, readers can skip most of them, with the only exception of Authentication and Authorization, and Communication with the server, which are also required by the simplest applications.

These Blazor advanced features are organized in subsections:

- References to components and HTML elements
- JavaScript interoperability
- Globalization and localization
- Authentication and authorization
- Communication with the server
- AOT compilation

Because of a lack of space, we can't give all the details of each feature, but the details are covered by links in the *Further reading* section. We start with how to reference components and HTML elements defined in Razor markup.

References to components and HTML elements

Sometimes we might need a reference to a component in order to call some of its methods. This is the case, for instance, for a component that implements a modal window:

```
<Modal @ref="myModal">
...
</Modal>
...
<button type="button" class="btn btn-primary"
   @onclick="() => myModal.Show()">
   Open modal
</button>
...
@code{
private Modal  myModal {get; set;}
 ...
}
```

As the preceding example shows, references are captured with the `@ref` directive. The same `@ref` directive can also be used to capture references to HTML elements. HTML references have an `ElementReference` type and are typically used to call JavaScript functions on HTML elements, as explained in the next subsection.

JavaScript interoperability

Since Blazor doesn't expose all JavaScript features to C# code, and since it is convenient to take advantage of the huge JavaScript code base, sometimes it is necessary to invoke JavaScript functions. Blazor allows this through the `IJSRuntime` interface that can be injected into a component via dependency injection.

Once we have a `IJSRuntime` instance, a JavaScript function that returns a value can be called as shown here:

```
T result = await jsRuntime.InvokeAsync<T>(
   "<name of JavaScript function or method>", arg1, arg2....);
```

Functions that do not return any result can be invoked as shown here:

```
await jsRuntime.InvokeAsync(
   "<name of JavaScript function or method>", arg1, arg2....);
```

Arguments can be either basic types or objects that can be serialized in JSON, while the name of the JavaScript function is a string that can contain dots that represent access to properties, sub-properties, and method names, such as the `"myJavaScriptObject.myProperty.myMethod"` string.

Thus, for instance, we can save a string in the browser's local storage with the following code:

```
await jsRuntime
    .InvokeVoidAsync("window.localStorage.setItem",
       myLocalStorageKey, myStringToSave);
```

Arguments can also be `ElementReference` instances captured with the `@ref` directive, in which case they are received as HTML elements on the JavaScript side.

The JavaScript functions invoked must be defined either in the `Index.html` file or in JavaScript files referenced in `Index.html`.

If you are writing a component library with a Razor library project, JavaScript files can be embedded together with CSS files as resources in the DLL library. You just need to add a `wwwroot` folder in the project root and place the needed CSS and JavaScript files in that folder or in some subfolder of it. After that, these files can be referenced as follows:

```
_content/<dll name>/<file path relative to wwwroot>
```

Accordingly, if the filename is `myJsFile.js`, the DLL name is `MyCompany.MyLibrary`, and the file is placed in a `js` folder inside `wwwroot`, then its reference will be:

```
_content/MyCompany.MyLibrary/js/myJsFile.js
```

It is worth pointing out also that all CSS files added to components (CSS isolation) we mentioned earlier in this chapter, are compiled into a unique CSS file that is added as a DLL resource. This file must be referenced in the `index.html` page as:

```
<assembly name>.Client.styles.css
```

If your JavaScript files are organized as ES6 modules, you can avoid referencing them in `Index.html` and can load the modules directly, as shown here:

```
// _content/MyCompany.MyLibrary/js/myJsFile.js  JavaScript file
export function myFunction ()
{
...
}
...
//C# code
var module = await jsRuntime.InvokeAsync<JSObjectReference>(
    "import", "./_content/MyCompany.MyLibrary/js/myJsFile.js");
...
T res= await module.InvokeAsync<T>("myFunction")
```

In addition, instance methods of C# objects can be called from JavaScript code by taking the following steps:

1. Say the C# method is called `MyMethod`. Decorate the `MyMethod` method with the `[JSInvokable]` attribute.
2. Enclose the C# object in a `DotNetObjectReference` instance and pass it to JavaScript with a JavaScript call:

```
var objRef = DotNetObjectReference.Create(myObjectInstance);
//pass objRef to JavaScript
....
//dispose the DotNetObjectReference
objRef.Dispose()
```

3. On the JavaScript side, say the C# object is in a parameter called `dotnetObject`. Then we just need to invoke:

```
dotnetObject.invokeMethodAsync("<dll name>", "MyMethod", arg1, ...).
then(result => {...})
```

The Awesome Blazor project (`https://github.com/AdrienTorris/awesome-blazor`) lists a lot of open-source projects that use JavaScript's interoperability to build .NET wrappers for well-known JavaScript libraries. There, you can find wrappers for 3D graphics JavaScript libraries, plot JavaScript libraries, and so on.

The next section explains how to handle content and number/date localization.

Globalization and Localization

As soon as the Blazor application starts, both the application culture and the application UI culture are set to the browser culture. However, the developer can change both of them by assigning the chosen cultures to `CultureInfo.DefaultThreadCurrentCulture` and `CultureInfo.DefaultThreadCurrentUICulture`. Typically, the application lets the user choose one of its supported cultures, or it accepts the browser culture only if it is supported; otherwise, it falls back to a supported culture. In fact, it is possible to support just a reasonable number of cultures because all application strings must be translated into all supported cultures.

If the application must support a single culture, this culture can be set once and for all in `Program.cs` after the host has been built but before the host is run.

This can be done by replacing await builder.Build().RunAsync() with:

```
var host = builder.Build();
…
CultureInfo.DefaultThreadCurrentCulture = new CultureInfo(…);
CultureInfo.DefaultThreadCurrentUICulture = new CultureInfo(…);
…
await host.RunAsync();
```

In case the application must support several languages, the code is similar, but the culture information must be taken from the browser local storage, where the user must be given the option to store it in some application's option page.

Once the `CurrentCulture` is set, dates and numbers are automatically formatted according to the conventions of the chosen culture. For the UI culture, the developer must manually provide resource files with the translations of all application strings in all supported cultures. Blazor uses the same localization/globalization techniques of ASP.NET Core server-side projects, so the user is referred to the *ASP.NET Core globalization* section of *Chapter 16, Presenting ASP.NET Core,* for more details.

There are two ways to use resource files:

1. You create a resource file, say, `myResource.resx`, and then add all language-specific files: `myResource.it.resx`, `myResource.pt.resx`, and so on. In this case, Visual Studio creates a static class named `myResource` whose static properties are the keys of each resource file. These properties will automatically contain the localized strings corresponding to the current UI culture. You can use these static properties wherever you like, and you can use pairs composed of a resource type and a resource name to set the `ErrorMessageResourceType` and the `ErrorMessageResourceName` properties of validation attributes or similar properties of other attributes. This way, the attributes will use an automatically localized string.
2. You add only language-specific resource files (`myResource.it.resx`, `myResource.pt.resx`, and so on). In this case, Visual Studio doesn't create any class associated with the resource file, and you can use resource files together with `IStringLocalizer` and `IStringLocalizer<T>` injected in components as you use them in ASP.NET Core MVC views (see the *ASP.NET Core globalization* section of *Chapter 16, Presenting ASP.NET Core*).

Let's move to the next advanced feature that is fundamental in all applications: authentication and authorization.

Authentication and Authorization

In the Routing subsection, we discussed how the `CascadingAuthenticationState` and `AuthorizeRouteView` components prevent unauthorized users from accessing pages protected with an `[Authorize]` attribute. Let's go deeper into the details of how page authorization works.

In .NET applications, authentication and authorization information is usually contained in a `ClaimsPrincipal` instance. In server applications, this instance is built when the user logs in, taking the required information from a database. In Blazor WebAssembly, such information must be provided by some remote server that takes care of SPA authentication, too. Since there are several ways to provide authentication and authorization to a Blazor WebAssembly application, Blazor defines the `AuthenticationStateProvider` abstraction.

Authentication and authorization providers inherit from the `AuthenticationStateProvider` abstract class and override its `GetAuthenticationStateAsync` method, which returns `Task<AuthenticationState>`, where `AuthenticationState` contains the authentication and authorization information. Actually, `AuthenticationState` contains just a `User` property with a `ClaimsPrincipal`.

Once we've defined a concrete implementation of `AuthenticationStateProvider`, we must register it in the dependency engine container in the application `Program.cs` file:

```
builder.services.AddScoped<AuthenticationStateProvider,
   MyAuthStateProvider>();
```

We will return to the predefined implementations of `AuthenticationStateProvider` offered by Blazor after having described how Blazor uses authentication and authorization information provided by a registered `AuthenticationStateProvider`.

The `CascadingAuthenticationState` component calls the `GetAuthenticationStateAsync` method of the registered `AuthenticationStateProvider` and cascades the returned `Task<AuthenticationState>`. You can intercept this cascading value with a `[CascadingParameter]` defined as follows in your components:

```
[CascadingParameter]
private Task<AuthenticationState>myAuthenticationStateTask { get; set; }
......
ClaimsPrincipal user = (await myAuthenticationStateTask).User;
```

Note

However, Blazor applications typically use `AuthorizeRouteView` and `AuthorizeView` components to control user access to content.

`AuthorizeRouteView` prevents access to pages if the user doesn't satisfy the prescriptions of the page `[Authorize]` attribute; otherwise, the content in the `NotAuthorized` template is rendered. `AuthorizeRouteView` also has an `Authorizing` template that is shown while user information is being retrieved.

`AuthorizeView` can be used within components to show the markup it encloses only to authorized users. It contains the same `Roles` and `Policy` parameters as the `[Authorize]` attribute that you can use to specify the constraints the user must satisfy to access the content:

```
<AuthorizeView Roles="Admin,SuperUser">
//authorized content
</AuthorizeView>
AuthorizeView can also specify NotAuthorized and an Authorizing template:
<AuthorizeView>
  <Authorized>
    ...
  </Authorized>
  <Authorizing>
    ...
  </Authorizing>
```

```
  <NotAuthorized>
    ...
  </NotAuthorized>
</AuthorizeView>
```

However, the main point in SPA authorization is how to get authorization information. This information must be provided by the server after user has logged in. While we may provide our custom login, authentication, and `AuthenticationStateProvider`, Blazor offers an out-of-the-box solution.

Namely, if one adds authorization while creating a Blazor WebAssembly project, the following method call is added to the application dependency engine:

```
builder.Services.AddOidcAuthentication(options =>
{
    // Configure your authentication provider options here.
    // For more information, see https://aka.ms/blazor-standalone-auth
    builder.Configuration.Bind("Local", options.ProviderOptions);
});
```

This method adds an `AuthenticationStateProvider` that extracts the user information from the authentication cookie of an OAuth provider. The OAuth protocol with the OAuth provider is performed with the help of the `AuthenticationService.js` JavaScript file we saw in the Loading and starting the application subsection of this chapter. The OAuth provider endpoint returns user information in the form of a bearer token that can also be used to authenticate communications with the server's web API. Bearer tokens are described in detail in *Chapter 20, Securing Data and Applications*. Blazor WebAssembly communication is described in the next subsection.

The previous code takes the OAuth parameters from a configuration file you must add as `wwwroot/appsettings.json`:

```
{
  "Local": {
    "Authority": "{AUTHORITY}",
    "ClientId": "{CLIENT ID}"
  }
}
```

In case you use Google as an authentication provider, `AUTHORITY` is `https://accounts.google.com/` while `CLIENT ID` is the client ID you receive when you register your Blazor application with the Google developers program.

Google needs some more parameters, namely the return URL where to return once the authentication process is completed, and the page where to return after a logout:

```
{
  "Local": {
```

```
      "Authority": "https://accounts.google.com/",
      "ClientId": "2...7-e...q.apps.googleusercontent.com",
      "PostLogoutRedirectUri": "https://localhost:5001/authentication/logout-callback",
      "RedirectUri": "https://localhost:5001/authentication/login-callback",
      "ResponseType": "id_token"
    }
  }
```

Where `https://localhost:5001` must be replaced by the actual domain of the Blazor application.

Before any authentication or if the authentication fails, an unauthenticated `ClaimsPrincipal` is created. This way, when the user tries to access a page that is protected by an `[Authorize]` attribute, the `AuthorizeRouteView` component invokes the `RedirectToLogin` component, which, in turn, navigates to the `Authentication.razor` page, passing it a login request in its action route parameter:

```
@page "/authentication/{action}"
@using Microsoft.AspNetCore.Components.WebAssembly.Authentication
<RemoteAuthenticatorView Action="@Action" />

@code{
    [Parameter] public string? Action { get; set; }
}
```

The `RemoteAuthenticatorView` acts as an interface with the usual ASP.NET Core user login/registration system, and whenever it receives an "action" to perform it redirects the user from the Blazor application to the proper ASP.NET Core server page (login, registration, logout, user profile).

Once the user logs in, they are redirected to the Blazor application page that caused the login request. The redirect URL is computed by the `BlazorReview.Layout->RedirectToLogin.razor` component, which extracts it from the `NavigationManager` and passes it to the `RemoteAuthenticatorView` component. This time, the `AuthenticationStateProvider` is able to get the user information from the authentication cookie that has been created by the login operation.

It is possible both to design a custom OAuth provider for your Blazor application or to design a completely custom way to get a bearer token with an internal login Blazor page without leaving the Blazor application. In this last case, you must provide a custom implementation of the `AuthenticationStateProvider`. More details on these advanced custom scenarios are available in the official documentation reference in the *Further reading* section.

Having learned how to authenticate with an external OAuth provider, and how to handle authorization within the Blazor application we are ready to learn how to exchange data and how to authenticate with a REST API.

The next subsection describes a Blazor WebAssembly-specific implementation of the `HttpClient` class and related types.

Communication with the server

Blazor WebAssembly supports the same .NET `HttpClient` and `HttpClientFactory` classes described in the *.NET HTTP clients* section of *Chapter 15, Applying Service-Oriented Architectures with .NET*. However, due to the communication limitations of browsers, their implementations are different and rely on the browser `fetch` API.

In fact, for security reasons, all browsers do not allow direct opening of generic TCP/IP connections, but force all server communications to pass either through Ajax or through the fetch API. This way, when you attempt a communication toward a URL that differs from the domain where the browser downloaded the SPA application, the browser automatically switches to the CORS protocol, thus informing the server that the communication was started by a browser application that was downloaded from a different domain and that might potentially be a phishing web site.

In turn, the server, accepts CORS communications just from well-known domains that are pre-listed in its code. This way, the server is sure that the request can't come from a phishing Web Site.

In *Chapter 15, Applying Service-Oriented Architectures with .NET*, we analyzed how to take advantage of `HttpClientFactory` to define typed clients. You can also define typed clients in Blazor with exactly the same syntax.

However, since an authenticated Blazor application needs to send the bearer token created during the authentication process in each request to the application server, it is common to define a named client as shown here:

```
builder.Services.AddHttpClient("BlazorReview.ServerAPI", client =>
         client.BaseAddress = new Uri("https://<web api URL>"))
.AddHttpMessageHandler<BaseAddressAuthorizationMessageHandler>();
```

`AddHttpMessageHandler` adds a `DelegatingHandler`, that is, a subclass of the `DelegatingHandler` abstract class. Implementations of `DelegatingHandler` override its `SendAsync` method in order to process each request and each relative response:

```
protected override async Task<HttpResponseMessage> SendAsync(
        HttpRequestMessage request,
        CancellationToken cancellationToken)
{
//modify request
   ...
HttpResponseMessage= response = await base.SendAsync(
   request, cancellationToken);
//modify response
   ...
return response;
}
```

`BaseAddressAuthorizationMessageHandler` automatically adds any bearer token previously obtained by an authentication process. If this bearer token is expired or is not found at all, it tries to get a new bearer token by using the authentication cookie received when the user manually logged in with the OAuth provider. This way it can obtain a fresh bearer token without requesting a new manual login. If this attempt also fails, an `AccessTokenNotAvailableException` is thrown. Typically, this exception is captured and used to trigger a redirection to the login page by calling its Redirect method, as shown below:

```
try
{
        //server call here
}
catch (AccessTokenNotAvailableException exception)
{
        exception.Redirect();
}
```

If both the Blazor application and the Web Api are deployed in different subfolders of the same domain, Blazor requests are issued without the CORS protocol, so they are automatically accepted by the server. Otherwise, the ASP.NET Core sever must enable CORS requests, and must list the Blazor application URL among the allowed CORS domains with something like:

```
builder.Services.AddCors(o => {
    o.AddDefaultPolicy(pbuilder =>
    {
        pbuilder.AllowAnyMethod();
        pbuilder.WithHeaders(HeaderNames.ContentType, HeaderNames.Authorization);
        pbuilder.WithOrigins(https://<Blazor client url>, …, https://<Another client
url>);
    });
 });
```

Then you must place also the `app.UseCors()` middleware in the ASP.NET Core pipeline.

The example data shown in the Weather page of the ReviewBlazor application are downloaded from a static file located in the `wwwroot/sample-data` folder of the same Blazor application, so a normal, not-CORS request is issued and no bearer token is needed to make the request. Accordingly, the `Weather` page uses a default `HttpClient` defined in `Program.cs` as:

```
builder.Services.AddScoped(sp => new HttpClient { BaseAddress = new
Uri(builder.HostEnvironment.BaseAddress) });
```

Summing up, architecting Blazor WebAssembly communication with the server requires the following steps:

1. Definition of adequate server CORS policies

2. Definition of adequate `HttpClients`
3. Defining how to pass adequate bearer tokens to the `HttpClients` through an authorization message handler. The simplest choice being the usage of the out-of-the-box `BaseAddressAuthorizationMessageHandler`.
4. Defining policies for redirecting to the login page when a bearer token is expired and when there is no automatic way of getting another valid token

The next subsection explains how to improve the performance of compute-intensive applications with Blazor AOT compilation.

AOT compilation

Once uploaded in the browser, .NET assemblies are not compiled Just-In-Time (JIT) at their first execution, as is the case for other platforms. Instead, they are interpreted by a very fast interpreter. Only the .NET runtime is pre-compiled and uploaded to the browser directly in WebAssembly.

JIT compilation is avoided since it would considerably increase the application start time, which is already quite high because of the high application download size (about 10 MB). In turn, the download size is large due to the .NET libraries that any Blazor application needs to work properly.

In order to reduce download size, during the compilation in release mode, Blazor .NET assemblies are tree-shaken to remove all unused types and methods. However, notwithstanding this tree-shaking, the typical download size remains quite high. A good download improvement is achieved with the default caching of the .NET runtime, which reduces the download size to 2-4 MB. However, the download size still remains high the first time a Blazor application is visited.

Starting from .NET 6, Blazor offers an alternative to JIT compilation: Ahead-Of-Time (AOT) compilation. With AOT, all application assemblies are compiled into a unique WebAssembly file during the application publication.

AOT compilation is very slow and may last something like 10-30 minutes, even in the case of small applications. On the other hand, it must be executed only once when the application is published, so the compilation time doesn't impact the application start time.

Unfortunately, AOT compilation more than doubles the download size, since the compiled code is more verbose than the source .NET code. Therefore, AOT should be adopted only in performance-critical applications that can trade a higher start time for better performance.

.NET WebAssembly AOT compilation requires an additional build tool that must be installed as an optional .NET SDK workload in order to use it. This can be done by selecting the **.NET WebAssembly build tools** option from the list of optional components when Visual Studio is installed.

.NET WebAssembly build tools can also be installed after the Visual Studio installation. More specifically, the first time, you can install them with the following shell command:

```
dotnet workload install wasm-tools
```

Instead, when a new .NET version is installed, we just need to launch the following command to update all previously installed workloads:

```
dotnet workload update
```

Once the AOT workload has been installed, AOT compilation can be enabled on a per-project basis by adding the `<RunAOTCompilation>true</RunAOTCompilation>` declaration to the Blazor project file, as shown here:

```
<Project Sdk="Microsoft.NET.Sdk.BlazorWebAssembly">
  <PropertyGroup>
    <TargetFramework>net10.0</TargetFramework>
    <RunAOTCompilation>true</RunAOTCompilation>
  </PropertyGroup>
  ...
```

The next section briefly discusses some of the most relevant third-party tools and libraries that complement Blazor's official features and help increase productivity in Blazor projects.

Third-party tools for Blazor WebAssembly

Notwithstanding Blazor being a young enough product, its third-party tool and product ecosystem is already quite rich. However, before deciding on the adoption of third-party libraries, it is necessary to assess both the libraries and the team that maintains them. First of all, we must be sure the library is adequate to our needs and can be integrated in our project without issues. Then we must verify the availability of adequate documentation and support.

Last but not least, we must be sure the library will be maintained for the whole lifetime of our Blazor client.

Among the open source, free products, it is worth mentioning the **Blazorise** project (`https://github.com/stsrki/Blazorise`), which contains various free basic Blazor components (inputs, tabs, modals, and so on) that can be styled with various CSS frameworks, such as Bootstrap and Material. It also contains a simple editable grid and a simple tree view.

Also worth mentioning is **BlazorStrap** (`https://github.com/chanan/BlazorStrap`), which contains pure Blazor implementations of all Bootstrap 4 and 5 components and widgets.

Among all the commercial products, it is worth mentioning **Blazor Controls Toolkit** (`https://blazorct.azurewebsites.net/`), which is a complete toolset for implementing commercial applications. It contains all input types with their fallbacks in case they are not supported by the browser; all Bootstrap components; other basic components; a complete, advanced drag-and-drop framework; and advanced customizable and editable components, like detail views, detail lists, grids, and a tree-repeater (a generalization of the tree view). All components are based on a sophisticated metadata representation system that enables the user to design the markup in a declarative way using data annotations and inline Razor declarations.

Moreover, it contains additional sophisticated validation attributes, tools for undoing user input, tools for computing changes to send to the server, sophisticated client-side and server-side query tools based on the OData protocol, and tools to maintain and save the whole application state.

It is also worth mentioning the **bUnit** open source project (`https://github.com/egil/bUnit`), which provides tools for testing Blazor components.

The Awesome Blazor project (https://github.com/AdrienTorris/awesome-blazor) lists thousands of open source and commercial Blazor resources, such as tutorials, posts, libraries, and example projects.

A complete example of a Blazor WebAssembly application based on the WWTravelClub book use case can be found in the *Using Client Technologies section* of *Chapter 22, Case Study: Practical Usage of .NET Aspire*. The actual code is contained in the folder associated with this chapter in the GitHub repository of the book.

The next section explains how to use Blazor to implement cross-platform applications.

.NET MAUI Blazor

Everything you've learned about Blazor WebAssembly—like components, routing, forms—applies to .NET MAUI Blazor. The only differences are deployment (native apps instead of browsers) and device API access.

.NET MAUI is Microsoft's recommended choice to implement cross-platform applications. In fact, .NET MAUI applications can be just-in-time compiled on all Windows, Android, iOS, and other Linux-based devices. .NET MAUI contains a common abstraction of all target devices, and at the same time takes advantage of each device's peculiarities by offering platform-specific libraries, each containing all platform-specific features of a target platform.

We may consider .NET MAUI whenever a browser client is not adequate to our needs for the reasons discussed at the beginning of the chapter, and we would like to deploy on various platforms.

We will not describe in detail .NET MAUI, but after a short introduction on .NET MAUI we will focus just on .NET MAUI Blazor. This way, by learning just Blazor, you will be able to develop both Single Page Applications, Progressive Applications, and Cross-platform applications. Moreover, a .NET MAUI Blazor solution may be implemented alongside with a Blazor WebAssembly solution since most of the code of the two options is exactly the same.

What is .NET MAUI?

.NET MAUI extends `Xamarin.Forms` cross-platform capabilities from Android and iOS to include Windows and macOS. Thus, .NET MAUI is a cross-platform framework for creating both native mobile and desktop apps with C#.

The basis of .NET MAUI is `Xamarin.Forms`. In fact, Microsoft has provided a guide to migrate the original `Xamarin.Forms` apps to .NET MAUI, as can be verified at the following link: `https://docs.microsoft.com/en-us/dotnet/maui/get-started/migrate`. However, .NET MAUI has been conceived to be the new generation framework for any native/desktop app development in C#.

There is a specific difference between `Xamarin.Forms` and .NET MAUI. In `Xamarin.Forms`, there is a specific native project for any kind of device we would like to publish to on the app, while in .NET MAUI, this will be placed as a multi-target platform.

The next section explains how to use .NET MAUI to run a Blazor application as a native application.

Developing native applications with Blazor

.NET MAUI is not installed by default when you install Visual Studio 2026, but you need to select the .NET MAUI workload in the Visual Studio installer. Therefore, if you don't see MAUI projects when you start a new project in your Visual Studio installation, you need to run the Visual Studio installer and modify your existing installation with the addition of the .NET MAUI workload.

Once you have the MAUI workload installed, in the project creation wizard, you should be able to select **C#/All platforms/MAUI**, and then select **.NET MAUI Blazor Hybrid App**, as shown here:

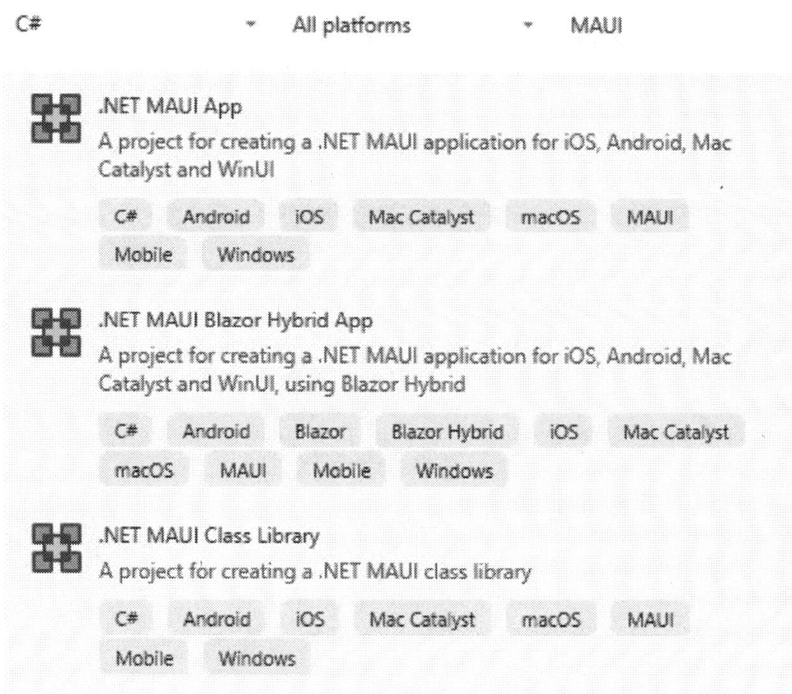

Figure 18.2: Creating a .NET MAUI Blazor application

Create a MAUI Blazor project and call it `MAUIBlazorReview`. The MAUI Blazor application contains the usual `Layout` and `Pages` folders, where you can place your Blazor components and pages, but they are placed inside a `Components` folder. It also contains a `wwwroot` folder containing the usual `index.html` page and all the CSS and JavaScript you might need. Finally, it also contains the usual `_Imports.razor` page, where you can place all your default using statements.

A MAUI Blazor application also uses layout pages that you can place in the `Layout` folder and may reference Razor libraries containing CSS components and JavaScript files. Figure 18.3 shows the file structure of a MAUI Blazor project.

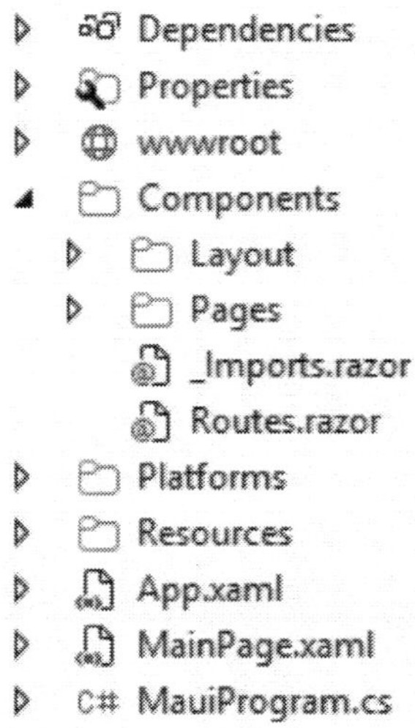

Figure 18.3: .NET MAUI Blazor project

The only difference with a Blazor WebAssembly project is that services, instead of being declared in a `Program.cs` file, are declared in `MauiProgram.cs` together with MAUI-specific code:

```
public static class MauiProgram
{
    public static MauiApp CreateMauiApp()
    {
        var builder = MauiApp.CreateBuilder();
        builder
            .UseMauiApp<App>()
            .ConfigureFonts(fonts =>
            {
                fonts.AddFont("OpenSans-Regular.ttf", "OpenSansRegular");
            });

        builder.Services.AddMauiBlazorWebView();

#if DEBUG
        builder.Services.AddBlazorWebViewDeveloperTools();
        builder.Logging.AddDebug();
#endif

        return builder.Build();
    }
}
```

Attention must be paid when using an `HttpClient` class to communicate with a server. Blazor web applications may use URLs relative to the domain where they were downloaded, while MAUI Blazor applications must use absolute URLs since they are not associated with any default URL. Therefore, an `HttpClient` definition is added to the services with something like this:

```
builder.Services.AddScoped(sp => new HttpClient
    { BaseAddress = new Uri("https://localhost:7215") });
```

The Platforms folder contains a subfolder for each platform supported by the application, where each subfolder contains platform-specific code, as shown in figure 18.4.

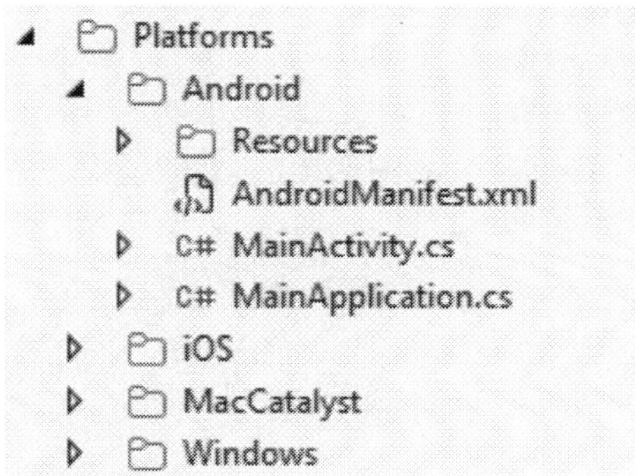

Figure 18.4: Platforms folder

Each platform folder contains predefined platform-specific files that you should not modify, so we will not describe them.

Supported folders can be changed by editing the `TargetFrameworks` element of the `MAUIBlazorReview.csproj` file:

```
<TargetFrameworks>net10.0-android;net10.0-ios;net10.0-maccatalyst</TargetFrameworks>
```

You can select the platform where to run the application from the dropdown next to the green Visual Studio run button. On a Windows machine you can select just Windows and Android. If you select Android an Android device simulator is launched.

In order to debug for iOS/Mac platforms on a Windows machine, you need to connect an iOS or Mac device to your computer.

When you build the project, the build may fail, asking you to install an Android SDK version. If this is the case, please follow the simple instructions in the error message.

A complete example of a .NET MAUI Blazor application based on the WWTravelClub book use case can be found in the *Using Client Technologies section* of *Chapter 22, Case Study: Practical Usage of .NET Aspire*. The actual code is contained in the folder associated with this chapter in the GitHub repository of the book.

Summing up, in this section you learned how to define a cross-platform application by reusing the Blazor WebAssembly code of a SPA, with the help of .NET MAUI Blazor. This is great, since you can always start with a

SPA, and then, if necessary, you can define a cross-platform version of the same applications by spending just a couple of days!

Summary

In this chapter you learned about client-side technologies. In particular, you learned what a SPA is and learned how to build a SPA based on the Blazor WebAssembly framework. The first part of the chapter described Blazor WebAssembly architecture, and then the chapter continues explaining how to exchange input/output with Blazor components and the concept of binding.

After having explained Blazor's general principles, the chapter focused on how to get user input while furnishing the user with adequate feedback and visual clues in the event of errors. Then, the chapter furnished a short description of advanced features, such as JavaScript interoperability, globalization, authentication with authorization, and client-server communication.

Finally, the last section explains how to use Blazor to implement cross-platform applications based on .NET MAUI, and how to transform a Blazor WebAssembly project into a .NET MAUI Blazor project.

Complete examples of Blazor applications based on the WWTravelClub book use case can be found in the *Using Client Technologies section* of *Chapter 22, Case Study: Practical Usage of .NET Aspire*.

Questions

1. What is WebAssembly?
2. What is an SPA?
3. What is the purpose of the Blazor router component?
4. What is a Blazor page?
5. What is the purpose of the `@namespace` directive?
6. What is an `EditContext`?
7. What is the right place to initialize a component?
8. What is the right place to process the user input?
9. What is the `IJSRuntime` interface?
10. What is the purpose of `@ref`?

Further reading

Here, you have some links that you may consider using to gather more information about this chapter.

- Blazor official documentation is available at `https://docs.microsoft.com/en-us/aspnet/core/blazor`
- Assemblies' lazy loading is described at `https://docs.microsoft.com/en-US/aspnet/core/blazor/webassembly-lazy-load-assemblies`
- All HTML events supported by Blazor together with their event arguments are listed at `https://learn.microsoft.com/en-us/aspnet/core/blazor/components/event-handling`

- Blazor supports the same validation attributes as ASP.NET MVC, with the exception of `RemoteAttribute`: `https://docs.microsoft.com/en-us/aspnet/core/mvc/models/validation#built-in-attributes`
- A description of the `InputFile` component, and how to use it, can be found here: `https://docs.microsoft.com/en-US/aspnet/core/blazor/file-uploads`
- More details on Blazor localization and globalization are available here: `https://docs.microsoft.com/en-US/aspnet/core/blazor/globalization-localization`
- More details on Blazor authentication, and on all its related URLs, are available here: `https://docs.microsoft.com/en-US/aspnet/core/blazor/security/webassembly/`
- **Blazorise** project: `https://github.com/stsrki/Blazorise`
- **BlazorStrap**: `https://github.com/chanan/BlazorStrap`
- **Blazor Controls Toolkit**: `https://blazorct.azurewebsites.net/`
- **bUnit**: `https://github.com/egil/bUnit`
- **Awesome Blazor** project: `https://github.com/AdrienTorris/awesome-blazor`

19

Orchestrators and .NET Aspire

Microservice architectures were conceived to both solve software production/maintenance problems and ensure resilience and fine-grained performance tuning. While software production/maintenance relies mainly on the adoption of Domain Driven Design (*see Chapter 7, Understanding the Different Domains in Software Solutions*) and related patterns, resilience and fine-grained performance tuning rely on network software called **orchestrators**.

More specifically, in order to fine-tune a microservice application, hardware resources must be allocated in a way that is proportional to each microservice's needs; this is achieved by replicating microservice instances. Moreover, we must ensure that at least one replica of each microservice is running to achieve zero downtime. This is achieved with at least 2-3 replicas and by allocating replicas on different machines so that some replicas might also survive hardware faults.

Finally, since microservice replicas can be moved from one computer to another because of possible hardware faults or performance optimizations, microservice instances have no stable network addresses. Therefore, we must track where each microservice instance is to be able to dispatch its messages.

Orchestrators face all the above problems by adequately handling microservices replication and allocation of replicas to available hardware. Moreover, messages are sent to a unique virtual address that is common to all undistinguishable microservice replicas, and then the orchestrator takes care of forwarding each message to an available replica independently of the physical machine where the replica is running, according to some load-balancing algorithm.

We can say that the main jobs of orchestrators are:

- ***Handling microservice replicas***. The number of replicas can be changed dynamically for fine-tuning the application performance, and the orchestrator takes care of creating and allocating to available machines the new replicas, and also of selecting the replicas to destroy when the number of replicas decreases. Moreover, whenever a replica crashes, it must be automatically restarted.
- ***Handling hardware faults***. In case of hardware failures, replicas are automatically moved from the failed hardware to other machines.
- ***Load balancing microservices load***. The load of all replicas of each microservice is balanced by adequately selecting the replica that receives each incoming message.

After a general review of orchestrators and their features, this chapter gives a short introduction to Kubernetes, which is the most popular orchestrator, and finally describes .NET Aspire, which is a .NET tool for simulating the job of an orchestrator on the developer machine, and which also compiles its code to the code for actual orchestrators. A practical example of .NET Aspire usage is described in the *Testing a Worker microservice with .NET Aspire* section of *Chapter 22, Case study: Practical Usage of .NET Aspire*. A more complete description of Kubernetes may be found in our monograph on microservices: *Practical Serverless and Microservices with C#* (`https://www.amazon.com/Microservices-Azure-microservices-serverless-development/dp/1836642016`) and in Kubernetes official documentation listed in the *Further reading section*.

More specifically, this chapter covers the following topics:

- A Primer on Orchestrators
- Orchestrating your Microservices with Kubernetes
- Developing Microservice applications with .NET Aspire

Technical requirements

This chapter requires the free Visual Studio 2026 Community edition or better, with all the database tools installed.

> **Note**
>
> All concepts are clarified with simple examples within the chapter and with a complete example application based on the WWtravelClub book use case that you can find in the *Testing a Worker microservice with .NET Aspire* and *Deploying a Worker microservice on Kubernetes* sections of *Chapter 22, Case Study: Practical Usage of .NET Aspire*.

If you would like to test Kubernetes as well, you need to install Docker Desktop following the instructions in the *Technical requirements* section of *Chapter 21, Applying a Microservice Architecture to Your Enterprise Application*.

The code for this chapter is available at `https://github.com/PacktPublishing/Software-Architecture-with-.NET-10-and-C-sharp-5E`.

A Primer on Orchestrators

This section will review the main features of orchestrators and will compare the most popular of them. A more detailed description of the most popular one, Kubernetes, will be given in the next section.

More specifically, this section will discuss the following topics:

1. Why and how do orchestrators use containers
2. How orchestrators handle microservice replicas and their network addresses
3. How orchestrators handle permanent storage
4. How do orchestrators ensure resiliency and zero downtime?

5. How orchestrators interface with the external world
6. The most popular orchestrators

Each topic will be discussed in a separate section. Let's start with containers.

Why and how orchestrators use containers

Containers are a kind of "*light virtual machine*" that we discussed in the *Containers and Docker* section of *Chapter 10, Applying a Microservice Architecture to Your Enterprise Application*.

Containers are the preferred choice of the most popular orchestrators, since they can be moved from one machine to another without imposing constraints on the software that must be installed on the machine. This way, they exploit the available hardware to the best.

Most orchestrators allow the grouping of several containers into units that run on the same machine. This means that if a container is moved from one machine to another, all other containers in the same unit are moved with it.

Orchestrators that support containers' grouping also give the possibility to decide the order in which all containers in the same unit are started.

Running on the same machine, containers in the same unit can exchange information both through `localhost` and through the permanent storage of the hosting machine. This capability, when available, enables the following useful microservices patterns:

- **Init Container**. In this case, one or many main containers are started only after a container defined as **Init Container** terminates execution. This way, the Init Container can perform some initialization tasks before the main containers are launched. For instance, an Init Container can verify if a database exists, and in case it doesn't already exist, it can create and populate it.
- **Sidecar**. In this case, a container defined as **sidecar** is started before one or many main containers. This way, all main containers can always rely on the existence of the sidecar. Sidecars are used either to enhance or to adapt existing containers to the application needs. This way, developers can use pre-existing open-source Docker images by adapting their interfaces with the remainder of the application with the help of an easy-to-write sidecar. Sidecars can also be used to monitor, and to collect statistics of the main containers.

Both Init Container and Sidecar have the purpose of modifying the behavior of an existing main container without modifying its code. Init containers perform some initialization tasks, while sidecars modify the main container interface with the remainder of the application. Both are useful when we have no access to the code of the main container or when we don't want to modify it for modularity constraints. For instance, the main container is a standard module used in various ways in other applications, so we don't want the peculiarity of a specific application to influence its code.

Orchestrators may also control the CPU and memory resources allocated to each container; more specifically, the developer can specify the minimum and maximum CPU and memory resources for each container, and the orchestrator imposes them as follows:

- The orchestrator allocates containers only on a machine with the minimum free resources they require.

- If a container exceeds the maximum allowed CPU resources, it is throttled to give more room to other containers.
- If a container exceeds its maximum allowed memory, an exception is thrown that causes the container to crash. As we will see in the *How orchestrators ensure resiliency and zero downtime* subsection, crashed containers are automatically restarted, thus releasing the memory excess possibly caused by a leak.

Summing up, you learned why to containerize your microservices, that you must adequately plan the resources each container can waste, and how to use init containers and sidecars to modify the behavior of preexisting containers. The next section explains the basics of replica handling.

How orchestrators handle microservice replicas and their network addresses

Replicating microservices is a MUST for performance tuning and for enforcing zero downtime. It is worth noting that we can create two different types of replicas:

undistinguishable replicas, and **differentiated replicas**.

Undistinguishable replicas are defined as replicas that are configured with exactly the same configuration parameters and that share the same permanent storage. Their purpose is to perform several copies of the same identical task in parallel, each on a different request, thus increasing the microservice performance. They are similar to the identical replicas of a classical Web application running on a Web farm that is behind a load-balancer.

> **Note**
>
> All microservices that encode business logic are indistinguishable. In fact, in this case, each replica has no private storage, but is just one of N identical processors that take care of a portion of the incoming requests. All replicas use the same database or a distributed database.

Differentiated replicas, instead, are defined as replicas that are configured differently and that may have different permanent storage.

> **Note**
>
> Differentiated replicas are used to implement distributed storage, distributed databases, and tools like distributed message brokers. In fact, microservices that handle parts of stored information (such as database records and message broker queues) are not undistinguishable.

Undistinguishable replicas are assigned a single network address where all other microservices can send their requests. At this address, a load-balancer assigns each request to an available replica.

The picture below summarizes how undistinguishable replicas are handled.

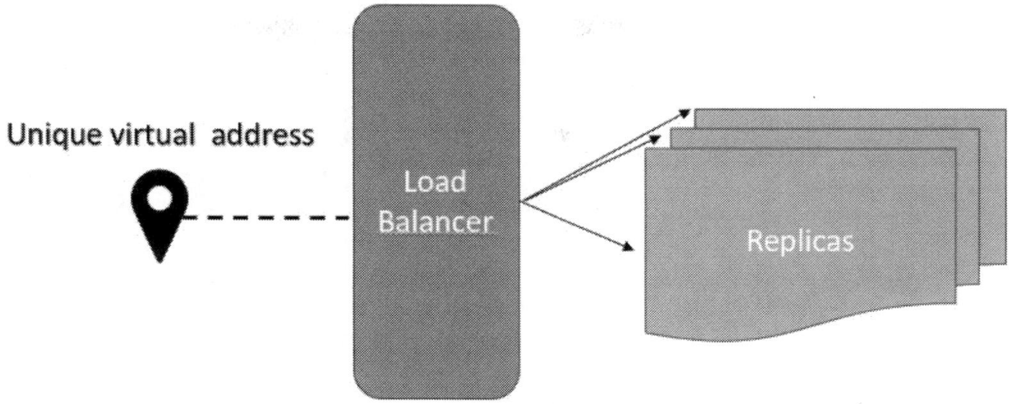

Figure 19.1: Handling undistinguishable replicas

Undistinguishable replicas increase performance by executing in-memory tasks in parallel, but they can't parallelize access to permanent storage since, in order to ensure application coherence, they must use exactly the same permanent storage (same database or same files).

Databases' parallelization can be achieved with database replication. Database replicas can be accessed as microservice replicas through a unique virtual address handled by an orchestrator-controlled load-balancer. However, in this case, each replica has its own private permanent storage, and it also needs its own private virtual address since the various replicas must synchronize their data by exchanging messages among them.

Similar arguments also apply to the implementation of efficient message brokers. That's why some orchestrators also allow differentiated replicas, where each replica has its private permanent storage and virtual address. Differentiated replicas may use either orchestrator-supplied load-balancing tools or they may implement custom load-balancing algorithms.

It is worth pointing out that application developers usually need just undistinguishable replicas, since differentiated replicas are used just to implement tools like distributed databases and distributed message brokers. That is why some cloud-based orchestrators conceived for easy deployment of microservice applications offer just undistinguishable replicas.

Let's move to a discussion on how orchestrators supply safe, permanent storage to containers.

How orchestrators handle permanent storage

Where do microservices store information? Containers can't use the permanent storage of the machines that host them because, in case they are moved to other machines they would lose their permanent data, therefore, they must necessarily use network storage units.

Accordingly, each orchestrator offers various mechanisms for allocating network storage to container nodes. In all cases, the allocated storage must be projected inside the file system of all containers that must share it. We refer to this process as *mounting a volume into a container*. *Figure 19.2* summarizes the whole process.

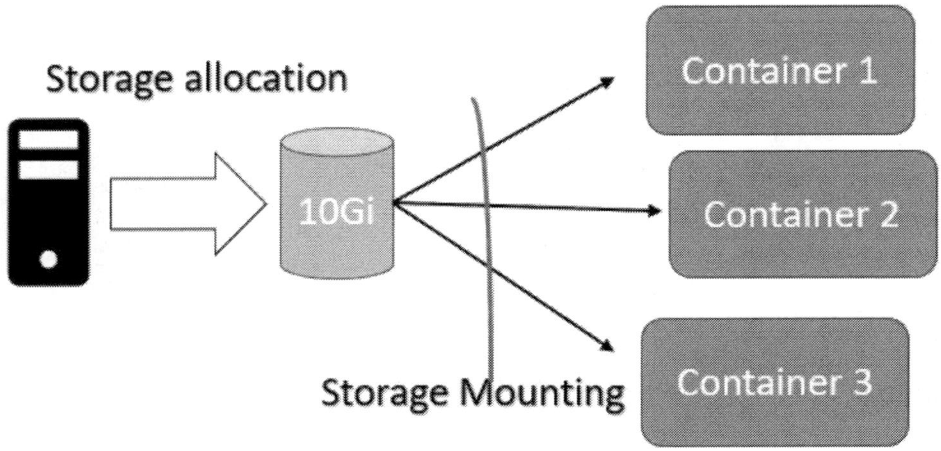

Figure 19.2: Allocating and mounting storage

After having learned orchestrator routine tasks, it is time to understand how they react to any kind of malfunctions. The next section explains how orchestrators can handle malfunctions with zero downtime.

How orchestrators ensure resiliency and zero downtime

One of the main goals of orchestrators is to handle any kind of malfunction with zero application downtime and with a fast recovery time.

Most orchestrators achieve this goal with the following services:

- In case of machine faults, replicas running on that machine are moved to a different machine.
- When a container crashes, it is restarted. If a container is part of a group, all containers in that group are restarted in the order and with the constraints configured by the developer (init containers, sidecars, etc.).
- Each microservice has replicas, and replicas are allocated on different machines. This way, during the recovery from a hardware or software fault, the application can continue running.
- The developer may configure endpoints where the orchestrator may get information on the container health and on the completion of the startup procedure. The result of these tests drives both the procedure that starts all containers in a group, and the procedure that detects crashed containers. Moreover, some orchestrators also have the concept of temporary failure (a congestion, for instance). When a temporary failure is detected, the container is not considered crashed but is removed from the load-balancing process that assigns requests to replicas. While crashes can be discovered both by testing a user-provided endpoint and by detecting the actual crash of the process that is run by the container, temporary failures are detected just through user-defined checks.
- Some cloud-based orchestrators also offer built-in tools for ensuring resilient communication through predefined sidecars.

Both the above services increase the application resiliency and ensure both zero downtime and automatic recovery from any kind of faults.

However, these services do not come at 0 cost for developers. In fact, microservices code must handle operating system kill signals to save the state before exiting, and all microservices must handle duplicate messages that might arise from the application of resiliency communication policies. In fact, as discussed in previous chapters, communication resiliency is achieved by resending messages if no reception confirmation arrives within a certain time, and this might cause message duplication.

Up to now we learned the "*internal life*" inside of an orchestrator. Let's also discover how orchestrators interact with the external world.

How orchestrators interface with the external world

All orchestrators must take the burden of handling the interaction of the application with the external world (the internet or a private network).

For this reason, they distinguish between communication inside the cluster that runs the application, which is called **internal**, and communication that goes in/out of the microservice application, which is called **external**.

External endpoints are assigned IP addresses and names visible outside of the application cluster. Moreover, they are usually assigned more robust load balancers that include typical Web server features.

In some orchestrators, like Kubernetes, for instance, one may serve external endpoints with a custom Web server that must be installed in the application cluster. This way, the application can be exposed with a unique endpoint, while typical Web server rules route traffic to several internal endpoints.

Having finished our short review of orchestrator features, we can move to a short review of the most popular orchestrators.

The most popular orchestrators

The simplest way to run an application based on several communicating containers is by using Docker networks. In fact, Docker, and Docker Desktop in particular, support virtual networks where running containers may be attached to their endpoints.

This feature was mainly conceived to furnish a simple way to test a microservice application during its development. Docker also includes a layer built on top of Docker called **Docker Compose** where you can configure the whole application with a `yaml` file (see next section for an introduction to `yaml` files). Here, you may define which container to include in the virtual network, mount permanent storage on it, pass parameters to containers, etc.

Being substantially a test and debug tool, Docker Compose doesn't offer all the orchestrator features we discussed in this section, but notwithstanding this, it can be used to run a simple container-based application on a single machine. Needless to say, this is a viable option when performance is not an issue.

Docker Compose became very popular thanks to its simplicity and its convenient learning curve. As a consequence, the Docker team evolved it into an actual Orchestrator called **Swarm** that can run several replicas of a microservice and that spans several machines.

Swarm brings with it the simplicity and simple learning curve of Docker Compose, but can't compete in flexibility and available features with full-featured orchestrators like Kubernetes.

Therefore, both Swarm and Docker Compose cannot be used to run complex microservice applications, but just for entry-level simple microservice applications.

Another simple and minimal orchestrator is **Nomad**. Nomad was initially designed by **CircleCI** team for running user jobs, and then it was released as open-source. It can be run either in cloud or on an on-premise network, but its focus is on scheduling tasks more than furnishing an adequate environment for running microservice applications.

At the moment, the more complete and popular orchestrator is Kubernetes, which will be described in the next section.

However, due to Kubernetes' high learning curve, all major Clouds together with Kubernetes offer simpler Cloud-only proprietary orchestrators. Some of them are implemented with Kubernetes itself.

Being application-oriented, they offer just undistinguishable replicas, since users can solve their database and message broker performance problems by adopting the distributed databases and message brokers available in the Cloud.

Configuring them is easy for simple applications, but as more advanced features are needed, configuring them becomes as difficult as configuring Kubernetes, and then even more difficult.

Moreover, they are tied to the Cloud that offers them, so after the application has grown too much, it is expensive to move to or integrate with a different Cloud. In our experience at the moment, they are good entry points when starting microservices development, but before applications become too complex, it is wise to move to Kubernetes.

Each of the big Cloud competitors has its Cloud offer, more specifically:

- *Azure* has *Azure Container Apps*
- *Google Cloud* has *Google Cloud Run*
- *AWS* has Amazon *Elastic Container Service*

They are all quite similar in the features they offer, so feel free to choose one of your favorite cloud providers.

The table below summarizes the features of all orchestrators described so far.

Orchestrators	Completeness	Learning curve	When to use
Docker compose, Swarm, Nomad	Minimal	Fast	Use when performance and zero downtime are not a priority
Azure Containers Apps, Google Cloud Run, elastic Container Service	Average	Fast	Use as an entry point when the application is still quite simple but performance and zero downtime are priorities

Kubernetes	High	Slow	Use with complex applications with critical non-functional requirements

Table 19.1: Orchestrators comparison

Let's dive into Kubernetes. More information on the other orchestrators listed in this subsection can be found in the *Further reading* section.

Up to now, you learned just the general features of most orchestrators and what the main orchestrators available are. However, a good understanding of how orchestrators work and how they can be used in practice requires basic knowledge of at least one complete orchestrator, like Kubernetes. Let's learn how Kubernetes works in the next section.

Orchestrating your Microservices with Kubernetes

At the time of writing, **Kubernetes** is the most popular orchestrator and a kind of standard for cluster orchestration that can be used with a wide ecosystem of tools and applications.

> **Note**
>
> Kubernetes implements all the orchestrator desirable features previously exposed in their complete form.

While not being tied to specific languages or frameworks, Kubernetes is a fundamental tool for managing hardware resources and communications in .NET distributed applications based on microservices. Kubernetes can be used on your private machine's cluster, or you can use hardware-scalable Kubernetes offerings from all main Cloud providers.

Below is the roadmap of our short tour in the world of Kubernetes.

1. Kubernetes basics and .yaml files
2. How Kubernetes handles microservices replicas
3. How Kubernetes handles communication and virtual addresses
4. How Kubernetes applications communicate with the external world
5. How developers and administrators can interact with a Kubernetes cluster
6. Advanced topics, such as using network storage, configuring your replicas, handling secrets, and how to define custom Health checks

Kubernetes basics

A **Kubernetes cluster** is a virtual network populated by virtual machines that runs the Kubernetes orchestrator. All machines of a Kubernetes cluster are called **nodes**. Kubernetes is installed on specific machines referred to as **control-plane nodes**, while all other machines simply run an interface software called **Kubelet** that connects with the software running on the control-plane nodes.

In Kubernetes, containers are grouped into units called **Pod**. A Pod is the smallest software unit we can deploy on a Kubernetes cluster. Moreover, Pods may be replicated to increase performance, so in general, it makes no sense to address a message to a specific Pod; instead, we address it to any of the identical replicas of the same Pod.

Cluster nodes and Pods are managed by control-plane nodes that communicate with cluster administrators through an API server, as shown in the following diagram:

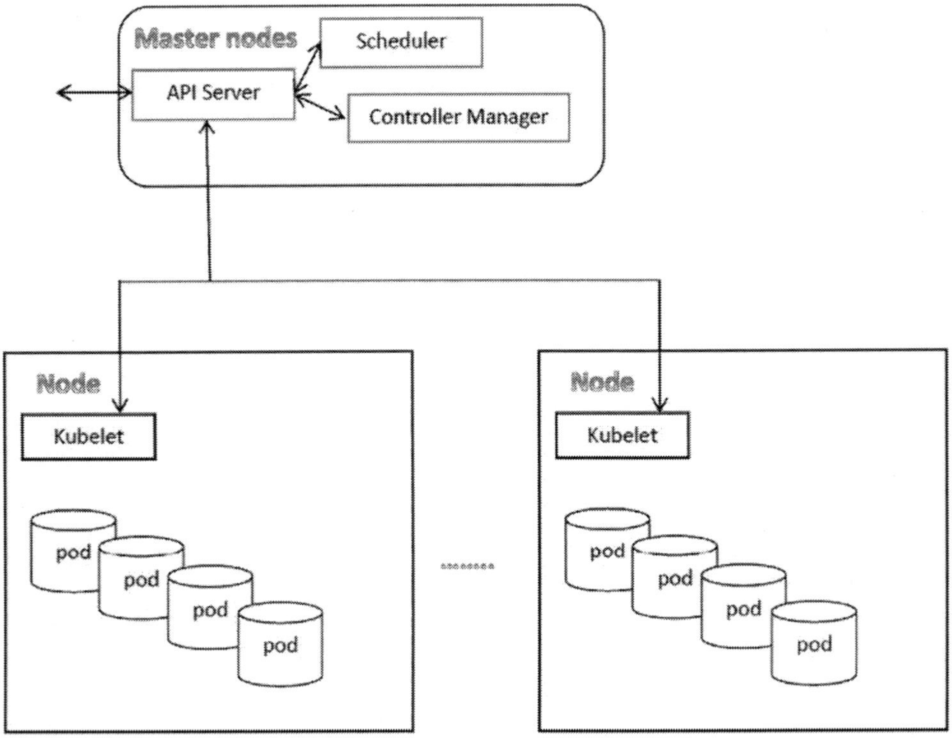

Figure 19.3: Kubernetes cluster

The scheduler allocates Pods to nodes according to the administrator constraints, while the controller manager groups several daemons that monitor the cluster's actual state and try to move it toward the desired state declared through the API server. There are controllers for several Kubernetes resources, from Pod replicas to communication facilities. In fact, each resource has some target objectives to be maintained while the application runs, and the controller verifies these objectives are actually achieved, possibly triggering corrective actions if not, such as moving some Pods running too slowly to less crowded nodes.

The Kubelet software manages the interaction of each non-control-plane node with the control-plane nodes.

In Kubernetes, communication between Pods is handled by resources called **Services** that are assigned virtual addresses by the Kubernetes infrastructure and that forward their communications to sets of identical Pods. In short, Services are Kubernetes' way of assigning consistent virtual addresses to sets of Pod replicas.

All Kubernetes entities may be assigned name-value pairs called **labels** that are used to reference them through a pattern-matching mechanism. More specifically, **selectors** select Kubernetes entities by listing labels they must have.

Thus, for instance, all Pods that receive traffic from the same **Service** are selected by specifying labels that they must have in the **Service** definition. The way a **Service** routes its traffic to all connected Pods depends on the way Pods are organized. Stateless Pods are organized in so-called **ReplicaSets** that correspond to the set of indistinguishable replicas discussed in the previous section. *ReplicaSets* have a unique virtual address assigned to the whole group, and traffic is equally split among all Pods of the ReplicaSet.

Stateful Kubernetes Pod replicas are organized into so-called **StatefulSets**. StatefulSets correspond to the differentiated replicas discussed in the previous section; therefore, Kubernetes Services assign a different name to each Pod of the StatefulSet they are connected to. These names look like the following:

```
basename-0.<base URL>, basename-1.<base URL>, ..., basename-n.<base URL>
```

All Kubernetes entities mentioned in this short introduction can be defined in a `.yaml` file, which, once deployed to a Kubernetes cluster, causes the creation of all entities defined in the file. The subsection that follows describes `.yaml` files, while the other subsections thereafter describe in detail all the basic Kubernetes objects mentioned so far, and explain how to define them in a `.yaml` file.

.YAML files

Since Kubernetes is coded by describing the final state desired for all entities in the cluster, it must be coded with a language that describes objects. The **YAML** language is preferred over JSON since it is more human-readable.

YAML instructions are packaged in files with a `.yaml` extension. `.yaml` files, like JSON files, can be used to describe nested objects and collections in a human-readable way, but they do it with a different syntax. You have objects and lists, but object properties are not surrounded by `{}`, and lists are not surrounded by `[]`. Instead, nested objects are declared by simply indenting their content with spaces. The number of spaces can be freely chosen, but once it has been chosen, spaces must be used consistently.

The remainder of this section is dedicated to a description of the YAML syntax, so readers who already know YAML can skip it.

List items can be distinguished from object properties by preceding them with a hyphen (`-`). Here is an example involving nested objects and collections:

```yaml
Name: John
Surname: Smith
Spouse:
  Name: Mary
  Surname: Smith
Addresses:
- Type: home
  Country: England
```

```
    Town: London
    Street: My home street
  - Type: office
    Country: England
    Town: London
    Street: My home street
```

The preceding `Person` object has a `Spouse` nested object and a nested collection of addresses. As you can see, the syntax is more readable than JSON since it avoids the overhead of parentheses.

`.yaml` files can contain several sections, each defining a different entity, that are separated by a line containing the `---` string. Comments are preceded by a # symbol, which must be repeated on each comment line.

Each section starts with the declaration of the Kubernetes API group and version. In fact, not all Kubernetes objects belong to the same API group. For objects that belong to the Core API group, we can specify just the API version, as in the following example:

```
apiVersion: v1
```

While objects belonging to different API groups must also specify the API name, as in the following example:

```
apiVersion: apps/v1
```

The next subsection starts a description of all Kubernetes objects and of how to define them. We begin with the most popular and useful Kubernetes objects, `ReplicaSets` and `Deployments` that are built on top of them.

ReplicaSets and Deployments

The most important building block of Kubernetes applications is the `ReplicaSets`, that is, a Pod replicated N times. Usually, however, you use a more complex object that is built on top of the `ReplicaSet` – the `Deployment`. `Deployments` not only create a `ReplicaSet`, but also monitor them to ensure that the number of replicas is kept constant regardless of any events that might involve the `ReplicaSets`. In other words, they are a declarative way of defining `ReplicaSets` and Pods.

Replicating the same functionalities, and thus the same Pods, is the simplest way to optimize for performance: the more replicas we create of the same Pod, the more hardware resources and threads are available for the functionality encoded by that Pod. Thus, when we discover that a functionality becomes a bottleneck in the system, we may just increase the number of replicas of the Pod that encodes that functionality.

Each `Deployment` has a name (`metadata->name`), an attribute that specifies the desired number of replicas (`spec->replicas`), a key-value pair (`spec -> selector-> matchLabels`) that selects the Pods to monitor, and a template (`spec->template`) that specifies how to create new Pod replicas:

```
apiVersion: apps/v1
kind: Deployment
metadata:
```

```
  name: my-deployment-name
  namespace: my-namespace #this is optional
spec:
  replicas: 3
  selector:
    matchLabels:
      my-Pod-label-name: my-Pod-label-value
      ...
  template:

  ...
```

namespace is optional and, if not provided, a namespace called default is assumed. Namespaces are a way of keeping the objects of a Kubernetes cluster separate. For instance, a cluster can host the objects of two completely independent applications, each placed in a separate namespace in order to prevent possible name collisions. In a few words, Kubernetes namespaces have the same purpose as .NET namespaces: preventing name collisions.

Indented inside the template is the definition of the Pod to replicate. Complex objects such as Deployments can also contain other kinds of templates, for instance, a template of disk-like memory required by the external environment. We will discuss this in more detail in the *Advanced Kubernetes concepts* sub-section.

In turn, the Pod template contains a metadata section with the labels used to select the Pods, and a spec section with a list of all of the containers:

```
metadata:
  labels:
    my-Pod-label-name: my-Pod-label-value
    ...
spec:
  containers:
  ...
  - name: my-container-name
    image: <Docker imagename>
    resources:
      requests:
         cpu: 100m
         memory: 128Mi
       limits:
         cpu: 250m
         memory: 256Mi
    ports:
    - containerPort: 6379
    env:
```

```
      - name: env-name
        value: env-value
```

Each container has a name and must specify the name of the Docker image to use to create the container. If the Docker image is not contained in the public Docker registry, the name must be a URI that also includes the repository's domain.

Then, containers must specify the memory and CPU resources that they need to be created in the `resources->requests` object. A Pod replica is created only if these resources are currently available on some machine.

The `resources->limits` object, instead, specifies the maximum resources a container replica can use. If, during the container execution, these limits are exceeded, an action is taken to limit them. More specifically, if the CPU limit is exceeded, the container is throttled (its execution is stopped to restore its CPU consumption), while if the memory limits are exceeded, an exception is thrown, and the container is restarted. CPU time is expressed in millicores; 1,000 millicores means 100% of the CPU time, while memory is expressed in mebibytes (1Mi = 1,024*1,024 bytes), or other units.

`containerPort` must be the port exposed by the container. Here, we can also specify further information, such as the protocol used.

`env` lists all the operating system environment variables to pass to the containers with their values.

Both containers and Pod templates can contain other fields, such as properties that define virtual files and properties that define commands that return the readiness and the health state of the container.

We will analyze these fields in the *Advanced Kubernetes concepts* subsection.

The following subsection describes Pod sets conceived to store state information, that is, `StatefulSets`.

StatefulSets

StatefulSets' Pod instances have ordinal numbers attached to them. They are started in sequence according to these numbers, and they are stopped in reverse order. If the `StatefulSet` contains N replicas, these numbers go from 0 to N-1. Moreover, a unique name for each instance is obtained by chaining the Pod name specified in the template with the instance ordinal, in the following way: `<Pod name>-<instance ordinal>`. Thus, instance names will be something like `myPodname-0`, `myPodname-1`, and so on. As we will see in the *Services* subsection, instance names are used to build unique cluster network URIs for all instances, so that other Pods can communicate with a specific instance of a `StateFulSet` Pod.

The definition of a `StatefulSet` is very similar to that of a `Deployment`:

```
apiVersion: apps/v1
kind: StatefulSet
metadata:
  name: my-stateful-set-name
spec:
  selector:
```

```
    matchLabels:
      my-Pod-label-name: my-Pod-label-value
      ...
  serviceName: "my-service-name"
  replicas: 3
  template:
  ...
```

The `template` part is the same as that of `Deployments`. The main difference between StatefulSets and Deployments is the `serviceName` field. This specifies the name of a service that must be connected with the `StatefulSet` to provide unique network addresses for all Pod instances. We will discuss this subject in more detail in the *Services* subsection. Moreover, usually, StatefulSets use some form of storage. We will discuss this in detail in the *Advanced Kubernetes concepts* section. It is also worth pointing out that the default order of the creation and stop strategy of StatefulSets can be changed by specifying an explicit `Parallel` value for the `spec->PodManagementPolicy` property (the default value is `OrderedReady`).

The next subsection describes how to provide stable network addresses to both `ReplicaSets` and `StatefulSets` through `Services`.

Services

Since Pod instances can be moved between nodes, they have no stable IP address attached to them. **Services** take care of assigning a unique and stable virtual address to a whole `ReplicaSet` and of load balancing the traffic to all its instances. `Services` are not software objects created in the cluster, but just an abstraction of the various settings and activities needed to implement their functionalities.

`Services` also handle assigning a unique virtual address to each instance of a `StatefulSet`. In fact, there are various kinds of Services; some were conceived for `ReplicaSets` and others for `StatefulSets`.

A **ClusterIP** service type is assigned a unique cluster internal IP address. In order to create virtual IP addresses for ClusterIP services, Kubernetes interferes with the **DHCP** protocol.

A ClusterIP service specifies the Pods it is connected to through label pattern matching. It uses tables maintained by the Kubernetes infrastructure to load balance the traffic it receives between all the Pod instances to which it is connected.

Therefore, other Pods can communicate with the Pods connected to a ClusterIP service by interacting with this service that is assigned a stable IP address and the stable network name `<service name>.<service namespace>.svc.cluster.local`. Since it is just assigned local IP addresses, a ClusterIP service can't be accessed from outside the Kubernetes cluster.

> **Note**
>
> A ClusterIP is the usual communication choice for Deployments and ReplicaSets that do not communicate with anything outside of their Kubernetes cluster.

Here is the definition of a typical ClusterIP service:

```
apiVersion: v1
kind: Service
metadata:
  name: my-service
  namespace: my-namespace
spec:
  selector:
    my-selector-label: my-selector-value
    ...
  ports:
  - name: http
    protocol: TCP
    port: 80
    targetPort: 9376
  - name: https
    protocol: TCP
    port: 443
    targetPort: 9377
```

Each ClusterIP service can work on several ports and can route any port (`port`) to the ports exposed by the containers (`targetPort`). However, it is very often the case that `port` = `targetPort`. Ports can be given names, but these names are optional. Also, the specification of the protocol is optional; when not explicitly specified, all supported level 4 protocols are allowed. The `spec->selector` property specifies all the name/value pairs that select the Pods to which to route the communications it receives.

Since a ClusterIP service can't be accessed from outside the Kubernetes cluster, we need other service types to expose a Kubernetes application on a public IP address.

The more convenient way to expose some Pods to the outside world is through a **LoadBalancer** service, in which case the Kubernetes cluster is exposed to the outside world through a layer 4 load-balancer.

The definition of a LoadBalancer service is similar to that of a ClusterIp service, the only difference being that the `spec->type` property must be set to `LoadBalancer`:

```
...
spec:
  type: LoadBalancer
  selector:
...
```

If no further specification is added, a dynamic public IP is randomly assigned. However, if a specific public IP address is required, it can be set as a public IP address for the cluster load balancer by specifying it in the `spec->loadBalancerIP` property:

```
...
spec:
  type: LoadBalancer
  loadBalancerIP: <your public ip>
  selector:
  ...
```

`StatefulSets` don't need any load balancing since each Pod instance has its own identity, but do require a unique URL address for each Pod instance. This unique URL is provided by the so-called **Headless** Services. Headless Services are defined like ClusterIP services, the only difference being that they have a `spec->clusterIP` property set to none:

```
...
spec:
  clusterIP: none
  selector:
...
```

All `StatefulSets` handled by a headless Service must place a headless service name in their `spec->serviceName` property, as already stated in the *StatefulSets* subsection.

The unique DNS name provided by a headless service to all `StatefulSets` Pod instances it handles is `<unique Pod name>.<service name>.<namespace>.svc.cluster.local`. Headless services provide these DNS names by dynamically manipulating DNS records, meaning that whenever a Pod is moved to another machine, its DNS record is automatically updated by the headless service.

The next subsection describes how to expose several frontend microservices through a unique load balancer with web-hosting capabilities.

Ingresses

Ingresses were conceived to enable each application running in a Kubernetes cluster to expose a unique HTTP-based interface. More specifically, several frontend microservices, instead of each having its own load balancer service, interface with the external world through a unique load balancer connected with a Web server that routes different URLs to different ClusterIP services. This way, the whole application needs a unique IP address and benefits from all the facilities of an advanced Web server.

Since rewriting all functionalities of an advanced Web server from scratch would be substantially impossible, Ingresses rely on existing Web servers to offer their services. More specifically, Kubernetes offers the possibility to add an interface module called **Ingress Controllers** to connect each Kubernetes cluster with an existing Web server, such as NGINX or Apache.

Ingress Controllers are custom Kubernetes objects that must be installed in the cluster. They handle the interface between Kubernetes and the pre-existing web server software, which can be either an external web server or a web server that is part of the Ingress Controller installation.

Ingress controllers are installed through `.yaml` files, and there are Ingress controllers based on all main web servers. Moreover, usually Cloud Kubernetes Clusters offer their custom preinstalled ingress controllers.

All ingress controllers offer name-based virtual hosting, that is, they associate several domain names with the same IP address and route each domain, or <domain>/<path prefix>, to a different ClusterIp Service.

Once installed, an ingress controller allows us to define **Ingress** objects with `.yaml` files like we define deployments or statefulSets.

Virtual hosting can be configured in the Ingress definition in a way that is independent of the chosen Ingress Controller. More specifically, name-based virtual hosting is defined in the `spec-> rules` section of the Ingress definition:

```
...
spec:
...
  rules:
  - host: *.mydomain.com
    http:
      paths:
      - path: /
        pathType: Prefix
        backend:
          service:
            name: my-service-name
            port:
              number: 80
  - host: my-subdomain.anotherdomain.com
...
```

Each rule specifies an optional hostname that can contain the * wildcard. If no hostname is provided, the rule matches all hostnames. For each rule, we can specify several paths, each redirected to a different `service/port` pair, where the service is referenced through its name. The way the match with each path is carried out depends on the value of `pathType`; if this value `is Prefix`, the specified

path must be a prefix of any matching path. Otherwise, if this value is `Exact`, the match must be exact. Matches are case-sensitive.

We can also associate an https certificate with one or several domains. Certificates are encoded in Kubernetes secrets (see the *Advanced Kubernetes concepts* subsection):

```
...
spec:
...
  tls:
  - hosts:
    - www.mydomain.com
    - subdomain.mydomain.com
    secretName: my-certificate1
- hosts:
  - www.anotherdomain.com
  secretName: my-certificate2
...
```

HTTPS certificates can be obtained free of charge at https://letsencrypt.org/. The procedure is explained on the website, but basically, as with all certificate authorities, you provide a key, and they return the certificate based on that key. It is also possible to install a certificate manager that takes care of automatically installing and renewing the certificate. The way a key/certificate pair is encoded in a Kubernetes secret string is detailed in the *Advanced Kubernetes concepts* subsection.

The whole Ingress definition is as follows:

```
apiVersion: networking.k8s.io/v1
kind: Ingress
metadata:
  name: my-example-ingress
  namespace: my-namespace
spec:
  tls:
  ...
  rules:
  ...
```

Here, the namespace is optional, and if not specified, it is assumed to be the default.

At this point, you have learned how to define your microservice replicas, how to define their interaction patterns through services, and how to expose your application to the external world.

In the next section, we will put into practice some of the concepts explained here by defining a local Kubernetes cluster simulator in Docker Desktop.

Using Docker Desktop Kubernetes and Kubectl

The simplest way to test Kubernetes is by exploiting Docker Desktop Kubernetes. You can activate it by entering Docker Desktop settings and then entering the **Kubernetes** tab. Once here, select **kind** as Kubernetes software, select at least 2 as the number of nodes, and finally start the cluster.

Once you've created a Kubernetes cluster, you can interact with it through the **kubectl** command-line tool. kubectl is integrated into Docker Desktop Kubernetes.

Usually, kubectl must be configured to interact with a specific cluster and with specific credentials, but Docker Desktop Kubernetes, once started, automatically configures kubectl to interact with it through default administrative credentials. kubectl commands can be run through any Windows console.

If you issue the `kubectl get nodes` command, you get a list of all your Kubernetes nodes. In general, `kubectl get <object type>` lists all objects of a given type. You can use it with nodes, Pods, statefulset, and so on. `kubectl get all` shows a list of all the objects created in your cluster. If you also add the name of a specific object, you will get information on just that specific object, as shown here:

```
kubectl get <object type>/<object name>
```

If you add the `--watch` option, the object list will be continuously updated, so you can see the state of all the selected objects changing over time. You can leave this watch state by hitting `Ctrl + C`. The following command shows a detailed report on a specific object:

```
kubectl describe <object type>/<object name>
```

The above commands display objects in the default namespace. If you would like to list objects in other namespaces, you need to add the `-n <namespace>` option.

All objects described in a `.yaml` file, say `myClusterConfiguration.yaml`, can be created with the following command:

```
kubectl apply -f myClusterConfiguration.yaml
```

Then, if you modify the `.yaml` file, you can reflect all the modifications in your cluster with the same apply command, as shown here:

```
kubectl apply -f myClusterConfiguration.yaml
```

You can destroy all objects that were created with a `.yaml` file by passing the same file to the delete command, as shown here:

```
kubectl delete -f myClusterConfiguration.yaml
```

The delete command can also be passed an object type and a list of names of objects of that type to destroy, as shown in the following example:

```
kubectl delete deployment deployment1 deployment2...
```

The preceding kubectl commands should suffice for most of your practical needs. For more details, the *Further reading* section contains a link to the official documentation.

The *Deploying a Worker microservice on Kubernetes* section of *Chapter 22, Case study: Practical Usage of .NET Aspire,* contains a complete example of how to deploy microservices to Kubernetes.

In the next section, we will analyze other important Kubernetes features.

Advanced Kubernetes concepts

In this section, we will discuss other important Kubernetes features, including how to assign permanent storage to StatefulSets; how to store secrets such as passwords, connection strings, or certificates; and how a container can inform Kubernetes about its health state. All of these subjects are organized into dedicated subsections. We will start with the problem of permanent storage. At first read, you can skip all but the first subsection, and then return to them after having practiced with Kubernetes.

Requiring permanent storage

Since Pods are moved between nodes, they can't store data on the disk storage offered by the current node where they are running, or they would lose that storage as soon as they are moved to a different node. This leaves us with two options:

- Using external or internal databases: ReplicaSets usually store information with the help of databases. Here, with internal databases, we mean databases installed directly in the Kubernetes cluster.
- Using cloud or network storage: not being tied to a physical cluster node, cloud or network storage can be associated permanently with specific Pod instances of StatefulSets.

Since access to databases doesn't require any Kubernetes-specific techniques but can be done with the usual connection strings, we will concentrate on cloud/network storage.

Kubernetes offers an abstraction of storage called **PersistentVolumeClaim (PVC)** that is independent of the underlying storage provider. More specifically, PVCs are allocation requests that are either matched to predefined resources or allocated dynamically.

Cloud providers such as Azure offer different storage classes with different performance and different costs. Moreover, the PVC can also specify the accessMode, which can be:

- **ReadWriteOnce**: The volume can be mounted as read-write by a single Pod
- **ReadOnlyMany**: The volume can be mounted as read-only by many Pods
- **ReadWriteMany**: The volume can be mounted as read-write by many Pods

If you have network storage connected to your on-premise Kubernetes cluster you can install an open-source dynamic storage provider also on your on-premise cluster.

Volume claims can be added to StatefulSets in a specific `spec->volumeClaimTemplates` object:

```
volumeClaimTemplates:
- metadata:
    name: my-claim-template-name
  spec:
    resources:
      request:
        storage: 5Gi
    volumeMode: Filesystem
    accessModes:
    - ReadWriteOnce
    storageClassName: my-optional-storage-class
```

The storage property contains the storage requirements. `volumeMode` set to `Filesystem` is a standard setting that means the storage will be available as a file path. The other possible value is `Block`, which allocates the memory as unformatted. `storageClassName` must be set to an existing storage class offered by the cloud provider or installed in the cluster. If it's omitted, the default storage class will be assumed.

All available storage classes can be listed with the following command:

```
kubectl get storageclass
```

Once `volumeClaimTemplates` has defined how to create permanent storage, each container must specify which file path to attach that permanent storage to in the `spec->containers->volumeMounts` property:

```
...
volumeMounts
- name: my-claim-template-name
  mountPath: /my/requested/storage
  readOnly: false
...
```

Here, name must correspond to the name given to the PVC.

The following subsection shows how to use Kubernetes secrets.

Kubernetes secrets

Some data, such as passwords and connection strings, cannot be exposed but need to be protected by some kind of encryption. Kubernetes handles private sensitive data that needs encryption through specific objects called secrets. Secrets are sets of key-value pairs that are encrypted to protect them.

They can be created by putting each value in a file, and then invoking the following kubectl command:

```
kubectl create secret generic my-secret-name \
--from-file=./secret1.bin \
--from-file=./secret2.bin
```

In this case, the filenames become the keys and the files' contents are the values.

When the values are strings, they can be specified directly in the kubectl command, as shown here:

```
kubectl create secret generic dev-db-secret \
--from-literal=username=devuser \
--from-literal=password='$dsd_weew1'
```

In this case, keys and values are listed one after the other, separated by the = character. In the previous example, the actual password is enclosed between single quotes to escape special characters like $ that are usually required to build strong passwords.

Once defined, secrets can be referred to in the `spec->volume` property of a Pod (Deployment or StatefulSet template), as shown here:

```
...
volumes:
- name: my-volume-with-secrets
  secret:
    secretName: my-secret-name
...
```

After that, each container can specify on which path to mount them in the `spec->containers->volumeMounts` property:

```
...
volumeMounts:
- name: my-volume-with-secrets
  mountPath: "/my/secrets"
  readOnly: true
...
```

In the preceding example, each key is seen as a file with the same name as the key.

When secrets contain strings, they can also be passed as environment variables in the `spec->containers->env` object:

```
env:
- name: SECRET_USERNAME
```

```
    valueFrom:
      secretKeyRef:
       name: dev-db-secret
       key: username
  - name: SECRET_PASSWORD
    valueFrom:
      secretKeyRef:
        name: dev-db-secret
        key: password
```

Here, the name property must match the secret's name. Passing secrets as environment variables is very convenient when containers host ASP.NET Core applications, since, in this case, environment variables are all immediately available in the configuration object (see the *Loading configuration data and using it with the options framework* section of *Chapter 16, Presenting ASP.NET Core*).

Secrets can also encode the key/certificate pair of an HTTPS certificate with the following kubectl command:

```
kubectl create secret tls test-tls --key="tls.key" --cert="tls.crt"
```

Secrets defined in this way can be used to provide HTTPS certificates in Ingresses. You can do this by placing the secret names in the `spec->tls->hosts->secretName` properties of an Ingress.

We are almost at the end of our trip in the world of Kubernetes. We need just the last piece: how to inform Kubernetes that our replica is ready to receive input and is in a good health state.

Liveness and readiness checks

Kubernetes automatically monitors all containers to ensure they are still alive and that they keep their resource consumption within the limits declared in the `spec->containers->resources->limits object`.

When some conditions are violated, the container is either throttled, restarted, or the whole Pod instance is restarted on a different node. How does Kubernetes know that a container is in a healthy state? While it can use the operating system to check the healthy state of nodes, it has no universal check that works with all containers.

Therefore, the containers themselves must inform Kubernetes of their health, otherwise Kubernetes cannot verify them. Containers can inform Kubernetes of their health in two ways: either by declaring a console command that returns their health or by declaring an endpoint that provides the same information.

Both declarations are provided in the `spec-> containers-> livenessProb` object. The console command check is declared as shown here:

```
...
livenessProbe:
  exec:
    command:
    - cat
```

```
        - /tmp/healthy
    initialDelaySeconds: 10
    periodSeconds: 5
    failureThreshold: 5
...
```

If the command returns 0, the container is considered healthy. In the preceding example, the software running in the container records its state of health in the `/tmp/healthy` file, so the `cat/tmp/healthy` command returns it. `PeriodSeconds` is the time between checks, while `initialDelaySeconds` is the initial delay before performing the first check. An initial delay is always necessary so as to give the container time to start.

`failureThreshold` is the number of consecutive times the check must fail to consider the container unhealthy. If not specified, it defaults to 3.

The endpoint check is quite similar:

```
...
livenessProbe:
  exec:
    httpGet:
      path: /healthz
      port: 8080
      httpHeaders:
      - name: Custom-Health-Header
      value: container-is-ok
  initialDelaySeconds: 10
  periodSeconds: 5
  failureThreshold: 5
...
```

The test is successful if the HTTP response contains the declared header with the declared value.

Similarly, the readiness of containers is monitored with a readiness check. A readiness failure implies just a temporary inability of the container, due, for instance, to congestion. Accordingly, no action is performed on the container, but it is excluded from the load-balancing performed by all connected services till the check is successful again.

The readiness check is defined in a similar way as the liveness check, the only difference being that `livenessProbe` is replaced with `readinessProbe`. Often, the `readinessProbe` is identical to the `livenessProbe` with the exception of having a lower `failureThreshold` (typically 1).

While a general knowledge of Kubernetes and other orchestrators is necessary to design microservices, the good news is that you don't need to test your microservices with actual orchestrators during development because .NET Aspire simulates all orchestration features needed to test your software in the development stage.

Developing Microservice applications with .NET Aspire

Debugging a microservice application during development is quite hard. No tool is able to debug all services deployed in a Kubernetes cluster simultaneously. The usage of Kubernetes simulators like Minikube and Kind that run on developer machines doesn't solve the problem. One can try to attach a debugger to a single service replica, but this option is also hard since it is difficult to connect to code that runs inside a container that runs inside a Kubernetes cluster.

The only feasible approach is to hack the application so that the traffic directed to the target service replica is redirected to a replica that runs outside of the cluster in Visual Studio (or in another IDE that allows debugging). However, this solution is also tricky and time-consuming, so using it during the continuous code and test that characterizes development is hard.

A more feasible option is to run all containers in a Docker network that runs on the development machine. This way, since Visual Studio supports Docker containers, all services can be debugged simultaneously. However, this solution also requires a non-negligible setup time in the error-prone task of configuring the whole network.

.NET Aspire furnishes a simpler alternative to the direct usage of Docker networks to test microservice applications on the development machines. Moreover, it offers a simple way to configure also the interaction among microservices and between each microservice and other resources. Finally, .NET Aspire projects can be compiled to produce instructions to both deploy all microservices on Azure Container Apps and to create also some of the resources which they use on Azure, or to create Kubernetes deployments and services.

More specifically, .NET Aspire takes care of the microservices interaction and offers also other services, namely:

- It handles the interaction with environment resources such as databases and message-brokers in a very simple way. You don't need to specify a connection string that might change when the microservice is deployed, but it is enough that you declare the interaction between a microservice and a resource together with some general configuration. This capability relies on a .NET feature called **local service discovery**, which will be discussed in detail in the *Service Discovery and its Role in .NET Aspire* subsection.
- It offers simulators of Cloud services, together with common disk and in-memory databases and message brokers.
- The interaction between microservices and other resources is configured declaratively in a dedicated .NET project, thus avoiding the use of virtual addresses and connection strings inside the microservices code.
- Once a .NET Aspire project is run, all microservices and resources are run, and interaction among microservices and resources is automatically handled.
- While microservices are run in the development environment, both logs and statistics are collected.
- As soon as a .NET Aspire project is run, a smart console appears in the browser that shows all collected statistics and logs, together with the links to access all microservice endpoints.

Interaction among microservices and among microservices and other resources is declared in a special type of project called **App Host**. You can find the App Host project and all other Aspire templates by typing "*Aspire*" in the Visual Studio search box, as shown in the image below:

Figure 19.4: Aspire projects and solution templates

Another Aspire-specific project type is the **.NET Aspire Service Defaults** project. It furnishes extension methods to configure various services. In order to ensure that some basic services are configured in exactly the same way in all microservices, we define them in this project and then call their extension methods in the `Program.cs` configuration of all microservice projects. Accordingly, all microservices' outermost layers must add a reference to this project.

As a default, all Aspire templates configure the following service defaults:

- `HttpClient` service discovery. In the App Host configuration, microservices and resources are given names, and thanks to this configuration `HttpClients` can use virtual URLs based on these names instead of the actual resource URLs that might depend on where the resources are deployed in the various environments (development, staging, production, etc.).
- `HttpClient` resiliency. Each `HttpClient` call is automatically applied all resiliency policies we discussed in the *Resilient Task Execution* subsection of *Chapter 11, Applying a Microservice Architecture to Your Enterprise Application*. More specifically, both retry, circuit break, timeout, and rate-limiting (bulkhead isolation) strategies are automatically applied and can be configured once and for all in the .NET Aspire Service Defaults project.
- Open telemetry, which will be discussed in a dedicated subsection.
- Public endpoints exposing microservices health conditions. Health checks are used both by the App Host orchestrator and by staging and production orchestrators like Kubernetes (see the *Liveness and readiness checks* subsection in this chapter). Two default endpoints are provided: `/health`, which returns a 200 HTTP code and a "*healthy*" test response if the microservice is healthy, and an */alive* endpoint, which returns a 200 HTTP code and a "*healthy*" test response if the microservice is running and has not crashed.

As a default, both endpoints are exposed only during development for security reasons. However, if the Microservice is not accessible to external users, it can also be safely exposed in production. You just need to remove the condition on the environment in the `MapDefaultEndpoints()` extension defined in the .NET Aspire Service Defaults project.

If, instead, the microservice is a frontend, these endpoints can be exposed only if they are protected by both authentication and a throttling strategy that prevents denial-of-service attacks.

You don't need to add all these configurations manually since they are automatically added when the project is created. Most of the time, you will need to change just some parameters, such as the parameters of the various resiliency strategies.

Each Microservice needs to call `builder.AddServiceDefaults()` and `app.MapDefaultEndpoints()` in order to apply all configured defaults, as shown below:

```
var builder = WebApplication.CreateBuilder(args);

// Add service defaults & Aspire client integrations.
builder.AddServiceDefaults();

// Add application specific services
builder.Services.....

...
// Build application host
var app = builder.Build();
//Configure application
```

```
app….
…
//Add default endpoints
app.MapDefaultEndpoints();

app.Run();
```

There is also a MAUI-specific version of the .NET Aspire Service Defaults project.

Available also are Aspire-specific testing projects based on `xUnit`, `NUnit`, and `MSTest`. They have all the needed references to create an App Host, launch the application, and communicate with microservices through URLs based on their names (service discovery).

As soon as you add a test project, it contains an initial example test with the whole code for creating the App Host and issuing a call to a microservice. You just need to adapt the code to the actual test you would like to perform:

```
// Arrange
 var cancellationToken = new CancellationTokenSource(DefaultTimeout).Token;

 var appHost = await DistributedApplicationTestingBuilder
  .CreateAsync<Projects.AspireApp1_AppHost>(cancellationToken);
 appHost.Services.AddLogging(logging =>
 {
     …
 });
 appHost.Services.ConfigureHttpClientDefaults(clientBuilder =>
 {
     clientBuilder.AddStandardResilienceHandler();
 });

 await using var app = await appHost.BuildAsync(cancellationToken)
  .WaitAsync(DefaultTimeout, cancellationToken);
 await app.StartAsync(cancellationToken)
  .WaitAsync(DefaultTimeout, cancellationToken);

 // Act
 var httpClient = app.CreateHttpClient("webfrontend");
 await app.ResourceNotifications
  .WaitForResourceHealthyAsync("webfrontend", cancellationToken)
  .WaitAsync(DefaultTimeout, cancellationToken);
 var response = await httpClient.GetAsync("/", cancellationToken);
```

```
// Assert
Assert.Equal(HttpStatusCode.OK, response.StatusCode);
```

In the code above, the microservice name that you might need to replace to test all various microservices is highlighted.

Also available is a template called **.Net Aspire Empty App** that creates both the App Host and Service Defaults projects, and a **.Net Aspire Starter App** template that also adds an example microservice and resources together with their App Host configurations.

The .NET Aspire Starter App template has a great didactic value because it immediately shows basic configurations and how to configure and use an `HttpClient` with service discovery. Moreover, it is a good way to explore the console that appears in the browser when the application is launched, with its statistics and logs, and the links to access all Microservice endpoints. All readers are encouraged to create, explore, and run this project.

Service discovery is not an Aspire-specific feature but is a general .NET feature. It relies on various providers to map service names to actual URLs. We will discuss it in more detail in the next subsection.

Service Discovery and its Role in .NET Aspire.

Service discovery is an `HttpClient` feature provided through extension methods defined in the `Microsoft.Extensions.ServiceDiscovery` NuGet package.

Service names are mapped to actual URLs by using maps defined in providers. As a default, just the `.NET Configuration` provider is added to the list of providers.

This provider tries to read these maps from the `Services` section of the client microservice project configuration, where they must be defined as follows:

```
"Services": {
    "myservice": {
      "https": [
        "10.46.24.91:80"
      ]
       "http": [
        "10.46.24.91:443"
      ]
    }
  }
```

When the service is called with `http://myservice`, the endpoint specified in the "*http*" subsection is chosen; otherwise, if it is called with `https://myservice`, the one in the "*https*" subsection is chosen.

The configuration-based provider is added with:

```
builder.Services.AddServiceDiscovery();
```

The above code also adds the **pass-through** provider, which simply resolves each service name to the service name itself. In a few words, the pass-through provider does nothing! It must be used when deploying to Kubernetes, since in Kubernetes, names are resolved by services.

Therefore, when deploying to Kubernetes, each microservice must have an associated service whose name is identical to the microservice name.

For instance, if we have a Microservice called `routes_planning` that is deployed in a Kubernetes `routes_planning_Deployment`, then communications to `routes_planning` must be passed through a Kubernetes service called `routes_planning`.

If a service name is not resolved by the configuration-based provider, it is passed to the next provider, which is the pass-through provider.

Suppose now we would like to deploy on Kubernetes but first, we need to test our application with .NET Aspire. Do we need two different service discovery settings for these two environments?

The answer is no! In fact, .NET Aspire doesn't use a configuration file to define the service maps. Instead, when the APP Host project launches a microservice, it injects all service resolution rules it needs into environment variables that are then merged with all other microservice configuration information.

When the application is published to a Kubernetes cluster, there will be no App Host, so no service resolution maps are injected in the configuration, and all resolutions are passed to the pass-through provider.

One can also use `AddServiceDiscoveryCore()`, which doesn't add any default provider, instead of `AddServiceDiscovery()`. In this case, providers must be added manually by calling `AddPassThroughServiceEndpointProvider()` and `AddConfigurationServiceEndpointProvider()`.

For instance, if we would like to add just the configuration-based provider, we can simply write:

```
builder.Services.AddServiceDiscoveryCore()
    .AddConfigurationServiceEndpointProvider();
```

Service discovery can also be customized by setting the properties of the `ConfigurationServiceEndPointResolverOptions` object. For instance, the code below changes the name of the `Services` section where to place all service name maps:

```
builder.Services.Configure<ConfigurationServiceEndPointResolverOptions>(
    static options =>
    {
        options.SectionName = "MyCustomResolverSection"
    });
```

Once added and configured, service discovery requires us to specify the Http clients that must use it. The code below applies service discovery to all Http clients:

```
builder.Services.ConfigureHttpClientDefaults(http =>
{
    http.AddServiceDiscovery();
});
```

`ConfigureHttpClientDefaults` can also be used to add and configure the various resiliency policies to all Http clients:

```
builder.Services.ConfigureHttpClientDefaults(http =>
{
    http.AddStandardResilienceHandler();
   http.AddServiceDiscovery();
});
```

The code above is the default `HttpClient` configuration added in all .NET Aspire Service Defaults projects.

Service discovery can also be added to a specific named HttpClient as shown below:

```
builder.Services.AddHttpClient("myclient", static client =>
{
    client.BaseAddress = new("https://myservice");
})
.AddServiceDiscovery();
```

When service discovery is in place, we can also write URIs like "https+http://myservice" or "http+https://myservice". In this case, service discovery would attempt to resolve the URI with the first protocol (https or http), and would move to the second protocol in case of failure.

This is useful when we use http during development and https in staging and production. For this purpose, it is enough to define just http endpoints in the launch settings of all microservice projects. In fact, the App Host uses each microservice's launch settings to create the service discovery maps that it injects into the environment variables. Therefore, only http maps would be generated during development, so https resolution will fail. After deployment, instead, just the pass-through provider will work so https resolution will succeed.

Up to this point, we have supposed that each microservice has just a single endpoint, but sometimes some services might have several endpoints, each on a different port. When a microservice has several endpoints, we must give names to all endpoints but one (the default endpoint). Endpoint names are given in the service definition and configuration that is in the App Host. Below is the definition of a microservice with a default endpoint and a named endpoint whose name is "aux":

```
var routesPlanning = builder.AddProject<Projects.RoutesPlanningService>("myservice ")
    .WithHttpsEndpoint(hostPort: 9999, name: "aux");
```

In this case, the generated configuration map will associate two URLs with the service name, one for the default endpoint and the other for the named endpoint, as shown below:

```
"Services": {
    "myservice ": {
      "https": ["https://localhost:8080"],
      "aux": ["https://localhost:8090"]
    }
  }
```

The default endpoint can be accessed with "https://myservice", while for the named endpoint we must also add the endpoint name to the URI, as shown below:

```
https://_aux. myservice
```

When using Aspire App Host the above configuration is automatically created and injected in all services that need it, so we don't need to worry about it.

However, if we deploy on Kubernetes, we must define a Kubernetes service that resolves correctly both "https://myservice" and "https://_aux.myservice". This result is easily achieved with named ports, as shown below:

```
apiVersion: v1
kind: Service
metadata:
  name: myservice
spec:
  selector:
    name: myservice
  ports:
  - name: default
    port: 8080
  - name: aux
    port: 8090
```

The port associated with the default endpoint must be given the default name, while all ports associated with named endpoints must be given the same name as the endpoint.

Now that we understand the magic behind actual service URLs discovery, let's move to the magic behind resources integration and connection string automatic handling.

Resources Integration and Automatic Resources Configuration

Resources needed by the various microservice projects can be simulated when the solution is run. It is enough to add the corresponding Aspire NuGet packages, and to declare and configure the resource in the App Host. There are extension methods for declaring the main databases, Redis, and the main message brokers like RabbitMQ, Kafka, and also an Azure Service Bus simulator. For a complete list of all resources that can be added to an Aspire project and configured in its App Host, please refer to the official documentation on integration `https://aspire.dev/integrations/gallery/`.

Behind the curtain, all these resources are implemented with Docker images, so most extension methods also give the possibility of choosing a specific Docker image and a specific version. Furthermore, since the App Host also supports generic Docker images, one can implement extension methods for a custom resource that is not supported yet. However, the list of supported resources grows quickly, so you should find all the resources you need already implemented.

When you configure a resource you give it a name, and if the resource supports a connection string, that name is assumed to be the name of the connection string. Accordingly, when the App Host creates a resource, it computes its connection string and passes it in the `ConnectionStrings` section of the configuration of all microservices that use that resource. This is done by placing the configuration string in an environment variable called `ConnectionStrings__<name>`, where `<name>` is the name that we gave to the resource.

For instance, suppose our application needs a SQL Server Instance containing a database called "mydatabase", in the App Host we may declare these resources with:

```
var builder = DistributedApplication.CreateBuilder(args);
var sql = builder.AddSqlServer("sql");
var db = sql.AddDatabase("mydatabase");
```

Now, if a microservice defined in the `MyExampleProject` project must use the "mydatabase" database, it must declare it as follows:

```
builder.AddProject<Projects.MyExampleProject>()
       .WithReference(db);
```

The `WithReference(db)` call causes the connection string for accessing "mydatabase" in the SQL Server instance to be injected in the `ConnectionStrings__mydatabase` environment variable of the `MyExampleProject` microservice.

Clearly, when we configure a resource, we can also specify the credentials to access it instead of using the default credentials created by the extension method.

More details on how to configure resources and microservices in the App Host will be given in the next subsection.

Usually, together with the connection string, the App Host passes a whole configuration section containing more details on the resources, such as username and password. The format of these auxiliary data depends on the specific resource type. The auxiliary info format of all supported resources is available in the official documentation.

If we would like to use an already existing resource, we don't need to declare it in the App Host, but we need to declare its connection string with `builder.AddConnectionString` so that the App Host can inject it into all microservices that need it. For instance, if the SQL Server database of the previous example already exists both in the development environment and in the deployment environment, the code must be modified as follows:

```
var builder = DistributedApplication.CreateBuilder(args);
var db = builder.AddConnectionString("parameterName", "database");
```

Where `parameterName` is the name of the parameter that contains the actual connection string in the App Host configuration file in the "Parameters" section, as shown below:

```
{
    "Parameters": {
         " parameterName ": " SERVER=XXX.XXX.X.XX;DATABASE=DATABASENAME ......"
    }
}
```

Needless to say, we can use .NET environments to provide different configurations in different environments.

The remainder of the code remains unchanged:

```
builder.AddProject<Projects.MyExampleProject>()
       .WithReference(db);
```

What happens to all connection strings, and to the auxiliary resource data when the application is deployed in production or staging?

If deployment is manual, the same environment variable inserted by the App Host must be defined in the configuration of the target orchestrator. Thus, for instance, if the target orchestrator is Kubernetes, it must be defined in the env section of a Deployment. As we will see in more detail in the Deploying a .NET Aspire Project section, when we use automatic tools for configuring the target orchestrator, there are two possibilities:

- If the automatic tool is also capable of provisioning the required resources, it will also configure all environment variables automatically, taking all the needed information from the created resources
- If the automatic tool doesn't generate the required resources but just the code for configuring all microservices, the tool will ask the environment variable values from the user

Well! You learned how to configure all microservice with .NET Aspire together with all resources they use. (databases, message brokers, etc.). The next subsection details how to handle telemetry during development and when the application is deployed.

Application Telemetry

It is quite easy to monitor what happens in a monolithic application and trace how each request evolves. The same is not true in a distributed environment since the state of each part is stored in a different computer, and since each request is split among several cooperating microservices. Moreover, since communications are asynchronous, the order events take place in the whole hardware doesn't necessarily correspond to the logical processing order of each request. For these reasons, microservice applications use **telemetry** to collect and reorganize data.

Telemetry enables the monitoring of a Microservice application as a whole, that is by connecting adequately related events taking place in different Microservices. More specifically, it collects the following data:

- ***Logging***. Individual logs of all microservices and resources are collected and classified according to their generation time and source.
- ***Tracing***. Traces correlate log events that are part of the same logical activity (e.g. the handling of a single request), even if they're spread across multiple machines or processes. Tracing is the starting point for diagnosing and debugging malfunctions.
- ***Metrics***. Various microservice metrics are collected by each executing microservice and are sent to a collection point.

When the application is run in the development environment and use the App Host as the orchestrator, each microservice's Telemetry is enabled by the `ConfigureOpenTelemetry()` call configured in the .NET Aspire Service Defaults project. This call enables the collection of metrics and the transmission of these metrics, together with the microservice logs, to an Open Telemetry endpoint that implements the **Open Telemetry protocol (OTLP)**.

During development, the Aspire console that opens when the solution is run works as an Open Telemetry Endpoint, and the data for connecting with this endpoint are injected as environment variables into all Microservices by the App Host. Therefore, all data we can see in this console comes from Telemetry.

When the application is deployed, the same environment variables must contain the data of an Open Telemetry endpoint available in the deployment environment. Azure supports OTLP, so if, for instance, the application is deployed to Azure Kubernetes, we must pass the data of the Telemetry endpoint that is created together with the Azure Kubernetes cluster. It is also possible to pass Open Telemetry data to third-party tools installed in the orchestrator.

The environment variables automatically injected in each microservice by the App Host that we must inject manually in the deployment environment are:

- `OTEL_EXPORTER_OTLP_ENDPOINT`, which contains the URL of the OTLP endpoint.
- `OTEL_SERVICE_NAME`, which contains the service name that the microservice must add to the data it sends. To avoid confusion, you should use the same name given to the microservice in the App Host configuration.
- `OTEL_RESOURCE_ATTRIBUTES`, which contains a unique ID that univocally identifies each service instance. It must be added to all data, too, and must have the format: `service.instance.id=<unique name>`. Typically, one uses GUIDs as service unique names.

Once all services offered by Aspire are clarified, and you know how to configure each microservice and resource, you just need to learn how to put everything together in the App Host definition.

Configuring Microservices and Resources

The App Host is the place where you put together all definitions of the microservices and resources of your application and where you configure all their inter-relations. More specifically, there you can configure the following entities:

1. ***.NET Projects***. They can be configured with:

```
var myService = builder.AddProject<Projects.MyProjectName>("myservicename");
```

2. ***Containers stored in some registry***. They can be configured with:

```
var myService = builder.AddContainer("myservicename", "ContainerNameOrUri");
```

3. ***Executables***. They can be configured with:

```
var myService = builder.AddExecutable("myservicename", "<shell command>",
"<executable working directory>");
```

4. ***Docker files to be built***. They can be configured as:

```
var myService = builder.AddDockerfile("myservicename ", "relative/context/path");
```

Where, "relative/context/path" is the folder containing the Docker file and all files needed to build the Docker file. This path must be relative to the directory that contains the App Host project file.

Each of the above commands can be followed by several configuration options, passed with a fluent interface, as shown in the example below:

```
var cache = builder.AddProject<Projects......
var apiService = builder.AddProject<Projects......
builder.AddProject<Projects.MyAspireProject>("webfrontend")
    .WithReference(cache)
    .WaitFor(cache)
    .WithReference(apiService)
    .WaitFor(apiService);
```

- `WithReference` declares that the service communicates with the resource or service passed as argument. It causes the injection of all environment variables containing the data needed by service discovery, connection strings or other auxiliary resource information.

- `WaitFor` declares that the microservice must be started after the service or resource passed as argument is running.
- `WithReplicas(int n)` is another important method of the configuration fluent interface. It declares that the microservice must be replicated `n` times. It is important if we plan to use an automatic tool for compiling App Host configuration into Kubernetes or Azure Container App configuration code.

Unluckily, often when in development mode, the limited power of our development machine doesn't allow the same number of replicas, we need in production. Therefore, we should execute different configuration instructions in these two cases.

The App Host configuration is executed both when we run the application on the development machine and when we use App Host configuration to generate code for other platforms. In the second case, we say that we are in publishing mode instead of running mode. Luckily, the builder object contains information on the execution environment in the `builder.ExecutionContext` property. In particular, we can use the `builder.ExecutionContext.IsPublishMode` and the `builder.ExecutionContext.IsRunMode` properties to differentiate the configuration in run mode and in publish mode.

As already mentioned, the in the *Service Discovery and its Role in .NET Aspire* subsection, we can also use the `WithEndpoint` fluent interface method to declare auxiliary endpoints available on other ports:

```
var MyService =
  builder.AddProject<Projects.MyService>("myservice ")
    .WithEndpoint(hostPort: 9999, name: "aux");
```

`WithEndpoint` can be replaced by `WithHttpsEndpoint` and `WithHttpEndpoint` to declare respectively https-only and http-only endpoints.

The `WithExternalHttpEndpoints()` fluent interface method declares that the microservice endpoint must be available outside of the application for application clients. These endpoints will be exposed with LoadBalancer services when publishing the application on Kubernetes and with external ingresses when publishing the application on Azure Container Apps.

Resources used by microservices can be declared and configured with the same fluent interface. Each resource type requires a dedicated NuGet package that provides the needed extension methods to the fluent interface. All these extension methods are built on the `builder.AddContainer` method since they use Docker images to implement the resources. Therefore, if a resource we need is not available yet, we can write ourselves the needed extension methods. However, as already mentioned, there are resources for all main databases, Redis, all main message brokers, and for most of the Azure services. Some Azure resources configurator provision and use actual Azure resources, while others use local simulator. There are simulators for Azure Storage and for Azure Service Bus.

The reader is referred to the official documentation for a list of all available resource integrations `https://aspire.dev/integrations/gallery/`.

As a default, when the App Host is shut down, all database data is lost since all Docker images use temporary storage. However, we can use the `WithDataVolume()` fluent interface method to force the usage of a permanent Docker volume storage:

```
var sql = builder.AddSqlServer("sql")
                 .WithDataVolume();
var db = sql.AddDatabase("database");
```

When this method is called, a Docker volume with an auto-generated name is created. For more control on the volume name and on the directory inside the container where it is mounted, one can use `WithBindMount`:

```
var sql = builder.AddSqlServer("sql")
                 .WithBindMount("MyVolumeName", "/var/opt/mssql");
var db = sql.AddDatabase("database");
```

Most resources use a default username, such as `sa`, and an autogenerated password. Both credentials are available through the **resources** info link of the App Host Browser console. However, if data is not persisted with a volume, this password may change at each run.

Luckily, all resources also give the possibility to specify some parameters, and username and password are always among them.

Needless to say, parameters are not inserted directly in the code, for obvious reasons. They are taken from the "*Parameter*" section of the App Host configuration. Therefore, they can be inserted in the App Host configuration file, so we can also provide a different value for each environment by using the usual .NET environment-based configuration files override.

The first step is the definition of a parameter object with the name of the "*Parameters*" property that contains the actual value:

```
var password = builder.AddParameter("sqlpassword", secret: true);
```

By setting `secret` to `true`, we just enable the generation of a hint to store the parameter in a safe place when we run Aspire in publish mode.

Then, the parameter is placed in the right place of the resource extension method, that is resource-specific:

```
var sql = builder.AddSqlServer("sql", password)
                 .WithBindMount("MyVolumeName", "/var/opt/mssql");
var db = sql.AddDatabase("database");
```

The actual value must be placed in the App Host project configuration file as shown below:

```
{
  "Parameters": {
    "sqlpassword": "my_password_value",
```

```
    ...
  },
  ...
}
```

As you can see, parameter values are specified in a `Parameters` section of the App Host configuration file as label-value pairs.

This subsection completes our trip in the Aspire world. At this point, you are able to code and run your microservice application in Visual Studio. You need to learn just how to deploy your Aspire solution to your target orchestrator, first in staging/testing environments and then in production. You will learn how to do it in the next subsection.

Deploying a .NET Aspire Project

.NET Aspire can be used to test an application or a small part of a complex microservice application on the development machine, thus replacing Docker Kubernetes and Docker networks.

However, small applications can be completely implemented in Aspire and then the Aspire code can be used to generate the configuration of the target orchestrator. This, generation can be manual or based on automatic tools.

Both manual generation and automatic tools rely on a JSON manifest that can be created automatically and that describes the application configuration. The JSON manifest can be generated by adding the launch profile below to the App Host project `launchSettings.json`:

```
"profiles": {
  "generate-manifest": {
    "commandName": "Project",
    "launchBrowser": false,
    "dotnetRunMessages": true,
    "commandLineArgs": "--publisher manifest --output-path aspire-manifest.json"
  }
```

Once added to `launchSettings.json`, this profile appears in the Visual Studio profile-selection combo next to the run button. It is enough to select the "generate-manifest" profile and run the solution. When the solution runs, the application is compiled but instead of running, it creates the JSON manifest in the App Host project folder.

You can read this manifest manually and use the information it contains to configure your orchestrator, or you can use automatic tools that generate the manifest and use it to automatically configure an orchestrator.

Visual Studio supports natively the deployment to Azure Container Apps. Publishing to Azure Container Apps is straightforward. It is enough to right-click on the solution App Host project and select **"Publish"**. After that, you can select the Azure Container Apps publish target. The procedure will guide you to connect to your Azure subscription and to provide all information needed to publish the application.

The publish wizard will publish all microservices as Azure Container Apps applications, and will provision in Azure all other resources defined in the App Host, such as databases and other Azure resources.

Available also is an external tool called **Aspir8** (`https://prom3theu5.github.io/aspirational-manifests/getting-started.html`) capable of deploying the application on a Kubernetes cluster. However, in this case it will create just Kubernetes Deployments and Services.

Once installed Aspir8 supports the following commands:

- `aspirate init`: Initializes the Aspir8 project in the current directory
- `aspirate generate`: Generates Kubernetes manifests based on the .NET Aspire app host manifest
- `aspirate apply`: Applies the generated Kubernetes manifests to the Kubernetes cluster
- `aspirate destroy`: Deletes the resources created by the apply command

For simple applications, you can deploy directly on a Kubernetes cluster, and in the case of more complex applications, you can use the Kubernetes manifest as a starting point for designing the needed Kubernetes configuration.

The apply and destroy commands need a `Kubectl` installation, and all operations are performed using the current `Kubectl` context, that is, the current Kubernetes cluster and the current credentials.

If you would like to manually inspect the manifest generated by the App host, please refer to its official format documentation `https://learn.microsoft.com/en-us/dotnet/aspire/deployment/manifest-format`.

A practical example of .NET Aspire usage is described in the *Testing a Worker microservice with .NET Aspire* section of *Chapter 22, Case study: Practical Usage of .NET Aspire.*

This subsection completes our .Aspire learning path with the last step involved in Aspire development: deployment. While automatic deployment on Azure Containers Apps is a mature technology, Aspir8 is continuously improving but is a good starting point for the actual deployment.

Summing up .Aspire makes possible testing the application or part of it during development, and at the same time provides facilities for deploying and configuring properly the application in staging and production. Before leaving our Aspire learning path, it is worth summarizing the .NET Aspire development workflow:

1. Define an Aspire Visual Studio solution
2. Define all microservices' default settings (service, discovery, resiliency policies, health endpoints, and open telemetry), in the .NET Aspire Service Defaults project
3. Incrementally define all microservice projects
4. Incrementally define all resources (databases, message brokers, etc.) needed to run all defined services
5. Incrementally configure all defined projects and resources in the App Host
6. As soon as you have something that can run in the target orchestrator, deploy it to a testing environment, such as Minikube or Kind, with the help of Aspire deployment facilities
7. As soon as you have something that can be used by actual users, deploy it to a staging environment
8. When you are satisfied with staging results deploy to the production environments

That's all! Now you are ready to start your Aspire professional experience.

Summary

After an introduction to the orchestrator's features and a short description of the most popular orchestrators, this chapter focuses on the Kubernetes orchestrator.

After a detailed but self-contained description of Kubernetes, the chapter explains how to test microservice applications during development with the help of .NET Aspire.

Finally, the chapter explains how to use the .NET Aspire configuration to generate configuration code for actual orchestrators like Azure Container Apps and Kubernetes.

Questions

1. What is the difference between a ReplicaSet and a StatefulSet?
2. Why are Kubernetes Services needed?
3. Why is a Kubernetes Ingress needed?
4. What are the Aspire specific .NET SDK projects?
5. Is Service Discovery an Aspire-specific feature?
6. How many Service Discovery providers come with the Aspire default settings?
7. What is the best way to handle pre-existing resources that are not defined with the App Host but are shared by several Microservices?
8. Does Aspir8 provision Azure resources, too?
9. What is the purpose of the `WithReference` fluent interface method?

Further reading

Here, you have some links you may consider using to gather more information about this chapter:

- The official documentation for Azure Container Apps can be found here: `https://learn.microsoft.com/en-us/azure/container-apps/`.
- The official documentation on AWS Amazon Elastic Container Service can be found here: `https://docs.aws.amazon.com/ecs/`.
- The official documentation on Google Cloud Run can be found here: `https://docs.cloud.google.com/run/docs?hl=en`.
- A more complete but at the same time self-contained description of Kubernetes may be found in our monograph on microservices "Practical Serverless and Microservices with C#": `https://www.amazon.com/Microservices-Azure-microservices-serverless-development/dp/1836642016`.
- The official documentation on Nomad can be found here: `https://developer.hashicorp.com/nomad`.
- The official documentation on Swarm can be found here: `https://docs.docker.com/engine/swarm/`.
- The official documentation for Kubernetes can be found here: `https://kubernetes.io/docs/home/`.

- More information on Helm and Helm charts can be found in the official documentation. This is extremely well written and contains some good tutorials: `https://helm.sh/`.
- The official documentation for Azure Kubernetes can be found here: `https://docs.microsoft.com/en-US/azure/aks/`.
- Official Aspire documentation: `https://learn.microsoft.com/en-us/dotnet/aspire/get-started/aspire-overview`
- All available Aspire integrations: `https://aspire.dev/integrations/gallery/`
- App Host configuration manifest format: `https://learn.microsoft.com/en-us/dotnet/aspire/deployment/manifest-format`
- Aspir8: `https://prom3theu5.github.io/aspirational-manifests/getting-started.html`

Get this book's PDF version and more

Scan the QR code (or go to `packtpub.com/unlock`). Search for this book by name, confirm the edition, and then follow the steps on the page.

UNLOCK NOW

Note: Keep your invoice handy. Purchases made directly from Packt don't require an invoice.

20

Securing Data and Applications

This chapter is dedicated to enterprise application security. Security is not an isolated feature we can add at any time, but the result of several techniques coordinated by a well-designed overall strategy that creates a solid wall around all application resources. Therefore, it must be taken into account in all of the application development stages, and both architects and developers must have a clear understanding of why and how all security techniques work and contribute to the overall application security.

Privacy, non-modifiability, and proof of identity are the main ingredients of all security strategies, so we will first analyze how cryptography can be used to ensure them, and then how they can cooperate in more complex security strategies to secure communication and to verify user and software authorizations.

The chapter also discusses the practical implementation of both secured communications and authentication/authorization in .NET.

Finally, we give a short description of how to secure table fields in Cloud databases without necessarily trusting the Cloud provider. More specifically, this chapter covers the following topics:

- A Primer on Cryptography
- Securing communications
- Authentication and Authorization
- Encrypting database fields in the Cloud

Technical requirements

This chapter requires the free Visual Studio 2026 Community edition or better, with all the database tools installed. The code for this chapter is available at `https://github.com/PacktPublishing/Software-Architecture-with-.NET-10-and-C-sharp-5E`.

A Primer on Cryptography

Cryptography is the building block of most security techniques. It uses a secret to transform an initial message (we say the message is **encrypted**) into a way that only those who know that secret or another connected secret can reconstruct the original message (we say the message is **decrypted**). The secrets used to encrypt and decrypt the messages are called **keys**.

Cryptography has a fundamental role in all applications since it ensures the privacy of communication and can also be used to verify the identity of all participants, thus preventing spoofing and man-in-the-middle attacks. In particular, it has a fundamental role in HTTPS-secured Web communication and in all authentication techniques.

If both encryption and decryption use the same key, the encryption is called **symmetric**; if the two keys are different, the encryption is called **asymmetric**. Therefore, symmetric encryption is based on a single key, while asymmetric encryption is based on 2 different keys. Both symmetric and asymmetric encryption underpin TLS, authentication flows, and other advanced security techniques discussed later on in the chapter.

Typically, one of the two keys of an asymmetric encryption is kept public, while the other one is known only by the entity that must encrypt or decrypt the messages. Therefore, asymmetric encryption is useful in the two scenarios below:

- Anyone can encrypt a message with a public encryption key, but the message can be decrypted only by someone who knows the private decryption key. Encrypted e-mails are a typical usage of this arrangement: each possible recipient has a private decryption key, while the associated encryption keys are kept public and are associated with the recipient's email address. Whoever would like to send a secure email to a recipient uses the public encryption key associated with the recipient's email address to encrypt it. This way, anyone can send messages to a recipient, but these messages can be decrypted and understood only by the intended recipient. If anyone else somehow intercepts the email, he can't decrypt or understand it. *Figure 20.1* gives a visual picture of the whole process of sending/receiving an encrypted message:

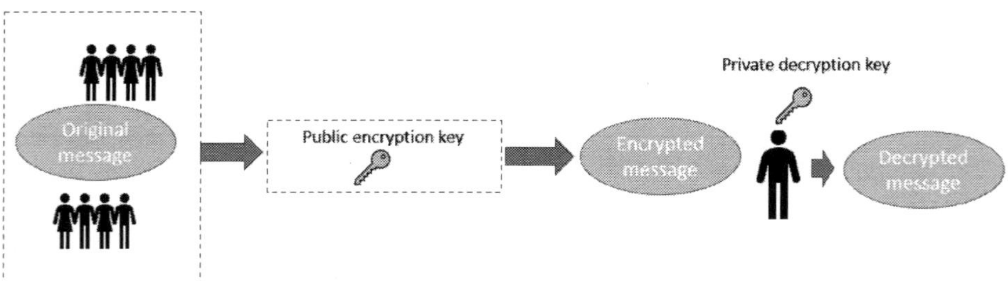

Figure 20.1: Public encryption with private decryption

- Just an entity that knows the private encryption key can encrypt a message, but everyone can decrypt it by using the associated public decryption key. This way, whoever receives the encrypted message is sure it was encrypted by the owner of the private encryption key, and is sure that no one else modified the original message because any subsequent modification would require the private encryption key. A digital signature is based on this arrangement. Below is a picture that shows this arrangement:

Figure 20.2: Private encryption with public decryption

Symmetric encryption, instead, admits just one possible arrangement: both sender and recipient must share a common secret, that is, the encryption/decryption **symmetric key**.

This poses the following question: how can a couple of people agree on a common symmetric key, being sure that no one else spies on them?

Of course, two people can agree on a safe symmetric key in a physical meeting, where no one else can spy on them. Below is a picture that shows this arrangement:

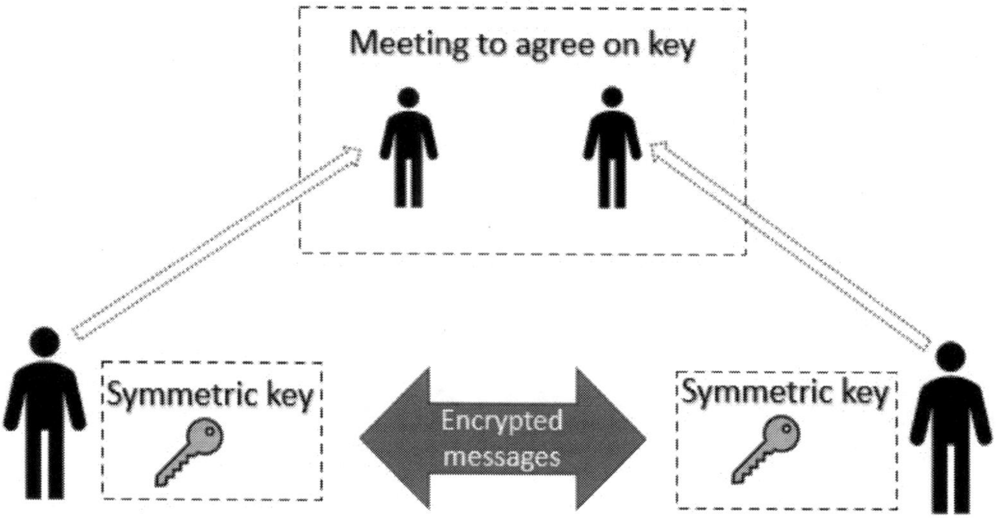

Figure 20.3: Symmetric key with simple agreement

Note

However, if at least one of them, say John, has a private decryption key, the other one, say Mary, may decide on the symmetric key and may use the public encryption key to encrypt a message containing the symmetric key. The message containing the symmetric key can be safely sent to John with any media since only John can decrypt it. As we will see in the *Securing communications* section, this arrangement is adopted for securing the TLS communications (HTTPS).

Below is a picture that shows how this arrangement works:

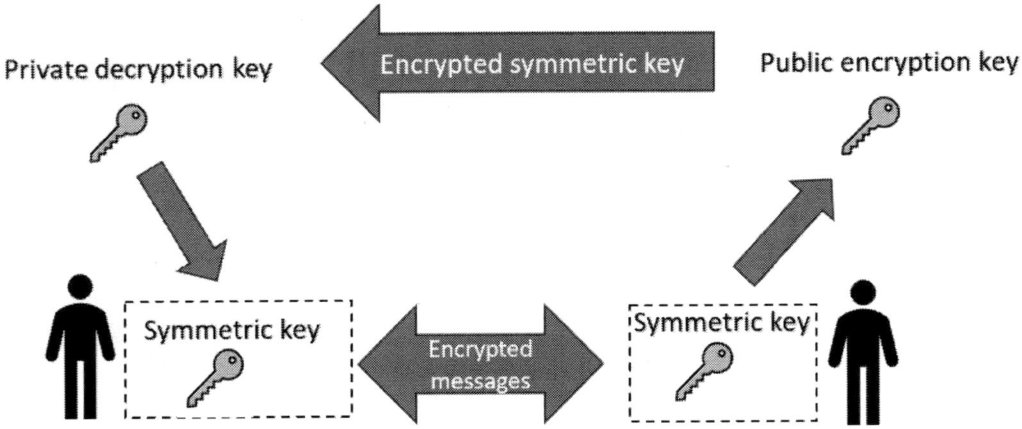

Figure 20.4: Using an asymmetric key to agree on a symmetric key

Well, you just learned the basics of cryptography, all security techniques are based on! So, you are ready to learn all the secrets of security techniques. Let's start our trip in the world of security techniques.

Encrypting for privacy

If our main purpose is preventing others from reading a message, the simplest solution is the usage of symmetric encryption. In fact, once a couple of people have agreed on a symmetric key, they can exchange secure messages with no risk their messages might be understood or modified by other people because both decryption and modification require the knowledge of the symmetric key.

Privacy is ensured also by a public encryption/private decryption arrangement, but in this, the message might be modified by other people since the encryption key is public.

Furthermore, usually, asymmetric encryption algorithms are also less efficient.

> **Note**
>
> Therefore, all applications based on a continuous and fast exchange of data secure communication with symmetric keys and use asymmetric keys just to come to an agreement on the symmetric key when the communication starts.
>
> On the other side, applications that can't rely on an initial negotiation for agreeing on a symmetric key must necessarily use a public encryption/private decryption arrangement.

Thus, for instance, HTTPS communication uses symmetric encryption after a negotiation stage, while emails that can't rely on an initial negotiation for agreeing on a symmetric key, secure emails with a public encryption/ private decryption arrangement.

In the case of emails, modifications performed by unauthorized users and impersonation are prevented by applying a digital signature. We explore this concept in the next subsection.

Digital signature: preventing unauthorized modification

Sometimes we don't want to encrypt a message because we want to enable everyone to read it. However, we might want to prevent unauthorized modifications and impersonation of the actual message author.

This is the case of a library distributed as a DLL: we don't want anyone but the author to be able to modify the DLL.

Unauthorized modifications and impersonation are easily prevented if the author has a private asymmetric encryption key by creating a **digital signature** and adding it to the message. The digital signature algorithm works as follows:

1. The whole message is processed to produce a short message called the hash of the message, with the following features:
    a. It is not computationally feasible to find messages that produce a given hash
    b. All hashes have substantially the same probability, that is, hashes are uniformly distributed on the space of all possible messages
2. The computed hash is encrypted by the author with his asymmetric encryption key

Once the computed signature is added somehow at the end of the message.

Now, whoever gets the message can verify it was actually produced by the declared author, that is, by the possessor of the private encryption key, as follows:

1. It decrypts the hash using the author's public decryption key
2. It recomputes the hash by processing the messages with the same algorithm used by the author
3. If the computed and decrypted hashes are the same, we are sure that the author is the possessor of the private encryption key and that no one modified the message. In fact, if a malicious actor modifies the message before it arrives at one of the intended users, they can't produce a new valid hash since they don't know the private encryption key needed to adapt the signature to the new content. Moreover, a malicious user can't apply modifications that leave the hash unchanged because of the constraints a and b on the hashing algorithm.

When you create a .NET library, Visual Studio gives you the possibility to sign the compiled DLL. In this case, we say that the library has a *strong name*. A signature can be applied by right-clicking on the DLL project name in Visual Studio Solution Explorer and then choosing **Properties**. Then, select **Strong naming** in the left menu. If another project references your strong-named DLL, the signature is verified before using the library, so it wouldn't be possible to replace your library with a modified version of it.

In the various arrangements analyzed up to now, it appears we may feel safe if "*something can be done only by the possessor of a private key*." However, are we always sure that the possessor of a given private key actually is our intended interlocutor?

For instance, let's say we somehow get Microsoft's public decryption key. Can we safely use it to verify the digital signature of a Microsoft DLL is correct?

The challenge here is that a malicious agent might have modified the DLL, and then he might have hijacked us on a fake Microsoft public decryption key. In the next subsection, we will describe why digital signatures actually work and how it overcomes the previous issue.

Proof of identity and chains of certificate authorities

In most situations, when we receive a message or when we are starting a communication session, we need proof that our interlocutor actually is the intended one. In cryptography, this problem is known as **proof of identity**. It can be factored out into two subproblems:

a. Proving that our interlocutor knows a private asymmetric key ***Kp***

b. Proving that the unique possessor of ***Kp*** actually is our intended interlocutor

Problem ***a*** is easily solved if each message of our interlocutor is digitally signed with ***Kp***. This technique suffices if the "*message*" is a DLL or an email, but if we are starting a communication session where we both receive and send secrets, we need a priori proof before any payload is exchanged.

An a priori proof of knowledge of a private asymmetric key ***Kp*** can be obtained by asking our interlocutor to encrypt with ***Kp*** a short test message we send him. Then, we decrypt the encrypted message with the public key associated with ***Kp***, and if we get back our initial test message, we have the desired proof that our interlocutor knows ***Kp***.

After that, a trusted third party should confirm the identity of the unique possessor of ***Kp***. In a few words, we need a kind of notary that certifies the identity of the unique possessor of ***Kp***. Similar notaries exist and are called certification authorities. They produce electronic documents called certificates that associate a private key with its unique owner. What is the content of a similar ***Kp*** certificate? The certificate can't contain ***Kp*** because it, being private, can't be exposed, but it can contain the unique public key associated to ***Kp***, say ***PKp***, together with data expressing somehow the identity of the ***Kp*** owner.

Certificates are digitally signed by the certification authority with a private key, say ***Ka***. Together with the ***Ka*** digital signature, the certification authority also includes the public key corresponding to ***Ka***, say ***PKa***, so that its signature can be easily verified.

Figure 20.5 summarizes the whole process:

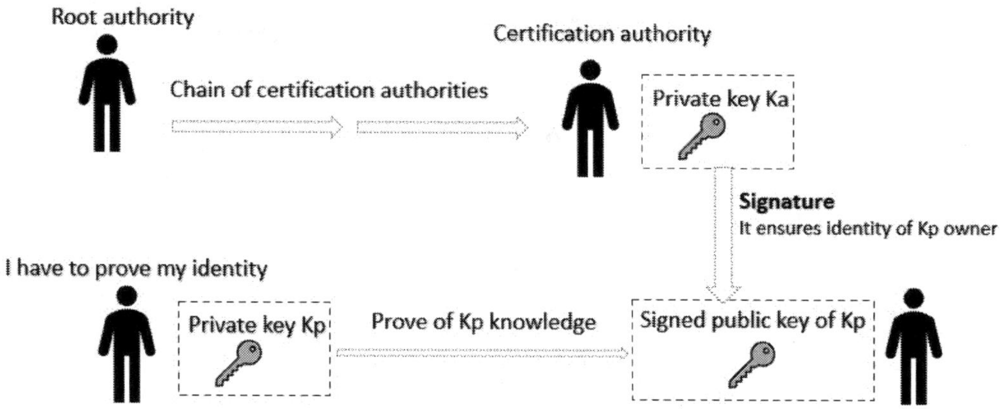

Figure 20.5: Using an asymmetric key to agree on a symmetric key

However, how do we ensure that the possessor of ***Ka*** and ***PKa*** is an actual certification authority? The fact is that there is also a certificate associated with ***PKa***, which is, in turn, signed by a higher-level certificate authority, and so on, until we reach root certificate authorities that, being well known, don't need to be certified by anyone else. Being well-known trivially means that their certificates are added to the pool of **trusted certificates** of all computers.

The certificates' chain that connects our interlocutor to some root authority can be verified because the certificates of all authorities are available online.

For security reasons, each certificate has an expiration date (including those of all certification authorities), but each certificate can also be revoked before its expiration date if its associated private key is compromised, or if there are suspicions it has been compromised. The list of all revoked certificates is available online and is automatically consulted together with the full certificate chain each time a proof of identity is required. This includes, for instance, the verification of a DLL signature, the verification of an email signature, and the identity verification performed each time a browser connects with the HTTPS protocol.

Let's take a look at the procedure we must follow to get a private key and a signed certificate for that key:

1. We use a cryptography library to generate a private key of a given length and based on a given algorithm. Typically, private keys are stored in files with a .key extension.
2. We use the same software to extract a **Certificate Signing Request** (CSR) from the previous .key file. This request contains the public key associated with the input .key file, together with the information we want to certify (proof of identity). The information to certify depends on the purpose and kind of certificate. It can be the ownership of a Web domain, or the actual name of our company, or some of our personal data.
3. The CSR is typically stored in a .csr file.
4. We submit the CSR to the certification authority, which, after having verified the information it must certify, emits the certificate. If the information to certify is simply the ownership of a web domain, the whole procedure can be performed electronically, since we can prove the ownership by simply putting

something on our website. However, if the information to certify involves personal data or company data, an interaction with a human is unavoidable.

5. After all needed verification, the authority returns an *X.509* certificate, which has a .crt or .cer file extension

The format and what can be included in an X.509 certificate is described in the *RFC 5280 §4* specification (`https://datatracker.ietf.org/doc/html/rfc5280#section-4`).

Now you know what an X.509 certificate is, how to get one and how to process it for proving and verifying identities. However, you also need to learn how to choose the cryptography algorithms and key lengths for your target level of security.

Keeping our encryption safe

Cryptography can be broken both by computing a private key from its associated public key or by analyzing the encrypted messages with various cryptanalysis techniques.

In fact, in theory, it is always possible to compute the private key given its associated public key, but the computation is unfeasible. However, actual unfeasibility depends on the length of the keys, because with short keys it is always possible to discover the private key with a try and verify approach or with more sophisticated techniques that depend on the mathematical properties of the adopted algorithm.

At the moment, the more popular asymmetric algorithm is RSA, but it has been proven that RSA can be broken with quantum computing, so new techniques have been developed, such as **elliptic cryptography** and **lattice-based cryptography,** that are already available in all main cryptographic libraries.

Cryptanalysis uses the probability of occurrence of observed patterns and, when available, the knowledge of the original message to guess the keys. Again, the main defense is the key length. However, in the long run, recurrent patterns and the knowledge of some original messages might enable an attacker to break the cryptography.

Therefore, all practical techniques include the so-called **probabilistic encryption**. In a few words, they add some noise to the encrypted message so that the same pattern is always encrypted with different bits. This way, probabilistic occurrence analysis is not possible anymore.

The simplest way to turn a deterministic encryption algorithm into a probabilistic one is to concatenate the original message with a random short message before encryption.

We have finished our short introduction to cryptography, so you can start learning its practical applications in the design of enterprise software. We start with the most important application in the domain of Web and microservices: how to secure communications.

Securing communications

In this section, we will learn how both symmetric and asymmetric cryptography, as well as the proof of identity you studied so far, can be used to secure TCP/IP communication with TLS.

As a first step, let's start analyzing why communications must be secured with TLS or other similar protocols. Then we will focus on the TLS protocol itself and on how it can be used in practice in .NET applications.

Secured communication prevents third parties from spying on the communication, but this is not its only purpose. It has another important purpose: proving the identity of the server!

One might object that the client doesn't need a proof of identity by the server, since the client himself decides the domain and IP address to which to connect to! This is false! The client does need a proof of identity from the server because it might be the victim of a **man-in-the-middle** attack!

This means a third party might somehow intercept its communication with the server and might replace the role of the server in the communication. In a similar situation, we are convinced that we are communicating with the chosen domain, and our browser would also show that domain name in its bar, but we are actually communicating with a malicious agent!

Luckily, the malicious agent would fail a proof of identity! Now if we use the server public key to send an encrypted symmetric key to be used for encrypting all subsequent messages, then only our intended server will be able to decrypt this message to continue the communication with us.

Actually, there is no a priori proof of server identity, but the server's ability to decrypt the symmetric key and continue the communication is itself a proof of identity.

This is the basic idea behind the TLS protocol, which acts at level 4 of the communication protocol, that is, at the level of the TCP/IP connection. Below is a short summary of the **handshaking** procedure for starting a TLS secured communication:

1. **Client "Hello"**. Client contacts the server and sends it a list of the supported security protocols (TLS version, asymmetric algorithms, symmetric algorithms, and hashing algorithms and their versions). Client also sends a random string called "*client random*" that will be used later on.
2. **Server "Hello"**. The server answers with the safest protocols in the list it supports. From that instant on, client and server agree to use them in the subsequent steps. Server also sends a random string called "*server random*" that will be used later on.
3. **Server identity**. The server sends its certificate, but at this time it doesn't supply any proof that it knows the associated private key.
4. **Server identity verification**. The client verifies the validity of the server certificate and confirms it belongs to its intended interlocutor.
5. **Client symmetric key generation**. The client sends a random master secret to the server, encrypted with the server's public key. Then computes a Symmetric Key by chaining client random, the server random and the master secret.
6. **Server symmetric key computation**. Server decrypts the master secrets and performs the same computation performed by the client to compute the same symmetric key. Please notice that the server can successfully compute the symmetric key only if it actually knows the private key declared in its certificate.
7. **Handshake termination**. Both server and client send a termination message encrypted with the newly computed symmetric key and with the symmetric algorithm negotiated at the beginning. This way, each of them proves to the other it has correctly computed the symmetric key.
8. **Actual communication**. Server and client start the secured communication, encrypting all messages with the computed symmetric key and the negotiated symmetric algorithm.

It is worth clarifying the role of the client and server randoms. They ensure both parties that the symmetric key is unique for that session, otherwise a malicious agent might replace the server and might reuse previously spied messages to answer to the client. This might work if the client requests are the same as the ones of an old request. We need both a server random and a client random because a malicious agent might also replay all messages of another client, so both parties must ensure the uniqueness of the symmetric key.

There is also a variant called **mTLS,** where the client also has a certificate and uses it to prove its identity to the server. mTLS can replace client application-based login/authentication that will be discussed in the next section.

mTLS adds the following extra steps:

- ***4a. Client Identity. Client*** sends its certificate to the server.
- ***4b. Server verifies the client certificate.*** Server verifies the expiration date of the client certificate and processes the chain of certificate authorities to verify that the client certificate is valid.
- ***5a. Client proof of identity***. The client proves it knows the private key associated with the certificate it sent to the server by computing a signature of all messages exchanged so far, and sending it to the server.
- ***5b. Server verifies client signature***. Server computes the hash of the messages sent to the client and compares it with the hash contained in the client's signature to verify they are the same.

Usually, TLS server certificates are installed on Web servers like IIS, Apache or NGINX, but what if we want to secure internal communications between all microservices of our application? While the communication with the external world is usually mediated by a distributed Web server, internal communications are not. For instance, in a Kubernetes cluster there is a unique Web server that interfaces with the external world, but no web server that handles internal communications.

Therefore, in case of internal communications, each microservice must have and use its private TLS certificate directly. From an implementation perspective if our microservices are implemented with ASP.NET Core these private certificates can be handled by ASP.NET Core micro-Web-server: Kestrel.

Next subsection describes how to handle TLS certificates with Kestrel in practice.

Using server certificates with Kestrel

Adding HTTPS certificates to each microservice is necessary to secure inter-application communications. In turn, securing inter-application communication is a MUST if **0-trust** is among the application requirements, that is if each application part must protect itself from other application parts that might be infected by a malicious user. When using ASP.NET Core, certificates may be installed on Kestrel which is ASP.NET Core micro-Web-server.

The first time you create an ASP.NET Core project with HTTPS support .NET SDK automatically creates a self-signed certificate with its associated private key, which will then be used in all subsequent projects. The private counterpart of this certificate is not added as a file but is added to a so-called **Certificate Store**. Certificate stores are safe places each operating system uses to store certificates.

Each operating system has various stores. An important store used by .NET SDK running on Windows is `CurrentUser\My` (that is equivalent to `CurrentUser\Personal`).

The first part of the path is called the *location*, while the second part is called the *store*. The CurrentUser location contains all certificates that are specific to the currently logged user. There are other locations such as LocalMachine that contain the certificates shared by all users.

The My (or equivalently Personal) store contains all owned certificates, that is, all certificates whose private key is known.

The certificate created by the .NET SDK is issued for the "*localhost*" domain. We say that its *Subject* is "*localhost*". Being self-signed, to make your browser trust it, the public part of this certificate must be added to all trusted certificates as if it were a root certificate.

In Windows, trusted certificates are contained in the Root store, so in our case, the .NET SDK adds the public part of the certificate to CurrentUser\Root.

In Kestrel, HTTPS can be enabled by specifying a port in the HTTPS->PORTS setting, which can be done by assigning that port to the ASPNETCORE_HTTPS_PORTS environment variable. Also possible is assigning an https complete URL to the semicolon-separated list in the URLS setting (ASPNETCORE_URLS environment variable).

When no other information is supplied, Kestrel assumes it is in development mode and looks for a certificate whose subject is localhost in CurrentUser\My.

Complete information that includes certificate location in a file or in a certificate store can be specified by configuring endpoints. Endpoints can be specified either in configuration or by setting a property of an option object in the code. Below is an endpoint specified in the configuration file based on a certificate placed in a certificate store:

```
"Kestrel": {
    "Endpoints": {
      "Http": {
        "Url": "http://localhost:8080"
      },
      ...
      "HttpsCertStore": {
        "Url": "https://localhost:8081",
        "Certificate": {
          "Subject": "mydomain.com",
          "Store": " Personal",
          "Location": " CurrentUser",
          "AllowInvalid": "false"
        }
      },
```

Where AllowInvalid set to false causes an exception if the certificate is expired, revoked or not rooted in a trusted certificate authority.

The same setting can be passed in code as follows:

```
var builder = WebApplication.CreateBuilder(args);
builder.WebHost.ConfigureKestrel((context, serverOptions) =>
{
    serverOptions.Listen(IPAddress.Loopback, 8080);
    serverOptions.Listen(IPAddress.Loopback, 8081, listenOptions =>
    {
        listenOptions.UseHttps(StoreName.My,
          "mydomain.com",
          false,
          StoreLocation.CurrentUser);

    });
});
```

Certificates can also be taken by usual files. In this case, both public and private parts are stored in a unique `.pfx` file protected by a password.

The `.pfx` file can be created from both a `.key` and a `.crt` file by opening a Linux console (you need WSL2 installed) and typing the following command:

```
openssl pkcs12 -export -out MyCertificate.pfx -inkey MyCertificate.key -in
MyCertificate.crt -password mypassword
```

Once we have a `.pfx` file, we can use it in the configuration file:

```
{
  "Kestrel": {
    "Endpoints": {
      "Http": {
        "Url": "http://localhost:8080"
      },
    ...
      "HttpsCertFile": {
        "Url": "https://localhost:8081",
        "Certificate": {
          "Path": "MyCertificate.pfx",
          "Password": "MyPassword"
        }
      },
      ...
```

We can do the same with code, too:

```
var builder = WebApplication.CreateBuilder(args);
builder.WebHost.ConfigureKestrel((context, serverOptions) =>
{
    serverOptions.Listen(IPAddress.Loopback, 8080);
    serverOptions.Listen(IPAddress.Loopback, 8081, listenOptions =>
    {
        listenOptions.UseHttps("MyCertificate.pfx", "mypassword");

    });
});
```

Note

In case of microservices running in Docker containers, the best option is to take the certificate from a file that is mounted from a Kubernetes secret (see the *Advanced Kubernetes concepts* subsection of *Chapter 19, Orchestrators and .NET Aspire*).

We can also enable mTLS as obligatory or optional by adding another configuration to `listenOptions`:

```
...
listenOptions.UseHttps(o =>
{
    o.ClientCertificateMode = ClientCertificateMode.RequireCertificate
  //or ClientCertificateMode.AllowCertificate for optional
});
```

`ClientCertificateMode.RequireCertificate` forces the server to pretend a valid client certificate to accept the communication.

At this point, you need to learn the last piece needed for enabling an mTLS-enabled communication: how a .NET client can handle its mTLS client certificate.

Using client certificates with .NET HttpClient

If we are using `IHttpClientFactory` to configure our HttpClients, we may first read the certificate and then create a message handler that adds the certificate:

```
//Load certificate from file
var clientCertificate=X509CertificateLoader
    .LoadPkcs12FromFile("MyCertificate.pfx", "MyPassword");
//create handler with certificate
var handler = new HttpClientHandler();
handler.ClientCertificates.Add(clientCertificate);
```

```
builder.Services.AddHttpClient("namedClient", c =>
{
  //configure HttpClient instances
    ...
})
//Add handler to HttpClient instances
.ConfigurePrimaryHttpMessageHandler(() => handler);
```

We will describe how to handle authentication with clients that authenticate with client certificates in the *Handling client certificate authentication in ASP.NET Core* subsection.

Securing communication with TLS is not enough to protect communication between a user and the application because data may be stolen in the browser before it is sent. We will analyze how to prevent this possibility in the next subsection.

Preventing the execution of malicious scripts in the browser

If a malicious agent is able to inject malicious scripts in the browser while the user is on a Web page, they can spy the content of page fields, cookies, data stored in local storage, and other locations, and can also force the browser application to perform undesired actions. These kinds of attacks are known as **Cross-Site Scripting** (XSS).

We can prevent JavaScript variables from being spied on by enclosing every piece of JavaScript code in a function scope, so that its variables are not accessible from other functions. It is also possible to organize the code as JavaScript modules since each module is locally scoped.

However, the JavaScript files we are using might be modified themselves, so we must verify the JavaScript files' integrity.

Below are some possible sources of malicious scripts:

- Modifications of script files either on the server where they were deployed or during the download process. Modifications, during download, can be prevented by using TLS. While the overall integrity of files can be verified by checking their hashes in the browser.
- Injection of HTML code containing in-line scripts. HTML injection can be prevented by HTML-encoding all user-originated content shown in the UI, so that HTML is turned into plain text that can't cause damage.
- Malicious extensions, somehow installed in the browser.
- Modification of the page while it is downloaded. This attack is prevented with the use of TLS.

Therefore, we may conclude that some of the above attacks can be prevented with techniques specific to the attack. However, together with these techniques, it is wise to add general strategies that avoid the execution of malicious scripts independently of their source.

Luckily, the HTTP protocol includes the `Content-Security-Policy` (**CSP**) header for both listing the trusted sources of scripts and verifying the script integrity.

The `Content-Security-Policy` header can be added to each HTTP response header as shown below:

```
Content-Security-Policy: default-src 'self'; ….
```

It can also be included in the HTML header with a `meta http-equiv` tag as shown below:

```
<html >
    <head>
        <meta charset="UTF-8">
        <!-- CSP Meta Tag Implementation -->
        <meta http-equiv="Content-Security-Policy" content="default-src 'self'; ….>
…
```

The `Content-Security-Policy` header value is a semicolon-separated set of instructions. In turn, each instruction is composed of a name and several space-separated values. For instance, let's analyze the header below:

```
Content-Security-Policy: default-src 'self'; script-src 'self' https://*.mytrusted.com"
```

- `default-src` specifies the generally allowed sources of content. The `'self'` values means that the only allowed source is the domain from which the response whose issued. Content-type specific instructions can override this value.
- `script-src` specifies the allowed origins for scripts. Being more specific it overrides the prescriptions of `default-src`. The * char works as a wildcard.

`img-src` specifies the allowed sources for images, `font-src` the allowed sources for fonts, `media-src` the allowed sources for media, `frame-src` the allowed sources for frames, `object-src` for external objects. Setting `object-src` to `'none'` (as is advised) means external objects are prohibited.

With these instructions specified, any in-line script is not allowed. Moreover, the usage of the JavaScript `eval` function is also prohibited. In-line scripts can be enabled by adding the `'unsafe-inline'` value, while `eval` can be enabled with the `'unsafe-eval'` value.

Script integrity can be verified with hashes. The hash of each script is computed and converted to base-64 and prefixed with the name of the hash algorithm, followed by a - char. Thus, a hash computed with sha256 would look like the following:

```
sha256-ax207MWO…….
```

These hashes are then copied into the integrity property of each script tag as shown below:

```
<script src="./main.js" integrity ="sha256-ax207MWO……."></script>
```

Finally, all computed hashes must replace their sources in the `script-src` instruction, as shown below:

```
Content-Security-Policy: "sha256-ax207MWO......"  "sha256- ......"...
```

Usually, most JavaScript libraries furnish their hashes, so one needs to compute just the hashes of the custom JavaScript code.

All Content-Security-Policy instructions can be found here: `https://developer.mozilla.org/en-US/docs/Web/HTTP/Reference/Headers/Content-Security-Policy` while a more detailed description of CSP can be found here: `https://developer.mozilla.org/en-US/docs/Web/HTTP/Guides/CSP`.

You learned how to prevent the execution of malicious scripts in client applications running in a browser that are based on both WebAssembly and JavaScript. Once communication and client integrity are secured users can safely send their credentials (both login information and authentication tokens), so now you are ready to face application authentication.

Authentication and Authorization

Authentication is the process of recognizing a legitimate application user before its request is executed. Please don't confuse authentication with log-in. Log-in is the process of requesting a secret that proves one's identity by using long-lived credentials, such as a username-password pair. Then, each subsequent request is authenticated with the secret received as a consequence of a successful login.

Authorization is the process of verifying if an authenticated user has the required features for accessing a specific service. In general, each user who successfully authenticates their request is authorized to request just a subset of the services offered by the application.

ASP.NET Core authorization was described in the *ASP.NET Core service authorization* subsection of *Chapter 15, Applying Service-Oriented Architectures with .NET*, therefore this section focuses mainly on authentication and on how to handle all user information needed for the authorization.

The next subsection describes the features of the secret used to authenticate and how to use it to configure authorization, too.

Tokens and Claims

Secrets used to authenticate are called **authentication tokens**, or simply **tokens** when the context is clear. Authentication tokens must not be created or forged by unauthorized entities, so they must be either encrypted with a private encryption key or signed by the authority that emits them. However, their content must be accessible to the software component that performs the authentication and that must extract the information they contain to drive authorization.

Applications either have dedicated endpoints that take care of handling authorization tokens and the associated users' information, or delegate this task to a dedicated API called **authentication server**.

In the first case, we can use symmetric cryptography to sign or encrypt authorization tokens, while in the other case, the authentication server must encrypt or sign tokens with a private key whose public counterpart is known by all other applications that rely on that authentication server so that they can both verify token authenticity and extract all information they contain to drive authorization.

All popular authentication algorithms rely on claims-based tokens, that is, on tokens that contain information on the authenticated user in the form of attribute-value pairs called claims.

Including claims in the authentication tokens is fundamental for the following reasons:

- The information contained in the claims can be used to drive user authorization based on user features such as his role in the company, his age, his level of reliability, his responsibilities, and so on
- It avoids the extraction of all needed user information from a database at each request, since this information is available in the authentication token itself
- All sensitive user data can be concentrated into a unique, well-protected authentication server, thus reducing the risk of attacks and data leaks

The names of standard claims are URIs whose domain part belongs to some international normative. The most popular claims, such as Name (the username), GivenName (the actual user name), and Email, belong to a normative initially conceived for SOAP, so their URIs look like this:

`http://schemas.xmlsoap.org/ws/2005/05/identity/claims/emailaddress`

Anyone can define their application-specific claims with a name that is not necessarily a URI. However, defining it with a URI based on a domain one owns ensures their uniqueness.

Since claim values are represented as strings, each claim has an associated type that specifies its intended data type, so if needed, each application can convert it to the appropriate data type.

In .NET, claims are represented by instances of the `System.Security.Claims` type:

```
new Claim(ClaimTypes.Name, myData.UserName)
```

The claim name can be taken from the `ClaimTypes` static class that contains properties for all popular claims whose value is their URI. The constructor also accepts an optional string that may specify the value type.

Once extracted from an authentication token and converted into Claim instances, claims are packaged in a `ClaimsPrincipal` instance as follows:

```
Var claims = new[]
    {
        ...
        new Claim(ClaimTypes.Name, data.UserName),
        new Claim(ClaimTypes.Role, ...)
        ...
    };
var myPrincipal=new ClaimsPrincipal(new ClaimsIdentity(
      claims, myAuthenticationSchemaName))
```

Where myAuthenticationName contains the name associated with the authentication source. In fact, each application may handle several sources of authentication tokens. For instance, N sources based on different kinds of authentication cookies, another one based on client certificates, and so on.

Once built, the ClaimsPrincipal is placed in the User property of the ASP.NET Core HttpContext associated to the current request, that is available in the dependency injection engine. From there the ClaimsPrincipal is automatically passed to the properties of other ASP.NET Core classes, and in particular to the User property of the selected controller.

Moreover, HttpContext.User is processed by the AuthorizeAttribute to implement ASP.NET Core attribute-based authorization explained in the *ASP.NET Core service authorization* subsection of *Chapter 15, Applying Service-Oriented Architectures with .NET*.

When the authentication token is created, a ClaimsPrincipal is built in the same way by taking all claims values from a user record.

Then the ClaimsPrincipal is processed by methods that create the specific type of authentication token.

ASP.NET Core authorization and authentication require the addition of the UseAuthentication() and UseAuthorization() middleware placed in the ASP.NET Core pipeline in Program. Cs as shown below:

```
...
app.UseAuthentication();
app.UseRouting();
app.UseAuthorization();
...
```

Both authentication and authorization options are configured in the services part of Program.cs. Below is the authentication configuration:

```
builder.Services.AddAuthentication(
    <default authentication schema name>)
    .Add<authettication type 1>(o =>
    {
        ...
    })
    .Add<authentication type 2>(o =>
    {
        ...
    })
    ...
    .;
```

Where, Add<authetication type 1> and Add<authetication type 2> stand for different kinds of authentication techniques supported, since each application may support several authentication mechanisms.

Each authentication schema has an associated option object the developer can use to fine-tune its features, and must have a unique name.

<default authentication schema name> must be a name associated with one of the schemas that is added, and define which schema to use as default.

The default schema is the only one used to fill `HttpContext.User`. Moreover, if an authorization is based on the default schema, there is no need to specify any schema name in the `AuthorizeAttribute`; otherwise, the `AuthorizeAttribute` must explicitly list all schemas it uses to test authorization as shown in the example below:

```
[Authorize(Roles="…", AuthenticationSchemes = AuthSchemes)]
public class MyExampleController : Controller
{
 private const string AuthSchemes =
  CookieAuthenticationDefaults.AuthenticationScheme + "," +
  JwtBearerDefaults.AuthenticationScheme;
  …
```

If one uses policies instead of roles, all schemas to use can be specified directly in the policy definition, and we may omit them in all `AuthorizeAttribute` instances based on that policy:

```
builder.Services.AddAuthorization(options =>
{
   options.AddPolicy("CanDrive", policy =>
   {
      policy.AuthenticationSchemes.Add("myschema1");
      policy.AuthenticationSchemes.Add("myschema2");
      …
      policy.RequireAssertion(context =>
       context.User.HasClaim(c => c.Type == "HasDrivingLicense"))
   });
});
```

We may also mix all claims coming from different schemas into a unique default policy and avoid the specification of schema names in policies and `AutorizeAttribute` instances with the following setting in the authorization options:

```
builder.Services.AddAuthorization(options =>
{
    var defaultAuthorizationPolicyBuilder =
        new AuthorizationPolicyBuilder(
           "mySchem1", "mySchem2", …);
    defaultAuthorizationPolicyBuilder =
```

```
        defaultAuthorizationPolicyBuilder.RequireAuthenticatedUser();
    options.DefaultPolicy = defaultAuthorizationPolicyBuilder.Build();
    //place below policy definitions
    ...
});
```

There are Add... methods for cookie-based authentication, for bearer-token based authentication, and for OAuth-based authentication. Let's start with cookie-based authentication.

Cookie-based authentication

Cookie-based tokens are typically used in Web applications based on server-side rendering because cookies, once sent to the browser, persist through page changes. Moreover, they are automatically sent back to the server each time a request to *the same domain that emitted them* is issued. Therefore, they can be used to automatically add an authentication token to all requests that target a given domain.

Each cookie has a name and a value. Names must be unique for each web domain; thus, if a cookie with the same name is sent from the server, it replaces the previous cookie.

The cookie name informs the server it is an authentication cookie, while its value contains the authentication token.

If a cookie has an expiration date, it is called a **persistent cookie,** and it is valid till that expiration date, and then it ceases to be sent to its target domain. If a cookie has no expiration date, it is considered a **session cookie** that is valid till the browser application is closed.

Since cookies remain in the browser cache, they can be stolen by malicious agents who can clone them and use them to perform unwanted authentications. They can also be stolen while they are being exchanged between the client and server. The last possibility is prevented if the client-server communication is secured by TLS. Luckily, cookies have attributes that can be used to prevent their theft:

- ***HttpOnly.*** It prevents manipulation on the client side, so the only action allowed is to send the cookie with each request to its target domain. This attribute is enough to prevent cookie theft in the browser.
- ***Secure.*** When this attribute is set, the cookie is sent to the server only if the connection with the server is secure. This attribute is enough to prevent cookie theft during communication. However, it also prevents the possibility to authenticate the user when the connection is not secure.

Another issue with cookies is that a cookie is sent to the server each time a request is made to each target domain. Therefore, it is also sent when a form that is in a page belonging to a malicious agent is posted to the cookie target domain. This way the malicious user can authenticate a form submission that might contain a malicious request.

Luckily, the `SameSite=<option>` cookie setting can prevent this kind of attack. There `<option>` is one of the values below.

- **Strict.** The cookie is sent to its target domain only if the request comes from a page that is in the cookie target domain, too. This setting prevents the previous cross-domain attack, but has also negative effects. For instance, suppose one clicks a link in a page from the `otherpage.com` domain, and suppose this link goes to a page in the cookie target domain, say `mytargetdomain.com`. The cookie is not sent, so the user receives a login request and is forced to log in again, even if they already have the needed authentication cookie.

- **Lax**. This setting applies the same limitations as the `Strict` setting, but it applies them only to POST, PUT, and DELETE requests, thus excluding GET requests. As a consequence, it solves the issue of the link in `otherpage.com` page that goes to the cookie target domain, but avoids malicious actions since no action should be performed as a consequence of a GET action. Moreover, cookies are not sent also when the request comes from frames nested in the main browser page. This setting prevents any cross-domain attack and should always be set for authentication cookies.

Summing up, authentication cookies are safe and cause no problems when they contain the following settings: `HttpOnly`, `Secure`, `Samesite=Lax`.

Next subsection explains how authentication cookies are handled in ASP.NET Core.

Handling cookie authentication in ASP.NET Core

In ASP.NET Core authentication cookies are created as a consequence of login requests by first building a `ClaimsPrincipal` as explained in the previous *Tokens and claims* subsection, and then by executing a code like the one below:

```
var claimsPrincipal = new ClaimsPrincipal(....);
var authProperties = new AuthenticationProperties
{
    ExpiresUtc = DateTime.UtcNow.AddDays(30),
    IsPersistent = model.RememberMe,
    IssuedUtc = DateTime.UtcNow,
    AllowRefresh = true
};
await HttpContext.SignInAsync(
    <Authentication schema name>,
    claimsPrincipal,
    authProperties);
```

Where:

- `ExpireUTC` is the cookie expiration time.
- `IsPersistent` set if the cookie is a persistent cookie or a session cookie. `AllowRefresh` enables the cookie to be refreshed with a new expiration time at each new request from the same user. This way, as long as the user issues frequent requests the cookie never expires. However, `AllowRefresh` just enables the cookie refresh, while the actual refresh setting must be set in the cookie authentications options in `Program.cs` that should look like the following:

```
builder.Services.AddAuthentication(
CookieAuthenticationDefaults.AuthenticationScheme)
```

```
.AddCookie(o =>
{
    o.LoginPath = "/account/login";
    o.SlidingExpiration = true;
    o.Cookie = new CookieBuilder
    {
        SameSite = SameSiteMode.Lax,
        HttpOnly = true,
        SecurePolicy = CookieSecurePolicy.Always
    };
});
```

Where:

- `LoginPath` specifies the path to the login page, so that the authentication middleware can automatically redirect each unlogged user to the login page.
- `SlidingExpiration` activates cookie automatic refresh. This setting works only if we enabled cookie refresh when the cookie was created.
- `Cookie` allows the specification of each cookie attribute. The example code enabled all settings needed to keep the cookie safe, that is: `HttpOnly`, `Secure`, `Samesite=Lax`.

An example containing a practical usage of cookie authentication is contained in the `ch17` folder of the GitHub repository associated with the book. The code of this example is discussed in the *A Frontend Microservice* section of *Chapter 22, Case Study: Practical Usage of .NET Aspire.*

The next section explains how to perform authentication with Web tokens.

Web token authentication

Bearer tokens are the preferred way to authenticate Web API endpoints since they can be easily added to HTTP headers by all HTTP clients. Bearer tokens are inserted in the HTTP Authorization header of all requests that need authentication as follows:

```
Authorization: Bearer <bearer token string>
```

Bearer tokens can be implemented in several ways. REST services typically use JWTs that are strings with a Base64 URL encoding of JSON objects. More specifically, JWT creation starts with a JSON header, as well as a JSON payload. The JSON header specifies the kind of token and how it is signed, while the payload consists of a JSON object that contains all the claims as property/value pairs. The following is an example header:

```
{
  "alg": "RS256",
  "typ": "JWT"
}
```

The following is an example payload:

```
{
  "iss": "wwtravelclub.com"
  "sub": "example",
  "aud": ["S1", "S2"],
  "roles": [
  "ADMIN",
  "USER"
  ],
  "exp": 1512975450,
  "iat": 1512968250230
}
```

Then, the header and payload are Base64-encoded, and the corresponding strings are concatenated as follows:

```
<header BASE64 string>.<payload base64 string>
```

The preceding string is then signed with the algorithm specified in the header, which, in our example, is RSA+SHA256, and the signature string is concatenated with the original string as follows:

```
<header BASE64 string>.<payload base64 string>.<signature string>
```

The preceding code is the final bearer token string. A symmetric signature can be used instead of RSA, but, in this case, both the JWT issuer and all the services using it for authorization must share a common secret, while, with RSA, the private key of the JWT issuer does not need to be shared with anyone, since the signature can be verified with just the issuer's public key.

Some payload properties are standard, such as the following:

- `iss`: Issuer of the JWT. Often represented by a Web domain.
- `aud`: The audience, that is, the services and/or operations that can use the token for authorization. If a service does not see its identifier within this list, it should reject the token. The audience is often represented as a Web domain, too.
- `sub`: A string that identifies the principal (that is, the user) to which the JWT was issued.
- `iat`, `exp`, and `nbf`: These are the time the JWT was issued, its expiration time, and, if set, the time after which the token is valid, respectively. All the times are expressed as seconds from midnight UTC on January 1, 1970. Here, all the days are considered as having exactly 86,400 seconds in them.

Other claims may be defined as public if we represent them with a unique URI; otherwise, they are considered private to the issuer and to the services known to the issuer.

The next section explains how JWTs are handled in ASP.NET Core.

Handling web token authentication in ASP.NET Core

JWTs are returned as a consequence of a login, a conversion of another kind of token, or as a consequence of renewal requests. In fact, JWTs are typically short-lived, so in order to avoid frequent login requests to the user when a JWT is about to expire, it is used to authenticate a renewal request to a renewal endpoint, which returns a fresh new JWT.

Like the creation of authentication cookies, the creation of a JWT also starts from a previously built set of claims. However, in this case, we need an additional NuGet package: `Microsoft.AspNetCore.Authentication.JwtBearer`.

Once we have all our claims, we may proceed as follows:

```
var claims = new List<Claim>
{
  new Claim(...),
  new Claim(...) ,
  ...
};
var token = new JwtSecurityToken(
  issuer: "MyIssuer",
  audience: ...,
  claims: claims,
  expires: DateTime.UtcNow.AddMinutes(expiryInMinutes),
  signingCredentials:
    new SigningCredentials(
     key: new
       SymmetricSecurityKey(Encoding.ASCII.GetBytes("MySecret")),
     algorithm: SecurityAlgorithms.HmacSha256Signature
    )
);
string stringToken = new JwtSecurityTokenHandler().WriteToken(token);
```

Where `stringToken` is the JWT in its final string format.

The example above uses a symmetric key, but when tokens are emitted by a dedicated authentication server that serves several applications, the authentication must use a private key of an asymmetric pair while each application must use the associated public key to verify the authentication server signature. In this case, the `SigningCredentials` must be created as follows:

```
new SigningCredentials(
      key: new RsaSecurityKey(cert.GetRSAPrivateKey()),
      algorithm: SecurityAlgorithms.RsaSha256
     )
 );
```

Where cert is an RSA certificate loaded with something like:

```
var cert = X509CertificateLoader
    .LoadPkcs12FromFile("MyCertificate.pfx", "MyPassword");
```

The application that must authenticate users with tokens emitted by the authentication server needs the `Microsoft.AspNetCore.Authentication.JwtBearer` NuGet package, too. Its authentication services section should be something like the following:

```
builder.Services.AddAuthentication(JwtBearerDefaults.AuthenticationScheme)
  .AddJwtBearer(options => {
        options.TokenValidationParameters =
         new TokenValidationParameters
        {
           ValidateIssuer = true,
           ValidateAudience = true,
           ValidateLifetime = true,
           ValidateIssuerSigningKey = true,
           ValidIssuer = "My.Issuer",
           ValidAudience = "This.Website.Audience",
           IssuerSigningKey = new
              SymmetricSecurityKey(Encoding.ASCII.GetBytes("MySecret"))
        };
});
```

The preceding code provides a name to the authentication scheme, that is, a default name. Then, it specifies JWT authentication options. Usually, we require that the authentication middleware verifies that the JWT is not expired (`ValidateLifetime = true`), that it has the right issuer and audience, and that its signature is valid.

The preceding example uses a symmetric signing key generated from a string. This means that the same key is used to sign and verify the signature. This is an acceptable choice if JWTs are created by the same website that uses them, but it is not an acceptable choice if there is a unique JWT issuer that controls access to several web API sites.

Here, we should use an asymmetric key (typically, an `RsaSecurityKey`), so JWT verification requires just the knowledge of the public key associated with the actual private signing key:

```
...
IssuerSigningKey = new RsaSecurityKey(
    X509CertificateLoader
    .LoadCertificateFromFile("MyCertificate.crt").GetRSAPublicKey())

...
```

The next section explains how to authenticate with client certificates.

Client certificate authentication

In the *Securing communications* section, we have seen that a client can participate in the TLS protocol with a client certificate. The client certificate can be used as proof of the identity of the client, but no standard certification authority might certify all application-specific claims we need to drive the client authorization.

This means we may use client certificates to authenticate the user, but we must find a way to get all the claims needed by our application. We are left with two options:

1. We create a custom certification authority that might be our authentication server, and supply it with a self-signed certificate it can use to sign all client certificates we need in our application. This self-signed certificate must be added to the trusted certificate store of all computers served by the authentication server. This way, we would enable our authentication server to emit trusted certificates. Typically, client certificates generated this way contain the client's unique name (username if the client is a human or a URL if the client is an application) and the group it belongs to. Then, either groups are used to generate role claims, or groups and some names are mapped to claims with the help of fast in-memory data structures.
2. We support client certificates issued by standard certification authorities, and then use some unique identifier associated with the certificate as a key in a user's database that contains all claims associated with each user. Each certificate has a **thumbprint** that can be used as a key.

Technique 1 is the most practical, and it is the actual technique used by Kubernetes clusters. Each Kubernetes user submits a certificate containing the group it is assigned to the cluster administrator. The cluster administrator verifies the user actually belongs to the declared group, and then submits the user request to the cluster certification authority that signs it with its certificate. Then the user can register their client certificate in the kubectl configuration file with the help of the adequate `kubectl config` commands.

In Kubernetes, groups and usernames can be mapped to Kubernetes permissions with the help of **Role** objects that contain a set of permissions, and with the help of **RoleBinding** objects that associate groups and usernames to Roles.

Technique 2 requires a database access at each request to retrieve all user claims, so it is practical to use it just for authenticating the user to an endpoint that emits bearer tokens. This way, client certificates are used just as login credentials, while the remainder of the solution uses bearer tokens whose claims are stored in the token itself and do not require database accesses in the authentication stage.

The next subsection explains how to implement client certificate authentication in practice, in ASP.NET Core.

Handling client certificate authentication in ASP.NET Core

In order to configure client certificates in ASP.NET Core we need the `Microsoft.AspNetCore.Authentication.Certificate` NuGet package.

Then we need to configure Kestrel or IIS for accepting client certificates, either as obligatory or as optional. The optional setting is useful if our application also supports other authentication techniques. Please refer to the *Using server certificates with Kestrel* subsection of this chapter for configuring client certificates in Kestrel.

Then, you need to configure client certificate authentication in the authentication options:

```
builder.Services.AddAuthentication(
        CertificateAuthenticationDefaults.AuthenticationScheme)
    .AddCertificate(options =>
    {
        options.Events = new CertificateAuthenticationEvents
        {
            OnCertificateValidated = context =>
            {
                if (!Valid(context.ClientCertificate))
                {
                    context.Fail("Unknown Client");
                   return Task.CompletedTask;
                }
                 var claims =
                   ExtractClaims(context.ClientCertificate.Subject);
                 context.Principal = new ClaimsPrincipal(
                     new ClaimsIdentity(claims, context.Scheme.Name));
                 context.Success();

                 return Task.CompletedTask;
            }
        };
    });
```

You must manually validate the certificate, any user with a certificate signed by a certificate authority might be able to authenticate. The code above factors out the whole validation logic in a `Validate` function that, in case of failure, breaks the authentication process, returning a failure result. If one uses a custom certificate authority, the validation process might simply verify the name of the certificate issuer, that is, *context.ClientCertificate*. The *issuer* corresponds to the so-called **Distinguished Name** of the custom certificate authority, and the certificate chain is rooted in a trusted authority. The Distinguished Name is the content of the `Subject` field of an X.509 certificate.

The check that the certificate is rooted in a trusted certificate authority is automatically performed when establishing the mTLS connection and is performed by calling the `Verify` method of the client certificate instance.

The previous code uses an `ExtractClaims` method to extract claims from the certificate `Subject`. The `Subject` field of a certificate contains some attribute-value pairs that should identify the owner. They must be chosen from the ones mentioned in the table below:

Field	Field Symbol	Length constraints
CountryCode	*C*	2
Organization	*O*	*1–64*
OrganizationUnit	*OU*	*1–32*
CommonName	*CN*	*1–64*
Location	*L*	*1–64*
StateOrProvince	*S*	*1–64*

Table 20.1: Properties contained in the Subject field of an X.509 certificate

In string format, each pair contains the field symbol, an `=`, and finally the value. All pairs are separated by a `/`, and a `/` must also be applied before the first pair.

When the certificate is used for authentication, one typically uses the `CommonName` as the username and `Organization` as a group that is transformed into a role. Therefore, in this case, the Subject string format is:

`"/O=MyGroup/CN=MyUserName"`

each `/` mark may optionally be followed by a space.

The easiest way to get all certificate attributes for creating the needed claims is the usage of the `SubjectName` properties that contain the whole Subject data in rough format, and a method that enumerates all pairs:

```
var attributes=context.ClientCertificate.SubjectName
    .EnumerateRelativeDistinguishedNames()
    .Where(m => m.GetSingleElementType()?.FriendlyName is not null)
    .ToDictionary(
    m => m.GetSingleElementType().FriendlyName!,
    m => m.GetSingleElementValue());
var name = attributes["CN"]??string.Empty;
var group= attributes["O"]??string.Empty;
...
```

The `ch20` folder of the GitHub repository associated with the book contains an example of an MVC website that requires data from an API Server and uses a client certificate to authenticate. The client certificate was signed with the server certificate, so the client certificate is trusted if we add the server certificate to the list of trusted certificates.

This can be done with the Windows snap-in for managing certificates:

1. Open a Windows console and execute the `mmc` command
2. In the application that opens, select **File->Add / remove snap-in**

3. Add the Certificates snap-in
4. Among all possible locations, select **user account**
5. Click **Ok**
6. In the left panel, select the trusted root certificate authority folder, and then its certificates subfolder. Right-click on it and select **All activities->Import**.
7. Follow the guided procedure, and when you are required to select a file, locate and select the `root_cc.pfx` certificate that is in the example
8. Complete the import and close the application (you don't need to save the settings)

After a successful import, you can launch the Visual Studio solution. However, before doing so, place a breakpoint at line 48 of `ClientAuthentication->Progam.cs` so you can follow step by step how the client is authenticated and how client claims are built.

The client certificate contains just the `CN` attribute, so we have just the client's name. The client certificate is validated by verifying that the issuer subject is the right one:

```
if (context.ClientCertificate.Issuer!= "CN=localhost")
 {
     context.Fail("Unknown Client");
     return Task.CompletedTask;
 }
...
```

The MVC application invokes the API Server in the `Index` Action of the `HomeController`. Please inspect that code and place some breakpoints there, too. Also, take a look at the named `HttpClient` definition in the `Program.cs` of the MVC application.

That's all! Let's move to OAuth-based authentication.

OAuth authentication

The **OAuth** protocol enables a user to authenticate to an application without furnishing their login credentials to that application but furnishing them to a trusted **authorization server**. Actually, OAuth is used for emitting authorization tokens in general; when it is used specifically for user authentication, we speak of **OpenID-Connect** (**OIDC**) over OAuth.

In a few words, the user can authenticate to several applications by exploiting credentials of a single server that offers OAuth authentication services, like Google, GitHub, Facebook, etc.

The peculiarity of OAuth is that you can authenticate to your target application with your authorization server credentials without revealing your credentials to the target application. This is a fundamental point since the same credentials are used across several applications, so a malicious application might use your credentials to access the other applications.

From a user perspective, OAuth authentication works this way:

1. User tries to access a protected page of the target application

2. User is redirected to the login page of the authorization server. This is an important step also in single-page and native applications because the user can verify that he is on the authorization server URL, so he is sure his credentials will not be shared with anyone else.
3. User inserts his credentials there and logs in. This way, his credentials do not pass through the target application but are always inserted in a page of the trusted authorization server.
4. The user is asked permission to share some personal data with the target application. Typically, the user can choose which data to share.
5. User is redirected back to the requested page of the target application

If the user is already logged into the authorization server with a valid persistent authentication cookie, steps 3-4 are skipped, and the user sees just a series of redirects that lead them to the requested page.

Suppose now that your enterprise information system is made of N web applications that use a unique authentication server. Usually, your credentials are collected by each of the N applications and sent to the authentication server, so you reveal your credentials to each of the N applications.

Does it make sense to adopt OAuth in the above information system so that the credentials are revealed just to the authentication server?

Obviously, since all applications belong to the same organization, if the user trusts the authorization server, they should also trust all N applications. However, notwithstanding this, the adoption of OAuth might make sense because it reduces the possibility of stealing users' credentials.

Fewer applications handle the credentials, so there is less possibility that credentials are stolen because one of the N applications is compromised. Moreover, if credentials are handled by just one application, most of the security investments might be concentrated on just that application.

However, if the N target applications are single-page applications that typically have quite a high loading time, being redirected to the authorization server and then back to the application has the cost of loading the application another time. Moreover, the current single-application global state is lost. In several scenarios, all this is simply unacceptable, so it is better to renounce the OAuth adoption.

Furthermore, in the case of single-page applications, credentials are shared with the target application just on the client-side and are never sent to the application running on the server, since the client issues the login request directly to the authentication server. Accordingly, if the user trusts the application as they trust the authentication server, there is no advantage in the adoption of OAuth.

If the N applications are native applications, an adequate implementation of OAuth should require the opening of a browser page on the authorization server URL, so the user can be sure their credentials are shared only with the authorization server. However, again, if the user trusts the application as they trust the authentication server because they belong to the same information system, verifying the URL of the credential recipient is not essential, so there is no advantage in the OAuth adoption.

Let's look for the details of the **OAuth 2 protocol**:

1. Browser is redirected to the authorization server's OAuth-specific page
2. If the client is not already logged in, the authorization server redirects the browser to the login page
3. Once logged in, the user is asked for permission to authorize the target application

4. Once user authorization is granted, the authorization server redirects the browser to a predefined application page and appends to the URL a one-time **authorization code**
5. The application uses the authorization code to get a bearer token from the authorization server by connecting to a dedicated endpoint. This is done on the application server-side in case of classical Web applications, and on the client side in case of single-page applications.
6. In the case of single-page applications, the bearer token is directly used as an authentication token. In the case of classical applications, the bearer token information is used to create an authentication cookie.

Native applications work similarly, but instead of redirecting the browser, they simply open a browser page on the authorization server's OAuth handling page. Then the flow is the same. It is important to point out that on the server side, the application must have a page where it can receive the **authorization code** via the redirection explained at point 4.

Once we have a clear understanding of how OAuth 2 works, we can move to its ASP.NET Core implementation.

Handling OAuth authentication in ASP.NET Core

The way Blazor WebAssembly handles OAuth was explained in the *Authentication and authorization* subsection of *Chapter 18, Client Frameworks: Blazor*. Basically, all parameters required by the OAuth 2 protocol, such as the authorization server OAuth URL page (*Authority*), the unique ID that identifies the application (*ClientId*), and the application URL where to return the authorization code, are specified in the services section of `Program.cs` with the code below:

```
builder.Services.AddOidcAuthentication(options =>
{
    // Configure your authentication provider options here.
    // For more information, see https://aka.ms/blazor-standalone-auth
    builder.Configuration.Bind("Local", options.ProviderOptions);
});
```

The above code takes all parameters from the configuration file. In the case of Google, the parameters are:

```
{
  "Local": {
    "Authority": "https://accounts.google.com/",
    "ClientId": "2...7-e...q.apps.googleusercontent.com",
    "PostLogoutRedirectUri": "https://localhost:5001/authentication/logout-callback",
    "RedirectUri": "https://localhost:5001/authentication/login-callback",
    "ResponseType": "id_token"
  }
}
```

In the case of an MVC application, OAuth must be configured as an authentication method:

```
builder.Services.AddAuthentication(options =>
{
    options.DefaultScheme =
      CookieAuthenticationDefaults.AuthenticationScheme;
    options.DefaultChallengeScheme =
      ...;//Name of the schema associated to the provider to use as
        // default
})
.AddCookie(...)
.AddGoogle(options =>
    {
        // Google configuration options
    })
    .AddFacebook(options =>
    {
        // Facebook configuration options
    })
    .AddMicrosoftAccount(options =>
    {
        // Microsoft Account configuration options
    })
    .AddTwitter(options =>
    {
        // Twitter configuration options
    })
    ...
;
```

There is an extension method for each well-known authorization server that is defined in dedicated NuGet packages. For instance, the NuGet package for using the Microsoft authorization server is:

```
Microsoft.AspNetCore.Authentication.MicrosoftAccount
```

The *Further Reading* section furnishes links to where all available OAuth providers can be found.

We must also configure cookie authentication because the token received at the end of the OAuth process is turned into a cookie. Moreover, the cookie authentication must be set as the default schema.

In order to add an OAuth provider to your application, you must register your application in a way that depends on the provider. Again, the *Further Reading* section furnishes links to where you can find how to register with the various providers.

Once registered, you should have all the information needed in the provider options, such as your `ClientId` and a secret to use.

With the configuration in place, in your login controller, the OAuth protocol can be triggered with:

```
await HttpContext.ChallengeAsync("provider schema name",
       new AuthenticationProperties { RedirectUri = returnUrl });
```

Where the first parameter must be the schema name you associated with the provider you would like to log in. The first parameter may be omitted, in which case the schema is specified in `options.DefaultChallengeScheme` is taken.

`returnUrl` is the application page where to return after a successful login, and must be specified as an absolute URL since it will be passed to the authorization server.

The `ChallengeAsync` instruction should be the last one in your login action methods.

In order to log out, you must sign out from both cookie authentication and from the chosen OAuth provider with:

```
return SignOut(new AuthenticationProperties
        {
            RedirectUri = "/SignedOut"
            //page for unauthenticated users
        },
        // Clear auth cookie
        CookieAuthenticationDefaults.AuthenticationScheme,
        // Redirect to provider signout endpoint
        "provider schema name");
```

Some providers also have an information endpoint where you can get user attributes useful for creating claims. In this case, the middleware takes care of retrieving them and using them to generate claims. Please refer to each OAuth provider's documentation in the *Further reading* section for how to configure and get claims from each specific OAuth provider.

We finished our description of authentication techniques; let's move on to how to protect our data in the cloud.

Encrypting database fields in the Cloud

In order to store sensitive data in Cloud databases, we must trust the Cloud provider, and also, when we trust it, we must verify that the probability of successful attacks is below an acceptable threshold.

In order to decrease the total risk, we may decide to encrypt sensitive data with a key that is not accessible to the Cloud provider. However, if our software also runs in the same cloud, this key must necessarily be used by the code that runs on the Cloud machines, so while the software is running, it could be stolen from these machines' RAM by an attacker who somehow gains administrative or SYSTEM privileges.

The only protection against these attacks is preventing the execution of malicious instructions that might allow a malicious user to control of a machine. The best prevention consists of both applying all security patches as soon as they are available and controlling each external input to avoid your code crashing and starting to interpret data as if it were instructions.

Data exposed in permanent storage has a higher risk of being spied on than data exposed in the computer RAM. In the worst case, permanent storage data can be stolen by people working for the Cloud provider itself.

The encryption of database fields with a key that is not known by the cloud provider decreases the total risk almost to 0. However, encryption prevents some database operations on encrypted data. In particular, identity checks that might be necessary to perform JOIN operations would fail because, for security reasons, encryption must be probabilistic, so two original values usually turn into different encrypted values.

As a conclusion, join and search operations are not possible on encrypted fields, so we can't encrypt all data. Therefore, the best option one has at the moment is to concentrate all sensitive data in fields that do not need to be processed by the database engine.

Summary

In this chapter, after a self-contained introduction to cryptography, we described techniques for securing communication and their practical implementation in .NET.

Comprehensive security requires multiple layers: (1) Encrypt data in transit with TLS, (2) Verify identity and permissions through authentication and authorization, (3) Encrypt sensitive data at rest. No single layer is sufficient—attackers will probe every weakness. Combine all three to create robust protection.

Questions

1. What technique is used to prove the identity of a DLL author?
2. After TLS or mTLS handshake, how are session messages encrypted?
3. In a TLS session, how does the server prove it knows the private key associated with its certificate?
4. How does TLS prevent man-in-the-middle attacks?
5. What is the difference between TLS and mTLS?
6. What is the best practice for passing a TLS certificate to a container?
7. What are the preferred authentication techniques for Web API?
8. What are the main techniques for preventing authentication cookies cross-site attacks?
9. How ASP.NET Core handles claims-based authorization? Describe the advised techniques.
10. Are you able to characterize OAuth authentication with a few words?

Further reading

The following are some links you may consider reading to gather more information in relation to this chapter:

- Kestrel configuration: `https://learn.microsoft.com/en-us/aspnet/core/fundamentals/servers/kestrel/endpoints?view=aspnetcore-10.0`

- X.509 certificates specifications: `https://datatracker.ietf.org/doc/html/rfc5280`
- Content Security Policy: `https://developer.mozilla.org/en-US/docs/Web/HTTP/Reference/Headers/Content-Security-Policy` `https://developer.mozilla.org/en-US/docs/Web/HTTP/Guides/CSP`
- ASP.NET Core OAuth: `https://learn.microsoft.com/en-us/aspnet/core/security/authentication/social/?view=aspnetcore-10.0&tabs=visual-studio`
- ASP.NET Core OAuth providers: `https://learn.microsoft.com/en-us/aspnet/core/security/authentication/social/?view=aspnetcore-10.0&tabs=visual-studio`
- JSON Web Tokens: `https://www.jwt.io/introduction#what-is-json-web-token`
- Cookie attributes: `https://developer.mozilla.org/en-US/docs/Web/HTTP/Guides/Cookies`
- Cookie authentication options: `https://learn.microsoft.com/it-it/dotnet/api/microsoft.aspnetcore.authentication.cookies.cookieauthenticationoptions?view=aspnetcore-10.0`
- Microsoft SEAL library:`https://www.nuget.org/packages/Microsoft.Research.SEALNet`
- Cross-Site Request Forgery: `https://learn.microsoft.com/it-it/aspnet/core/security/anti-request-forgery?view=aspnetcore-10.0`

21

Hardening Cloud-Based Solutions

In modern software architecture, reliability and cybersecurity are deeply connected. It is no longer enough to think only about whether the application code is correct or whether the business logic behaves as expected. Architects must also consider the environment in which the system runs, since weak configurations, permissive defaults, and poor operational controls can undermine even well-designed applications.

In *Chapter 20, Securing Data and Applications*, the focus presented was application-level secure coding, OWASP concerns, and data-handling logic inside your services. This chapter is about *hardening the cloud environment your system runs* in through guardrails, secure defaults, configuration baselines, and continuous verification.

So, while the last chapter focused on making sure the application does not leave the door unlocked from the inside, this chapter focuses on making sure the building around it has controlled entrances, security cameras, access policies, and alarms.

For example, secure coding may prevent an API from accepting malicious input, while cloud hardening helps ensure that the API is deployed behind appropriate network controls, uses managed identities instead of exposed secrets, follows baseline configuration rules, and is continuously checked for drift or misconfiguration.

One way to understand this shift is to think of the previous chapter as focusing on the protection of what happens inside the application itself, while this chapter focuses on the protection of the environment surrounding it. In other words, the earlier discussion emphasized secure behavior in code and services, whereas this one emphasizes secure foundations, operational safeguards, and cloud-level controls that help prevent exposure caused by misconfiguration or weak governance.

For that, the chapter covers:

- What hardening is and why it matters in the cloud
- Shared responsibility between you and your cloud provider
- Secure baseline with a landing zone
- Misconfiguration management and drift control using IaC
- Incident readiness and operational resilience

In modern software architecture, cybersecurity is part of the foundation of reliability, not a separate concern handled only at the end of the project. As a software architect, you must be ready to deliver reliable solutions, and there is no way to do so without thinking about cybersecurity nowadays. The following topics provide the foundation for that discussion by connecting security concerns to the architectural decisions that influence how systems are designed, deployed, monitored, and protected.

What is hardening and why does it matter in the cloud?

In cloud environments, the dominant class of failures is often not zero-day exploitation but *misconfiguration and over-permissive defaults*. Situations like a storage account accidentally exposed publicly, or even an admin identity with broad permissions and no just-in-time controls, are more likely to happen than many teams assume.

There are other aspects of misconfiguration that can cause exploitation of information, such as a database reachable from the public Internet or a Kubernetes cluster where workloads run privileged by default.

CI/CD can also be misconfigured in a way that can cause damage, like having an identity that can deploy anywhere, without guardrails. All these examples mentioned up to here are expanding the attack surface and should be treated to reduce it. These recurring patterns highlight why hardening becomes essential: it provides a systematic way to reduce unnecessary exposure, enforce safer defaults, and limit the impact of mistakes or misuse.

Hardening is the discipline of *reducing the attack surface* and *making the secure path the easy path*, so teams can move fast without repeatedly re-learning the same security lessons. Hardening in modern cloud environments strongly aligns with Zero Trust principles. So, you may consider hardening as a continuous capability, not a one-time checklist. Although it begins with secure setup decisions, it must continue through ongoing verification, policy enforcement, configuration review, and operational readiness. In a hardened solution, we have a secure baseline – called a **landing zone**. Besides that, the infrastructure is deployed using **Infrastructure as code** (IaC), and guardrails are enforced with policies and procedures. Finally, there is a continuous process for detecting drifts, and there are operational playbooks to run when things go wrong.

Hardening and Compliance

It is worth mentioning that hardening decisions are not driven only by technical risk, but also by regulatory and compliance requirements. Frameworks such as ISO/IEC 27001, SOC 2, the NIST Cybersecurity Framework, and CIS Benchmarks provide structured guidance on controls related to identity management, logging, configuration baselines, change management, and incident response.

Aligning your cloud hardening strategy with these standards not only reduces security risk but also simplifies audits, demonstrates due diligence, and builds trust with enterprise customers and regulators. In many organizations, hardening is the practical implementation layer that turns compliance objectives into enforceable technical controls.

These concerns exist because the software architect must clearly understand their responsibilities within the shared responsibility model. Let's check exactly what this means in the next topic.

Shared responsibility drives hardening priorities

Depending on the type of cloud solution you have chosen, as we have discussed in *Chapter 10, Deciding on the Best Cloud-Based Solution*, the **shared responsibility model** will change. This means that the hardening priorities will also change accordingly.

The table below summarizes how the hardening focus shifts across service models:

Service model	What the provider mainly handles	What you mainly harden	Typical hardening focus
IaaS	Physical data centers, hardware, virtualization stack	Guest OS, patching, host controls, configuration	Golden images, patch management, host firewall, EDR, service minimization
PaaS	OS, runtime lifecycle, platform patching, and much platform maintenance	Application configuration, identity, network exposure, and data protection settings	TLS enforcement, disabling legacy protocols, private access, restricted endpoints, auditing
Kubernetes/container platforms	Varies by platform; often parts of the control plane and sometimes worker node management in managed offerings	Cluster access, workload security, images, runtime policies, traffic	RBAC, admission controls, pod security, network policies, image signing, and scanning
Serverless	Runtime environment, scaling, and most infrastructure operations	Function configuration, identities, secrets, triggers, and event source exposure	Least privilege, secret handling, trigger exposure control, observability, and alerting

Table 21.1: Shared responsibility models

> **Note**
>
> The more the provider manages, the more hardening becomes about *configuration, identity, and network exposure* and less about OS patching.

In **Infrastructure as a Service** (IaaS), you operate closest to the traditional server model, so you are responsible for the guest OS, patching cadence, endpoint/EDR agents, configuration management, and host-based firewall rules. The cloud provider focuses on the physical data centers, hardware, and underlying virtualization stack. Because you control the OS layer, hardening usually centers on repeatable golden images, baseline configuration, disciplined patch management, and host-level controls such as local firewalls, file integrity, and service minimization.

A practical example is a virtual machine hosting an internal API: even if the cloud provider secures the underlying infrastructure, you still need to disable unnecessary services, keep the OS patched, enforce firewall restrictions, and ensure only approved administrative access paths are allowed. Hardening shifts here toward operating system discipline, repeatable server baselines, and strict control over administrative and network access.

On the other hand, with **Platform as a Service** (PaaS), you shift from managing servers to managing secure configuration, such as app settings, identity and authentication, network exposure, and data protection options. The provider typically owns the OS and much of the runtime lifecycle, including patching and underlying platform maintenance. Hardening here is often about selecting and enforcing the right secure settings toggles, like requiring TLS, disabling legacy protocols, enforcing private access, limiting public endpoints, and turning on control-plane auditing so you can detect risky configuration changes and suspicious administrative activity.

For example, when deploying a web application to a managed app service, the hardening effort is less about maintaining the operating system and more about enforcing HTTPS only, disabling public administrative access, integrating with strong identity controls, and restricting database access to private network paths. The focus is on securing platform configuration, identity enforcement, controlled exposure, and continuous auditing of configuration changes.

Now in **container platforms** *(Kubernetes)*, you own what runs inside the cluster, such as image content, runtime security policies, Role-Based Access Control (RBAC) design, and how workloads communicate. Depending on whether you use managed Kubernetes, the provider may take on more of the worker node management, but you still carry responsibility for cluster access and workload security posture. Hardening typically focuses on strong RBAC and least privilege, admission and policy controls to prevent unsafe deployments, pod security and runtime restrictions, network policies for segmentation, and image supply-chain controls like signing, scanning, and provenance validation.

A concrete example is preventing teams from deploying privileged containers or images from untrusted registries. Even in a managed Kubernetes service, those protections still depend on your policies, admission controls, and workload governance. Cluster access control, runtime restrictions, and supply-chain protection are key points in this case.

Lastly, in **serverless** scenarios, your footprint is mostly configuration and permissions. Function settings, identities, secrets, triggers, and the surface area of event sources are your focus. The provider handles the runtime environment, scaling, and most infrastructure operations, which reduces some operational burden but doesn't remove security ownership. Hardening targets commonly trigger exposure, avoiding overly permissive endpoints, strict least privilege for function identities, safe secret handling with managed secret stores, rotation, no plaintext config, and strong observability with logs, traces, and alerts. The idea is that you can quickly detect anomalous invocations, abuse of credentials, or unexpected downstream access.

For example, a serverless function triggered by an HTTP endpoint may scale automatically and run on a managed platform, but it can still be exposed if anonymous access is enabled unnecessarily, secrets are stored in plain text, or the function identity has excessive access to storage and messaging services. In short, here hardening shifts toward permissions, trigger exposure, secret handling, and observability of event-driven behavior.

As a software architect, the decision about which type of cloud solution to use may change due to the level of configuration and operational discipline needed to harden the solution effectively. It is worth noting that the main architectural difference is not whether hardening is required, but where it must be concentrated.

This is why the choice of cloud model should also lead to a discussion about the baseline that will guide deployments. Once the team understands where hardening responsibilities are concentrated, it needs a repeatable foundation that defines approved configurations, security guardrails, network patterns, identity controls, and governance expectations.

Establish a secure baseline with a landing zone

A **landing zone** is the minimum set of cloud foundations that make every workload safer by default. There are several aspects to achieving this.

Before checking them out, to make this section easier to navigate, it helps to think about the landing zone in a practical order of attention. First, define the organizational structure that separates environments and responsibilities. Then, establish the identity baseline that controls who can operate the cloud and how workloads authenticate. After that, ensure visibility through logging, reduce exposure through the network baseline, and finally adapt runtime hardening to the selected computing model. This progression helps show that a landing zone is not a single control, but a layered foundation.

In other words, the landing zone defines both scope and priority. It begins with the structural decisions that affect every workload, then moves into the guardrails that protect access, visibility, communication paths, and runtime behavior. This ordering is useful because the team can understand where to start, what comes next, and how the different baseline areas reinforce one another.

Organizational Structure

A clear account, subscription, or project structure is foundational. For example, a company may decide that production APIs, development workloads, shared networking, and security monitoring must not live in the same subscription or project because they have different owners, risk levels, access needs, and compliance expectations. The common pattern for that is to separate production from non-production with strong isolation. This means separating shared platform (networking, security tooling, identity integration) from workloads and using separate environments for dev/test/staging/prod with distinct access policies.

A practical way to visualize this is to imagine a company using one subscription or project space for shared networking and central security services, another for production workloads, and others for development, testing, and staging. In the same way, application teams may deploy only into their own workload boundaries, while the platform team manages shared services such as connectivity, logging, or identity integration.

It is worth noting that organizational structure is not only about grouping resources, but also about enforcing clearer ownership and safer isolation.

As practical guardrails, you should consider restricting which regions can be used, requiring tags/labels (*owner*, *data classification*, *environment*, *cost center*), and applying resource naming conventions to support auditing and automation.

So restricting regions may prevent accidental deployment into locations that are not approved for compliance or latency reasons. Requiring tags and labels makes it easier to identify who owns a resource, what type of data it handles, and which environment it belongs to. Naming conventions, in turn, support automated checks, reporting, and faster operational investigation when something goes wrong.

Identity Baseline

Before going into detailed controls, it is useful to read identity hardening as a progression. First, control who can operate the cloud. Second, control how privileged access is granted. Third, control how workloads authenticate. Finally, separate responsibilities so that human operators, application teams, and deployment identities do not have unnecessary overlap. This progression creates a clearer hierarchy and reinforces that the **identity baseline** is a structured set of guardrails rather than a collection of isolated practices.

1. Control human administrative access with minimal roles and time-bound elevation
2. Protect privileged access with stronger approval, monitoring, and emergency access practices
3. Ensure workloads authenticate using safer platform-native mechanisms instead of embedded credentials
4. Separate operational responsibilities so guardrails cannot be casually bypassed

It is also important to create identity hardening as guardrails. We are not talking about application authentication here. The focus is on who can operate the cloud and how workloads authenticate. For instance, engineers should not be permanent admins, and their elevation should be time-bound, audited, and deliberate. To do so, use **role-based access control** (RBAC) with minimal roles. Besides that, use privileged identity management with JIT elevation, approval workflows, and MFA.

Maintaining break-glass accounts with strict controls and monitored use is also good practice. Besides that, workloads should authenticate using platform-native identities, like managed identities presented in Azure. It is also recommended to have short-lived tokens, not embedded secrets, with no credentials in repos, no static cloud keys in containers, and rotation policies for any unavoidable secrets.

To finish, it is also recommended to split responsibilities between the security team who manages guardrails and policies, the app teams who manage application config within permitted boundaries, and the CI/CD identities that can deploy but not change guardrails or disable logging.

This layered view is important because identity is one of the most common ways hardening can fail in practice. If administrative roles are too broad, if privileged access is persistent, or if workloads depend on static credentials, the security posture becomes fragile even when other controls are present. That is why the identity baseline is often one of the highest-priority parts of a landing zone.

Logging Baseline

Logging baseline is what turns the landing zone into something observable and auditable. Without it, teams may define policies and structures but still lack the evidence needed to understand changes, detect misuse, investigate incidents, or prove compliance. For this reason, it is helpful to connect each type of log not only with what is being collected, but also with why it matters operationally.

It is good practice to turn on and centralize control plane logs, who changed what in cloud resources, network flow logs wherever they are supported, identity sign-in logs, and resource configuration snapshots. Good advice here is to store logs in a protected, immutable location with retention appropriate for your risk and compliance needs.

Each of these log categories supports a different operational purpose. Control plane logs help explain who changed resources and when, which is essential for tracing administrative actions. Network flow logs help identify unexpected traffic patterns, support segmentation validation, and assist with incident investigation. Identity sign-in logs help reveal suspicious access attempts, unusual locations, or risky authentication behavior. Resource configuration snapshots help teams compare expected versus actual state and understand how drift or unauthorized changes emerged over time. Adding this purpose makes the logging baseline easier to understand as an operational tool, not just a storage requirement.

Network Baseline

The **network baseline** can be understood through three complementary concerns: reducing public exposure, controlling private communication paths, and enforcing safer defaults.

The first concern is exposure at the edge. The main goal here is to reduce the number of places where external traffic can directly reach the environment.

The idea here is to control exposure and constrain movement, once a hardened cloud solution assumes the network is hostile and designs for a limited blast radius. To do this, you should work on reducing public exposure, preferring a small number of public entry points with the help of an API gateway or an ingress tool with WAF, which will protect you by DDoS mitigation where applicable, and by rate limiting and bot protection at the edge.

The second concern is how internal and service-to-service connectivity is handled. In other words, once traffic enters the environment, the design should reduce unnecessary openness and keep communication paths as private and restricted as possible.

It is important to have private access to managed services, using private connectivity to managed databases, message brokers, storage, and secret stores; disabling public endpoints for these services; and using private DNS zones to keep resolution internal. Besides, forcing outbound traffic through a firewall or proxy to restrict outbound destinations by policy and monitoring unusual outbound volume or destinations is also important. It is worth noting that segmentation by environment and the creation of trust zones will make your network safer.

The third concern is the use of default platform decisions that prevent unsafe deployment patterns from becoming common. These defaults reduce the chance that teams accidentally choose permissive or legacy options when provisioning resources.

It is also a good idea to define platform defaults such as *Public access disabled* for databases/storage unless explicitly approved, TLS minimum versions enforced, and approved SKUs/tiers only, which avoids unsupported or legacy offerings.

Seen together, these three areas improve scannability because they show a clear sequence: first, limit what is exposed publicly, then constrain how private connectivity works, and finally standardize secure defaults so those decisions are repeatable. This framing also reinforces the idea that network hardening is about both architecture and operational consistency.

In short, network hardening is about designing the environment so that exposure is intentional, private communication is constrained, and unsafe defaults are difficult to deploy accidentally.

Runtime hardening by the computing model

Earlier, the shared responsibility discussion explained why hardening priorities change depending on the service model. This subsection adds something different: it translates that architectural idea into concrete runtime controls. In other words, the earlier section explained where responsibility sits, while this shows what hardening looks like in practice once the computing model has already been chosen.

The way we harden the solution varies according to the computing model selected. For IaaS (Virtual Machines), the focus is to secure the host, using golden images with hardened OS settings, automatic patching and vulnerability scanning, disabling password logins, restricting SSH/RDP, host firewall with deny-by-default inbound, and enabling endpoint detection and response agent where supported.

Now, for PaaS, we need to harden configuration, not the OS, so hardening is about secure toggles and safe defaults, like enforcing TLS minimum versions, disabling public access to backing services, restricting inbound by IP ranges or private endpoints, disabling debug/diagnostic settings that expose secrets, and turning on platform logs, access logs, and alerts.

For Kubernetes, hardening is mainly about preventing unsafe workloads and limiting cluster access, so policy-driven hardening is a good option. Security defaults, such as running as non-root, dropping Linux capabilities, using a read-only root filesystem where feasible, preventing noisy neighbors and some DoS patterns, setting resource limits, and disallowing privileged pods, are good practices to follow. For accessing the cluster, the usage of RBAC (Role-Based Access Control) with minimal roles and avoiding cluster-admin is desired. Additionally, separate admin actions from app deployment identities and audit cluster events and API calls.

At this point, the landing zone has established the baseline structure, access controls, visibility, network posture, and runtime expectations. Even so, a secure baseline does not guarantee that the environment will remain aligned over time. Teams change configurations, infrastructure evolves, new services are deployed, and exceptions accumulate. That is why the next topic becomes a natural continuation of this one.

Even with a secure baseline in place, misconfiguration remains difficult to avoid completely, especially as environments evolve through deployments, exceptions, emergency changes, and manual adjustments. The next challenge, therefore, is preserving the intended state over time. Misconfiguration management and drift control using IaC help keep the intended state and the actual state from diverging, extending the same hardening logic into day-to-day operational change. Let's understand how to deal with it.

Misconfiguration management and drift control using IaC

Even if you start your application with the proper security, drift happens in some circumstances, such as manual hotfixes, emergency changes, or even *temporary* public exposure that never gets reverted.

This exposes one of the central paradoxes of cloud operations: environments must evolve quickly, but they must also remain secure and controlled. The more teams rely on manual adjustments to gain speed, the harder it becomes to preserve a stable and auditable baseline. Hardening addresses this tension through regular posture scans, continuous drift detection, and **Infrastructure as Code** (IaC), which makes change both faster and more disciplined. Low-risk issues can be remediated automatically, while high-risk changes can require review and approval before they are applied.

A strong practice is to treat the cloud as immutable by making changes go through IaC and pipelines, and exceptions need to be logged and reconciled quickly. Relying on people to remember security rules does not scale, so guardrails must be enforced through automation.

For example, instead of manually opening a database to public access during troubleshooting and trusting someone to close it later, the change should go through the IaC definition and deployment pipeline, so it is tracked, reviewed, and reconciled with the intended baseline.

There are many benefits of IaC, such as repeatability, reviewability, and easier drift detection. To facilitate its implementation, we can consider as best practices: environment parameterization, module reuse with approved templates, avoiding secrets in templates, and separating state and configuration for production and non-production environments.

When it comes to hardening a pipeline, this includes a process to validate IaC using a static analysis tool, a scan for misconfigurations (public exposure, open security groups, etc.), policy checks, plan and preview changes, approval for production, deployment, and post-deployment verification. For policy checks, you can enforce simple rules like:

- Storage must not be public
- Databases must use private networking
- Kubernetes workloads must be non-root
- All resources must have required tags
- Production accepts only artifacts that are built by your pipeline, scanned, and signed

In practice, enforcement means that these rules are evaluated automatically during the pipeline, before deployment is allowed to continue. If a template tries to create a public storage account, attach a database to a public endpoint, run a Kubernetes workload as root, or omit required tags, the pipeline can fail the validation stage and block the change. In the same way, production promotion can be denied when artifacts are not scanned, signed, or produced by the approved pipeline. This makes policy enforcement preventive rather than reactive.

The main goal of this kind of rule is to prevent insecure resources from ever being created. To help with that, another critical aspect is to guarantee observability of what is being changed in your environment. So, controlling resource creation or changes, logging policy, or IAM changes are best practices.

Besides that, visibility is required into service access logs, network flows, and workload logs. Monitoring and alerting are also important, especially in cases such as public exposure changes (new public IP, opened ports, public storage), IAM changes (new role assignments, elevated privileges, new access keys), disabled logging or policy changes, unusual outbound traffic spikes, or deployments from unknown identities.

But remember that these alerts should not exist in isolation. Each important alert should be connected to a defined response procedure, so teams know how to investigate, contain, and recover from the event. For example, a public exposure change may require immediate validation and rollback, an unexpected IAM privilege escalation may require access review and credential rotation, and disabled logging may require urgent restoration of visibility before normal operations continue.

To conclude, do not forget to have logs centralized and protected, in a dedicated environment, with limited access to writing data, and a defined retention policy, ensuring that critical logs aren't easily deleted. This approach will guide you as a software architect toward a more resilient and secure environment that avoids misconfiguration and reduces inevitable drifts that may occur.

However, even with strong preventive controls, secure baselines, and drift reduction practices, no environment can be considered fully protected from incidents. Hardening, therefore, must go beyond prevention and include the ability to detect, contain, and respond when something goes wrong. This is where incident readiness and operational resilience become essential.

Incident readiness and operational resilience

In today's threat landscape, it is widely understood that organizations are not debating if they will be attacked, but rather when the incident will occur. So hardening isn't complete until you can respond effectively to an incident.

This perspective is important because it shifts the goal from the unrealistic idea of preventing every possible incident to the more practical goal of responding quickly, consistently, and effectively when one happens. In other words, resilience is not about assuming failure of security controls, but about recognizing that strong architecture must include prepared response paths when preventive measures are not enough.

Considering this scenario, it is best practice to prepare playbooks for different kinds of incidents, such as:

- ***Credential leak***: In this case, revoking tokens and keys, rotating secrets, and invalidating sessions will be necessary
- ***Public exposure***: Revert configurations, block ingress, and confirm data access logs need to be defined in the playbook
- ***Compromised workload***: For this scenario, the isolation of the environment, blocking egress, and redeploying a new and clean workload can be an alternative
- ***Suspicious Identity and Access Management (IAM) changes***: If this happens, the best alternative is to freeze risky roles, review audit logs, and require re-authentication

Preparing playbooks is only part of the work. These playbooks should also be tested periodically so the team can validate whether the response steps are still realistic, whether the required permissions and tools are available, and whether the expected roles and responsibilities are clear during an incident. This kind of exercise helps reveal gaps before a real event occurs and turns the playbook from a document into an operational capability.

Up to this point, the focus has been mainly on security incidents that involve compromise, exposure, or unauthorized access. However, operational resilience also requires attention to another type of scenario: incidents in which the availability of the application is affected, whether by cybersecurity attacks or by the operational impact they create.

Beyond security incidents involving compromise or exposure, availability must also be treated as part of the hardening discussion, because attacks, misconfigurations, and operational failures can prevent the system from serving users. This is one of the situations where a disaster recovery playbook may be necessary. To do so, you must have backups with tested restores. Besides that, considering the risk of being unavailable, a multi-zone deployment may be justified, and this also needs to be tested. Rate limiting and autoscaling guardrails are also important for preventing unavailability.

As a software architect, you may incentivize the execution of these playbooks periodically to guarantee your team is ready for an incident that may occur, protecting the solution you are delivering.

Summary

Hardening cloud-based solutions is about turning security from a best effort into a system property. You do that by:

- Building a secure baseline (landing zone)
- Enforcing guardrails via policy and pipelines
- Minimizing exposure through identity and network controls
- Hardening runtime defaults across IaaS/PaaS/Kubernetes
- Monitoring the right signals
- And preparing for incidents as a normal operational concern

So hardening is not about adding controls everywhere; it is about deliberately reducing optionality in ways that lower systemic risk.

Questions

1. Why does hardening in cloud computing focus so heavily on misconfiguration and guardrails?
2. What changes in your hardening responsibilities when moving from IaaS to PaaS?
3. What are the most important high-signal alerts to detect dangerous posture changes?
4. How does IaC reduce the burden on developers while improving security?
5. What are the concerns of a team that wants to be ready for a possible cybersecurity incident?

Further reading

The following resource provides additional insight into the topics covered in this chapter:

- Architecture strategies for hardening resources at `https://learn.microsoft.com/en-us/azure/well-architected/security/harden-resources`

Get this book's PDF version and more

Scan the QR code (or go to `packtpub.com/unlock`). Search for this book by name, confirm the edition, and then follow the steps on the page.

UNLOCK NOW

Note: Keep your invoice handy. Purchases made directly from Packt don't require an invoice.

22

Case Study: Practical Usage of .NET Aspire

The case study of the book – World Wild Travel Club (WWTravelClub) was well-accepted as a book chapter in the last edition and we decided to maintain it. This case study will take you through the process of creating software architecture for a travel agency.

So, this chapter serves as the architectural synthesis of the book, bringing together the concepts explored throughout previous chapters into a complete enterprise-scale solution. Through the WWTravelClub case study, we will examine how architectural decisions involving scalability, distributed systems, DevSecOps, cloud-native services, messaging, and domain-driven design interact in a realistic software platform.

The purpose of this case study is not to provide exhaustive framework training or a production-ready implementation. Instead, the goal is to help you understand how architectural principles, trade-off evaluation, system integration, and enterprise design decisions can be applied when building modern distributed applications with .NET and Azure technologies.

Let's start with a description of what our case study application is. Then, we will gradually move to formal specifications.

Technical requirements

This chapter requires the free Visual Studio 2026 Community edition or better.

The code for this chapter is available at `https://github.com/PacktPublishing/Software-Architecture-with-.NET-10-and-C-sharp-5E`.

Introducing World Wild Travel Club

WWTravelClub is a travel agency that was created to revolutionize vacation planning and travel experiences globally. To do so, they are developing an online service, where each aspect of a trip is meticulously curated and supported by a dedicated team of destination-specific experts.

The concept of this platform is that you can be both a visitor and a destination expert at the same time. The more you participate as an expert in a destination, the more points you score. These points can then be redeemed for tickets that people buy online using the platform.

Imagine a traveler searching for personalized vacation packages while simultaneously interacting with destination experts who provide recommendations and local insights. At the same time, administrators must manage packages, users, and operational workflows at scale. These scenarios help illustrate the different responsibilities and interactions that shape the WWTravelClub platform requirements. The person responsible for the WWTravelClub project came with the following requirements list for the platform:

- Common user view:
- Promotional packages on the home page
- Get a recommendation
- Search for packages
- Details of each package:
- Buy a package
- Buy a package with a club of experts included
- Comment on your experience
- Ask an expert
- Evaluate an expert
- Register as a common user
- Destination expert view:
- The same view as the common user view
- Answer questions asking for your destination expertise
- Manage the points you scored by answering questions
- Exchange points for tickets
- Administrator's view:
- Manage packages
- Manage common users
- Manage destination experts

Besides the functionalities asked for on the platform, it is important to note that WWTravelClub intends to have more than 100 destination experts per package and will offer around 1,000 different packages all over the world. These scalability and operational expectations directly influence several architectural decisions discussed later in this chapter, including the adoption of distributed services, asynchronous communication patterns, cloud-native infrastructure, and scalable storage technologies.

It is important to know that, in general, customers do not bring the requirements ready for development. That is why the process of gathering requirements is so important, as described in *Chapter 1, Understanding the Importance of Software Architecture*. This process will transform the list presented above into user needs and system requirements. Let's check how this will work in the next section.

User needs and system requirements

As presented in *Chapter 1, Understanding the Importance of Software Architecture*, to summarize the user needs, you may use the User Story Pattern. We have used this approach here so that you can read the following user stories for WWTravelClub. To improve clarity, the user stories were grouped into domains that represent the primary business capabilities of the platform. These categories help organize the requirements according to customer experience, expert collaboration, administrative operations, scalability and performance, security and compliance, and localization and accessibility.

Customer experience

- US_001: As a common user, I want to view promotional packages on the home page so that I can easily find my next vacation
- US_002: As a common user, I want to search for packages I cannot find on the home page so that I can explore other trip opportunities
- US_003: As a common user, I want to see the details of a package so that I can decide which package to buy
- US_004: As a common user, I want to register myself so that I can start buying the package
- US_005: As a registered user, I want to process the payment so that I can buy a package
- US_006: As a registered user, I want to buy a package with an expert recommendation included so that I can have an exclusive trip experience
- US_007: As a registered user, I want to comment on my experience so that I can give feedback on my trip
- US_008: As a user, I want to get a recommendation of a good place to visit according to other people from my city, so I can find out about new places that fit my style

Expert collaboration

- US_009: As a registered user, I want to ask for an expert so that I can find out the best things to do on my trip
- US_010: As a registered user, I want to review an expert who has helped me so that I can share with others how fantastic he was
- US_011: As a registered user, I want to register as a destination expert view so that I can help people who travel to my city
- US_012: As an expert user, I want to answer questions about my city so that I can score points to be exchanged in the future
- US_013: As an expert user, I want to exchange points for tickets so that I can travel around the world more

Administrative operations

- US_014: As an administrator user, I want to manage packages so that users can have fantastic opportunities to travel

- US_015: As an administrator user, I want to manage registered users so that WWTravelClub can guarantee good service quality
- US_016: As an administrator user, I want to manage expert users so that all the questions regarding our destinations are answered
- US_017: As an administrator user, I want to offer more than 1,000 packages around the world so that different countries can experience the WWTravelClub service

Scalability and performance

- US_018: As the CEO, I want to have more than 1,000 users simultaneously accessing the website so that the business can scale effectively

Security and compliance

- US_019: As a user, I want to know if my credit card information is stored securely, so I can buy packages safely

Localization and accessibility

- US_020: As a user, I want to access WWTravelClub in my native language so that I can easily understand the package offered
- US_021: As a user, I want to access WWTravelClub in Chrome, Firefox, and Edge web browsers so that I can use the web browser of my preference

Notice that while you start writing the stories, information related to non-functional requirements such as security, environment, performance, and scalability can be included.

However, some system requirements may be omitted when you write user stories and need to be included in the software specification. These requirements can be related to legal aspects, hardware and software prerequisites, or even points of attention for the correct system delivery. We discussed them in *Chapter 2, Non-Function Requirements*. So non-function requirements need to be mapped and listed, as well as the user stories. The WWTravelClub system requirements are presented in the following list. Note that requirements are written in the future tense because the system does not exist yet:

- SR_001: The system shall use cloud computing components to deliver the scalability required
- SR_002: The system shall respect *General Data Protection Regulation (GDPR)* requirements
- SR_003: Any web page of this system shall respond within at least 2 seconds when 1,000 users are accessing it concurrently

The idea of having this list of user stories and system requirements is to help you understand how complex the development of a platform might be if you think about it from an architectural perspective.

Considering we now have the list of user stories for the platform, it is time to start selecting the .NET project types that will be used at WWTravelClub. Let's check them in the next topic.

Main types of .NET projects used at WWTravelClub

The development of this book's use case will be based on various kinds of .NET Core Visual Studio projects. This section describes all of them. Let us select **New project** in the Visual Studio File menu.

For instance, you can filter .NET Core project types by typing them into the search engine as follows. The choice of project type is not simply a development preference but an architectural decision. Different project templates support different operational and scalability goals, such as front-end decoupling, service isolation, distributed deployment, testing strategies, and long-term maintainability:

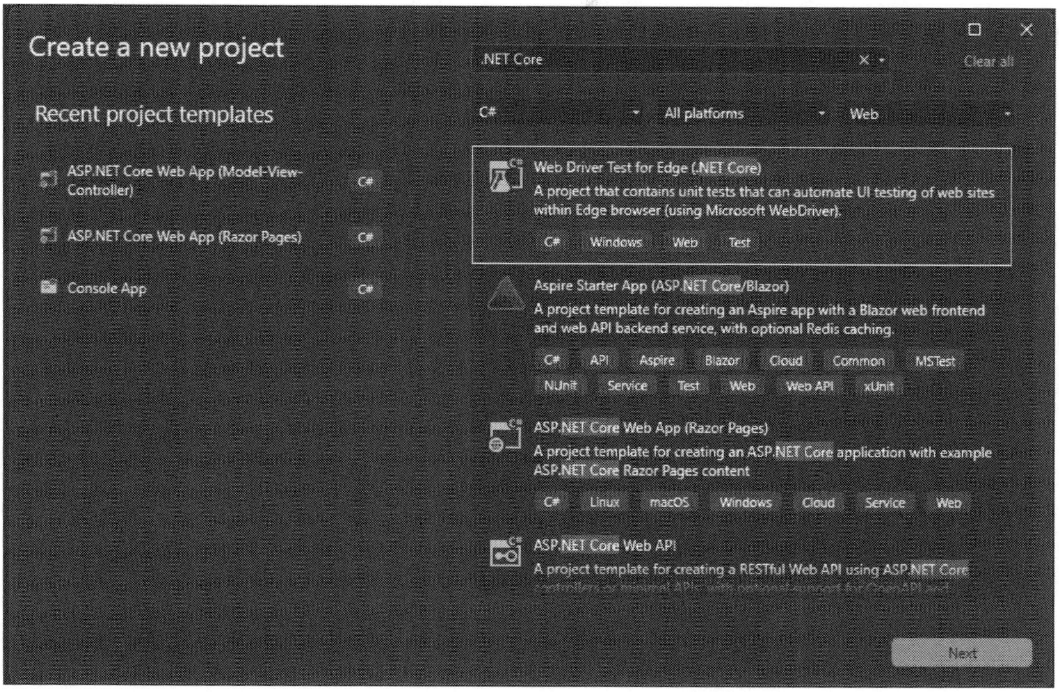

Figure 22.1: Searching for types of .NET Core projects in Visual Studio

There, you will find common C# projects (console, a class library, Windows Form, WPF), and various types of test projects, each based on a different test framework: xUnit, NUnit, and MSTest. Choosing among the various testing frameworks is just a matter of preference since they all offer comparable features. Adding tests to each piece of software that composes a solution is a common practice and allows the software to be modified frequently without jeopardizing its reliability.

You may also want to define your class library projects under the .NET Standard, which were discussed in *Chapter 5, Implementing Code Reusability in C#*. These class libraries are based on standards that make them compatible with several .NET versions. For instance, libraries based on 2.0 standards are compatible with all .NET Core versions greater than or equal to 2.0, with all .NET versions greater than 5, and with all .NET Framework versions greater than 4.6. This compatibility advantage comes at the price of having fewer available features.

Besides filtering Project Types to the Cloud, we have several more project types. Some of them will enable us to define microservices. Microservice-based architecture allows an application to be split into several independent microservices. Several instances of the same microservice can be created and distributed across several machines to fine-tune the performance of each application part. If you want to learn about microservices, we have talked about them in the following chapters:

- *Chapter 11, Applying a Microservice Architecture to Your Enterprise Application*
- *Chapter 14, Implementing Microservices with .NET*

In *Chapter 2, Non-Functional Requirements*, we have an ASP.NET Core application project described in the subsection Creating a scalable web app with .NET 10. There, we defined an ASP.NET Core application, but Visual Studio also contains project templates for projects based on RESTful APIs and the most important single-page application frameworks, such as Angular, React, Vue.js, and the Blazor framework based on WebAssembly, which was discussed in *Chapter 18, Client Frameworks: Blazor*. Some of them are available with the standard Visual Studio installation, while others require the installation of an SPA package, called ASP.NET and web development workload. For more information, please visit `https://learn.microsoft.com/en-us/aspnet/core/client-side/spa/intro`

To finish, testing projects are discussed in detail in *Chapter 9, Testing Your Enterprise Application*. We suggest you as a software architect try all the templates available in Visual Studio by creating proof of concepts that may help you define the best project types for your solution.

Now that we have checked these different project types, let's have a look at GitHub and how it can be helpful to manage WWTravelClub requirements.

Managing WWTravelClub requirements using GitHub

As discussed in *Chapter 3, Managing Requirements*, an important step for a software development project is where and how the team will organize the User Stories mapped from the user needs. There, as described in the *Introducing GitHub projects* section, GitHub is also an alternative to document system requirements using issues in GitHub Projects, which are mainly tasks or actions that need to be completed to deliver a product or service.

From an architectural governance perspective, requirement traceability and workflow visibility are essential for coordinating distributed teams and ensuring that business requirements remain connected to implementation tasks throughout the software lifecycle.

So, considering the scenario described for WWTravelClub, we decided to use **Team planning** as template:

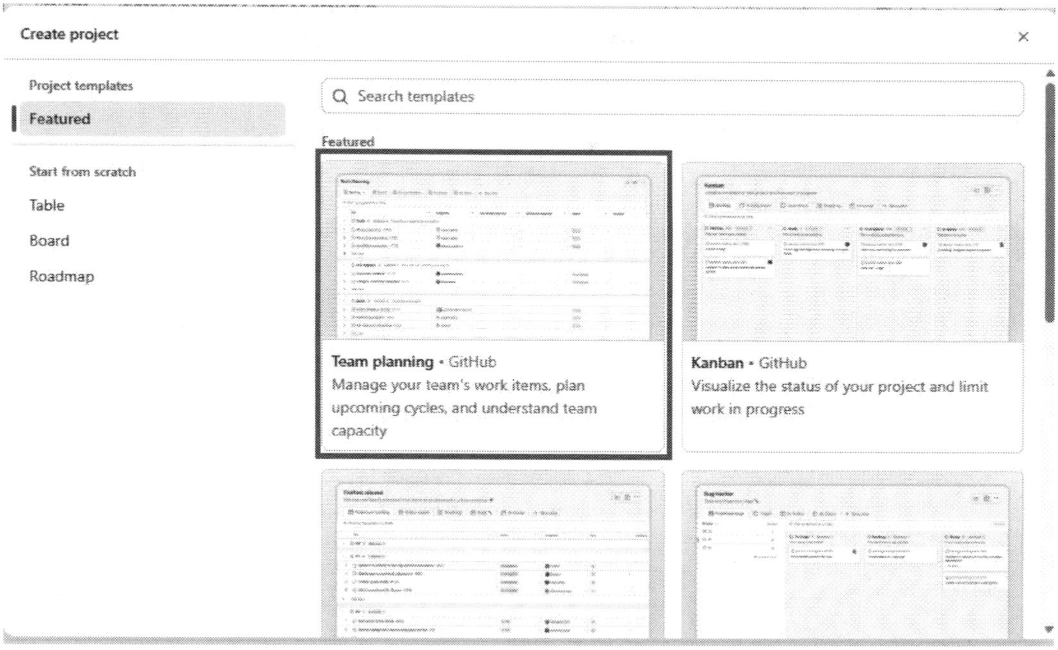

Figure 22.2: Creating a GitHub Project Using Templates

After that, the creation of **Todo** tasks is quite simple:

- Inside each issue, we **create sub-issues**, as you can see in *Figure 22.3*
- It is important to determine that the connections between work items are useful during software development. Hence, as a software architect, you must provide this knowledge to your team, and, more than that, you must motivate them to make these connections:

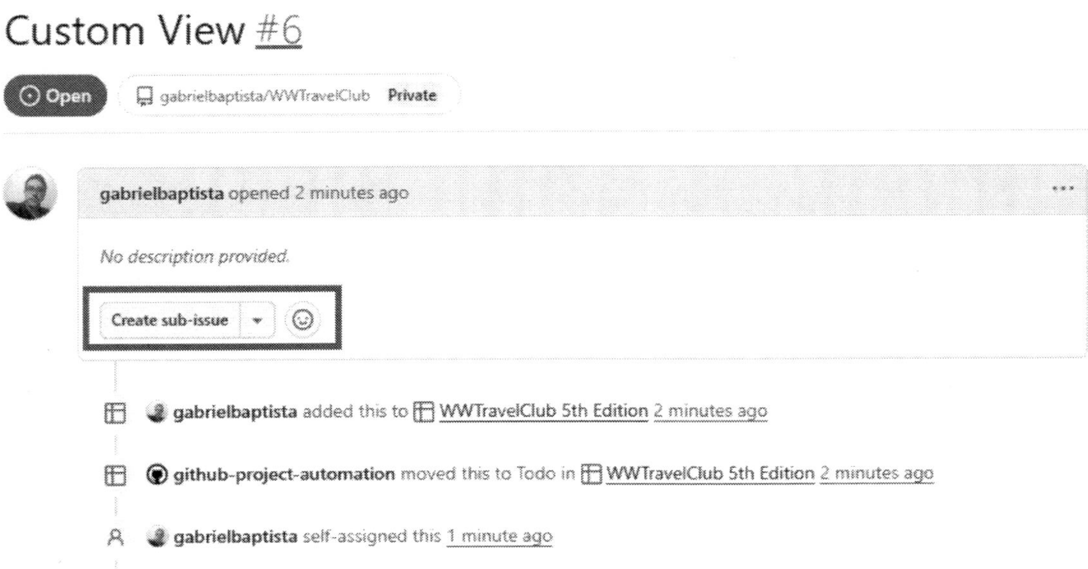

Figure 22.3: Defining a sub-issue to an Epic issue selected

As soon as you create a sub-issue, you will be able to connect it to several User Stories that detail its specifications. The following screenshot shows the details:

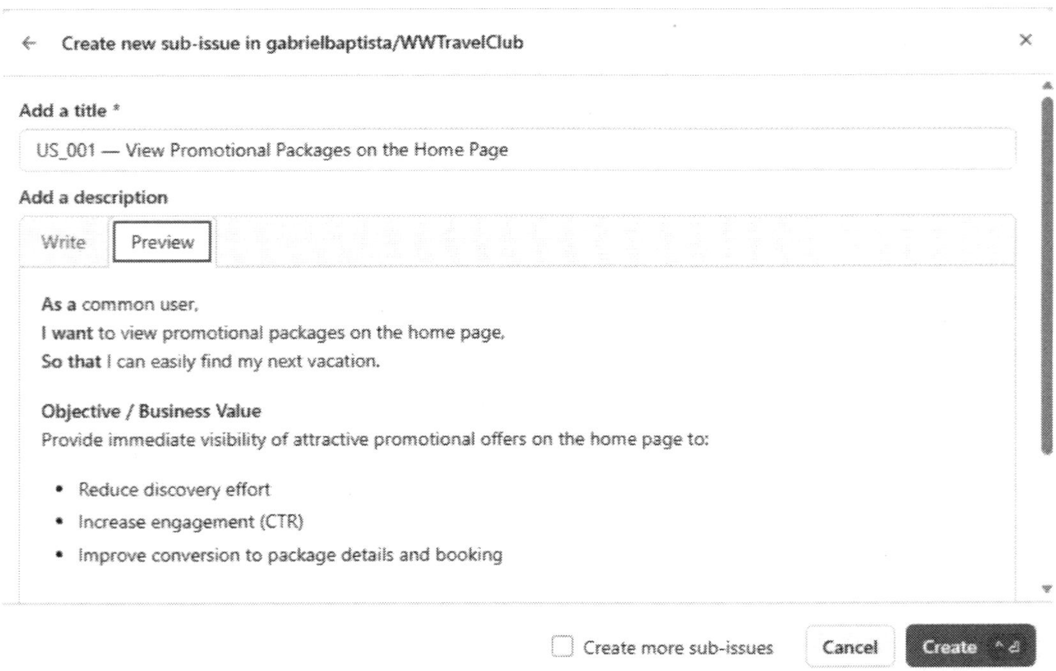

Figure 22.4: User Story Issue

After that, any kind of task can be created as issues for each User Story. The user interface provided by GitHub is efficacious because it enables you to track the chain of functionalities and the relationships between them:

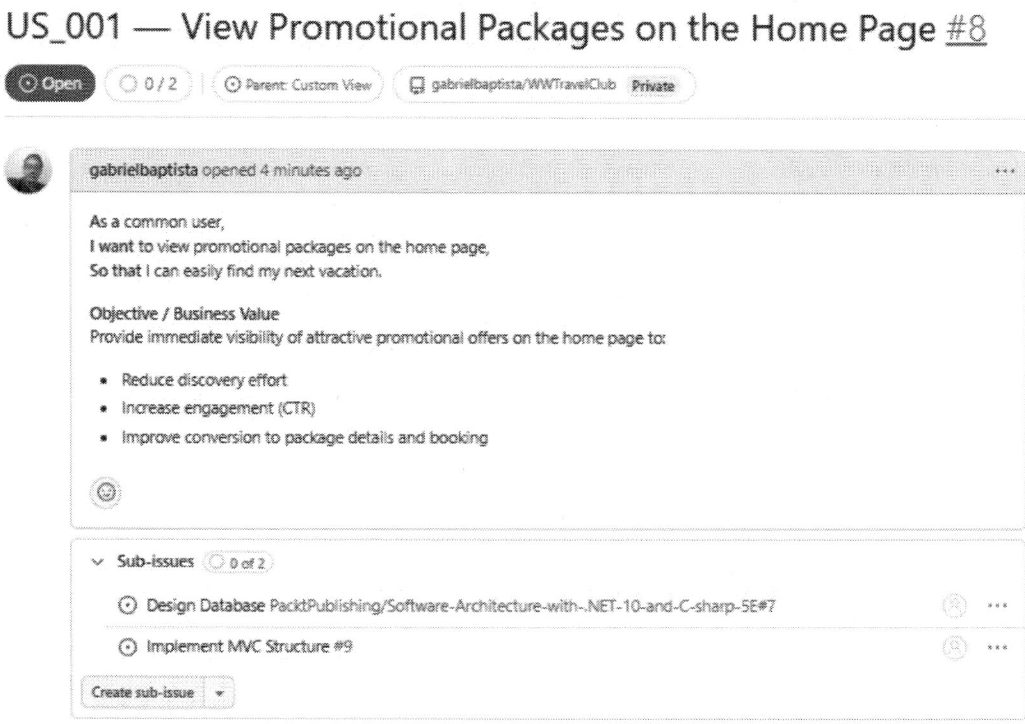

Figure 22.5: Sub-issues view

Considering we are using Scrum as a basis, as soon as you complete the input of the issues, you will be able to plan the project sprints together with your team. The **Backlog** view enables you to define in which sprint/ iteration issues will be developed:

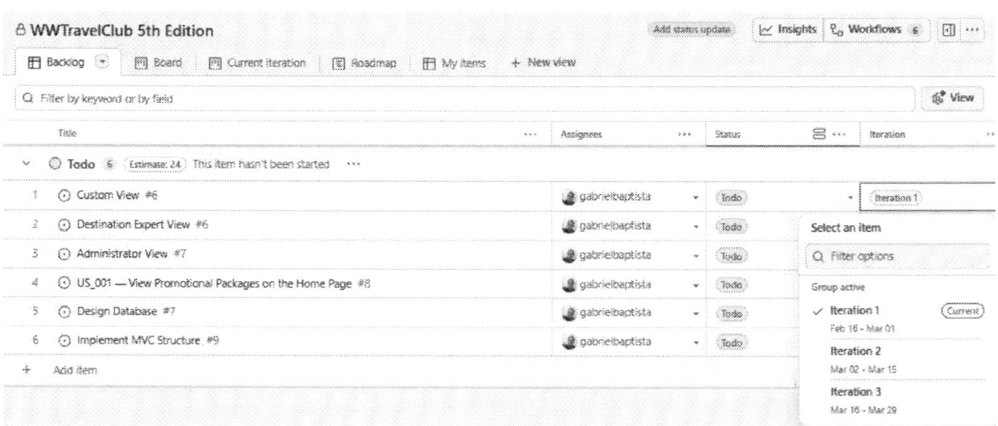

Figure 22.6: Backlog view

By clicking on the **Current Iteration**, you will see just the work items assigned to that sprint. Each sprint page is quite like the backlog page but contains more tabs, where you can define Sprint Period and Team Capacity, for instance:

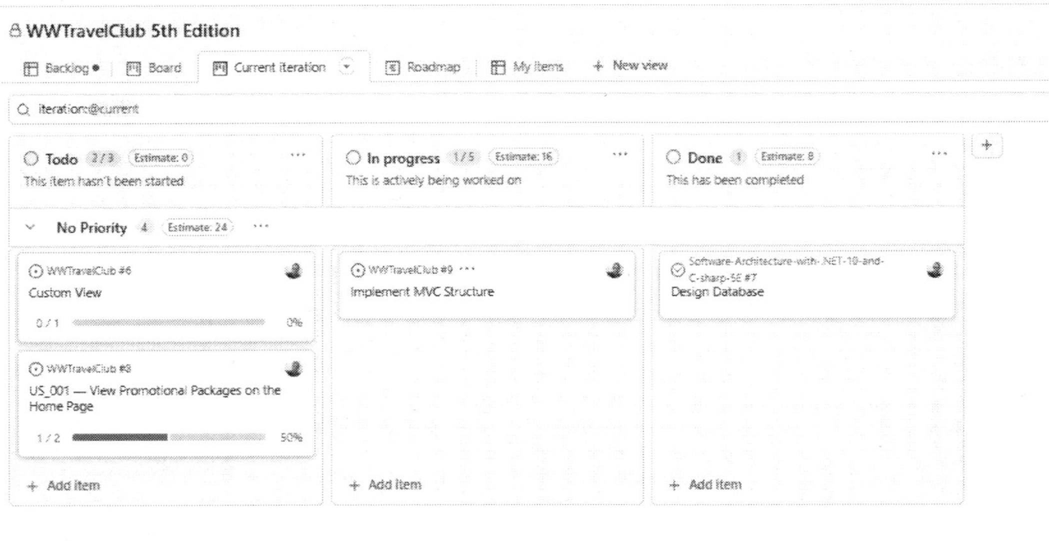

Figure 22.7: Planning view

Also useful is the **Roadmap** menu that enables a view of when the issues are planned to be delivered, as shown below:

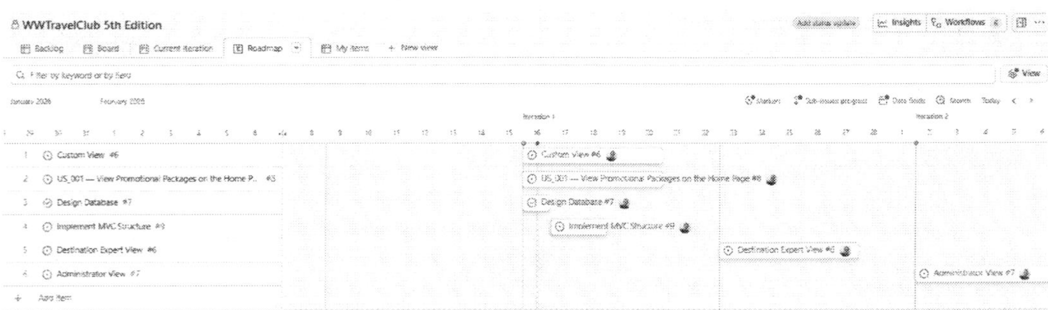

Figure 22.8: Roadmap view

Once you understand this mechanism, you will be able to create and plan any software project. It is worth mentioning that the tool itself will not solve problems related to team management. However, the tool is a great way to incentivize the team to update the project status, so you can maintain a clear perspective of how the project is evolving.

Now that we have defined how we will manage WWTravelClub requirements, it is time to start thinking about the code standard that will be followed by the developers. Let's check this out in the next section.

Code standard for WWTravelClub - DOs and DON'Ts when writing code

In *Chapter 4, Best Practices in Coding C#,* we learned that, as a software architect, you must define a code standard that matches the needs of the company you are working for.

In the sample project of this book, this is no different. The way we decided to present the standard for it is by describing a list of DOs and DON'Ts. We have followed this list while writing the samples we produced. It is worth mentioning that the list is a good way to start your standard and, as a software architect, you should discuss this list with the developers you have in the team so that you can develop it in a practical and good manner.

It is also important to remember that we have discussed in the section *Understanding and applying tools that can evaluate C# code*, some good tools that can help you define a coding style for your team.

In addition, the statements below are designed to clarify communication between team members and improve the performance and maintenance of the software you are developing.

You may consider the list below a waste of space in the book, since we have great C# community coding standards without the need of enforcing a standard. However, how can you guarantee maintainability without it? If defining coding standards were not necessary, we wouldn't have so many projects with difficulty for maintenance all over the world.

In distributed enterprise environments, coding standards are not only about stylistic consistency. They also help reduce operational risk, improve maintainability across teams, simplify onboarding, and ensure that services remain understandable as the platform evolves. So, let's check the list of DOs and DON'Ts defined for the WWTravelClub Project:

- DO write your code in English
- DO use PascalCasing for all public member, type, and namespace names consisting of multiple words
- DO use camelCasing for parameter names
- DO write classes, methods, and variables with understandable names
- DO comment public classes, methods, and properties
- DO use the using statement whenever possible
- DO use async implementation whenever possible
- DON'T write empty try-catch statements
- DON'T write methods with a cyclomatic complexity score of more than 10
- DON'T use break and continue inside for/while/do-while/foreach statements

These DOs and DON'Ts are simple to follow and, better than that, will yield great results for the code your team produces. It is worth mentioning that these DOs and DON'Ts are a guide, not a set of hard-and-fast rules to be followed by every team. They can be adapted as needed for the specific needs of a team before they are sent out to the team members. As a software architect, it is essential that all team members follow the same DOs and DON'Ts.

Considering we now have a defined Coding Standard, let's learn how to apply SonarCloud as a tool for helping us in code analysis.

Applying SonarCloud at WWTravelClub APIs

Now that we have already created the WWTravelClub repository, we can evolve the code quality as discussed in *Chapter 4, Best Practices in Coding C#*. As we saw in that chapter, Azure DevOps enables continuous integration, and this can be useful. In this section, we will discuss more reasons why the DevOps concept and the Azure DevOps platform are so useful.

For now, the only thing we would like to introduce is the possibility of analyzing code after it is committed by the developers but before it has been published. Nowadays, in the SaaS world for application life cycle tools, this is only possible because of some of the SaaS code analysis platforms that we have. This use case will use SonarCloud.

Sonar Cloud is the SaaS version provided by Sonar. It is free for open-source code and can analyze code stored in GitHub, Bitbucket, and Azure DevOps. The user needs to register for these platforms. As soon as you log in, assuming your code is stored in Azure DevOps, you can follow the steps described in the following article to create a connection between your Azure DevOps and Sonar Cloud: `https://docs.sonarcloud.io/`.

> **Tip**
>
> Sonar also provides a self-managed edition that can be useful for scenarios where Sonar Cloud cannot be used. Please check `https://www.sonarsource.com/` for more details.

It is important to mention that automated code analysis is a key component of a mature DevSecOps pipeline because it enables quality validation and security checks to occur continuously throughout the development lifecycle instead of only during final release stages. Considering this scenario, after setting up the connection between your project in Azure DevOps and Sonar Cloud, you will have a build pipeline like the one that follows:

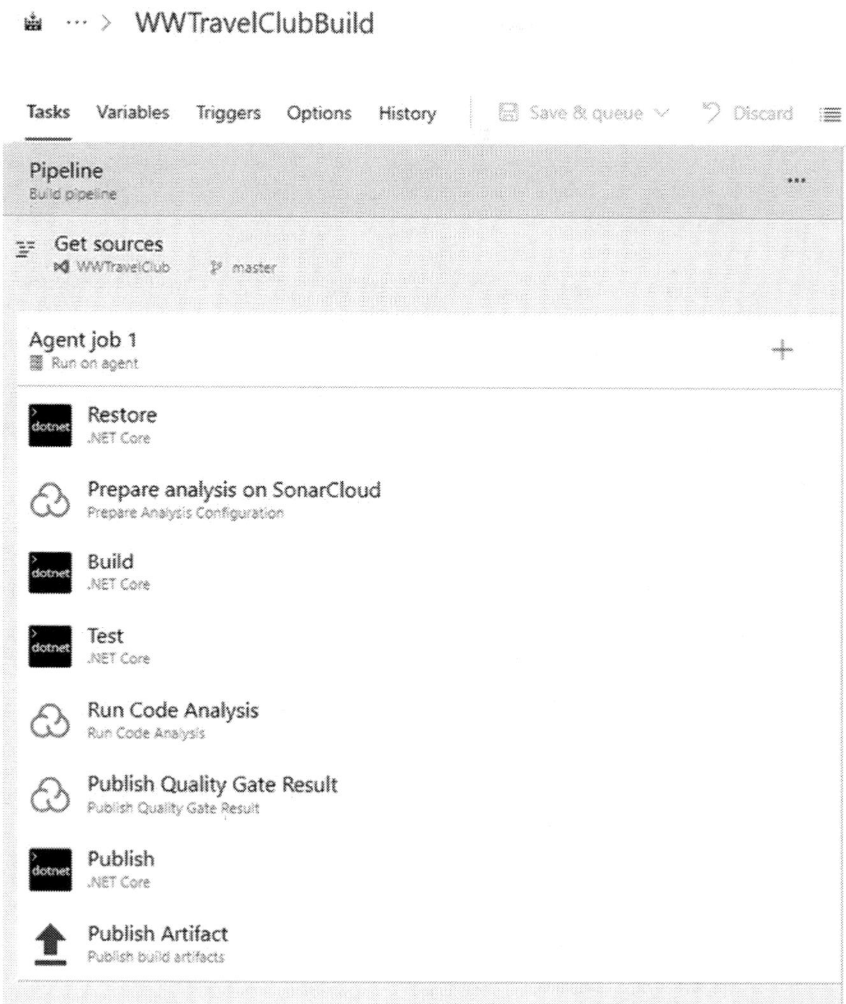

Figure 22.9: Sonar Cloud configuration in the Azure build pipeline

It is worth mentioning that C# projects do not have a GUID number, and this is required by Sonar Cloud. You can easily generate one using this link: `https://www.guidgenerator.com/` or using the Create GUID tool in Visual Studio (**Tools** -> **Create GUID**). The GUID will need to be placed in the project file:

```
<Project Sdk="Microsoft.NET.Sdk.Web">
  <PropertyGroup>
    <TargetFramework>net10.0</TargetFramework>
    <Nullable>enable</Nullable>
    <ImplicitUsings>enable</ImplicitUsings>
    <ProjectGuid>6CFF4331-0C5A-40D9-8603-AC01BB36697C</ProjectGuid>
  </PropertyGroup>
</Project>
```

As soon as you finish the build, the result of the code analysis will be presented in Sonar Cloud, as can be seen in the following screenshot.

Figure 22.10: SonarCloud results

Also, by this time, the code analyzed is not yet in the release, so this can be useful for getting the next step of quality before releasing your system. You can use this approach as a reference for automating code analysis during committal.

It is worth noting that if you use GitHub as your code repository, there is an automatic mode where Sonar can monitor your code. Considering you are working in an open-source environment, this can be an alternative. You can also set up a GitHub Action to do so, if necessary.

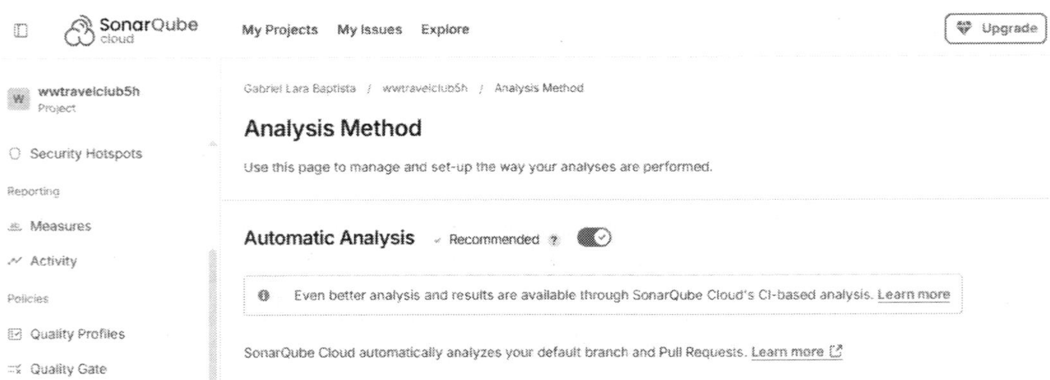

Figure 22.11: SonarCloud Automatic Analysis setup for GitHub Projects

Considering we have implemented a way to continuously evaluate code quality, it is time to design reusable software. Let's look at this in the next section.

Reusing code as a fast way to deliver good and safe software

As we checked in *Chapter 5, Implementing Code Reusability in C#*, a good approach for accelerating the delivery of good software is creating reusable components. The final design of the solution for evaluating content for WWTravelClub can be checked in the picture below. This approach consists of using many topics that were discussed in the chapter. First, all the code is placed in a .NET 10 class library. This means that you can add this code to different types of solutions, such as ASP.NET Core web apps and .NET MAUI apps for the Android and iOS platforms.

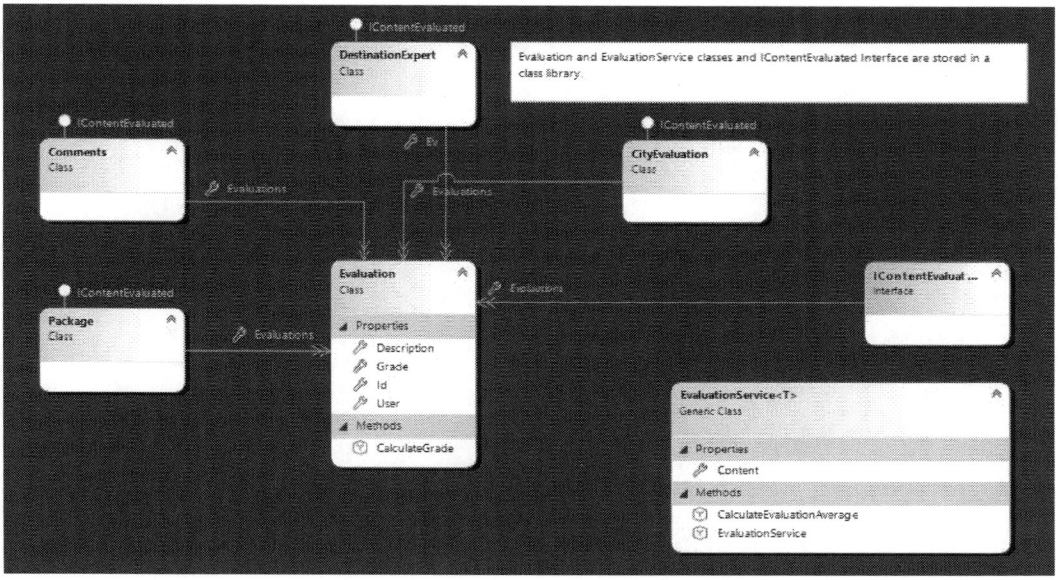

Figure 22.12: WWTravelClub reuse approach

This design makes use of object-oriented principles such as inheritance, so you do not need to write properties and methods more than once that can be used in many classes. The design also makes use of the polymorphism principle so that you can change the behavior of the code without changing the name of the method.

To finish, the design abstracts the idea of the content by introducing generics as a tool that can facilitate the manipulation of similar classes, such as the ones we have in WWTravelClub to evaluate content regarding cities, comments, destination experts, and travel packages.

The big difference between a team that incentivizes code reuse and one that does not is the speed of delivering good software to end users. Of course, beginning this approach is not easy, but rest assured that you will get good results after some time working with it.

Since we have covered the possibilities of code reuse using object-oriented principles, what about organizing the application using domains created by *Domain-driven design (DDD)*? We will check this in the next section.

Understanding the domains of the WWTravelClub application

In this section we will perform the DDD analysis of the WWTravelClub system, trying to identify all its domains (also called Bounded Contexts), that is the subsystems characterized by different languages used by the experts. Once identified each domain might be assigned to a different development team and will give rise to a different microservice.

From the requirements listed in the *Introducing World Wild Travel Club* and *Understanding user needs and system requirements* sections, we know that the WWTravelClub system is composed of the following parts:

- Information about the available destinations and packages.
- Reservation/purchase orders subsystem.
- Communication with the experts/review subsystem.
- Payment subsystem. We briefly analyzed the features of this subsystem and its relationship with the reservation purchase subsystem at the beginning of *Chapter 7, Understanding the Different Domains in Software Solutions*, Understanding domain-driven design section.
- User accounts subsystem.
- Statistics reporting subsystem.

Do the preceding subsystems represent different Bounded Contexts? Can some subsystems be split into different Bounded Contexts? The answers to these questions are given by the languages that are spoken in each subsystem:

- The language that's spoken in subsystem 1 is the language of travel agencies. There is no concept of a customer, just of locations, packages, and their features.
- The language that's spoken in subsystem 2 is common to all service purchases, such as the available resources, reservations, and purchase orders. This is a separate Bounded Context.
- The language that's spoken in subsystem 3 has a lot in common with subsystem 1's language. However, there are also typical social media concepts, such as ratings, chats, post sharing, media sharing, and so on. This subsystem can be split into two parts: a social media subsystem that has a new Bounded Context and an available information subsystem that is part of the Bounded Context of subsystem 1.
- In subsystem 4, we speak the language of banking. This subsystem communicates with the reservation purchase subsystem and executes tasks that are needed to carry out a purchase. From these observations, we can see that it is a different Bounded Context and has a customer/supplier relationship with the purchase/reservation system.
- Subsystem 5 is a separate Bounded Context (as in almost all web applications). It has a relationship with all the Bounded Contexts that have either the concept of a user or the concept of a customer because the concept of user accounts always maps to these concepts. You must be wondering how. Well, it's quite simple—the currently logged-in user is assumed to be the social media user of the social

media Bounded Context, the customer of the reservation/purchase Bounded Context, and the payer of the payment Bounded Context.

- The query-only subsystem, that is, 6, speaks the language of analytics and statistics and differs a lot from the languages that are spoken in the other subsystems. However, it has a connection with almost all the Bounded Contexts since it takes all its input from them. The preceding constraints force us to adopt CQRS in its strong form, thereby considering it a query-only separated Bounded Context.

In conclusion, each of the listed subsystems defines a different Bounded Context, but part of the communication with the experts/review subsystem must be included in the information about the available destinations and the package's Bounded Context.

As the analysis continues and a prototype is implemented, some Bounded Contexts may split and some others may be added, but it is fundamental to immediately start modeling the system and to immediately start analyzing the relations among the Bounded Contexts with the partial information we have since this will drive further investigations and will help us define the communication protocols and Ubiquitous Languages that are needed so that we can interact with the domain experts.

The following is a basic first sketch of the domain map:

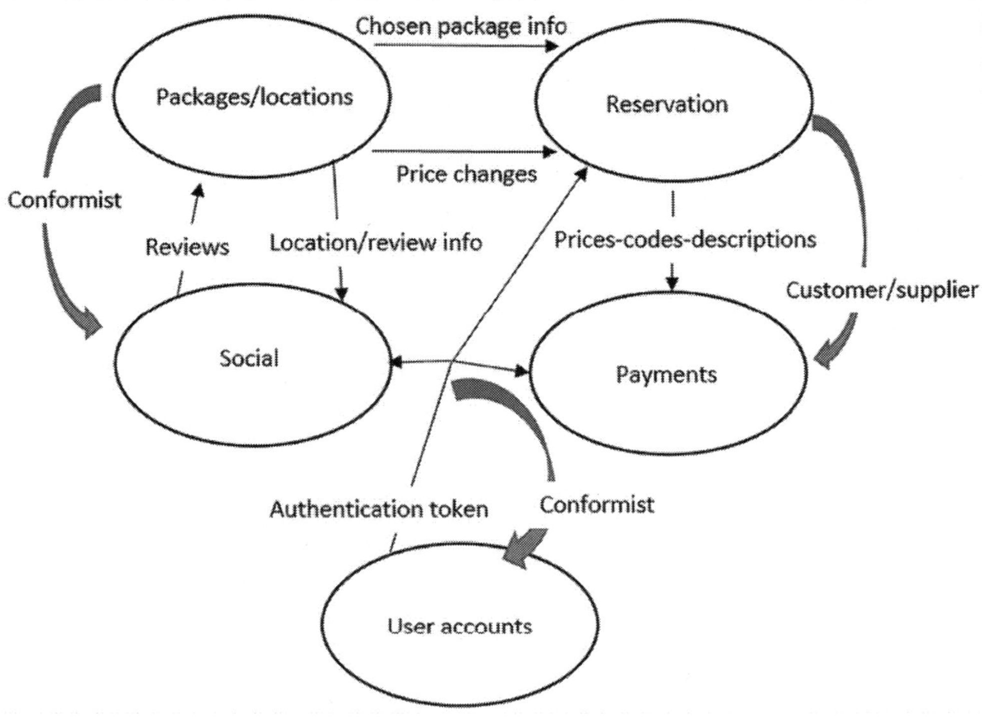

Figure 22.13: WWTravelClub domain map. Thin black arrows represent data exchanged between Bounded Contexts, while thick blue arrows represent the relationships between Bounded Contexts (conformist, customer/supplier, and so on)

For simplicity, we've omitted the *Statistics reporting Bounded Context*. We say just that it collects statistics on the daily purchases of each package.

Here, we're assuming that the *User accounts* and *Social Bounded Contexts* have a *conformist* relationship with all the other Bounded Contexts that communicate with them because they are implemented with already existing software, so all the other components must adapt to them.

As we mentioned previously, the relationship between *Reservation* and *Payments* is *customer/supplier* because *Payments* provides services that are used to execute the tasks of **Reservation**. All the other relationships are classified as **Partners**. The various concepts of customer/user that most Bounded Contexts have are coordinated by the *User accounts* authorization token arrow, which indirectly takes care of mapping these concepts between all the Bounded Contexts.

The **Packages/locations** subsystem communicates the following information to **Reservation**:

- Chosen Package Info which contains the package information that's needed to carry out a reservation/purchase
- Price changes which take care of informing pending purchase orders of possible price changes

Social interactions are started from an existing review provided by users (**Reviews** arrow between **Packages/locations** and **Social**) and are supported by *Location/review* info communications from **Packages/locations** to **Social**.

Finally, **Reservation** communicates purchase codes, descriptions, and prices to *Payments* through the *Prices-codes-descriptions* arrow.

Once we have identified our application Bounded Contexts, we can organize the application DevSecOps cycle.

The WWTravelClub DevSecOps approach

During *Chapter 8, Understanding DevSecOps Principles and CI/CD*, screenshots from the WWTravelClub project have shown the steps needed to implement a good DevSecOps cycle. The WWTravelClub team has decided to use GitHub because they understand that the tool is essential for getting the best current DevSecOps experience for the whole cycle.

The requirements were written using user stories, connected to a GitHub Project. The code is placed in the GitHub repo. Both concepts are explained in *Chapter 3, Managing Requirements.*

The management life cycle used for getting things done is Scrum, presented in *Chapter 1, Understanding the Importance of Software Architecture*. This approach divides the implementation into Sprints, which forces value to be delivered by the end of each cycle. Using the CI facilities we learned in this chapter, code will be compiled each time the team merges new code into the master branch of the repository.

Once the code is compiled and tested, the first stage of the deployment is done. The first stage is named *Development* because you enable it for internal tests. Both Application Insights and Test and Feedback can be used to get the first feedback on the new release.

If the tests and the feedback of the new release pass, it is time to go to the second stage, called **Staging**. Application Insights and Test and Feedback can be used again, but now in a more stable environment.

The cycle ends with the authorization to deploy in the **Production** stage. This certainly is a tough decision, but DevOps indicates that you must do it continuously so you can get better feedback from customers. Application

Insights remains a useful tool since you can monitor the evolution of the new release in production, even comparing it to past releases.

The WWTravelClub project approach described here can be used in many other modern application development life cycles. Together, GitHub Projects, CI/CD pipelines, automated testing, code analysis, peer reviews, and staged deployments form a unified DevSecOps strategy that supports both rapid delivery and operational reliability for enterprise systems. As a software architect, you must oversee the process. The tools are ready to go, and it depends on you to make things right!

For this reason, even considering WWTravelClub as a hypothetical scenario, some concerns were considered while building it:

- CI is enabled, but a multi-stage scenario is enabled too.
- Security checks are made by GitHub Advanced Security.
- Even with a multi-stage scenario, the *PR (Pull Request)* is a way to guarantee that only good-quality code will be presented in the first stage.
- To do a good job in the PR, peer reviews are undertaken. The usage of GitHub Copilot Agent is allowed to help with understanding and debugging PRs.
- The peer reviews check, for instance, the presence of a feature flag when creating a new feature.
- The peer reviews check both unit and functional tests developed during the creation of the new feature.

The preceding steps are not exclusively for WWTravelClub. You, as a software architect, will need to define the approach to guarantee a safe CI/CD scenario. You may use this as a starting point. It is worth pointing out that both in Azure DevOps and GitHub we can completely disable pushing on the master branch, thus forcing the usage of PR for merging modifications on the master branch.

In the next section we will start with the actual code, by showing how to choose among various data storage options.

How to Choose Your Data Storage in the Cloud

In *Chapter 12, How to Choose Your Data Storage in the Cloud*, we have learned how to use NoSQL. Now we must decide whether NoSQL databases are adequate for this book's use case, the WWTravelClub application. We need to store the following families of data:

- ***Information about available destinations and packages:*** Relevant operations for this data are read since packages and destinations do not change very often. However, they must be accessed as fast as possible from all over the world to ensure a pleasant user experience when users browse the available options. Therefore, a distributed relational database with geographically distributed replicas is possible, but not necessary since packages can be stored inside their destinations in a cheaper NoSQL database.
- ***Destination reviews:*** In this case, distributed write operations have a non-negligible impact. Moreover, most writes are additions since reviews are not usually updated. Additions benefit a lot from sharding and do not cause consistency issues like updates do. Accordingly, the best option for this data is a NoSQL collection.
- ***Reservations:*** In this case, consistency errors are not acceptable because they may cause overbooking. Reads and writes have a comparable impact, but we need reliable transactions and good consistency

checks. Luckily, data can be organized in a multi-tenant database where tenants are destinations since reservation information belonging to different destinations is completely unrelated. Accordingly, we may use sharded SQL Azure database instances.

In conclusion, the best option for data in the first and second bullet points is Cosmos DB, while the best option for the third point is Azure SQL Server. Actual applications may require a more detailed analysis of all data operations and their frequencies. In some cases, it is worth implementing prototypes for various possible options and executing performance tests with typical workloads on all of them.

In the ch12 folder of the GitHub repository associated with the book, you can find the migration of the destinations/packages data layer we looked at in *Chapter 13, Interacting with Data in C# – Entity Framework Core,* to Cosmos DB.

This section finishes the application requirements and preparation stage of our sample application. Let's move to the implementation of the first worker microservice.

Worker microservice based on RabbitMQ

This section explains the modifications needed to use a message broker. This kind of solution is usually more difficult to test and design but allows for better horizontal scaling and also enables more extra features at almost no cost since they are offered by the message broker itself.

At this stage, the architectural focus shifts from requirement analysis to operational scalability. The following implementation demonstrates how asynchronous messaging and worker microservices can improve resiliency, throughput, and workload distribution for enterprise applications such as WWTravelClub.

We assume that RabbitMQ has already been installed and adequately prepared as explained in the *Installing RabbitMQ* subsection of *Chapter 14, Implementing Microservices with .NET*.

Let's create a copy of the previous section solution and rename `GrpcMicroServiceRabbitProto` as the solution folder.

First, the ASP.NET Core project must be replaced by another **Worker** Service project with the same `GrpcMicroService` name. Also, this project must add the connection string to its configuration file and must call the `AddDbDriver` and `AddApplicationServices` extension methods to add all the database and application layer services to the dependency injection engine. Below is the full content of the `Program.cs` file:

```
using DBDriver.Extensions;
using DDD.ApplicationLayer;
using GrpcMicroService.HostedServices;
using Microsoft.Extensions.Configuration;
using Microsoft.Extensions.DependencyInjection;
using Microsoft.Extensions.Hosting;

IHost host = Host.CreateDefaultBuilder(args)
    .ConfigureServices((hostContext, services) =>
    {
```

```
        services.AddApplicationServices();
        services.AddDbDriver(hostContext.Configuration
            .GetConnectionString("DefaultConnection")??string.Empty);
        services.AddHostedService<ProcessPurchases>();
    })
    .Build();

await host.RunAsync();
```

We just need ProtoBuf for the binary messages, so both the FakeSource process and the GrpcMicroService projects must add just the Google.Protobuf and Grpc.Tools NuGet packages. Both projects need the following messages.proto file, which defines just the purchase message:

```
syntax = "proto3";
option csharp_namespace = "GrpcMicroService";
import "google/protobuf/timestamp.proto";
package purchase;
message PurchaseMessage {
  string id = 1;
  google.protobuf.Timestamp time = 2;
  string location = 3;
  int32 cost =4;
  google.protobuf.Timestamp purchaseTime = 5;
}
```

The automatic generation of the message classes is enabled in both projects with the same XML declaration in their project files:

```
<ItemGroup>
    <Protobuf Include="Protos\messages.proto" GrpcServices="Client" />
</ItemGroup>
```

In fact, both projects need to specify Client code generation since no service needs to be created. However, the FakeSource project uses just a link to the actual .proto file, so its reference is:

```
<ItemGroup>
  <Protobuf Include="..\GrpcMicroService\Protos\messages.proto"
      GrpcServices="Client">
    <Link>Protos\messages.proto</Link>
  </Protobuf>
</ItemGroup>
```

To communicate with the RabbitMQ server, both projects must add the RabbitMQ.Client NuGet package.

Finally, FakeSource also adds the Polly NuGet package because we will use Polly to define reliable communication strategies.

The ExecuteAsync method of the client project is a little bit different:

```
protected override async Task ExecuteAsync(
CancellationToken stoppingToken)
{
    var channelOpts = new CreateChannelOptions(
        publisherConfirmationsEnabled: true,
        publisherConfirmationTrackingEnabled: true,
        outstandingPublisherConfirmationsRateLimiter:
          new ThrottlingRateLimiter(MAX_OUTSTANDING_CONFIRMS)
    );
    Random random = new Random();
    var factory = new ConnectionFactory() { HostName = "localhost" };

    IConnection? connection = null;
    IChannel? channel = null;
    try
    {
        while (!stoppingToken.IsCancellationRequested)
        {
        ...
        }
    }
    finally
    {
        if (connection != null)
        {
            if(channel != null)
                channel.Dispose();
            connection.Dispose();
            channel = null;
            connection = null;
        }
    }
}
```

Communication requires the creation of a connection factory, then the connection factory generates a connection, and the connection generates a channel. The connection factory is created outside of the main loop since it can be reused several times, and it is not invalidated by communication errors.

For the connection and channel, outside of the main loop, we just define the variables and where to place them, since they are invalidated in the case of communication exceptions, so we must dispose of them and recreate them from scratch after each exception.

`channelOpts` are the channel creation options and must be passed to the method that creates a channel. In our case, we required confirmation of reception and fixed a maximum number of tracked confirmations. When this limit is hit, communications automatically slow down to avoid congestion.

The main loop is enclosed in `try/finally` to ensure that any channel/connection pair is disposed of before leaving the method.

Inside the main loop, as a first step, we create the purchase message:

```
var purchaseDay = DateTime.UtcNow.Date;
//randomize a little bit purchase day
purchaseDay = purchaseDay.AddDays(random.Next(0, 3) - 1);

var purchase = new PurchaseMessage
{
    //message time
    PurchaseTime = Timestamp.FromDateTime(purchaseDay),
    Time = Timestamp.FromDateTime(DateTime.UtcNow),
    Id = Guid.NewGuid().ToString(),
    //add random location
    Location = locations[random.Next(0, locations.Length)],
    //add random cost
    Cost = 200 * random.Next(1, 4)
};
byte[]? body = null;
using (var stream = new MemoryStream())
{
    purchase.WriteTo(stream);
    stream.Flush();
    body = stream.ToArray();
}
```

Before executing the communication, we define a Polly strategy pipeline:

```
ResiliencePipeline pipeline = new ResiliencePipelineBuilder()
    .AddRetry(new RetryStrategyOptions
    {
        ShouldHandle = new PredicateBuilder().Handle<Exception>(),
        BackoffType = DelayBackoffType.Exponential,
        UseJitter = true,  // Adds a random factor to the delay
        MaxRetryAttempts = 4,
```

```
        Delay = TimeSpan.FromSeconds(3),
    })
    .Build();
```

The above pipeline contains just an exponential retry strategy, which in the case of an exception waits for an exponentially growing amount of time. So, if six attempts are made, then the second attempt is made after 2 seconds, the third after 4 seconds, the fourth after 8 seconds, and so on. If all attempts fail, the exception is rethrown and causes the message to be lost. If it's important that messages can't be lost, we can combine this strategy with a circuit breaker strategy (see *Resilient task execution* in *Chapter 11, Applying a Microservice Architecture to Your Enterprise Application*).

Once we have defined the Polly pipeline, we can execute all the communication steps in the context of this pipeline:

```
await pipeline.ExecuteAsync(async (token) =>
{
    try
    {
        if (connection == null || channel == null)
        {
            connection = await factory.CreateConnectionAsync();
            channel = await
               connection.CreateChannelAsync(channelOpts);

        }
        //Actual communication is here
        //and will be detailed into another code block
    }
    catch
    {
        if(channel != null)
            channel.Dispose();
        if(connection != null)
            connection.Dispose();
        channel = null;
        connection = null;
        throw;
    }

}, stoppingToken);
```

If there are no valid connections or channels, they are created. In the case that an exception is thrown, both the channel and the connection are disposed of, since they might have been corrupted by the exception. This way, the next communication attempt will use a fresh connection and a new channel. After the disposal, the exception is rethrown so it can be handled by Polly strategies.

Finally, below are the actual communication steps:

1. First, if the queue doesn't already exist, it is created. The queue is created as durable; that is, it must be stored on disk and not be exclusive so that several servers can extract messages from the queue in parallel:

```
await channel.QueueDeclareAsync(queue: "purchase_queue",
    durable: true,
    exclusive: false,
    autoDelete: false,
    arguments: null);
```

2. Then, each message is declared as persistent; that is, it must be stored on disk:

```
var properties = new BasicProperties();
properties.Persistent = true;
```

3. Finally, the message is sent through the default exchange, which sends it to a specific named queue:

```
await channel.BasicPublishAsync(exchange: "",
        routingKey: "purchase_queue",
        mandatory: true,
        basicProperties: properties,
        body: body);
```

If a confirmation doesn't arrive within a default timeout, an exception is thrown that triggers the Polly retry policy. When messages are taken from a local database queue, we can also use a non-blocking confirmation that triggers the removal of the message from the local queue.

The `ExecuteAsync` method of the server-hosted process is defined in the `HostedServices/ProcessPurchase.cs` file:

```
protected override async Task ExecuteAsync(CancellationToken stoppingToken)
{
    var channelOpts = new CreateChannelOptions(
        publisherConfirmationsEnabled: true,
        publisherConfirmationTrackingEnabled: true,
        outstandingPublisherConfirmationsRateLimiter:
          new ThrottlingRateLimiter(MAX_OUTSTANDING_CONFIRMS)
    );

    while (!stoppingToken.IsCancellationRequested)
```

```
    {
        try
        {
            var factory = new ConnectionFactory()
                  { HostName = "localhost" };
            using (var connection = await
              factory.CreateConnectionAsync())
            using (var channel = await
              connection.CreateChannelAsync(channelOpts))
            {
                await channel.QueueDeclareAsync(
                  queue: "purchase_queue",
                  durable: true,
                  exclusive: false,
                  autoDelete: false,
                  arguments: null);
                await channel.BasicQosAsync(
                  prefetchSize: 0, prefetchCount: 1, global: false);

                var consumer =
                  new AsyncEventingBasicConsumer(channel);
                consumer.ReceivedAsync += async (sender, ea) =>
                {
                    …
                };

                await channel.BasicConsumeAsync(
                  queue: "purchase_queue",
                  autoAck: false,
                  consumer: consumer,
                  cancellationToken: stoppingToken);
                await Task.Delay(1000, stoppingToken);
            }
        }
        catch { }
    }
}
```

Inside the main loop, if an exception is thrown, it is intercepted by the empty catch. Since the two using statements are left, both the connection and channel are disposed of. Therefore, after the exception, a new loop is executed that creates a new fresh connection and a new channel.

In the using statement body, we ensure that our queue exists and then set `prefetch` to 1. This means that each server must extract just one message at a time, which ensures a fair distribution of the load among all servers.

However, setting prefetch to 1 might not be convenient when servers are based on several parallel threads since it sacrifices thread usage optimization in favor of fair distribution among servers. Therefore, threads that could successfully process further messages (after the first) might remain idle.

Then, we define a message received event handler. `BasicConsumeAsync` starts the actual message reception. With `autoAck` set to false, when a message is read from the queue, it is not removed but just blocked, so it is not available to other servers that read from the same queue. The message is actually removed when a confirmation that it has been successfully processed is sent to RabbitMQ. We can also send a failure confirmation, in which case the message is unblocked and becomes available for processing again.

If no confirmation is received, the message remains blocked until the connection and channel are disposed of.

`BasicConsumeAsync` remains blocked until `stoppingToken` is signalled, that is, until the application is shut down.

Let's move on to the code inside the 'message received' event. This is the place where the actual message processing takes place.

As a first step, the code verifies if the application is being shut down, in which case it disposes of the channel and connection and returns without performing any further operations:

```
if (stoppingToken.IsCancellationRequested)
{
    channel.Dispose();
    connection.Dispose();
    return;
}
```

Then, a session scope is created to access all session-scoped dependency injection services:

```
using (var scope = services.CreateScope())
{
  try
  {
  // actual message processing
  ...
  }
  catch {
    try
    {
      await ((AsyncEventingBasicConsumer)sender)
        .Channel.BasicNackAsync(ea.DeliveryTag, false, true);
    }
    catch { }
  }
}
```

When an exception is thrown during the message processing, a `Nack` message is sent to RabbitMQ to inform it that the message processing failed. `ea.DeliveryTag` is a tag that uniquely identifies the message. The second argument set to `false` informs RabbitMQ that the Nack is just for the message identified by `ea.DeliveryTag` and doesn't also involve all other messages waiting for confirmation from this server. Finally, the last argument set to `true` asks RabbitMQ to requeue the message whose processing failed.

Inside the try block, we get an instance of the command handler:

```
var handler = scope.ServiceProvider
  .GetRequiredService<ICommandHandler<PurchaseCommand>>();
```

Then, we deserialize the message body to get a `PurchaseMessage` instance and pass it to the command handler:

```
var body = ea.Body.ToArray();
PurchaseMessage? message = null;
using (var stream = new MemoryStream(body))
{
    message = PurchaseMessage.Parser.ParseFrom(stream);
}
bool success = false;
try
{
    await handler.HandleAsync(new PurchaseCommand(new PurchaseInfoDTO
    {
        Cost = message.Cost,
        MessageId = Guid.Parse(message.Id),
        Location = message.Location,
        PurchaseTime = message.PurchaseTime.ToDateTimeOffset(),
        Time = message.Time.ToDateTimeOffset()
    }));
    success=true;
}
catch
{
    success = false;
}
```

If the operation fails, we send a Nack; otherwise, we send an Ack:

```
if (success)
    await ((AsyncEventingBasicConsumer)sender).Channel
        .BasicAckAsync(ea.DeliveryTag, false);
else
```

```
    await ((AsyncEventingBasicConsumer)sender).Channel
        .BasicNackAsync(ea.DeliveryTag, false, true);
```

That's all! The full code is in the `GrpcMicroServiceRabbitProto` subfolder of the `ch14` folder in the GitHub repository of this book. You can test the code by setting both the client and server projects as the start project and running the solution. After 1-2 minutes, the database should be populated with new purchases and new daily totals. In a staging/production environment, you can run several copies of both the client and server.

Now that we have created a microservice connected to a message broker, it is also important to learn how to expose packages from WWTravelClub using Web APIs. Let's see this in the next section.

Exposing WWTravelClub packages using Web APIs

Exposing WWTravelClub functionalities through Web APIs is not simply a technical integration choice, but an architectural strategy that enables scalability, service decoupling, interoperability, and independent evolution of distributed components. APIs define stable communication boundaries between frontend applications, external consumers, mobile clients, and backend services, helping the platform evolve without tightly coupling all application layers together.

In the WWTravelClub scenario, APIs also support operational flexibility by enabling independent deployment cycles, horizontal scaling, centralized security policies, and integration with cloud-native monitoring and gateway solutions. These characteristics become especially important as the platform grows in both geographic reach and number of concurrent users.

For this reason, we will implement an ASP.NET REST service that lists all the packages that are available for a given vacation's start and end dates. For didactic purposes, we will not structure the application according to the best practices described in *Chapter 7, Understanding the Different Domains in Software Solutions*; instead, we will simply generate the results with a LINQ query that will be directly placed in the controller action method. Well-structured ASP.NET Core applications have been presented in *Chapter 14, Implementing Microservices with .NET* and *Chapter 17, Implementing Frontend Microservices with ASP.NET Core.*

Let us make a copy of the `WWTravelClubDB` solution folder and rename the new folder `WWTravelClubWebAPI`. The `WWTravelClubDB` project was built step by step in the various sections of *Chapter 13, Interacting with Data in C# – Entity Framework Core.* Let us open the new solution and add a new ASP.NET Core API project to it named `WWTravelClubWebAPI` (the same name as the new solution folder). For simplicity, select **No Authentication**. However, ensure that **Enable OpenApi support** and **Use controllers** are checked.

Right-click on the newly created project and select **Set as Startup project** to make it the default project that is launched when the solution is run.

Finally, we need to add a reference to the `WWTravelClubDB` project.

ASP.NET Core projects store configuration constants in the `appsettings.json` file. Let's open this file and add the database connection string for the database we created in the `WWTravelClubDB` project to it as shown here:

```
{
    "ConnectionStrings": {
```

```
        "DefaultConnection": "Server=
    (localdb)\\mssqllocaldb;Database=wwtravelclub;
Trusted_Connection=True;MultipleActiveResultSets=true"
    },
    ...
    ...
}
```

Now, we must add the `WWTravelClubDB` entity framework database context to `Program.cs` as shown here:

```
builder.Services.AddDbContext<WWTravelClubDB.MainDBContext>(options =>
    options.UseSqlServer(
      builder.Configuration.GetConnectionString("DefaultConnection"),
            b =>b.MigrationsAssembly("WWTravelClubDB")))
```

The option object settings that are passed to `AddDbContext` specify the usage of SQL Server with a connection string that is extracted from the `ConnectionStrings` section of the `appsettings.json` configuration file with the `Configuration.GetConnectionString("DefaultConnection")` method. The `b =>b.MigrationsAssembly("WWTravelClubDB")` lambda function declares the name of the assembly that contains the database migrations (see *Chapter 13, Interacting with Data in C# – Entity Framework Core*), which, in our case, is the DLL that was generated by the `WWTravelClubDB` project. For the preceding code to compile, you should add the `Microsoft.EntityFrameworkCore` and `WWTravelClubDB` namespaces.

To test our API interactively, we must add a NuGet package that uses the OpenApi document generated by ASP.net Core to automatically create a web interface for interacting with our Web API.

The most popular packages are **SwaggerUI** and **Scalar**. We will use SwaggerUI, so let's add a reference to the `Swashbuckle.AspNetCore.SwaggerUi` NuGet package.

The user interface endpoint is added through a `app.UseSwaggerU(…)` call in `Program.cs`. Since the UI interface must be added only in development mode, we may modify the `Program.cs` code as follows:

```
var app = builder.Build();
…
if (app.Environment.IsDevelopment())
{
    app.MapOpenApi();

    app.UseSwaggerUI(options =>
    {
        options.SwaggerEndpoint("/openapi/v1.json", "v1");
    });

}
```

```
...
app.Run();
```

The two SwaggerEndpoint arguments specify, respectively, the path to the OpenApi documentation and the name shown in the user interface.

Now, we are ready to encode our service. Let's delete the WeatherForecastController, which is automatically scaffolded by Visual Studio. Then, right-click on the **Controllers** folder and select **Add | Controller**. Now, choose an empty API controller and name it, PackagesController. First, let's modify the code as follows:

```
[Route("api/packages")]
[ApiController]
public class PackagesController : ControllerBase
{
    [HttpGet("bydate/{start}/{stop}")]
    [ProducesResponseType<IEnumerable<PackagesListDTO>>(200)]
    [ProducesResponseType<ValidationProblem>(400)]
    [ProducesResponseType(500)]
    public async Task<IActionResult> GetPackagesByDate(
        [FromServices] WWTravelClubDB.MainDBContext ctx,
        DateTime start, DateTime stop)
    {
    }
}
```

The Route attribute declares that the basic path for our service will be api/packages. The unique action method that we implement is GetPackagesByDate, which is invoked on HttpGet requests on paths of the bydate/{start}/{stop} type, where start and stop are the DateTime parameters that are passed as input to GetPackagesByDate. The ProduceResponseType<> and ProduceResponseType attributes declare the following:

- When a request is successful, a 200 code is returned, and the body contains an IEnumerable of the PackagesListDTO (which we will soon define) type containing the required package information.
- When the request is ill-formed, a 400 code is returned. Bad requests are automatically handled by the ASP.NET Core validation component which return a ValidationProblem instance that contains all detected errors.
- In the case of unexpected errors, a 500 code is returned with the exception error message.

Now, let's define the PackagesListDTO class in a new DTOs folder:

```
namespace WWTravelClubWebAPI.DTOs;
public record PackagesListDTO
{
    public int Id { get; set; }
    public required string Name { get; set; }
```

```
    public decimal Price { get; set; }
    public int DurationInDays { get; set; }
    public DateTime? StartValidityDate { get; set; }
    public DateTime? EndValidityDate { get; set; }
    public required string DestinationName { get; set; }
    public int DestinationId { get; set; }
}
```

Finally, let's add the following using clauses to our controller code so that we can easily refer to our DTO, to Entity Framework LINQ methods, and to predefined controller results:

```
using Microsoft.EntityFrameworkCore;
using WWTravelClubWebAPI.DTOs;
using Microsoft.AspNetCore.Http.HttpResults;
```

Now, we are ready to fill the body of the `GetPackagesByDate` method with the following code.

```
try
{
    var res = await ctx.Packages
        .Where(m => start >= m.StartValidityDate
&&stop<= m.EndValidityDate)
        .Select(m => new PackagesListDTO
        {
            StartValidityDate = m.StartValidityDate,
            EndValidityDate = m.EndValidityDate,
            Name = m.Name,
            DurationInDays = m.DurationInDays,
            Id = m.Id,
            Price = m.Price,
            DestinationName = m.MyDestination.Name,
            DestinationId = m.DestinationId
        })
        .ToListAsync();
    return Ok(res);
}
catch (Exception err)
{
    return StatusCode(500, err.ToString());
}
```

The LINQ query is like the one contained in the `WWTravelClubDBTest` project we tested in *Chapter 13, Interacting with Data in C# – Entity Framework Core*. Once the result has been computed, it is returned with an `OK` call. The method's code handles internal server errors by catching exceptions and returning a 500-status code. Since bad requests are automatically handled bay ASP.NET Core validation before the Controller method is called we don't need to add code for handling bad requests.

Let's run the solution and open the browser on `https://localhost:<service port>/swagger`. It is worth mentioning that you can also configure your local settings file to either launch or go to the Swagger UI URL automatically.

The user interface of the OpenAPI documentation will look as follows:

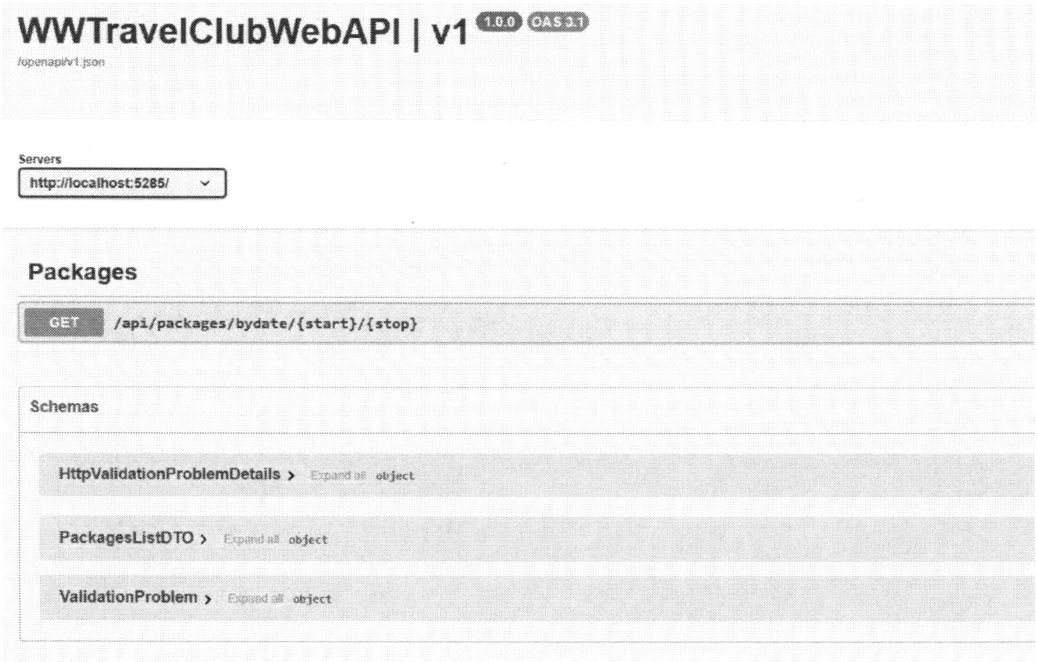

Figure 22.14: Swagger UI

`PackagesListDTO` is the model we defined to list the packages, while `ProblemDetails` is the model that is used to report errors in the event of bad requests. By clicking the GET button, we can get more details about our GET method and we can also test it, as shown in the following screenshot:

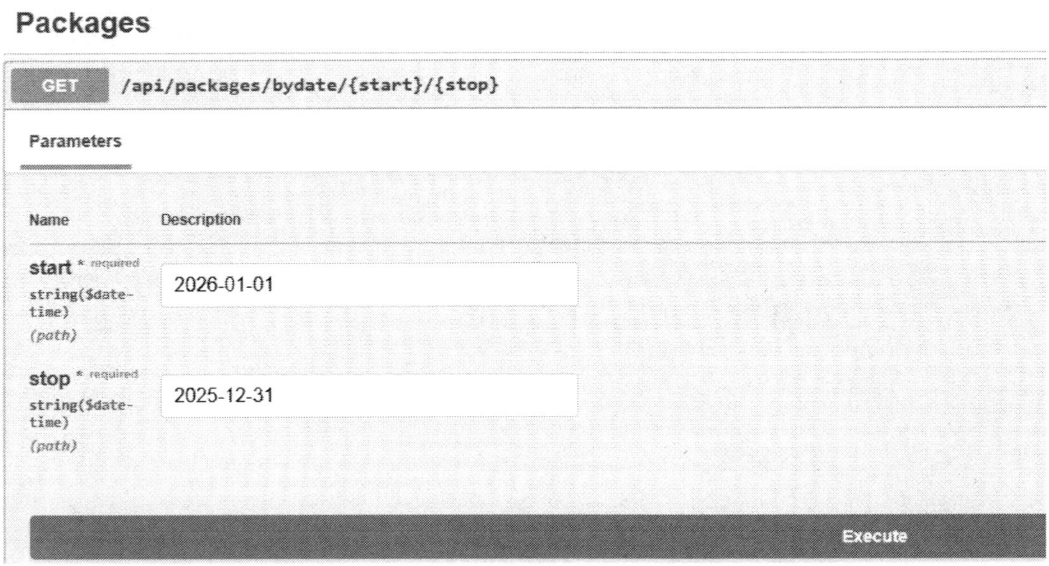

Figure 22.15: GET method details

Pay attention when it comes to inserting dates that are covered by packages in the database; otherwise, an empty list will be returned.

Dates must be entered in a correct JSON format; otherwise, a 400 Bad Request error is returned, like the one shown in the following code:

```
{
  "type": "https://tools.ietf.org/html/rfc9110#section-15.5.1",
  "title": "One or more validation errors occurred.",
  "status": 400,
  "errors": {
    "start": [
      "The value '2026' is not valid."
    ]
  },
  "traceId": "00-5a79f74eb3a95d67029a6956d9e3d635-de742b5240fa8253-00"
}
```

If you insert the correct input parameters, the Swagger UI returns the packages that satisfy the query in JSON format.

That is all! You have implemented your first API with OpenAPI documentation!

It is time to move to the implementation of a worker microservice with ASP.NET core.

A worker microservice with ASP.NET Core

In this section, we will show you how to implement a microservice that receives communications through gRPC and an internal queue based on a database table. The example is a part of the WWTravelClub book use case. The first subsection briefly describes the microservice specifications and the overall architecture. The reader is encouraged to review *Chapter 15, Implementing Microservices with .NET*, which contains all the theory behind this example.

The specifications and architecture

Our example microservice is required to compute the daily sums of all purchases. According to the data-driven approach, we suppose that all daily sums are pre-computed by receiving messages that are sent as soon as a new purchase is finalized. The purpose of the microservice is to maintain a database of all purchases and of all daily sums that can be queried by an administrative user. We will implement just the functionalities needed to fill the two database tables.

The implementation described in this section is based on an ASP.NET Core application that hosts a gRPC service. The gRPC service simply fills a message queue and immediately returns to avoid the sender remaining blocked for the whole time of the computation.

The actual processing is performed by an ASP.NET Core-hosted service declared in the dependency injection engine associated with the application host. The worker-hosted service executes an endless loop where it extracts N messages from the queue and passes them to N parallel threads that process them.

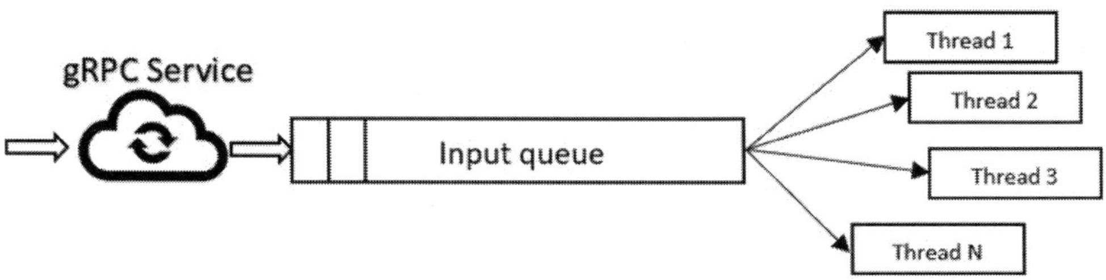

Figure 22.16: gRPC microservice architecture

When the N messages are taken from the queue, they are not immediately removed but are simply marked with the extraction time. Since messages can only be extracted from the queue if their last extraction time is far enough ahead (say, a time T), no other worker thread can extract them again while they are being processed. When message processing is successfully completed, the message is removed from the queue. If the processing fails, no action is taken on the message, so the message remains blocked in the queue until the T interval expires, and then it can be picked up again by the worker thread.

The microservice can be scaled vertically by increasing the processor cores and the number N of threads. It can be scaled horizontally, too, by using a load balancer that splits the loads to several identical copies of the ASP.NET Core application. This kind of horizontal scaling increases the number of threads that can receive messages and the number of worker threads, but since all ASP.NET Core applications share the same database, it is limited by database performance.

The service will be implemented with Onion Architecture and related patterns described in *Chapter 7, Understanding the Different Domains in Software Solutions.*

The domain model layer is implemented in a separate DLL and contains three aggregates: one that abstracts the request queue, and the others that abstract each purchase and each daily purchase information. The domain services layer, implemented with another DLL, defines the three repository interfaces associated with the three aggregates defined in the domain model layer.

Application services contain two commands with their implementation, one for adding a new queue item and the other for updating purchases and daily purchases.

Finally, the outermost layer takes care of communications, and of attaching the domain layer with a DBDriver based on Entity Framework Core. It is implemented with an ASP .NET gRPC service project template.

The full code is available in the `ch14/GrpcMicroService` folder of the GitHub repository associated with the book.

Let's start creating the whole code! As a first step, let's create an empty Visual Studio Solution called `GrpcMicroService`, then we will add all project libraries that implement the various layers and drivers of the Onion Architecture. Creating an empty solution is easy: just select **Create a new project** and then write "*Blank*" in the search box; the **Blank Solution** template should appear in the list of project templates.

Next subsection describes the domain layer, that is both domain model and model services. We will not give all the details since the focus of the example is the microservice architecture and the communication technique. However, the full code is available in the `ch14/GrpcMicroService` folder of the GitHub repository associated with the book.

The Domain Layer

Let's add two C# library projects called `WorkerMDomainModel` and `WorkerMDomainServices` to the previously created solution; they will implement respectively the Domain Model and Domain Services layers. Delete the two Class1.cs files automatically scaffolded by Visual Studio and do the following:

1. Add `WorkerMDomainServices` as a reference to `WorkerMDomainModel`
2. Copy the content of the GitHub repository `ch07/OnionArchitecture/ DomainModel` folder and paste it in the root of the `WorkerMDomainModel` project
3. Copy the content of the GitHub repository `ch07/OnionArchitecture/ DomainServices` folder and paste it in the root of the `WorkerMDomainServices` project

You should obtain the following structure:

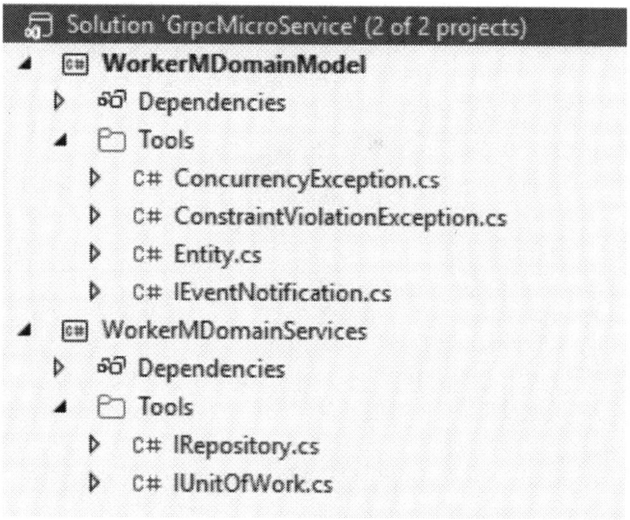

Figure 22.17: gRPC worker microservice Domain layer

The two exceptions are just useful tools to signal database concurrency and constraint violation database errors.

`Entity.cs` contains the `Entity<T>` abstract generic class that factors out all common features of all aggregates. All our aggregates will inherit from this class. `Entity<T>` was described in the *DDD Entities in .NET* and *Command handlers and Aggregate events* subsections of *Chapter 7, Understanding the Different Domains in Software Solutions*. `IEventNotification`, instead, is an empty interface that represents the domain events described in *Domain events* and *Command handlers and Aggregate events* subsections of *Chapter 7, Understanding the Different Domains in Software Solutions*.

In the `WorkerMDomainServices` project, `IRepository` is an empty interface that marks all repository interfaces so they can be easily found by automatic repository discovery tools based on reflection. All repository interfaces defined in the `WorkerMDomainServices` will inherit from it. `IUnitOfWork` is the interface described in the *Unit of work pattern* section of *Chapter 7, Understanding the Different Domains in Software Solutions*.

Purchase Information received through messages is moved to the Domain layer through a **DTO** (Data Transfer Object) called `PurchaseInfoDTO`:

```
public class PurchaseInfoDTO
{
    public DateTimeOffset Time { get; set; }
    public DateTimeOffset PurchaseTime { get; set; }
    public required string Location { get; set; }
    public decimal Cost { get; set; }
    public Guid MessageId { get; set; }
}
```

Where PurchaseTime, Location, and Cost are purchase-specific data, while Time is the time the message was created, and MessageId is a Guid that univocally identifies each message.

We will add the above class to a DTOs folder created in the WorkerMDomainServices project.

Let's add also a Models folder to WorkerMDomainModel. We will place there our aggregates together with their state interfaces.

Our aggregates are:

- QueueItemAggregate that represents a queue item. Its associated state interface is IQueueItem.
- PurchaseAggregate that represents a single purchase. Its associated state interface is IPurchase.
- DayTotalAggregate that represents the total of all purchases performed in each day. Its associated state interface is IDayTotal.

As an example, we give the definition of QueueItemAggregate and its state interface; all other aggregates are available with the complete microservice project in the ch14 folder of the GitHub repository associated with the book:

```
public interface IQueueItem
{
    long Id {get; set;}
    DateTimeOffset Time {get; set;}
    DateTimeOffset PurchaseTime {get; set;}
    DateTimeOffset ExtractionTime {get; set;}
    public string Location {get; set;}
    public decimal Cost {get; set;}
    public Guid MessageId {get; set;}
}
public class QueueItemAggregate(IQueueItem state)
{
    public long Id => state.Id;
    public DateTimeOffset Time => state.Time;
    public DateTimeOffset PurchaseTime => state.PurchaseTime;
    public DateTimeOffset ExtractionTime => state.ExtractionTime;
    public string Location => state.Location;
    public decimal Cost => state.Cost;
    public Guid MessageId => state.MessageId;
    public void MarkExtraction(DateTimeOffset time)
    {
        state.ExtractionTime = time;
    }
}
```

Just the `ExtractionTime` property of the aggregate can be modified through the `MarkExtraction` method, which is set with the time the item is extracted by the queue. It is needed for the algorithm that ensures a safe queue item processing we will explain later on in this section. All other properties belong to the original message and can't be modified.

Together with DTOs, `WorkerMDomainServices` contains all repository interfaces that are placed in a `IRepositories` folder. Below is the `IQueueItemRepository` interface associated with the `QueueItemAggregate` aggregate:

```
public interface IQueueItemRepository: IRepository
{
    public Task<IList<QueueItemAggregate>> Top(int n, int minutesBlocked);
    public Task Dequeue(IEnumerable<QueueItemAggregate> items);
    public QueueItemAggregate Enqueue(PurchaseInfoDTO messageInfo);
}
```

`Top` extracts the N messages to pass to a maximum of N different threads. `minutesBlocked` is the number of minutes a queue item remains inaccessible after it has been extracted. After this timeout expires, the service assumes that its processing failed and makes the queue item available for another processing attempt. This is our service's main technique to prevent data losses.

`Enqueue` creates a new queue item and adds it to the queue. It takes the needed message info from the `PurchaseInfoDTO` instance that is passed.

Finally, `Dequeue` removes the items that have been successfully processed from the queue.

Each repository inherits from the empty `IRepository` interface, which is used to mark all repository implementations so that they can be easily found through reflection and automatically added to the dependency injection engine.

The interface that updates the daily purchase totals is defined as shown below:

```
public interface IDayTotalRepository: IRepository
{
    DayTotalAggregate New(DateTimeOffset day);
    Task<DayTotalAggregate?> Get(DateTimeOffset day);
}
```

While `New` creates a new daily total, `Get` retrieves an existing one. In both cases, the `Add` method of the aggregate can be used to add a new purchase to the running total:

```
public  class DayTotalAggregate(IDayTotal state)
{
    public DateTimeOffset Id => state.Id;
    public decimal Total => state.Total;
```

```
    public void Add(decimal purchaseCost)
    {
        state.Total += purchaseCost;
    }
    public void Reset()
    {
        state.Total = 0m;
    }
}
```

The `IPurchaseRepository` associated with `PurchaseAggregate` is similar:

```
public interface IPurchaseRepository: IRepository
{
    PurchaseAggregate New(PurchaseInfoDTO message);
    Task<PurchaseAggregate?> Get(Guid messageId);
}
```

While `New` creates a new purchase, taking the needed information from a `PurchaseInfoDTO` instance, `Get` retrieves an existing purchase from its message id.

The next subsection describes the DB driver that is based on Entity Framework Core.

The DB driver

The DB driver can be implemented with an Entity Framework Core-based library, so let's add a new library project called `WorkerMDBDriver` to our solution. Then let's add a reference to `WorkerMDomainServices` so it can implement all interfaces of both the Domain model and Domain services.

Now, as in all Entity Framework Core projects based on SQL Server, add a reference to the `Microsoft.EntityFrameworkCore.SqlServer` and `Microsoft.EntityFrameworkCore.Tools` NuGet packages.

Finally, delete the class that Visual Studio automatically creates, and copy the content of the GitHub repository `ch07/OnionArchitecture/DBDriver` folder into its root.

We will have a `DBContext` called `MainDbContext` that already implements the `IUnitOfWork` interface.

The `Extensions` folder contains the `AddDbDriver` extension method that add all DB driver implementations to the dependency injection engine. We will call it in the gRPC ASP.NET Core projects that implements the outermost level of our microservice Onion architecture:

```
    public static IServiceCollection AddDbDriver(
        this IServiceCollection services,
        string connectionString)
    {
        services.AddDbContext<IUnitOfWork, MainDbContext>(options =>
            options.UseSqlServer(connectionString,
```

```
                b =>
                b.MigrationsAssembly(typeof(DBExtensions)
                 .Assembly.GetName().Name)));
        services.AddAllRepositories(typeof(DBExtensions).Assembly);
        return services;
    }
}
```

There, we call `AddDbContext` to activate all Entity Framework functionalities. `MainDbContext` has been declared internal and is injected behind the `IUnitOfWork` interface to keep all layers independent from the DB driver. The first argument of `UseSqlServer` is passed the connection string, while its second argument specifies which library contains the database migrations. In our case, we specify the assembly that contains the `DBExtensions` type, that is, the `WorkerMDBDriver` dll itself.

The `AddAllRepositories` method uses reflection to add all repository interfaces whose implementations are contained in the assembly it is passed as an argument. Its code is contained in the `Extensions/RepositoryExtensions.cs` file. There, repository implementations are recognized by the fact that they implement `IRepository`:

```
var repositories = assembly.GetTypes()
    .Where(x => !x.IsAbstract && x.IsClass
&&typeof(IRepository).IsAssignableFrom(x));
```

Let's add a folder called `Models` where we will place all database entities. Each entity must implement the state interface of its associated aggregate. Below is the definition of the `QueueItem` entity; all other entities are available with the full microservice code in the `ch14` folder of the GitHub repository associated with the book:

```
[Index(nameof(Time))]
[Index(nameof(ExtractionTime))]

public class QueueItem:IQueueItem
{
    public long Id { get; set; }
    public DateTimeOffset Time { get; set; }
    public DateTimeOffset PurchaseTime { get; set; }
    public DateTimeOffset ExtractionTime { get; set; }
    [MaxLength(128), Required]
    public required string Location { get; set; }
    public decimal Cost { get; set; }
    public Guid MessageId { get; set; }
}
```

After adding all entities, we can add the following properties to the `MainDbContext` class:

```
public DbSet<DayTotal> DayTotals { get; set; }
public DbSet<QueueItem> QueueItems { get; set; }
public DbSet<Purchase> Purchases { get; set; }
```

Before generating database migrations we must add a `IDesignTimeDbContextFactory<MainDbContext>` implementation. You can find its code together with the whole microservice code in the `ch14` folder of the Book GitHub repository (check if the SQL instance name in the connection string corresponds to the instance you have on your computer).

The database project, called `WorkerMDBDriver`, is contained in the `ch14/GrpcMicroService` folder of the GitHub repository associated with the book. It already contains all the necessary database migrations, so if you copy the DB driver from there, you can create the needed database with the steps below:

1. In the Visual Studio Package Manager Console, select the `WorkerMDBDriver` project
2. In Visual Studio Solution Explorer, right-click on the `WorkerMDBDriver` project and set it as the startup project
3. In the Visual Studio Package Manager Console, issue the `Update-Database` command

If instead, you implemented the DB driver yourself, you must execute the following command immediately after step 2 and before step 3:

```
Add-Migration initial
```

Let's also add a Repositories folder where we can place all repository implementations. Here, we will describe just the `IQueueItemRepository` implementation:

```
internal class QueueItemRepository : IQueueItemRepository
{
    private readonly MainDbContext ctx;
    public QueueItemRepository(IUnitOfWork uw)
    {
        ctx = (MainDbContext)uw;
    }
    public async Task Dequeue(IEnumerable<QueueItemAggregate> items)
    {
     ...
    }

    public QueueItemAggregate Enqueue(PurchaseInfoDTO messageInfo)
    {
...
    }
```

```
    public async Task<IList<QueueItemAggregate>>
  Top(int n, int minutesBlocked)
    {
...
    }
}
```

In its constructor, the repository implementation is injected the `IUnityOfWork` interface, which it casts to its implementation `MainDbContext`. This is the only way to get a proper `MainDbContext` instance since `MainDbContext` is exposed in the dependency injection engine behind the `IUnityOfWork` interface.

Top extracts just the queue items that weren't already extracted before `minutesBlocked`:

```
public async Task<IList<QueueItemAggregate>> Top(int n, int minutesBlocked)
{
    var limit = DateTimeOffset.Now.AddMinutes(-minutesBlocked);
    var states = await ctx.QueueItems
        .OrderByDescending(m => m.Time)
        .Where(m => m.ExtractionTime < limit)
        .ToListAsync();
    return states.Select(m => new QueueItemAggregate(m)).ToList();
}
```

Before being returned all items are transformed into aggregates by calling the aggregate constructor and passing the entity in its constructor.

Once successfully processed items are removed from the queue with `Dequeue`:

```
public async Task Dequeue(IEnumerable<QueueItemAggregate> items)
{
    var states = items.Select(async m => await ctx.QueueItems.FindAsync(new
object[m.Id])).ToList();
    foreach (var tItem in states)
    {
        var item = await tItem;
        if(item != null)
            ctx.QueueItems.Remove(item);
    }
}
```

Since the method is passed the aggregates instead of the actual entity, it must retrieve the entities to delete through their principal keys, which are the same as the aggregate principal key. It does this job with `FindAsync`.

The Enqueue method just creates an entity, adds it to the in-memory table cache and returns its associated aggregate:

```
public QueueItemAggregate Enqueue(PurchaseInfoDTO messageInfo)
{
    var toAdd = new QueueItem
    {
        Cost= messageInfo.Cost,
        ExtractionTime= DateTimeOffset.MinValue,
        MessageId= messageInfo.MessageId,
        Location= messageInfo.Location,
        Time= messageInfo.Time,
        PurchaseTime= messageInfo.PurchaseTime,
    };
    ctx.QueueItems.Add(toAdd);
    return new QueueItemAggregate(toAdd);
}
```

Please notice that no method passes changes to the database by calling `await ctx.SaveChangesAsync` because handling transactions is the responsibility of the Application services layer that we are going to discuss in the next subsection.

Application services

Application services are implemented as another class library added to our solution. Let's call it `WorkerMApplicationServices`. As a first step, remove the class automatically scaffolded by Visual Studio, and copy the content of the GitHub repository `ch07/OnionArchitecture/ApplicationServices` folder into the project root. The `Extensions/HandlersDIExtensions.cs` contains the `AddApplicationServices` extension method that uses reflection to retrieve all command handlers, event handlers, and queries contained in an assembly to the dependency injection engine. It also adds the `EventMediator` defined in the `tools/EventMediator.cs` file to the dependency injection engine.

The `EventMediator` must be injected in all command handlers that need to trigger all event handlers associated with some aggregates. It is enough to call its `TriggerEvents(IEnumerable<IEventNotification>events)` passing it all events associated with any aggregate.

The other classes and interfaces defined in the `tools` folder are:

- `EventTrigger`, that is a class needed by `EventMediator`
- `ICommand` which is an empty interface that marks all commans so that they can be easily found with reflection

- `ICommandHandler<T>` is the interface that must be implemented by all command handlers, where `T` is the associated `ICommand`
- `IEventHandler<T>` is the interface that must be implemented by all event handlers, where `T` is the associated event (`IEventNotification`)

Since the dependency injection extension methods defined in `Extensions/HandlersDIExtensions.cs` need an abstraction of the dependency injection, we must add a reference to the `Microsoft.Extensions.DependencyInjection.Abstractions` NuGet package.

Finally, we must add a reference to the `WorkerMDomainServices` project so that all command and event handlers can use all repository interfaces and can manipulate all event handlers.

Let's add a `Commands` folder to place all commands, and a `Handlers` folder to place all command and event handlers.

Our simple microservice has no events and a single command that processes an incoming purchase message:

```
public class PurchaseCommand(PurchaseInfoDTO purchase): ICommand
{
    public PurchaseInfoDTO Purchase => purchase;
}
```

The associated handler is:

```
internal class PurchaseCommandHandler(
    IPurchaseRepository purchaseRepo,
    IDayTotalRepository dayTotalRepo,
    IUnitOfWork uow) : ICommandHandler<PurchaseCommand>
{
    public async Task HandleAsync(PurchaseCommand command)
    {
        var purchase=command.Purchase;
        await uow.StartAsync();
        try
        {
            var existing = await purchaseRepo.Get(purchase.MessageId);
            if (existing != null)
            {
                await uow.RollbackAsync();
                return;
            }
            else
            {
                var day = await
                    dayTotalRepo.Get(purchase.PurchaseTime);
```

```
                if (day == null)
                    day = dayTotalRepo.New(purchase.PurchaseTime);
                day.Add(purchase.Cost);
                purchaseRepo.New(purchase);
                await uow.SaveEntitiesAsync();
                await uow.CommitAsync();
            }
        }
        catch
        {
            await uow.RollbackAsync();
            throw;
        }

    }
}
```

The whole processing must be performed in a transaction scope to prevent interference from other threads that process other purchases.

If the purchase is already in the database, the message received is a duplicate and must not be processed.

Otherwise, the day associated with the purchase is retrieved, or created if it doesn't already exist, and the purchase cost is added to the day statistics. At this point all changes are passed to the database with await `uow.SaveEntitiesAsync()` and the transaction is committed.

In case of errors, the transaction is rolled back and any exception is passed to the caller.

The whole queue handling is not part of the business logic, so it must be included in the application services, but must be moved to the outermost layer that contains all environment dependencies and that will be described in the next subsection.

The Outermost Layer

The outermost layer is an ASP.NET Core gRPC service project called `GrpcMicroService`. Let's add it to our solution. Then, let's add it a reference to both `WorkerMApplicationServices` and `WorkerMDBDriver`.

When the project is scaffolded by Visual Studio, it contains a `.proto` file in its `Protos` folder. This file needs to be deleted and replaced by a file called `counting.proto`, whose content must be

```
syntax = "proto3";
option csharp_namespace = "GrpcMicroService";
import "google/protobuf/timestamp.proto";
package counting;
service Counter {
  // Accepts a conting request
  rpc Count (CountingRequest) returns (CountingReply);
```

```
}
message CountingRequest {
  string id = 1;
  google.protobuf.Timestamp time = 2;
  string location = 3;
  sint32 cost =4;
  google.protobuf.Timestamp purchaseTime = 5;
}.
message CountingReply {}
```

The above code defines the gRPC service with its input and output messages and the .NET namespace where to place them. We import the "google/protobuf/timestamp.proto" predefined .proto file because we need the TimeStamp type. The request contains purchase data, the time when the request message was created, and a unique message id that is used to force message idempotency.

Automatic code generation for this file is enabled by replacing the existing protobuf XML tag with:

```
<Protobuf Include="Protos\counting.proto" GrpcServices="Server" />
```

The Grpc attribute set to "Server" enables server-side code generation.

In the Services project folder, the predefined gRPC service scaffolded by Visual Studio must be replaced with a file named CounterService.cs with the content below:

```
public class CounterService: Counter.CounterBase
{
    private readonly IQueueItemRepository _queue;
    private readonly IUnitOfWork _uow;
    public CounterService(IQueueItemRepository queue,
        IUnitOfWork uow)
    {
        _queue = queue;
        _uow = uow;
    }
    public override async Task<CountingReply> Count(
        CountingRequest request,
        ServerCallContext context)
    {
        _queue.Enqueue(
          new WorkerMDomainServices.DTOs.PurchaseInfoDTO
          {
              Cost = request.Cost,
              MessageId = Guid.Parse(request.Id),
              Location = request.Location,
```

```
                PurchaseTime =
                 request.PurchaseTime.ToDateTimeOffset(),
                Time = request.Time.ToDateTimeOffset()
            });
        await _uow.SaveEntitiesAsync();
        return new CountingReply { };
    }

}
```

The actual service that receives the purchase messages inherits from the `Counter.CounterBase` abstract class created by the code generator from the `counting.proto` file. It receives the `IMessageQueue` repository interface and the `IUnitOfWork` interface through dependency injection and overrides the abstract `Count` method inherited from `Counter.CounterBase`. Then, `Count` uses `IMessageQueue` to enqueue each received message.

Before compiling, a few other steps are necessary:

1. In `Program.cs` we must call the application services dependency injection extension method:

    ```
    builder.Services.AddApplicationServices();
    ```

2. We must add the database connection string to the appsettings.json settings file:

    ```
    "ConnectionStrings": {
            "DefaultConnection": "Server=(localdb)\
    \MSSQLLocalDB;Database=workermicroservice;Trusted_Connection=True;MultipleActiveR
    esultSets=true"
    }
    ```

3. We must add all the necessary database layer interfaces to the dependency injection by calling the `AddStorage` database layer extension method:

    ```
    builder.Services.AddStorage(
      builder.Configuration.
        GetConnectionString("DefaultConnection"));
    ```

4. In `Program.cs`, we must remove the declaration of the gRPC service scaffolded by Visual Studio, and we must replace it with:

    ```
    app.MapGrpcService<CounterService>();
    ```

At this point, compilation should succeed. Having completed the application layer infrastructure, we can move to the hosted service that performs the actual queue processing.

Processing the queued requests

The actual request processing is performed by a worker-hosted service that runs in parallel with the ASP.NET Core pipeline. It is implemented with the hosted services we discussed in the *Using generic hosts* section of *Chapter 11, Applying a Microservice Architecture to Your Enterprise Application*. It is worth recalling that hosted services are implementations of the `IHostedService` interface added to the dependency injection engine as follows:

```
builder.Services.AddHostedService<MyHostedService>();
```

We already described how to implement hosted services for the implementation of ASP.NET Core-based worker microservices in the *Implementing worker microservices with ASP.NET core section* of *Chapter 14, Implementing Microservices with .NET*.

Below we repeat the whole code with all details that are specific to our example. The hosted service is defined in the `ProcessPurchases.cs` file placed in the `HostedServices` folder:

```
public class ProcessPurchases: BackgroundService
{
    private const int MinuteBlocked = 3;
    readonly IServiceProvider _services;
    public ProcessPurchases(IServiceProvider services)
    {
        _services = services;
    }
    protected override async Task ExecuteAsync(CancellationToken stoppingToken)
    {
        bool queueEmpty = false;
        while (!stoppingToken.IsCancellationRequested && !queueEmpty)
        {
            // Code execution
            ...

            if (queueEmpty)
            {
                await Task.Delay(100, stoppingToken);
                queueEmpty = false;
            }
        }
    }
}
```

Below is the content of the inner loop:

```
using (var scope = _services.CreateScope())
{
    IQueueItemRepository queue = scope.ServiceProvider
          .GetRequiredService<IQueueItemRepository>();
    IUnitOfWork uow = scope.ServiceProvider
          .GetRequiredService<IUnitOfWork>();
    var toProcess = await queue.Top(10, MinuteBlocked);
    if (toProcess.Count > 0)
    {
        Task<QueueItemAggregate>[] tasks =
        new Task<QueueItemAggregate>[toProcess.Count];
        for (int i = 0; i < tasks.Length; i++)
        {
            var toExecute = async () =>
            {
                QueueItemAggregate item = toProcess[i];
                using (var sc = _services.CreateScope())
                {
                    var handler = sc.ServiceProvider
                      .GetRequiredService
                           <ICommandHandler<PurchaseCommand>>();
                    try
                    {
                        await handler.HandleAsync(
                         new PurchaseCommand(new PurchaseInfoDTO
                        {
                            Cost = item.Cost,
                            Location = item.Location,
                            MessageId = item.MessageId,
                            PurchaseTime = item.PurchaseTime,
                            Time = item.Time
                        }));
                        return item;
                    }
                    catch
                    {
                        return null;
                    }
                }
            };
            tasks[i] = toExecute();
        }
```

```
            await Task.WhenAll(tasks);
            var processed = tasks.Select(m => m.Result)
                .Where(m => m !=          null).ToList();
            if (processed.Count > 0)
            {
                await queue.Dequeue(processed);
                await uow.SaveEntitiesAsync();
            }
        }
        else queueEmpty = true;
    }
```

The above code was already explained microservices in the *Implementing worker microservices with ASP.NET Core* section of *Chapter 14, Implementing Microservices with .NET*. Therefore, here, we will analyze just the `toExecute` lambda that is specific to our example:

```
var toExecute = async () =>
{
    QueueItemAggregate item = toProcess[i];
    using (var sc = _services.CreateScope())
    {
        var handler = sc.ServiceProvider
         .GetRequiredService<ICommandHandler<PurchaseCommand>>();
        try
        {
            await handler.HandleAsync(
            new PurchaseCommand(new PurchaseInfoDTO
            {
                Cost = item.Cost,
                Location = item.Location,
                MessageId = item.MessageId,
                PurchaseTime = item.PurchaseTime,
                Time = item.Time
            }));
            return item;
        }
        catch
        {
            return null;
        }
    }
};
```

Each task creates a different session scope, so it can have a private copy of all repositories and command handlers, and then processes its request with `await handler.HandleAsync(…)`.

When a processing fails and throws an exception, `toExecute` returns null; otherwise, it returns the processed queue items.

Therefore, it is enough to filter all non-null results for deciding which queue items to remove from the queue:

```
var processed = tasks.Select(m => m.Result)
            .Where(m => m != null).ToList();
if (processed.Count > 0)
{
    await queue.Dequeue(processed);
    await uow.SaveEntitiesAsync();
}
```

That's all! Now we need a source of purchase data to test our code. In the next subsection, we will create a fake microservice that randomly creates purchase data and passes it to the Counter gRPC service.

Testing the gRPC Microservice project with a fake purchase request generator

Let's implement another microservice that feeds the previous microservice with randomly generated requests. The right project for a worker service that is not based on ASP.NET Core is the Worker Service project template. This project template automatically scaffolds a host containing a unique hosted service called `Worker`. We called this project `FakeSource`. In order to enable gRPC client usage, we must add the following NuGet packages: `Google.Protobuf`, `Grpc.NET.Client`, and `Grpc.Tools`.

Then, we must add the same `counting.proto` file as was added to the previous project. However, this time we must require client code generation by placing the code below in the `FakeSource` project file:

```
<ItemGroup>
    <Protobuf Include="..\GrpcMicroService\Protos\counting.proto" GrpcServices="Client">
      <Link>Protos\counting.proto</Link>
    </Protobuf>
 </ItemGroup>
```

The `GrpcServices` attribute set to Client is what enables client code generation instead of server code generation. The link tag appears since we added the same `counting.proto` file of the `GrpcMicroService` project as a link instead of copying it into the new project.

The hosted service is defined with the usual endless loop:

```
namespace FakeSource;
public class Worker : BackgroundService
{
```

```
    private readonly string[] locations = new string[]
           { "Florence", "London", "New York", "Paris" };
    protected override async Task ExecuteAsync(CancellationToken stoppingToken)
    {
        Random random = new Random();
        while (!stoppingToken.IsCancellationRequested)
        {
          try
          {
             ...
             await Task.Delay(2000, stoppingToken);
          }
          catch (OperationCanceledException)
          {
             return;
          }
          catch { }
        }
    }
}
```

The locations array contains locations that will be randomly selected. As soon as the `ExecuteAsync` method starts, it creates the `Random` instance that will be used in all random generations.

Each loop is enclosed in a `try/catch`; if an `OperationCanceledException` is generated, the method exits, since a similar exception is created when the application is being shut down and the thread is killed. In the case of other exceptions, the code tries to recover by simply moving to the next loop. In an actual production application, the final `catch` should contain instructions to log the intercepted exception and/or instructions for a better recovery strategy. In the next example, we will see more sophisticated exception handling that is adequate for actual production applications.

Inside the `try`, the code creates a purchase message and sends it to the Counter service, and then sleeps for 2 seconds.

Below is the code that sends the requests:

```
var purchaseDay = new DateTimeOffset(DateTime.UtcNow.Date, TimeSpan.Zero);
//randomize a little bit purchase day
purchaseDay = purchaseDay.AddDays(random.Next(0, 3) - 1);
//message time
var now = DateTimeOffset.UtcNow;
//add random location
var location = locations[random.Next(0, locations.Length)];
var messageId = Guid.NewGuid().ToString();
//add random cost
```

```
int cost = 200 * random.Next(1, 4);
//send message
using var channel = GrpcChannel.ForAddress("http://localhost:5071");
var client = new Counter.CounterClient(channel);
//since this is a fake random source
//in case of errors we simply do nothing.
//An actual client should use Polly
//to define retry policies
try
{
    await client.CountAsync(new CountingRequest
    {
        Id = messageId,
        Location = location,
        PurchaseTime = Timestamp.FromDateTimeOffset(purchaseDay),
        Time = Timestamp.FromDateTimeOffset(now),
        Cost = cost
    });

}
catch {}
```

The code just prepares the message with random data; then, it creates a communication channel for the gRPC server address and passes it to the constructor of the `Counter` service proxy.

Tip

Please, replace the port in the server address with the actual port used for HTTP in your server. You may find it in the `launchSettings.json` file of the `GrpcMicroservice` project.

Finally, the `Count` method is called on the proxy. The call is enclosed in a `try/catch`, and in the case of an error, the error is simply ignored, since we are just sending random data. Instead, an actual production application should use Polly to retry the communication with predefined strategies. Polly was described in the `Resilient task execution` section of *Chapter 11, Applying a Microservice Architecture to Your Enterprise Application*. We will show you how to use Polly in the example in the next section.

And there you have it! Now it is time to test everything. Right-click on the solution and select **Set Startup Projects**, then set both `FakeSource` and `GrpcMicroService` to start. This way, both projects will be launched simultaneously when the solution is run. Set the `GrpcMicroService` debug target to http.

Launch Visual Studio and then let both processes run for a couple of minutes, then go to **SQL Server Object Explorer** and look for a database called **workermicroservice**. If the **SQL Server Object Explorer** window is not available in the left menu of Visual Studio, go to the top **Window** menu and select it.

Once you have located the database, show the content of the `DayTotals` and `Purchases` tables. You should see all computed daily sums and all processed purchases.

You can also inspect what happens in the server project by opening the `HostedServices/ProcessPurchases.cs` file and placing breakpoints on the `queue.Top(10, MinuteBlocked)` and `await queue.Dequeue(...)` instructions.

You can also move `FakeSource` into a different Visual Studio solution so that you can simultaneously run several copies of `FakeSource`, each in a different Visual Studio instance. It is also possible to double-click on the `FakeSource` project, which gives the option to save a new Visual Studio solution containing just a reference to the `FakeSource` project.

The full code is in the `GrpcMicroService` subfolder of the `ch14` folder of the book's GitHub repository. The next section shows you how to solve the same problem with queued communication using the RabbitMQ message broker.

It is time to move to the implementation of a fundamental frontend microservice for our sample application.

A Frontend Microservice

In this section, as an example of an ASP.NET Core MVC frontend microservice described in *Chapter 17, Implementing Frontend Microservices with ASP.NET Core*, we will implement the administrative panel for managing the destinations and packages of the WWTravelClub book use case. The application will be implemented with the Domain-Driven Design (DDD) approach and associated patterns described in *Chapter 7, Understanding the Different Domains in Software Solutions*. So, having a good understanding of that chapter is a fundamental prerequisite to reading this chapter.

At this point, the architectural concerns discussed throughout the chapter begin to surface directly in the user-facing experience. Decisions related to CQRS, microservices, authentication, scalability, and service separation now influence not only backend processing but also responsiveness, usability, and maintainability from the frontend perspective.

The subsections that follow describe the overall application specifications and organization. The full code of the example can be found in the `ch17` folder of the GitHub repository associated with the book.

As usual, let's start by stating clearly our frontend microservice specifications.

Defining application specifications

The destinations and packages entities were described in *Chapter 13, Interacting with Data in C# – Entity Framework Core*. Here, we will use the same data model, with the necessary modifications to adapt it to the DDD approach. The administrative panel must allow packages/destination listing and CRUD operations on them. To simplify the application, the two listings will be quite simple: the application will show all destinations sorted according to their names, while all packages will be sorted starting from the ones with a later validity date.

Furthermore, we make the following assumptions:

- The application that shows destinations and packages to the user shares the same database used by the administrative panel. Since only the administrative panel application needs to modify data, there will be just one write copy of the database with several read-only replicas.
- Price modifications and package deletions are immediately used to update the user's shopping carts. For this reason, the administrative application must send asynchronous communications about price changes and package removals. We will not implement all the communication logic here, but we will just add all such events to an event table, which should be used as input to a parallel thread that's in charge of sending these events to all relevant microservices.

Here, we will give the full code for just package management; most of the code for destination management is designed as an exercise for you. The full code is available in the `ch17` folder of the GitHub repository associated with this book. In the remainder of this section, we will describe the application's overall organization and discuss some relevant samples of code. We start with an overall description of the application architecture.

Defining the application architecture

The application is organized based on the guidelines described in *Chapter 7, Understanding the Different Domains in Software Solutions*, while considering the DDD approach and related patterns. That is, the application is organized into a DB Driver and four layers, each implemented as a different project:

- There's a DB driver, which contains the repository's implementation and the classes describing database entities. It is a .NET library project.
- There are also domain services and domain models layers, which contain respectively repository specifications, that is, interfaces that describe repository implementations and DDD aggregates. In our implementation, we decided to implement aggregates as independent classes that store information in a state object. Each state object implements an interface that is defined in the domain models and that is implemented by a DB Driver entity. Hence, for instance, the `PackageAggregate` aggregate stores its state in a corresponding `IPackage` interface defined in the domain model layer. In turn, `IPackage` is implemented by the Entity Framework Core `Package` entity defined in the DB Driver. The domain model layer also contains the definitions of all the domain events, while the event handlers that will subscribe to these events are defined in the application layer. `PackageAggregateas`, as all other aggregates, also has an associated `IPackageRepository` repository interface in the domain services.
- All repository interfaces inherit from the empty `IRepository` interface.

> **Tip**
>
> This way they declare of being a repository interfaces, so that, all repository interfaces can be automatically discovered with reflection and added to the dependency injection engine together with their implementations.

- There is an application services layer that contains all commands and query definitions together with their handlers and all event handlers.
- Finally, there's outermost layer – that is, the ASP.NET Core MVC application. Controllers fill query objects and execute them to get ViewModels they can pass to Views. They update storage by filling command objects and executing their associated command handlers. In turn, command handlers use repository interfaces and `IUnitOfWork` instances coming from the domain layer to manage and coordinate transactions. The outermost layer takes the burden of connecting all abstract interfaces (repository interfaces, aggregate state interfaces, etc.) with their implementations.

The application uses the **Command Query Responsibility Segregation** (CQRS) pattern; therefore, it uses command objects to modify the storage and query objects to query it.

The query is simple to use and implement: controllers fill their parameters and then call their execution methods. In turn, execution methods use repository methods to interact with the database.

It is beneficial to encapsulate query objects behind interfaces so that their implementations can be replaced by fake implementations when you test controllers.

The chain of objects and calls involved in the execution of commands is more complex. This is because it requires the construction and modification of aggregates, as well as a definition of the interaction between several aggregates and between aggregates and other applications through domain events to be provided.

The following diagram is a sketch of how storage update operations are performed. The circles are data being exchanged between the various layers, while rectangles are the procedures that process them. Moreover, dotted arrows connect implementations with either interfaces they implement or with types that require them in their constructors:

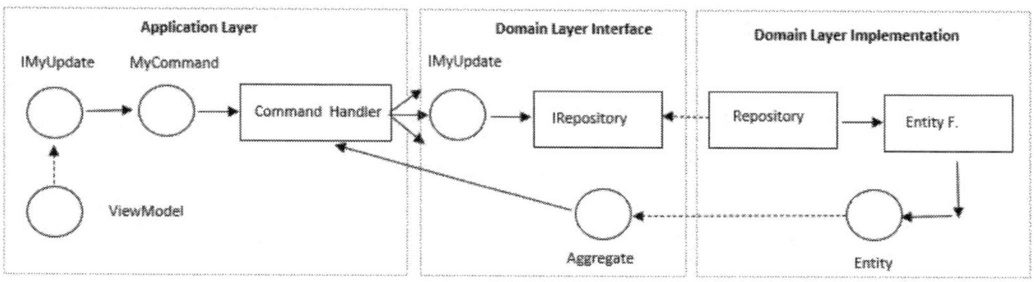

Figure 22.18: Diagram of command execution

Here's the flow of action through *Figure 22.18* as a list of steps:

1. A controller's action method receives one or more ViewModels and performs validation
2. One or more ViewModels containing changes to apply are hidden behind interfaces (`IMyUpdate`) defined in the domain layer or are copied in different classes. They are used to fill the properties of a command object. These interfaces must be defined in the domain layer since they will be used as arguments of the repository aggregate methods defined there.
3. At this point the application services layer comes into play. A command handler matching the previous command is retrieved via Dependency Injection (DI) in the controller action method. Then, the handler

is executed. During its execution, the handler interacts with various repository interface methods and with the aggregates they return.

4. When creating the command handler discussed in step 3, the ASP.NET Core DI engine automatically injects all parameters declared in its constructor. In particular, it injects all repository interface implementations needed to perform all command handler transactions. The command handler performs its job by calling the methods of the repository implementations received in its constructor to build aggregates and by modifying the built aggregates. Aggregates either represent already-existing entities or newly created ones. Handlers use the `IUnitOfWork` interface, as well as the concurrency exceptions returned by the domain layer, to organize their operations as transactions. It is worth pointing out that each aggregate has its own associated repository interface, and that the whole logic for updating each aggregate is defined in the aggregate itself, not in its associated repository interface, to keep the code more modular.
5. Behind the scenes, in the DB driver, repository implementations use Entity Framework to perform their job. Aggregates are created by passing entities that implement their state interfaces in their constructors. `IUnitOfWork` methods, which handle transactions and pass changes to the database, are implemented with `DbContext` methods. In other words, `IUnitOfWork` is implemented with the application's Entity Framework Core `DbContext`.
6. Domain events are generated during each aggregate processing and are added to the aggregates themselves by us calling their `AddDomainEvent` methods. However, they are not triggered immediately. Usually, they are triggered at the end of all the aggregates' processing and before changes are passed to the database; however, this is not a general rule.

The application handles errors by throwing exceptions.

> **Tip**
>
> A more efficient approach would be to define a request-scoped object in the dependency engine, where each application subpart may add its errors as domain events. However, while this approach is more efficient, it increases the complexity of the code and the application development time.

The Visual Studio solution is composed of 5 projects:

- There's a project, called `PackagesManagementDomainModel`, containing the domain model, which is a .NET library.
- There's a project, called `PackagesManagementDomainServices`, containing the domain services, which is a .NET library.
- There's a project, called `PackagesManagementApplicationServices`, containing the application services, which is a .NET library.
- There's a project, called `PackagesManagementDB`, containing the DB Driver which is a .NET library based on Entity Framework Core.
- Finally, there's an ASP.NET Core MVC project, called `PackagesManagement`, that contains the onion architecture outermost layer. When you define this project, select **No Authentication**; otherwise, the

user database will be added directly to the ASP.NET Core MVC project instead of to the database layer. We will add a simplified authentication manually.

Let's start by creating the `PackagesManagement` ASP.NET Core MVC project so that the whole solution has the same name as the ASP.NET Core MVC project. Then, we'll add the other library projects to the same solution.

Finally, let the ASP.NET Core MVC project reference both `PackagesManagementApplicationServices` and `PackagesManagementDB`, while `PackagesManagementDB` references `PackagesManagementDomainServices` and `PackagesManagementDomainServices` references `PackagesManagementDomainModel`. We suggest you define your own projects and then copy the code of this book's GitHub repository into them as you read this section.

The next subsection describes the code of the `PackagesManagementDomainModel` project.

The Domain Model

As a first step, create a library project called `PackagesManagementDomainModel` and delete the class automatically scaffolded by Visual Studio. Then, copy the content of the GitHub `ch07/OnionArchitecture/DomainModel` folder into the project root. It is just a tools folder containing some DDD tools that were described in *Chapter 7, Understanding the Different Domains in Software Solutions*, namely:

- The `Entity<T>` class all aggregates must inherit from
- A couple of exceptions needed by the DB Driver to report constraint violations and concurrency exceptions to the Domain Model
- The `IEventNotification` empty interface that marks all domain events so they can be found by reflection

Now let's add an `Aggregates` folder where we can place all aggregates and their state interfaces.

Here we place aggregates that correspond to the database entities we already introduced in *Chapter 13, Interacting with Data in C# – Entity Framework Core*. Namely, `PackageAggregate` and `DestinationAggregate`. We also have a `PackageEventAggregate` that is the aggregate associated with the table where we will place events to be propagated to other microservices. For each aggregate, we also define an interface that represents its state; thus, we have `IPackage`, `IDestination` and `IPackageEvent`.

As an example, let's analyze `PackageAggregate`:

```
public class PackageAggregate(IPackage state): Entity<int>
{
    public override int Id => state.Id;
    public string Name { get {return state.Name; }
        set { state.Name = value; } }
    public string Description { get { return state.Description; }
        set { state.Description = value; } }
    public decimal Price { get { return state.Price; }
          set {
        if (value != state.Price)
        {
```

```
            AddDomainEvent(new PackagePriceChangedEvent(
                    Id, value, EntityVersion, EntityVersion + 1));
            state.EntityVersion = state.EntityVersion + 1;
        }
        state.Price = value;
      } }
  public int DurationInDays { get { return state.DurationInDays; }
        set { state.DurationInDays = value; } }
    public DateTime? StartValidityDate {
    get { return state.StartValidityDate; }
        set { state.StartValidityDate = value; } }
    public DateTime? EndValidityDate {
        get { return state.EndValidityDate; }
        set { state.EndValidityDate = value; } }
    public int DestinationId => state.DestinationId;
    public long EntityVersion => state.EntityVersion;
}
```

It contains the same properties as the Package entity, which we saw in *Chapter 13, Interacting with Data in C# – Entity Framework Core*. The only differences are the following:

It inherits from `Entity<int>`, which furnishes all basic functionalities of aggregates.

Some properties are read-only, namely `EntityVersion`, `Id` and `DestinationId`. This is because aggregates must enforce business update rules and neither the package id nor its associated destination can't be changed once a package has been created. Moreover, `EntityVersion` is automatically increased whenever price changes.

When a package is deleted or when its price changes, other microservices that interact with the customers must be informed of these changes. Accordingly, when a `PackageAggregate` is deleted or when its price is changed, domain events are generated. These events trigger the creation of `PackageEventAggregate` instances, which, in turn, populate a database table of messages to be sent to other interested microservices.

Below, the definition of `PackageEventAggregate`:

```
public enum PackageEventType { Deleted, CostChanged }
public  class PackageEventAggregate(IPackageEvent state): Entity<long>
{
    public override long Id => state.Id;
    public PackageEventType Type => state.Type;
    public int PackageId => state.PackageId;
    public decimal NewPrice => state.NewPrice;
    public long? OldVersion => state.OldVersion;
    public long? NewVersion => state.NewVersion;
}
```

All properties are read-only because once created package events can't be changed.

Domain events are defined in an Event folder. We have two kinds of events: one for package deletion and one for price change:

```
public class PackageDeleteEvent : IEventNotification
{
    public PackageDeleteEvent(int id, long oldVersion)
    {
        PackageId = id;
        OldVersion = oldVersion;
    }
    public int PackageId { get; }
    public long OldVersion { get; }
}

public class PackagePriceChangedEvent : IEventNotification
{
    public PackagePriceChangedEvent(int id, decimal price,
        long oldVersion, long newVersion)
    {
        PackageId = id;
        NewPrice = price;
        OldVersion = oldVersion;
        NewVersion = newVersion;
    }
    public int PackageId { get; }
    public decimal NewPrice { get; }
    public long OldVersion { get; }
    public long NewVersion { get; }
}
```

All domain events are marked with the empty `IEventNotification` interface so they can be easily found with reflection.

When an aggregate sends all its changes to another application, it should have a version property. The application that receives the changes uses this version property to apply all changes in the right order. An explicit version number is necessary because changes are sent asynchronously, so the order they are received in may differ from the order they were sent in. For this purpose, events that are used to publish changes outside of the application have both `OldVersion` (the version before the change) and `NewVersion` (the version after the change) properties. Events associated with delete events have no `NewVersion` since, after being deleted, an entity can't store any versions.

For more details on how to use and process version information to restore the right order of incoming messages, please refer to the *A worker microservices with ASP.NET core* section of this chapter.

Let's move to the Domain Services.

Domain Services

The Domain services layer contains just repository interface definitions. Before going into the details of our repositories, let's copy the content of the GitHub `ch07/OnionArchitecture/DomainServices` folder into the root of our `PackagesManagementDomainServices` project. It is a Tools folder that contains just the definitions of the `IUnitOfWork` interface we defined in *Chapter 7, Understanding the Different Domains in Software Solutions*, and the empty `IRepository` interface that marks all repositories, so they can be easily found with reflection.

Repositories are placed in a `IRepositories` folder. In our case we have `IDestinationRepository`, `IPackageRepository`, and `IPackageEventRepository`. As an example, let's have a look at the `IPackageRepository` repository:

```
public interface IPackageRepository : IRepository
{
Task<IList<PackageInfosDTO>> GetAllInfo();
Task<IPackage?> GetAsync(int id);
PackageAggregate New(string name, string description, decimal price).
int durationInDays, DateTime? startValidityDate,
DateTime? endValidityDate, int DestinationId);
Task<PackageAggregate?> Delete(int id);
}
```

`PackageInfosDTO` is a DTO defined in the domain services. In fact, domain services also contain DTOs used to return query results instead of aggregates. These query results are returned by repository methods called by application services **Query** objects.

Repositories always contain just a few methods since all business logic should be represented as aggregate methods – in our case, just the methods to create a new package, to retrieve an existing package, and to delete an existing package. The logic to modify an existing package is included in the `PackageAggregate` itself.

Let's move to the actual database implementation of the whole domain layer.

The DB driver

The data layer project is named `PackagesManagementDB` and contains references to the `Microsoft.EntityFrameworkCore.SqlServer` NuGet packages, since we are using Entity Framework Core with SQL Server. It also references `Microsoft.EntityFrameworkCore.Tools`, which is needed to generate database migrations, as explained in the Entity Framework Core migrations section of *Chapter 13, Interacting with Data in C# – Entity Framework Core.*

`PackagesManagementDB` needs a reference to `PackagesManagementDomainServices` and must be referenced by `PackagesManagement`, which, being the outermost layer, has the burden of connecting all interfaces with their implementations.

Before going starting the entity definitions let copy the content of the GitHub `ch07/OnionArchitecture/DBdriver` folder in the root of our `PackagesManagementDB` project. It adds a `DBContext` that already implements `IUnitOfWork` and an extension method to be called by the outermost layer to connect all interfaces with their implementations. More details, on the added functionalities can be found in the *A worker microservices with ASP.NET core -> The DB Driver* subsection of this chapter.

`PackagesManagementDB` has a `Models` folder that contains all database entities. When needed, each entity has an associated `IEntityTypeConfiguration`-based configuration class. Entity definitions are similar to the ones in *Chapter 13, Interacting with Data in C# – Entity Framework Core*. However, some entities might have an `EntityVersion` property decorated with the `[ConcurrencyCheck]` attribute. It contains the entity version that is needed for sending changes to other microservices. The `ConcurrencyCheck` attribute is needed to prevent concurrency errors while updating the entity version. This prevents suffering the performance penalty implied by a transaction.

More specifically, when saving entity changes, if the value of a field marked with the `ConcurrencyCheck` attribute is different from the one that was read when the entity was loaded in memory, a concurrency exception is thrown to inform the calling method that someone else modified this value after the entity was read but before we attempted to save its changes. This way, the calling method can repeat the whole operation with the hope that, this time, no one will write the same entity in the database during its execution.

The only alternative to the `ConcurrencyCheck` attribute would be:

1. Start a transaction
2. Read the interested aggregate
3. Increment its `EntityVersion` property
4. Update the aggregate
5. Save all changes
6. Close the transaction

The transaction duration would be unacceptably long since the transaction should be maintained for the time of various database commands, namely from the initial read to the final update. Thus, preventing other requests from accessing the involved tables/records for too long a time.

On the contrary, by using the `ConcurrencyCheck` attribute, we open just a very short single-command transaction when the aggregate is saved to the database:

1. Read the interested aggregate
2. Increment the value of the `EntityVersion` property
3. Update the aggregate
4. Save all changes with a fast single-command transaction

It is worth analyzing the code of the Package entity:

```
public class Package : IPackage
{
```

```
    public int Id { get; set; }
    [MaxLength(128)]
    public required string Name { get; set; }
    [MaxLength(128)]
    public string? Description { get; set; }
    public decimal Price { get; set; }
    public int DurationInDays { get; set; }
    public DateTime? StartValidityDate { get; set; }
    public DateTime? EndValidityDate { get; set; }
    public Destination MyDestination { get; set; } = null!;
    [ConcurrencyCheck]
    public long EntityVersion { get; set; }

    public int DestinationId { get; set; }
}
```

The relation among destinations and packages is defined in the `OnModelCreating` method of the `MainDbContext` class that also recalls all entity configurations:

```
protected override void OnModelCreating(ModelBuilder
builder)
{
    builder.Entity<Destination>()
        .HasMany(m => m.Packages)
        .WithOne(m => m.MyDestination)
        .HasForeignKey(m => m.DestinationId)
        .OnDelete(DeleteBehavior.Cascade);

    new DestinationConfiguration()
        .Configure(builder.Entity<Destination>());
    new PackageConfiguration()
        .Configure(builder.Entity<Package>());
}
```

It is worth analyzing also the `MainDbContext` implementation of `IUnitOfWork. SaveEntitiesAsync()`:

```
public async Task<bool> SaveEntitiesAsync()
{
    try
    {
        return await SaveChangesAsync() > 0;
    }
    catch (DbUpdateConcurrencyException ex)
    {
```

```
        foreach (var entry in ex.Entries) await entry.ReloadAsync();
        throw new ConcurrencyException(ex);
    }
    catch (DbUpdateException ex)
    {
        throw new ConstraintViolationException(ex);
    }
}
```

The preceding implementation just calls the `SaveChangesAsync` `DbContext` context method, which saves all changes to the database, but then it intercepts all concurrency exceptions caused by `[ConcurrencyCheck]` violations and reloads all involved entities, so that the next attempt will work on updated entities and may succeed. The method also performs exception translation since it translates Entity Framework Core specific exceptions into classes defined in the domain model library.

The `Repositories` folder contains all repository implementations. As a significant example, it is worth analyzing the implementation of the `IPackageRepository.Delete` method:

```
public async Task<PackageAggregate?> Delete(int id)
{
    var model = await _context.Packages.Where(m => m.Id == id)
        .FirstOrDefaultAsync();
    if (model is not Package package) return null;
    _context.Packages.Remove(package);
    var result=new PackageAggregate(package);
    result.AddDomainEvent(
        new PackageDeleteEvent(
            model.Id, package.EntityVersion));
    return result;
}
```

It reads the entity from the database and formally removes it from the `Packages` dataset. This will force the entity to be deleted in the database when changes are saved to the database. Moreover, it adds a `PackageDeleteEvent` to the list of domain events of the aggregate it returns.

The `Extensions` folder contains the `DBExtensions` static class, which, in turn, defines the `AddDbDriver` `IServiceCollection` extension method. This method takes care of connecting all domain layer interfaces with their DB driver implementations in the dependency injection engine. It must be called in the `Program.cs` file of the `PackageManagement` project as shown below:

```
...
builder.Services.AddControllersWithViews();
builder.Services.AddDbDriver(
        builder.Configuration
```

```
            .GetConnectionString("DefaultConnection")??string.Empty);
...
```

Then, we must add the connection string to the `PackageManagementappsettings.json` file, as shown here:

```
{
  "ConnectionStrings": {
    "DefaultConnection": "Server=(localdb)\
\mssqllocaldb;Database=wwtravelclubadmin;Trusted_Connection=True;MultipleActiveResultSets
=true"
  },
```

At this point, if you have not copied the whole code from the GitHub repository, you must create database migrations (in the GitHub repository code, migrations have already been created). Let's open Visual Studio Package Manager Console, select `PackagesManagementDB` as the default project in its dropdown, and then launch the following command:

```
Add-Migration Initial -Project PackagesManagementDB
```

The preceding command will scaffold the first migration. We may apply it to the database with the `Update-Database-Project PackagesManagementDB` command. Please note that if you copy the project from GitHub, you don't need to scaffold migrations since they have already been created, but you still need to update the database, so you need to issue the `Update-Database-Project PackagesManagementDB` command.

If you would like to create the database automatically when the application is run in production or staging, we must add an `UseDatabase` extension method to the `DBExtensions` class located in the `Extensions/DBextensions.cs` file:

```
private static async Task Seed(MainDbContext context)
{
    ...
}
public static async Task<IServiceProvider> UseDatabase(
    IServiceProvider serviceProvider)
{
    using var serviceScope = serviceProvider.CreateScope();
    var context = serviceScope.ServiceProvider
        .GetRequiredService<IUnitOfWork>() as MainDbContext;
    if (context != null)
    {
        await context.Database.MigrateAsync();
        await Seed(context);
    }
```

```
    return serviceProvider;
}
```

The `UseDatabase` extension method ensures migrations are applied to the database by calling `context.Database.MigrateAsync()` and then populates the database with some initial data. Database seeding is useful for creating some initial users, or some other kind of default entities. In our case, we just create some sample destinations and packages.

`context.Database.MigrateAsync()` is useful to quickly set up and update staging and test environments. When deploying in production, in case we don't have the credentials for creating a new database or for modifying its structure, we can also produce an SQL script from the migrations using the migration tools. Then, this script should be examined before being applied by the person in charge of maintaining the database and finally applied with his credentials.

The `UseDatabase` method must be added in the `Program.cs` file of the `PackagesManagement` outermost layer just before `app.Run()` as shown below:

```
...
await app.Services.UseDatabase();
app.Run();
```

Let's move to the application services.

Defining the application services

As a first step let copy the content of the GitHub `ch07/OnionArchitecture/ApplicationServices` folder in the root of our `PackagesManagementApplicationServices` project. The `Tools` folder contains:

- The `IQuery` and `ICommand` are empty interfaces that mark all commands so that they can be easily found with reflection and added with their handlers to the dependency injection engine.
- The `IEventHandler<Event>` interface that marks all event handlers associated with the same event `Event` so that they can be easily found with reflection and added to the dependency injection engine.
- The `ICommandHandler<Command>` interface that marks all command handlers associated with the same command `Command` so that they can be easily found with reflection and added to the dependency injection engine.
- The `EventMediator` class is added to the dependency injection engine and used by all command handlers to trigger all events added to any aggregate. It uses the `EventTrigger` to retrieve all event handlers associated with the same event from the dependency injection engine.

The `Extensions` folder contains the extension methods that add command handlers, event handlers, queries and `EventMediator` to the dependency injection engine. They must be called by `Program.cs` in the `PackagesManagement` project, as shown below:

```
...
builder.Services.AddDbDriver(...)
```

```
builder.Services.AddApplicationServices();
...
```

Then, we must add a `Queries` folder to place all queries and their associated interfaces. We have two queries, one that retrieves information on all packages, and another that retrieves the key and name of all destinations. The first query is needed to show all packages to the user, and the other query is needed to populate the selection logic for choosing a destination during a package definition.

As an example, let's have a look at the query that lists all packages:

```
public class PackagesListQuery(IPackageRepository repo):
    IPackagesListQuery
{
    public async Task<IList<PackageInfosDTO>> GetAllPackages()
    {
        return await repo.GetAllInfo();
    }
}
```

In our simple application, the query class just calls a method of the repository that is automatically injected in its constructor without further processing. However, in general, more than one repository call is needed, followed by processing of all results.

All commands are placed in a `Command` folder. As an example, let's have a look at the command used to modify packages:

```
public class UpdatePackageCommand : ICommand
{
    public int Id { get; init; }
    public required string Name { get; init; }
    public required string Description { get; init; }
    public decimal Price { get; init; }
    public int DurationInDays { get; init; }
    public DateTime? StartValidityDate { get; init; }
    public DateTime? EndValidityDate { get; init; }
}
```

It contains just the package properties that can be modified plus the package `Id`.

The command for creating a new package is similar but also contains a `DestinationId` property and doesn't contain an `Id`, because the package `Id` is autogenerated by the database.

Command handlers are placed in the Handlers folder. It is worth analyzing the command that updates packages:

```
public class UpdatePackageCommandHandler(IPackageRepository repo,
 IEventMediator mediator)
```

Its principal constructor has automatically injected the IPackageRepository repository and an EventMediator instance needed to trigger event handlers. The following code also shows the implementation of the standard HandleAsync command handler method:

```
public async Task HandleAsync(UpdatePackageCommand command)
{
    bool done = false;
    PackageAggregate? model;
    while (!done)
    {
        try
        {
            model = await repo.GetAsync(command.Id);
            if (model is null) return;
            model.Name= command.Name;
            model.Description = command.Description;
            model.DurationInDays = command.DurationInDays;
            model.Price = command.Price;
            model.StartValidityDate = command.StartValidityDate;
            model.EndValidityDate = command.EndValidityDate;

            await mediator.TriggerEvents(model.DomainEvents);
            await repo.UnitOfWork.SaveEntitiesAsync();
            done = true;
        }
        catch (ConcurrencyException)
        {
            //add here some Logging
        }
    }
}
```

HandleAsync uses the repository to get an instance of the aggregate to modify. If the aggregate is not found (it has been deleted), the command stops its execution. Otherwise, all changes are passed to the retrieved aggregate. Immediately after the update, all events contained in the aggregate are triggered. In particular, if the price has changed, the event handler associated with the price change is executed. The concurrency check declared with the [ConcurrencyCheck] attribute on the EntityVersion property of the Package entity ensures that the package version is updated properly (by incrementing its previous version number by 1), as well as that the price-changed event is passed the right version numbers.

Also, event handlers are placed in the Handlers folder. As an example, let's have a look at the price-changed event handler:

```
public class PackagePriceChangedEventHandler(
IPackageEventRepository repo):
    IEventHandler<PackagePriceChangedEvent>
{

    public Task HandleAsync(PackagePriceChangedEvent ev)
    {
        repo.New(PackageEventType.CostChanged, ev.PackageId,
            ev.OldVersion, ev.NewVersion, ev.NewPrice);
        return Task.CompletedTask;
    }
}
```

The principal constructor has automatically injected the `IPackageEventRepository` repository, which handles the database table and all the events to send to other applications. The `HandleAsync` implementation simply calls the repository method that adds a new `IPackageEvent` to a queue of events to be sent to other microservices.

The `IPackageEvent` records should be extracted by the above queue and sent to all interested microservices by a parallel task that is not implemented in the GitHub code associated with this section. It can be implemented as a hosted service (thus inheriting from the `BackgroundService` class) and then added to the DI engine with a call such as `builder.Services.AddHostedService<MyHostedService>()`, as detailed in the Using generic hosts subsection of *Chapter 11, Applying Microservice Architecture to Your Enterprise Application.*

We are almost finished! Just the outermost layer is missing, that in the case of an MVC-based applications consists of controllers and views. The next subsection discusses the ASP.NET Core MVC `PackagesManagement` project.

Defining the ASP.NET Core MVC outermost layer

We already discussed the extension methods to add to `Program.cs` for populating the dependency injection engine and for automatically creating the database. We just need to discuss:

- Globalization
- Authentication and authorization
- Controllers and Views

Let's discuss each subject in a separate subsection, starting with globalization.

Packages Management globalization

In an actual production application, we should discuss all cultures to support, and we should furnish ways to select the desired culture plus reasonable defaults based on the browser culture.

In our simple example let suppose we supports just the `en-US` culture. Accordingly, let's freeze the application culture to `en-US` by adding the following code to the ASP.NET Core pipeline in `Program.cs`:

```
...
app.UseAuthorization();

var ci = new CultureInfo("en-US");
app.UseRequestLocalization(new RequestLocalizationOptions
{
    DefaultRequestCulture = new RequestCulture(ci),
    SupportedCultures = new List<CultureInfo>
    {
        ci,
    },
    SupportedUICultures = new List<CultureInfo>
    {
        ci,
    }
});
...
```

Let's move to authentication and authorization.

PackageManagement authentication and authorization

Authentication and authorization are not merely security implementation details but central architectural concerns in distributed enterprise systems. Decisions involving token propagation, identity boundaries, authorization strategies, and service trust relationships directly affect scalability, operational governance, and long-term maintainability.

In a microservice application containing several frontend microservices, both login and authentication must be defined by a unique module working as an authentication server.

If each HTML-based frontend is directly accessible to the users, then the best solution is the adoption of an authentication server together with an OAuth protocol that transforms the authentication token provided by the authentication server into a cookie-based authentication token suitable for the frontend that needs user authentication. Then, each frontend uses that token to decide user authorizations on the various operations.

If, on the other side, all frontends are behind a unique microservice that takes care of interfacing all requests, then that microservice can take care of handling login, authenticating each request, and authorizing or not the operation contained in the request. However, also in this case an authorization token must be forwarded to each destination frontend for the following reasons:

- The interface microservice can base its operation authorization just on the URL format, but sometimes authorization may depend also on the values of parameters contained in the URL
- When an operation is authorized to a user, the result of the operation may depend on the user and on its claims. For instance, in a customer's listing the actual customers listed might depend on the user: a manager might see all customers, while other employed might see just the customers assigned to them

In this case the interface microservice might add a bearer token to each request to enable each frontend to fine-tune authorization.

In our case, we may suppose we get authentication through OAuth. However, in order to test the application easily with no need to set up an authentication server, we may add a login page and a fake login based on hardwired usernames and passwords.

The authorization middleware is already in place also in projects without authentication, so we must add just the middleware that detects the authentication token, verifies it, and extracts all claims from it:

```
...
app.UseAuthentication();
app.UseRouting();
...
```

All authentication options, including the type of authentication chosen, which in our case is cookie-based, are specified in the services definition area of `Program.cs`:

```
builder.Services.AddAuthentication(
    CookieAuthenticationDefaults.AuthenticationScheme)
    .AddCookie(o =>
    {
        o.LoginPath = "/account/login";
        o.SlidingExpiration = true;
    });
```

We added cookie authentication and named it with its default name, `CookieAuthenticationDefaults.AuthenticationScheme`. Then we defined some cookie-specific options, namely the path where to redirect unauthenticated requests—that is, the path to the login page—and the automatic renewal of the cookie expiration time at each new request.

Login/logout operations are taken care of by an `AccountController` which uses the `HttpContext.SignInAsync` and `HttpContext.SignOutAsync` methods to log in and out the user. These methods simply create and destroy the authentication cookie.

The `Logout` action method is quite simple and is shown here (for more information on authentication in ASP.NET Core please refer to the Defining the ASP.NET Core pipeline section of *Chapter 20, Securing Data and Applications*):

```
[HttpPost]
[ValidateAntiForgeryToken]
public async Task<IActionResult> Logout()
{
    await HttpContext

      .SignOutAsync(CookieAuthenticationDefaults.AuthenticationScheme);

    return RedirectToAction(nameof(HomeController.Index), "Home");
}
```

It just calls the `SignOutAsync` method and then redirects the browser to the home page. To avoid it being called by clicking a link, it is decorated with HttpPost, so it can only be invoked via a form submit.

Tip

All requests that cause modifications must never use a GET verb, otherwise someone might erroneously trigger those actions either by clicking a link or by writing the wrong URL in the browser. An action triggered by a GET might also be exploited by a phishing web site that might adequately "*camouflage*" a link that triggers a dangerous GET action. The GET verb should be used just for retrieving information.

Login, on the other hand, requires two action methods. The first one is invoked via Get and shows the login form, where the user must enter their username and password. It is shown here:

```
[HttpGet]
public async Task<IActionResult> Login(string? returnUrl = null)
{
    // Clear the existing  cookie
    //to ensure a clean login process
    await HttpContext

      .SignOutAsync(CookieAuthenticationDefaults.AuthenticationScheme);

    ViewData["ReturnUrl"] = returnUrl;
    return View();
}
```

It receives `returnUrl` as its parameter when the browser is automatically redirected to the login page by the authorization middleware. This happens when an unlogged-in user tries to access a protected page. `returnUrl` is stored in the ViewState dictionary that is passed to the login view. The form in the login view passes it back, together with the username and password, to the controller when it is submitted, as shown in this code:

```
<form asp-route-returnurl="@ViewData["ReturnUrl"]" method="post">
...
</form>
```

The form post is intercepted by an action method with the same Login name but decorated with the [HttpPost] attribute, as shown here:

```
[HttpPost]
[ValidateAntiForgeryToken]
public async Task<IActionResult> Login(
    LoginViewModel model,
   string? returnUrl = null)
{
  ...
```

The preceding method receives the LoginViewModel used by the login view, together with the returnUrl query string parameter. The ValidateAntiForgeryToken attribute verifies a token (called an anti-forgery token) that MVC forms automatically. This is then added to a hidden field to prevent XSRF/CSRF attacks.

Note

Forgery attacks exploit authentication cookies stored in the victim's browser to submit a legitimate authenticated request to a Web application. They do this by inducing the user to click a button of a phishing website that causes a submit to the target web application. The fraudulent request is accepted since once a form is submitted the authentication cookies for the target URL are automatically sent by the browser. There are just two defenses against this kind of attacks:

Authentication cookies are defined as same-origin, that is, they are sent from other domains only in the case of GET requests. Thus, when a form is submitted from a phishing web site to the target application, they are not sent.

AntiForgery tokens added to forms. In this case, also if authentication cookies are sent together with the submitted form, the application understands that the request comes from a different website and block it, since it is missing a valid AntiForgery token.

As a first step, the action method logs the user out if they are already logged in:

```
if (User?.Identity?.IsAuthenticated??false)
{
    await HttpContext.SignOutAsync();
}
```

Otherwise, it verifies whether there are validation errors, in which case it shows the same view filled with the data of the ViewModel to let the user correct their errors:

```
if (ModelState.IsValid)
{
    ...
}
else
 // If we got this far, something failed, redisplay form
 return View(model);
```

If the model is valid, the controller verifies user credentials after having extracted the user record by a database. In our fake case we simply compare user credentials with hardwired username and password:

```
var result = model.UserName=="admin"&&model.Password=="admin";
```

If the operation is successful, the action method signs in the user and redirects the browser to `returnUrl` if it's not null; otherwise, it redirects the browser to the home page. Otherwise, it returns a wrong-credentials error:

```
if (result)
{
    //signing in code omitted
    ...
    if (!string.IsNullOrEmpty(returnUrl))
        return LocalRedirect(returnUrl);
    else
        return RedirectToAction(nameof(HomeController.Index), "Home");
}
else
{
    ModelState.AddModelError(string.Empty,
 "wrong user name or password");
    return View(model);
}
```

The sign-in operation requires the previous packaging of all user claims into a `ClaimsIdentity` instance and the specification of the authentication token properties:

```
var claims = new[]
{
    new Claim(ClaimTypes.Name, model.UserName),
    new Claim(ClaimTypes.Role, "Administrator")
};
var claimsIdentity = new ClaimsIdentity(
```

```
        claims, CookieAuthenticationDefaults.AuthenticationScheme);
var authProperties = new AuthenticationProperties
{
    ExpiresUtc = DateTime.UtcNow.AddDays(30),
    IsPersistent = model.RememberMe,
    IssuedUtc = DateTime.UtcNow,
    AllowRefresh = true
};
```

After that, we have all the information to perform the signing operation:

```
await HttpContext.SignInAsync(
    CookieAuthenticationDefaults.AuthenticationScheme,
    new ClaimsPrincipal(claimsIdentity),
    authProperties);
```

That's all! More details can be inspected directly in the GitHub repository code.

Let's move to the remaining controllers and Views.

Defining controllers and views

`ManagePackagesController` contains an `Index` method that shows all packages in table format (for more details on controllers, views and on the MVC pattern in general, please refer to the *The MVC pattern* section of *Chapter 16, Presenting ASP.NET Core*):

```
[HttpGet]
public async Task<IActionResult> Index([FromServices] IPackagesListQuery query)
{
    var results = await query.GetAllPackages();
    var vm = new PackagesListViewModel
       { Items = new ReadOnlyCollection<PackageInfosDTO>(results) };    return View(vm);
}
```

The query object is injected into the action method by DI. Then, the action method invokes it and inserts the resulting `IEnumerable` into the Items property of a `PackagesListViewModel` instance. It is a good practice to include `IEnumerables` in ViewModels instead of passing them directly to the views so that, if necessary, other properties can be added without the need to modify the existing view code.

Moreover, it is good practice to define enumerable properties of ViewModels as `IReadOnlyCollection<T>` if the `IEnumerables` are read-only or as `IList<T>` if the `IEnumerables` can be modified or if they are involved in model binding. In fact, `ICollection<T>` has a `Count` property, which may be very useful when rendering ViewModels in views, while `IList<T>` also has indexers that are necessary for rendering all items with appropriate names for model binding to succeed (see this Phil Haack post: `http://haacked.com/archive/2008/10/23/model-binding-`

to-a-list.aspx). `IEnumerable<T>` should be preferred only in the case that one needs the typical lazy evaluation of `IEnumerable<T>`.

The results are shown in a Bootstrap table since Bootstrap CSS is automatically scaffolded by Visual Studio. Bootstrap is a good choice for a CSS framework, since it is quite simple and extensible, and is not connected to any particular company, but is handled by an independent team. The result is shown here:

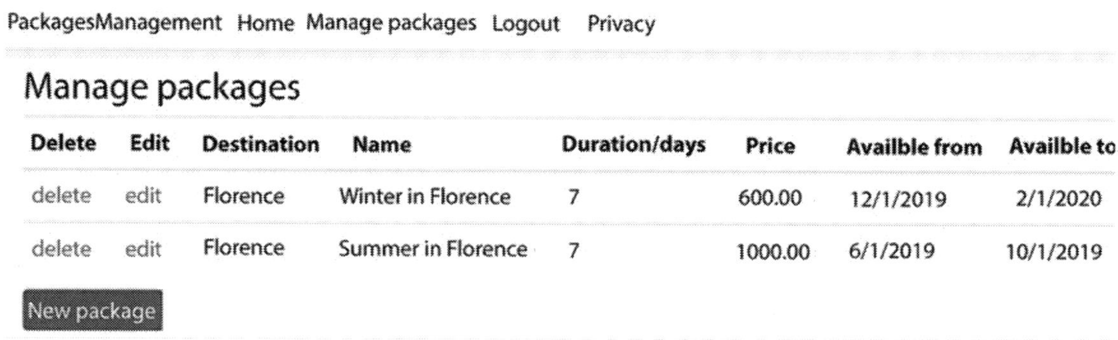

Figure 22.19: Application packages handling page

The **New package** link (it is shaped like a Bootstrap button, but it is a link) invokes a controller `Create` action method, while the **delete** and **edit** links in each row invoke a `Delete` and `Edit` action method, respectively, and pass them the ID of the package shown in the row.

Here is the implementation of the two-row links:

```
@foreach(var package in Model.Items)
{
<tr>
    <td>
        <a asp-controller="ManagePackages"
            asp-action="@nameof(ManagePackagesController.Delete)"
            asp-route-id="@package.Id">
            delete
        </a>
    </td>
    <td>
        <a asp-controller="ManagePackages"
            asp-action="@nameof(ManagePackagesController.Edit)"
            asp-route-id="@package.Id">
            edit
        </a>
    </td>
    ...
    ...
```

It is worth describing the code of the HttpGet and HttpPost Edit action methods:

```
[HttpGet]
public async Task<IActionResult> Edit(
    int id,
    [FromServices] IPackageRepository repo)
{
    if (id == 0) return RedirectToAction(
        nameof(ManagePackagesController.Index));
    var aggregate = await repo.GetAsync(id);
    if (aggregate is null) return RedirectToAction(
        nameof(ManagePackagesController.Index));
    var vm = new PackageFullEditViewModel
    {
        Id = aggregate.Id,
        Name = aggregate.Name,
        Description=aggregate.Description??string.Empty,
        Price=aggregate.Price,
        DurationInDays=aggregate.DurationInDays,
        StartValidityDate=aggregate.StartValidityDate,
        EndValidityDate=aggregate.EndValidityDate

    };
    return View(vm);
}
```

The HttpGet Edit method uses IPackageRepository to retrieve the existing package aggregate. If the package is not found, that means it has been deleted by some other user, and the browser is redirected again to the list page to show the updated list of packages. Otherwise, the aggregate is used to fill the PackageFullEditViewModel ViewModel, which is rendered by the Edit view.

The action method that processes the post of the view form is given here:

```
[HttpPost]
public async Task<IActionResult> Edit(
    PackageFullEditViewModel vm,
    [FromServices] ICommandHandler<UpdatePackageCommand> command)
{
    if (ModelState.IsValid)
    {
        await command.HandleAsync(new UpdatePackageCommand {
            Id = vm.Id,
            Name = vm.Name,
            Description = vm.Description,
```

```
            Price = vm.Price,
            DurationInDays=vm.DurationInDays,
            StartValidityDate=vm.StartValidityDate,
            EndValidityDate=vm.EndValidityDate
        });
        return RedirectToAction(
            nameof(ManagePackagesController.Index));
    }
    else
        return View(vm);
}
```

If `ModelState` is valid, `UpdatePackageCommand` is created, filled with the ViewModel data and its associated handler is invoked; otherwise, the View is displayed again to the user to enable him to correct all the errors.

Links to the package list page and login page must be added to the main menu, which is in the `_Layout` view, as shown here:

```
@if (User.Identity.IsAuthenticated)
{
    <li class="nav-item">
            <a class="nav-link text-dark"
                asp-controller="ManagePackages"
                    asp-action="Index">Manage packages</a>
    </li>

        <li class="nav-item">
        <a class="nav-link text-dark"
href="javascript:document.getElementById('logoutForm').submit()">
            Logout
        </a>
    </li>
}
else
{
    <li class="nav-item">
        <a class="nav-link text-dark"
            asp-controller="Account" asp-action="Login">Login</a>
    </li>
}
```

`logoutForm` is an empty form whose only purpose is to send a post to the `Logout` action method. It has been added to the end of the body, as shown here:

```
@if (User.Identity.IsAuthenticated)
{
    <form asp-area="" asp-controller="Account"
            asp-action="Logout" method="post"
            id="logoutForm" ></form>
}
```

Now, the application is ready! You can run it, log in, and start to manage packages.

After having learned how to implement, in practice, a presentation layer with server-side technologies in this section, we just need to learn how to implement it also with client-side technologies. We will do it in the next section.

Using Client Technologies

In this section, we will implement a package search application for the WWTravelClub book use case. The first subsection explains how to set up the solution by exploiting the application services, domain layer and DB Driver of the MVC application we implemented in the previous section of this chapter.

Preparing the solution

We will modify the `PackagesManagement` project both to save coding time and to show how to transform a solution based on server-side MVC technology into a solution based on the Blazor client-side technology.

First, create a copy of the `PackagesManagement` solution folder we created in the previous section and rename it `PackagesManagementBlazor`.

To open the solution, right-click on the web project (the one named `PackagesManagement`) and remove it (**Remove** menu item). Then, go to the solution folder and delete the whole web project folder (the one named `PackagesManagement`).

Now, right-click on the solution and select **Add -> New Project**. Add a new **Blazor WebAssembly Standalone App** project called `PackagesManagementBlazor.Client`. Select **none** for authentication type, **Configure for https**, and **Include Sample Pages**. We don't need authentication since the search-by-location feature we are going to implement must also be available to unregistered users.

Now, add a `PackagesManagementBlazor.Server` **ASP.NET Core Web API** project. Select **none** for authentication type, **Configure for https**, **Enable OpenAPI support**, and **Use Controllers**.

Finally, add a `PackagesManagementBlazor.Shared` **Class Library** project, delete the default `Class1` class created by Visual Studio, and add this project to both `PackagesManagementBlazor.Client` and `PackagesManagementBlazor.Server` as references.

The server project needs to reference both the DB Driver (PackagesManagementDB) and the application services (PackagesManagementApplicationServices) projects, so please add them as references.

Both PackagesManagementBlazor.Client and PackagesManagementBlazor.Server must start simultaneously, so define them as starting projects by right-clicking on the solution, selecting **Configure Startup Projects**, and choosing them as startup projects.

Now, launch the solution to verify that everything works properly. Two console windows should open together with a browser window containing a Blazor application.

Take note of the Blazor application URL (https://localhost:7257/ in my case) since we will need it.

The Blazor web site will exchange data with the REST API web site that runs on a different domain (a domain is identified by both hostname and port number). REST API calls coming from browsers running on different domains are clues of potential phishing attacks; therefore, the receiving server accepts them only if they come from well-known domains (this way they are sure they don't come from phishing web sites).

On the other side, when a browser application tries to communicate with a different URL, the browser detects it and issues the call with a different protocol called CORS. Therefore, the receiving server, as soon as it detects the CORS protocol, understands it is coping with a request coming from a different website, and serves the request only if the other domain has been registered with a so-called CORS policy.

In ASP.NET, Core CORS policies are registered with the builder.Services.AddCors extension method in Program.cs.

Therefore, in our case, we need to register a CORS policy for the domain of the PackagesManagementBlazor.Client web application in the PackagesManagementBlazor.Server web application, since all REST API calls of PackagesManagementBlazor.Client will be issued to PackagesManagementBlazor.Server.

Accordingly, open Program.cs of the PackagesManagementBlazor.Server project and enable it for CORS by adding this:

```
builder.Services.AddCors(o => {
    o.AddDefaultPolicy(pbuilder =>
    {
        pbuilder.AllowAnyMethod();
        pbuilder.WithHeaders(HeaderNames.ContentType,
          HeaderNames.Authorization);
        pbuilder.WithOrigins("https://localhost:7257");
    });
});
```

Also, add app.UseCors(); in the ASP.NET Core pipeline, immediately before app.UseAuthorization().

Now, we must enable the Blazor application to communicate with this server. Launch the solution again and take note of the REST API URL from its associated console window (in my case, https://localhost:7049/), and then replace the URL in the HttpClient configuration in the Program.cs file of the Blazor application with this URL:

```
builder.Services.AddScoped(sp => new HttpClient {
 BaseAddress = new Uri("https://localhost:7049/")});
```

Let's also copy the same connection string of the old web project into the PackagesManagementBlazor.Serverappsettings.json file:

```
"ConnectionStrings": {
  "DefaultConnection": "Server=(localdb)\
\mssqllocaldb;Database=wwtravelclubadmin;Trusted_Connection=True;MultipleActiveResultSets
=true"
},
...
```

This way, we can reuse the database we have created. We also need to connect PackagesManagementBlazor.Server with the DB driver by adding the following code at the end of the services configuration code in the Program.cs file:

```
builder.Services.AddDbDriver(
        builder.Configuration
         .GetConnectionString("DefaultConnection")??string.Empty);
```

We also need to add all queries and command/event handlers defined in the application services to the dependency injection engine with:

```
builder.Services.AddApplicationServices();
```

At this point we have the project completely configured. We just need to implement server-side code and client-side code that implements our package search.

The next subsection explains how to design the server-side REST API.

Implementing the required ASP.NET Core REST APIs

As the first step, let's define the ViewModels used in the communication between the server and the client applications. They must be defined in the PackagesManagementBlazor.Shared project that is referenced by both applications.

Let's start with the PackageInfosViewModel ViewModel, which will be the data structure used by the Blazor application to exchange package info with the server-side REST API:

```
public class PackageInfosViewModel
{
```

```
    public int Id { get; set; }
    public required string Name { get; set; }
    public decimal Price { get; set; }
    public int DurationInDays { get; set; }
    public DateTime? StartValidityDate { get; set; }
    public DateTime? EndValidityDate { get; set; }
    public required string DestinationName { get; set; }
    public int DestinationId { get; set; }
}
```

Then, add the ViewModel that encloses all packages to return to the Blazor application:

```
namespace PackagesManagementBlazor.Shared
{
    public class PackagesListViewModel
    {
        Public required IReadOnlyCollection<PackageInfosViewModel>
            Items { get; set; }
    }
}
```

Now, we can also add our query that searches packages by location. Let's add it to the Queries folder in the root of the `PackagesManagementApplicationServices` project. Let's start with its interface `IPackagesListByLocationQuery`:

```
using PackagesManagementDomainServices.DTOs;
using System.Collections.ObjectModel;


namespace PackagesManagementApplicationServices.Queries
{
    public interface IPackagesListByLocationQuery: IQuery
    {
        Task<IReadOnlyCollection<PackageInfosDTO>>
            GetPackagesOf(string location);

    }
}
```

In order to implement this interface, we must add another repository method to the domain services `IPackageRepository`:

```
public interface IPackageRepository: IRepository
{
    Task<IList<PackageInfosDTO>> GetAllInfo();
    Task<IList<PackageInfosDTO>> GetInfoByDestination(string search);
    …
```

Now we must also add the implementation of this new method in the `PackageRepository` class of the DB Driver:

```
public async Task<IList<PackageInfosDTO>> GetInfoByDestination(string search)
{
    return await _context.Packages
    .Where(m => m.MyDestination.Name.Contains(search))
    .Select(m => new PackageInfosDTO
    {
        StartValidityDate = m.StartValidityDate,
        EndValidityDate = m.EndValidityDate,
        Name = m.Name,
        DurationInDays = m.DurationInDays,
        Id = m.Id,
        Price = m.Price,
        DestinationName = m.MyDestination.Name,
        DestinationId = m.DestinationId
    })
    .OrderByDescending(m => m.EndValidityDate)
    .ToListAsync();
}
```

Finally, we are ready for the `IPackagesListByLocationQuery` implementation:

```
using PackagesManagementDomainServices.DTOs;
using PackagesManagementDomainServices.IRepositories;
using System.Collections.ObjectModel;

namespace PackagesManagementApplicationServices.Queries
{
  public class PackagesListByLocationQuery(IPackageRepository repo) :
        IPackagesListByLocationQuery
    {
        public async Task<IReadOnlyCollection<PackageInfosDTO>>
```

```
            GetPackagesOf(string search)
        {
            return new ReadOnlyCollection<PackageInfosDTO> (
                await repo.GetInfoByDestination(search));
        }
    }
}
```

Now we are finally ready to define our `PackagesController`:

```
using Microsoft.AspNetCore.Mvc;
using PackagesManagementApplicationServices.Queries;
using PackagesManagementBlazor.Shared;
using System.Collections.Immutable;

namespace PackagesManagementBlazor.Server.Controllers
{
    [Route("[controller]")]
    [ApiController]
    public class PackagesController : ControllerBase
    {
        [HttpGet("{search}")]
        public async Task<PackagesListViewModel>
        GetAsync(string search,
            [FromServices] IPackagesListByLocationQuery query)
        {
            return new PackagesListViewModel
            {
                Items = (await query.GetPackagesOf(search))
                 .Select(m => new PackageInfosViewModel
                 {
                     Id = m.Id,
                     Name = m.Name,
                     DestinationName = m.DestinationName,
                     DestinationId = m.DestinationId,
                     Price = m.Price,
                     DurationInDays = m.DurationInDays,
                     StartValidityDate = m.StartValidityDate,
                     EndValidityDate = m.EndValidityDate

                 }).ToImmutableList()
            };
        }
```

```
    }
}
```

The server-side code is finished! Let's move on to the definition of the Blazor service that communicates with the server.

Implementing the client-side business logic in a service

Let's add a `ViewModels` and a `Services` folder to the `PackagesManagementBlazor.Client` project. Most of the ViewModels we need were defined in the `PackagesManagementBlazor.Shared` project. We only need a ViewModel for the search form. Let's add it to the newly defined `ViewModels` folder:

```
using System.ComponentModel.DataAnnotations;
namespace PackagesManagementBlazor.Client.ViewModels
{
    public class SearchViewModel
    {
        [Required]
        public string? Location { get; set; }
    }
}
```

Let's call our service `PackagesClient`, and let's add it to the Services folder:

```
using PackagesManagementBlazor.Shared;
using System.Net.Http.Json;

namespace PackagesManagementBlazor.Client.Services
{
    public class PackagesClient(HttpClient client)
    {
        public async Task<IEnumerable<PackageInfosViewModel>>
            GetByLocationAsync(string location)
        {
            var result =
                await client.GetFromJsonAsync<PackagesListViewModel>
                    ("Packages/" + Uri.EscapeDataString(location));
            return result?.Items??new List<PackageInfosViewModel>();
        }
    }
}
```

The code is straightforward! The `Uri.EscapeDataString` method URL-encodes the parameter so it can be safely appended to the URL.

Finally, let's register the service in the dependency injection in the Blazor `Program.cs` file:

```
builder.Services.AddScoped<PackagesClient>();
```

It is worth pointing out that in a commercial application, we should have registered the service through an `IPackagesClient` interface, in order to be able to mock it in the tests ((`.AddScoped<IPackagesClient, PackagesClient>()`).

With everything in place, we just need to build the user interface (UI).

Implementing the user interface

As the first step, let's delete the application pages we don't need, namely, `Pages->Counter.razor` and `Pages->Weather.razor`. Let's also remove their links from the side menu in `Shared->NavMenu.razor`.

We will put our code in the `Pages->Home.razor` page. Let's replace the code of this page with this:

```
@using PackagesManagementBlazor.Client.ViewModels
@using PackagesManagementBlazor.Shared
@using PackagesManagementBlazor.Client.Services
@inject PackagesClient client
@page "/"
<PageTitle>Packages</PageTitle>
<h1>Search packages by location</h1>
<EditForm Model="search"
          OnValidSubmit="Search">
  <DataAnnotationsValidator />
  <div class="form-group">
    <label for="integerfixed">Insert location starting chars</label>
    <InputText @bind-Value="search.Location" />
    <ValidationMessage For="@(() => search.Location)" />
  </div>
  <button type="submit" class="btn btn-primary">
        Search
  </button>
</EditForm>
@code{
    SearchViewModel search { get; set; } = new SearchViewModel();
    async Task Search()
    {
        ...
    }
}
```

The preceding code adds the needed `@using`, injects our `PackagesClient` service into the page and defines the search form. When the form is successfully submitted, it invokes the `Search` callback, where we will place the code that retrieves all the results.

It is time to add the logic to display all the results and to complete the `@code` block. The following code must be placed immediately after the search form:

```
@if (packages != null)
{
...
}
else if (loading)
{
    <p><em>Loading...</em></p>
}
@code{
    SearchViewModel search { get; set; } = new SearchViewModel();
    private IEnumerable<PackageInfosViewModel> packages;
    bool loading;
    async Task Search()
    {
        packages = null;
        loading = true;
        await InvokeAsync(StateHasChanged);
        packages = await client.GetByLocationAsync(search.Location);
        loading = false;
    }
}
```

The omitted code in the `if` block is responsible for rendering a table with all results. We will show it after we have commented on the preceding code.

Before retrieving the results with the `PackagesClient` service, we remove all previous results and set the loading field so the Razor code selects the `else if` path that replaces the previous table with a loading message. Once we've set these variables, we are forced to call `StateHasChanged` to trigger change detection and refresh the page. After all the results have been retrieved and the callback returns, there is no need to call `StateHasChanged` again because the termination of the callback itself triggers change detection and causes the needed page refresh.

Here is the code that renders the table with all results:

```
<div class="table-responsive">
  <table class="table">
    <thead>
```

```
        <tr>
          <th scope="col">Destination</th>
          <th scope="col">Name</th>
          <th scope="col">Duration/days</th>
          <th scope="col">Price</th>
          <th scope="col">Available from</th>
          <th scope="col">Available to</th>
        </tr>
      </thead>
      <tbody>
        @foreach (var package in packages)
        {
          <tr>
            <td>
              @package.DestinationName
            </td>
            <td>
              @package.Name
            </td>
            <td>
              @package.DurationInDays
            </td>
            <td>
              @package.Price
            </td>
            <td>
              @(package.StartValidityDate.HasValue ?
                package.StartValidityDate.Value.ToString("d")
                :
                String.Empty)
            </td>
            <td>
              @(package.EndValidityDate.HasValue ?
                package.EndValidityDate.Value.ToString("d")
                :
                String.Empty)
            </td>
          </tr>
        }
      </tbody>
    </table>
  </div>
```

Run the project and write the initial characters of Florence. Since we inserted Florence as a location in the same database in previous chapters (see the *A Frontend Microservice* section of this chapter), some results should appear. If you inserted different data, please try with different starting words.

Usually, together with a web-based client, all applications also furnish a mobile native application to get better performance with possibly slow mobile devices. So let's design a mobile native client application as well!

Adding a Blazor MAUI Version

In this section we explain how to add a Blazor MAUI version to the application of the previous solution.

First of all, right-click on the solution icon in Solution Explorer and add a new project to the solution. Select a MAUI Blazor application and call it `PackagesManagementMAUI`.

Open the `PackagesManagementMAUI` project file and remove all the platforms you don't want to support (I removed Android, iOS, and MacCatalyst, and remained with just Windows):

```
<TargetFrameworks Condition="$([MSBuild]::IsOSPlatform('windows'))">$
(TargetFrameworks);net10.0-windows10.0.19041.0
</TargetFrameworks>
```

Then, add a reference to the `PackagesManagementBlazor.Shared` project.

Now, right-click on the client WebAssembly project and select Open Folder in File Explorer. Then, copy the `ViewModels` and `Services` folders, and paste them in Visual Studio Solution Explorer under the newly created `PackagesManagementMAUI` node.

Then, change the namespaces of the files contained in these folders to be, respectively, `PackagesManagementMAUI.ViewModels` and `PackagesManagementMAUI.Services`.

Now, replace the content of the `Layout` and `Pages` folders of the newly created project with the content of the `Layout` and `Pages` folders of the client Blazor WebAssembly project.

Edit the newly copied `Home.razor` file and replace its header with:

```
@using PackagesManagementMAUI.Services
@using PackagesManagementBlazor.Shared
@using PackagesManagementMAUI.ViewModels
@inject PackagesClient client
@page "/"
```

Finally, add the same `HttpClient` and `PackagesClient` configurations of the WebAssembly project to `MAUIProgram.cs`:

```
builder.Services.AddScoped(sp => new HttpClient
    { BaseAddress = new Uri("https://localhost: 7049/") });
builder.Services.AddScoped<PackagesClient>();
```

With this, you must add PackagesManagementMAUI to the projects to start. Right-click on the solution and select **Configure Startup Projects**.

In the windows that open, select also the newly created MAUI Blazor project, and select **Windows Machine** (or some other device you configured) as **Debug Target**.

Now, you can launch the application. Two interface windows should open, a browser window, and a Windows window, but both client projects' windows should show exactly the same application.

After having discussed all components of our WWTravelClub applications, we just need to describe how to test it.

Testing the WWTravelClub application

In this section, we add some unit and functional test projects to the PackagesManagement frontend microservice we described in the *A Frontend Microservices* section of this chapter. If you don't have it, you can download it from the section of the GitHub repository associated with the book in the ch17 folder. It is worth pointing out that in real world projects, unit test batteries would be enhanced also with integration tests, while acceptance tests do not include just functional tests but also various kinds of performance tests.

The reader is encouraged to review *Chapter 9, Testing Your Enterprise Application* before continuing with this section.

As a first step, let's make a new copy of the solution folder and name it PackagesManagementWithTests. Then, open the solution and add it an **xUnit** .NET C# test project named PackagesManagementTest. Finally, add a reference to the ASP.NET Core project (PackagesManagement), since we will test it, and a reference to the latest version of the Moq NuGet package, since we require mocking capabilities. It is worth remembering that Moq is a mocking library and that the purpose of mocking is to decouple dependencies between classes by replacing actual classes with mocked classes whose behavior is under the complete control of the test code. This way each class can be unit tested independently from the behavior of other classes it references. For more details about Moq please refer to *Chapter 9, Testing Your Enterprise Application.*

At this point, we are ready to write our tests.

As an example, we will write unit tests for the Edit method decorated with [HttpPost] of the ManagePackagesController controller, which is shown below:

```
[HttpPost]
public async Task<IActionResult> Edit(
    PackageFullEditViewModel vm,
    [FromServices] ICommandHandler<UpdatePackageCommand> command)
{
    if (ModelState.IsValid)
    {
        await command.HandleAsync(new UpdatePackageCommand {
            Id = vm.Id,
            Name = vm.Name,
```

```
                Description = vm.Description,
                Price = vm.Price,
                DurationInDays=vm.DurationInDays,
                StartValidityDate=vm.StartValidityDate,
                EndValidityDate=vm.EndValidityDate
            });
            return RedirectToAction(
                nameof(ManagePackagesController.Index));
        }
        else
            return View(vm);
    }
```

Before writing our test methods, let's rename the test class that was automatically included in the test project as `ManagePackagesControllerTests`.

The first test verifies that if there are errors in `ModelState`, the action method renders a view with the same model it received as an argument so that the user can correct all errors. We need to test all possibilities. Let's delete the existing test method and write an empty `DeletePostValidationFailedTest` method, as follows:

```
[Fact]
public async Task DeletePostValidationFailedTest()
{
}
```

The method must be async and the return type must be Task since the Edit method that we have to test is async. As a preparation for the test, we need to create a controller instance, and we must add an error to `ModelState` as follows:

```
var controller = new ManagePackagesController();
controller.ModelState
    .AddModelError("Name", "fake error");
```

Then we invoke the method, injecting ViewModel and a mocked command handler as its arguments that do nothing, since it will not be invoked:

```
var vm = new PackageFullEditViewModel();
var commandDependency =
                new Mock<ICommandHandler<UpdatePackageCommand>>();
var result = await controller.Edit(vm, commandDependency.Object);
```

In the verification stage, we verify that the result is ViewResult and that it contains the same model that was injected into the controller:

```
var viewResult = Assert.IsType<ViewResult>(result);
Assert.Equal(vm, viewResult.Model);
```

Now, we also need a test to verify that if there are no errors, the command handler is called and then the browser is redirected to the Index controller action method. We call the `DeletePostSuccessTest` method:

```
[Fact]
public async Task DeletePostSuccessTest()
{
}
```

This time, we must adequately prepare a command handler mock:

```
var controller = new ManagePackagesController();
var commandDependency =
    new Mock<ICommandHandler<UpdatePackageCommand>>();
commandDependency
    .Setup(m =>
    m.HandleAsync(It.IsAny<UpdatePackageCommand>()))
    .Returns(Task.CompletedTask);
var vm = new PackageFullEditViewModel();
```

Since the handler `HandleAsync` method returns no async value, we can't use `ReturnsAsync`, but we have to return just a completed Task (`Task.Complete`) with the `Returns` method.

There is no need to fill the ViewModel with fake data, since the ViewModel is validated by ASP.NET Core before calling the action method. Fake, data will be needed just in the tests for the command handler.

The method to test is called with both the ViewModel and the mocked handler:

```
var result = await controller.Edit(vm,
    commandDependency.Object);
```

In this case, the verification code is as follows:

```
commandDependency.Verify(m => m.HandleAsync(
    It.IsAny<UpdatePackageCommand>()),
    Times.Once);
var redirectResult = Assert.IsType<RedirectToActionResult>(result);
Assert.Equal(nameof(ManagePackagesController.Index),
```

```
    redirectResult.ActionName);
Assert.Null(redirectResult.ControllerName);
```

As the first step, we verify that the command handler has actually been invoked once. Then we verify that the action method returns a `RedirectToActionResult` with the right action method name and with no controller name specified.

Once all the tests are ready, if the test window does not appear on the left bar of Visual Studio, we may simply select the Run all tests item from the Visual Studio Test menu. Once the test window appears, further invocations can be launched from within this window.

If a test fails, we can add a breakpoint to its code, so we can launch a debug session on it by right-clicking on it in the test window and then selecting **Debug selected tests**. It is worth remembering that failures do not necessarily depend on errors in the code under test but might also depend on errors in the testing code itself.

Once all microservices that compose an application have been implemented it is time to start their integration with tools like .NET Aspire, and their test into an actual orchestrator like Kubernetes. Next section shows how to do this in practice.

Testing a Worker microservice with .NET Aspire

In this section we will adapt the example of *A worker microservices with ASP.NET core* section to run with .NET Aspire. As a first step let copy the whole solution folder in a different location, so we can modify it without destroying the previous version, and rename the solution folder, `GrpcMicroServiceAspire`.

Then let's execute the following steps to prepare the overall solution:

1. Let's add a new App Host project to the solution, and let's call it `GrpcMicroServiceAppHost`
2. Let add a new .NET Aspire Service Defaults project to the solution and let call it `GrpcMicroServiceServiceDefaults`
3. Add a reference to the `FakeSource` and `GrpcMicroService` projects to the `GrpcMicroServiceAppHost` project
4. Vice versa, add a reference to the `GrpcMicroServiceServiceDefaults` project to the `FakeSource` and `GrpcMicroService` projects
5. Right click on the `GrpcMicroServiceAppHost` project and, in the menu that appears, select **Set as Startup Project**

The above steps prepare the solution for .NET Aspire. Now let start modifying the code. As a first step you must add service defaults to all our microservices. Therefore, let add `builder.AddServiceDefaults();` to the `Program.cs` file of the `GrpcMicroService` projects and the following code snippet in the services definition of the `FakeSource` project:

```
services.AddServiceDiscovery();

services.ConfigureHttpClientDefaults(http =>
```

```
{
    // Turn on resilience by default
    http.AddStandardResilienceHandler();

    // Turn on service discovery by default
    http.AddServiceDiscovery();
});
```

In fact, we can't add `builder.AddServiceDefaults()` to it since it is not a Web project, so we add just service discovery and resiliency policies.

Then, we must add the `app.MapDefaultEndpoints()` that adds Health endpoints just to the `program.cs` file of the `GrpcMicroService` project, since it is the only Web project that we have among our microservices. It must be placed as shown below:

```
...
var app = builder.Build();
app.MapDefaultEndpoints();
...
```

In order to enable service discovery also on Grpc communication, we must force Grpc channels to use http clients taken from the dependency injection engine. Accordingly, let's modify `FakeSource` hosted service constructor in `FakeSource->HostedServices->ProcessPurchases.cs` as follows:

```
HttpClient _client;
public Worker(ILogger<Worker> logger, HttpClient client)
{
    _logger = logger;
    _client= client;
}
```

Then, the channel creation code in the same file must be replaced with:

```
using var channel = GrpcChannel.ForAddress("http://grpcmicroservice",
    new GrpcChannelOptions
    {
        HttpClient= _client
    });
```

We passed the injected http client to the channel and replaced the actual service URL with a virtual URL based on the name assigned to the service in the App Host.

Instead of using the SQL server installation that come with Visual Studio we will configure also a SQL Server instance and a database with .NET Aspire. However, if we would like to start with a new instance and with empty database, we must configure so that it applies database migrations at start.

Let's add the following extension method to the `WorkerMDBDriver` project, in its `WorkerMDBDriver->Extensions->DBExtensions.cs` file:

```
public static async Task<IServiceProvider> UseDatabase(this
    IServiceProvider serviceProvider)
{
    using var serviceScope = serviceProvider.CreateScope();
    var context = serviceScope.ServiceProvider
        .GetRequiredService<IUnitOfWork>() as MainDbContext;
    if (context != null)
    {
        await context.Database.MigrateAsync();

    }
    return serviceProvider;
}
```

Now let's call this extension method from the `Program.cs` of the `GrpcMicroService` project as shown below:

```
...
await app.Services.UseDatabase();
app.Run();
```

Let's move to the App Host project and start the Aspire configuration. In the `AppHost.cs` file, let's declare the database:

```
var builder = DistributedApplication.CreateBuilder(args);
var sql = builder.AddSqlServer("sql");
var db = sql.AddDatabase("DefaultConnection");
```

If we don't want to lose all database data once the solution is stopped, we can chain `WithDataVolume()` after `AddSqlServer` as shown below:

```
var sql = builder.AddSqlServer("sql")
   . WithDataVolume();
```

Then, we declare the `GrpcMicroService` microservice with a dependency on the database:

```
var grpcMicroService = builder.AddProject<Projects.GrpcMicroService>("grpcmicroservice")
    .WithReference(db)
    .WaitFor(db);
```

At this point we can remove the `DefaultConnection` old connection string from `GrpcMicroService->Appsettings.json` file, since the connection string of the new database will be passed by the App Host in the `ConnectionStrings__DefaultConnection` environment variable.

Finally, let's declare the `FakeSource` microservice with a dependency on `GrpcMicroService`:

```
var fakeSource = builder.AddProject<Projects.FakeSource>("fakesource")
    .WithReference(grpcMicroService)
    .WaitFor(grpcMicroService);
builder.Build().Run();
```

Done!

> **Note**
>
> Before running the solution, please verify Docker Desktop is running; otherwise, Aspire will not be able to create an SQL Server container.

Now we can launch the solution. At the beginning, the `.WaitFor` we placed in the configuration prevents all microservices from starting while the database is being created:

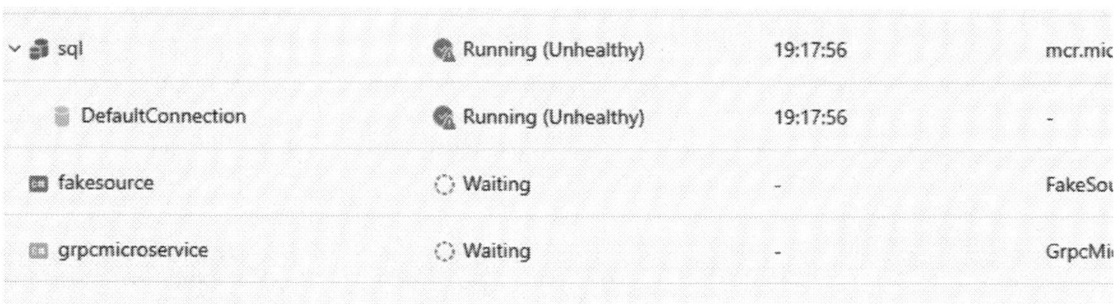

Figure 22.20: Services wait for the SQL Server instance to be ready

After a few seconds, the SQL Server instance enters a healthy state, and all services successfully start:

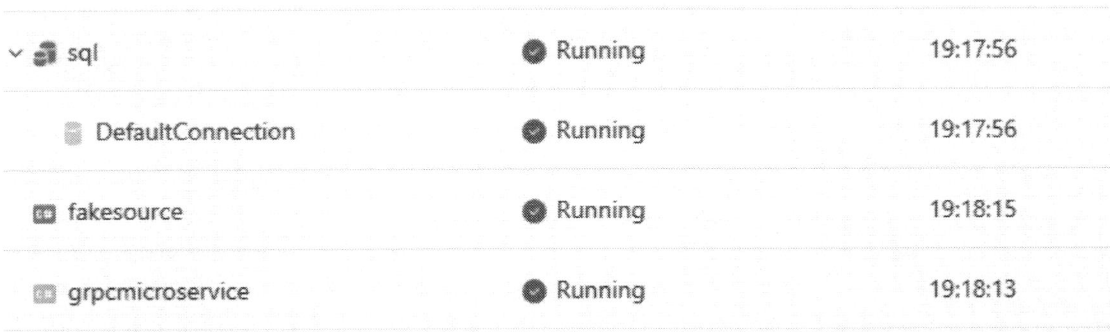

Figure 22.21: All services and resources running

At this point, let's click on the console icon of **grpcmicroservice** to inspect its log. You will see the updates being sent to the database:

Figure 22.22: Database updates issued by grpcmicroservice

Now that the worker microservice is functioning locally and interacting correctly with the database, the next step is to deploy it in a production-oriented orchestration environment.

Deploying a Worker microservice on Kubernetes

In this section, we will use the solution prepared in the previous section to create Docker images and to run them in Docker Desktop Kubernetes.

First, we need an SQL Server instance that accepts TCP/IP connections, so we cannot use the instance that comes with the Visual Studio installation. The simplest solution is to run it as a docker container in Docker Desktop:

```
docker run -e "ACCEPT_EULA=Y" -e "MSSQL_SA_PASSWORD=myP@ssw0rd" -p 1433:1433 -d --name
dockerSql --hostname dockerSql mcr.microsoft.com/mssql/server:2022-latest
```

Since during development we don't want to upload our development images to an actual image registry, we are left with two options: either we install a local registry as a container in Docker Desktop as we have done with SQL Server, or we push our Docker images to the Kind nodes with a Kind command.

The first option is quite complex because neither Kubernetes nor Docker trust registries with no HTTPS support or with a self-signed HTTPS certificate, so we need to change settings to remove this limitation.

On the other side, Docker Desktop Kind doesn't come with a console client that supports Kind commands; therefore, we need to perform a complete Kind installation.

The complete Kind installation appears more attractive since it enhances our Docker Desktop installation with the possibility to create several Kubernetes clusters and to perform several more customization tasks.

On Windows, Kind can be installed with the **Chocolatey** package manager using the command below:

```
choco install kind
```

> **Note**
>
> The above command must be issued by a PowerShell console opened with administrative privileges. Moreover, during the installation you will be asked for permission to run PowerShell command files, and you must grant this permission.

If you don't have Chocolatey installed, you can install it as follows:

1. Search PowerShell in the Windows search box
2. Right-click on the PowerShell link and select to execute it as an administrator
3. Finally, execute the PowerShell command suggested on the official Chocolatey page: `https://chocolatey.org/install#individual`.
4. With this in place deploying our application on Kubernetes is as easy as:
5. Creating Docker images for the `Fakesource` and `GrpcMicroService` application
6. Pushing these images into Docker Kubernetes cluster nodes
7. Defining Kubernetes Deployments based on the `FakeSource` and `GrpcMicroService` images and a `ClusterIp` Service for `GrpcMicroService`

Let's discuss each of the above points in a dedicated subsection.

Creating Docker images

Right click on the GrpcMicroService project and choose **Add -> Container Support** from the menu that appears. In the window that appears, choose the settings below:

Figure 22.23: Container image settings

After you confirm the settings, a Dockerfile is added to the project. The Dockerfile contains all instructions needed to create an appropriate Docker image.

Repeat the same operation on the FakeSource project. However, in this case we must modify the Dockerfile a little since it is not a Web project and is based on the `dotnet runtime` image instead of the `aspnet` image. We need to change its base images; otherwise, FakeSource will not be able to start once deployed.

We must perform the following line replacement:

```
//original line
FROM mcr.microsoft.com/dotnet/runtime:10.0 AS base
...
//replacement line
FROM mcr.microsoft.com/dotnet/aspnet:10.0 AS base
...
```

Now, you need just to click on the two newly created Dockerfiles and select **Build Image** from the menu that appears.

Two new images should appear in your Docker Desktop user interface: `grpcmicroservice:latest` and `fakesource:latest`.

Now let's push these images into our cluster.

Pushing images into Docker Kubernetes

As a first step, let's discover the name of our Kubernetes cluster by issuing the command below:

```
kind get clusters
```

The name should be `desktop`.

The two images can be pushed with the two commands below:

```
kind load docker-image fakesource:latest --name desktop
kind load docker-image grpcmicroservice:latest --name desktop
```

Done! Let's create all needed Kubernetes objects.

Defining Kubernetes objects

Below is the definition of the `grpcmicroservice` deployment:

```
apiVersion: apps/v1
kind: Deployment
metadata:
  name: grpcmicroservice
  labels:
```

```
    app: statistics
spec:
  selector:
    matchLabels:
      app: statistics
      role: worker
  replicas: 1
  template:
    metadata:
      labels:
        app: statistics
        role: worker
    spec:
      containers:
      - name: grpcmicroservice
        image: grpcmicroservice:latest
        imagePullPolicy: Never
        resources:
          requests:
            cpu: 10m
            memory: 10Mi
        env:
        - name: ASPNETCORE_HTTP_PORTS
          value: "8080"
        - name: ConnectionStrings__DefaultConnection
          value: "Server=host.docker.internal;Database=DefaultConnection;User
Id=sa;Password=myP@ssw0rd;Trust Server Certificate=True;MultipleActiveResultSets=true"
        ports:
        - containerPort: 8080
          name: http
```

`imagePullPolicy: Never` prevents Kubernetes nodes from requiring an updated version of the images we manually pushed in the nodes, because there is no registry containing them, so a similar attempt would fail. This setting must always be added whenever we manually push our images.

We indexed both PODs and Deployment with the labels:

```
app: statistics
role: worker
```

They are connected with the semantics and role of the microservice. You should always choose labels this way.

The `ASPNETCORE_HTTP_PORTS` environment variable is a standard ASP.NET setting that instructs ASP.NET on the port where to listen for HTTP requests. 8080 corresponds to one of the ports declared in the Dockerfile. There is an analogous `ASPNETCORE_HTTPS_PORTS` variable, but we don't use encrypted communication since it would require the installation of an HTTP certificate inside the container (the operation can be carried out with a volume mount).

The other environment variable is the default connection string. Adopting the `ConnectionStrings__DefaultConnection` name corresponds to placing the connection string in the `ConnectionStrings->DefaultConnection` property of the `AppSettings.json` file. `host.docker.internal` in the connection string is a trick used by Kind to refer to the computer that hosts Docker Desktop, and in fact in all Kubernetes nodes it resolves to the IP address assigned to your computer by Docker Desktop in all its virtual networks. In fact, the Sql Server instance we installed as a Docker container is exposed on your computer on `localhost:1433`, where `1433` is the default Sql Server port.

`fakesource` deployment is similar, but it declares no ports and doesn't need any environment variable.

Finally, below is the ClusterIp service that routes traffic to `grpcmicroservice`:

```
apiVersion: v1
kind: Service
metadata:
  name: grpcmicroservice
  labels:
    app: contract
    role: worker
spec:
  ports:
  - port: 80
    targetPort: 8080
  selector:
    app: statistics
    role: worker
```

The service must have the same name we assigned to `grpcmicroservice` in the App Host, otherwise all links like `http://grpcmicroservice` we use in all clients wouldn't work properly. For the same reason, the service must listen on the `80` port, since this is the port referred by `http://grpcmicroservice`. However, since `grpcmicroservice` listens on the `8080` port, the service must specify `8080` as `targetPort`.

All needed objects were inserted in the same `kubernetesdeploy.yaml` file in the `ch19` folder of the GitHub repository associated with the book.

Now we are ready to test our microservices on Kubernetes. Verify Docker Desktop is running and that the container containing our Sql server instance is running, too.

Connect from Visual Studio to the containerized Sql Server so you can inspect the data being written there. The connection settings are shown below:

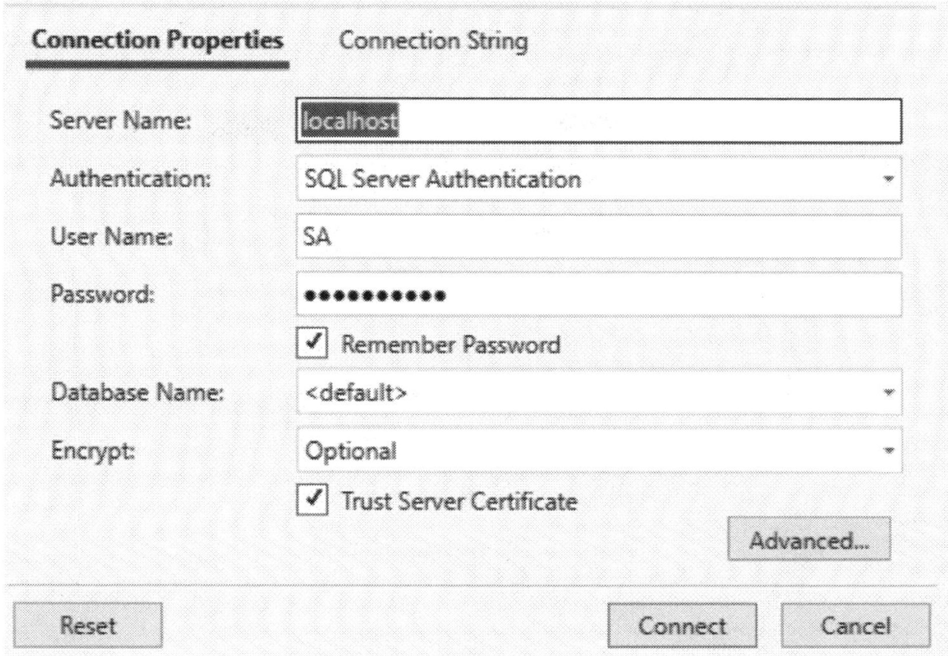

Figure 22.24: Connecting to the containerized SQL Server instance

Now open a console in the same folder that contains the `kubernetesdeploy.yaml` file, and issue the command below:

```
kubectl apply -f kubernetesdeploy.yaml
```

Wait a few seconds and then issue the `kubectl get all` command to verify that all objects have been created properly and that both PODs are in the ready state. Repeat the command a few times until everything is working properly.

Then inspect the Sql Server instance. A new database called `DefaultConnection` has been created. Inspect the `dbo.DayTotals` table by right-clicking on it and selecting **View Data**. You should see all daily totals computed so far by our worker microservice:

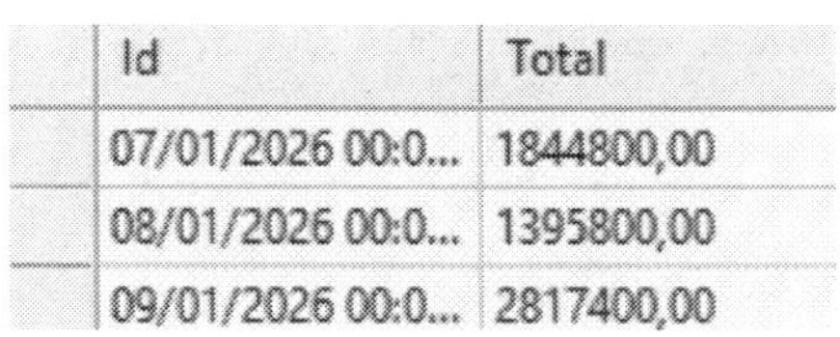

Id	Total
07/01/2026 00:0...	1844800,00
08/01/2026 00:0...	1395800,00
09/01/2026 00:0...	2817400,00

Figure 22.25: Computed daily totals

Now let's clean up our cluster with:

```
kubectl delete -f kubernetesdeploy.yaml
```

Done. You have run your first Kubernetes application!

This completes our tour of the practical implementation of a microservice enterprise application. We hope you enjoyed it and that you enjoyed the whole book as much as we enjoyed writing it!

Summary

Although WWTravelClub is intentionally simplified for educational purposes, the architectural decisions presented throughout this chapter reflect many of the trade-offs commonly encountered in real enterprise systems. Scalability, resiliency, distributed communication, DevSecOps practices, cloud-native infrastructure, and domain-driven design all interact continuously throughout the software lifecycle.

Rather than presenting a single "*correct*" architecture, this case study demonstrates how modern software architecture requires balancing technical flexibility, operational reliability, maintainability, security, and business evolution. The technologies used throughout the chapter are important, but the most critical skill for a software architect remains the ability to evaluate trade-offs and make decisions that align technical solutions with long-term organizational goals.

So the main purpose of this chapter is to deliver to you some pieces of implementation that could be useful to start the challenge of delivering a software solution for an enterprise. This is not a software implementation itself, but we are sure this content can help you with some great ideas of how to achieve a better architectural design of your solution, considering what we understand as the main purpose of a software architect – to help the team achieve the software implemented as the user really needs.

Part 3

Appendices

In this part, you will find the answers to the exercises provided throughout the chapters, along with additional resources to help you make the most of your learning experience.

This part of the book includes the following chapters:

- *Appendix A, Answers*
- *Appendix B, Unlock Your Exclusive Benefits*

A

Answers

Chapter 1

1. A software architect needs to be aware of any technology that can help them solve problems faster and ensure they can create better quality software, as well as guide architectural decisions, support the development team, and make trade-offs involving quality, cost, time, and future evolution.
2. Azure provides, and keeps improving, lots of components that a software architect can implement in solutions, especially for building, deploying, scaling, and maintaining modern cloud-based software architectures.
3. The best software development process model depends on the kind of project, team, and budget you have. As a software architect, you need to consider all these variables and understand different process models so you can fit the environment's needs, including traditional, incremental, agile, Scrum, XP, lean, and scaled agile approaches.
4. A software architect pays attention to any user or system requirement that can influence performance, security, usability, and so on, and helps stakeholders gather, analyze, specify, and review those requirements so they can guide the architecture and implementation.
5. All of them, but the non-functional requirements need to be given more attention, because they strongly influence architectural decisions. This includes requirements related to scalability, robustness, security, performance, usability, availability, and maintainability.
6. Design Thinking and Design Sprint are tools that help software architects define exactly what users need, validate ideas early, create prototypes, collect user feedback, and reduce the risk of building the wrong solution
7. User Stories are good when we want to define functional requirements. They can be written quickly and commonly deliver not only the feature required, but also the acceptance criteria for the solution, while also explaining who needs the feature, what they need, and why they need it.
8. Caching, asynchronous programming, and correct object allocation, as well as clear performance requirements, proper resource disposal, optimized database access, filtering only the required data, and performance testing under realistic load conditions.

9. To check that the implementation is correct, a software architect compares it with models and prototypes that have already been designed and validated, as well as the requirements specification, user stories, acceptance criteria, data flows, code inspections, tests, and stakeholder feedback.
10. AI can help during the requirements gathering process by summarizing collected material, generating meeting summaries and transcripts, helping review requirements for completeness, improving requirement documentation, and accelerating the creation or refinement of specifications and user stories. However, it must be used responsibly, especially when confidential project or customer information is involved

Chapter 2

1. Vertically and horizontally, also known as scaling up and scaling out. Vertical scaling means increasing the power of the hardware that hosts the application, while horizontal scaling means adding more servers or instances and balancing the load between them.
2. Yes, you can deploy automatically to an already-defined web app or create a new one directly using Visual Studio, and Visual Studio can connect to Azure to publish the application. For real-world projects, a CI/CD flow such as GitHub Actions is usually a better deployment strategy.
3. To take advantage of available hardware resources by minimizing the time they remain idle, so that when one thread is waiting for an operation to be finished, the application can use the CPU to work on other threads or tasks instead of wasting processing time.
4. Code behavior is deterministic, so it is easy to debug. The execution flow mimics the flow of sequential code, which means it is easier to design and understand, test, debug, and maintain. It also keeps many performance advantages of parallel programming while reducing the need to manually manage the thread lifecycle.
5. Because the right order minimizes the number of gestures that are needed to fill in a form, improves usability, reduces user effort, and allows users to move naturally between fields using keys such as Tab or Enter.
6. Because it allows for the manipulation of path files in a way that is independent of the operating system, helping the application handle differences between platforms, such as Windows and Linux path separators, and making the code more portable across Windows, Linux, and macOS.

Chapter 3

1. No, it is available for several platforms, not only for .NET projects. Azure DevOps can support different technologies, repositories, package types, test strategies, and deployment targets.
2. Automatic, manual, and load test plans, including manual acceptance tests, automatic unit tests, and load tests that can be defined, executed, tracked, and reported through Azure DevOps Test Plans.
3. Yes, they can – through Azure DevOps feeds, using Azure Artifacts. These feeds can host private packages, including NuGet packages, and can also connect to public package sources such as nuget.org.
4. To manage requirements and to organize the whole development process, by transforming requirements into manageable, assignable, trackable, and traceable units of work.

5. Epic work items represent high-level system subparts that are made up of several features. A Feature is more specific: it represents a shippable software component or functionality that usually belongs to one Epic and can be implemented across a smaller number of sprints.
6. A parent-child relationship, where Task work items are children of Product Backlog items or User Story work items. Tasks describe the specific work needed to implement the requirement described by the parent item.
7. They can organize projects using the same concept we have in Azure DevOps, but in a more flexible and simpler way. GitHub Projects can use issues, milestones, custom fields, labels, linked pull requests, reviewers, repositories, iterations, and views such as Table, Board, and Roadmap to plan and track work.
8. Both options are great tools for running agile projects. The best option depends on your team experience, the objective of the project, and the kind of solution being developed. GitHub is often a better option for open-source and repository-centered collaboration, while Azure DevOps is a strong option for enterprise projects that need integrated planning, repositories, artifacts, test plans, and pipelines.
9. GitHub Code Agent works as an autonomous development agent inside GitHub. You can assign it a task through a GitHub issue or Copilot prompt, and it can research the repository, prepare an implementation plan, make code changes in a branch, and optionally open a pull request for human review. It runs on GitHub in a GitHub Actions-powered environment and works best when the requirements are clear, structured, and traceable.

Chapter 4

1. Maintainability gives you the opportunity to deliver the software you designed quickly. It also allows you to fix bugs easily, reduce technical debt, make future changes safer, and keep the code understandable as the system evolves.
2. Cyclomatic complexity is a metric that detects the number of possible execution paths a method has. The higher the number, the worse the effect, because the method becomes harder to understand, test, debug, and maintain. A high value usually indicates that the code should be refactored into smaller methods or classes.
3. A version control system will guarantee the integrity of your source code, giving you the opportunity to analyze the history of each modification that you've made, collaborate safely with other developers, use branches and pull requests, review changes before merging, protect architectural decisions, track versions, and recover previous states of the code when necessary.
4. A garbage collector is a .NET Core/.NET (5+)/.NET Framework system, which monitors your application and detects objects that you aren't using anymore. It disposes of these objects to release memory, but it mainly manages memory for managed objects. It does not automatically release unmanaged resources such as files, streams, sockets, or operating system handles at the exact time they are no longer needed. For this reason, unmanaged resources must be released explicitly using patterns such as try-finally, using, or IDisposable.
5. The IDisposable interface is important firstly because it is a good pattern for deterministic cleanup. Secondly, it is required in classes that instantiate objects that need to be disposed of by the programmer since the garbage collector cannot dispose of them or cannot release their unmanaged resources

immediately and predictably. Implementing IDisposable helps avoid memory leaks, resource exhaustion, and unstable application behavior.

6. .NET 10 encapsulates some design patterns in some of its libraries in a way that can guarantee safer code, such as with dependency injection and Builder. It also supports modern C# features, nullable reference types, logging integration through ILogger, safer object creation patterns, and built-in practices that help developers write cleaner, more maintainable, and more reliable code.
7. Well-written code is code that any person skilled in that programming language can handle, modify, and evolve, and that follows agreed coding standards, has clear names, low complexity, low coupling, high cohesion, appropriate error handling, good resource management, and is safe to replicate as a pattern across the codebase.
8. Roslyn is the .NET compiler that's used for code analysis inside Visual Studio, and it is important because it exposes compiler information through APIs, allowing tools to inspect syntax trees, symbols, and semantic models while the developer is coding.
9. Code analysis is a practice that considers the way the code is written to detect bad practices before compilation or during build and review processes. Its importance is that it helps detect problems such as memory leaks, unsafe exception handling, bad programming practices, maintainability issues, style violations, and possible design weaknesses before they reach production.
10. Roslyn is an engine that provides an API that enables analyzers to inspect your code for style, quality, maintainability, design, and other issues. This is done during design time, so you can check the mistakes before compiling your code, and it also supports live diagnostics, refactoring, custom analyzers, and automatic enforcement of coding standards through tools integrated into Visual Studio and the .NET build process.
11. Visual Studio extensions are tools that have been programmed to run inside Visual Studio. These tools can help you out in some cases where the Visual Studio IDE doesn't have the appropriate feature for you to use, including tools for productivity, code analysis, formatting, refactoring, security checks, and quality improvement.
12. SonarLint, and the SonarAnalyzer.CSharp NuGet package, as well as built-in .NET analyzers, Visual Studio Code Style tools, Code Cleanup, Roslyn analyzers, and other third-party analyzers available as Visual Studio extensions or NuGet packages.
13. AI-assisted tools complement static analyzers by adding contextual and explanatory feedback during coding and pull request reviews. Static analyzers are good at enforcing predefined rules, while AI tools such as GitHub Copilot can suggest refactoring, explain problems, improve readability, check whether code follows team standards, help review pull requests, and propose cleaner alternatives. They should not replace static analysis; instead, they add another layer of support for quality, consistency, and architectural governance.

Chapter 5

1. No, since you will have lots of duplicate code in this approach, which will cause difficulties when it comes to maintenance, bug fixing, consistency, and future evolution. Copy-and-paste may look faster at first, but if the same logic changes later, every copied version must be found and updated. If one copy is missed, the system can behave inconsistently.

2. The best approach for code reuse is creating libraries, centralizing reusable logic in shared components, services, base classes, interfaces, or APIs, depending on architectural need. The main idea is to avoid duplication by placing stable behavior behind clear abstractions that can be reused safely.
3. Yes. You can find components that have already been created in the libraries you've created before and then increase these libraries by creating new components that can be reused in the future. The chapter describes a reuse lifecycle: use existing reusable components, identify new library candidates, modify the specification for reuse, design components with stable interfaces, build the architecture with the library version, and document/socialize the library.
4. The .NET Standard is a specification that allows compatibility between different frameworks of .NET, from .NET Framework to Unity. .NET 10, on the other hand, is a modern unified .NET implementation and should be considered the foundation for sharing code in new applications. .NET Standard is mainly useful as a compatibility target when you need to support older or diverse consumers, such as legacy .NET Framework projects.
5. By creating a .NET Standard library, you will be able to use it in different .NET implementations, such as .NET Core, .NET, the .NET Framework, and Xamarin, if those platforms support the selected .NET Standard version. This is useful when a library must be consumed by older or cross-platform .NET implementations.
6. You can enable code reuse using object-oriented principles, such as inheritance, encapsulation, abstraction, and polymorphism. These principles help centralize common behavior, hide implementation details, create clear contracts, and allow different classes to share or specialize behavior. However, deep inheritance should be avoided when it increases coupling; composition may be a better option in many cases.
7. Generics is a sophisticated implementation that simplifies how objects with the same characteristics are treated, by defining a placeholder that will be replaced with the specific type at compile time, which allows the same class, method, interface, delegate, or service to work with different types while preserving type safety and performance.
8. The answer for this question is well explained by Immo Landwerth on the .NET blog: https://devblogs.microsoft.com/dotnet/the-future-of-net-standard/. The basic answer is that .NET versions 5 and above need to be thought of as the foundation for sharing code moving forward. For new libraries, you should usually target .NET 10 when your consumers are modern .NET applications. You should target .NET Standard 2.0 only when you need broad compatibility with older or diverse .NET implementations, especially the legacy .NET Framework. The decision depends on the consumers of the library, required APIs, platform compatibility, support expectations, and whether you need modern .NET features.
9. When you are refactoring code, you are writing it in a better way, respecting the contract of input and output of data that this code will process. The main challenges are avoiding behavior changes, preventing regressions, having enough unit tests, eliminating duplication safely, reducing complexity without breaking functionality, cleaning up design, and ensuring the code is stable before it becomes reused across many projects.
10. AI can help evolve the documentation and distribution of .NET libraries by generating XML documentation comments, creating or improving README files, suggesting NuGet metadata, helping

prepare project files for packaging, explaining how to publish packages, and supporting library usage examples. AI can accelerate these tasks, but the architect and team still need to review the results for accuracy, security, licensing, and consistency with the library's purpose.

Chapter 6

1. Design patterns are good solutions to common problems in software development, providing proven structures that help improve maintainability, reusability, consistency, and efficiency when designing software.
2. While design patterns give you code implementation for typical problems we face in development, design principles help you select the best options when it comes to implementing the software architecture. In other words, design patterns are reusable solution structures, while design principles, such as SOLID, are broader guidelines that help you design software with good structure, low coupling, high cohesion, and long-term maintainability.
3. The Builder pattern will help you generate sophisticated objects without the need to define them in the class where you are going to use them. It is a good idea when object creation is complex, involves several configuration steps, supports different final representations, or when you want to separate object construction from object usage.
4. The Factory pattern is useful in situations where you have multiple kinds of objects from the same abstraction, and you don't know which of them needs to be created at compile time. It is especially useful when the concrete object must be selected at runtime according to configuration, business rules, platform, country, provider, or execution context.
5. The Singleton pattern is useful when you need a class that has only one instance during the software's execution. It can be useful for shared configuration or application-wide infrastructure, but in modern .NET applications, this need is often handled better through dependency injection lifetimes, especially by registering a service as a singleton. Care is needed with shared state and concurrency.
6. The Proxy pattern is used when you need to provide an object that controls access to another object, especially when the real object is expensive to create, load, or access. It can be used to implement lazy loading, caching, access control, or delayed retrieval of data until it is really needed.
7. The Command pattern is used when you need to execute a command that will affect the behavior of an object. It is useful when a request should be encapsulated as an object, allowing actions to be queued, logged, retried, reused, extended, or even undone and redone. It also helps decouple the code that requests an action from the code that performs it.
8. The Publisher/Subscriber pattern is useful when you need to provide information about an object to a group of other objects. It is especially useful when communication should be asynchronous, loosely coupled, scalable, and able to support multiple independent subscribers. In distributed systems, this is commonly implemented through a message broker, such as Azure Service Bus or RabbitMQ.
9. The DI pattern is useful if you want to implement the Inversion of Control principle. Instead of creating instances of the objects that the component depends on, you just need to define their dependencies, declare their interfaces, and enable the reception of the objects by injection. You can do this by using the constructor of the class to receive the objects, tagging some class properties to receive the objects, or defining an interface with a method to inject all the necessary components. In modern .NET,

dependency injection is also important for service composition, lifetime management, testability, modularity, and maintainability. Constructor injection is usually preferred for mandatory dependencies, while property and method injection are better suited to optional or action-specific dependencies.

10. The Builder pattern is justified when constructors or object initializers would make object creation hard to read, hard to validate, or hard to evolve. I would use it when the object has many optional parameters, requires a sequence of construction steps, needs validation during creation, or must support different final representations. However, if the object can be created clearly with a simple constructor or object initializer, using Builder may add unnecessary complexity and become overengineered.
11. I would use Publisher/Subscriber when the services need loose coupling, asynchronous communication, scalability, or multiple independent consumers reacting to the same event. It is a good fit when the publisher should not know who consumes the message, or when consumers can process the message later. However, I would prefer direct synchronous interaction when an immediate response is required, the interaction is simple, or the services are tightly related. The trade-offs include latency, operational complexity, message reliability, retries, ordering, monitoring, eventual consistency, and the extra infrastructure needed for a message broker.

Chapter 7

1. Changes in the language used by experts and changes in the meaning of words.
2. Domain mapping.
3. No; the whole communication passes through the entity, that is, the aggregate root.
4. Because aggregates represent part-subpart hierarchies.
5. Just one since repositories are aggregate-centric.
6. The application layer manipulates repository interfaces. Repository implementations are registered in the dependency injection engine.
7. To coordinate operations on several aggregates in single transactions.
8. The specifications for updates and queries are usually quite different, especially in simple CRUD systems. The reason in its strongest form is mainly the optimization of query response times.
9. Dependency injection.
10. No; a serious impact analysis must be performed before we can adopt it.

Chapter 8

1. DevOps is the approach of delivering value to the end user continuously. To do this successfully, continuous integration, continuous delivery, and continuous feedback must be undertaken. DevSecOps extends this idea by adding security as a continuous responsibility throughout the whole software delivery lifecycle. It combines people, processes, products, automation, feedback, and security practices to deliver value safely and continuously.

2. Continuous integration allows you to check the quality of the software you are delivering every single time you make a change. You can implement this by turning on this feature in Azure DevOps or GitHub Actions. CI automatically builds and tests the application after code changes, helping the team detect problems earlier, reduce merge conflicts, and keep the main branch stable.
3. Continuous delivery allows you to deploy a solution once you are sure that all the quality checks have passed the tests you designed. Azure DevOps helps you with that by providing you with relevant tools, and GitHub Actions can also be used for the same purpose. CD creates a controlled path for moving validated changes through environments such as development, staging, and production.
4. Continuous security is the practice of including security checks and controls throughout the software lifecycle, especially inside the CI/CD process. It helps detect insecure code, vulnerable dependencies, exposed secrets, weak configurations, and other risks as early as possible, instead of treating security as a final activity before release.
5. Continuous feedback is the adoption of tools in the DevOps life cycle that enable fast feedback when it comes to performance, usability, and other aspects of the application you are developing. In DevSecOps, continuous feedback also helps the team learn from production behavior, monitor stability and security, detect incidents early, and use real operational data to improve the solution.
6. Yes, you can have DevOps separately and then enable Continuous Integration later. You can also have Continuous Integration enabled without Continuous Delivery enabled. Your team and process need to be ready and attentive for this to happen. So, yes, DevSecOps can exist without CI/CD, but CI/CD makes DevSecOps faster, more consistent, and easier to automate.
7. You may misunderstand CI as a continuous delivery process. In this case, you may cause damage to your production environment. In the worst scenario, you can have, for example, a feature that isn't ready but has been deployed, you can cause a stop at a bad time for your customers, or you can even suffer a bad collateral effect due to an incorrect fix. Other risks include insecure code, moving too quickly through the pipeline, unstable releases, poor test coverage, lack of review, weak deployment controls, and a bad understanding of DevSecOps by the team.
8. A multi-stage environment protects production from bad releases when a fully automated build and deployment pipeline is in place, because changes can be validated first in development and staging before they reach production. It also allows approvals, quality checks, testing, and business validation to happen at each stage, reducing deployment risk.
9. Automated tests anticipate bugs and bad behaviors in preview scenarios. They help CI/CD by validating code automatically during the pipeline, detecting business logic errors, regression problems, and functional failures before deployment reaches later environments or production.
10. Pull requests allow code reviews before commits are made in the master branch or main branch. They help CI/CD by creating a controlled review point before code is merged, allowing developers, reviewers, automated checks, static analysis tools, and even AI-assisted review tools to evaluate the quality and safety of the change.
11. No; pull requests can help you in any development approach where you have Git as your source control, even when CI/CD is not enabled. They are useful for collaboration, review, discussion, quality control, and protecting the main branch.

12. Application Insights is a helpful tool for monitoring the health of the system you've deployed, which makes it a fantastic continuous feedback tool. Its main purpose in DevSecOps is to provide production feedback about requests, failures, response times, dependencies, exceptions, availability, performance, and possible abnormal behavior, helping the team improve the application continuously.
13. To maximize the value that the software provides for the target organization. Service design thinking treats software as an evolving service, not just as a finished product. Its goal is to keep the solution aligned with user needs, business outcomes, operational quality, and continuous improvement.
14. You would choose not to enable continuous production deployment when the team, process, tests, monitoring, approval flow, security controls, or rollback strategy is not mature enough. It may also be inappropriate when production changes require strict governance, user notification, change management, regulatory approval, database coordination, or scheduled release windows.
15. I would assess CI/CD readiness by checking whether the team has strong version control practices, frequent integration habits, reliable automated tests, pull request reviews, branch protection, secure coding practices, static analysis, dependency and secret scanning, multi-stage environments, deployment approvals, monitoring, rollback plans, and enough maturity to respond quickly when a pipeline or deployment fails.

Chapter 9

1. Because the probability of the same error occurring in a unit test and in its associated application code is very low.
2. Because most of the tests must be repeated after any software change occurs.
3. `[Theory]` is used when the test method defines several tests, while `[Fact]` is used when the test method defines just one test.
4. Assert.
5. `Setup`, `Returns`, and `ReturnsAsync`.
6. Yes, with `ReturnAsync`.
7. No; it depends on the complexity of the user interface and how often it changes.
8. The ASP.NET Core pipeline isn't executed, but inputs are passed directly to controllers.
9. Usage of the `Microsoft.AspNetCore.Mvc.Testing` NuGet package.
10. The usage of Selenium or Playwright.

Chapter 10

1. IaaS is a good option when you are migrating from an on-premises solution or if you have an infrastructure team.
2. PaaS is the best option for fast and safe software delivery in systems where the team is focused on software development.
3. If the solution you intend to deliver is provided by a well-known player, as a SaaS, you should consider using it because this way you have the smallest possible time-to-market and a very low investment, with almost no drawbacks.

4. FaaS.
5. Azure SQL Server Database can be up in minutes, and you will have all the power of Microsoft SQL Server afterward. More than that, Microsoft will handle the database server infrastructure.
6. In a hybrid scenario, you have the flexibility to decide on the best solution for each part of your system, while respecting the solution's development path in the future.

Chapter 11

1. The modularity of code and deployment modularity.
2. No. Other important advantages include handling the development team and the whole CI/CD cycle well, and the possibility of mixing heterogeneous technologies easily and effectively.
3. A library that helps us implement resilient communication.
4. Once you've installed Docker on your development machine, you can develop, debug, and deploy Dockerized .NET applications.
5. Orchestrators are software that manage microservices and nodes in microservice clusters. Azure supports two relevant orchestrators: Azure Kubernetes Service and Azure Service Fabric.
6. With communication based on the publisher-subscriber pattern. This way, no changes are needed to the sending microservices when a new microservice is added, because the added microservice just needs to subscribe to already existing events created by the senders.
7. A message broker. It takes care of service-to-service communication and events.
8. The same message can be received several times because the sender doesn't receive a confirmation of reception before its time-out period, and so the sender resends the message again. Protection against duplicate messages consists of turning all messages into idempotent messages. Deletes and modifications are typically idempotent, but additions are not. Therefore, they must be made idempotent by storing information about received messages and verifying if the messages were already received.

Chapter 12

1. Redis is a distributed in-memory storage based on key-value pairs and supports distributed queuing. Its most well-known usage is for distributed caching, but it can be used as an alternative to relational databases since it is able to persist data to disk. However, it is not usually a full replacement for relational databases when the system requires complex relationships, rich querying, strong transactional modeling, or relational constraints. It is better suited to caching, session storage, queues, very low-latency key-value access, and some newer AI-related scenarios, such as semantic cache or vector search.
2. Yes, they are. Most of this chapter's sections are dedicated to explaining why. NoSQL databases are especially valid when the system needs flexible schemas, document-oriented data, horizontal scaling, high performance in distributed environments, or efficient handling of semi-structured data. However, relational databases remain a better default when strong consistency, transactions, joins, and structured schemas are central to the solution.

3. Write operations, because all copies or replicas of the same data must be updated. Read operations scale more naturally because different replicas can serve different read requests, but distributed writes require partitioning, coordination, or sharding to scale efficiently.
4. The main weaknesses of NoSQL databases are their consistency and transactions, while their main advantage is performance, especially when it comes to handling distributed writes. They also usually require the application to take more responsibility for maintaining references, data coherence, and model evolution. Their main advantage is that they can scale horizontally and handle flexible, distributed, document-oriented data more naturally than relational databases.
5. Eventual, Consistent Prefix, Session, Bounded Staleness, Strong. Ordered from strongest to weakest, they are: Strong, Bounded Staleness, Session, Consistent Prefix, and Eventual consistency.
6. No, they are not efficient in a distributed environment. GUID-based strings perform better since their uniqueness is automatic and don't require synchronization operations. Cosmos DB primary keys should be generated explicitly by the application, commonly as strings using values such as Guid.NewGuid().ToString(), instead of relying on auto-increment integer keys.
7. OwnsMany and OwnsOne. In Entity Framework Core, these methods configure owned entities, so they are stored inside the parent, or "father," document instead of being treated as separate, independent documents.
8. Yes, they can. Once you use SelectMany, indices can be used to search for nested objects. Cosmos DB can index nested paths, including paths inside arrays, so nested collections can be queried efficiently when the indexing policy supports those paths.
9. I would choose Session consistency. In this shopping cart scenario, each user must immediately see their own updates, but other users do not need to see those changes instantly. Session consistency guarantees read-your-own-writes behavior for the same user session, while avoiding the extra latency and throughput cost of Strong consistency.
10. Eventual consistency would likely be sufficient for showing like counts, because exact immediate freshness is usually not critical for this kind of high-scale social signal. The trade-off is that users may briefly see stale or slightly different counts across regions, but the system gains better latency, availability, throughput, and scalability.
11. I would usually choose tenantId as the partition key or include it in a hierarchical or synthetic partition key, because tenant-level queries are common in SaaS systems. This keeps each tenant's data logically grouped and makes tenant-scoped queries efficient. However, I would also check tenant size and traffic distribution: if a few tenants are much larger or busier than others, using only tenantId could create hot partitions, so a composite or hierarchical strategy may be needed.
12. I would evolve the data model in the application layer rather than through relational migrations. The application should be able to read both the old and new JSON structures during a transition period, usually by adding a schema version field, writing new documents in the new format, and gradually updating or backfilling older documents. This allows the system to keep running while documents are migrated incrementally and safely.

Chapter 13

1. With the help of database-dependent providers.

2. Either by calling them Id or by decorating them with the Key attribute. This can also be done with a fluent configuration approach.
3. With the MaxLength and MinLength attributes, or with their equivalent fluent configuration methods.
4. With something similar to builder.Entity<Package>().HasIndex(m => m.Name);.
5. With something similar to:

```
builder.Entity<Destination>()
.HasMany(m => m.Packages)
.WithOne(m => m.MyDestination)
.HasForeignKey(m => m.DestinationId)
.OnDelete(DeleteBehavior.Cascade);
```

6. `Add-Migration` and `Update-Database`.
7. No, but you can forcefully include them with the `Include` LINQ. With `Include`, related entities are loaded together with the main entities.
8. Yes, it is, thanks to the `Select` LINQ clause.
9. By calling `context.Database.Migrate()`.

Chapter 14

1. Because using queues is the only way to avoid time-consuming blocking calls.
2. With the import declaration.
3. With the standard Duration message.
4. Version compatibility and interoperability.
5. Better horizontal scalability and support for the Publisher/Subscriber pattern.
6. For two reasons: the operation is very fast, and the insertion in the first queue of a communication path must necessarily be a blocking operation.
7. With the following XML code:

```
<ItemGroup>
    <Protobuf Include="Protos\file1.proto" GrpcServices="Server/Client" />
   <Protobuf Include="Protos\file2.proto" GrpcServices="Server/Client" />
   ...
</ItemGroup>
```

8. With channel.BasicPublish(...).
9. With channel.WaitForConfirmsOrDie(timeout).

Chapter 15

1. No, since this would violate the principle that a service reaction to a request must depend on the request itself, and not on other messages/requests that have previously been exchanged with the client.
2. No, because this would undermine interoperability.
3. Yes, it can. The primary action of a POST must be creation, but deletion can be performed as a side effect. The HTTP verb to use is determined by the virtual table named in the URL (in our case, a POST, since the operation is an addition), but other operations can be performed on other virtual tables that are not mentioned in the URL as side effects.
4. From the request body
5. The `ApiController` attribute sets up some default behaviors that help in the implementation of REST services.
6. When using API controllers, they are declared with the Route and `Http<verb>` attributes. When using a minimal API, they are declared in the first argument of `MapGet`, `MapPost`, ... `Map{Http verb}`.
7. By adding something like `builder.Services.AddHttpClient<MyProxy>()` in the dependency injection part of the host configuration.

Chapter 16

1. Yes. The standard ASP.NET Core project pipeline scaffolded by Visual Studio includes middleware/modules such as error handling with UseExceptionHandler, HSTS with UseHsts, HTTPS redirection with UseHttpsRedirection, routing with UseRouting, authorization with UseAuthorization, static assets with MapStaticAssets, and Razor Pages with MapRazorPages().WithStaticAssets(). In development, UseDeveloperExceptionPage can also be used to show detailed error information.
2. No. An ASP.NET Core pipeline module does not need to inherit from a base class or implement a specific interface. A middleware module can be any class with a constructor that receives a RequestDelegate and an Invoke or InvokeAsync method that receives an HttpContext. It can also be written directly as a lambda passed to app.Use.
3. No. Several tag helpers may be defined for the same tag. They are executed in a configurable order, and they can cooperate by using a shared data structure while the tag is being processed.
4. Yes. In a controller, validation errors can be checked by testing ModelState.IsValid. If it is false, validation errors have occurred, and the controller usually returns the same ViewModel to the same view so the user can correct the input.
5. The instruction is @RenderBody(). It is placed in the layout view where the output of the main view should be inserted.
6. Secondary sections of the main view are invoked in a layout view with @RenderSection("SectionName", required: false) or with required: true if the section is mandatory. The main view defines the section with @section SectionName { ... }.

7. A controller invokes a view by returning a ViewResult, usually with the View method, such as return View("ViewName", viewModel). If the view name is the same as the action method, the controller can simply call return View(viewModel).
8. By default, the globalization module uses three providers: query string parameters, the .AspNetCore.Culture cookie, and the Accept-Language request header sent by the browser.
9. No. ViewModels are the main and recommended way for controllers to communicate structured data to views, but they are not the only way. Controllers can also use ViewData, ViewBag, and TempData to pass additional information to views or between requests.

Chapter 17

1. API Gateways interface WEB APIs, while frontends produce directly the HTML to be sent to the client.
2. Because they are exposed to the world outside of the application.
3. Because they slow down access to the database by blocking database objects.
4. Whenever the probability of interference during a database operation is not high.
5. Domain events increase code modularity.

Chapter 18

1. It is a W3C standard: the assembly of a virtual machine running in W3C-compliant browsers.
2. A web UI where dynamic HTML is created in the browser itself.
3. Selecting a page based on the current browser URL.
4. A Blazor component with routes attached to it. For this reason, the Blazor router can select it.
5. Defining the .NET namespace of a Blazor component class.
6. A local service that takes care of storing and handling all forms-related information, such as validation errors and changes in HTML inputs.
7. Either `OnInitialized` or `OnInitializedAsync`.
8. Callbacks and services.
9. Blazor way to interact with JavaScript.
10. Getting a reference to a component or HTML element instance.

Chapter 19

1. Each POD of a StateFulSet has a unique virtual address, while PODs of a ReplicaSet can be reached only through services that assign requests to them according to load-balancing strategies
2. Services are needed to furnish stable addresses to PODs notwithstanding they might be moved from one machine to another. Moreover, they are needed also to perform load balancing among replicas.
3. Ingresses are needed to perform HTTPS termination and virtual hosting.

4. The basic Aspire projects are AppHost, Servicedefaults, and various test projects (one for each supported testing framework). Then, there are also starter projects and empty Aspire solutions that include the basic projects needed to code an Aspire solution (AppHost, and Servicedefaults).
5. No, it is a general .NET feature.
6. Just 2. One that does not translate virtual URLs and that is useful for deploying on Kubernetes, and the other one that performs a configuration-based translation.
7. The usage of `AddConnectionString`.
8. No, it doesn't.
9. A `WithReference(myResource)` call causes the configuration data for accessing "`myResource`" to be injected as environment variables in the project that performs the call, so that they can be used by service discovery to access "`myResource`".

Chapter 20

1. Electronic Signature.
2. They are encrypted with symmetric encryption based on a common key agreed during the handshake stage.
3. Server proves its identity by encrypting a message provided by the client with its private key.
4. Man-in-the-middle attacks are prevented because the server must prove its identity, and no man-in-the-middle can prove it is the server.
5. In TLSm, not only the server, but also the client proves their identity. Therefore, TLSm, can be used as a way to authenticate the client.
6. Using a TLS secret.
7. Authentication tokens inserted in each request header.
8. Using HTTP-only cookies with a Same-Site policy, that is, cookies that can't be manipulated by either JavaScript or WebAssembly code and that are sent to the server only if the browser page is on the same domain where the cookie should be sent.
9. With the help of the `AuthorizationAttribute` and the possible definition of authorization policies. In turn, authorization policies analyze user claims to decide on authorization.
10. With OAuth authentication, users can authenticate to N different WEB applications by furnishing their credentials to a trusted authentication server instead of furnishing them to the N different, possibly untrusted target applications.

Chapter 21

1. Hardening in cloud computing focuses heavily on misconfiguration and guardrails because many cloud security failures come from exposed resources, overly permissive identities, public endpoints, weak defaults, or uncontrolled changes, rather than only from application bugs. Guardrails help make the secure path the default path, preventing teams from accidentally creating insecure resources or drifting away from the approved baseline.

2. When moving from IaaS to PaaS, your responsibility shifts from hardening the operating system and host to hardening configuration, identity, access, networking, and data protection settings. In IaaS, you must manage guest OS patching, host firewalls, EDR, services, and server baselines. In PaaS, the provider handles more of the OS and runtime lifecycle, so your focus becomes enforcing TLS, disabling legacy protocols, restricting public access, using private endpoints, enabling auditing, and applying least privilege.
3. The most important high-signal alerts are alerts that detect dangerous posture changes, such as new public IPs, opened inbound ports, public storage access, databases exposed to the internet, new role assignments, elevated privileges, new access keys, disabled logging, disabled policies, unusual outbound traffic spikes, and deployments from unknown identities. These alerts matter because they point to changes that can immediately increase exposure or reduce visibility.
4. IaC reduces the burden on developers by turning infrastructure setup into reusable, reviewed, automated templates instead of manual configuration. It improves security because changes can go through pipelines, static analysis, policy checks, approval gates, preview plans, and post-deployment verification. This helps prevent insecure resources from being created, detects drift, and makes environments repeatable, auditable, and easier to correct.
5. A team that wants to be ready for a possible cybersecurity incident must prepare playbooks, monitoring, logs, access controls, backups, and recovery procedures before an incident happens. The team should be ready for scenarios such as credential leaks, public exposure, compromised workloads, suspicious IAM changes, and availability problems. They also need protected centralized logs, tested restores, incident response roles, periodic playbook exercises, secret rotation procedures, containment steps, rollback plans, and disaster recovery options such as multi-zone deployment when justified.

Download the example code files

The code bundle for the book is hosted on GitHub at `https://github.com/PacktPublishing/Software-Architecture-with-.NET-10-and-C-sharp-5E/`

B

Unlock Your Exclusive Benefits

Your copy of this book includes the following exclusive benefits:

DRM-Free PDF Version

Download DRM-free PDF and ePub copies of this book.

7-Day Packt Library Access

Get 7-day unlimited access to 8,000+ books and videos. No credit card required.

Available for first-time Packt+ trial users only.

Next-Gen Reader Access

Read this book on Packt Reader with progress sync, dark mode and note-taking.

Follow the guide below to unlock them. The process takes only a few minutes and needs to be completed once.

Unlock this Book's Free Benefits in 3 Easy Steps

Step 1

Keep your purchase invoice ready for *Step 3*. If you have a physical copy, scan it using your phone and save it as a PDF, JPG, or PNG.

For more help on finding your invoice, visit `https://www.packtpub.com/en-us/unlock?step=1`.

> Note
>
> **Note**: If you bought this book directly from Packt, no invoice is required. After *Step 2*, you can access your exclusive content right away.

Step 2

Scan the QR code or go to `packtpub.com/unlock`.

On the page that opens (similar to *Figure B.1* on desktop), search for this book by name and select the correct edition.

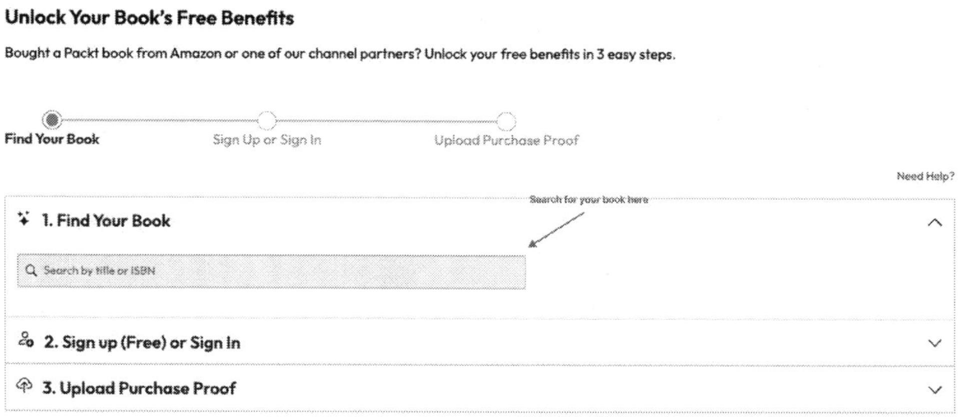

Figure B.1: Packt unlock landing page on desktop

Step 3

After selecting your book, sign in to your Packt account or create one for free. Then upload your invoice (PDF, PNG, or JPG, up to 10 MB). Follow the on-screen instructions to finish the process.

Need Help

If you get stuck and need help, visit `https://www.packtpub.com/unlock-benefits/help` for a detailed FAQ on how to find your invoices and more. This QR code will take you to the help page.

> Note
>
> **Note:** If you are still facing issues, reach out to `customercare@packt.com`.

Other Books You May Enjoy

If you enjoyed this book, you may be interested in these other books by Packt:

Software Architecture with C++

Adrian Ostrowski, Piotr Gaczkowski

ISBN: 9781789612462

- Understand how to apply the principles of software architecture
- Apply design patterns and best practices to meet your architectural goals
- Write elegant, safe, and performant code using the latest C++ features
- Build applications that are easy to maintain and deploy
- Explore the different architectural approaches and learn to apply them as per your requirement
- Simplify development and operations using application containers
- Discover various techniques to solve common problems in software design and development

The C++ Programmer's Mindset

Sam Morley

ISBN: 9781835888438

- Apply computational thinking to complex C++ problems
- Break problems into components using abstraction
- Use algorithms and data structures effectively in C++
- Design modular and reusable C++ code
- Analyze and improve algorithmic performance
- Parse, transform, and interpret data in multiple formats
- Scale up with concurrency, GPUs, and profiling tools

Packt is searching for authors like you

If you're interested in becoming an author for Packt, please visit `authors.packt.com` and apply today. We have worked with thousands of developers and tech professionals, just like you, to help them share their insight with the global tech community. You can make a general application, apply for a specific hot topic that we are recruiting an author for, or submit your own idea.

Share your thoughts

Now you've finished *Software Architecture with C# 14 and .NET 10*, we'd love to hear your thoughts! Scan the QR code below to go straight to the Amazon review page for this book and share your feedback or leave a review on the site that you purchased it from.

https://packt.link/r/1806663554

Your review is important to us and the tech community and will help us make sure we're delivering excellent quality content.

Index

Symbols

.NET
- communication facilities 288, 289
- design patterns 160, 161
- interoperability with 52, 53
- used, for dealing with microservices 287

.NET 10
- scalable web app, creating 35 – 44
- tips and tricks, for coding 106, 107

.NET Aspire
- application telemetry 587, 588
- microservices and resources, configuring 589 – 592
- project, deploying 592, 593
- resource integration and automatic resources configuration 585 – 587
- service discovery 582 – 585
- service discovery, role 582 – 585
- used, for developing Microservice applications 578 – 582

.NET Aspire Service Defaults project 579

.NET Generic Host
- reference link 160

.NET HttpClient
- client certificates, using with 609

.NET MAUI 546

.NET MAUI Blazor 546

.NET Standard 337

.NET WebAssembly build tools option 544

.NET communication facilities 288, 289
- hosts, using 292 – 297
- resilient task execution 290, 291
- Visual Studio support, for Docker 297

.NET libraries
- documenting 135 – 139
- promoting 134
- publishing 135 – 139

.NET, using for code reuse 127, 128
- C#, dealing with 130
- considerations 133, 134
- libraries, promoting 134
- reusable class library, creating 129, 130

.NET, with SOA 416
- .NET HTTP clients 427 – 430
- ASP.NET Core 418, 419
- ASP.NET Core authorization 423, 424
- ASP.NET Core support, for OpenAPI 425 – 427
- gRPC support 417
- REST services 418
- REST services, implementing with ASP.NET Core 419 – 422
- SOAP client support 416

.Net Aspire Empty App 582

.Net Aspire Starter App template 582

A

AI agents design patterns 162

AI impact
- on requirement management and implementation 80 – 82

AOT compilation 544

API gateway 282

API management systems 482

ASP.NET Core
- basics 435, 436
- configuration data, loading 440
- configuration data, using with options framework 440
- controllers and ViewModels, defining 449 – 453
- environment access, at runtime 444
- middleware 436 – 440
- pipeline, defining 446 – 449
- publish profiles and project files, using 443
- worker microservices, implementing with 389 – 392

ASP.NET Core MVC

and design principles, connection between 468, 469
Razor Views 454 – 456
response HTML, creating 454
view code, reusing 464

ASP.NET Core MVC outermost layer
controllers and views, defining 720 – 724
defining 714
PackageManagement, authentication and authorization 715 – 719
Packages Management globalization 715

ASP.NET Core Web **139**

ASP.NET Core configuration
files 440, 441
environment name, setting 442
mapping, to .NET objects 445, 446, 450
publish profiles and project files, using 443, 444
sources 441, 442

ASP.NET Core pipeline **437**
advantages 469
globalization 471 – 475
MVC pattern 475, 476
server-side and client-side validation 470, 471

Access Control **65**

Advanced Message Queuing Protocol (AMQP) **394**

Agile Manifesto **9**
URL 9

App Host **578**

Application insights **213 - 217**

Aspir8 **593**

Avalonia platform
reference link 505

Azure
scalable web app, creating 30 – 33
storage accounts 315

Azure Cosmos DB **319**
account, creating 320, 321
container, creating 321 – 323
Cosmos DB client 328, 329
Cosmos DB Entity Framework Core provider 329, 330
data, accessing 323, 324
database consistency, defining 324 – 327

Azure DevOps **62, 212, 213**
boards menu 64
project, creating 62 – 64
reference link 65
requirements connection, to artifacts 66
system requirements 64, 65

Azure Key Vault **57**

Azure Service Bus **393**
reference link 288

Azure account
creating 5 – 7

acceptance tests **223**
writing 225, 226

action methods **420**

advanced concepts, Kubernetes
liveness and readiness checks 576, 577
permanent storage, requiring 573, 574
secrets 574 – 576

aggregates **177**

agile
scaling 14

agile software development process models **9, 10**
Extreme Programming (XP) 12, 13
lean software development 11
scrum model 13, 14

application layer **493**

application services **180**
defining 493 – 495

application telemetry **587**
logging 588
metrics 588
tracing 588

asymmetric encryption **598**

asynchronous programming **23**

authentication **56, 612**
client certificate authentication 622
cookie authentication, handling 617, 618
cookie-based authentication 616
default schema 615
OAuth authentication 625 – 627
servers 612
tokens 612 – 614
web token authentication 618, 619

authentication strategy

- defining 495, 496

authorization 612

authorization code 627

authorization model
- claims-based 57
- policy-based 57
- role-based 56
- simple 56

authorization server 625

automated unit
- writing 224

automatic tuning 260

availability 30

B

Behavior-Driven Development (BDD) 233 - 235

BenchmarkDotNet
- URL 44

Blazor
- advanced features 534
- bindings 525 – 527
- component lifecycle 528 – 530
- component structure 514 – 518
- error handling 522, 523
- events 523 – 525
- forms and validation 530 – 532
- native application, developing with 547 – 549
- pages and components 514
- templates and cascading parameters 519 – 522
- used, for updating HTML 527, 528

Blazor Controls Toolkit
- reference link 545

Blazor Forms 531

Blazor WebAssembly
- architecture 506
- third-party tools 545

Blazor WebAssembly architecture 506, 507
- application, loading 509, 510
- application, starting 509, 510
- routing 511 – 513
- Single-Page Applications (SPA) 507 – 509

Blazor advanced features
- AOT compilation 544
- authentication and authorization 538 – 541
- communication, with server 542 – 544
- globalization and localization 537, 538
- JavaScript interoperability 535 – 537
- references, to components and HTML elements 535

BlazorStrap
- reference link 545

Blazorise project
- reference link 545

Bootstrap CSS 509

Bounded Contexts 169, 274, 660
- relations 171, 172

Brighter
- reference link 289

Builder pattern 146 - 148, 293

bUnit
- reference link 546

backend caching 23

bank language 167

binary serialization
- issues 373 – 380

binary serializers
- issues 374

binding 525

C

C# 5
- functional tests, automating 243

C# 14 5

C# programming, performance issues
- exceptions 45, 46
- string concatenation 45

C# test projects
- advanced test preparation 238 – 240
- defining, in Visual Studio 235, 236
- GitHub Copilot 242
- interfaces, mocking with Moq 240, 241
- teardown scenarios 238 – 240
- xUnit test framework, using 236 – 238

CI/CD cycle 270

CI/CD methodology 64

Certificate Store 606

CircleCI team 560

Cloud databases
- fields, encrypting 629

ClusterIP service type 567

Code Cleanup 111

Code Metrics 86

Command Query Responsibility Segregation (CQRS) 161

Command pattern 155, 156, 189 - 192

Concurrency Checks 491

Context Map 171

Cosmos DB provider 363

Cross-Origin Resource Sharing (CORS) 479

Cross-Site Scripting (XSS) 610

Cucumber
- reference link 233

caching 23

change detection 527

classic layers architecture, DDD 179, 180

classical repositories 184

client certificate authentication 622
- handling, in ASP.NET Core 622 – 625

client technologies 502, 724
- Blazor MAUI Version, adding 734, 735
- choosing, for application 505, 506
- client-side business logic, implementing in service 730, 731
- cross-platform applications 505
- native applications 505
- progressive web applications 504
- required ASP.NET Core REST APIs, implementing 726 – 730
- Single-Page Applications (SPA) 503
- solution, preparing 724 – 726, 732
- user interface, implementing 731 – 734

cloud architecture resiliency patterns
- reference link 30

cloud architecture security patterns
- reference link 57

cloud computing design patterns 161
- Bulkhead Isolation 161
- Cache Aside 161
- circuit-breaker 161
- Command Query Responsibility Segregation (CQRS) 161
- Publisher/Subscriber 161
- Retry 161

code
- reusing, for safe software 659

code agents 81

code reusability
- features 125, 126
- in development lifecycle 127
- limitations 124, 125
- principles 123, 124

coding, in C#
- class coupling 94, 95
- cyclomatic complexity 87 – 92
- depth of inheritance 92, 93
- maintainability index 87
- number of lines 95, 96
- simple coding 86

command query responsibility segregation (CQRS) pattern 186 - 188, 701

communications 373

communications, securing 604 - 606
- client certificates, using with .NET HttpClient 609
- malicious scripts execution, preventing in browser 610, 611
- server certificates, using with Kestrel 606 – 609

compiled models 350

connectors 335

containers 285

continuous delivery (CD) 195, 199
- development stage 199
- production stage 200
- staging 199

continuous feedback (CF) 211

continuous integration (CI) 195, 198

continuous security (CS) 200
- continuous production deployment, applying with control 201 – 203
- incomplete features 203 – 206
- insecure code, applying in repository 201
- unstable solution for testing 207 – 211

control-plane nodes 561

controlled application
- testing 246 – 248

controllers
- defining 497, 498

cookie-based authentication 616
- handling, in ASP.NET Core 617, 618

persistent cookie 616
session cookie 616

cross-platform applications 505

cryptanalysis 604

cryptography 597 - 600
asymmetric encryption 598
chains of certificate authorities 602 – 604
digital signature 601
elliptic cryptography 604
lattice-based cryptography 604
privacy, encrypting for 600
proof of identity 602 – 604
public encryption, with private decryption 598
safe encryption 604
symmetric encryption 598
symmetric key 600

custom events 508

D

DB Driver 181
defining 490 – 492

DDD architectures 178
classic layered architecture 179, 180
onion architecture 180 – 184

DDD entities 172, 173
entity-level validation 173, 174
in .NET 174 – 176

DDD patterns
aggregate events 189 – 192
Command pattern 189 – 192
CQRS pattern 186 – 188
event sourcing 189
repository pattern 184
Unit of Work pattern 185, 186

DDD-adapted repositories 184

DHCP protocol 567

DRY principle 125

Data Transfer Objects (DTOs) 183, 187, 355

Database Transaction Units (DTUs) 310

Dependency injection pattern 158, 159

DevSecOps 195 - 197
continuous delivery (CD) 199
principles 198

DevSecOps principles 198
continuous delivery (CD) 199, 200
continuous feedback (CF) 211
continuous integration (CI) 198
continuous security (CS) 200

Development Team 13

Distinguished Name 623

Docker 286, 287

Docker Compose 559

Docker Kubernetes
images, pushing into 744

Docker Registry
reference link 301

Document-Oriented Database 312

Domain Model 181

Domain Services 181

DrawIO
URL 17

data layer
deploying 361, 362

data serialization 371

data storage
choosing, in cloud 663, 664

data-driven asynchronous communication 372, 384 - 386

database access 24

dependency injection (DI) 106, 296

design patterns 143
Builder pattern 146 – 148
Command pattern 155, 156
Dependency injection pattern 158, 159
Factory pattern 148 – 150
in .NET 160, 161
Proxy pattern 153 – 155
Publisher/Subscriber pattern 157, 158
Singleton pattern 150 – 152

design sprint 22

design sprints 21

design thinking 21

differentiated replicas 556

digital signature 601

direct SQL commands 349
issuing 359 – 361

distributed transactions 386 - 389

documentation 124

domain events 170, 178

domain layer
defining 488, 489

domain-driven design (DDD) 165, 169, 170, 485
- aggregates 177
- Bounded Context implementation 170, 171
- domain events 178
- value objects 176

dynamic link libraries (DLLs) 127, 272

E

Entity Framework Core
- advanced features 364 – 366
- configuring 337, 338
- data, querying 351 – 355
- data, updating 351 – 355
- DB entities, defining 338 – 341
- entities, turning into aggregates 357 – 359
- mapped collections, defining 341
- mapping configuration 342 – 346
- migrations 346 – 349
- query results, returning to outer layer 355 – 357

Erlang 393

Extreme Programming (XP) 11 - 13
- URL 12

elicitation 16

elliptic cryptography 604

envelope 405

event sourcing 189, 387

exceptions 45, 46

external application 559

extreme programming 226

F

Factory pattern 148 - 150

Figma
- URL 17

FluentValidation library 471

Function as a Service (FaaS) 254, 264

fast selection logic
- designing 50, 51
- example 51, 52

fault element 405

feature 65

fluent configuration interface 335

formatter 451

frontend microservice 282, 699
- application architecture, defining 700 – 703
- application services, defining 711 – 714
- application specifications, defining 699, 700
- ASP.NET Core MVC outermost layer, defining 714
- DB Driver 706 – 711
- Domain Model 703 – 705
- Domain Services 706

frontends 480, 481

functional tests 223, 230 - 232
- automating, in C# 242, 243
- Behavior-Driven Development (BDD) 233
- controlled application, testing 246 – 248
- recording, with Selenium IDE 248, 249
- staging application, testing with Selenium 244 – 246

G

Gang of Four (GoF) 144

Gherkin 233

GitHub 213

GitHub Code Agent 81, 82

GitHub Copilot 242
- applying, for code analysis 117 – 119

GitHub projects 74 - 80

Graph Database 312

gRPC 370

garbage collector (GC) 24, 104

gateways 183

generics 132, 133

H

HTML micro-frontends 483 - 485

Headless Services 569

handshaking procedure 605

hardening 634
- compliance requirements 634
- importance, in cloud 634

horizontal scaling 34

hosted services 292

hosts 292
hybrid applications
uses 266

I

IISExpress 444
Infrastructure as a Service (IaaS) 254, 265, 635
and Azure opportunities 255 – 257
security responsibilities 257, 258
Infrastructure as code (IaC) 634
misconfiguration management and drift control 641, 642
Ingress Controllers 569
Init Container 555
Inversion of Control (IoC) container 159
identity baseline 638
incident readiness and operational resilience 642, 643
incremental model
analyzing 9
integration tests 222
automating 223
writing 224
internal application 559
internal queues
replacing, with RabbitMQ 395 – 399
interoperability
with .NET 52, 53

K

Kanban 14
Kanban board 14
Kestrel 436
server certificates, using with 606 – 609
Key-Value Database 313
Kubelet 561
Kubernetes
.YAML files 563, 564
advanced concepts 573
basics 561 – 563
Docker Desktop Kubernetes, using 572
Ingresses 569 – 571
Kubectl, using 572
microservices, orchestrating with 561
ReplicaSets and deployments 564 – 566
services 567 – 569
StatefulSets 566
worker microservice, deploying 742, 743
Kubernetes cluster 561
Kubernetes objects
defining 744 – 748

L

Language Integrated Query (LINQ) 336
Linux
service, creating 54
Liskov substitution principle 144
Load Balancers 283
LoadBalancer service 568
labels 563
landing zone 634, 637
secure baseline, establishing with 637
lattice-based cryptography 604
lazy loading technique 155
lean software development 11
lift and shift 258
local service discovery 578
logging baseline 638
long-term support (LTS) versions 4
loose coupling 276

M

MQTT 394
MVC Razor 433
MVC pattern 475
MassTransit
reference link 289
Memento 155
Mermaid 18
URL 18
Message Broker 384
Micro-Frontends 284, 480, 481
Microsoft Authentication Library (MSAL) 56
Microsoft Azure 5

Minimum Viable Product (MVP) **21**
Model View Controller (MVC) **433**
Moq
interfaces, mocking with 240, 241
Multi-Factor Authentication (MFA) **56**
mTLS **606**
man-in-the-middle attack **605**
microservice architecture
defining 485 – 488
microservices **270, 271**
and evolution of concept of modules 272, 273
and layered architectures 280, 281
dealing, with .NET 287
design principles 274
interacting, with container registry 301, 302
managing, with tools 301
orchestrating, with Kubernetes 561
user interface 282, 283
microservices architectures
considerations 284
microservices design principles **274**
chained requests/responses, avoiding 276 – 279
independence, of choices 274, 275
independence, of deployment environment 275
loose coupling 275, 276
microservices implementation, with .NET worker services and message brokers **393**
RabbitMQ, installing 393
middleware **437**
reference link 447
modularity **123**
multithreading environments
do's and don'ts 47 – 49

N

NServiceBus
reference link 289
NoSQL databases **312 – 314**
NoSQL document-oriented databases
versus SQL document-oriented databases 316 – 319
Nomad **560**
native applications **505**
network baseline **639, 640**
nodes **278, 561**

O

OAuth 2 protocol **626**
OAuth authentication **625**
handling, in ASP.NET Core 627 – 629
working 625, 626
OAuth protocol **625**
Object-Relational Mapping (ORM)
basics 334 – 337
Observer pattern **157**
Ocelot
reference link 482
Open Telemetry protocol (OTLP) **588**
Open Web Application Security ProjectÂ® (OWASP)
URL 55
OpenAPI **413**
reference link 414
OpenAPI Specification **139**
OpenID-Connect (OIDC) **625**
Orchestrators **287, 561**
Docker Compose 559
Nomad 560
Swarm 559
object allocation **24**
object initializer **339**
object-oriented analysis approach **130 – 132**
object-relational mappings (ORMs) **168**
onion architecture, DDD **180 – 184**
application services 181
domain layer 181
orchestrators
containers, using in 555
features 554
interfacing, with external world 559
microservice replicas, handling 556
network addresses, handling 556, 557
permanent storage, handling 557

resiliency and zero downtime. ensuring 558

P

Package Manager Console **346**

PersistentVolumeClaim (PVC) **573**

Platform as a Service (PaaS) **254, 258, 264, 265, 636**
- SQL databases 259 – 262
- web apps 259

Playwright
- reference link 225

Pod **562**

Polly **289**

Product Owner **13**

Protocol Buffer (Protobuf) **374**

Proxy pattern **153 - 155**

Publisher/Subscriber pattern **157, 158, 183**

package management systems **273**

packages **273**

pages **508**

parameters **508**

pass-through provider **583**

performance **20**

performance tests **223 - 225**

persistent cookie **616**

private asymmetric key **602**

probabilistic encryption **604**

professional development project
- tasks 4

progressive web applications **504**

proof of identity **602**

protobuf serialization **380, 381**

prototypes **17**

providers **335**
- reference link 335

public Web APIs **481 - 483**

Q

query objects **490**

R

REST web services **408**
- API versioning 415, 416
- authentication 414, 415
- authorization 414, 415
- methods example 413
- native HTTP features 410 – 412
- OpenAPI standard 413, 414
- service type compatibility rules 409, 410

RPC approach **381 - 384**

RabbitMQ **289, 393**
- basics 394, 395
- installing 393
- reference link 394
- used, for replacing internal queues 395 – 399

Razor Views **454 - 456**
- flow of control statements 456 – 458
- properties 458, 459
- tag helpers, using 459 – 464

Redis **314, 315**

Remote Desktop Protocol (RDP) **256**

Remote Procedure Calls (RPC) **371**

ReplicaSets **563**

Reqnroll/SpecFlow **233**

Role objects **622**

RoleBinding objects **622**

relational databases **309 - 312**

repository **184**

repository options **308**
- Azure storage accounts 315, 316
- NoSQL databases 312 – 314
- Redis 314, 315
- relational databases 309 – 312

repository pattern **184**

requirement management, in Azure DevOps **64**
- AI impact 80 – 82
- epic work items 65
- feature work items 65
- product backlog items 66
- user story work items 66

requirements
- analyzing 17

requirements connection, to artifacts **66**
- Azure DevOps repository 66 – 70
- package feeds 70 – 72
- pipelines 73, 74

test plans 72, 73

requirements engineering process **15**

requirements gathering process, impact on system results

use cases 22 – 26

requirements-gathering process **15, 16**

resiliency **30**

resource groups **255**

robustness **20**

role-based access control (RBAC) **638**

router **507**

routers **508**

S

SAFeÂ® **14**

URL 15

SOAP Web services **405, 406**

specifications 406 – 408

SOLID principles

dependency inversion 145

interface segregation 145

Liskov substitution principle 145

open-closed 144

single responsibility 144

using, as guardrails for design patterns 144

SQL databases **259 - 262**

SQL document-oriented databases

versus NoSQL document-oriented databases 316 – 319

Scalar **674**

Scrum Master **13**

Scrum Team **13**

Scrum framework **11**

URL 13

Selenium

staging application, testing with Selenium 245, 246

Selenium IDE

reference link 225

used, for recording tests 248, 249

Separation of Concerns principle **472**

Service Design Thinking **197, 198**

Service definition **563**

Service-Oriented Architecture (SOA) **273, 401**

communication stack 404

selection checklist

features 405

fundamental features 404

principles 402, 403

Services **562**

Simple Object Access Protocol (SOAP) **405**

Single-Page Applications (SPA) **479, 503, 507**

Single-Page Applications (SPAs) **434**

Singleton pattern **150 - 152**

Software as a Service (SaaS) **62, 254, 262, 265**

using, scenarios 263

SonarCloud

applying, at WWTravelClub APIs 656 – 658

SonarQube for Visual Studio **114**

applying, for code analysis 114, 115

Sprint **13**

StatefulSets **563**

Swagger

web API, documenting with 139, 140

Swagger UI **139, 674**

Swarm **559**

Swashbuckle **139**

safe architecture, practices

authentication 56

sensitive data 57

web security 57

safe code, in C#

IDisposable interface 105, 106

try-catch 102, 103

try-finally 104, 105

writing 102

saga transactions

choreography 388

orchestration 388

scalability **20, 30**

scalable web app

creating, in Azure 30 – 33

creating, with .NET 10 35 – 44

scrum model **13, 14**

secure baseline, with landing zone

establishing 637

identity baseline 638
logging baseline 638, 639
network baseline 639, 640
organizational structure 637
runtime hardening, by computing model 640

security **20**

security by design **55, 56**

serialization **373**

server random **605**

serverless computing **254, 264**

service
creating, in Linux 54

session cookie **616**

shared responsibility model **635**
hardening priorities, driving 635 – 637

sidecar **555**

software architecture **4**

software deployment models **254**
IaaS 254
PaaS 254
SaaS 254
serverless (FaaS) 254

software development lifecycle (SDLC) **4**

software development process model **7**

software domains **166 - 168**
unique model 167

specifications
reviewing 20
writing 18, 19

standardization **124**

stored procedures **349**

string concatenation **45**

subcutaneous tests **232**

symmetric encryption **598**

symmetric key **599**

T

Task Parallel Library (TPL) **47**

Task-Based Asynchronous Patterns **48**

Team Foundation Server (TFS) **263**

Test-Driven Development (TDD) **13, 226 - 228**

target framework moniker (TFM) **129**

template syntax **520**

templates **511**

tenants **318**

test-driven development (TDD)
green stage 228
red stage 228
refactoring stage 229, 230

tests
organization 222

tools, for facilitating DevSecOps implementation
application insights 213 – 217
Azure DevOps 212
GitHub 213

traditional software development process models **8**
incremental model 9
waterfall model 8

transactions
handling 361

U

UNO platform
reference link 505

Ubiquitous Language **169**

Unified Modeling Language (UML) **17**

Unit of Work pattern **186**

undistinguishable replicas **556**

unit tests **222**
automating 223

usability **49, 50**

use cases **17**

user interface (UI) **49**

user needs and system requirements **647**
administrative operations 647
customer experience 647
detecting 16, 17
localization and accessibility 648
scalability and performance 648
security and compliance 648

V

ViewModel **452, 475**

Visual Studio

C# test projects, defining 235, 236
Code Metrics 86

Visual Studio support, for Docker
Docker file, analyzing 298, 299
project, publishing 299 – 301

version control system 96
dealing with, in teams 100 – 102
with AI support 96 – 100

vertical scaling 33, 34

view code, reusing 464
partial views 466, 467
shared page structure 464 – 466
view components 467, 468

view components 467

virtual hosting 483

W

WWTravelClub
.NET projects, types 648 – 650
code standard 655
domains 660 – 662
managing, with GitHub 650 – 654
testing 735 – 738

WWTravelClub APIs
SonarCloud, applying 656 – 658

WWTravelClub DevSecOps approach 662, 663
Production stage 662
Staging. Application Insights and Test and Feedback 662

WWTravelClub packages
exposing, with Web APIs 673 – 678

WWTravelClub use case 166

Wide-Column Store Database 313

Worker Service 396

World Wild Travel Club 646

waterfall model 8

web API
documenting, with Swagger 139, 140

web applications
presentation layers 434, 435

web apps 259

web token authentication 618, 619
handling, in ASP.NET Core 620 – 622

well-written code identification 108, 109
code analysis tools 109 – 113
code check, after static analysis tools 115, 116
extension tools, applying 113, 114
GitHub Copilot, applying for code analysis 117 – 119
SonarQube for Visual Studio, applying 114, 115

worker microservice
based, on RabbitMQ 664 – 673
deploying, on Kubernetes 742, 743
Docker images, creating 743, 744
images, pushing into Docker Kubernetes 744
Kubernetes objects, defining 744 – 748
testing, with .NET Aspire 738 – 742

worker microservice, with ASP.NET Core 679
application services 688 – 690
DB Driver 684 – 687
domain layer 680 – 684
gRPC Microservice project, testing with fake purchase request generator 696 – 698
outermost layer 690 – 692
queued requests, processing 693 – 696
specifications and architecture 679, 680

worker microservices
implementing, with ASP.NET Core 389 – 392

X

xUnit test framework 236

Y

YAML 563

Made in the USA
Coppell, TX
18 October 2026

93262785R00450